—

Film Actors Guide:
WESTERN EUROPE

v. 1

by

JAMES ROBERT PARISH

with

Kingsley Canham, Hervé Dumont,
Jeanne Passalacqua, Linda J. Sandahl
and Florence Solomon

The Scarecrow Press, Inc.
Metuchen, N.J. & London
1977

Library of Congress Cataloging in Publication Data

Parish, James Robert.
   Film actors guide.

   Includes index.
   CONTENTS: [1] Western Europe.
   1. Moving-picture actors and actresses--Registers.
I. Title.
PN1998.A2P389   791.43'028'0922   77-22485
ISBN 0-8108-1044-1

CONTENTS

1985631

CONTENTS

PREFACE

The goal in this volume is to provide a single compendium of motion-picture actors--in this instance, those based in Western Europe exclusive of Scandinavia--who have performed in feature-length films. It is hoped that the following checklists will offer film enthusiasts a useful research tool.

Entries include only full-length films of over four reels or forty minutes. So long as the major reputation was first obtained in Europe, actors/actresses who made films in the United States are included, along with their American credits. An index to all actors and actresses appearing in the 129 photographs in this book follows the Preface.

The selection of performers has been based on a desire to offer in a manageably-sized book a wide spectrum of professional actors who have been employed in the film industries throughout Western Europe. Naturally the volume does not attempt to be all-inclusive. The cut-off date for inclusion in this work is the end of 1975; if a film's release date is after then it will not appear in an individual's listing. Some Hungarian, Czechoslovakian, and other Eastern European films appear in this volume because of the player's major subsequent identification with Western Europe (Germany in a great many cases). Beginning arbitrarily with film release dates of 1946, German credits are given as "W Ger" (West German) and, few in the present volume, "E Ger."

Alphabetization of actors/actresses' names that are compounds has been according to one Anglo-American practice--i.e., that of entry under Da, De, Van, etc.--as an aid for those unfamiliar with European practice. Cross references are entered from alternate forms.

English language titles given in square brackets are those supplied a foreign film by British or U.S. distributors and are not to be considered translations. Occasionally the distributors' titles change between one release engagement and another year's re-release. Often, too, a foreign film is released in Britain or America under its foreign title; and occasionally one is released under two different English-language titles, one in Britain, one in the U.S.

The author and his co-workers would be most appreciative of any suggestions, corrections, or additions that any reader may care to provide.

James Robert Parish

EUROPEAN COUNTRIES
NOT COVERED IN THIS VOLUME*

Albania	Latvia
Bulgaria	Lithuania
Czechoslovakia	Norway
Denmark	Poland
East Germany	Sweden
Estonia	Turkey
Finland	USSR
Greece	Yugoslavia
Hungary	

---

*The current work, Film Actors Guide: Western Europe, is the first in a projected series that will eventually also cover Eastern Europe (and the USSR), Asia, Africa, and Australia. In the case of Scandinavia the designation "Eastern Europe" is for convenience only.

ABBREVIATIONS

Note: Only for American- or British-made feature
films/documentaries/serials/telefeatures are releasing companies designated; for film products elsewhere
only the countries of origin are designated.

*	denotes a serial
AA	Allied Artists Pictures Corporation Anglo-Amalgamated Film Distributors (N. B. some releases bear only "Anglo" as distributors)
ABC-TV	American Broadcasting Corporation television network
ABFD	Associated British Film Distributors
ABP/ABPC	Associated British Picture Corporation
AFT	American Film Theatre
AFU	Army Film Unit
AIP	American International Pictures
AKU	Army Kinematograph Unit
Alg	Algerian
AP & D	Associated Producers and Distributors
Arg	Argentinian
Associated FN	Associated First National Pictures, Inc. (later part of Warner Bros. , Inc.)
Aus	Austrian
Avco Emb	Avco Embassy Pictures Corporation
b.	born
B & D	British and Dominions Film Corporation
Bel	Belgian
BFI	British Film Institute
BIED	British Independent Exhibitors' Distributors
BL/BLFC	British Lion Film Corporation

Br	British
Braz	Brazilian
Bry	Bryanston Films
Bul	Bulgarian
Butcher	Butcher's Film Service
BV	Buena Vista Distribution Co., Inc.
Can	Canadian
CBS	Columbia Broadcasting System television network
CFF	Children's Film Foundation
CFU	Crown Film Unit
Cin	Cinerama Releasing Corporation
Col	Columbia Pictures Industries, Inc.
CUE	Commonwealth United Entertainment
Czech	Czechoslovakian
d.	died
Dan	Danish
Dut	Dutch
E Ger	East German
Egy	Egyptian
EL	Eagle Lion Film Distributors
Emb	Embassy Pictures Corporation
EMI	Electrical and Musical Industries
Eng	English (the language)
ep	episode
Ex	Exclusive Films
FBO	Film Booking Offices
Fin	Finnish
FN	First National Pictures, Inc. (later part of Warner Bros., Inc.)
FNP	First National-Pathé (British)
FOB	Festival of Britain
Fox	Fox Film Corporation
Fr	French
GB	Great Britain
GEF	Golden Era Film Distributors
Ger	German

GFD	General Film Distributors
GN	Grand National
GPO	General Post Office
Hun	Hungarian
IFD	Independent Film Distributors
IFR	International Film Renters
Isr	Israeli
It	Italian
Jap	Japanese
JMG	Jury-Metro-Goldwyn
Liech	Liechtenstein
LIP	Lippert Pictures, Inc.
	London Independent Producers
Metro-Goldwyn	Metro-Goldwyn Distributing Corporation (later part of Metro-Goldwyn-Mayer, Inc.)
Mex	Mexican
MGM	Metro-Goldwyn-Mayer, Inc.
MOI	Ministry of Information
Mon	Monogram Pictures Corporation
MRA	Moral Rearmament
Nat Gen	National General Pictures, Inc.
NBC-TV	National Broadcasting Company television network
Nor	Norwegian
Par	Paramount Pictures Corporation
PDC	Producers Distributing Corporation
Pol	Polish
Por	Portuguese
PRC	Producers Releasing Corporation
Rep	Republic Pictures Corporation
RFD	Rank Film Distributors
Rum	Rumanian
Rus	Russian
SC	Sound City Films
Sp	Spanish
Swe	Swedish
Swi	Swiss

TFD	Twickenham Film Distributors
Tun	Tunisian
Tur	Turkish
TV	Television
20th	Twentieth Century-Fox Film Corporation
UA	United Artists Corporation
UNFS/UNESCO	United Nations Film Service
Univ	Universal Pictures, Inc.
USA	United States of America
W & F	Woolf and Freedman Film Service
W Ger	West German
WB	Warner Bros., Inc.
WB-7 Arts	Warner Bros.-Seven Arts, Inc.
WPD	Warner-Pathé Distributors
Yug	Yugoslavian

ACKNOWLEDGMENTS

Ruud Bischoff

Jean Canham

John Robert Cocchi

Lorenzo Codelli

Peter Cowie

Goswin Doerfler

Geoff Donaldson

Morris Everett, Jr.

Pierre Guinle

Christian Hette

Doug McClelland

Norman Miller

Jorge Pelayo

Michael R. Pitts

Francisco Rialp

Mel Schuster

Henri Sonet

Tantivy Press

T. Allan Taylor

Theatre Collection at Lincoln Center Library for the Performing Arts (Paul Myers and his staff)

INDEX TO
ACTORS AND ACTRESSES
IN THE PHOTOGRAPHS

THE GUIDE

ADJANI, ISABELLE, b. June 17, 1955, Paris
Le Petit Bougnat (Fr 1969)
Faustine et le bel été (Fr 1971)
La Gifle [The Slap] (Fr-It 1974)
L'Histoire d'Adèle H (Fr 1975)

AGREN, JANET, b. 1950
Il giovane normale (It 1969)
Du soleil plein les yeux (Fr 1969)
Io non vedo, tu non parli, lui non sente (It 1971)
Io non spezzo, rompo (It 1971)
La più bella serata della mia vita (It 1972)
Avanti! (UA 1972)
Pulp (GB-It 1972)
La vita a volte e molto dura, vero Provvidenza? [Providenza...
Mause-falle für zwei schräge Vögel] (It-W Ger 1972)
Racconti proibiti di niente vestiti (It 1972)
Fiorina la vacca (It 1972)
Ingrid sulla strada (It 1973)
Tecnica di un amore (It 1973)
Il saprofita (It 1974)
Paolo Barca, maestro elementare, praticamente nudista (It 1975)
Sensualidad (Sp 1975)

AIMEE, ANOUK (Françoise Sorya), b. April 27, 1932, Paris
La Maison sous la mer (Fr 1946)
La Fleur de l'âge (Fr 1947) [unfinished]
Les Amants de Vérone (Fr 1948)
Golden Salamander (GFD 1950)
La Bergère et le ramoneur (Fr 1950) (voice only)
Noche de tormenta [Nuit d'Orage] (Sp-Fr 1951)
Les Crimes de l'amour (ep "La Rideau cramoisi") (Fr 1952)
Conquêtes du froid (Fr 1952)
The Man Who Watched Trains Go By [Paris Express] (Eros 1953)
Forever My Heart (ep "Happy Birthday") (BL 1954)
Contraband Spain (ABP 1955)
Les Mauvaise Rencontres (Fr 1955)
Ich suche Dich (W Ger 1956)
Nina (W Ger 1956)
Stresemann (W Ger 1957)
Tous peuvent me tuer [Anyone Can Kill Me] (Fr-It 1957)
Pot-Bouille [The Noise of Lovers] (Fr-It 1957)

1

Aimee and Michael York in Justine (1969).

Montparnasse 19 (Fr-It 1957)
La Tête contre les murs [The Keepers] (Fr 1958)
The Journey (MGM 1959)
Les Dragueurs [The Young Have No Morals] (Fr 1959)
La dolce vita [The Sweet Life] (It-Fr 1960)
Le Farceur [The Joker] (Fr 1960)
Lola (It-Fr 1960)
L'imprevisto [L'Imprévu] (It-Fr 1961)
Quai Notre-Dame (Fr 1961)
Il giudizio universale [The Last Judgment] (It-Fr 1961)
Sodoma e Gomorra [Sodom and Gomorrah] (It-USA 1962)
Otto e mezzo [$8\frac{1}{2}$] (It 1962)
Les Grands Chemins [Flesh and Blood] (Fr-It 1963)
I giorno più corto [The Shortest Day] (It-Fr 1963)
Il terrorista (It-Fr 1963)
Il successo (It 1963)
Liolà--Le coq du village (It-Fr 1964)
Le voci bianche (It 1965)
La fuga (It-Fr 1965)
Il Morbidone (It 1965)
Le stagioni del nostro amore [Seasons of Our Love] (It 1966)

Un Homme et une femme [A Man and a Woman] (Fr 1966)
Lo scandalo (It 1966)
Un Soir, un train (Fr-Bel 1968)
The Appointment (MGM 1969)
The Model Shop (Col 1969)
Justine (20th 1969)
Si c'était à refaire (Fr 1976)

ALBERS, HANS, b. Sept. 22, 1892, Hamburg; d. July 24, 1960
Die Jahreszeiten des Lebens (Ger ?)
Im grossen Augenblick (Ger 1911)
Die Sünden ver Väter (Ger 1911)
Zigeunerblut (Ger 1911)
Komödianten (Ger 1912)
Die Macht des Goldes [Gulden magt] (Ger-Dan 1912)
Der Totentanz [Dødedansen] (Ger-Dan 1912)
Wenn die Maske fällt [Naar masken falder] (Ger-Dan 1912)
Zu Tode gehetzt [Dødens gaade] (Ger-Dan 1912)
Rache des Gefallenen (Ger 1917)
Rauschgold (Ger 1917)
Baronchen auf Urlaub (Ger 1917)
1000 Nacht (Ger 1918)
Die Prinzessin von Urbino (Ger 1919)
Der Fürst (Ger 1919)
Berlin W. (Ger 1920)
Die Marquise von O. (Ger 1920)
Der Falschspieler (Ger 1921)
Madeleine (Ger 1921)
Der böse Geist Lumpazivagabundus (Ger 1922)
Lydia Sanin (Ger 1922)
Menschenopfer (Ger 1922)
Die Geliebte des Königs (Ger 1922)
Der falsche Dimitri (Ger 1922)
Söhne der Nacht (Ger 1922)
Der Tiger des Zirkus Farini (Ger 1922)
Versunkene Welten (Ger 1922)
Fräulein Raffke (Ger 1923)
Das Testament des Joe Sievers (Ger 1923)
Auf Befehl der Pompadour (Ger 1924)
Das schöne Abenteuer (Ger 1924)
Gehetzte Menschen (Ger 1924)
Taumel (Ger 1924)
Guillotine (Ger 1924)
Der Bankraub unter den Linden (Ger 1925)
Athleten (Ger 1925)
Der König und das kleine Mädchen (Ger 1925)
Vorderhaus und Hinterhaus (Ger 1925)
Der Mann aus dem Jenseits (Ger 1925)
Deutsche Herzen am deutschen Rhein (Ger 1925)
Die Gesunkenen (Ger 1925)
Die Venus von Montmartre (Ger 1925)
Ein Sommernachtstraum (Ger 1925)
Halbseide (Ger 1925)

Luxusweibchen (Ger 1925)
Mein Freund--der Chauffeur (Ger 1925)
An der schönen blauen Donau (Ger 1926)
Nur eine Tänzzerin [Bara en danserska] (Ger-Swe 1926)
Husarenliebe (Ger 1926)
Seeschlacht beim skagerrak (Ger 1926)
Der lachende Ehemann (Ger 1926)
Der Prinz und die Tänzerin (Ger 1926)
Der Soldat der Marie (Ger 1926)
Die drei Mannequins (Ger 1926)
Die Frau, die nicht "nein" sagen kann (Ger 1926)
Die versunkene Flotte (Ger 1926)
Die Villa im Tiergarten (Ger 1926)
Die Warenhausprinzessin (Ger 1926)
Eine Dubarry von heute (Ger 1926)
Ich hatt einen Kameraden (Ger 1926)
Jagd auf Menschen (Ger 1926)
Kussen ist keine Sünde (Ger 1926)
Nixchen (Ger 1926)
Schatz, mach kasse (Ger 1926)
Wir sind vom H. U. H. Infanterie-Regiment (Ger 1926)
Der goldene Abgrund (Ger 1927)
Die Dollarprinzessin und ihre 6 freier (Ger 1927)
Eszogen 3 Burschen (Ger 1927)
Die glühende Gasse (Ger 1927)
Drei Seelen ein Gedanke (Ger 1927)
Eine kleine Freundin braucht jeder Mann (Ger 1927)
En perfekt gentleman [Överste Jacques Renard] (Swe 1927)
Der grösste Gauner des Jahrhunderts (Ger 1927)
Primanerliebe (Ger 1927)
Finaldo Rinaldini (Ger 1927)
Das Fräulein aus Argentinien (Ger 1928)
Der Rote Kreis (Ger 1928)
Dornenweg einer Fürstin (Ger 1928)
Frauenarzt Dr. Schäfer (Ger 1928)
Herr Meister und Frau Meisterin (Ger 1928)
Heut war ich bei der Frieda (Ger 1928)
Prinzessin Olala (Ger 1928)
Rasputin's Liebesabenteuer (Ger 1928)
Saxophon-Susi (Ger 1928)
Weib in Flammen (Ger 1928)
Wer das Scheiden hat erfunden (Ger 1928)
Asphalt (Ger 1929)
Ja Ja, die Frau sind meine schwache Seite (Ger 1929)
Mascottchen (Ger 1929)
Möblierte Zimmer (Ger 1929)
Die Nacht Gehört Uns (Ger 1929)
Teure Heimat (Ger 1929)
Verebte Triebe: Der Kampf ums Neue Geschlecht (Ger 1929)
Der blaue Engel (Ger 1929)
The Blue Angel (Eng lang version of Der blaue Engel) (Ger 1930)
Der Greifer (Ger 1930)
Hans in Allen Gassen (Ger 1930)

Drei Tage Liebe (Ger 1931)
Der Sieger (Ger 1931)
Bomben auf Monte Carlo (Ger 1931)
Monte Carlo Madness (Eng lang version of Bomben auf Monte
  Carlo) (Ger 1931)
Der Draufgänger (Ger 1931)
Heut Kommt's Drauf an (Ger 1932)
Quick (Ger 1932)
Der Weisse Dämon [Ranschgift] (Ger 1932)
Ein Gewisser Herr Gran (Ger 1933)
Flüchtlinge (Ger 1933)
F. P. I. Antwortet Nicht (Ger 1933)
Peer Gynt (Ger 1934)
Gold (Ger 1934)
Henker, Frauen and Soldaten (Ger 1935)
Varieté (Ger 1936)
Savoy-Hotel 217 (Ger 1936)
Der Mann, der Sherlock Holmes War [Two Jolly Adventurers]
  (Ger 1936)
Unter heissem Himmel (Ger 1936)
Fahrendes Volk (Ger version of Les Gens du voyage) (Ger 1937)
Die gelbe Flagge (Ger 1937)
Sergeant Berry (Ger 1938)
Wasser für Canitoga (Ger 1939)
Ein Mann auf Abwegen (Ger 1939)
Trenck, Der Pandur (Ger 1940)
Carl Peters (Ger 1941)
Münchhausen (Ger 1942)
Grosse Freiheit Nr. 7 [La Paloma] (Ger 1944)
Shiva und die Galgenblume (Ger 1944)
...Und über uns der Himmel (W Ger 1947)
Föhn (W Ger 1950)
Von Teufel gejagt (W Ger 1950)
Blaubart (Ger version of Barbe-bleu) (W Ger 1951)
Nachts auf den Strassen (W Ger 1952)
Kapt'n Bay'Bay (W Ger 1952)
Johnny Rettet Nebrador (W Ger 1953)
Auf der Reeperbahn Nachts um Halb Eins (W Ger 1953)
Am Jedem Finger Zehn (W Ger 1954)
Der Letste Mann (W Ger 1955)
Vor Sonnenuntergang (W Ger 1956)
I fidanzati della morte (It 1956)
Das Herz von St. Pauli (W Ger 1957)
Der tolle Bomberg (W Ger 1957)
Das gab's nur einmal (W Ger 1957)
Der Greifer (W Ger 1958)
Der Mann im Strom. CCC (W Ger 1958)
Dreizehn Alte Esel (W Ger 1958)
Kein Engel ist so rein (W Ger 1959)

ALVES, LAURA (Laura Alves Magno), b. Sept. 8, 1922, Lisbon
  O pai tirano (Por 1941)
  O pátio das cantigas (Por 1942)

Laura Alves

O leão da estrela (Por 1947)
Sonhar (Por 1951)
Fácil (Por 1951)
Um marido solteiro (Por 1952)
O costo de África (Por 1954)
Perdeu-se um marido (Por 1956)
O parque das ilusões (Por 1963)
O ladrão de quem se fala (Por 1969)

ALVES DA COSTA, JOAQUIM, b. May 26, 1903
Táxi 9297 (Por 1927)
Rito ou Rita? (Por 1927)
Hipnotismo aos domicílios (Por 1927)
Vigário Foot-Ball Club (Por 1927)
A canção do berço (Por 1930)
A mulher que ri (Por 1930)
Maria Papoila (Por 1937)
Amanhã como hoje (Sp 1947)
Ribatejo (Por 1949)
Cantiga da rua (Por 1949)
Eram duzentos irmãos (Por 1951)
Um marido solteiro (Por 1952)
Rosa de Alfama (Por 1953)
O cerro dos enforcados (Por 1954)
Quando o mar galgou a terra (Por 1954)

Joaquim Alves da Costa

Perdeu-se um marido (Por 1956)
Dois dias no paraiso (Por 1957)
O homem do dia (Por 1958)
Um dia de vida (Por 1962)
Nove rapazes e um cão (Por 1963)
O amor desceu em pára-quedas (Por 1968)
O diabo era outro (Por 1969)

ALVES DA CUNHA, JOSE MARIA, b. Aug. 19, 1889, Lisbon; d.
      Sept. 23, 1956
Uratau (Fr 1926)
Maria do mar (Por 1930)
Lisboa, crónica anedótica (Por 1930)
Tragédia rústica (Por 1931)
O feitico do império (Por 1940)
A garça (Por 1952)
A serpente (Por 1952)
Duas causas (Por 1952)
Rosa de Alfama (Por 1953)

ALVINA, ANICEE, b. Jan. 28, 1953, Boulogne-Billancourt, France
   Elle boit pas, elle fume pas, elle drague pas, mais elle cause
      (Fr 1969)
   Friends [Deux enfants qui s'aiment] (GB-Fr 1971)
   Le Rempart des béguines [Gli amori impossibili/Rampart of
      Desire] (Fr-It 1972)

José Maria Alves da Cunha

Les Grands Sentiments font les bons guenletons (Fr 1973)
Glissements progressifs du plaisir (Fr 1973)
Paul and Michelle [Paul et Michelle] (GB-Fr 1974)
Le Jeu avec le feu [Giochi di fuoco] (Fr-It 1974)
Isabelle devant le désir (Fr-Bel 1975)
Une Femme fatale (W Ger-Fr 1975)

AMMELROOY, WILLEKE VAN see VAN AMMELROOY, WILLEKE

ANDERGAST, MARIA, b. June 4, 1912, Brunnthal, Bayern, Germany
    Der verlorene Sohn (Ger 1934)
    Abenteuer eines jungen Herrn in Polen (Ger 1934)
    Endstation (Ger 1935)
    Mein Leben für Maria Isabell (Ger 1935)
    Der Vogelhändler (Ger 1935)
    Der Kurier des Zaren (Ger-Fr 1936)
    Skandal un die Fledermaus (Ger 1936)
    Seine Tochter ist der Peter (Aus 1936)
    Manja Valewska (Aus 1936)
    Donaumelodien (Ger-Hung 1936)
    Die Drei um Christine (Ger 1936)
    Drei Mäderl um Schubert [Dreimäderlhaus] (Ger 1936)
    Husaren, heraus! (Ger 1936)
    Die glücklichste Ehe von Wien (Aus 1937)
    Das Geheimnis um Betty Bonn (Ger 1938)

Das grosse Abenteuer (Ger 1938)
Monika (Ger 1938)
Schüsse in Kabine 7 (Ger 1938)
Die Pfingstorgel (Ger 1939)
Hochzeitsreise zu Dritt (Ger 1939)
Unsterblicher Walzer (Ger 1939)
Roman eines Arztes (Ger 1939)
Das Glück wohnt nebenan (Ger 1939)
Polterabend (Ger 1940)
Ihr Privatsekretär (Ger 1940)
Der Herr im Haus (Ger 1940)
Ein Leben lang (Ger 1940)
Der liebe Augustin (Ger 1940)
Der laufende Berg (Ger 1941)
Sechs Tage Heimaturlaub (Ger 1941)
So ein Früchten (Ger 1942)
Das grosse Spiel (Ger 1942)
Abenteuer im Grandhotel (Ger 1943)
...und die Musik spielt dazu [Saison in Salzburg] (Ger 1943)
Ein Mann gehört ins Haus (Ger 1945) [Not released until 1948]
Der weite Weg (Aus 1946)
Der Hofrat Geiger (Aus 1947)
Zyankali (Aus 1948)
Kleine Melodie aus Wien (Aus 1948)
Auf der Alm, da gibts ka Suend (Aus 1950)
Die Mitternachtsvenus (W Ger 1951)
Der alte Sünder (Aus 1951)
Eva erbt das Paradies (Aus 1951)
Hallo, Dienstmann! (Aus 1952)
Der Mann in der Wanne (Aus 1952)
Die Wirtin von Maria-Wörth (Aus 1952)
Junggesellenfalle (W Ger 1953)
Der Verschwender (Aus 1953)
Sanatorium total verrückt (W Ger 1954)
Wenn die Alpenrosen blühn (W Ger 1955)
Die fröliche Wallfahrt (W Ger 1956)
Kaiserball (Aus 1956)
Verlobung am Wolfgangsee (Aus 1956)
Das Schloss in Tirol (W Ger 1957)
Almenrausch und Edelweiss (Aus 1957)
Wetterleuchten über dem Zillertal [Der gestohlene Himmel]
     (W Ger-It 1974)

ANDRESS, URSULA, b. March 19, 1936, Berne, Switzerland
     Le avventure ed amori di Giacomo Casanova (It 1954)
     Un Americano a Roma (It 1954)
     La catena dell'odio (It 1955)
     Dr. No (UA 1962)
     Four for Texas (WB 1963)
     Fun in Acapulco (Par 1963)
     Nightmare in the Sun (Zodiak Films 1964)
     She (WPD 1965)
     What's New Pussycat? (UA 1965)

Les Tribulations d'un chinois en Chine [Up to His Ears] (Fr-
It 1965)
La decima vittima [The Tenth Victim] (It 1965)
The Blue Max (20th 1966)
Once Before I Die (Seven Arts 1966)
Casino Royale (Col 1967)
No Toys for Christmas (It 1967)
Le dolci signore (It 1967)
The Southern Star (Col 1968)
Anyone Can Play (It 1968)
Perfect Friday (London Screenplays 1970)
Soleil rouge [Red Sun] (Fr-It-Sp 1971)
L'ultima occasione [Last Chance for a Born Loser] (It-Fr 1973)
Colpo in canna (It 1974)
Scaramouche (It 1975)
Africa Express (It 1975)

Harry Andrews in Entertaining Mr. Sloane (1970).

ANDREWS, HARRY, b. Nov. 10, 1911, Tonbridge, Kent, England
The Red Beret [Paratrooper/The Big Jump] (Col 1953)
The Black Knight (Col 1954)
The Man Who Loved Redheads (BL 1955)
Helen of Troy (WB 1956)

Alexander the Great (UA 1956)
Moby Dick (WB 1956)
A Hill in Korea [Hell in Korea] (BL 1956)
St. Joan (UA 1957)
I Accuse! (MGM Br 1958)
Ice Cold in Alex [Desert Attack] (ABPC 1958)
The Devil's Disciple (UA 1959)
Solomon and Sheba (UA 1959)
A Touch of Larceny (Par 1960)
In the Nick (Col 1960)
Circle of Deception (20th 1960)
I Due Nemici [The Best of Enemies] (It-USA 1961)
Barabba [Barabbas] (It-USA 1962)
The Inspector [Lisa] (20th 1962)
Reach for Glory (Gala 1962)
Cleopatra (20th 1963)
Nine Hours to Rama (20th 1963)
55 Days at Peking (AA 1963)
The Informers [Underworld Informers] (RFD 1963)
Nothing but the Best (AA 1964)
The System [The Girl Getters] (Bry 1964)
633 Squadron (UA 1964)
The Hill (MGM 1965)
The Agony and the Ecstasy (20th 1965)
The Truth About Spring (Univ 1965)
Sands of the Kalahari (Emb 1965)
Modesty Blaise (20th 1966)
The Jokers (RFD 1966)
The Deadly Affair (Col 1966)
The Night of the Generals (GB-Fr 1967)
The Long Duel (RFD 1967)
Danger Route (UA 1967)
I'll Never Forget What's'isname (RFD 1967)
The Charge of the Light Brigade (UA 1968)
The Night They Raided Minsky's (UA 1968)
A Dandy in Aspic (Col 1968)
Play Dirty (UA 1968)
L'Etoile du Sud (Fr-GB 1969)
Battle of Britain (UA 1969)
A Nice Girl Like Me (Avco Emb 1969)
The Seagull (WPD 1969)
Too Late the Hero (Cin 1970)
Entertaining Mr. Sloane (WPD 1970)
Destiny of a Spy (TVM 1970) (filmed in 1969 as The Gaunt
    Woman)
Wuthering Heights (Anglo-EMI 1970)
Country Dance [Brotherly Love; (MGM-EMI 1970) made in 1969]
Nicholas and Alexandra (Col 1971)
Burke and Hare (UA 1972)
The Nightcomers (Avco Emb 1972)
I Want What I Want (Cin 1972)
The Ruling Class (UA 1972)
Man of La Mancha (It 1972)

Theatre of Blood (UA 1973)
Man at the Top (MGM-EMI 1973)
The Mackintosh Man (WB 1973)
Night Hair Child (RFD 1973) [made in 1971]
The Internecine Project (BL 1974)

ANNABELLA (Suzanne Georgette Charpentier), b. July 14, 1909,
    Varenne-Saint-Hilaire (Seine), France
Napoléon (Fr 1927) (sound added for 1934 release)
Maldone (Fr 1927)
Romance à l'inconnue (Fr 1929)
Deux fois vingt ans (Fr 1929)
Trois Jeunes Filles nues (Fr 1929)
La Maison de la flèche (Fr 1930)
Un Soir de rafle (Fr 1930)
Barcarolle d'amour (Fr 1931)
Autour d'une enquête (Fr 1931)
Le Million (Fr 1931)
Son altesse l'amour (Fr 1931)
Un Fils d'Amérique (Fr 1932)
Paris Méditerranée (Fr 1932)
Marie "Légende Hongroise" (Fr 1932)
Gardez le sourire (Fr 1932)
Mademoiselle Josette, ma femme (Fr 1932)
Sonnenstrahl (Aus 1933)
Quartorze juillet (Fr 1933)
La Bataille (Fr 1934)
Les Nuits moscovites (Fr 1934)
Caravane [Fr version of Caravan] (Fr 1934)
L'Equipage (Fr 1935)
Variétès (Fr 1935)
Veille d'armes (Fr 1935)
La Bandera (Fr 1935)
Anne-Marie (Fr 1936)
Wings of the Morning (20th Br 1937)
Under the Red Robe (20th Br 1937)
Dinner at the Ritz (20th Br 1937)
La Citadelle du silence (Fr 1937)
Hotel du Nord (Fr 1938)
The Baroness and the Butler (20th 1938)
Suez (20th 1938)
Bridal Suite (MGM 1939)
Tonight We Raid Calais (20th 1943)
Bomber's Moon (20th 1943)
13 Rue Madeleine (20th 1946)
Eternel Conflit (Fr 1947)
Dernier Amour (Fr 1948)
L'Homme qui revient de loin (Fr 1949)
Don Juan (Sp 1950)
Quema el suelo (Sp 1950)

ANTONELLI, LAURA, b. 1941 [1946?], Pola, Yugoslavia
    Dr. Goldfoot and the Girl Bombs [Le spie vengona dal semi-
    freddo] (USA-It 1966)

Un detective [Macchie di belletto] (It 1967)
L'arcangelo (It 1967)
La rivoluzione sessuale (It 1968)
Satyricon (It 1968)
Venere in pellicia [Venus im Pelz] (It-W Ger 1969)
Sledge (USA-It 1969)
Incontro d'amore a Bali [Avventura a Bali] (It 1969)
Verushka (It 1970)
Gradiva (It 1970)
Les mariés de l'an II [Gli sposi dell'anno secondo] (Fr-It 1970)
All'onorevole piacciono le donne (It 1971)
Il merlo maschio (It 1971)
Sans mobile apparent [Senza movente] (Fr-It 1971)
Docteur Popaul [Trappola per un lupo] (Fr-It 1972)
Malizia (It 1972)
A Man Called Jericho (USA-It 1972)
Histoire de l'oeil [Simona] (Bel-It 1973)
Peccato veniale (It 1973)
Sesso matto (It 1974)
Mio Dio, come sono caduta in basso (It 1974)
Incontro d'amore (It 1975)
La divina creatura (It 1975)
La malizia di venere (It 1975)

ARLETTY (Leonie Bathiat), b. Aug. 15, 1898
Un Chien qui rapporte (Fr 1930)
Mais n'te promène donc pas toute nue (Fr 1931)
Enlevez-moi (Fr 1932)
Feue la Mère de Madame (Fr 1932)
Un Idée Folle (Fr 1933)
Un Soir de réveillon (Fr 1933)
Je ne te confie pas ma femme (Fr 1933)
La Guerre des valses (Fr 1933)
Pension Mimosa (Fr 1934)
Le Voyage de M. Perrichon (Fr 1934)
La Fille de Madame Angot (Fr 1934)
L'Ecole des cocottes (Fr 1934)
Amants et Voleurs (Fr 1935)
Le Vertige (Fr 1935)
La Garçonne (Fr 1936)
Un Mari rêvé (Fr 1936)
Aventure à Paris (Fr 1936)
Faisons un rêvé (Fr 1937)
Mirages (Fr 1937)
Aloha, ou le chant des îles (Fr 1937)
Les Perles de la Couronne (Fr 1937)
Messieurs Les-Ronds-de-Cuir (Fr 1937)
Le Petit Chose (Fr 1938)
Désire (Fr 1938)
La Chaleur du sein (Fr 1938)
Hôtel du Nord (Fr 1938)
Si tu m'aimes (Fr 1938)
Le Jour se lève (Fr 1939)
Fric-frac (Fr 1939)

Circonstances atténuantes (Fr 1939)
Tempête (Fr 1940)
Madame sans gêne (Fr 1941)
La Femme que j'ai le plus aimée (Fr 1942)
Bolero (Fr 1942)
L'Amant de Borneo (Fr 1942)
Les Visiteurs du soir (Fr 1942)
Les Enfants du paradis [Children of Paradise] (Fr 1945)
La Fleur de l'âge (unfinished 1947)
Buffalo Bill et la bergère (Fr 1948) [unfinished]
Portrait d'un assassin (Fr 1949)
L'Amour, madame (Fr 1951)
Gibier de potence [Gigolo] (Fr 1951)
Le Père de Mademoiselle [The Father of the Girl] (Fr 1953)
Le Grand Jeu [The Card of Fate] (It-Fr 1954)
L'Air de Paris (Fr-It 1955)
Mon curé chez les pauvres (Fr 1956)
Vacances explosives (Fr 1957)
Le Passager clandestin (Fr-Australian 1958)
Et ta soeur? (Fr 1958)
Maxime (Fr 1958)
Un Drôle de dimanche (Fr 1958)
Les Petits Matins [Girl on the Road] (Fr 1961)
La Loi des hommes (Fr 1962)
La Gamberge (Fr 1962)
The Longest Day (20th 1962)
Tempo di Roma (It-Fr 1963)
Le Voyage à Biarritz (Fr-It 1963)

ATTENBOROUGH, RICHARD, b. Aug. 29, 1923, Cambridge, England
In Which We Serve (BL 1942)
The Hundred Pound Window (WB-FN 1942)
Schweik's New Adventures [It Started at Midnight] (Coronel 1943)
Journey Together (RKO 1945)
A Matter of Life and Death [Stairway to Heaven] (GFD 1946)
School for Secrets [Secret Flight] (GFD 1946)
The Man Within [The Smugglers] (GFD 1947)
Dancing with Crime (Par 1947)
Brighton Rock [Young Scarface] (Pathe 1947)
London Belongs to Me [Dulcimer Street] (GFD 1948)
The Guinea Pig [The Outsider] (Pathe 1948)
The Lost People (GFD 1949)
Boys in Brown (GFD 1949)
Morning Departure [Operation Disaster] (GFD 1950)
Hell Is Sold Out (Eros 1951)
The Magic Box (BL 1951)
The Gift Horse [Glory at Sea] (IFD 1952)
Father's Doing Fine (ABP 1952)
Eight O'Clock Walk (BL 1954)
The Ship That Died of Shame [PT Raiders] (GFD 1955)
Private's Progress (BL 1956)
The Baby and the Battleship (BL 1956)

Brothers in Law (BL 1957)
The Scamp (GN 1957)
Dunkirk (MGM 1958)
The Man Upstairs (BL 1958)
Sea of Sand [Desert Patrol] (RFD 1958)
Danger Within [Breakout] (BL 1959)
I'm All Right, Jack (BL 1959)
Jet Storm (Britannia 1959)
S. O. S. Pacific (RFD 1959)
The Angry Silence (BL 1960)
The League of Gentlemen (RFD 1960)
Only Two Can Play (BL 1962)
All Night Long (RFD 1962)
The Dock Brief [Trial and Error] (MGM 1962)
The Great Escape (UA 1963)
Seance on a Wet Afternoon (RFD 1964)
The Third Secret (20th 1964)
Guns at Batasi (20th 1964)
The Flight of the Phoenix (20th 1965)
The Sand Pebbles (20th 1966)
Doctor Dolittle (20th 1967)
The Bliss of Mrs. Blossom (Par 1968)
Only When I Larf (Par 1968)
The Magic Christian (CUE 1969)
David Copperfield (20th 1969)
The Last Grenade (CIRO 1970)
Loot (BL 1970)
A Severed Head (Col 1970)
10 Rillington Place (Col 1970)
Rosebud (UA 1974)
Brannigan (UA 1975)
Conduct Unbecoming (BL 1975)
And Then There Were None (EMI 1975)

AUDRAN, STEPHANE, b. 1939, Versailles, France
La Bonne Tisane [Kill or Cure] (Fr 1957)
Les Cousins (Fr 1959)
Le Signe du lion (Fr 1959)
Les Bonnes Femmes (Fr-It 1959)
Les Godelureaux (Fr-It 1960)
Saint-Tropez blues (Fr-It 1960)
L'Oeil du malin (It-Fr 1961)
Landru (Fr-It 1962)
Le Tigre aime la chair fraîche [The Tiger Likes Fresh Meat]
    (Fr 1964)
Les Durs à cuire (Fr 1964)
Paris vu Par (ep "La Muette") (Fr 1964)
Marie-Chantal contre Dr Kah (Fr-Sp-It-Moroccan 1965)
La Ligne de démarcation (Fr 1966)
Le Scandale [The Champagne Murders] (Fr 1966)
Les Biches (Fr-It 1968)
La Femme infidèle [The Unfaithful Wife] (Fr-It 1968)
La Peau de torpédo [Pill of Death] (Fr-W Ger-It 1969)

Stéphane Audran appearing in Le Scandale (1967).

Le Boucher [The Butcher] (Fr-It 1969)
La Dame dans l'auto avec des lunettes et un fusil [The Lady in the Car with Glasses and a Gun] (Fr 1970)
La Rupture (Fr-It-Bel 1970)
Juste avant la nuit [Just Before Nightfall] (Fr-It 1971)
Sans mobile apparent senza movente (Fr-It 1971)
Aussi loin qui l'amour (Fr 1971)
Un Meurtre est un meurtre (Fr 1972)
Kressu und die tote Taube in der Beethovenstrasse [Dead Pigeon on Beethovenstrasse] (W Ger 1972)
Le Charme discret de la bourgeoisie [The Discreet Charm of the Bourgeoisie] (Fr 1972)
Les Noces rouges [Blood Wedding] (Fr-It 1973)
Comment reussir dans la vie quand on est con et pleurnichard (Fr 1973)
Hay que matar A. B. (Sp 1973)
Le Cri du coeur (Fr 1974)
Vincent, François, Paul et les autres (Fr 1974)
Chi dice donna dice...danno (It 1975)

AULIN, EWA, b. Feb. 13, 1950, Stockholm
Don Giovanni in Sicilia (It 1967)

Col cuore in gola [Deadly Sweet] (It-Fr 1967)
La morte ha fatto l'uovo [La mort a pondu un oeuf/Plucked]
    (It-Fr 1968)
Candy [Candy e il suo pazzo mondo] (USA-It-Fr 1969)
Start the Revolution Without Me (WB 1969)
La controfigura (It 1971)
Questa specie d'amore (It 1972)
Rosina Fumo viene in città per farsi il corredo (It 1972)
Sette strani cadaveri (It 1972)
Ceremonia sangrienta [The Legend of Blood Castle] (Sp 1972)
Fiorina la vacca (It 1972)
Il tuo piacere e il mio (It 1973)
La morte sorride all'assassino (It 1973)
Quando l'amore è sensualita (It 1973)
Una vita lunga un giorno (It 1974)

AUMONT, JEAN-PIERRE (Jean Pierre Salomon), b. Jan. 5, 1909,
    Paris
Echec et Mat (Fr 1931)
Jean de la lune (Fr 1932)
Eve cherche un père (Fr 1932)
Faut-il les marier? (Fr 1932)
La Tragédie de Lourdes (Fr 1933)
Dans les rues (Fr 1933)
Lac aux dames (Fr 1934)
Le Voleur (Fr 1934)
Maria Chapdelaine (Fr 1934)
Un Jour viendra (Fr 1935)
Les Yeux noirs (Fr 1935)
L'Equipage (Fr 1935)
Les Beaux Jours (Fr 1935)
Tarass Boulba (Fr 1936)
La Porte du large (Fr 1936)
Cargaison Blanche (Fr 1936)
Le Messager (Fr 1937)
Drôle de drame (Fr 1937)
Maman Colibri (Fr 1937)
La Femme du bout du monde (Fr 1937)
Chéri Bibi (Fr 1938)
Le Paradis de Satan (Fr 1938)
Hôtel du nord (Fr 1938)
La Belle Etoile (Fr 1938)
S.O.S. Sahara (Fr 1938)
Je t'attendrai [Le Déserter] (Fr 1939)
Bizarre Bizarre (Fr 1939)
Song of the Street (Mayer-Burstyn 1939)
Assignment in Brittany (MGM 1943)
The Cross of Lorraine (MGM 1944)
Heartbeat (RKO 1946)
Song of Scheherazade (Univ 1947)
Siren of Atlantis (UA 1948)
The First Gentleman [Affairs of a Rogue] (Col Br 1948)
Hans le marin (Fr 1949)
Golden Arrow [Three Men and a Girl; The Gay Adventure]

(Renown 1949)
La Vie commence demain (Fr 1949)
L'Homme de joie (Fr 1950)
L'Amant de paille (Fr 1950)
La vendetta del corsaro [The Pirates' Vengeance] (It 1950)
Ultimo incontro (It-Fr 1951)
Les Loups chassent la nuit (Fr 1951)
Lili (MGM 1953)
Moineaux de Paris (Fr 1953)
Königsmark (Fr-It 1953)
Si Versailles m'etait conté (Fr 1953)
Dix-huit Heures d'escale (Fr 1954)
Charge of the Lancers (Col 1954)
Napoléon (Fr 1954)
Mademoiselle de Paris (Fr 1955)
Hilda Crane [The Many Loves of Hilda Crane] (20th 1956)
The Seventh Sin (MGM 1957)
La Passe dangereuse (Fr 1958)
John Paul Jones (WB 1959)
La Verte Moisson (Fr 1959)
Domenica d'estate (It 1959)
La Blonde de Buenos Aires [The Blonde of Buenos Aires] (Arg 1959)
The Enemy General (Col 1960)
The Devil at Four O'Clock (Col 1961)
Les Sept Péchés capitaux [Seven Capital Sins] (Fr-It 1961)
Le Couteau dans la plaie [Five Miles to Midnight] (Fr 1962)
Un Dimanche d'été [Always on Sunday] (It-Fr 1962)
Vacances Portugaises (Fr 1963)
El coleccionista de cadavres [Cauldron of Blood/Blind Man's Bluff] (Sp-USA 1967)
Castle Keep (Col 1969)
L'Homme au cerveau greffe (Fr-It-W Ger 1972)
La Nuit américaine [Day for Night] (Fr 1973)
Porgi l'altra guancia [Turn the Other Cheek] (Fr-It 1974)
The Man in the Iron Mask (Fr 1975)
The Happy Hooker (Cannon 1975)
Catherine et Cie (Fr-It 1975)

AZNAVOUR, CHARLES (Charles Aznavourian), b. May 28, 1924, Paris
Les Disparus de St. Agil (Fr 1938)
Music Hall (documentary) (Fr 1942)
Une Gosse "sensass" (Fr 1956)
Paris Music-Hall (Fr 1957)
C'est arrivé à Chandelles (Fr 1957)
La Tête contre les murs [The Keepers] (Fr 1958)
Les Dragueurs [The Young Have No Morals] (Fr 1959)
Le Testament d'Orphée (Fr 1960)
Tirez sur le pianiste [Shoot the Piano Player] (Fr 1960)
Le Passage du Rhin [The Crossing of the Rhine] (Fr-W Ger 1960)
Un Taxi pour Tobrouk [Taxi for Tobruk] (Fr-W Ger-Sp 1960)
Horace 62 (Fr 1962)

Le Diable et les dix commandements (Fr-It 1962)
Pourquoi Paris? (Fr-It 1962)
Les Quatre Vérités (Fr-It-Sp 1963)
Le Rat d'Amérique (Fr-It 1963)
Cherchez l'idole (Fr-It 1963)
Les Vierges (Fr 1963)
Tempo di Roma (It-Fr 1963)
La Métamorphose des cloportes (Fr 1964)
Altà infedeltà [High Infidelity] (ep "Peccato nel pomeriggio")
    (It-Fr 1964)

Charles Aznavour with Claire Bloom in High Infidelity (1964).

Paris au mois d'août (Fr 1965)
Le Facteur s'en va-t-en guerre [The Postman Goes to War]
    (Fr 1967)
Caroline chérie (Fr-It-W Ger 1967)
Candy (USA-It-Fr 1968)
The Games (20th 1969)
Le Temps des loups [Carbon Copy] (Fr-It 1969)
The Adventurers (Par 1970)
Un Beau Monstre (Fr-It 1970)

La Part des lions (Fr 1971)
Les Intrus (Fr 1971)
The Blockhouse (Hemdale 1973)

BAAL, KARIN, b. 1940, Berlin
Die Halbstarken (W Ger 1956)
Jede Nacht in einem andern Bett (W Ger 1957)
Das Herz von St. Pauli (W Ger 1957)
Der müde Theodor (W Ger 1957)
Das Mädchen Rosemarie (W Ger 1958)
Der eiserne Gustav (W Ger 1958)
So angelt man keinen Mann (W Ger 1959)
Jons und Erdme (W Ger 1959)
Bobby Dodd greift ein (W Ger 1959)
Der Jugendrichter (W Ger 1959)
Arzt ohne Gewissen (W Ger 1959)
Wir Kellerkinder (W Ger 1960)
Die junge Sünderin (W Ger 1960)
Vertauschtes Leben (W Ger 1961)
Die toten Augen von London (W Ger 1961)
Blond muss man sein auf Capri (W Ger 1961)
Das letzte Kapitel (W Ger 1961)
Und so was nennt sich Leben (W Ger 1961)
Zwischen Shanghai und St. Pauli (W Ger-It 1962)
Strasse der Verheissung (W Ger 1962)
So toll wie anno dazumal (W Ger 1962)
Mord am Canale Grande (W Ger 1964)
Ganovenehre (W Ger 1966)
Der Hund von Blackwood Castle (W Ger 1967)
Hannibal Brooks (UA 1969)
Cosa avete fatto a Solange (It-W Ger 1970)
Das Geheimnis der grünen Stecknadel (W Ger-It 1972)

BAKER, STANLEY, b. Feb. 28, 1928, Ferndale, Glamorganshire,
        Wales; d. June 28, 1976
Undercover [Underground Guerrillas] (UA 1943)
All Over Town (GFD 1949)
Your Witness [Eye Witness] (WB 1950)
Lilli Marlene (Monarch 1950)
The Rossiter Case (Ex 1951)
Cloudburst (Ex 1951)
Captain Horatio Hornblower, R. N. (WB Br 1951)
Home to Danger (Eros 1951)
Whispering Smith Hits London [Whispering Smith versus Scotland
        Yard] (Ex 1952)
The Cruel Sea (GFD 1953)
The Red Beret [Paratrooper] (Col 1953)
Hell Below Zero (Col 1954)
The Good Die Young (IFD 1954)
Beautiful Stranger [Twist of Fate] (BL 1954)
Knights of the Round Table (MGM 1954)
Helen of Troy (WB 1955)
Richard III (IFD 1955)

Stanley Baker

Alexander the Great (UA 1956)
Child in the House (Eros 1956)
A Hill in Korea [Hell in Korea] (BL 1956)
Checkpoint (RFD 1956)
Hell Drivers (RFD 1957)
Campbell's Kingdom (RFD 1957)
Violent Playground (RFD 1958)
Sea Fury (RFD 1958)
The Angry Hills (MGM 1959)
Yesterday's Enemy (Col 1959)
Jet Storm (Britannia 1959)
Blind Date [Chance Meeting] (RFD 1959)
Hell Is a City (WPD 1960)
The Criminal [The Concrete Jungle] (AA 1960)
The Guns of Navarone (Col 1961)
Sodoma e Gomorra [Sodom and Gomorrah] (It-USA 1962)
Eva [Eve] (It 1962)
In the French Style (Col 1963)
A Prize of Arms (Bry 1962)
The Man Who Finally Died (Magna 1962)
Zulu (Par 1963)
Dingaka [S. Africa 1965]
Sands of the Kalahari (Par 1965)
La ragazza con la pistola [The Girl with the Pistol] (It 1967)
Accident (LIP 1967)
Robbery (Par 1967)
Where's Jack? (Par 1969)
The Games (20th 1969)

The Last Grenade (CIRO 1970)
Perfect Friday (London Screenplays 1970)
Popsy Pop [The 21 Carat Snatch] (Fr-It 1970)
Una lucertola con la pelle di donna [A Lizard with a Woman's
    Skin] (It-Fr 1971)
Innocent Bystanders (Par 1972)
Zorro (Fr-It 1975)

BANKS, LESLIE, b. June 9, 1890, West Derby, England; d. April
    21, 1952
The Most Dangerous Game [The Hounds of Zaroff] (RKO 1932)
Strange Evidence (Par 1933)
The Fire Raisers (W & F 1933)
I Am Suzanne (Fox 1934)
The Night of the Party (Gaumont 1934)
Red Ensign [Strike!] (Gaumont 1934)
The Man Who Knew Too Much (Gaumont 1934)
Sanders of the River (UA Br 1935)
The Tunnel [Transatlantic Tunnel] (Gaumont 1935)
Debt of Honour (GFD 1936)
The Three Maxims [The Show Goes On] (GFD 1936)
Fire Over England (UA Br 1937)
Wings of the Morning (20th Br 1937)
Farewell Again [Troopship] (UA Br 1937)
21 Days [21 Days Together] (Col Br 1937)
Jamaica Inn (ABPC 1939)
Dead Man's Shoes (ABPC 1939)
The Arsenal Stadium Mystery (GFD 1939)
Sons of the Sea (GN 1939)
The Door with Seven Locks [Chamber of Horrors] (Pathe 1940)
Busman's Honeymoon [Haunted Honeymoon] (MGM Br 1940)
Neutral Port (GFD 1940)
Cottage to Let [Bombsight Stolen] (GFD 1941)
Ships with Wings (UA Br 1941)
The Big Blockade (UA Br 1942)
Went the Day Well? [48 Hours] (UA Br 1942)
Henry V (EL 1945)
Mrs. Fitzherbert (Pathe 1947)
The Small Back Room [Hour of Glory] (BL 1949)
Your Witness [Eye Witness] (WB Br 1950)
Madeleine [Strange Case of Madeleine] (GFD 1950)

BANNEN, IAN, b. June 29, 1928, Airdrie, Lanarkshire, Scotland
Private's Progress (BL 1956)
The Long Arm [The Third Key] (RFD 1956)
Miracle in Soho (RFD 1957)
Yangtse Incident [Battle Hell] (BL 1957)
The Birthday Present (BL 1957)
A Tale of Two Cities (RFD 1958)
She Didn't Say No! (ABP 1958)
Behind the Mask (BL 1958)
Carlton-Browne of the F.O. [Man in a Cocked Hat] (BL 1959)
A French Mistress (BL 1960)

Suspect (BL 1960)
On Friday at Eleven [The World in My Pocket] (GB-W Ger 1961)
Macbeth (BL 1961)
Station Six Sahara (BL 1962)
Psyche 59 (Col 1963)
Mister Moses (UA 1964)
The Hill (MGM 1965)
Rotten to the Core (BL 1965)
The Flight of the Phoenix (20th 1965)
Penelope (MGM 1966)
The Sailor from Gibraltar (UA 1967)
Lock Up Your Daughters! (Col 1969)
Too Late the Hero (Cin 1970)
La spina dorsale del diavolo [The Deserter] (It-Yug-USA 1970)
Jane Eyre (BL 1971)
Fright (BL 1971)
Doomwatch [Something Like the Truth] (Tigon 1972)
The Offence (UA 1972)
The Mackintosh Man (WB 1973)
From Beyond the Grave (ep "An Act of Kindness") (Col-War 1974)
Identikit (It 1974)
Il viaggio [The Voyage] (It 1974)
Bite the Bullet (Col 1975)

BARDOT, BRIGITTE, b. Sept. 28, 1934, Paris
Le Trou normand [Crazy for Love] (Fr 1952)
Manina, la fille sans voile [The Girl in the Bikini] (Fr 1952)
Les Dents longues (Fr 1952) [cameo]
Le Portrait de son père (Fr 1953)
Si Versailles m'était conté (Fr 1953)
Act of Love (USA-Fr 1954)
Tradita [Night of Love] (Fr-It 1954)
Le Fils de Caroline chérie (Fr 1954)
Helen of Troy (WB 1954)
Futures vedettes (Fr 1955)
Doctor at Sea (GFD 1955)
Les Grandes Manoeuvres [Summer Manoeuvres] (Fr-It 1955)
La lumière d'en face [The Light Across the Street] (Fr 1955)
Cette Sacrée Gamine [Mam'zelle Pigalle] (Fr 1955)
Mio figlio Nerone (It-Fr 1956)
En effeuillant la Marguerite [Please, Mr. Balzac] (Fr 1956)
Et Dieu créa la femme [And God Created Woman] (Fr 1956)
La Mariée est trop belle [The Bride Is Much Too Beautiful]
   (Fr 1956)
Une Parisienne [Parisienne] (Fr-It 1957)
Les Bijoutiers du clair de lune [The Night Heaven Fell] (Fr-It
   1957)
En cas de malheur [Love Is My Profession] (Fr-It 1958)
La Femme et le pantin [The Female] (Fr-It 1958)
Babette s'en va-t-en guerre [Babette Goes to War] (Fr 1959)
Voulez-vous danser avec moi? [Come Dance with Me] (Fr-It
   1959)
La Vérité [The Truth] (Fr-It 1960)

Brigitte Bardot (left) and Jeanne Moreau in <u>Viva Maria!</u> (1965).

L'Affaire d'une nuit (Fr 1960)
La Bride sur le cou [Only for Love] (Fr-It 1961)
Vie privée [A Very Private Affair] (Fr-It 1961)
Amours célèbres (ep "Agnes Bernauer") (Fr-It 1961)
Le Repos du guerrier [Love on a Pillow] (Fr-It 1962)
Le Mépris [Contempt] (Fr-It 1963)
Marie Soleil (Fr 1964) [uncredited cameo]
Une Ravissante Idiote [Adorable Idiot] (Fr-It 1964)
Viva Maria! (Fr-It 1965)
Dear Brigitte (20th 1965) (cameo)
Masculin-feminin [Masculine-Feminine] (Fr-Swe 1966) (cameo)
A coeur joie [Two Weeks in September] (Fr-GB 1967)
Histoires extraordinaires [Spirits of the Dead] (ep "William
    Wilson") (Fr-It 1967)
Shalako (Cin 1968)
L'Ours et la poupée [The Bear and the Doll] (Fr 1969)
Les Femmes (Fr-It 1969)
Les Novices (Fr-It 1970)
Les Pétroleuses (Fr-Sp-GB-It 1971)
Boulevard du Rhum (Fr 1971)
Don Juan 1973 (Fr-It 1973)
L'Histoire très bonne et très joyeuse de Colinot Trousse-
    Chemise (Fr-It 1973)

BARRAULT, JEAN-LOUIS, b. Sept. 9, 1910, Le Vesinet, Seine,
    France
Les Beaux Jours (Fr 1935)
Sous les yeux d'Occident (Fr 1936)
A nous deux, madame la vie (Fr 1936)
Un Grand Amour de Beethoven (Fr 1936)
Helene (Fr 1936)
Jenny (Fr 1936)
Mademoiselle Docteur (Fr 1937)
Police mondaine (Fr 1937)
Le Puritain (Fr 1937)
Les Perles de la Couronne (Fr 1937)
Mirages (Fr 1937)
Drôle de drame (Fr 1937)
Altitude 3200 (Fr 1937)
Nous les jeunes (Fr 1938)
Orage (Fr 1938)
La Piste du Sud (Fr 1938)
Farinet oder das falsche Geld (Ger 1939)
Le Destin fabuleux de Desirée Clary (Fr 1941)
Parade en sept nuits (Fr 1941)
Montmartre-sur-Seine (Fr 1941)
La Symphonie fantastique (Fr 1942)
Lumière d'été (Fr 1943)
L'Ange de la nuit (Fr 1943)
Les Enfants du paradis [Children of Paradise] (Fr 1945)
La Part de l'ombre (Fr 1945)
Le Cocu magnifique (Bel 1946)
D'homme à hommes (Fr 1948)

La Ronde (Fr 1950)
Si Versailles m'était conté (Fr 1953)
Le Dialogue de Carmélites (Fr-It 1959)
Le Miracle des loups [Blood on His Sword] (Fr-It 1961)
Le Testament du Docteur Cordelier (Fr 1961)
Architecture, art de l'espoir (Bel 1961) (narrator)
The Longest Day (20th 1962)
La Grande Frousse/La Cité de l'indicible peur (Fr 1964)
Chappaqua (Hunter 1966)

BATES, ALAN, b. 1934, Allestree, Derbyshire, England
The Entertainer (Bry 1960)
Whistle Down the Wind (RFD 1961)
A Kind of Loving (AA 1962)
The Running Man (Col 1963)
The Caretaker [The Guest] (BL 1963)
Nothing but the Best (AA 1963)
Zorba the Greek (20th 1964)
Georgy Girl (Col 1966)
Le Roi de coeur [King of Hearts] (Fr-It 1966)
Far from the Madding Crowd (MGM 1967)
The Fixer (MGM 1968)
Women in Love (UA 1969)
Three Sisters (BL 1970)
The Go-Between (MGM-EMI 1971)
A Day in the Death of Joe Egg (Col 1972)
L'Impossible Objet [Impossible Object] (Fr 1973)
Bartley (AFT 1974)
In Celebration (AFT 1974)
Royal Flash (Fox-Rank 1975)

BAUR, HARRY, b. 1880, Montrouge, France; d. April 20, 1943
Shylock (Fr 1913)
Le Solitaire (Fr 1913)
L'Ame du bronze (Fr 1916)
La Voyante (Fr 1923)
Le Juif polonais (Fr 1931)
Poil de carotte (Fr 1932)
La Tête d'un homme (Fr 1933)
Cette Vieille canaille (Fr 1933)
Les Misérables (Fr 1934) [3 parts]
Un Homme en or (Fr 1934)
Rotchild (Fr 1934)
Le Greluchon delicat (Fr 1934)
Nuits moscovites (Fr 1934)
Moscow Nights [I Stand Condemned; Eng lang version of Nuits
    moscovites] (GFD 1935)
Crime et châtiment (Fr 1935)
Les Yeux noirs (Fr 1935)
Golgotha (Fr 1935)
Samson (Fr 1936)
Tarass Boulba (Fr 1936)
Le Golem (Fr 1936)

Harry Baur

Nitchevo (Fr 1936)
Un Grand Amour de Beethoven (Fr 1936)
Paris (Fr 1937)
Sarati le terrible (Fr 1937)
Un Carnet de bal (Fr 1937)
Les Secrets de la Mer Rouge (Fr 1937)
Mollenard (Fr 1938)
Le Patriote (Fr 1938)
Tragédie impériale (Fr 1938)
Le President Haudecoeur (Fr 1938)
Volpone (Fr 1939)
L'Assassinat du Père Noël (Fr 1941)
Pêchés de jeunesse (Fr 1942)
Symphonie eines Lebens (Ger 1943)

BEATTY, ROBERT, b. Oct. 19, 1909, Hamilton, Ontario, Canada
    Murder in Soho [Murder in the Night] (ABPC 1939)
    Mein Kampf [My Struggle] (ABPC 1940)
    Dangerous Moonlight [Suicide Squadron] (RKO-Radio 1941)
    49th Parallel [The Invaders] (GFD 1941)
    One of Our Aircraft Is Missing (Anglo 1942)
    Suspected Person (Pathe 1942)

San Demetrio-London (Ealing 1943)
It Happened One Sunday (Pathe 1944)
Appointment with Crime (Anglo 1946)
Odd Man Out (GFD 1947)
Green Fingers (Anglo 1947)
Against the Wind (GFD 1948)
Counterblast (Pathe 1948)
Another Shore (GFD 1948)
Portrait from Life [The Girl in the Painting] (GFD 1948)
The Twenty Questions Murder Mystery [Murder on the Air]*
     (GN 1950)
Her Favourite Husband [The Taming of Dorothy] (Renown 1950)
Captain Horatio Hornblower, R. N. (WB Br 1951)
Calling Bulldog Drummond (MGM Br 1951)
The Magic Box (BL 1951)
Wings of Danger [Dead on Course] (Ex 1952)
The Gentle Gunman (GFD 1952)
The Net [Project M7] (GFD 1953)
The Oracle [The Horse's Mouth] (ABFD 1953)
The Square Ring (GFD 1953)
The Broken Horseshoe (Butcher 1953)
The Master of Ballantrae (WB 1953)
Albert, R. N. [Break to Freedom] (Eros 1953)
L'amanti di Paridi [The Face That Launched a Thousand Ships]
     (Fr-It 1953)
Out of the Clouds (GFD 1955)
Portrait of Alison [Postmark for Danger] (AA 1955)
Time Lock (IFD 1957)
Tarzan and the Lost Safari (MGM 1957)
The Shakedown (RFD 1960)
The Amorous Prawn (BL 1962)
Bikini Paradise (AIP 1964)
One Million Years B. C. (20th 1966) (voice only)
2001: A Space Odyssey (MGM 1968)
Where Eagles Dare (MGM 1968)
Sitting Target (MGM-EMI 1972)
Pope Joan [The Devil's Impostor] (Col Br 1972) (role cut from
     British release print)
The Spikes Gang (UA 1974)

BELL, MARIE (Marie-Jeanne Bellon-Downey), b. Dec. 23, 1900,
          Bègles (Gironde), France
     Paris (Fr 1924)
     La Valse de l'adieu (Fr 1926)
     Madame Récamier (Fr 1928)
     Figaro (Fr 1929)
     La Nuit est à nous (Fr 1929)
     Le Soker (Swe 1930)
     L'Homme qui assassina (Fr 1930)
     La Folle Aventure (Fr 1930)
     La Chance (Fr 1931)
     L'Homme à l'hispano (Fr 1932)
     Caprices de princesse (Fr 1933)

Le Grand Jeu (Fr 1934)
Fédora (Fr 1934)
Poliche (Fr 1934)
Le Roman d'un jeune homme pauvre (Fr 1935)
Sous la terreur (Fr 1935)
La Garçonne (Fr 1936)
Quand minuit sonnera (Fr 1936)
La Tentation (Fr 1936)
Blanchette (Fr 1936)
Les Demi-Vierges (Fr 1936)
Pantins d'amour (Fr 1936)
La Glu (Fr 1936)
Un Carnet de bal (Fr 1937)
Legion d'honneur (Fr 1938)
Vidocq (Fr 1938)
La Charrette Fantôme (Fr 1939)
Noix de coco (Fr 1939)
Ceux du ciel (Fr 1940)
Vie privée (Fr 1942)
Le Colonel Chabert (Fr 1943)
La Bonne Soupe (Fr-It 1963)
Vaghe stelle dell'orsa (It 1965)

BELLI, AGOSTINA (Agostina Maria Magnoni), b. April 13, 1947,
   Milan
Banditi a Milano [Bandits at Milan] (It-Fr 1968)
Cran d'Arrêt (Fr 1969)
Il terribile ispettore (It 1969)
Angeli senza paradiso (It 1970)
Ivanna (Sp-It 1971)

Agostina Belli

Mimi Metallurgico, ferito nell'onore [The Seduction of Mimi]
    (It 1972)
La Calandria (It 1972)
La notte dei diavoli (It 1972)
Baciamo le mani (It 1972)
Barbablu (It 1972)
Ma che musica, maestro (It 1972)
Quando l'amore è sensualità (It 1972)
All'onorevole piacciono le donne (It 1972)
Giornata nera par l'Ariete [Le Jour Malefique] (It-Bel 1972)
L'ultima neve di primavera (It 1973)
La sepolta viva (It 1973)
Revolver [La Poursuite Implacable] (It-Fr 1973)
Virilità (It 1973)
Milano odia: la polizia non puo sparare (It 1974)
La governante (It 1974)
La coppià dispari (It 1974)
Le Jeu avec le feu (Fr-It 1974)
Il piatto piange (It 1974)
Profumo di Donna [Parfum de femmes] (It-Fr 1974)
Il lumacone (It 1974)
Conviene far bene l'amore (It 1974)
Due cuori e una cappella (It 1975)

BELMONDO, JEAN-PAUL, b. April 9, 1933, Neuilly-sur-Seine,
    France
A pied, à cheval et en voiture (Fr-It 1957)
Sois belle et tais-toi [Blonde for Danger] (Fr 1958)
Drôle de dimanche (Fr 1958)
Les Tricheurs [Youthful Sinners] (Fr 1958)
Les Copains du dimanche (Fr 1958) (unreleased)
Ein Engel auf Erden (W Ger-Fr 1959)
A bout de souffle [Breathless] (Fr 1959)
A Double Tour [Leda] (Fr-It 1959)
Classe tous risques [The Big Risk] (Fr-It 1960)
Les Distractions [Trapped by Fear] (Fr-It 1960)
La Française et l'Amour [Love and the Frenchwoman] (ep
    "L'Adultere") (Fr 1960)
Lettere di una novizia (It-Fr 1960)
Moderato Cantabile [Seven Days... Seven Nights] (Fr 1960)
La ciociara [Two Women] (It-Fr 1961)
La viaccia [The Love Maker] (It-Fr 1961)
Leon Morin, prêtre (Fr-It 1961)
Une Femme est une femme [A Woman Is a Woman] (Fr 1961)
Amours célèbres (Fr-It 1961)
Un Nommé La Rocca (Fr-It 1961)
Cartouche [Swords of Blood] (Fr-It 1961)
Un Singe en hiver [It's Hot in Hell] (Fr 1962)
Le Doulos [Doulos the Finger Man] (Fr 1962)
I Don Giovanni della Costa Azzura (It 1962)
L'Ainé des Ferchaux (Fr 1962)
Un Coeur gros comme ça [The Winner] (Fr 1962) [documentary]
Mare matto (It-Fr 1963)

Jean-Paul Belmondo

I giorno più corto [The Shortest Day] (It-Fr 1963)
Dragées au poivre [Sweet and Sour] (Fr-It 1963)
Peau de banane [Banana Skin] (Fr-It 1963)
L'Homme de Rio [That Man from Rio] (Fr-It 1963)
Cent Mille Dollars au soleil [Greed in the Sun] (Fr-It 1963)
Echappement libre [Backfire] (Fr-It-Sp 1964)
La Chasse à l'homme [Male Hunt] (Fr-It 1964)
Weekend à Zuydcoote [Weekend at Dunkirk] (Fr 1964)
Par un beau matin d'été (Fr-It-Sp 1964)
Les Tribulations d'un chinois en Chine [Up to His Ears] (Fr-It
    1965)
Pierrot le fou (Fr-It 1965)
Paris brûle-t-il? [Is Paris Burning?] (Par 1966)
Tendre voyou (Fr-It 1966)
Le Voleur [The Thief of Paris] (Fr-It 1966)
Casino Royale (Col 1967)
Ho! [Ho "Criminal Face"] (Fr-It 1968)
Le Cerveau (Fr-It 1969)
La Sirène du Mississippi [Mississippi Mermaid] (Fr-It 1969)
Un Homme qui me plaît (Fr 1969)
Dieu a choisi Paris [God Chose Paris] (Fr 1969)
Borsalino (Fr-It 1970)
Les Mariés de l'an II [The Scoundrel] (Fr-It-Rum 1970)
Le Casse [The Burglars] (Fr-It 1971)
Docteur Popaul (Fr 1972)
La Scoumoune [Hit Man] (Fr-It 1972)
L'Héritier [The Inheritor] (Fr-It 1973)
Le Magnifique [How to Destroy the Reputation of the World's
    Greatest Secret Agent] (Fr-It 1973)

Stavisky (Fr 1973)
Peur sur la ville (Fr 1975)
L'Incorrigible (Fr 1975)
L'Alpagueur (Fr 1975)

BENUSSI, FEMI (Eufemia Benussi), b. 1948, Yugoslavia
Il boia scarlatto (It 1965)
Uccellacci e uccellini (It 1966)
Un brivido sulla pelle (It 1966)
A suon di lupara [The Biggest Bundle of Them All] (It-USA 1966)
Omicidio per appuntamento (It 1967)
OO (It 1967)
Radhapura [Endstation der Verdammten] (W Ger 1967)
Nato per uccidere (It 1967)
Omicidio per vocazione (It 1968)
Frau Wirtin hat auch einen Grafen [Susanna ed i suoi dolci vizi
    alla corte del re] (W Ger-It 1968)
Vacanze sulla Costa Smeralda (It 1968)
L'uomo venuto per uccidere (It-Sp 1968)
Le calde notti di Poppea (It 1968)
Samoa, regina della giungla (It 1968)
El Zorro (It 1968)
Il rosso segno della follia [Un hacha para la luna de miel] (It-
    Sp 1968)
Requiem per un gringo [Requiem para el gringo] (It-Sp 1968)
Tarzana, sesso selvaggio (It 1969)
Quintana (It-Sp 1969)
Homo eroticus (It 1969)
I tre Supermen della giungla [Los tres Supermen en la selva]
    (It-Sp 1969)
Rivelazioni di un maniaco sessuale al capo della squadra mobile
    (It 1970)
La morte bussa due volte [Blonde Köder für den Mörder] (It-
    W Ger 1971)
Questa libertà di avere le ali bagnate (It 1971)
Se ti incontro, ti ammazzo (It 1971)
Le belve (It 1971)
Un apprezzato professionista di sicuro avvenire (It 1972)
Le calde notti del Decamerone (It 1972)
I giochi proibiti dell'Aretino Pietro [Di Pietro l'Aretino si rac-
    conta] (It 1972)
Il prode Anselmo (It 1972)
Blood Story (It 1972)
L'ultimo Decamerone (It 1972)
Finalmente le mille e una notte (It 1972)
Canterbury proibito (It 1972)
Poppea, prostituta al servizio dell'impero (It 1972)
Paolo il caldo (It 1973)
La ragazza di Via Condotti (It-Sp 1973)
Leva lo diavolo tuo dal convento (It 1973)
Quando l'amore e sensualita (It 1973)
La mala ordina [Der Mafia-Boss--sie töteten wie Schakale]
    (It-W Ger 1973)

Il tuo piacere è il mio (It 1973)
Adolescence pervertie [Adolescenza perversa] (Fr-It 1973)
Il figlioccio del padrino (It 1973)
Ingrid sulla strada (It 1973)
Carnalità (It 1974)
Bruna formosa cerca superdotato [La Partouze] (It 1974)
C'est plus facile de garder la bouche ouverte (Fr-It 1974)
A pugni nudi (It 1974)
L'infedele nuda (It 1974)
La dove non batte il sole [Blood Money] (It-Hong Kong 1974)
Il domestico (It 1974)
La sanguisuga conduce la danza (It 1975)
So Sweet, So Dead (It 1975)
Lezioni private (It 1975)

BERGER, HELMUT (Helmut Steinberger), b. May 29, 1944, Salz-
    burg, Austria
As Helmut Steinberger:
    Le streghe [The Witches] (ep "La strega bruciata viva") (It 1967)
As Helmut Berger:
    I giovani tigri [The Young Tigers] (It 1968)
    La caduta degli Dei [Götterdämmerung/The Damned] (It 1969)
    Sai cosa faceva Stalin alle donne? [Do You Know What Stalin
        Did to Women?] (It-Fr 1969)
    Das Bildnis des Dorian Gray [Il dio chiamato Dorian/Dorian
        Gray] (W Ger-It 1970)
    Il giardino dei Finzi-Contini [The Garden of the Finzi-Continis]
        It 1971)
    Un Beau Monstre [A Strange Love Affair] (Fr-It 1971)
    Una farfalla con le ali insanguinate [A Butterfly with Bloody
        Wings] (It 1971)
    La colonna infame (It 1972)
    Ludwig II [Le Crepuscule des Dieux/Ludwig] (W Ger-Fr-It 1973)
    Les Voraces [Così bello, così corrotto, così conteso/The Greedy
        Ones] (Fr-It 1973)
    Ash Wednesday (Par 1973)
    Reigen (W Ger 1973)
    La testa del serpente [El clan de los immorales/Ordine di ucci-
        cere/Order to Kill] (Sp-It 1975)
    Gruppo di famiglia in un interno [Conversation Piece] (It 1975)
    The Romantic Englishwoman (GB-Fr 1975)

BERGER, SENTA, b. May 13, 1943, Vienna
    Die unentschuldigte Stunde (Aus 1957)
    Die Lindenwirtin vom Donaustrand (W Ger 1957)
    The Journey (MGM 1958)
    Der veruntreute Himmel (W Ger 1958)
    Der brave Soldat Schweik (W Ger 1960)
    Ich heirate Herrn Direktor (Aus 1960)
    O sole Mio (W Ger 1960)
    Adieu, Lebewohl, good bye (W Ger 1961)
    Eine hübscher als die andere (W Ger 1961)
    Es muss nicht immer Kaviar sein (W Ger 1961)

Diesmal muss es Kaviar sein (W Ger-Fr 1961)
The Secret Ways (Univ 1961)
Immer Aerger mit dem Bett (W Ger 1961)
Junge Leute brauchen Liebe (Aus 1961)
Ramona (W Ger 1961)
Das Wunder des Malachias (W Ger 1961)
Frauenarzt Dr. Sibelius (W Ger 1962)
Das Geheimnis der schwarzen Koffer (W Ger 1962)
Sherlock Holmes und das Halsband des Todes (W Ger-It-Fr
    1962)
Das Testament des Dr. Mabuse (W Ger 1962)
The Waltz King (BV 1963)
Jack und Jenny (W Ger 1963)
The Victors (Col 1963)
Kali Yug I--Göttin der Rache [Kali-Yug, la dea della vendetta/Kali-
    Yug, déesse de la vengeance] (W Ger-It-Fr 1964)
Kali Yug II--Das Geheimnis des indischen Tempels [Il misterio
    del tempio indiano/Le mystere du temple hindou] (W Ger-It-
    Fr 1964)
Major Dundee (Col 1965)
The Glory Guys (UA 1965)
Schüsse im 3/4 Takt [Du suif dans l'Orient-Express] (Aus-Fr
    1965)
The Spy with My Face (MGM 1966)
Lange Beine, lange Finger (W Ger 1966)
Unser Boss ist eine Dame [Operazione San Gennaro] (W Ger-It-
    Fr 1966)
Cast a Giant Shadow (UA 1966)
Our Man in Marrakesh [Bang Bang...You're Dead] (AA 1966)
The Poppy Is Also a Flower (Comet 1966)
The Quiller Memorandum (20th 1966)
Peau d'espion [Congiura di spie/Der grausame Job/To Commit
    a Murder] (Fr-It-W Ger 1966)
Diaboliquement votre [Mit teuflischen Grüssen/Diabolically Yours]
    (Fr-W Ger 1967)
The Ambushers (Col 1967)
Cuori solitari (It 1968)
Geier könner warten [Les Etrangers/Quelli che sanno uccidere]
    (W Ger-Fr-It 1968)
Infanzia, vocazione e prime esperienze di Giacomo Casanova,
    veneziano (It 1968)
If It's Tuesday, This Must Be Belgium (UA 1969)
De Sade (AIP 1969)
Un anguilla da trecento milioni (It 1970)
Quando le donne avevano la coda (It 1970)
Le Saut de l'ange [Da parte degli amici firmato mafia] (Fr-It
    1971)
Wer im Glashaus lebt...der Graben (W Ger 1971)
Quando le donne persero la coda (It 1972)
Die Moral der Ruth Halbfass (W Ger 1972)
Roma Bene [Liebe und Sex in Rom] (It-W Ger-Fr 1972)
Causa di divorzio (It 1972)
Amore e ginnastica (It 1973)

Reigen (W Ger 1973)
Bisturi, la mafia bianca (It 1973)
Die scharlachrote Buchstabe [La lettera scarlatta] (W Ger-It
    1973)
Di mamma non ce n'è una sola (It 1973)
L'uomo senza memoria (It 1974)
La bellissima estate (It 1974)
Frühlingsfluten (W Ger 1974)
The Swiss Conspiracy (USA-W Ger 1975)
Il ventre nero della signora (It 1975)
Mitgift (W Ger 1975)   1985631
La guardia del corpo (It 1975)

BERGNER, ELISABETH, b. Aug. 22, 1897, Drohobycz, Germany
    Der Evangelimann (Ger 1923)
    Nju (Ger 1924)
    Der Geiger von Florenz (Ger 1926)
    Liebe (Ger 1926)
    Dona Juana (Ger 1927)
    Fräulein Else (Ger 1928)
    Ariane (Ger 1931)
    Loves of Ariane (Ger 1931) [Eng lang version of Ariane]
    Der träumende Mund (Ger 1932)
    Catherine the Great (UA Br 1934)
    Escape Me Never (UA Br 1935)
    As You Like It (20th Br 1936)
    Dreaming Lips (UA Br 1937)
    A Stolen Life (Par Br 1939)
    Paris Calling (Univ 1941)
    Die glücklichen Jahre der Thornwalds (W Ger 1952)
    Cry of the Banshee (AIP 1970)
    Strogoff [Michel Strogoff] (It-Fr-Bul 1970)
    Der Fussgänger (W Ger 1973)

BERRY, JULES (Jules Paufichet), b. Feb. 9, 1889, Poitiers,
    France; d. April 20, 1951
    L'Argent (Fr 1928)
    Monsieur Personne (Fr 1932)
    Quick (Fr 1932)
    Arlette et ses papas (Fr 1934)
    Jeunes Filles à marier (Fr 1935)
    Le crime de M. Lange (Fr 1935)
    Baccara (Fr 1935)
    Une Poule sur un mur (Fr 1936)
    Les Loups entre eux (Fr 1936)
    Touche à tout (Fr 1936)
    27, rue de la Paix (Fr 1936)
    Le Mort en fuite (Fr 1936)
    Aventure à Paris (Fr 1936)
    Le Club des Aristocrates (Fr 1937)
    Arsène Lupin, detective (Fr 1937)
    Rendez-vous aux Champs-Elysées (Fr 1937)
    Un Homme à abattre (Fr 1937)

Le Voleur de femmes (Fr 1937)
L'Avion de minuit (Fr 1938)
Clodoche (Fr 1938)
Hercule (Fr 1938)
Cafe de Paris (Fr 1938)
Cas de conscience (Fr 1938)
Carrefour (Fr 1938)
L'Inconnue de Monte Carlo (Fr 1938)
Son oncle de Normandie (Fr 1938)
Le Jour se Lève (Fr 1939)
Derrière la façade (Fr 1939)
Parade en sept nuits (Fr 1941)
Chambre 13 (Fr 1941)
Après l'Orage (Fr 1942)
Symphonie fantastique (Fr 1942)
L'Assassin à peur la nuit (Fr 1942)
La Troisième Dalle (Fr 1942)
Les Visiteurs du soir (Fr 1942-1945)
Felicie Nanteuil (Fr 1942)
Le Grand Combat (Fr 1942)
Le Camion blanc (Fr 1942)
Marie-Martine (Fr 1942)
Le Voyageur de la Toussaint (Fr 1942)
L'Homme de Londres (Fr 1943)
Le Soleil de Minuit (Fr 1943)
L'Enfant de la tourmente (Fr 1944)
Etoile sans lumière (Fr 1946)
Messieurs Ludovic (Fr 1946)
Dorothéa cherche l'amour (Fr 1946)
Si jeunesse savait (Fr 1947)
Portrait d'un assassin (Fr 1949)
Histoires extraordinaires (Fr 1950)
Le Gang des tractions arrière (Fr 1951)
Les Maîtres nageurs (Fr 1951)
Pas de week-end pour notre amour (Fr 1951)
Sans tambour ni trompette (Fr 1951)
Tête blonde (Fr 1951)

BERTINI, FRANCESCA (Elena Seracini Vitiello), b. April 11, 1888,
     Naples
Re Lear (It 1910)
Tristano e Isotta (It 1911)
La Contessa di Challant (It 1911)
Manon Lescaut (It 1911)
Il mercante di Venezia (It 1911)
La rosa di Tebe (It 1912)
La suonatrice ambulante (It 1912)
Il pappagallo della zia Berta (It 1912)
Lagrime e sorrisi (It 1912)
Idillio tragico (It 1912)
La maestrina (It 1913)
Tramonto (It 1913)
L'arma dei vigliacchi (It 1913)

Francesca Bertini

In faccio al destino (It 1913)
Terra promessa (It 1913)
L'avvoltoio (It 1913)
La gloria (It 1913)
L'anima del demi-monde (It 1913)
La bufera (It 1913)
L'arrivista (It 1913)
L'ultima carta [L'ultimo atout] (It 1913)
La cricca dorato (It 1913)
Idolo infranto (It 1913)
La vigilia di Natale (It 1913)
Per la sua gioia (It 1913)
L'Histoire d'un Pierrot (It 1913)
L'onesta che uccide (It 1914)
L'amazzone mascherata (It 1914)
La canzone (It 1914)
La principessa straniera (It 1914)
Sangue bleu (It 1914)
Una donna (It 1914)
Rose e spine (It 1914)
Per il blasone (It 1914)

Nelly la gigolette (It 1914)
Una buona lezione (It 1914)
Il veleno della parola (It 1914)
Diana l'affascinatrice (It 1915)
Assunta spina (It 1915)
Nella fornace (It 1915)
Il capestro degli Asburgo (It 1915)
Yvonne, la bella della (It 1915)
La signora delle camelie (It 1915)
Don Pietro Caruso (It 1916)
Colpa altrui [Eroismo d'amore] (It 1916)
Odette (It 1916)
La perla del cinema (It 1916)
Fedora (It 1916)
Vittima dell'ideale (It 1916)
Maligno riflesso (It 1916)
Il patto (It 1916)
Destino (It 1916)
I Carbonari (It 1916)
Baby l'indiavolata (It 1916)
L'educanda monella (It 1916)
Nel gorgo della vita (It 1916)
La piccola fonte (It 1917)
Malea (It 1917)
Anima redenta (It 1917)
Andreina (It 1917)
Tosca (It 1918)
Il processo Clemenceau [L'Affaire Clemenceau] (It-Fr 1918)
Frou-Frou (It 1918)
Mariunte (It 1918)
La piovra (It 1918)
La donna nuda (It 1918)
Spiritismo (It 1918)
Eugenia Grandet (It 1918)
Saracinesca (It 1919)
Anima allegra (It 1919)
L'orgoglio (It 1919)
L'avarizia (It 1919)
La gola (It 1919)
L'accidia (It 1919)
La lussuria (It 1919)
L'invidia (It 1919)
Beatrice (It 1919)
La contessa Saura (It 1919)
Lisa Fleuron (It 1919)
La legge (It 1919)
La principessa (It 1919)
L'ombra (It 1919)
La sfinge (It 1919)
Il conquistatore del mondo (It 1919)
La principessa Giorgio (It 1919)
Anima selvaggia (It 1920)
Maddalena Ferrat (It 1920)

Amore di donno (It 1920)
La blessure la ferita (It 1920)
Marion (It 1920)
Ultimo sogno (It 1920)
La giovinezza del diavolo (It 1920)
Amore vince sempre (It 1921)
La blessure (It 1921)
La donna, il diavolo, il tempo (It 1921)
La fanciulla d'Amalfi (It 1921)
Conseulita (It 1921)
Monte-Carlo (It 1927)
Odette (It 1927)
Tu m'appartiens [Tu mi appartieni] (Fr-It 1928)
La Possession (Fr 1929)
La Femme d'une nuit [La donna di una notte] (Fr-It 1930)
Déchéance [Odette] (Fr-It 1934)
Dora, la espia (Sp 1943)
A sud niente di nuovo (It 1956)
Una ragazza di Praga (It 1969)

BIBERTI, LEOPOLD, b. Sept. 18, 1897, Berlin; d. Nov. 24, 1969
Kleine Scheidegg (Swi 1937)
Der achti Schwyzer (Swi 1940)
Dilemna (Swi 1940)
Das Menschlein Matthias (Swi 1941)
Der doppelte Matthias und seine Tochter (Swi 1941)
Landammann Stauffacher (Swi 1941)
Der Schuss von der Kanzel (Swi 1942)
Dr. Wyberfind (Swi 1943)
Die letzte Chance (Swi 1945)
Swiss Tour (Swi 1949)
Uli der Pächter (Swi 1955)
Zwischen uns die Berge (Swi 1956)
Rose Berndt (W Ger 1957)
Gluck meus mer ha (Swi 1957)
S. O. S. Gletscherpilot (Swi 1959)
An heiligen Wassern (W Ger-Swi 1960)
Wilhelm Tell (Swi 1961)

BIDEAU, JEAN-LUC, b. Oct. 1, 1940, Geneva
Le Voleur (Fr 1966)
Les Bons Vivants (Fr 1966)
Charles mort ou vif (Swi 1969)
James ou pas (Swi 1970)
La Salamandre (Swi 1971)
Les Arpenteurs (Swi 1972)
Le Petit Poucet (Fr 1972)
L'Invitation (Swi 1973)
Last Tango in Paris (Fr-It-USA 1973)
Etat de siège (Fr 1973)
Belle (Bel 1973)
La Fille au violoncelle (Swi 1973)

Projection privée (Fr 1974)
Voyage en Grande Tartarie (Fr 1974)
L'Homme du fleuve (Fr 1974)
Nuit d'or (Fr 1975)

BIRGEL, WILLY, b. Sept. 19, 1891, Köln; d. 1974
    Fürst Woronzeff (Ger 1934)
    Ein Mann will nach Deutschland (Ger 1934)
    Barcarole (Ger 1935)
    Schwarze Rosen (Ger 1935)
    Einer zuviel an Bord (Ger 1935)
    Das Mädchen Johanna (Ger 1935)
    Schlussakkord (Ger 1936)
    Ritt in die Freiheit (Ger 1936)
    Verräter (Ger 1936)
    Zu neuen Ufern (Ger 1937)
    Fanny Eissler (Ger 1937)
    Menschen ohne Vaterland (Ger 1937)
    Unternehmen Michael (Ger 1938)
    Geheimzeichen LB 17 (Ger 1938)
    Der Blaufuchs (Ger 1938)
    Der Fall Deruga (Ger 1938)
    Verklungene Melodie (Ger 1938)
    Der Gouverneur (Ger 1939)
    Kongo-Express (Ger 1939)
    Maria-Ilona (Ger 1939)
    Hotel Sacher (Ger 1939)
    Feinde (Ger 1940)
    Das Herz der Königin (Ger 1940)
    ...Reitet für Deutschland (Ger 1941)
    Kameraden (Ger 1941)
    Diesel (Ger 1942)
    Du gehörst zu mir (Ger 1943)
    Der dunkle Tag (Ger 1943)
    Ich brauche dich (Ger 1944)
    Der Majoratsherr (Ger 1944)
    Musik in Salzburg (Ger 1944)
    Mit meinen Augen (Ger 1944)
    Die Brüder Noltenius (Ger 1945)
    Leb' wohl Christina (Ger 1945)
    Zwischen gestern und morgen (W Ger 1947)
    Vom Teufel gejagt (W Ger 1950)
    Das ewige Spiel (W Ger 1951)
    Wenn die Abendglocken läuten (W Ger 1951)
    Der Kaplan von San Lorenzo (W Ger 1953)
    Mein Herz darfst du nicht fragen (W Ger 1953)
    Sterne über Colombo (W Ger 1953)
    Die Gefangene des Maharadscha (W Ger 1954)
    Konsul Strotthoff (W Ger 1954)
    Rittmeister Wronski (W Ger 1955)
    Ein Mann vergisst die Liebe (W Ger 1955)
    Rosenmontag (W Ger 1955)
    Die Toteninsel (W Ger 1955)

Rosen für Bettina (W Ger 1956)
Ein Herz kehrt heim (W Ger 1956)
Heidi und Peter (Swi 1956)
Zwischen Zeit und Ewigkeit (W Ger 1956)
Johannisnacht (W Ger 1956)
Die Heilige und ihr Narr (Aus 1957)
Frauenarzt Dr. Bertram (W Ger 1957)
Liebe kann wie Gift sein (W Ger 1958)
Der Priester und das Mädchen (Aus 1958)
Geliebte Bestie (Aus 1959)
Arzt aus Leidenschaft (W Ger 1959)
Wenn die Glocken hell erklingen (Aus 1959)
Frau Cheney's Ende (W Ger-Swi 1961)
Die blonde Frau des Maharadscha (W Ger 1962)
Romanze in Venedig (W Ger 1962)
Ein Sarg aus Hongkong (W Ger-Fr 1964)
Agent 505--Todesfalle Beirut (W Ger 1966)
Schonzeit für Füchse (W Ger 1966)

Jane Birkin

BIRKIN, JANE, b. Dec. 14, 1947, London
   The Knack... and How to Get It (UA 1965)
   Blow-Up (MGM 1966)
   Kaleidoscope (WB 1966)
   Wonderwall (Cinecenta 1968)
   La Piscine (Fr 1968)
   Slogan (Fr 1968)
   Les Chemins de Katmandou (Fr 1969)
   Trop petit, mon ami (Fr 1969)

Alba pagana [May Morning] (It 1969)
Sex Power (Fr 1970)
Delitto a Oxford (It 1970)
Romance of a Horse Thief [Le Voleur de Chevaux] (AA 1970)
Cannabis (Fr 1970)
Dix-Neuf Jeunes Filles et un matelot (Fr 1971)
Trop jolies pour être honnêtes (Fr 1972)
Corringa [Les Diablesses/Seven Dead in the Cat's Eyes] (It-Fr 1972)
Don Juan 73 (Fr 1972)
Projection privée (Fr 1973)
Le Mouton enragé (Fr 1973)
Comment réussir dans la vie quand on est con et pleurnichard (Fr 1974)
Dark Place (It 1974)
La Moutarde me monte au nez (Fr 1974)
Sérieux comme le plaisir (Fr 1974)
Sept morts sur ordonnance (Fr 1975)
La Course à l'echalote (Fr 1975)
Catherine et Cie (Fr 1975)
Je t'aime moi non plus (Fr 1975)

BLACKMAN, HONOR, b. Aug. 22, 1926, London
Fame Is the Spur (GFD 1947)
Daughter of Darkness (Par 1948)
Quartet (ep "The Alien Corn") (GFD 1948)
A Boy, a Girl and a Bike (GFD 1949)
Conspirator (MGM Br 1949)
Diamond City (GFD 1949)
So Long at the Fair (GFD 1950)
Green Grow the Rushes [Brandy Ashore] (BL 1951)
The Rainbow Jacket (GFD 1954)
The Delavine Affair (Monarch 1954)
Diplomatic Passport (Eros 1954)
The Yellow Robe (ABPC 1955)
The Glass Cage [The Glass Tomb] (Ex 1955)
Breakaway (RKO 1956)
Suspended Alibi (RFD 1957)
You Pay Your Money (Butcher 1957)
Account Rendered (RFD 1957)
A Night to Remember (RFD 1958)
The Square Peg (RFD 1958)
A Matter of WHO (MGM 1961)
Serena (Butcher 1962)
Jason and the Argonauts (Col 1963)
Goldfinger (UA 1964)
The Secret of My Success (MGM 1965)
Life at the Top (Col 1965)
Moment to Moment (Univ 1965)
A Twist of Sand (UA 1967)
Shalako (WPD 1968)
Twinky [Lola] (RFD 1969)
The Virgin and the Gipsy (London Screenplays 1970)

The Last Grenade (CIRO 1970)
Something Big (20th 1971)
Fright (BL 1971)

BLAIN, GERARD, b. 1930, Paris
    Les Fruits sauvages [Wild Fruit] (Fr 1953)
    Avant le déluge (Fr-It 1953)
    Escalier de service (Fr 1954)
    Voici le temps des assassins [Deadlier Than the Male] (Fr
        1955)
    Crime et châtiment [Crime and Punishment] (Fr 1956)
    Le Désir mene les hommes (Fr 1957)
    Giovanni Mariti (It-Fr 1957)
    Le Beau Serge (Fr 1958)
    Les Cousins (Fr 1959)
    Match contre la mort (Fr-It 1959)
    Via Margutta [Run with the Devil] (It 1960)
    La Peau et les os [The Mazur File] (Fr 1960)
    I delfini (It 1960)
    Il gobbo (It-Fr 1960)
    Traqués par la Gestapo (Fr 1961)
    L'oro di Roma (It-Fr 1961)
    Hatari! (Par 1962)
    Lo sgarro (It-Fr 1962)
    Les Vierges (Fr 1962)
    La Soupe aux poulets (Fr 1963)
    La Bonne Soupe (Fr-It 1963)
    Amori pericolosi (It-Fr 1964)
    Via Veneto (Fr-It 1965)
    Un Amore (It-Fr 1966)
    Missione mortale molo 83 (It 1966)
    Du suif chez les dabes (Fr 1966)
    Un Homme de trop [Shock Troops] (Fr 1967)
    Joe Caligula (Fr 1968)
    Les Amis (Fr 1971)
    Le Pélican (Fr 1974)

BLANC, ANNE-MARIE, b. Sept. 2, 1921, Vevey, Switzerland
    Wachtmeister Studer (Swi 1939)
    Die missbrauchten Liebesbriefe (Swi 1940)
    Gilberte de Courgenay (Swi 1941)
    Landammann Stauffacher (Swi 1941)
    Maturareise (Swi 1942)
    Marie-Louise (Swi 1943)
    On ne meurt pas comme ça (Fr 1946)
    White Cradle Inn [High Fury] (BL 1947)
    Das Kuckucksei (W Ger 1948)
    Palace-Hotel (Swi-W Ger 1951)
    Gefangene Seele (W Ger 1951)
    Ich warte auf Dich (W Ger 1952)
    Mit 17 beginnt das Leben (W Ger 1953)
    Hoheit lassen bitten (W Ger 1954)
    Frühlingslied [S'Vreneli am Guggisberg] (Swi-W Ger 1954)

Roman eines Frauenarztes (W Ger 1954)
Ein Herz kehrt heim (W Ger 1954)
S. O. S. Gletscherpilot (Swi 1959)
Via Mala (W Ger 1961)
La Blonde de Pekin (Swi-Fr 1966)
Riedland (Swi 1975)

BLANCHAR, PIERRE, b. June 30, 1896, Philippeville, Algeria;
    d. 1963
Papa bon coeur (Fr 1920)
Jocelyn (Fr 1922)
Geneviève (Fr 1922)
Terre promise (Fr 1924)
Aux Jardins de Murcie (Fr 1924)
L'Arriviste (Fr 1924)
Le Juge d'instruction (Fr 1924)
Le Tombeau sous l'Arc de Triomphe (Fr 1926)
La Valse de l'adieu (Fr 1926)
Le Joueur d'echecs (Fr 1927)
La Capitaine Fracasse (Fr 1927)
En 1812 (Ger 1928)
La Marche nuptiale (Fr 1928)
L'Atlantide (Fr 1931)
La Couturière de Lunéville (Fr 1931)
Les Croix de bois (Fr 1932)
La Belle Marinière (Fr 1932)
Mélo (Fr 1932)
Iris perdue et retrouvée (Fr 1933)
Cette vieille canaille (Fr 1933)
Au bout du monde (Fr-Ger 1934)
Turandot (Fr 1934)
Le Diable en bouteille (Fr 1934)
L'Or (Fr 1934)
Crime et châtiment (Fr 1935)
Amants et voleurs (Fr 1935)
Le Coupable (Fr 1936)
Le Secret d'une vie (Fr 1936)
Mademoiselle Docteur (Fr 1937)
L'Homme de nulle part (Fr 1937)
La Dame de pique (Fr 1937)
Un Carnet de bal (Fr 1937)
Une Femme sans importance (Fr 1937)
L'Affaire du courier de Lyon (Fr 1937)
Les Bateliers de la Volga (Fr 1938)
Le Joueur [The Gambler] (Fr 1938)
L'Etrange Monsieur Victor (Fr 1938)
A Royal Divorce (Par 1938)
Nuit de décembre (Fr 1939)
L'Empreinte du Dieu (Fr 1940)
La Neige sur les pas (Fr 1941)
La Prière aux étoiles (Fr 1941) [unfinished]
Pont carral (Fr 1942)

Secrets (Fr 1942)
Un Seul Amour (Fr 1943)
Le Bossu (Fr 1944)
Patrie (Fr 1945)
Le Bataillon du ciel (Fr 1946)
La Symphonie pastorale (Fr 1946)
Après l'amour (Fr 1947)
Docteur Laennec (Fr 1948)
Bal cupidon (Fr 1948)
Mon ami Sainfoin (Fr 1949)
Du Rififi chez les femmes (Fr 1959)
Katia [The Magnificent Sinner] (Fr 1959)
Le Monocle noir (Fr 1960)

BLECH, HANS CHRISTIAN, b. Feb. 20, 1925, Darmstadt, Germany
Affäre Blum (E Ger 1948)
Epilog (W Ger 1950)
Lockende Gefahr (W Ger 1950)
08/15 I (W Ger 1954)
Decision Before Dawn (20th 1952)
Geständnis unter vier Augen (W Ger 1954)
Sauerbruch [Das war mein Leben] (W Ger 1954)
Phantom des grossen Zeltes (W Ger 1954)
08/15 II (W Ger 1955)
Kinder, Mütter und ein General (W Ger 1955)
Banditen der Autobahn (W Ger 1955)
08/15 in der Heimat (W Ger 1955)
Weil Du arm bist, musst Du Früher sterben (W Ger 1956)
Schwarzer Stern in weisser Nacht (W Ger-Fr 1958)
Solange das Herz schlägt (W Ger 1958)
Das Erbe von Björndal (W Ger 1960)
Ich schwöre und gelobe (W Ger 1960)
L'Enclos [Ograda] (Fr-Yug 1961)
The Longest Day (20th 1962)
Der Besuch [The Visit] (W Ger-Fr-It-USA 1964)
Morituri (20th 1965)
Battle of the Bulge (WB 1965)
La Voleuse [Schornstein Nr. 4] (Fr-W Ger 1966)
Cardillac (W Ger 1970)
Le Client de la morte Saison (Fr-Israeli 1970)
Ansichten eines Clowns (W Ger 1975)
Falsche Bewegung (W Ger 1975)
Les Innocents aux mains sales (Fr-It-W Ger 1975)
La Chaîr de l'orchidée (Fr 1975)
Il faut vivre dangereusement (Fr 1975)

BLIER, BERNARD, b. Jan. 11, 1916, Buenos Aires
Trois-six-neuf (Fr 1937)
Le Messager (Fr 1937)
La Dame de Malacca (Fr 1937)
Gribouille (Fr 1937)
L'Habit vert (Fr 1937)
Altitude 3200 (Fr 1938)

Grisou (Fr 1938)
Entrée des artistes (Fr 1938)
Double crime sur la Ligne Maginot (Fr 1938)
Place de la Concorde (Fr 1938)
Hôtel du nord (Fr 1938)
L'Enfer des anges (Fr 1939)
Quartier Latin (Fr 1939)
Le Jour se lève (Fr 1939)
Tourelle 3 (Fr 1939) [unfinished]
Nuit de décembre (Fr 1939)
Le Pavillon brûle (Fr 1941)
L'Assassinat du Père Noël (Fr 1941)
Premier Bal (Fr 1941)
Caprices (Fr 1941)
La Symphonie fantastique (Fr 1942)
La Femme que j'ai le plus aimée (Fr 1942)
Romance à trois (Fr 1942)
La Nuit fantastique (Fr 1942)
Carmen (Fr 1942)
Le Journal tombe à cinq heures (Fr 1942)
Marie-Martine (Fr 1942)
Domino (Fr 1943)
Les Petites du Quai aux Fleurs (Fr 1943)
Je suis avec toi (Fr 1943)
Farandole (Fr 1944)
Seul dans la nuit (Fr 1945)
Monsieur Grégoire s'évade (Fr 1945)
Messieurs Ludovic (Fr 1946)
Le Café du Cadran (Fr 1946)
Quai des Orfèvres (Fr 1947)
Dédée d'Anvers (Fr 1947)
D'Homme à hommes (Fr 1948)
Les Casse-pieds [Spice of Life] (Fr 1949)
L'Ecole Buissonnière (Fr 1949)
Retour à la vie [Return to Life] (Fr 1949)
Monseigneur (Fr 1949)
La Souricière (Fr 1949)
Manèges [The Wanton] (Fr 1949)
L'Invité du mardi (Fr 1950)
Les Anciens de Saint-Loup (Fr 1950)
Souvenirs perdus [Lost Property] (Fr 1951)
Sans laisser d'adresse (Fr 1951)
La Maison Bonnadieu (Fr 1951)
Agence matrimoniale (Fr 1952)
Je l'ai été trois fois (Fr 1952)
Suivez cet homme (Fr 1953)
Secrets d'alcove [The Bed] (Fr-It 1953)
Avant le déluge (Fr-It 1953)
Scènes de ménage (Fr 1954)
Le Dossier noir (Fr-It 1955)
Les Hussards (Fr 1955)
Mère Courage (Fr-W Ger 1955) [unfinished]
Rivelazione (It 1956)

Crime et châtiment [Crime and Punishment] (Fr 1956)
Quand la femme s'en mêle (Fr-It-W Ger 1957)
Retour de manivelle [There's Always a Price Tag] (Fr-It 1957)
La Bonne Tisane (Fr 1957)
Les Misérables (Fr-It-E Ger 1957)
Sans famille [The Adventures of Remi] (Fr-It 1957)
L'Ecole des cocottes (Fr 1957)
La Chatte [The Face of the Cat] (Fr 1958)
En Légitime Défense (Fr 1958)
Archimède le Clochard (Fr 1958)
Les grandes familles (Fr 1958)
Le Joueur [The Gambler] (Fr-It 1958)
Marie-Octobre (Fr 1958)
Marche ou crève (Fr-Bel 1959)
Le Secret du Chevalier d'Eon (Fr 1959)
Les Yeux de l'amour (Fr 1959)
La grande guerra (Fr-It 1959)
Histoires d'amour défendues (Fr-It 1959)
Vive Henri IV, vive l'amour (Fr-It 1960)
Arrêtez les tambours (Fr 1960)
Crimen (It-Fr 1960)
Il gobbo (It-Fr 1960)
Le Président (Fr-It 1961)
Le Cave se rebiffe (Fr-It 1961)
Le Monocle noir (Fr 1961)
I briganti italiani (It-Fr 1961)
Les Petits Matins [Girl on the Road] (Fr 1961)
Le Septième Juré [The Seventh Juror] (Fr 1961)
Mathias Sandorf (Fr-It-Sp 1962)
Pourquoi Paris? (Fr-It 1962)
Les Jeunes Filles de bonnes familles (Fr-It 1962)
Germinal (Fr 1962)
I compagni (It-Fr 1963)
Les Tontons flingueurs (Fr 1963)
La Bonne Soupe (Fr-It 1963)
La Chance et l'amour (Fr-It 1964)
Alta infedeltà (It-Fr 1964)
Les Barbouzes [Undercover Men] (Fr 1964)
Cent Mille Dollars au soleil (Fr-It 1964)
La Chasse à l'homme [Male Hunt] (Fr-It 1964)
Les Bons Vivants (Fr-It 1965)
Quand passent les faisans (Fr 1966)
Le Grand Restaurant (Fr 1966)
Una questione d'onore (It-Fr 1966)
Delitto quasi perfetto [Imperfect Murder] (It-Fr 1966)
Duello nel mondo (It 1966)
Un Idiot à Paris [An Idiot in Paris] (Fr 1966)
Peau d'espion [To Commit a Murder] (Fr-W Ger-It 1967)
Si j'étais un espion [Breakdown] (Fr 1967)
Lo straniero [The Stranger] (It-Fr-Alg 1967)
Du mou dans la gâchette (Fr-It 1967)
Le fou du Labo 4 [The Madman of Laboratory 4] (Fr 1967)
Coplan sauve sa peau [The Devil's Garden] (Fr-It 1968)

Caroline chérie (Fr-It-W Ger 1969)
Faut pas prendre les enfants du Bon Dieu pour des canards
   sauvages (Fr 1969)
Riusciranne i nostri eroi a ritrovare l'amico misteriosamente
   scomparso in Africa? (It 1969)
Mon oncle Benjamin (Fr-It 1969)
Appelez-moi Mathilde (Fr 1970)
Biribi (Fr-Tun 1970)
Le Distrait (Fr 1970)
Le Cri du cormoran le soir au-dessus des jonques (Fr 1971)
Jo (Fr 1971)
Tout le monde il est beau, tout le monde il est gentil (Fr-It
   1972)
Elle cause plus... elle flingue (Fr-It 1972)
Le Grand Blond avec une chaussure noire (Fr 1972)
Moi y en à vouloir des sous (Fr 1973)
Par le sang des autres (Fr-Canada-It 1973)
La Main à couper (Fr-Canada 1973)
Bons Baisers à lundi (Fr 1974)
C'est pas parce qu'on à rien à dire qu'il faut fermer sa gueule
   (Fr-It 1974)
C'est dur pour tout le monde (Fr 1974)
Ce cher Victor (Fr 1975)
Le Faux-cul (Fr 1975)
Amici miei (It 1975)

BLOOM, CLAIRE, b. Feb. 15, 1931, London
   The Blind Goddess (GFD 1948)
   Limelight (UA 1952)
   La Bergère et le ramoneur [Mr. Wonderbird] (Fr 1952) [voice
      only in Eng lang version]
   The Man Between (BL 1953)
   Innocents in Paris (IFD 1953)
   Ballettens born [Ballet Girl] (Den 1954) [narrator of Eng lang
      version]
   Richard III (IFD 1955)
   Alexander the Great (UA 1956)
   The Brothers Karamazov (MGM 1958)
   The Buccaneer (Par 1958)
   Look Back in Anger (ABP 1959)
   Schachnovelle [Brainwashed] (W Ger 1960)
   The Chapman Report (WB 1962)
   The Wonderful World of the Brothers Grimm (MGM 1962)
   The Haunting (MGM 1963)
   80,000 Suspects (RFD 1963)
   Il maestro di Vigevano [The Teacher from Vigevano] (It 1963)
   Alta infedeltà [Sex in the Afternoon] (ep "Peccato nel pomeriggio")
      (It 1964)
   The Outrage (MGM 1964)
   The Spy Who Came in from the Cold (Par 1965)
   Charly (Cin 1968)
   Three into Two Won't Go (RFD 1969)
   The Illustrated Man (WB-7 Arts 1969)

Red Sky at Morning (Univ 1970)
A Severed Head (Col 1970)
A Doll's House (MGM-EMI 1973)

BOGARDE, DIRK (Derek Niven Van Den Bogaerde), b. March 28,
   1921, Hampstead, London
Come On George (ABFD 1939) (extra)
Dancing with Crime (Par 1947) (bit)
Esther Waters (GFD 1948)
Quartet (ep "The Alien Corn") (GFD 1948)
Once a Jolly Swagman [Maniac on Wheels] (GFD 1948)
Dear Mr. Prohack (GFD 1949)
Boys in Brown (GFD 1949)
The Blue Lamp (GFD 1950)
So Long at the Fair (GFD 1950)
The Woman in Question [Five Angles on Murder] (GFD 1950)
Blackmailed [Mr. Christopher] (GFD 1951)
Hunted [The Stranger in Between] (GFD 1952)
Penny Princess (GFD 1952)
The Gentle Gunman (GFD 1952)
Appointment in London (BL 1953)

Kay Kendall and Dirk Bogarde in Doctor in the House (1954).

Desperate Moment (GFD 1953)
They Who Dare (BL 1954)
Doctor in the House (GFD 1954)
The Sleeping Tiger (AA 1954)
For Better, for Worse [Cocktails in the Kitchen] (ABP 1954)
The Sea Shall Not Have Them (Eros 1955)
Simba (GFD 1955)
Doctor at Sea (RFD 1955)
Cast a Dark Shadow (Eros 1955)
The Spanish Gardener (RFD 1956)
Ill Met by Moonlight [Night Ambush] (RFD 1957)
Doctor at Large (RFD 1957)
Campbell's Kingdom (RFD 1957)
A Tale of Two Cities (RFD 1958)
The Wind Cannot Read (RFD 1958)
The Doctor's Dilemma (MGM 1959)
Libel (MGM 1959)
Song Without End (Col 1960)
The Angel Wore Red (MGM 1960)
The Singer Not the Song (RFD 1961)
Victim (RFD 1961)
HMS Defiant [Damn the Defiant!] (Col 1962)
The Password Is Courage (MGM 1962)
The Mind Benders (AA 1962)
We Joined the Navy (WPD 1962) (cameo)
I Could Go On Singing (UA 1962)
Doctor in Distress (RFD 1963)
The Servant (Elstree 1963)
Hot Enough for June [Agent 8-3/4] (RFD 1963)
King and Country (WPD 1964)
The High Bright Sun [McGuire Go Home!] (RFD 1964)
Darling... (AA 1965)
Modesty Blaise (20th 1966)
Accident (LIP 1967)
Our Mother's House (MGM 1967)
Sebastian (Par 1967)
The Fixer (MGM 1968)
Oh! What a Lovely War (Par 1969)
Justine (20th 1969)
La caduta degli Dei [The Damned] (It-W Ger 1969)
Upon This Rock (Marstan 1970)
Morte a Venezia [Death in Venice] (It 1971)
Le Serpent [The Serpent] (Fr-It-W Ger 1973)
Il portiere di notte [The Night Porter] (It 1973)
La testa del serpents [El clan de los immorales/Ordine di uc-
    cicere/Order to Kill] (Sp-It 75)

BÖHM, KARL-HEINZ, b. March 16, 1928, Darmstadt, Germany
    Haus des Lebens (W Ger 1952)
    Alraune (W Ger 1952)
    Der Tag vor der Hochzeit (W Ger 1952)
    Der Weibertausch (W Ger 1952)
    Salto mortale (W Ger 1953)

Arlette erobert Paris (W Ger 1953)
Der unsterbliche Lump (W Ger 1953)
Hochzeit auf Reisen (W Ger 1953)
Die Sonne von St. Moritz (W Ger 1954)
...und ewig bleibt die Liebe (W Ger 1954)
Die Hexe (W Ger 1954)
Die goldene Pest (W Ger 1954)
Die heilige Lüge (W Ger 1955)
Ich war ein hässliches Mädchen (W Ger 1955)
Unternehmen Schlafsack (W Ger 1955)
Schwedenmädel (W Ger 1955)
Dunja (Aus 1955)
Sissi (W Ger 1955)
Die Ehe des Dr. med. Danwitz (W Ger 1955)
Sissi, die junge Kaiserin (W Ger 1955)
Nina, Kitty und die grosse Welt (W Ger 1956)
Blaue Jungs (W Ger 1957)
Sissi--Schicksalsjahre einer Kaiserin (W Ger 1957)
Das Schloss in Tirol (W Ger 1958)
Le Passager clandestin (Fr-Australian 1958)
The Stowaway [Eng lang version of Le Passager clandestin] (Fr-
    Australian 1958)
Man müsste nochmal zwanzig sein (W Ger 1958)
Das haut einen Seemann doch nicht um (W Ger 1958)
Das Dreimäderlhaus (Aus 1958)
La Paloma (W Ger 1959)
Der Gauner und der Liebe Gott (W Ger 1959)
Kriegsgericht (W Ger 1959)
Peeping Tom (AA 1959)
Too Hot to Handle (WPD 1960)
Magnificent Rebel (W Ger 1960)
La Croix des vivants (Fr 1961)
Four Horsemen of the Apocalypse (MGM 1962)
Rififi à Tokyo (Fr-It 1962)
The Wonderful World of the Brothers Grimm (MGM 1962)
Come Fly with Me (MGM 1963)
The Venetian Affair (MGM 1967)
Der amerikanische Soldat (W Ger 1970)
Schloss Hubertus (W Ger 1973)
Effi Briest (W Ger 1974)
Faustrecht der Freiheit (W Ger 1975)
Mutter Küsters Fahrt zum Himmel (W Ger 1975)

BONI, CARMEN (Carmelo Bonicatti), b. April 17, 1904, Rome; d.
    Nov. 18, 1963
    La scimitarra di Barbarossa (It 1919)
    Ave Maria, gratia plena! (It 1919)
    Il fiore del Caucaso (It 1920)
    Ma non è una cosa seria (It 1920)
    Miss Dorothy (It 1920)
    Monella di strada (It 1920)
    Mon Oncle Barbassou (It 1921)
    La preda (It 1921)

La dame de chez Maxim's (It 1923)
La piccola ignota (It 1923)
Il riscatto (It 1923)
La bocca chiusa (It 1924)
La moglie bella (It 1924)
Il focolare spento [Il più grande amore] (It 1925)
L'ultimo Lord (It 1926)
Addio, giovinezza! (It 1927)
Die Gefangene von Shanghai (Ger 1927)
Die Geschichte einer kleiner Pariserin [Sprung in Glück/La
  storia di una piccola parigina] (Ger-It 1927)
Grand Hotel Atlantic (Ger 1927)
Prinzessin Olalà (Ger 1927)
Meine Tante von Monaco (Ger 1927)
Der Fidele Bauer (Ger 1927)
Venus im Frack (Ger 1927)
Liebeskarnaval [Mascherata d'amore] (Ger-It 1928)
Scampolo (Ger-It 1928)
Adjutant des Zaren [Al zervizio dello zar] (Ger-It 1928)
Katharine Knie [Danzatrice di corda] (Ger-It 1929)
Quartier Latin (Fr 1929)
Paramount on Parade [Ger version of Paramount on Parade]
  (Ger 1930)
Il richiamo del cuore (It 1930)
La riva dei bruti (It 1930)
La vacanza del diavolo (It 1931)
La femme en homme (Fr 1931)
Ne sois pas jalouse (Fr 1932)
Quelle vecchia canaglia (It 1934)
Cléo, robes et manteaux (It 1935)
Le comte de Monte-Cristo (Fr 1942)
D'homme à hommes (Fr 1948)

BORELLI, LYDA, b. March 22, 1884, Rivarolo Ligure, Italy; d.
  June 2, 1959
Ma l'amor mio non muore (It 1913)
Memoria dell'altro (It 1913)
La donne nuda (It 1914)
Il bosco Sacro (It 1915)
Fior di male (It 1915)
Rapsodia satanica (It 1915)
Marcia nuziale (It 1915)
La falena (It 1916)
Malombra (It 1916)
Madame Tallien (It 1916)
Carnevalesca (It 1917)
Il dramma di una notte (It 1917)
La storia dei tredici (It 1917)
Una notte a Calcutta (It 1918)
La leggenda di Santa Barbara (It 1918)

BORSCHE, DIETER, b. Oct. 25, 1909, Hannover, Germany
Alles weg'n dem Hund (Ger 1935)
Wie einst im Mai (Ger 1937)

Preussische Liebesgeschichte (Ger 1938)
Die kluge Schwiegermutter (Ger 1939)
Die Geliebte (Ger 1939)
Nachtwache (W Ger 1949)
Es kommt ein Tag (W Ger 1949)
Der fallende Stern (W Ger 1949)
Dr. Holl (W Ger 1951)
Fanfaren der Liebe (W Ger 1950)
Sündige Grenze (W Ger 1951)
Herz der Welt (W Ger 1952)
Vater braucht eine Frau (W Ger 1953)
Le Guérisseur (Fr 1953)
Die grosse Versuchung (W Ger 1953)
Der Kaplan von San Lorenzo (W Ger 1953)
Fanfaren der Ehe (W Ger 1953)
Königliche Hoheit (W Ger 1953)
Ali Baba et les quarante voleurs (Fr 1954)
Zwischenlandung in Paris [Escale à Orly] (Fr-W Ger 1955)
Ich war ein hässliches Mädchen (W Ger 1955)
Die Barrings (W Ger 1955)
San Salvatore (W Ger 1956)
Wenn wir alle Engel wären (W Ger 1956)
Rot ist die Liebe (W Ger 1956)
Nachts im grünen Kakadu (W Ger 1957)
Zwei Herzen im Mai (W Ger 1958)
A Time to Love and a Time to Die (Univ 1958)
U 47--Kapitänleutnant Prien (W Ger 1959)
Das hab' ich im Paris gelernt (W Ger 1959)
Sabine und die 100 Männer (W Ger 1960)
Ein Thron für Christine (W Ger-Sp 1960)
Die toten Augen von London (W Ger 1961)
Die glücklichen Jahre der Thorwalds (W Ger 1962)
Muss i. denn zum Städtele hinaus (W Ger 1962)
Der rote Rausch (W Ger 1962)
Ein Toter sucht seinen Mörder (W Ger 1962)
Das Feuerschiff (W Ger 1963)
Der Henker von London (W Ger 1963)
Der schwarze Abt (W Ger 1963)
Scotland Yard jagt Dr. Mabuse (W Ger 1963)
Ein Frauenarzt klagt an (W Ger 1963)
Die Goldsucher von Arkansas (W Ger-It-Fr 1964)
Das Phantom von Soho (W Ger 1964)
Der Schut (W Ger-It-Fr-Yug 1964)
Durchs wilde Kurdistan [El salvaje Kurdistan] (W Ger-Sp 1965)
Der Arzt stellt fest (W Ger-Sp 1966)
Wenn Ludwig ins Manöver zieht (W Ger 1967)
Der Arzt von St. Pauli (W Ger 1968)
Lady Hamilton (W Ger-It-Fr 1968)
Der Pfarrer von St. Pauli (W Ger-It-Fr 1970)

BOS, ANNIE, b. Dec. 10, 1886, Amsterdam; d. Aug. 3, 1975
    Gebroken Levens (Dut 1914)
    Weergevonden (Dut 1914)

De Vloek van het Testament (Dut 1915)
Liefdesstrijd (Dut 1915)
Het Geheim van den Vuurtoren (Dut 1916)
Vogelvrij (Dut 1916)
Liefdesoffer (Dut 1916)
Majoor Frans (Dut 1916)
La Renzoni (Dut 1916)
Het Geheim van Delft (Dut 1917)
Madame Pinkette & Co. (Dut 1917)
Gouden Ketenen (Dut 1917)
Ulbo Garvema (Dut 1917)
De Kroon der Schande (Dut 1918)
Toen 't Licht Verdween (Dut 1918)
Oorlog en Vrede I--1914--Erfelijk Belast (Dut 1918)
Oorlog en Vrede II--1916--Ontvluchting (Dut 1918)
Oorlog en Vrede III--1918--Gewetenswroeging (Dut 1918)
Op Hoop van Zegen (Dut 1918)
American Girls (Dut 1919)
Een Carmen van het Noorden (Dut 1919)
Het Goudvischje (Dut 1919)
Schakels (Dut 1920)
Het Verborgen Leven [Hidden Lives] (Dut-GB 1920)
Zonnetje [Joy] (Dut-GB 1920)
De Vrouw van de Minister [John Heriot's Wife] (Dut-GB 1920)
Rechten der Jeugd (Dut 1921)
Without Fear (USA) (Fox 1922)
Mooi Juultje van Volendam (Dut 1924)

BOSE, LUCIA, b. Jan. 28, 1931, Milan
Non c'è pace tra gli ulivi (It 1950)
Çronaca di un amore (It 1950)
E l'amor che mi rovina (It 1951)
Parigi è sempre Parigi (It 1951)
Le ragazze di Piazza di Spagna (It 1951)
Le due verità (It 1951)
Roma, ore 11 [Rome, 11 o'clock] (It 1952)
Era lei che lo voleva (It 1953)
Accadde al commissariato (It 1954)
Questa è la vita (ep "La marsina stretta") (It 1954)
La signora senza camelie [La traviata/The Lost One] (It 1954)
Tradita (It 1954)
Vacanze d'amore [Le Village magique] (It-Fr 1954)
Muerte de un ciclista (Sp 1955)
Sinfonia d'amore (It 1955)
Gli sbandati (It 1956)
Amanti di domani [Cela s'appelle l'aurore] (It-Fr 1957)
Le testament d'Orphèe [The Testament of Orpheus] (Fr 1959)
No somos de piedra (Sp 1968)
Nocturno 29 (Sp 1968)
Sotto il segno dello scorpione (It 1968)
Del amor y otras soledades (Sp 1968)
Fellini Satyricon (It 1968)
Jurtzenka [Un invierno en Mallorca] (Sp 1969)

Ciao Gulliver (It 1970)
Metello (It 1970)
Qualcosa striscia nel buio (It 1970)
Arcana (It 1971)
Nathalie Grangier (Fr 1972)
La casa de las palomas [Un solo grande amore] (Sp-It 1972)
La controfigura (It (1972)
La colonna infame (It 1973)
Ceremonia sangrienta (Sp 1973)
La Messe dorée [Nella profonda luce dei sensi] (Fr-It 1975)

BOUCHET, BARBARA (Bärbel Gutcher), b. Aug. 15, 1943, Reichen-
  burg, Germany
A Global Affair (MGM 1964)
The Best Man (UA 1964)
What a Way to Go! (20th 1964)
Sex and the Single Girl (WB 1965)
In Harm's Way (Par 1965)
John Goldfarb, Please Come Home! (20th 1965)
Agent for H. A. R. M. (Univ 1966)
Casino Royale (Col 1967)
Danger Route (UA 1968)
Sweet Charity (Univ 1969)
Colpo Rovente [Red Hot Shot] (It 1970)
L'asino d'oro: processo per fatti strani contro Lucius Apuleio,
  cittadino romano (It 1970)
Brancaleone alle crociate (It 1970)
Cerca di capirmi (It 1970)
Il debito coniugale (It 1970)
Il prete sposato (It 1970)
Le calde notti di Don Giovanni [Le avventure e gli amori di Don
  Giovanni] (It 1971)
La tarantola dal ventre nero (It 1971)
Non commettere atti impuri (It 1971)
L'uomo dagli occhi di ghiaccio (It 1972)
Sette orchidee macchiate di rosso (It 1972)
Milano Calibro 9 (It 1972)
Una cavalla tutta nuda (It 1972)
Non si sevizia un paperino (It 1972)
Valeria dentro e fuori (It 1972)
Finalmente le mille e una notte (It 1972)
Forza G [Winged Devils] (It 1972)
Casa d'appuntamento (It 1972)
Anche se volessi lavorare, che faccio? (It 1972)
Racconti proibiti di niente vestiti (It 1972)
La Calandria (It 1972)
Alla ricerca del piacere (It 1972)
La dama rossa uccide sette volte [Il cadavere che non voleva
  morire] (It 1972)
Una ragazza tutta nuda assassinata nel parco (It 1972)
Donne sopra femmine sotto (It 1972)
Ancora una volta prima di lasciarci (It 1973)
Un tipo con una faccia strana ti cerca per ucciderti [Ricco]

(It-Sp 1973)
Quelli che contano (It 1974)
La badessa di Castro (It 1974)
Il tuo piacere è il mio (It 1974)
La svergognata (It 1974)
Per le antiche scale (It 1975)
L'adulterà [To anghistri] (It-Greek 1975)
L'anatra all'arancia (It 1975)
40 gradi all'ombra del lenzuolo (It 1975)
Brogliaccio d'amore (It 1975)
L'amica di mia madre (It 1975)

BOUQUET, MICHEL, b. 1926, Paris
Monsieur Vincent (Fr 1947)
Brigade criminelle (Fr 1947)
Pattes blanches (Fr 1948)
Manon (Fr 1949)
Deux sous de violettes (Fr 1951)
Trois Femmes, trois âmes (ep "Coralie") (Fr 1951)
Mina de Vanghel (Fr 1952) (narrator)
Plein Ciel Malgache (Fr 1954) (narrator)
La Tour de Nesle [The Tower of Lust] (Fr-It 1954)
Nuit et brouillard (Fr 1955) (narrator)
Le Piège [The Trap] (Fr-It 1958)
Katia [The Magnificent Sinner] (Fr 1960)
Regard sur la folie (Fr 1962) (narrator)
Egypte, o Egypte (Fr 1962) (narrator of ep "Images du ciel")
Les Amitiés particulières [This Special Friendship] (Fr 1964)
Le Tigre se parfume à la dynamite [An Orchid for the Tiger]
  (Fr-It-Sp 1965)
Lamiel (Fr-It 1967)
La Route de Corinthe [The Road to Corinth] (Fr-It W Ger
  1967)
La mariée était en noir [The Bride Wore Black] (Fr-It 1967)
La Femme infidèle [The Unfaithful Wife] (Fr-It 1968)
Un Mur à Jérusalem (Fr 1968)
La Sirène du Mississippi [Mississippi Mermaid] (Fr-It 1969)
Le Dernier Saut (Fr 1969)
Dieu a choisi Paris [God Chose Paris] (Fr 1969) (narrator)
Borsalino (Fr-It 1970)
Un Condé [The Cop] (Fr-It 1970)
La Rupture (Fr-Bel-It 1970)
Comptes à rebours (Fr-It 1971)
Juste avant la nuit [Just Before Nightfall] (Fr-It 1971)
L'Humeur vagabonde (Fr 1971)
Le Bonheur dans vingt ans: Prague 1948-1968 (Fr 1971)
  (narrator)
La Route romane (Fr 1971) (narrator)
Papa les petits bateaux (Fr 1971)
Paulina 1880 (Fr 1972)
Malpertuis (Bel 1972)
L'Attentat [Plot] (Fr-It-W Ger 1972)
Trois Milliards sans ascenseur (Fr-It 1972)

La Sainte famille (Fr-Swi 1972)
Les Anges (Fr 1972)
Il n'y a pas de fumée sans feu (Fr-It 1972)
Le Serpent [The Serpent] (Fr-It-W Ger 1973)
Le Complot (Fr-Sp-It 1973)
Défense de savoir (Fr-It 1973)
Les Grands Sentiments font les bons gueuletons (Fr 1973)
Deux Hommes dans la ville (Fr-It 1973)
France S. A. (Fr 1973)
La Main à couper (Fr-Can 1973)
La Dynamite est bonne à boire (Fr-Sp 1974)
La Pieuvre (Fr-It 1974)
Thomas (Fr 1974)
Au delà de la peur [La paura dietro la porta] (It-Fr 1975)
Vincent mit l'âne dans un pré (Fr 1975)

BOURBER, AAF (Aafje ten Hoope), b. Oct. 17, 1885, Amsterdam;
d. May 23, 1974
Het Wrak in de Noordzee (Dut 1915)
Genie Tegen Geweld (Dut 1916)
Cirque Hollandais (Dut 1924)
Oranje Hein (Dut 1925)
Waar een Wil Is, Is een Weg (Dut 1931)
Op Hoop van Zegen (Dut 1934)
De Jantjes (Dut 1924)
Bleeke Bet (Dut 1934)
Suikerfreule (Dut 1935)
Het Leven Is Niet Zo Kwaad (Dut 1935)
Oranje Hein (Dut 1936)
Merijntje Gijzen's Jeugd (Dut 1936)
Drie Wenschen (Dut 1937)
Veertig Jaren (Dut 1938)
Vadertje Langbeen (Dut 1938)
De Laatste Dagen van een Eiland (Dut 1938)
Morgen Gaat het Beter (Dut 1939)
Ergens in Nederland (Dut 1940)
Sterren Stralen Overal (Dut 1953)

BOURVIL (André Raimbourg), b. July 27, 1917, Pétrot-Vicquemere,
France; d. Nov. 8, 1970
La Ferme du pendu (Fr 1945)
Pas si bête! (Fr 1946)
Blanc comme neige (Fr 1947)
Par la fenêtre (Fr 1947)
Le Coeur sur la main (Fr 1948)
Le Roi Pandore (Fr 1949)
Miquette et sa mère (Fr 1949)
Le Rosier de Madame Husson (Fr 1950)
Le Passe-muraille (Fr 1950)
Seul dans Paris (Fr 1951)
Le Trou normand [Crazy for Love] (Fr 1952)
Les Trois Mousquetaires (Fr-It 1953)

Si Versailles m'était conté (Fr 1953)
Poisson d'avril (Fr 1954)
Cadet Rousselle (Fr 1954)
Si Paris nous était conté (Fr 1955)
Un Fil à la patte (Fr 1955)
Les Hussards (Fr 1955)
La Traversée de Paris [A Pig Across Paris] (Fr-It 1956)
Le Chanteur de Mexico (Fr-Sp 1957)
Les Misérables (Fr-E Ger-It 1957)
Le Miroir à deux faces [The Mirror Has Two Faces] (Fr-It
    1958)
Sérénade au Texas (Fr 1958)
Un drôle de dimanche (Fr 1958)
La Jument verte (Fr-It 1959)
Le Chemin des écoliers (Fr-It 1959)
Le Bossu (Fr-It 1959)
Fortunat (Fr-It 1960)
Le Capitan (Fr-It 1960)
Tout l'or du monde [All the Gold in the World] (Fr-It 1961)
Les Culottes rouges (Fr 1962)
Tartarin de Tarascon (Fr 1962)
Un Clair de lune à Mauberge (Fr 1962)
The Longest Day (20th 1962)
Un drôle de paroissien [Thank Heaven for Small Favors] (Fr
    1963)
Le Tracassin (Fr 1963) [made in 1961]
La Foire aux cancres (Fr 1963)
Les Bonnes Causes (Fr 1963)
Le Magot de Josefa (Fr-It 1964)
La Grande Frousse (Fr 1964)
La Cuisine au beurre (Fr-It 1964)
Guerra segreta [Guerre secrète/The Dirty Game] (It-Fr-W Ger 1965)
L'Âge ingrat (Fr 1965)
La Grosse Caisse (Fr 1965)
Le Corniaud [The Sucker] (Fr-It 1965)
Les Grandes Gueules [The Wise Guys] (Fr-It 1966)
Trois Enfants... dans le désordre (Fr 1966)
La Grande Vadrouille (Fr 1966)
Voglio vivere la mia vita (It-Fr 1967)
Les Arnaud (Fr-It 1967)
Les Cracks (Fr-It 1967)
La Grande Lessive (Fr 1968)
Quei temerari sulle loro pazze, scatenate, scalcinate carriole
    [Gonflés à bloc/Monte Carlo or Bust] (It-Fr 1969)
Le Cerveau (Fr-It 1969)
L'Arbre de Noël [The Christmas Tree] (Fr-It 1969)
L'Etalon (Fr 1970)
Le Mur de l'Atlantique (Fr-It 1970)
Le Cercle rouge (Fr-It 1970)

BOYD, STEPHEN, b. June 4, 1928, Belfast
    An Alligator Named Daisy (RFD 1955)
    The Man Who Never Was (20th 1956)

A Hill in Korea [Hell in Korea] (BL 1956)
Seven Waves Away [Abandon Ship!] (Col 1957)
Island in the Sun (20th 1957)
Seven Thunders [Beasts of Marseilles] (RFD 1957)
Les Bijoutiers du clair de lune [Heaven Fell That Night] (Fr
  1958)
The Bravados (20th 1958)
Ben-Hur (MGM 1959)
Woman Obsessed (20th 1959)
The Best of Everything (20th 1959)
The Big Gamble (20th 1960)
The Inspector [Lisa] (20th 1962)
Billy Rose's Jumbo (MGM 1962)
Venus imperiale [Imperial Venus] (It 1962)
The Fall of the Roman Empire (Par 1964)
The Third Secret (20th 1964)
The Oscar (Emb 1966)
The Bible... In the Beginning (20th 1966)
Fantastic Voyage (20th 1966)
The Caper of the Golden Bulls (Emb 1967)
Department K (Col 1967)
Shalako (WPD 1968)
The Slaves (WB 1969)
Carter's Army (ABC-TV 1970)
Marta (Sp-It 1970)
Kill! [Kill Kill Kill] (Fr-Sp 1972)
Historia de una traicion (Sp-It 1972)
The Man Called Noon (GB-Sp-It 1973)
Key West (NBC-TV 1973)
The Lives of Jenny Dolan (NBC-TV 1975)

BOYER, CHARLES, b. Aug 28, 1897, Figeac, France
L'Homme du large (Fr 1920)
Le Grillon du foyer (Fr 1920)
Chantelouve (Fr 1921)
L'esclave (Fr 1922)
La Ronde infernale (Fr 1927)
Le Capitaine Fracasse (Fr 1928)
Le Procès de Mary Dugan [Fr version of The Trial of Mary
  Dugan] (MGM 1929)
Barcarolle d'amour [Fr version of Ger film Brand in der Oper]
  (Ger 1930)
Révolte dans la Prison [Fr version of The Big House] (MGM
  1930)
The Magnificent Lie (Par 1931)
Quand on est belle [Fr version of The Easiest Way] (MGM 1931)
Men Call It Love [Fr version of Men Call It Love] (MGM 1931)
Tumultes [Fr version of Ger film Sturme der Leidenschaft]
  (Fr 1931)
I. F. 1 ne repond plus [Fr version of Ger film F. P. 1 antwortet
  nicht] (Ger 1931)
The Man from Yesterday (Par 1932)
Red-Headed Woman (MGM 1932)

Charles Boyer (left), Brigitte Bardot and Henri Vidal in La Parisienne (1957).

L'Epervier [Les Amoureux] (Fr 1933)
Moi et l'impèratrice [Fr version of Ger film Ich und die Kaiser-
    in] (Ger 1933)
The Only Girl [Heart Song] [Eng lang version of Ger film Ich
    und die Kaiserin] (Ger 1933)
Liliom (Fr 1933)
La Bataille (Fr 1934)
The Battle [Hara-Kiri/Thunder in the East] [Eng lang version
    of La Bataille] (Fr 1934)
Caravan (Fox 1934)
Caravane [Fr version of Caravan] (Fox 1934)
Le Bonheur (Fr 1934)
Private Worlds (Par 1935)
Break of Hearts (RKO 1935)
Shanghai (Par 1935)
Mayerling (Fr 1936)
The Garden of Allah (UA 1936)
Tovarich (WB 1937)
Conquest [Marie Waleska] (MGM 1937)
History Is Made at Night (UA 1937)

Orage (Fr 1937)
Algiers (UA 1938)
Love Affair (RKO 1939)
When Tomorrow Comes (Univ 1939)
Le Corsaire (Fr 1939) [unfinished]
All This, and Heaven Too (WB 1940)
Untel père et fils/The Heart of a Nation (Fr-USA 1940) [com-
    pleted in USA] (narrator)
Back Street (Univ 1941)
Hold Back the Dawn (Par 1941)
Appointment for Love (Univ 1941)
Tales of Manhattan (20th 1942)
The Constant Nymph (WB 1943)
Flesh and Fantasy (Univ 1943)
Gaslight [The Murder in Thornton Square] (MGM 1944)
Together Again (Col 1944)
Bataille de Russie [Fr version of The Battle of Russia] (US War
    Dept 1945) [documentary; narrator]
Le combattant [Fr version of The Fighting Lady] (US War Dept
    1945) [documentary; narrator]
Confidential Agent (WB 1945)
Cluny Brown (20th 1946)
A Woman's Vengeance (Univ 1948)
Arch of Triumph (UA 1948)
The Thirteenth Letter (20th 1951)
The First Legion (UA 1951)
The Happy Time (Col 1952)
Thunder in the East (Par 1953) [filmed in 1951]
Madame de... [The Earrings of Madame De] (Fr-It 1953)
Nana (Fr-It 1954)
The Cobweb (MGM 1955)
La fortuna di essere donna (It-Fr 1956)
Paris-Palace Hôtel (Fr-It 1956)
Around the World in 80 Days (UA 1956)
La Parisienne (Fr-It 1957)
The Buccaneer (Par 1958)
Maxime (Fr 1958)
La Grande Rencontre [Fr version of Windjammer] (Fr 1958)
    [narrator]
Fanny (WB 1961)
The Four Horsemen of the Apocalypse (MGM 1962)
Les Démons de minuit [Midnight Folly] (Fr-It 1961)
Julia, Du bist zauberhaft [Adorable Julia] (Aus-Fr 1961)
Love Is a Ball [All This and Money Too] (UA 1963)
A Very Special Favor (Univ 1964)
How to Steal a Million (20th 1966)
Paris brûle-t-il? [Is Paris Burning?] (Fr 1966)
Casino Royale (Col 1967)
Barefoot in the Park (Par 1967)
The April Fools (National General 1969)
The Madwoman of Chaillot (WPD 1969)
Rublo de las dos caras [The Day the Hot Line Got Hot] (Sp-Fr-
    It 1969)

Lost Horizon (Col 1973)
Stavisky (Fr-It 1974)

BRASSEUR, CLAUDE (Claude Espinasse), b. June 15, 1936, Paris
Le Pays d'où je viens (Fr 1956)
L'Eau vive [The Girl on the River] (Fr 1956)
L'Amour descend du ciel (Fr 1957)
Rue des Prairies (Fr-It 1959)
La Verte Moisson (Fr 1959)
Pierrot la tendresse (Fr 1960)
Les Distractions [Trapped by Fear] (Fr-It 1960)
La Bride sur le cou [Please, Not Now] (Fr-It 1961)
Les Menteurs [House of Sin] (Fr 1961)
Les Sept Péchés capitaux [Seven Capital Sins] (ep "L'Envie")
   (Fr-It 1961)
Les Ennemis (Fr 1961)
Le Caporal épinglé [The Vanishing Corporal] (Fr 1962)
Nous irons à Deauville (Fr 1962)
Un Clair de lune à Mauberge (Fr 1962)
Germinal (Fr-It 1962)
Peau de banane [Banana Skin] (Fr-It 1963)
Dragées au poivre [Sweet and Sour] (Fr-It 1963)
La Soupe aux poulets (Fr 1963)
Lucky Jo (Fr 1964)
Bande à part (Fr 1964)
La Bonne Occase (Fr-It 1965)
Du Rififi à Paname [Rififi in Paris] (Fr-W Ger-It 1965)
Le Chien fou [The Mad Dog] (Fr 1966)
Un Homme de trop [Shock Troops] (Fr-It 1967)
La Chasse royale (Fr-Czech 1969)
Catherine--Il suffit d'un amour (Fr-It 1970)
Trop petit, mon ami (Fr 1970)
Le Viager (Fr 1972)
Une Belle Fille comme moi (Fr 1972)
Bel Ordure (Fr 1973)
Les Seins de glace (Fr-It 1974)
L'Agression (Fr 1975)
Il faut vivre dangereusement (Fr-It 1975)

BRASSEUR, PIERRE (Pierre Espinasse), b. Dec. 22, 1905, Paris;
   d. Aug. 14, 1972
Madame Sans-Gêne (Fr 1925)
Feu (Fr 1928)
Un Trou dans le mur (Fr 1930)
Circulez! (Fr 1931)
I. F. 1 ne répond plus (Fr 1931)
Mon ami Victor (Fr 1932)
Le Vainqueur (Fr 1932)
Un Rêve blond (Fr 1932)
Quick (Ger-Fr 1932)
Voyage de noces (Sp-Fr 1932)
Papa sans le savoir (Fr 1932)

Chanson d'une nuit (Fr 1933)
Moi et l'impératrice (Fr 1933)
Le Sexe faible (Fr 1933)
Incognito (Fr 1933)
Caravane (Fr-USA 1934)
La Garnison amoureuse (Fr 1934)
Le Miroir aux alouettes (Fr 1934)
Johnny Haute Couture (Fr 1934)
L'Oncle de Pékin (Fr 1934)
Le Bébé de l'escadron [Quand la vie était belle] (Fr 1935)
Bout-de-chou (Fr 1935)
Un Oiseau rare (Fr 1935)
La Valse eternelle (Fr 1935)
Quadrille d'amour (Fr 1935)
Jeunesse d'abord (Fr 1936)
Pattes de mouches (Fr 1936)
Le Mari rêvé (Fr 1936)
La Reine des requilleuses (Fr 1936)
Prête-moi ta femme (Fr 1936)
Passe à vendre (Fr 1936)
Vous n'avez rien a déclarer? (Fr 1936)
Claudine a l'école (Fr 1937)
Hercule [L'Incorruptible] (Fr 1937)
Mademoiselle ma mère (Fr 1937)
Une Femme qui se partage (Fr 1937)
Café de Paris (Fr 1938)
Gosse de riche (Fr 1938)
Grisou (Fr 1938)
Le Quai des brumes (Fr 1938)
Le Schpountz (Fr 1938)
Visages de femmes (Fr 1938)
Frères corses (Fr 1938)
Giuseppe Verdi (It-Fr 1938)
Trois Argentins à Montmartre (Fr 1939)
Dernière jeunesse (Fr 1939)
Le père Lebonnard (Fr 1939)
Le Chemin de l'honneur (Fr 1939)
Sixième étage (Fr 1939)
Tobie est un ange (Fr 1941) [destroyed]
Le Soleil a toujours raison (Fr 1941)
Les Deux Timides (Fr 1941)
Promesse à l'inconnue (Fr 1942)
La Croisée des chemins (Fr 1942)
Lumière d'été (Fr 1942)
Adieu Léonard (Fr 1943)
Les Enfants du paradis [Children of Paradise] (Fr 1945)
Le Pays sans étoiles (Fr 1945)
Jericho (Fr 1945)
La Femme fatale (Fr 1945)
Les Portes de la nuit (Fr 1946)
Pétrus (Fr 1946)
Rocambole (Fr 1946)
La Revanche de Baccarat (Fr 1946)

L'Arche de Noé (Fr 1946)
L'Amour autour de la maison (Fr 1946)
Croisière pour l'inconnu (Fr 1947)
La Nuit blanche (Fr 1948)
Le Secret de Monte-Cristo (Fr 1948)
Les Amants de Vérone (Fr 1948)
Portrait d'un assassin (Fr 1949)
Millionaires d'un jour (Fr 1949)
Julie de Carneilhan (Fr 1949)
Souvenirs perdus (ep "La Statuette") (Fr 1950)
L'Homme de la Jamaïque (Fr 1950)
Maître après Dieu (Fr 1950)
De Renoir à Picasso (Bel 1950)
Barbe-bleue (Fr 1951)
Le Plaisir (ep "La Maison Tellier") (Fr 1951)
Les Mains sales (Fr 1951)
Le Rideau rouge [The Red Curtain] (Fr 1952)
La Pocharde [The Drunkard] (Fr 1952)
La Bergère et le ramoneur (Fr 1952) [voice only]
Jouons le jeu (ep "L'Impatience") (Fr 1952) [interviewee]
Raspoutine (Fr-It 1954)
Vestire gli ignudi (It 1954)
La Tour de Nesle [The Tower of Lust] (Fr-It 1954)
Napoléon (Fr 1954)
Oasis (Fr-W Ger 1954)
Porte des Lilas (Fr-It 1957)
La Vie à deux (Fr 1958)
Les Grandes Familles (Fr 1958)
Sans famille [The Adventures of Remi] (Fr-It 1958)
La Tête contre les murs [The Keepers] (Fr 1958)
La Loi (Fr-It 1958)
Cartagine i fiamme [Carthage in Flames] (It 1958)
Messieurs les ronds-de-cuir (Fr 1958)
Le Dialogue des Carmélites (Fr-It 1958)
Candide, ou l'optimisme au XXe siècle [Candide] (Fr 1960)
Les Yeux sans visage [Eyes Without a Face] (Fr 1960)
Il bell'Antonio (It 1960)
L'Affaire Nina B (W Ger-Fr 1961)
Les Petits Matins [Girl on the Road] (Fr 1961)
Pleins feux sur l'assassin (Fr 1961)
Les Amours célèbres (ep "Agnès Bernauer") (Fr-It 1961)
Le crime ne paie pas (ep "L'Affaire Fenayrou") (Fr-It 1962)
Rencontres (Fr 1962)
Vive Henri IV, vive l'amour (Fr-It 1962)
Le Bateau d'Emile (Fr-It 1962)
L'Abominable Homme des douanes (Fr 1963)
Les Bonnes Causes [Don't Tempt the Devil] (Fr-It 1963)
Liolà/Le coq du village (It 1963)
Un soir... par hasard (Fr 1964)
Le Magot de Joséfa (Fr-It 1964)
Humour noir (ep "Le Fournui") (Fr-It 1964)
La Métamorphose des cloportes (Fr 1964)
Lucky Jo (Fr 1964)

L'Or du Duc (Fr-It 1965)
Grain de sable (Fr-It-W Ger-Por 1965)
Pas de panique (Fr 1965)
Un Monde nouveau (Fr-It 1965)
Pas de caviar pour Tante Olga (Fr 1965)
La Vie de château (Fr 1965)
Deux Heures à tuer (Fr-Bel 1965)
La Fille de la Mer Morte (Isr-Fr 1966)
Le Roi de coeur [The King of Hearts] (Fr-It 1966)
Le Fou du labo 4 [The Madman in Laboratory 4] (Fr 1967)
La Petite Vertu (Fr 1967)
Les Oiseaux vont mourir au Pérou [The Birds Come to Die in
    Peru] (Fr 1967)
Sous le signe de Monte-Cristo (Fr-It 1968)
Goto, l'île d'amour (Fr 1968)
Macédoine (Fr 1970)
Les Mariés de l'an II [The Scoundrel] (Fr-It-Rum 1970)
La più bella serata della mia vita (It 1972)

BRAZZI, ROSSANO, b. Sept. 18, 1917, Bologna
Processo e morte di Socrate (It 1939)
Il Ponte di vetro (It 1940)
Kean (It 1940)
Ritorno (It 1940)
La forza bruta (It 1940)
Tosca [The Story of Tosca] (It 1940)
È caduta una donna (It 1941)
Il re si diverte [The King's Jester] (It 1941)
Il bravo di Venezia (It 1941)
Una signora dell'ovest (It 1941)
I due foscari (It 1942)
La gorgona (It 1942)
Redenzione (It 1942)
Noi vivi (It 1942)
Baruffe chiozzotte [Paese senza pace] (It 1943)
Silenzio, si gira! (It 1943)
La casa senza tempo (It 1943)
Maria Malibran (It 1943)
Il treno crociato (It 1943)
Piazza Sepolcro [Cronaca di due secoli] (It 1943) [unreleased]
Aquila nera (It 1945)
Malia (It 1945)
La resa di Titì [The Merry Chase] (It 1945)
Furia (It 1946)
Il passatore (It 1947)
Il corriere del re (It 1948)
Il diavolo bianco (It 1948)
La grande aurora [The Great Dawn] (It 1948)
I contrabbandieri del mare (It 1949)
Eleanora Duse (It 1949)
Little Women (MGM 1949)
Romanzo d'amore [Toselli] (It-Fr 1950)
Vulcano (It 1950)

Incantesimo tragico [Olivia] (It 1951)
Gli inesorabili (It 1951)
La leggenda di Genoveffa (It 1952)
La donna che invento l'amore (It 1952)
L'ingiusta condanna [Quelli che non muoino/Guilt Is Not Mine]
    (It 1952)
Eran trecento (It 1952)
Il figlio di Lagardere (It 1952)
La vendetta di Aquila nera (It 1952)
Il boia di Lilla (It 1953)
C'erà una volta Angelo Musco (It 1953)
La corona nera (It 1953)
La prigioniera della terra di fuoco (It 1953)
Angela (It-USA 1954)
Carne de horca [Il terrore dell'Andalusia] (Sp-It 1954)
Three Coins in the Fountain (20th 1954)
The Barefoot Contessa (UA 1954)
La contessa di Castiglione [La Castiglione] (It-Fr 1955)
Faccia da mascalzone (It 1955)
La chair et le diable [Fuoco nelle vene] (Fr-It 1955)
Gli ultimo cinque minuti [The Last Five Minutes] (It 1955)
Summertime (UA 1955)
Il conte Aquila (It 1956)
Loser Takes All (BL 1956)
The Story of Esther Costello [The Golden Virgin] (Col 1957)
Interlude (Univ 1957)
The Legend of the Lost (UA 1957)
South Pacific (Magna Pictures 1958)
A Certain Smile (20th 1958)
Count Your Blessings (MGM 1959)
L'assedio di Siracusa [La charge de Syracuse/The Siege of
    Syracuse] (It-Fr 1960)
Austerlitz [Napoleone ad Austerlitz] (Fr-It 1960)
La monaca di Monza (It 1962)
Rome Adventure (WB 1962)
La rossa [Die Rote] (It-W Ger 1962)
L'intrigo [Meurtre par accident/Dark Purpose] (It-Fr 1962)
Light in the Piazza (MGM 1962)
Le quattro verità [Les quatre vérités/Las cuatro verdades/
    Three Fables of Love] (ep "La lepre e la tartaruga") (It-Fr-
    Sp 1963)
Il marito latino (It 1964)
The Battle of the Villa Fiorita (WB-7 Arts 1965)
Un amore [Une garce inconsciente] (It-Fr 1965)
La ragazza in prestito [Engagement italiano] (It-Fr 1965)
Il natale che quasi non fu [The Christmas that Almost Wasn't]
    (It-USA 1966)
La ragazza del bersagliere (It 1967)
Per amore...per maggia (It 1967)
The Bobo (WB-7 Arts 1967)
Woman Times Seven (ep "Amateur Night") (Emb 1967)
Krakatoa--East of Java (Cin 1968)
Andante (It 1968)

Diario segreto di una minorenne (It 1968)
Rey de Africa [Caccia ai violenti/One Step to Hell] (Sp-It-USA
  1968)
Salvare la faccia [Psychout for Murder] (It 1969)
The Italian Job (Par 1969)
Assignment Istanbul (It 1969)
Sette uomini ed un cervello (It 1969)
Honeymoon with a Stranger (ABC-TV 1969)
The Adventurers (Par 1970)
Intimita proibita di una giovane sposa (It 1970)
Il sesso del diavolo (It 1971)
Il giorno del giudizio (It 1971)
The Great Waltz (MGM 1972)
Racconti proibiti... di niente vestiti (It 1972)
Morir por amar (Sp 1972)
Il castello della paura (It 1973)

BRIALY, JEAN-CLAUDE, b. March 30, 1933, Aumale, Algeria
Die Kreutzersonate (W Ger 1956)
Eléna et les hommes [Paris Does Strange Things] (Fr-It 1956)
  (role cut from release print)
L'Ami de la famille (Fr 1957)
Tous peuvent me tuer [Anyone Can Kill Me] (Fr-It 1957)
Le Triporteur [The Screwball] (Fr 1957)
Ascenseur pour l'echafaud [Frantic] (Fr 1957)
Un Amour de poche (Fr 1957)
Cargaison blanche [Traffic in Souls] (Fr 1957)
L'Ecole des cocottes [In 6 Easy Lessons] (Fr 1958)
Et ta soeur? (Fr 1958)
Christine (Fr-It 1958)
Le Beau Serge (Fr 1958)
Les 400 coups (Fr 1958) (cameo)
Le Bel Âge [Love Is Where You Find It] (Fr-It 1958)
Le Chemin des ecoliers (Fr 1959)
Les Cousins (Fr 1959)
Le Gigolo (Fr 1959)
Les Yeux de l'amour (Fr 1959)
La notte brava [Night Heat] (It-Fr 1959)
Les Godelureaux (Fr-It 1960)
Le Puits aux trois vérités (Fr 1960)
Paris nous appartient (Fr 1960)
Les Petits Matins [Girl on the Road] (Fr 1961) (cameo)
Une Femme est une femme [A Woman Is a Woman] (Fr 1961)
L'Education sentimentale (Fr 1961)
Les Lions sont lâchés (Fr-It 1961)
Amours célèbres (ep "Agnes Bernauer") (Fr-It 1961)
Les Sept Péchés capitaux [Seven Capital Sins] (ep "L'Avarice")
  (Fr-It 1961)
La Chambre ardente [The Curse and the Coffin] (Fr-It 1961)
Cléo de 5 à 7 [Cleo from 5 to 7] (Fr-It 1962) (cameo)
Arsène Lupin contre Arsène Lupin (Fr-It 1962)
Le Diable et les dix commandements (ep "Le Bien d'autrui tu ne
  prendras") (Fr-It 1962)

Jean-Claude Brialy

Le Glaive et la balance [Two Are Guilty] (Fr-It 1962)
La banda Casaroli (It 1962)
Adieu Philippine (Fr-It 1962) (cameo)
Carambolages (Fr 1962)
La Bonne Soupe (Fr-It 1963)
Château en Suède [Nutty Naughty Chateau] (Fr-It 1963)
La Chasse à l'homme [Male Hunt] (Fr-It 1964)
La Ronde [Circle of Love] (Fr-It 1964)
Tonio Kröger (W Ger 1964)
Viheltäjät (Fin 1964) (cameo)
Un Monsieur de compagnie (Fr-It 1964)
L'Amour à la mer (Fr 1964)
La Bonne Occase (Fr-It 1964)
Comment epouser un premier ministre (Fr-It 1964)
Cent Briques et des tuiles [How Not to Rob a Department Store]
    (Fr-It 1965)
Io la conoscevo bene (It 1965)
Il morbidone (It 1965)

La mandragola (It-Fr 1965)
I nostri mariti (ep "Le Complexe d'Angelotto") (It 1966)
Le Roi de coeur [King of Hearts] (Fr-It 1966)
Un Homme de trop [Shock Troops] (Fr-It 1967)
Le Plus Vieux Métier du monde (ep "Mamselle Mimi") (Fr-
     W Ger-It 1967)
Lamiel (Fr-It 1967)
La Mariée était en noir [The Bride Wore Black] (Fr-It
     1967)
Operazione San Pietro [Au diable, les Anges] (It-Fr 1967)
Caroline chérie (Fr-It-W Ger 1967)
Manon 70 (Fr-It-W Ger 1968)
Le Bal du Comte d'Orgel (Fr 1970)
Cose di Cosa Nostra! (It 1970)
Le Genou de Claire [Claire's Knee] (Fr-It 1970)
Una stagione all'inferno [Une Saison en enfer] (It-Fr 1971)
Un meurtre est un meurtre (Fr 1972)
L'Oiseau rare (Fr-It 1973)
Comme un pot de fraises (Fr 1974)
Le Fantôme de la Liberté [The Phantom of Liberty] (Fr 1974)
Un Animal doué de deraison (Bra-Fr 1975)
Catherine et Cie (Fr-It 1975)

BRION, FRANÇOISE (Françoise de Ribon), b. Jan. 29, 1934, Paris
Donnez-moi ma chance (Fr 1957)
Nathalie [The Foxiest Girl in Paris] (Fr-It 1957)
Cette nuit-là (Fr 1958)
Le Petit Prof (Fr 1959)
Katia [The Magnificent Sinner] (Fr 1959)
L'Eau à la Bouche (Fr 1959)
Un Temoin dans la ville (Fr-It 1959)
Le Bel Âge (Fr 1960)
Le Saint Mène la danse (Fr 1960)
Coeur battant [The French Game] (Fr 1960)
Comment qu'elle est [Women Are Like That] (Fr 1960)
Les Parisiennes [Tales of Paris] (Fr-It 1961)
La Dénonciation (Fr 1961)
Lemmy pour les dames [Ladies Man] (Fr 1962)
Et Satan conduit le bal (Fr 1962)
L'Immortelle (Fr-It-Tur 1962)
Codine (Rum 1962)
Dragées au Poivre [Sweet and Sour] (Fr-It 1963)
Vacances portugaises (Fr 1963)
De Cuerpo Presente (Sp 1965)
El Salario del Crimen (Sp 1965)
Un Monde nouveau (Fr-It 1965)
Cartes sur table (Sp-Fr 1966)
La Blonde de Pékin (Fr-W Ger-It 1966)
Alexandre le Bienheureux (Fr 1967)
Les Gommes (Fr-Bel 1968)
To Grab the Ring (Holl 1968)
Un Beau Monstre [A Strange Love Affair] (Fr-It 1970)
Je, tu, elles (Fr 1971)

Les soleils de l'île de Pâques (Fr-Bra-Chile 1972)
Adieu Poulet (Fr 1975)

BROOK, CLIVE (Clifford Hardman Brook), b. June 1, 1887, London; d. Nov. 17, 1974
Trent's Last Case (Walturdaw 1920)
Kissing Cup's Race (Butcher 1920)
Her Penalty (Walturdaw 1921)
The Loudwater Mystery (Walturdaw 1921)
Daniel Deronda (Butcher 1921)
A Sportsman's Wife (Walturdaw 1921)
Sonia (Ideal 1921)
Christie Johnstone (Walturdaw 1921)
Shirley (Ideal 1922)
Married to a Mormon (Astral 1922)
Stable Companions (Jury 1922)
The Experiment (Stoll 1922)
A Debt of Honour (Stoll 1922)
Love and a Whirlwind (Cosmograph 1922)
Through Fire and Water (Ideal 1923)
This Freedom (Ideal 1923)
Out to Win (Ideal 1923)
The Royal Oak (Stoll 1923)
Woman to Woman (W & F 1923)
The Money Habit (Granger 1924)
The White Shadows [White Shadows] (W & F 1924)
The Wine of Life (Butcher 1924)
The Passionate Adventure (Gaumont 1924)
Love's Bargain [Human Desires] (Gaumont 1924)
Christine of the Hungry Heart (FN 1924)
The Recoil (Metro-Goldwyn 1924)
The Mirage (PDC 1924)
Enticement (FN 1925)
When Love Grows Cold (FBO 1925)
Playing with Souls (FN 1925)
Declassee (FN 1925)
The Woman Hater (WB 1925)
The Home Maker (Univ 1925)
If Marriage Fails (FBO 1925)
The Pleasure Buyers (WB 1925)
Seven Sinners (WB 1925)
Compromise (WB 1925)
Three Faces East (PDC 1925)
Why Girls Go Back Home (WB 1926)
For Alimony Only (PDC 1926)
You Never Know Women (Par 1926)
The Popular Sin (Par 1926)
Afraid to Love (Par 1927)
Barbed Wire (Par 1927)
Paying the Penalty Underworld [Paying the Penalty] (Par 1927)
Hula (Par 1927)
The Devil Dancer (UA 1927)
French Dressing [Lessons for Wives] (FN 1927)

Midnight Madness (Pathé 1928)
The Yellow Lily (FN 1928)
The Perfect Crime (FBO 1928)
Forgotten Faces (Par 1928)
Interference (Par 1929)
A Dangerous Woman (Par 1929)
The Four Feathers (Par 1929)
Charming Sinners (Par 1929)
The Laughing Lady (Par 1929)
The Return of Sherlock Holmes (Par 1929)
Slightly Scarlet (Par 1930)
Paramount on Parade (ep "Murder Will Out") (Par 1930)
Sweethearts and Wives (FN 1930)
Anybody's Woman (Par 1930)
East Lynne (Fox 1931)
Scandal Sheet (Par 1931)
Tarnished Lady (Par 1931)
The Lawyer's Secret (Par 1931)
Silence (Par 1931)
24 Hours [The Hours Between] (Par 1931)
Husband's Holiday (Par 1932)
Shanghai Express (Par 1932)
The Man from Yesterday (Par 1932)
The Night of June 13 (Par 1932)
Sherlock Holmes (Fox 1932)
Make Me a Star (Par 1932)
Cavalcade (Fox 1933)
Midnight Club (Par 1933)
If I Were Free [Behold We Live] (RKO 1933)
Gallant Lady (UA 1933)
Where Sinners Meet [The Dover Road] (Rep 1934)
Let's Try Again [Marriage Symphony] (RKO 1934)
Dressed to Thrill (Fox 1935)
The Dictator [The Love Affair of a Dictator/For the Love
    of a Queen/The Loves of a Dictator] (Gaumont 1935)
Love in Exile (GFD 1936)
The Lonely Road [Scotland Yard Commands] (ABFD 1936)
Action for Slander (UA Br 1937)
The Ware Case (ABFD 1938)
Return to Yesterday (ABFD 1940)
Convoy (ABFD 1940)
Freedom Radio [The Voice in the Night] (Col Br 1941)
Breach of Promise [Adventure in Blackmail] (MGM Br 1941)
The Flemish Farm (GFD 1943)
The Shipbuilders (Anglo 1943)
On Approval (GFD 1944)
The List of Adrian Messenger (Univ 1963)

BRUSSE, KEES, b. Feb. 26, 1925, Rotterdam
    Merijntje Gijzen's Jeugd (Dut 1936)
    De Dijk Is Dicht (Dut 1950)
    Ciske de rat [Ciske, ein Kind Braucht Liebe] (Dut-W Ger 1955)

Kleren Maken de Man (Dut 1957)
Jenny (Dut 1958)
Acht Mädels im Boot (Dut-W Ger 1958)
De Overval (Dut 1962)
Blue Movie (Dut-W Ger 1971)
V. D. (Dut 1972)
Jonny en Jessy (Bel 1973)
Dakota (Dut 1974)
Rooie Sien (Dut 1975)
Dokter Pulder Zaait Papavers (Dut 1975)

BUCHANAN, JACK, b. April 2, 1891, Helensburgh, Scotland; d.
    Oct. 20, 1957
Auld Lang Syne (Unicorn 1917)
Her Heritage (Ward's 1919)
The Audacious Mr. Squire (B & C 1923)
The Happy Ending (Gaumont 1925)
Settled Out of Court (Gaumont 1925)
Bulldog Drummond's Third Round (Astra-National 1925)
Confetti (FN-Pathé 1927)
Toni (Wardour 1928)
Paris (FN 1929)
The Show of Shows (WB 1929)
Monte Carlo (Par 1930)
Man of Mayfair (Par Br 1931)
Goodnight Vienna [Magic Night] (W & F 1932)
Yes Mr. Brown (W & F 1933)
That's a Good Girl (UA Br 1933)
Brewster's Millions (UA Br 1935)
Come Out of the Pantry (UA Br 1935)
Limelight [Backstage] (GFD 1936)
When Knights Were Bold (GFD 1936)
This'll Make You Whistle (GFD 1936)
Smash and Grab (GFD 1937)
The Sky's the Limit (GFD 1937)
Break the News (GFD 1938)
The Gang's All Here [The Amazing Mr. Forrest] (ABPC 1939)
The Middle Watch (ABPC 1939)
Bulldog Sees It Through (ABPC 1940)
The Band Wagon (MGM 1953)
As Long As They're Happy (GFD 1955)
Josephine and Men (BL 1955)
Les Carnets du Major Thompson [The Diary of Major Thompson]
    (Fr 1955)

BUCHHOLZ, HORST, b. Dec. 4, 1932, Berlin
Marianne [Marianne de ma jeunesse/Marianne of My Youth]
    (W Ger-Fr 1954)
Himmel ohne Sterne [Sky Without Stars] (W Ger 1955)
Regine (W Ger 1956)
Die Halbstarken [Teenage Wolf Pack] (W Ger 1956)
Herrscher ohne Krone [King in the Shadows] (W Ger 1957)
Robinson soll nicht sterben (W Ger 1957)

Horst Buchholz and Gina Lollobrigida in Cervantes, The Young Rebel
(1969).

Die Bekenntnisse des Hochstaplers Felix Krull [The Confessions
    of Felix Krull] (W Ger 1957)
Monpti (W Ger 1957)
Endstation Liebe (W Ger 1957)
Nasser Asphalt (W Ger 1958)
Auferstehung [Resurrezione/Resurrection] (W Ger-It-Fr 1958)
Tiger Bay (RFD 1959)
Das Totenschiff (W Ger 1959)
The Magnificent Seven (UA 1960)
Fanny (WB 1961)
One, Two, Three (UA 1961)
Nine Hours to Rama   (20th 1961)
La noia [L'Ennui/The Empty Canvas] (It-Fr 1964)
Operacion Estambul [Colpo grosso a Galata Bridge/L'homme
    d'Istamboul/That Man in Istanbul] (Sp-It-Fr 1965)
La Fabuleuse Aventure de Marco Polo [Le meravigliose avven-
    ture di Marco Polo/Marko Polo/Marco the Magnificent] (Fr-
    It-Yug-Egy-Afghanistan 1966)
Cervantes [Le avventure e gli amori di Miguel Cervantes/Les

aventures extraordinaires de Cervantes/Cervantes, The Young
Rebel] (Sp-It-Fr 1966)
Jonny Banco, geliebter Taugenichts [Johnny Banco]   (W Ger-Fr-
It 1967)
Come quando perche (It 1968)
La colomba non deve volare (It 1969)
Le sauveur (Fr 1970)
The Great Waltz (MGM 1972)
Aber Jonny... (W Ger 1973)
Lohngelder für Pittsville [The Catamount Killing] (W Ger-USA-
Pol 1974)

Richard Burton (right) and Peter O'Toole in Becket (1964).

BURTON, RICHARD (Richard Jenkins), b. Nov. 10, 1925, Pontrhyd-
fen, South Wales
The Last Days of Dolwyn [Woman of Dolwyn] (BL 1949)
Now Barabbas Was a Robber... (WB 1949)
Waterfront [Waterfront Women] (GFD 1950)
The Woman with No Name [Her Panelled Door] (ABP 1950)
Green Grow the Rushes (BL 1951)
My Cousin Rachel (20th 1952)

The Desert Rats (20th 1953)
The Robe (20th 1953)
Demetrius and the Gladiators (20th 1954) [cameo]
Prince of Players (20th 1955)
The Rains of Ranchipur (20th 1955)
Alexander the Great (UA 1956)
Sea Wife (20th 1956)
Amère Victoire [Bitter Victory] (Fr 1957)
Look Back in Anger (ABP 1959)
The Bramble Bush (WB 1960)
Ice Palace (WB 1960)
A Midsummer Night's Dream [Br release of dubbed Czech film,
    Sen Noci Svatojánské] (ABP 1961) (voice only)
The Longest Day (20th 1962)
Cleopatra (20th 1963)
The V. I. P. 's (MGM 1963)
Zulu (Par 1963) [narrator]
Becket (Par 1964)
The Night of the Iguana (MGM 1964)
The Sandpiper (MGM 1965)
What's New Pussycat? (UA 1965) [cameo]
The Spy Who Came In from the Cold (Par 1965)
Hamlet (WB 1965)
Who's Afraid of Virginia Woolf? (WB 1966)
The Taming of the Shrew (Col 1966)
The Comedians (MGM 1967)
Doctor Faustus (Col 1967)
Boom! (RFD 1968)
Candy (Cin 1968)
Where Eagles Dare (MGM 1968)
Staircase (20th 1969)
Anne of the Thousand Days (RFD 1970)
Villain (MGM-EMI 1971)
Raid on Rommel (Univ 1971)
Under Milk Wood (RFD 1972)
The Assassination of Trotsky [L'Assassinat de Trotsky] (Fr-It-
    GB 1972)
Hammersmith Is Out (Cin 1972)
Barbe-Bleue [Bluebeard] (Fr 1972)
Divorce His; Divorce Hers (ABC-TV 1973)
Rappresaglia [Massacre in Rome] (It 1973)
Sutjeska (Yug 1973)
Il viaggio [The Journey] (It 1974)
The Klansman (Par 1974)

BUZZANCA, LANDO, b. Italy
    Divorzio all'italiana [Divorce, Italian Style] (It 1961)
    I giorni contati (It 1962)
    Le monachine (It 1963)
    I mostri (It 1963)
    La parmigiana (It 1963)
    Sedotta e abandonata [Seduced and Abandoned] (It 1964)
    Cadavere per signora (It 1964)

L'idea fissa (ep "La prima notte") (It 1964)
I marziani hanno dodici mani (It 1964)
Senza sole ne luna (It 1964)
Su e giu (ep "Questione di principio") (It 1965)
Made in Italy (It 1965)
Colpo grosso ma non troppo (It 1965)
Extraconiugale (It 1965)
James Tont, operazione U. N. O. (It 1965)
Letti sbagliati (It 1965)
James Tont, operazione D. U. E. (It 1966)
Ringo e Gringo contro tutti (It 1966)
Per qualche dollaro in meno (It 1966)
Le lit à deux places [Racconti a due piazze] (ep "Morire per
    vivere") (Fr-It 1966)
I nostri mariti (ep "Il marito di Olga") (It 1966)
Caccia alla volpe [After the Fox] (It-USA 1966)
Una rosa per tutti (It 1967)
Le dolci signore (It 1967)
Don Giovanni in Sicilia (It 1967)
Spia spione [Una ladrone para un espia] (It 1967)
Operazione San Pietro (It 1968)
Meglio vedova (It 1968)
Ringo e Gringo contro tutti [Heroes a la fuerza] (It 1968)
Frau Wirtin hat auch eine Nichte (W Ger 1969)
Professione bigamo [Warum hab' ich bloss zweimal ja gesagt]
    (It-W Ger 1969)
Puro siccome un angelo papa mi fece monaco (It 1969)
Un caso di coscienza (It 1970)
Il debito conjugale (It 1970)
Fermate il mondo, voglio scendere (It 1970)
Quando le donne avevano la coda (It 1970)
Nel giorno del Signore (It 1970)
Il prete sposato (It 1970)
La prima notte del Dr. Danieli, industriale col complesso del
    giocattolo (It 1970)
Le belve (It 1971)
Homo eroticus (It 1971)
Il merlo maschio (It 1971)
Il vichingo venuto dal sud [Mia moglie Karen] (It 1971)
All onorevole piacciono le donne (It 1972)
La calandria (It 1972)
Jus primae noctis (It 1972)
Quando le donne persero la coda (It 1972)
Il sindicalista (It 1972)
L'uccello migratore (It 1972)
Io e lui (It 1973)
Il magnate (It 1973)
La schiava io ce l'ho e tu no (It 1973)
L'arbitro (It 1974)
Bello come un arcangelo (It 1974)
Il domestico (It 1974)
Il fidanzamento (It 1975)

CAINE, MICHAEL (Maurice Micklewhite), b. March 14, 1933, London
  A Hill in Korea [Hell in Korea] (BL 1956)
  How to Murder a Rich Uncle (Col Br 1957)
  The Key (Col 1958)
  The Two-Headed Spy (Col Br 1958)
  Blind Spot (Butcher 1958)
  Passport to Shame [Room 43] (BL 1959)
  The Day the Earth Caught Fire (Pax 1959)
  Foxhole in Cairo (Britannia 1960)
  The Bulldog Breed (RFD 1960)
  Solo for Sparrow (AA 1962)
  The Wrong Arm of the Law (BL 1962)
  Zulu (Par 1963)
  The Ipcress File (RFD 1965)
  Gambit (Univ 1965)

Michael Caine in Alfie (1966).

Alfie (Par 1966)
The Wrong Box (Col 1966)
Funeral in Berlin (Par 1966)
Hurry Sundown (Par 1966)
Sette volte donne [Woman Times Seven] (Emb 1967)
Billion Dollar Brain (UA 1967)
Deadfall (20th 1967)
Tonite Let's All Make Love in London (Lorrimer 1967) (as himself)
Play Dirty (UA 1968)
The Magus (20th 1968)
The Italian Job (Par 1969)
Battle of Britain (UA 1969)
Too Late the Hero (Cin 1969)
Simon, Simon (Tigon 1970)
Get Carter (MGM-EMI 1970)
The Last Valley (Cin 1970)
Zee & Co. [X, Y & Zee] (Col 1971)
Kidnapped (RFD 1971)
Pulp (UA 1973)
Sleuth (Fox-Rank 1973)
The Black Windmill (CIC 1974)
The Marseille Contract [The Destructors] (GB-Fr 1974)
The Wilby Conspiracy (UA 1975)
The Romantic Englishwoman (GB-Fr 1975)

CALAMAI, CLARA, b. Sept. 7, 1915, Prato, Italy
Pietro Micca (It 1937)
Ettore Fieramosca (It 1938)
Il Fornaretto di Venezia (It 1939)
Io, suo padre (It 1939)
Il socio invisibile (It 1939)
L'eredita in corsa (It 1939)
Le sorprese del vagone letto (It 1939)
Boccaccio (It 1940)
Capitan Fracassa (It 1940)
Manovre d'amore (It 1940)
Addio giovinezza! (It 1940)
Il re del circo (It 1940)
Caravaggio, il pittore maledetto (It 1941)
I mariti tempesta d'amore (It 1941)
L'avventuriera del piano di sopra (It 1941)
I pirati della Malesia (It 1941)
Luce nelle tenebre (It 1941)
Brivido (It 1941)
La regina di Navarra (It 1941)
La guardia del corpo (It 1942)
Le vie del cuore (It 1942)
Ossessione (It 1942)
Addio amore! (It 1942)
Don Cesare di Bazan (It 1942)
Le sorelle Materassi (It 1942)
Enrico IV (It 1943)
Una piccola moglie (It 1943)

Sorelle Materassi (It 1943)
Dieci minuti di vita (It 1943--unreleased)
Due lettere anonime (It 1944)
L'adultera (It 1945)
La resa di Titi (It 1946)
Il tiranno di Padova (It 1946)
L'ultimo amore (It 1946)
Il mondo vuole così (It 1946)
Quando gli angeli dormono [Cuando los angéles duermen] (Sp-It 1947)
Amanti senza amore (It 1947)
Vespro siciliano (It 1949)
Romanticismo (It 1951)
Carne inquieta (It 1952)
Il moschettiere fantasma (It 1954)
Nuits blanches [Le notti bianche/White Nights] (Fr-It 1957)
Afrodite, dea dell'amore (It 1958)
Le streghe [The Witches] (It 1967)

CALVERT, PHYLLIS (Phyllis Bickle), b. Feb. 18, 1915, London
Two Days to Live (Anglo 1939)
They Came by Night (20th Br 1940)
Let George Do It (ABFD 1940)
Charley's Bighearted Aunt (GFD 1940)
Neutral Port (GFD 1940)
Inspector Hornleigh Goes To It [Mail Train] (20th Br 1941)
Kipps [The Remarkable Mr. Kipps] (20th Br 1941)
The Young Mr. Pitt (20th Br 1942)
Uncensored (GFD 1942)
The Man in Grey (GFD 1943)
Fanny by Gaslight [Man of Evil] (GFD 1944)
2,000 Women (GFD 1944)
Madonna of the Seven Moons (EL 1944)
They Were Sisters (GFD 1945)
Men of Two Worlds (GFD 1946)
The Magic Bow (GFD 1946)
The Root of All Evil (GFD 1947)
Time Out of Mind (Univ Br 1947)
Broken Journey (GFD 1948)
My Own True Love (Par Br 1949)
The Golden Madonna (IFD 1949)
The Woman with No Name [Her Panelled Door] (ABP 1950)
Appointment with Danger (Par 1951)
Mr. Denning Drives North (BL 1951)
Mandy [Crash of Silence] (GFD 1952)
The Net [Project M7] (GFD 1953)
It's Never Too Late (ABP 1956)
Child in the House (Eros 1956)
The Young and the Guilty (ABP 1958)
Indiscreet (WB 1958)
A Lady Mislaid (ABP 1958)
Oscar Wilde (20th 1960)
The Battle of the Villa Fiorita (WPD 1965)
Twisted Nerve (BL 1968)

Oh! What a Lovely War (Par 1969)
The Walking Stick (MGM 1970)

CAPRIOLI, VITTORIO, b. Aug. 15, 1921, Naples
O sole mio (It 1946)
Manu il contrabbandiere (It 1948)
Luci del varietà (It 1950)
Altri tempi (ep "Il processo di Frine") (It 1952)
Totò a colori (It 1952)
Febbre di vivere (It 1953)
Villa Borghese (It 1954)
Carosello napoletano (It 1954)
Domanda di grazia (It 1954)
Tempi nostri (It 1954)
Bella non piangere (It 1955)
Buonanotte... avvocato! (It 1955)
Arrangiatevi (It 1959)
Recours en grâce [Tra due donne] (Fr-It 1959)
Il generale Della Rovere (It 1959)
La legge (It 1959)
Where the Hot Wind Blows (Emb 1960)
A porte chiuse (It 1961)
Leoni al sole (It 1961)
Cinque ore in contanti (It 1961)
Zazie dans le metro [Zazie nel metro] (Fr-It 1961)
I giorni contati (It 1962)
Adieu, Philippine (Fr-It 1962)
Parigi o cara (It 1962)
Tra due donne (It 63)
I cuori infranti (It 1963)
Amore facile (ep "Il vedovo bianco) (It 1964)
Le voci bianche [Voci Blanche/White Voices] (It 1964)
I maniaci (It 1964)
Una vergine per il principe (It 1965)
Desidere nel sole (It 1965)
Io, io, io... e gli altri (It 1966)
Adulterio all'italiana (It 1966)
Ischia, operazione amore (It 1966)
Come imparai ad amare le donne [Das gewisse Etwas der
    Frauen] (It-W Ger 1966)
La donna è una cosa meravigliosa (It 1966)
Assicurasi vergine (It 1967)
Le dolci signore (It 1967)
La violenza e l'amore [Il mito] (ep "La solitudine") (It 1967)
La violenza d'amore (It 1967)
Bersaglio mobile (It 1967)
Il marito è mio e l'ammazzo quando mi pare (It 1968)
La matriarca (It 1968)
Scusi, facciao l'amore? (It 1968)
Metti, una sera a cena (It 1969)
Splendori e miserie di Madame Royale (It 1970)
Er più--Storia d'amore e di coltello (It 1971)
Ettore lo fusto (It 1971)
Roma bene (It 1971)

Vittorio Caprioli (right) and Salvo Randone in I giorni contati (1962).

Anche se volessi lavorare, che faccio? (It 1972)
Quando gli uomini armarono la clava e con le donne fecero din
    don (It 1972)
Quando le donne si chiamavano Madonne (It 1972)
La colonna infame (It 1972)
Tont va bien (Fr 1972)
Trastevere (It 1972)
Il Boss (It 1973)
Io e lui (It 1973)
Paslo il caldo (It 1973)
Le magnifique [Come si distrugge la reputazione del più grande
    agente segreto del mondo] (Fr-It 1973)
Une journée bien remplie [Una giornata spesa bene] (Fr-It 1973)
Innocenza e turbamento (It 1974)
La governante (It 1974)
La montarde me monte an nez (Fr 1974)
Il messia [La Messie] (It-Fr 1975)
Domani saremo ricchi e onesti (It 1975)

CARDINALE, CLAUDIA, b. April 15, 1939, Tunisia
   Goha (Fr 1958)
   I soliti ignoti (It 1958)
   Audace colpo dei soliti ignoti (It 1959)
   Il magistrato [El magistrado] (It-Sp 1959)
   Un maledetto imbroglio (It 1959)
   Tre straniere a Roma (It 1959)

Claudia Cardinale

La prima notte [Les Nuits vénitiennes] (It-Fr 1959)
Upstairs and Downstairs (RFD 1959)
Su e giù per le scale (It 1959)
Vento del sud (It 1959)
Austerlitz [Napoleone ad Austerlitz] (Fr-It 1960)
Rocco e i suoi fratelli [Rocco and His Brothers] (It 1960)
I delfini (It 1960)
Il bell'Antonio (It 1960)
La ragazza con la valiagia (It 1961)
Les Lions sont lâches [I leoni scaterrati] (Fr-It 1961)
La viaccia (It 1961)
Cartouche (Fr 1962)
Senilità (It 1962)
Il gattopardo [The Leopard] (20th 1963)
La ragazza di Bube (It 1963)
Otto e mezzo (It 1963)
The Pink Panther (UA 1964)
Circus World (Par 1964)
Gli indifferenti (It 1964)

Il magnifico cornuto (It 1964)
I leoni scatenati (It 1965)
Blindfold (Univ 1965)
Vaghe stelle dell'Orsa (It 1965)
Lost Command (Col 1966)
The Professionals (Col 1966)
Le fate (ep "Fata Armenia") (It 1966)
Una rosa per tutti (It 1967)
Don't Make Waves (MGM 1967)
The Hell with Heroes (Univ 1968)
Il giorno della civettà (It 1968)
Ruba al prossimo tuo [A Fine Pair] (It-USA 1968)
C'erà una volta il West [Once Upon a Time in the West] (It 1968)
Certo, certissimo, anzi...probabile (It 1969)
Nell'anno del signore (It 1969)
La tenda rossa [Krasnaya palatka] (It-USSR 1969)
The Adventures of Gerard (UA 1970)
L'udienza (It 1971)
Bello, onesto, emigrato Australia sposerebbe compaesana illibata
    (It 1971)
Popsy Pop [Fuori il malloppo] (Fr-It 1971)
Le pistolere (It-Fr 1971)
La scoumoune [Il clan dei Marsigliesi] (Fr-It 1972)
Il giorno del furore (It 1972)
I guappi (It 1974)
Gruppo di famiglia in un interno (It 1974)
A mezzanotte va la ronda del piacere (It 1975)
Libera, amore mio (It 1975)

CARERE, CHRISTINE (Christine de Borde), b. July 27, 1930, Dijon,
    France
Folie douce (Fr 1950)
Olivia (Fr 1950)
Le Passage de Vénus (Fr 1951)
Paris chante toujours (Fr 1951)
Terza liceo [L'amour au collège] (It 1952)
Un Caprice de Caroline Chérie (Fr 1952)
Anatole chéri (Fr 1953)
Sang et lumières (Fr 1953)
Cadet-Rousselle (Fr 1954)
Tout chante autour de moi (Fr 1954)
Don Juan [El amor de Don Juan] (Fr-Sp 1955)
L'Affaire des poisons [Il processo dei veleni] (Fr-It 1955)
Una donna libera [Femmes libres] (It-Fr 1955)
Le Chemin du paradis (Fr-W Ger 1955)
Printemps à Paris (Fr 1956)
Bonjour jeunesse (Fr 1956)
Les Délinquants [Delincuentes] (Fr-Sp 1957)
Nuit blanche et rouge à lèvres [Quelle sacree soirée] (Fr 1957)
L'Amour descend u ciel (Fr 1957)
Les collègiennes [The Twilight Girls] (Fr 1957)
La Nuit des suspectes (Fr 1958)
A Certain Smile (20th 1958)
Mardi Gras (20th 1958)

A Private's Affair (20th 1959)
I Deal in Danger (20th 1966)

CARMICHAEL, IAN, b. June 18, 1920, Hull, England
Bond Street (Pathé 1948)
Dear Mr. Prohack (GFD 1949)
Trottie True [Gay Lady] (GFD 1949)
Ghost Ship (AA 1952)
Time Gentlemen Please! (ABFD 1952)
Meet Mr. Lucifer (GFD 1953)
Betrayed (MGM 1954)
The Colditz Story (BL 1955)
Storm Over the Nile (IFD 1955)
Simon and Laura (RFD 1955)
Private's Progress (BL 1956)
The Big Money (RFD 1956)
Brothers in Law (BL 1957)
Lucky Jim (BL 1957)
Happy Is the Bride (BL 1958)
Left, Right and Centre (BL 1959)
I'm All Right Jack (BL 1959)
School for Scoundrels (WPD 1960)
Light Up the Sky (Bry 1960)
Double Bunk (Bry 1961)
The Amorous Prawn (BL 1962)
Heavens Above! (BL-Romulus 1963)
Hide and Seek (Albion 1963)
Smashing Time (Par 1967)
The Magnificent Seven Deadly Sins (ep "Pride") (Tigon 1971)
From Beyond the Grave (ep "The Elemental") (Col-Warner 1974)

CARMINATI, TULLIO (Conte Tulli Carminati de Brambilla), b. Sept.
21, 1895, Zara, Yugoslavia; d. Feb. 26, 1971
Il bacio di Margherita da Cortona (It 1912)
La mia vita per la tua (It 1914)
La maschera di Caino (It 1915)
Val d'Olivi (It 1915)
Romanticismo (It 1915)
L'Aigrette (It 1916)
Il presagio (It 1916)
Tramonto triste (It 1916)
Il romanzo di una domatrice (It 1916)
La donna abbandonata (It 1917)
L'aigrette (It 1917)
Bimbi lontani (It 1917)
La vie più lunga (It 1917)
La via della luce (It 1917)
Il volto del passato (It 1918)
Madame Flirt (It 1918)
Kilda (It 1918)
La fibra del dolore (It 1918)
Il trono e la seggiola (It 1918)
Vertigine (It 1919)

Tullio Carminati

Chimere (It 1919)
La vita senza scopo (It 1919)
La belle Madame Hebert (It 1919)
Raffiche (It 1920)
Follia (It 1920)
Il segreto (It 1920)
Il tuo rivale (It 1920)
Al di là della vila (It 1920)
Amore stanco (It 1920)
La bambole e l'amore (It 1920)
La perfetta ebbrezza (It 1920)
La principessa d'Azzurro (It 1921)
La locanda delle ombre (It 1923)
Mensch gegen Mensch (Ger 1923)
Sybil (FN 1926)
The Bat (UA 1926)
The Duchess of Buffalo (FN 1926)
Stage Madness (Fox 1927)
The Patriot (Par 1927)
Three Sinners (Par 1928)
Gallant Lady (UA 1933)
Moulin Rouge (UA 1934)
One Night of Love (Col 1934)

Let's Live Tonight (Col 1935)
Paris in Spring (Par 1935)
La marcia miziale (It 1936)
The Three Maxims [The Show Goes On] (GFD 1936)
Sunset in Vienna (GFD 1937)
London Melody [Girls in the Street] (GFD 1937)
Safari (Par 1940)
La vita torna (It 1942)
Sinfonia fatale (It 1947)
L'apocalisse (It 1947)
La certosa di Parma (It 1947)
La madonnina d'oro [The Golden Madonna] (It 1949)
Gli uomini non guardano il cielo (It 1951)
La bellezza del diavolo [Beauty and the Devil] (It 1951)
Roman Holiday (Par 1953)
Giovanna al rogo (It 1954)
Ulisse [Ulysses] (It-USA 1954)
Good Bye, Sevilla (Sp 1955)
War and Peace (Par 1956)
Saint Joan (Col 1957)
Io, Caterina (It 1958)
Olympia [A Breath of Scandal] (It-USA 1958)
El Cid (AA 1961)
Hemingway's Adventures of a Young Man (20th 1962)
The Cardinal (Col 1963)
La congiura dei clieci [Le Mercenaire/Swordsman of Siena]
    (It-Fr 1963)

CAROL, MARTINE (Maryse Mourer), b. May 16, 1922, Biarritz;
    d. Feb. 6, 1967
La Ferme aux loups (Fr 1943)
Bifur III (Fr 1944)
Trente en quarante (Fr 1945)
L'Extravagant Mission (Fr 1945)
Voyage-surprise (Fr 1946)
En êtes-vous bien sûr (Bel 1946)
Miroir (Fr 1947)
La Fleur de l'âge (unfinished 1947)
Carré de Valets (Fr 1947)
Les Amants de Vérone (Fr 1948)
Un Nuit de noces [Wedding Night] (Fr 1949)
Je n'aime que toi (Fr 1949)
Nous irons à Paris (Fr 1949)
Méfiez-vous des blondes (Fr 1950)
Caroline Chérie (Fr 1950)
Le Desir et l'amour (Fr-Sp 1951)
Les Belles de nuit (Fr-It 1952)
Adorable Créatures (Fr 1952)
Un Caprice de Caroline Chérie (Fr 1952)
Lucrèce Borgia (It-Fr 1952)
La Pensionnaire (It-Fr 1953)
Destinées (ep "Lysistrata") (Fr-It 1953)
Secrets d'alcôve [The Bed] (ep "La lit de la Pompadour")

(Fr-It 1953)
Si Versailles m'était conté (Fr 1953)
Madame Du Barry [Mistress Du Barry] (Fr-It 1954)
Nana (Fr-It 1954)
Lola Montes (Fr-W Ger 1955)
Les Carnets du Major Thompson [The French They Are a Funny
Race] (Fr 1955)
Scandale à Milan (It-Fr 1956)
Action of the Tiger (Col 1956)
Around the World in 80 Days (UA 1956)
Nathalie [The Foxiest Girl in Paris] (Fr-It 1957)
Au bord du Volcan (Fr 1957)
Le Passager clandestin (Fr-Australian 1957)
Les Noces vénitiennes (Fr-It 1958)
Nathalie secret agent (Fr 1959)
Ten Seconds to Hell (UA 1959)
Austerlitz (Fr-It-Liech-Yug 1960)
La Française et l'amour [Love and the Frenchwoman] (ep "La
femme seule") (Fr 1960)
Un Soir sur la plage (Fr 1960)
L'Enlevement de Sabines [The Rape of the Sabine Women] (It-Fr
1961)
Vanina Vanini [The Betrayer] (It-Fr 1961)
La Cave se rebiffe (Fr-It 1961)
En plein cirage (Fr 1961)
Paradis de femmes (Fr-It 1964)
Hell Is Empty (GB-Czech 1970) [started in 1965, suspended when
Carol died, finished in 1967]

CAROTENUTO, MARIO, b. June 29, 1915, Rome
Marakatumba, ma non è una rumba (It 1949)
Miracolo a Viggiù (It 1951)
Bellezze a Capri (It 1952)
I due sergenti (It 1952)
Ci troviamo in galleria (It 1953)
Ieri, oggi, domani (It 1953)
Capitan Fantasma (It 1954)
Destini di donne (It 1954)
Lasciateci in pace (It 1954)
La spiaggia (It 1954)
Prima di sera (It 1954)
Non c'è amore più grande (It 1955)
Destinazione Piovarolo (It 1955)
Un eroe dei nostri tempi (It 1955)
Pane, amore e... (It 1955)
Racconti romani (It 1955)
Io piaccio (It 1955)
Scuola elementare (It 1955)
Quando tramonta il sole (It 1956)
I giorni più belli (It 1956)
A sud niente di nuovo (It 1956)
Poveri ma belli (It 1956)
Mio figlio Nerone (It 1956)

Montecarlo (It 1956)
Kean, genio e sregolatezza (It 1956)
Souvenir d'Italie (It 1956)
Vivendo, cantando... che male ti fo? (It 1957)
Susanna tutta panna (It 1957)
Femmine tre volte (It 1957)
Belle ma povere (It 1957)
Guardia, ladro e cameriera (It 1958)
La ballerina e buon Dio (It 1958)
Ladro lui, ladra lei (It 1958)
Mogli pericolose (It 1958)
Totò e Narcellino (It 1958)
Rascel marine (It 1958)
Il segreto delle rose (It 1958)
Gli zitelloni (It-Sp 1958)
Come te movi te fulmino (It 1958)
Pane, amore e Andalusia [Pan, amor y Andalucía] (It-Sp 1959)
L'amico del giaguaro (It 1959)
L'amore nasce a Roma (It 1959)
Primo amore (It 1959)
Uomini e nobiluomini (It 1959)
I ragazzi del juke-box (It 1959)
La cento chilometri (It 1959)
Le sorprese dell'amore (It 1959)
A qualcuna piace calvo (It 1959)
Juke-box, urli d'amore (It 1959)
Roulotte e roulette (Iy 1960)
Il terrore dell'Oklahoma (It 1960)
Cerasella (It 1960)
La grana [Le fric] (It-Fr 1960)
Genitori in blue jeans (It 1960)
Il mattatore (It 1960)
I piaceri dello scapolo (It 1960)
Urlatori alla sbarra (It 1960)
Le signore (It 1960)
Un dollaro di fifa (It 1960)
Caccia al marito (It 1960)
La banda del buco (It 1960)
Fontana di Trevi (It 1960)
Sanremo, la grande sfida (It 1960)
I teddy boys della canzone (It 1960)
Le svedesi (It 1961)
Mariti in pericolo (It 1961)
Che femmina e... che dollari! [Parlez-moi d'amour] (It-Fr 1961)
Ferragosto in bikini (It 1961)
Io bacio... tu baci (It 1961)
Vacanze alla baia d'argento (It 1961)
La ragazza sotto il lenzuolo (It 1961)
I soliti rapinatori a Milano (It 1961)
Cinque marines per cento ragazze (It 1961)
Bellezze sulla spiaggia (It 1961)
Le magnifiche sette (It 1961)
Scandali al mare (It 1961)
Il manetenuto (It 1961)

Peccati d'estate (It 1962)
Maciste contro Ercole nella valle dei guai (It 1962)
Il mio amico Benito (It 1962)
Colpo gobbo all'italiana (It 1962)
Gli eroi del doppio gioco (It 1962)
Pesci d'oro e bikini d'argento (It 1962)
Nerone '71 (It 1962)
Due marinai per cento geishe (It 1962)
La vendetta (Fr-It 1962)
Siamo tutti pomicioni (It 1963)
Tempo di Roma (It 1964)
Scandali... nudi (It 1964)
Sette monaci d'oro (It 1966)
Il padre di famiglia (It 1967)
Satryicon (It 1969)
Lisa dagli occhi blù (It 1969)
La ragazza del prete (It 1970)
Il debito coniugale (It 1970)
I due assi del guantone (It 1971)
La betía, ovvero in amore per ogni gaudenzia ci vuole sofferenza
(It-Yug 1971)
Rinscira l'Avv. Benenato a sconfiggere, il suo acerrimo nemico,
il Pretore Ciccio De Ingras (It 1971)
Correva l'anno di grazzia 1871 (It 1971)
Grando le donne si chiamavano "Madonne" (It-W Ger 1972)
Boccaccio (It-Fr 1972)
Girolimoni, il mostro di Roma (It 1972)
Il prode Anselmo e il suo scudiero (It 1972)
Storia di fila e di coltello (It 1972)
Fiorina la vacca (It 1973)
Furto di sera bel corpo di spera (It 1973)
Il sergente Rompiglioni (It 1973)
Racconti proibiti di niente vestiti (It 1973)
Quatre Zizis dans la marine (Fr 1974)
La liceale (It 1975)

CAROTENUTO, MEMMO, b. July 24, 1908, Rome
Umberto D (It 1951)
Processo contro ignoti (It 1952)
Stazione termini [Indiscretion of an American Wife] (It-USA 1953)
Tempi nostri (It 1953)
Via Padova 46 (It 1953)
Pane, amore e fantasia (It 1953)
Piovuto dal cielo (It 1953)
La domenica della buona gente (It 1953)
Prima di sera (It 1953)
Nerone e Messalina (It 1954) [made in 1949-1953]
Pane, amore e gelosia (It 1954)
L'allegro squadrone (It 1954)
Casa Ricordi (It 1954)
Le vacanze del sor Clemete (It 1954)
Peccato che sia una canaglia (It 1954)
Se vincessi cento milioni (It 1954)

Sei ore di tempo (It 1954)
Tempi nostri (It 1954)
I tre ladri (It 1954)
Bella non piangere (It 1954)
Cheri-Bibi (Fr-It 1954)
Accadde al penitenzario (It 1955)
La catena dell'odio (It 1955)
Carovana di canzoni (It 1955)
La ladra (It 1955)
Il bigamo (It 1955)
La fortuna di essere donna (It 1955)
Don Camillo e l'onorevole Peppone (It 1955)
Piccola posta (It 1955)
Gli ultimi cinque minuti (It 1955)
Addio sogni di gloria (It 1956)
La banda degli onesti (It 1956)
Cantando sotto le stelle (It 1956)
Guardia, guardia, scelta brigadiere, maresciallo (It 1956)
I giorni più belli (It 1956)
Mio figlio Nerone (It 1956)
Poveri ma belli (It 1956)
Il momento più bello (It 1956)
Padri e figli (It 1956)
Parola di ladro (It 1956)
Donne, amore e matrimonio (It 1956)
Tempo di villeggiatura (It 1956)
Totò, Peppino e i fuorilegge (It 1956)
A vent'anni è sempre festa (It 1957)
Addio alle armi (It 1957)
Belle ma povere (It 1957)
La canzone più bella (It 1957)
Classe di ferro (It 1957)
Il cocco di mamma (It 1957)
I dritti (It 1957)
Gente felice (It 1957)
Mariti in città (It 1957)
Mattino di primavera (It 1957)
Non cantare... baciami (It 1957)
Il sole tornera (It 1957)
Solo Dio mi fermerà (It 1957)
Susanna tutta panna (It 1957)
Totò e Marcellino (It 1958)
Un amore senza fine (It 1958)
Ballerina e buon Dio (It 1958)
Ragazzi della marina (It 1958)
L'uomo con i calzoni corti (It 1958)
Le dritte (It 1958)
Due sosia in allegria (It 1958)
E permesso maresciallo? (It 1958)
E arrivata la parigina (It 1958)
Gagliardi e pupe (It 1958)
Gambe d'oro (It 1958)
Io, mammeta e tu (It 1958)

Gli italiani sono matti [Los Italianos estan locos] (It-Sp 1958)
Ladra lei, ladro lui (It 1958)
Diez Fusiles esperan (Sp-It 1958)
L'amore più bello [Tal vez manana] (It-Sp 1959)
Il nemico di mia moglie (It 1959)
La Pica sul Pacifico (It 1959)
Poveri milionari [Pobres millonarios] (It-Sp 1959)
Psicanalista per signora [Le confident de ces donnes] (It-Fr 1959)
Le sorprese all'amore (It 1959)
Spavaldi e innamorati (It 1959)
Tutti innamorati (It 1959)
El lazarillo de Tormes (Sp 1959)
Agosto, donne mie non vi conosco (It 1960)
La notte dei teddy boys (It 1960)
Il principe fusto (It 1960)
I piaceri dello scapolo (It 1960)
Le ambizione (It 1961)
Akiko (It 1961)
Io bacio... tu baci (It 1961)
Mariti in pericolo (It 1961)
Rocco e le sorelle (It 1961)
Un branco di vigliacchi (It 1962)
Il segugio [Accorche-toi, y'a du vent] (It-Fr 1962)
Canzoni a tempo di twist (It 1962)
La ballata dei mariti (It 1963)
Gli onorevoli (It 1963)
Napoleone a Firenze (It 1964)
... poi ti sposero (It 1965)
Sette monaci d'oro (It 1966)
Il segreto del vestito rosso (It 1968)
Die Hochzeitsreise (W Ger-It 1969)
I due della formula [Alla corsa più pazza, pazza del mondo (It 1971)

CARREL, DANY (Suzanne Chazelles du Chavel), b. Sept. 20, 1935, Touzane, Indo-China
La Dortior des grandes [Girls' Dormitory] (Fr 1953)
Maternité clandestine (Fr 1953)
La Cage aux souris (Fr 1954)
La Patrouille des sables (Fr-Sp 1954)
Les Chiffoniers d'Emmäus (Fr 1954)
La melodía misteriosa (Sp-Fr 1955)
La Môme Pigalle (Fr 1955)
Les Indiscrètes (Fr 1955)
Les Grandes Manoeuvres (Fr-It 1955)
Les possedées [The Possessed] (Fr-It 1955)
Des gens sans importance (Fr 1955)
Elisa (Fr 1956)
Club de femmes (Fr-It 1956)
Que les hommes sont bêtes (Fr 1956)
Porte des Lilas (Fr-It 1957)
Escapade (Fr 1957)
Pot-Bouille [The House of Lovers] (Fr-It 1957)

La Moucharde (Fr 1958)
Ce corps tant désiré [Way of the Wicked] (Fr 1957)
Les Naufrageurs (Fr 1958)
Racconti d'estate (It-Fr 1958)
Les Dragueuers [The Young Have No Morals] (Fr 1959)
Die Gans von Sedan [W Ger-Fr 1959)
The Enemy General (Col 1960)
Quai du Pont du Jour (Fr 1960)
Il mulino delle donne di pietra (It-Fr 1960)
Les Mains d'Orlac [The Hands of Orlac] (Fr-GB 1960)
Les Ennemis (Fr 1961)
Le Cave est piégé (Fr 1961)
Carillons sans joie (Fr-It 1962)
Règlements de compte (Fr 1962)
Du grabuge chez les veuves (Fr-It 1963)
Le Bluffeur (Fr 1963)
Une Souris chez les hommes (Fr 1964)
Le Commissaire mene l'enquête (ep "Fermez votre porte") (Fr 1964)
L'Enfer (unfinished 1964)
Piège pour Cendrillon [A Trap for Cinderella] (Fr-It 1965)
Le Chien fou [The Mad Dog] (Fr 1966)
Un Idiot à Paris [An Idiot in Paris] (Fr 1966)
La Petite Vertu (Fr 1967)
Le Pacha [Showdown] (Fr-It 1967)
La Prisonnière [Woman in Chains] (Fr-It 1968)
Delphine (Fr 1968)
Clérambard (Fr 1969)
Les Portes de feu (Fr 1971)
Trois milliards sans ascenseur (Fr-It 1972)

CARRIERE, MATHIEU, b. Aug. 2, 1950, Hanover
Tonio Kröger (W Ger-Fr 1964)
Der junge Törless (W Ger-Fr 1966)
Gates to Paradise (GB-W Ger 1968)
Stado d'asside (It-Fr 1967)
La Maison des Bories (Fr 1970)
Petit Matin [The Virgin and the Soldier] (Fr 1971)
L'Homme aux cerveau greffé (Fr-It-W Ger 1972)
Malpertius (Bel 1972)
Rendez-vous à Bray (Fr-W Ger 1971)
Barbe-bleue [Bluebeard] (Fr-It-W Ger 1972)
Don Juan 1973 (Fr-It 1973)
Il n'y a pas de fumée sans feu [There Is No Smoke Without Fire] (Fr-It 1973)
La Jeune Fille assassinée (Fr-It-W Ger 1974)
India Song (Fr 1974)
Né pour l'Enfer (W Ger-It-Can-Fr 1975)
L'Appât (Fr-W Ger 1975)
Blondy (Fr-W Ger 1975)

CARROLL, MADELEINE (Marie Madeleine Bernadette O'Carroll), b. Feb. 6, 1906, West Bromwich
The Guns of Loos (New Era 1928)

What Money Can Buy (Gaumont 1928)
The First Born (W & F 1928)
The Crooked Billet (W & F 1929)
The American Prisoner (Wardour 1929)
Atlantic (Wardour 1929)
The 'W' Plan (Wardour 1930)
Young Woodley (Wardour 1930)
French Leave (Sterling 1930)
Escape (Radio 1930)
The School for Scandal (Par Br 1930)
Kissing Cup's Race (Butcher 1930)
Madame Guillotine (W & F 1931)
Fascination (Wardour 1931)
The Written Law (Ideal 1931)
Sleeping Car (Ideal 1933)
I Was a Spy (W & F 1933)
The World Moves On (Fox 1934)
The Love Affair of the Dictator [The Loves of a Dictator] (Gau-
    mont 1935)
The 39 Steps (Gaumont 1935)
The Secret Agent (Gaumont 1936)
The Case Against Mrs. Ames (Par 1936)
The General Died at Dawn (Par 1936)
Lloyds of London (20th 1936)
On the Avenue (20th 1937)
It's All Yours (Col 1937)
The Prisoner of Zenda (UA 1937)
Blockade (UA 1938)
Cafe Society (Par 1939)
Honeymoon in Bali [Husbands or Lovers] (Par 1939)
My Son, My Son (Col 1940)
Safari (Par 1940)
North West Mounted Police (Par 1940)
Virginia (Par 1941)
One Night in Lisbon (Par 1941)
Bahama Passage (Par 1941)
My Favorite Blonde (Par 1942)
White Cradle Inn [High Fury] (BL 1947)
An Innocent Affair [Don't Trust Your Husband] (UA 1948)
The Fan [Lady Windemere's Fan] (20th Br 1949)

CARTON, PAULINE (Pauline-Aimée Biarez), b. April 7, 1884,
        Geneva; d. June 17, 1974
    Le Pere Goriot (Fr 1921)
    Château historique (Fr 1923)
    Les Etrennes à travers les âges (Fr 1924)
    Le Petit Jacques (Fr 1925)
    Feu Mathias Pascal (Fr 1925)
    Le P'tit Parigot (Fr 1926)
    La Petite Fonctionnaire (Fr 1926)
    Education de prince (Fr 1927)
    Yvette (Fr 1927)
    Miss Edith, duchesse (Fr 1928)
    La Ronde infernale (Fr 1928)

L'Arpète (Fr 1929)
Mon Gosse de père (Fr 1929)
Le Blanc et le noir (Fr 1930)
Le Sang d'un poete (Fr 1930)
L'Amour à l'Américaine (Fr 1931)
Faubourg Montmartre (Fr 1931)
Sur la voie du bonheur (Fr 1931)
Criminel (Fr 1931)
Mon Curé chez les Riches (Fr 1932)
Ce Cochon de Morin (Fr 1932)
Suzanne (Fr 1932)
L'Abbé Constantin (Fr 1933)
Ame de clown (Fr 1933)
Bouton d'or (Fr 1933)
Ces Messieurs de la Santé (Fr 1933)
Du haut en bas (Fr 1933)
Miquette et sa mere (Fr 1933)
L'Ecole des cocottes (Fr 1934)
Les Anges noirs (Fr 1934)
Les Hommes de la côte (Fr 1934)
Les Misérables (Fr 1934)
Itto (Fr 1934)
Nous ne sommes plus des enfants (Fr 1934)
Le Petit Jacques (Fr 1934)
Tartarin de Tarascon (Fr 1934)
Mademoiselle Mozart (Fr 1935)
Le Nouveau Testament (Fr 1935)
Une Nuit de noces (Fr 1935)
Ferdinand le noceur (Fr 1935)
Bonne chance (Fr 1935)
Tarass Boulba (Fr 1935)
Train de plaisir (Fr 1935)
Paris-Camargue (Fr 1935)
Le Cauchemar de M. Berignon (Fr 1936)
Le Roman d'un jeune homme pauvre (Fr 1936)
Toi, c'est moi (Fr 1936)
Les Degourdis de la 11eme (Fr 1936)
Le Mioche (Fr 1936)
La Maison d'en face (Fr 1936)
Le Roman d'un tricheur (Fr 1936)
Vous n'avez rien a déclarer? (Fr 1936)
Courrier-Sud (Fr 1936)
Oeil-de-lynx, détective (Fr 1936)
Mon Pere avait raison (Fr 1936)
Les Anges noirs (Fr 1937)
A Venise, une nuit (Fr 1937)
La Belle de Montparnasse (Fr 1937)
Boissière (Fr 1937)
La Citadelle du silence (Fr 1937)
Gribouille (Fr 1937)
Mon Député et sa femme (Fr 1937)
Le Mot de Cambronne (Fr 1937)
Ne tirez pas Dolly (Fr 1937)

Desire (Fr 1937)
La Fille de la Madelon (Fr 1937)
Gardons notre sourire [Ersatz et Kommandantur] (Fr-Ger 1937)
M. Brelogue a disparu (Fr 1937)
Nuits de princes (Fr 1937)
Les perles de la couronne (Fr 1937)
Le Plus Beau Gosse de France [Le mari de la reine] (Fr 1937)
Conflit (Fr 1938)
Petite Peste (Fr 1938)
Les Gaîtés de l'exposition (Fr 1938)
La Marraine du regiment (Fr 1938)
Louise (Fr 1938)
Le Coeur ébloui (Fr 1938)
Un Fichu métier (Fr 1938)
Paix sur le Rhin (Fr 1938)
Quadrille (Fr 1938)
Mon oncle et mon cure (Fr 1938)
Remontons les Champs-Elysees (Fr 1938)
La Présidente (Fr 1938)
L'Etrange Nuit de Noël (Fr 1938)
La Belle Revanche (Fr 1939)
Conflit (Fr 1939)
Ils etaient neuf célibataires (Fr 1939)
Ma Tante dictateur (Fr 1939)
Vous seule que j'aime (Fr 1939)
Mobilisation (Fr 1939)
Le Monde tremblera [La révolte des vivants] (Fr 1939)
Narcisse (Fr 1939)
Sans lendemain (Fr 1939)
Sur le plancher des vaches (Fr 1939)
La Troisieme Dalle (Fr 1940)
La Prière aux étoiles (Fr 1941) [unfinished]
Six Petites Filles en blanc (Fr 1941)
La Neige sur les pas (Fr 1941)
Tobie est un ange (Fr 1941)
Manouche (Fr 1942)
La Belle Aventure (Fr 1942)
L'Amant de Borneo (Fr 1942)
Marie-Louise (Fr 1942)
Les Amants du Pont St-Jean (Fr 1947)
Blanc comme neige (Fr 1947)
Le Comédien (Fr 1947)
Tierce à coeur (Fr 1947)
L'Armoire volante (Fr 1948)
L'Ombre (Fr 1948)
Marlene (Fr 1948)
Barry (Fr 1948)
Le Diable boiteux (Fr 1948)
Amédée (Fr 1949)
Le Furet (Fr 1949)
Aux deux colombes (Fr 1949)
Miquette et sa mere (Fr 1949)
Les Branquignols (Fr 1949)
Je n'aime que toi (Fr 1949)

Menace de mort (Fr 1949)
Le 84 prend des vacances (Fr 1949)
Ronde de nuit (Fr 1949)
Tête blonde (Fr 1949)
Le Trésor de Cantenac (Fr 1949)
Aventure a Pigalle (Fr 1950)
Coueur-sur-Mer (Fr 1950)
Le Rosier de Mme. Husson (Fr 1950)
Le Tampon du Capiston (Fr 1950)
Minne, l'ingénue libertine (Fr 1950)
La Poison (Fr 1951)
Descendez, on vous demande (Fr 1951)
Ma Femme est formidable (Fr 1951)
Le Vrai Coupable (Fr 1951)
Je l'ai été trois fois (Fr 1952)
Monsieur Taxi (Fr 1952)
La Pocharde (Fr 1952)
La Vie d'une honnête homme (Fr 1952)
La Fille au fouet (Fr 1952)
Carnaval (Fr 1953)
Soyez les Bienvenus (Fr 1953)
Le Chasseur de chez Maxim's (Fr 1953)
Si Versailles m'etait conté (Fr 1953)
Les Fruits de l'été (Fr 1954)
Les Deux font la paire [Le Mort en fuite] (Fr 1954)
Pas de souris dans le bizness (Fr 1954)
Napoléon (Fr 1954)
Les Insoumises (Fr 1955)
Ces Sacrées Vacances (Fr 1955)
Rencontre à Paris (Fr 1955)
On déménage le colonel (Fr 1955)
Si Paris nous etait conte (Fr 1955)
Zaza (Fr 1955)
Assassins et voleurs (Fr 1956)
Baratin (Fr 1956)
Ah! Quelle équipe (Fr 1956)
Fric-frac en dentelles (Fr 1956)
Les Carottes sont cuites (Fr 1956)
Le Chanteur de Mexico [El Cantor de Mexico] (Fr-Sp 1956)
Mon Curé chez les pauvres (Fr 1956)
Les Trois font la paire (Fr 1957)
Déshabillez-vous, madame (Fr 1957)
Brigade des moeurs (Fr 1958)
En Bordée (Fr 1958)
A Pied, à cheval et en spoutnik (Fr 1958)
La Vie à deux (Fr 1958)
Les Gaîtes de l'escadrille (Fr 1958)
Messieurs les ronds-de-cuir (Fr 1959)
Vous n'avez rien a déclarer? (Fr 1959)
Business (Fr 1960)
La Fille du torrent (Fr-It 1960)
Interpol contre X (Fr 1960)
The Longest Day (USA-GB 1961)
Humour noir [Umorismo nero] (Fr-Sp-It 1965)

CARVALHO, RAUL DE see DE CARVALHO, RAUL

CARVALHO, RUI DE see DE CARVALHO, RUI

CASARÈS, MARIA, b. Nov. 21, 1922, La Coruna, Spain
   Les Enfants du Paradis [Children of Paradise] (Fr 1945)
   Les Dames du Bois de Boulogne (Fr 1946)
   Roger-la-Honte (Fr 1946)
   La Revanche de Roger-la-Honte (Fr 1946)
   La Septième Porte (Fr 1946) [filmed in Morocco]
   L'Amour autour de la maison [Love Locked Out] (Fr 1946)
   La Chartreuse de Parme (Fr 1948)
   Bagarres (Fr 1948)
   L'Homme qui revient de loin (Fr 1950)
   Orphée (Fr 1950)
   Ombre et Lumière (Fr 1951)
   La Vie de Jesus/En souvenir de moi (Fr 1952) [narrator]
   Le Testament d'Orphée (Fr 1960)
   Flavia la monaca mussulmana [The Rebel Nun] (It-Fr 1974)

CASSEL, JEAN-PIERRE (Jean-Pierre Crochon), b. Oct. 27, 1932,
   Paris
   Pigalle-Saint Germain-des Près (Fr 1950) [extra]
   La Route du bonheur (Fr-It 1953) [extra]
   The Happy Road (MGM 1957)
   A pied, à cheval et en voiture [Hold Tight for the Satellite]
      (Fr 1957)
   La Peau de l'ours (Fr 1957)
   Le Désordre et la nuit (Fr 1958)

Jean-Pierre Cassel

En cas de malheur [Love Is My Profession] (Fr-It 1958)
Et ta soeur? (Fr 1958)
Sacrée Jeunesse (Fr 1958)
La Marraine de Charley (Fr 1959)
Les Jeux de l'amour [Playing at Love] (Fr 1960)
Le Farceur [The Joker] (Fr 1960)
Candide ou l'optimisme au XXe siècle [Candide] (Fr 1960)
L'Amant de cinq jours [The Five Day Lover] (Fr-It 1961)
Les Sept Péchês Capitaux [Seven Capital Sins] (ep "L'Avarice")
   (Fr-It 1961)
La Gamberge (Fr 1961)
Napoleon II, l'aiglon (Fr 1961) [cameo]
Le caporal épinglé [The Vanishing Corporal] (Fr 1962)
Arsène Lupin contre Arsène Lupin (Fr-It 1962)
Cyrano et D'Artagnan (Sp-It-Fr 1963)
Nunca pasa nada (Sp-Fr 1963)
Les Plus Belles Escroqueries du monde (ep "L'Homme qui
   vendit la Tour Eiffel") (Fr-It-Japan 1963)
Alta infedeltà (ep "La sospirosa") (It-Fr 1964)
Un Monsieur de compagnie (Fr-It 1964)
Those Magnificent Men in Their Flying Machines, or How I Flew
   from London to Paris in 25 Hours and 11 Minutes (20th 1965)
Les Fêtes galantes (Fr-Rum 1965)
Paris brûle-t-il? [Is Paris Burning?] (Fr 1966)
Jeu de massacre (Fr 1967)
La dolci signore (It-Fr 1967)
Oh! What a Lovely War (Par 1969)
L'Armée des ombres (Fr-It 1969)
L'Ours et la poupée (Fr 1969)
La Rupture (Fr-It-Bel 1970)
La Bateau sur l'herbe (Fr 1971)
Malpertius (Bel 1972)
Le Charme discret de la bourgeoisie [The Discreet Charm of the
   Bourgeoisie] (Fr 1972)
Baxter! (MGM-EMI 1973)
Il magnate (It 1973)
The Three Musketeers [The Queen's Diamonds] (20th 1973)
Le Mouton enragé (Fr-It 1974)
Murder on the Orient Express (Par 1974)
The Four Musketeers [The Revenge of Milady] (20th 1974)
Docteur François Gailland (Fr 1975)

CASTELO, JULIETA (Maria Beatriz Pereira da Silva Macedo), b.
   Oct. 5, 1914, Viana do Castelo, Portugal
A ave de arribação (Por 1943)
Um homem às direitas (Por 1944)
Um homem do Ribatejo (Por 1946)
Camões (Por 1946)
Cais sodré (Por 1946)
Rainha santa (Sp 1947)
Ribatejo (Por 1949)
Chaimite (Por 1953)
Um cão (Por 1963)

Julieta Castelo

Dois destinos (Por 1964)
Vinte (Por 1965)
Nove irmãos (Por 1965)
Gil Vicente [Gil Vicente e o seu teatro] (Por 1966)
Cruz de ferro (Por 1967)
O amor desceu em pára-quedas (Por 1968)
O diabo era outro (Por 1969)
Derra pagem (Por 1974)

CATALA, MURIEL, b. July 20, 1952, Paris
Le Sauveur (Fr 1970)
Faustine et le bel été (Fr 1971)
Le Monache di Sant'Arcangelo [Les Religieuses du St-Archange]
(It-Fr 1972)
L'Histoire très bonne et très joyeuse de Colinot Trousse-Chemise
[Colinot, l'alzasottane] (Fr-It 1973)
Rocanegra [La loba y la paloma] (Sp 1973)
Vous interessez-vous à la chose? (Fr-W Ger 1974)
Verdict [L'accusa è: violenza carnale e omicidio] (Fr-It 1974)

CAVALIERI, LINA (Natalina Cavalieri), b. Dec. 25, 1874, Viterlo,
Italy; d. Feb. 7, 1944
Manon Lescaut (It 1914)

La sposa della morte (It 1915)
La rosa di Granata (It 1916)
The Eternal Temptress (Par 1917)
Love's Conquest (Par 1918)
A Woman of Impulse (Par 1918)
The Two Brides (Par 1919)
Amore che ritorna (It 1921)

CEGANI, ELISA, b. June 10, 1911, Turin, Italy
Aldebaràn (It 1935)
Ma non è una cosa seria (It 1936)
Cavalleria (It 1936)
La contessa di Parma (It 1937)
Ettore fieramosca (It 1938)
Napoli d'altri tempi (It 1938)
Retroscena (It 1939)
La corona di ferro (It 1940)
La cena della beffe (It 1941)
Gioco pericoloso (It 1942)
Harlem [Knockout] (It 1942)
Genti dell'aria (It 1943)
Nessuno torna indictro (It 1943)
I dieci comandamenti (It 1943)
Un giorno nella vita (It 1946)
La monaca di Monza (It 1947)
Fabiola (It 1947)
Eleonora Duse (It 1950) [made in 1947)
Le Château de verre [L'amante di una notte] (Fr-It 1951)
Messalina (It 1951)
Altri tempi [Quelques pas dans la vie] (It-Fr 1952)
La nemica (It 1952)
La fiammata (It 1952)
La prigioniera della Torre di Fuoco (It 1952)
Fanciulle di lusso (It 1952)
Amarti è il mio peccato (It 1953)
Canzone appassionata (It 1953)
Cento anni d'amore (It-Fr 1953)
Tempi nostri (It 1953)
Casa Ricordi (It 1954)
Nel gorgo del peccato (It 1954)
Graziella (It 1954)
Nanà (Fr-It 1955)
La fortuna di essere donna (It 1956)
Una donna libera (It 1956)
Il vetturale del Moncenisio (It 1956)
Amore e chiacchiere (It 1957)
La donna del giorno (It 1957)
Al servizio dell'imperatore [Si le roi savait ça] (It-Fr 1958)
Ciao, ciao, bambina (It 1959)
Constantine il grande [Constantine and the Cross] (It 1961)
Il giudizio universale (It 1961)
Cronache di un convento (It 1962)
Giacobbe ed Esaù (It 1963)

Perseo l'invincibile (It 1963)
Liolà (It 1964)
Saul e David (It 1965)
Io, io, io... e gli altri (It 1966)
Un killer per sua maestà [Faccia d'angelo/Face d'ange/Le
    Tueur aime les bonbons] (It-Fr 1968)
La rosa rossa (It 1973)

CELI, ADOLFO, b. July 27, 1922, Messina, Italy
Un americano in vacanza (It 1946)
Natale al campo 119 (It 1948)
Proibito rubare (It 1948)
Emigrantes (It 1949)
L'homme de Rio [L'uomo di Rio] (Fr-It 1964)
Tre notti d'amore (ep "La moglie bambina") (It 1964)
Un Monsieur de compagnie [Poi ti sposero] (Fr-It 1964)
Thunderball (UA 1965)
E venne un uomo (It 1965)
Le belle famiglie (ep "Amare è un po' morire") (It 1965)
Von Ryan's Express (20th 1965)
The Agony and the Ecstasy (20th 1965)
Rapina al sole (It 1965)
Slalom (It 1965)
El Greco (Fr-It 1966)
Grand Prix (MGM 1966)
Le piacevoli notti (It 1966)
El Yankee [Yankee] (It-Sp 1966)
Le Roi de coeur [Tutti pazzi meno io] (Fr-It 1967)
Ad ogni costo [Top Job/Diamantes a go-go/Grand Slam] (It-
    W Ger-Sp 1967)
Colpo maestro al servizio di Sua Maesta Britannica [Gran golpe
    al servicio de Su Majestad Britanica] (It-Sp 1967)
O. K. Connery [Operation Kid Brother] (It 1967)
Tiro a segno per uccidere (It 1967)
The Honey Pot (UA 1967)
The Bobo (WB-7 Arts 1967)
U atraco de ita y unetta [Sei simpatiche cargone/Uno scacco
    tutto matto] (Sp-It 1968)
Il padre di famiglia [Jeux d'adultes] (It-Fr 1968)
Dalle Ardenne all'inferno [La gloire des canailles/Und morgen
    fahrt ihr zur Hölle] (It-Fr-W Ger 1968)
Diabolik (It 1968)
Sentenza di morte (It 1968)
La donna, il sesso e il superuomo (It 1968)
Sette volte sette (It 1969)
L'alibi (It 1969)
Midas Run (Cin 1969)
L'arcangelo (It 1969)
La morte bussa due volte [Blonde Köder für den Mörder] (It-
    W Ger 1969)
Io Emanuelle (It 1969)
Un detective (It 1969)
Brancaleone alle crociate (It 1970)

Un condé [L'uomo venuto da Chicago] (Fr-It 1970)
In Search of Gregory [Alla ricerca di Gregory] (GB-It 1970)
Hanna cambiato faccia (It 1971)
Appuntamento col disonore (It 1971)
Murders in the Rue Morgue (AIP 1971)
Fragment of Fear (Col Br 1971)
Fratello Sole, Sorella Luna [Brother Sun, Sister Moon] (It-GB 1972)
L'occhio nel labirinto (It-W Ger 1972)
Chi l'ha vista morire? (It 1972)
Una chica casi decente (Sp 1972)
La "mala" ordina [Italian Connection/Der Mafia-Boss--Sie töteten wie Schakale] (It-W Ger 1972)
Una ragazza tutta nuda assassinata nel parco (It 1972)
Terza ipotesi su un caso di perfetta strategia criminale (It 1972)
Hitler: The Last Ten Days (GB-It 1973)
La villeggiatura (It 1973)
Piazza pulita [Pete, Pearl and the Pole] (It-USA 1973)
Le mataf [Tre per una grande rapina] (Fr-It 1974)
La mano spietata della legge (It 1974)
Il sorriso del grande tentatore [The Tempter] (It-GB 1974)
E poi non rimase nessuno [And Then There Were None] (It-GB 1974)
Le Fantôme de la liberté [Il fantasma della libertà] (Fr-It 1974)
Libera amore mio (It 1975)
Amici miei (It 1975)

CERVI, GINO, b. May 3, 1901, Bologna; d. Jan. 3, 1974
L'armata azzurra (It 1932)
Frontiere (It 1934)
Amore (It 1935)
Aldebaràn (It 1935)
I due sergenti (It 1937)
Ettore Fieramosca (It 1937)
Gli uomini non sono ingrati (It 1937)
Voglio vivere con Letizia! (It 1937)
L'argine (It 1938)
I figli del Marchese Lucera (It 1938)
Inventiamo l'amore (It 1938)
Un'avventura di Salvator Rosa (It 1939)
La peccatrice (It 1940)
Melodie eterne (It 1940)
Una romantica avventura (It 1940)
I promessi sposi (It 1941)
La corona di ferro (It 1941)
Il sogno di tutti (It 1941)
La regina di Navarra (It 1941)
Acque di primavera (It 1942)
Don Cesare di Bazan (It 1942)
L'ultimo addio (It 1942)
Quarta pagina (It 1942)
Gente dell'aria (It 1942)
Quattro passi fra le nuvole (It 1942)

Tristi amori (It 1943)
T'amerò sempre (It 1943)
Dieci minuti di vita (It 1943) [unreleased]
La locandiera (It 1944)
Quartetto pazzo (It 1944)
Racconti romani di Pietro l'Aretino [Racconti romani di un ex-novizia] (It 1944)
Che distinta famiglia! (It 1945)
Le miserie del signor Travet (It 1945)
Lo sbaglio d'essere vivo (It 1946)
Malia (It 1946)
Umanità (It 1946)
Un uomo ritorna (It 1946)
Aqulia nera (It 1946)
L'angelo e il diavolo (It 1946)
Furia (It 1947)
Cronaca nera (It 1947)
Quartetto pazzo (It 1947) [made in 1944]
Daniele Cortis (It 1947)
I miserabili (It 1947)
La signora dalle camelie (It 1948)
Guglielmo Tell [William Tell] (It 1948)
Anna Karenina (BL 1948)
Yvonne la nuit (Fr 1949)
La fiamme che non si spegne (It 1949)
Fabiola (It 1949)
La sposa non pue attendere (It 1949)
Donne senza nome [Women Without Names] (It 1950)
Il cielo è rosso (It 1950)
La scogliera del peccato (It 1951)
Cristo proibito (It 1951)
Il caimano del Piave (It 1951)
Sigillo rosso (It 1951)
Cameriera bella presenza offresi (It 1951)
O. K. Nerone (It 1951)
Tre storie proibite (It 1951)
Don Camillo (It 1952)
Moglie per una notte (It 1952)
La regina di Saba [The Queen of Sheba] (It 1952)
Stazione termini [Indiscretion of an American Wife] (It-USA 1953)
Si Versailles m'etait conté (Fr 1953)
Il ritorno di Don Camillo (It 1953)
Nerone e Messalina (It 1954)
La signora senza camelie (It 1954)
Maddelena (It 1954)
Napoleon (Fr 1954)
Addio mia bella signora (It 1954)
Les trois monsquetaires [Fate largo ai moschettieri (Fr-It 1954)
La grande avventura (It 1954)
Il cardinale Lambertini (It 1955)
Frou-Frou (Fr 1955)
Non c'è amore più grande (It 1955)
Don Camillo e l'onorevole Peppone (It 1955)

Gli innamorati (It 1955)
Il coraggio (It 1955)
Guardia, guardia scelta, brigadiere e maresciallo (It 1956)
Beatrice Cenci (It 1956)
Moglie e buoi... (It 1956)
Una donna libera (It 1956)
Cavallina storna (It 1956) [made in 1953]
Gli amanti del deserto [Los Amanto del deserto] (It-Sp 1956)
Amore e chiacchiere [Hablemos de amor] (It-Sp 1957)
Agguato a Tangeri [Un hombre en la red] (It-Sp 1958)
Le belle dell'aria [Muchachas en las nubes] (It-Sp 1958)
Thérèse Etienne (Fr-It 1958)
Le Grand Chef [Noi gangsters] (Fr-Sp 1958)
The Naked Maja (UA 1959)
Sans famille [Senza famiglia] (Fr-It 1959)
Nel segno di Roma (It 1959)
Brevi amori a Palma di Maiorca (It 1959)
Cartagine in fiamme (It 1959)
I sicari di Hitler (It 1960)
L'assedio di Siracusa [The Siege of Syracuse] (It 1960)
Il mistero dei tre continenti [Herrin der Welt/Les Mystères
    d'Angkor] (It-W Ger-Fr 1960)
La lunga notte del '43 (It 1960)
Le olimpiadi dei mariti (It 1960)
Femmine di lusso (It 1960)
La rivoltà degli schiavi [La rebelion de los esclavos] (It-Sp 1960)
Che gioia vivere [Quelle Joie de vivre!] (It-Fr 1961)
Un figlio d'oggi (It 1961)
Don Camillo, monsignore... ma non troppo (It 1961)
Gli attendenti (It 1961)
Le Crime ne paie pas [Il delitto non paga] (Fr-It 1962)
Dieci italiani per un tedesco (It 1962)
La monaca di Monza (It 1962)
Anni ruggenti (It 1962)
Il cambio della guardia [Avanti la muoica/En avant la musique]
    (It-Fr 1962)
Le Bon Roi Dagobert (Fr 1963)
La smania addosso (It 1963)
Gli onorevoli (It 1963)
Volles Herz und leere Taschen (W Ger-It 1963)
Becket (Par 1964)
Il compagno Don Camillo (It 1965)
Maigret à Pigalle (It 1967)
Fratello ladro (It 1972)
Uccidere in silenzio (It 1972)
La nanna (It 1973)

CHAPLIN, GERALDINE, b. July 31, 1944, Santa Monica, California
    Limelight (UA 1952)
    Par un beau matin d'ete (Fr-Sp-It 1964)
    Doctor Zhivago (MGM 1965)
    J'ai tue Raspoutine (Fr 1966)
    Andremo in citta (It 1966)

A Countess from Hong Kong (RFD 1966)
Stranger in the House [Cop-Out] (RFD 1967)
Peppermint Frappe (Sp 1967)
Stress es tres, tres (Sp 1968)
La madriguera (Sp 1969)
El jardin de las delicias (Sp 1970) (extra)
The Hawaiians [Master of the Islands] (UA 1970)
Sur un arbre perche (Fr 1971)
Zero Population Growth [Z. P. G.] (Univ 1971)
Innocent Bystanders (Scotia-Barber 1972)
La casa sin fronteras (Sp 1972)
Ana y los lobos (Sp 1972)
Verflucht Dies Amerika (W Ger-Sp 1973)
Le mariage a la mode (Fr 1973)
The Three Musketeers [The Queen's Diamonds] (20th 1973)
Y el projimo? (Sp 1973)
Sommer-flugene [Summer of Silence] (Nor 1974) [Eng lang version made simultaneously]
The Four Musketeers [The Revenge of Milady] (20th 1974)

CHARRIER, JACQUES, b. Nov. 11, 1936, Metz
Les Tricheurs [Youthful Sinners] (Fr 1958)
Les Dragueurs [The Young Have No Morals] (Fr 1959)
Babette s'en va-t-en guerre [Babette Goes to War] (Fr 1959)
La Main chaude [Eternal Ecstasy] (Fr-It 1959)
Tiro al Piccione [Pigeon Shoot] (It-Fr 1961)
Les Sept Péchés Capitaux [Seven Capital Sins] (ep "L'Avarice") (Fr-It 1961)
L'Oeil du Malin (Fr-It 1961)
A cause, à cause d'une femme [Because of a Woman] (Fr 1962)
Carmen di Trastevere (It 1962)
La Vie conjugale: Jean-Marc (Fr-It 1963)
La Vie conjugale: Françoise (Fr-It 1963)
Marie-Soleil (Fr 1964)
La Bonne Occase (Fr 1964)
Les Créatures (Fr-Swe 1966)
Le Plus Vieux Métier du monde (ep "Anticipation") (Fr-W Ger-It 1966)
A belles dents (W Ger-Fr 1966)
Money Money (Fr 1968)
Sirocco d'hiver [Sirocco] (Hun-Fr 1969)
Les Soleils de l'ile de Pâques (Fr-Bra-Chilean 1972)

CHECCHI, ANDREA, b. Oct. 21, 1916, Firenze, Italy; d. March 31, 1974
1860 (It 1933)
Vecchia guardia (It 1935)
Amore (It 1936)
Luciano Serra, pilota (It 1938)
Ettore Fieramosca (It 1938)
L'ultima carta (It 1938)
Grandi magazzini (It 1939)
Piccolo Hotel (It 1939)

La grande luce [Montevergine] (It 1939)
La conquista dell'aria (It 1939)
Giù il sipario (It 1940)
L'assedio dell'Alcazar (It 1940)
E sbarcato un marinaio (It 1940)
Incanto di mezzanotte (It 1940)
Senza cielo (It 1940)
Amiamoci cosi (It 1940)
Ore 9, lezione di chimica (It 1941)
Il re d'Inghilterra non paga (It 1941)
Ragazza che dorme (It 1941)
Tragica notte (It 1941)
Solitudine (It 1941)
Via delle cinque lune (It 1941)
Catene invisibili (It 1942)
La contessa Castiglione (It 1942)
Malombra (It 1942)
Avanti c'è posto (It 1942)
Giacomo l'idealista (It 1942)
Labbra serrate (It 1942)
M. A. S. (It 1942)
Tristi amori (It 1943)
Lettere al sottotenente (It 1943)
Tempesta sul golfo (It 1943)
La valle del diavolo (It 1943)
Dieci minuti di vita (It 1943 [unreleased]
Lacrime di sangue (It 1944)
Tutta la vita in ventiquattro'ore (It 1944)
Due lettere anonime (It 1945)
I dieci comandamenti (It 1945)
Un americano in vacanza (It 1946)
Le vie del peccato (It 1946)
Biraghin (It 1946)
L'ultimo amore (It 1946)
Roma città libera [La notte porta consiglio] (It 1946)
Albergo Luna camera 34 (It 1947)
Cronaca nera (It 1947)
La primula bianca (It 1947)
Caccia tragica (It 1947)
Marcia tragica (It 1948)
I fratelli Karamazoff (It 1948)
Carrefour des passions [Gli uomini sono nemici] (Fr-It 1948)
Le mure di Malapaga [Au delà des grilles] (It-Fr 1949)
La città dolente (It 1949)
Il grido della terra (It 1949)
Eleanora Duse (It 1950) [made in 1947]
Atto d'accusa (It 1950)
Gli uomini sono nemici (It 1950)
Il cielo è rosso (It 1950)
Rondini in volo (It 1950)
Paolo e Francesca (It 1950)
La strada finisce sul fiume (It 1950)
L'eroe sono io (It 1951)

Achtung, banditi! (It 1951)
Capitano nero (It 1951)
Altri tempi (It 1951)
Il sentiero dell'odio (It 1952)
Don Lorenzo (It 1952)
Sul ponte dei sospiri (It 1953)
La signora senza camelie [La traviata/The Lost One] (It 1954)
Amori di mezzo secolo (It 1954)
Pietà per chi cade (It 1954)
Casa Ricordi (It 1954)
Siluri umani (It 1954)
Tempi nostri (It 1954)
Addio Napoli (It 1954)
Il capitano di Venezia (It 1954) [made in 1952]
Tripoli bel suol d'amore (It 1954)
Rosso e nero [The Red and the Black/Rouge et Noir] (It 1954)
Appassionatamente (It 1954)
Se vincessi cento milioni (It 1954)
Le campane di San Giusto (It 1954)
Operazione notte (It 1955)
Buonanotte... avvocato! (It 1955)
I quattro del getto tonante (It 1955)
Le due orfanelle (It 1955)
L'intrusa (It 1955)
Il tesoro di Rommel (It 1956)
Disperato addio (It 1956)
Processo all'amore (It 1956)
Parola di ladro (It 1957)
Terrore sulla città (It 1957)
Mattino di primavera (It 1957)
Suprema confessione (It 1958)
Il... di mia moglie (It 1959)
Il terrore dei barbari (It 1959)
Il mondo dei miracoli (It 1959)
Le cameriere (It 1959)
L'impiegato (It 1959)
I piaceri dello scapolo (It 1960)
La strada dei giganti (It 1960)
La lunga notte del '43 (It 1960)
La maschera del demonio (It 1960)
Die 1000 Augen des Dr. Mabuse [Il diabolico dottor Mabuse]
    (W Ger-It 1960)
La ciociara (It 1960)
Le notti dei teddy boys (It 1960)
Il sicario (It 1961)
Akiko (It 1961)
Caccia all'uomo (It 1961)
Don Camillo, monsignore... ma non troppo (It 1961)
L'assassino (It 1961)
L'oro di Roma (It 1961)
Gli invasori (It 1961)
Dieci italiani per un tedesco (It 1962)
Colpo gobbo all'italiana (It 1962)

Cronache del '22 (It 1962)
Il mio amico Benito (It 1962)
Lo smemorato di Collegno (It 1962)
Il sangue e la sfida (It 1962)
Venere imperiale [Venus impériale] (It-Fr 1962)
Ultimatum alla vita (It 1963)
Il criminale (It 1963)
Il processo di Verona (It 1963)
Finche dura la tempesta [Beta som] (It 1964)
Italiani, brava gente (It 1964)
Io uccido, tu uccidi (ep "Giochi acerbi") (It 1965)
Super rapina a Milano (It 1965)
La vendetta dei gladiatori (It 1965)
Il gladiatore che sfido p'impero (It 1965)
Io, io, io... e gli altri (It 1966)
I soldi (It 1966)
Quien sabe? (It 1967)
El "Che" Guevara (It 1968)
I sette fratelli Cervi (It 1968)
Waterloo (It-USSR 1969)
Cerca di capirmi (It 1970)
Un apprezzato professionista di siuno avvenire (It 1972)
Baciamo le mani (It 1973)

CHEVALIER, MAURICE, b. Sept. 12, 1889, Menilmontant, Paris;
    d. Jan. 1, 1972
Le Mauvais Garçon (Fr 1921)
Goenzague (Fr 1923)
L'Aventure de la rue de Lourcine (Fr 1923)
Par habitude (Fr 1924)
Jim Bougne, boxeur (Fr 1924)
Bonjour, New York (Fr 1928) (cameo)
Innocents of Paris (Par 1929)
La Chanson de Paris (Par 1929) [Fr version of Innocents of
    Paris]
The Love Parade (Par 1929)
Parade d'Amour (Par 1929) [Fr version of The Love Parade]
Paramount on Parade (Par 1930) [also Fr version]
The Big Pond (Par 1930)
La Grande Mer (Par 1930) [Fr version of The Big Pond]
Playboy of Paris (Par 1930)
Le Petit Café (Par 1930) [Fr version of Playboy of Paris]
The Smiling Lieutenant (Par 1931)
Le Lieutenant souriant (Par 1931) [Fr version of The Smiling
    Lieutenant]
One Hour with You (Par 1932)
Une Heure près de toi (Par 1932) [Fr version of One Hour with
    You]
Make Me a Star (Par 1932) (cameo)
Love Me Tonight (Par 1932)
A Bedtime Story (Par 1933)
The Way to Love (Par 1933)
L'Amour guide (Par 1933) [Fr version of The Way to Love]

The Merry Widow (MGM 1934)
La Veuve joyeuse (MGM 1934) [Fr version of The Merry Widow]
Folies Bergère (UA 1935)
L'Homme des Folies Bergère (UA 1935) [Fr version of Folies Bergère]
L'Homme du Jour (Fr 1936)
Avec le sourire (Fr 1936)
The Beloved Vagabond (ABFD 1936)
Le Vagabond bien-aimé (ABFD 1936) [Fr version of The Beloved Vagabond]
Break the News (GFD 1937)
Pièges (Fr 1939)
Paris 1900 (Fr 1946)* (footage of Chevalier featured)
Le Silence est d'or [Man About Town] (Fr 1947)
Le Roi (Fr 1949)
Ma pomme (Fr 1950)
Schlager-Parade (W Ger 1953) (cameo)
Cento anni d'amore (ep "Amore 1954") (It 1953)
J'avais sept filles [I sette peccati di Papa] (It-Fr 1954)
Visite à Maurice Chevalier (Fr 1954) [documentary]
The Happy Road (MGM 1957) [sings title song only]
The Heart of Show Business (Staub 1957) [documentary] (cameo)
Gigi (MGM 1958)
Count Your Blessings (MGM 1959)
Can-Can (20th 1960)
Un, deux, trois, quatre! [Black Tights] (Fr 1960) (narrator)
A Breath of Scandal (Par 1960)
Pepe (Col 1960)
Les Années folles* (Fr 1960) (footage of Chevalier featured)
Fanny (WB 1961)
La Sage-femme, le curé et le bon Dieu [Jessica] (Fr 1961)
In Search of the Castaways (BV 1962)
A New Kind of Love (Par 1963)
La Bataille de France* (Fr 1963) [documentary] (footage of Chevalier featured)
Panic Button (Gorton 1964)
I'd Rather Be Rich (Univ 1964)
La chance et l'amour (Fr-It 1964) (interviewee)
Monkeys, Go Home! (BV 1967)
The Aristocats (BV 1970) (sings title song only)
La Naissance* (Fr 1970) (footage of Chevalier featured)
Le Chagrin et la pitié* (Fr 1972) (footage of Chevalier featured)

CHRISTIANS, MADY, b. Jan. 19, 1900, Vienna; d. Oct. 28, 1952
Audrey (Par 1916)
Die Krone von Kerkyra (Ger 1917)
Frau Marais Erlebnis (Ger 1917)
Das verlorene Paradies (Ger 1917)
Am Scheidewege (Ger 1918)
Die Verteidigerin (Ger 1918)
Am andern Ufer (Ger 1918)
Die Dreizehn (Ger 1918)
Nachtschatten (Ger 1918)

Fidelio (Ger 1919)
Eine junge Dame von Welt (Ger 1919)
Die Nacht des Grauens (Ger 1919)
Der goldene Klub (Ger 1919)
Not und Verbrechen (Ger 1919)
Die Peruanerin (Ger 1919)
Die Sühne der Martha Marx (Ger 1919)
Die Gesunkenen (Ger 1920)
Wer unter Euch ohne Sünde ist---- (Ger 1920)
Der Mann Ohne Namen (Ger 1920)*
Die Schicksalstag (Ger 1921)
Kinder der Zeit (Ger 1922)
Es leuchtet meine Liebe (Ger 1922)
Ein Glas Wasser [Ein Spiel der Königin] (Ger 1923)
Der Wetterwart (Ger 1923)
Die Buddenbrooks (Ger 1923)
Der verlorene Schuh (Ger 1923)
Die Finanzen des Grossherzogs (Ger 1923)
Mensch gegen Mensch (Ger 1924)
Soll und Haben (Ger 1924)
Die Verrufenen [Der Fünfte Stand/Slums of Berlin] (Ger 1925)
Der Farmer aus Texas (Ger 1925)
Die vom Niederrhein (Ger 1925)
Der Abenteuer (Ger 1925)
Ein Walzertraum [The Waltz Dream] (Ger 1925)
Nanette macht Alles (Ger 1926)
Die Welt will belogen sein [Der Mann mit dem Splitter] (Ger 1926)
Zopf und Schwert (Ger 1926)
Wien, Wie es Weint und Lacht (Ger 1926)
Die Geschiedene Frau (Ger 1926)
Die Königin vom Moulin Rouge (Aus 1926)
Der Sohn der Hagar (Ger 1927)
Grand Hotel [Hotel Boulevard] (Ger 1927)
Heimweh (Ger 1927)
Königin Luise (Ger 1928)
Fräulein Chauffeur (Ger 1928)
Le Duel (Fr 1928)
Eine Frau von Format (Ger 1928)
Priscillas Fahrt ins Glück [Princess Priscilla's Fortnight] (Ger-
     GB 1928)
Das Brennende Herz [The Burning Heart] (Ger 1929)
Metne Schwester und Ich (Ger 1928)
Liebe, Liebe (Ger 1928)
The Runaway Princess (JMG 1929)
Dich Hab'ich Geliebt [Because I Loved You] (Ger 1929)
Leutnant Warst du einst bei den Husaren [Mon Coeur incognito]
     (Ger-Fr 1930)
Das Schicksal der Renate Langen [Sein Letzter Brief] (Ger 1931)
Die Frau, von der Man spricht (Ger 1931)
Der schwarze Husar (Ger 1932)
Friederike (Ger 1932)
Salon Dora Green [Die Falle] (Ger 1933)
Ich und die Kaiserin (Ger 1932)
The Only Girl [Heart Song] (GB 1933) [Eng lang version of Ich

und die Kaiserin]
Manolescu, der Fürst der Diebe (Ger 1933)
A Wicked Woman (MGM 1934)
Escapade (MGM 1935)
Ship Cafe (Par 1935)
Come and Get It (UA 1936)
Seventh Heaven (20th 1937)
The Woman I Love (RKO 1937)
Heidi (20th 1937)
Tender Comrade (RKO 1943)
Address Unknown (Col 1944)
Letter from an Unknown Woman (Univ 1948)
All My Sons (Univ 1948)

CHRISTIE, JULIE, b. April 14, 1940, Chukua, Assam, India
Crooks Anonymous (AA 1962)
The Fast Lady (RFD 1962)
Billy Liar! (AA 1963)
Young Cassidy (MGM 1965)
Darling... (AA 1965)
Doctor Zhivago (MGM 1965)
Fahrenheit 451 (RFD 1966)
Far from the Madding Crowd (MGM 1967)
Tonite Let's All Make Love in London (Lorrimer Films 1967)
    (interviewee in documentary)
Petulia (WB 1968)
Star (Hunter 1968) [documentary made in 1966]
In Search of Gregory (GB-It 1970)
McCabe and Mrs. Miller (WB 1971)
The Go-Between (MGM-EMI 1971)
Don't Look Now (GB-It 1973)
Shampoo (Col 1975)
Nashville (Par 1975) (guest role playing herself)

CHRISTY, SUZANNE, b. 1904, Brussels
A la manière de Zorro (Bel 1923)
Dans Bruges la morte (Bel 1924)
L'Oeuvre immortelle (Bel 1924)
La Flamme du souvenir (Bel 1925)
La Forêt qui tue (Bel 1926)
Le Mariage de Melle Beulemans (Fr-Bel 1926)
La Divine Croisière (Fr 1927)
Rapacité (Fr 1927)
Ombre et lumière (Bel 1929)
Carillons et dentelles (Bel 1930)
Un Coup de téléphone (Fr 1931)
La Croix du Sud (Fr 1931)
Le Marchand de sable (Fr 1931)
Il a été perdu une mariée (Fr 1932)
Un Homme heureux (Fr 1932)
Jeunes Filles en liberté (Bel 1933)
La Femme invisible (Fr 1933)
C'était le bon temps (Bel 1936)

Gardons notre sourire (Bel 1936)
Le Mystère du 421 (Bel-Fr 1937)
Le P'tit Parigot (Fr--date unknown)
Un Foyer sans maman (Bel--date unknown)
Pan-pan (Fr--date unknown)

CILENTO, DIANE, b. Oct. 5, 1933, New Guinea
Wings of Danger [Dead on Course] (Ex 1952)
All Hallowe'en (ABFD 1953)
The Angel Who Pawned Her Harp (BL 1954)
The Passing Stranger (IFD 1954)
Passage Home (GFD 1955)
The Woman for Joe (RFD 1955)
The Admirable Crichton [Paradise Lagoon] (Modern Screenplays
    1957)
The Truth About Women (BL 1958)
Jet Storm (Britannia 1959)
The Full Treatment (Col 1961)
The Naked Edge (UA 1961)
I Thank a Fool (MGM 1962)
Tom Jones (UA 1963)
The Third Secret (20th 1964)
Rattle of a Simple Man (WPD 1964)
The Agony and the Ecstasy (20th 1965)
Hombre (20th 1967)
Negatives (Crispin 1968)
Zero Population Growth [Z. P. G.] (Univ 1971)
Hitler: The Last Ten Days (GB-It 1973)
The Wicker Man (BL 1973)

CLARK, PETULA, b. Nov. 15, 1932, West Ewell, Surrey, England
Medal for the General (Anglo 1944)
Strawberry Roan (Anglo 1945)
Murder in Reverse (Anglo 1945)
I Know Where I'm Going (GFD 1945)
London Town [My Heart Goes Crazy] (EL 1946)
Easy Money (GFD 1948)
Vice Versa (GFD 1948)
Here Come the Huggetts (GFD 1948)
Vote for Huggett (GFD 1949)
The Huggetts Abroad (GFD 1949)
Don't Ever Leave Me (GFD 1949)
The Romantic Age [Naughty Arlette] (GFD 1949)
Dance Hall (GFD 1950)
White Corridors (GFD 1951)
Madame Louise (Butcher 1951)
The Card [The Promoter] (GFD 1952)
Made in Heaven (GFD 1952)
The Runaway Bus (Eros 1954)
The Gay Dog (Eros 1954)
The Happiness of Three Women (Adelphi 1954)
Track the Man Down (Rep Br 1955)
That Woman Opposite [City After Midnight] (Monarch 1957)

6. 5 Special* [Calling All Cats] (AA 1958)
Goodbye Mr. Chips (MGM 1968)
Finian's Rainbow (WB-7 Arts 1968)

CLEMENTI, PIERRE, b. Sept. 28, 1942, Paris
    Le Chien de pique [The Jack of Spades] (It-Fr 1960)
    Adorable Menteuses (Fr 1961)
    Il gattopardo [The Leopard] (It-Fr 1962)
    Cent briques et des tuiles [How Not to Rob a Department Store]
        (Fr-It 1965)
    As ilhas encantadas (Por 1965)
    Brigade anti-gangs (It-Fr 1966)
    Un Homme de trop [Shock Troops] (Fr-It 1967)
    Lamiel (Fr-It 1967)
    Belle de jour (Fr-It 1967)
    Les Idoles (Fr 1968)
    Benjamin; ou Les Mémoires d'un puceau [Benjamin, or the
        Diary of an Innocent Young Man] (Fr 1968)
    Scusi, facciamo l'amore [Listen, Let's Make Love] (It-Fr 1968)
    Partner (It 1968)
    Wheel of Ashes (USA 1968)
    Les Roses de Tourlaville (Fr 1968)
    La Voie lactée [The Milky Way] (Fr-It 1969)
    Porcile [Pigsty] (It-Fr 1969)
    La sua giornata di gloria (It 1969) [introduction only]
    Le lit de la vierge [The Virgin's Bed] (Fr 1970)
    Il conformista [The Conformist] (It-Fr-W Ger 1970)
    I Cannibali [The Cannibals] (It 1970)
    Cabezas cortadas [Severed Heads] (Braz-Sp 1970)
    La Naissance (Fr 1970)
    La Leçon de choses ou les plaies ouvertes (Fr 1970)
    Nini Tirabuscio, la donna che invento la mossa (It 1970)
    Necropolis (It-GB 1970)
    Jupiter (Fr 1971)
    La Famille (Fr 1971)
    La pacifista (It-Fr-W Ger 1971) [orig made for It TV]
    La Cicatrice intérieure [Inner Scar] (Fr 1971)
    Crushproof (Parrot 1971)
    C. A. C. I. 71 (Swi 1971)
    Sweet Movie (Fr-Can-W Ger 1974)
    Steppenwolf (Swi-USA 1974)
    L'Ironie du sort (Fr 1974)
    De quoi s'agit-il? (Fr 1974)
    Le Fils d'Amr est mort [The Son of Amr Is Dead] (Bel-Fr-Tun
        1975)

CLIVE, COLIN (Colin Clive Greig), b. Jan. 20, 1900, St. Malo,
        France; d. June 25, 1937
    Journey's End (Tiffany 1930)
    The Stronger Sex (Ideal 1930)
    Frankenstein (Univ 1931)
    Lily Christine (Par Br 1932)
    Looking Forward (MGM 1933)

Christopher Strong (RKO 1933)
The Key (WB 1934)
One More River [Over the River] (Univ 1934)
Jane Eyre (Mon 1934)
Clive of India (UA 1935)
Bride of Frankenstein (Univ 1935)
The Girl from 10th Avenue (FN 1935)
The Man Who Broke the Bank at Monte Carlo (Fox 1935)
The Right to Live (WB 1935)
Mad Love [The Hands of Orlac] (MGM 1935)
The Widow from Monte Carlo (WB 1935)
History Is Made at Night (UA 1937)
The Woman I Love (RKO 1937)

COLLINS, JOAN, b. May 23, 1933, London
Lady Godiva Rides Again (BL 1951)
The Woman's Angle (ABP 1952)
Judgement Deferred (ABFD 1952)
I Believe in You (GFD 1952)
Decameron Nights (Eros 1952)
Cosh Boy [The Slasher] (IFD 1953)
Turn the Key Softly (GFD 1953)
The Square Ring (GFD 1953)

Joan Collins (standing) with Alexander Scourby (left), Rod Steiger, and Michael Dante in Seven Thieves (1960).

Our Girl Friday [The Adventures of Sadie] (Renown 1954)
The Good Die Young (IFD 1954)
Land of the Pharaohs (WB 1955)
The Virgin Queen (20th 1955)
The Girl in the Red Velvet Swing (20th 1955)
The Opposite Sex (20th 1956)
Sea Wife (20th 1957)
Island in the Sun (20th 1957)
The Wayward Bus (20th 1957)
Stopover Tokyo (20th 1957)
The Bravados (20th 1958)
Rally 'Round the Flag Boys! (20th 1959)
Seven Thieves (20th 1960)
Esther and the King (20th 1960)
The Road to Hong Kong (UA 1962)
Warning Shot (Par 1967)
If It's Tuesday, This Must Be Belgium (UA 1969)
Can Heironymus Merkin Ever Forget Mercy Humppe and Find
    True Happiness? (RFD 1969)
The Executioner (Col 1970)
Three in the Cellar [Up in the Cellar] (AIP 1970)
Subterfuge (RFD 1971) [made in 1968]
Quest for Love (RFD 1971)
Revenge (RFD 1971)
Fear in the Night (MGM-EMI 1972)
Asylum (CIC 1972)
Tales from the Crypt (Cin 1972)
Tales That Witness Murder (Par 1973)
Drive Hard, Drive Fast (ABC-TV 1973)
Alfie Darling (EMI 1975)
I Don't Want to Be Born (Fox-Rank 1975)
Dark Places (Bruton 1975) [made in 1973]

COMPTON, FAY, b. Sept. 18, 1894, London
She Stoops to Conquer (Gaumont 1914)
One Summer's Day (Int Ex 1917)
The Labour Leader (Int Ex 1917)
Judge Not (Jury 1920)
A Woman of No Importance (Ideal 1921)
The Old Wives' Tale (Ideal 1921)
The House of Peril (Astra Films 1922)
Diana of the Crossways (Ideal 1922)
A Bill of Divorcement (Ideal 1922)
This Freedom (Ideal 1923)
The Loves of Mary Queen of Scots (Ideal 1923)
Claude Duval (Gaumont 1924)
The Eleventh Commandment (Gaumont 1924)
The Happy Ending (Gaumont 1925)
Settled Out of Court (Gaumont 1925)
London Love (Gaumont 1926)
Robinson Crusoe (Epic Films 1927)
Somehow Good (Pathé 1927)
Zero (FNP 1928)

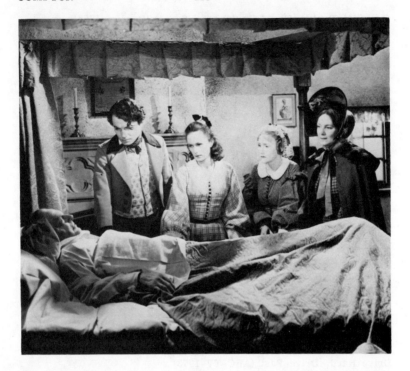

Fay Compton (second from right) with (left to right) Sam Livesy, James Mason, Geraldine Fitzgerald and Mary Clare in The Mill on the Floss (1937).

Fashions in Love (Par Br 1929)
Cape Forlorn [The Love Storm] (Wardour 1931)
Uneasy Virtue (Wardour 1931)
Tell England [The Battle of Gallipoli] (Wardour 1931)
Waltzes from Vienna [Strauss's Great Waltz] (Gaumont 1934)
Autumn Crocus (ABFD 1934)
Song at Eventide (Butcher 1934)
Wedding Group [Wrath of Jealousy] (Fox Br 1936)
The Mill on the Floss (NPFD 1937)
So This Is London (20th Br 1939)
The Prime Minister (WB Br 1941)
Odd Man Out (GFD 1947)
Nicholas Nickleby (GFD 1947)
London Belongs to Me [Dulcimer Street] (GFD 1948)
Esther Waters (GFD 1948)
Britannia Mews [Forbidden Street] (20th Br 1949)
Blackmailed [Mr. Christopher] (GFD 1951)
Laughter in Paradise (GFD 1951)
A Lady Possessed (Rep 1952)

Aunt Clara (BL 1954)
Othello (UA 1955)
Doublecross (BL 1956)
Town on Trial (Col 1957)
The Story of Esther Costello [The Golden Virgin] (Col 1957)
The Haunting (MGM 1963)
The Virgin and the Gypsy (London Screenplays 1970)

CONNERY, SEAN, b. Aug. 25, 1930, Edinburgh
No Road Back (RKO 1956)
Time Lock (IFD 1957)
Hell Drivers (RFD 1957)
Action of the Tiger (MGM 1957)
Another Time, Another Place (Par 1958)
Tarzan's Greatest Adventure (Par 1959)
Darby O'Gill and the Little People (BV 1959)
The Frightened City (AA 1961)
On the Fiddle [Operation Warhead] (AA 1961)
The Longest Day (20th 1962)
Dr. No (UA 1962)
From Russia with Love (UA 1963)
Woman of Straw (UA 1964)
Marnie (Univ 1964)
Goldfinger (UA 1964)
The Hill (MGM 1965)
Thunderball (UA 1965)
A Fine Madness (WB 1966)
You Only Live Twice (UA 1967)
Shalako (WPD 1968)
The Molly Maguires (Par 1969)
La tenda rossa [Krasnaya palatka/The Red Tent] (It-USSR 1969)
The Anderson Tapes (Col 1971)
Diamonds Are Forever (UA 1971)
The Offence (UA 1972)
Zardoz (Fox-Rank 1973)
Murder on the Orient Express (EMI 1974)
Ransom [The Terrorists] (BL 1974)
The Man Who Would Be King (AA 1975)

CONSTANTINE, EDDIE, b. Oct. 28, 1917, Los Angeles
Les Contes du Caire [Egypt by Three] (Egy 1953)
La Môme verte de gris [Gun Moll] (Fr 1953)
Cet Homme est dangereux [This Man Is Dangerous] (Fr 1953)
Les Femmes s'en balancent [Dames Don't Care] (Fr 1954)
Votre dévoué, Blake (Fr 1954)
Avanzi di Galera (It-Fr 1955)
Çà va barder! [Give 'em Hell] (Fr 1955)
Je suis un sentimental [Headlines of Destruction] (Fr-It 1955)
Signaux dans l'ombre (Fr 1955)
Vous Pigez? (Fr-It 1956)
Les Truands [Lock Up the Spoons] (Fr 1956)
L'Homme et l'enfant [Man and Child] (Fr-It 1956)
Folies-Bergère (Fr 1957)

Le Grand Bluff (Fr 1957)
Ces Dames préfèrent le mambo [Dishonorable Discharge] (Fr-It 1958)
Incognito (Fr 1958)
Hoppla, jetzt kommt Eddie! (W Ger 1958)
Passport to Shame [Room 43] (BL 1959)
Du Rififi chez les femmes [Riff Raff Girls] (Fr-It 1959)
S.O.S. Pacific (RFD 1959)
The Treasure of San Teresa [Hot Money Girl] (Britannia 1959)
Bomben auf Monte Carlo (W Ger 1960)
Comment qu'elle est! [Women Are Like That] (Fr 1960)
Le Chien de pique [The Jack of Spades] (It-Fr 1960)
Ça va être ta fête/Tout feu, tout flamme [It's Your Birthday] (Fr-It 1961)
Me faire ça à moi! [It Means That to Me] (Fr 1961)
Mani i alto [Destination Fury] (It-Fr 1961)
Cause Toujours, mon Lapin (Fr 1961)
Les Sept Péchés Capitaux [Seven Capital Sins] (ep "La Paresse" ["Sloth"]) (Fr-It 1961)
Lemmy pour les dames [Ladies Man] (Fr 1962)
Cleo de cinq à sept [Cleo from Five to Seven] (Fr-It 1962)
Une Grosse Tête [A Fat Head] (Fr 1962)
Bonne Chance, Charlie!/De la Poudre et des Balles (Fr 1962)
Nous irons à Deauville (Fr 1962) (uncredited cameo)
L'Empire de la nuit (Fr 1963)
Les Femmes d'abord (Fr-It 1963)
Comme s'il en pleuvait [As If It Were Raining] (Fr-Sp 1963)
A toi de faire, Mignonne [Your Turn, Darling] (Fr-It 1963)
De frissons partout (Fr-It 1964)
Nick Carter va tout casser/Nick Carter casse tout [License to Kill] (Fr-It 1964)
Laissez tirer les tireurs (Fr-It 1964)
Lucky Jo (Fr-It 1964)
Ces dames s'en mêlent (Fr-It 1965)
Alphaville; ou Une Etrange Aventure de Lemmy Caution (Fr-It 1965)
Faites vos jeux, Mesdames (Fr-Sp 1965)
Je vous salue, Mafia [Hail! Mafia] (Fr-It 1965)
Nick Carter et le trefle rouge (Fr-It 1965)
Du Rififi au Paname [The Upper Hand] (Fr-It-W Ger 1965)
Cartes sur table (Sp-Fr 1966)
Residencia para espias (Sp-Fr 1967)
A toute casser [No Holds Barred] (Fr-It 1968)
Ça barde chez les mignonnes (Fr-It 1969)
Les Gros Malins (Fr-It 1969)
Il était une fois un flic (Fr-It 1972)
Une Baleine qui avait mal aux dents (Fr 1973)
No Panic (Dut 1973)

COOPER, GLADYS, b. Dec. 18, 1888, Lewisham, London; d. Nov. 17, 1971
The Eleventh Commandment (Gerrard 1913)
Dandy Donovan, the Gentleman Cracksman (Jury 1914)

The Real Thing at Last (British Actors 1916)
The Sorrows of Satan (Walker 1917)
Masks and Faces (Ideal 1917)
My Lady's Dress (Moss 1917)
Unmarried (Granger's Exclusives 1920)
The Bohemian Girl (Astra 1922)
Bonnie Prince Charlie (Gaumont-British Screencraft 1923)
The Iron Duke (Gaumont 1935)
Kitty Foyle (RKO 1940)
Rebecca (UA 1940)
That Hamilton Woman [Lady Hamilton] (UA 1941)
The Black Cat (Univ 1941)
The Gay Falcon (RKO 1941)
This Above All (20th 1942)
Eagle Squadron (Univ 1942)
Now, Voyager (WB 1942)
Forever and a Day (RKO 1943)
Mr. Lucky (RKO 1943)
Princess O'Rourke (WB 1943)
The Song of Bernadette (20th 1943)
The White Cliffs of Dover (MGM 1944)
Mrs. Parkington (MGM 1944)
The Valley of Decision (MGM 1945)
Love Letters (Par 1945)
Beware of Pity (EL 1946)
The Green Years (MGM 1946)
The Cockeyed Miracle (MGM 1946)
Green Dolphin Street (MGM 1947)
The Bishop's Wife (RKO 1947)
Homecoming (MGM 1948)
The Pirate (MGM 1948)
The Secret Garden (MGM 1949)
Madame Bovary (MGM 1949)
Thunder on the Hill [Bonaventure] (Univ 1951)
At Sword's Point [Sons of the Musketeers] (RKO 1952) (made in
    1949)
The Man Who Loved Redheads (UA 1955)
Separate Tables (UA 1958)
The List of Adrian Messenger (Univ 1963)
My Fair Lady (WB 1964)
The Happiest Millionaire (BV 1967)
A Nice Girl Like Me (Avco Emb 1969)

CORDY, ANNIE (Leonie Correman), b. June 16, 1928, Brussels
    Si Versailles m'était conté (Fr 1953)
    Boum sur Paris (Fr 1953)
    Poisson d'Avril (Fr 1954)
    Bonjour sourire (Fr 1955)
    Le Chanteur de Mexico (Fr 1956)
    Viktor und Viktoria (W Ger 1957)
    Tabarin (Fr 1958)
    Cigarettes, whisky et p'tites pépées (Fr 1958)
    Tête folle (Fr 1959)

Ces Dames s'en mêlent (Fr 1964)
L'Or du Duc (Fr 1965)
Ces Messieurs de la famille (Fr 1969)
Le Passenger de la pluie (Fr 1969)
Ces Messieurs de la gâchette (Fr 1970)
La Rupture (Fr 1970)
Les Galets d'Etretat (Fr 1971)
Le Chat (Fr 1971)
Les Portes de feu (Fr 1971)
Elle court, elle court la Balnlieve (Fr 1972)
Commissarito di Notturno (It 1972)
Le Matef (Fr 1973)
La Dernière Bourrêe à Paris (Fr 1973)
Souvenir of Gibraltar (Bel 1975)
Isabelle devant le dêsir (Bel-Fr 1975)
Rue Haute (Bel-Fr 1975)

CORTESE, VALENTINA (a. k. a. Valentina Cortesa), b. Jan. 1,
      1925, Milan
Orizzonte dipinto (It 1940)
Il bravo di Venezia (It 1941)
La cena delle beffe (It 1941)
La Regina di Navarre (It 1941)
Primo amore (It 1941)
Soltanto un bacio (It 1942)
Una signora dell'Ouest (It 1942)
Orizzonte di sangue (It 1942)
Quarto pagino (It 1942)
Giorni felici (It 1942)
L'angelo biances (It 1942)
Quattro ragazze sognano (It 1943)
Chi l'ha visto? (It 1943)
Nessuno torna indietro (It 1943)
Un americano in vacanza [A Yank in Rome] (It 1945)
Il passatore (It 1947)
I miserabili [Les Misêrables] (It 1947)
Gli uomini sono nemici (It 1947)
L'ebreo errante (It 1947)
Il corriere del re (It 1947)
Roma, città libera (It 1948) [made in 1946]
Le Carrefour das passions [Crossroads of Passion] (Fr 1948)
The Glass Mountain (EL 1949)
La montagna di cristallo [It version of The Glass Mountain]
      (It 1949)
Donne senza nome [Unwanted Women] (It 1949)
Black Magic [Cagliastro] (USA-It 1949)
Thieves' Highway (20th 1949)
Malaya (MGM 1950)
Shadow of the Eagle (IFD 1950)
La rivale dell'imperatrice (It version of Shadow of the Eagle]
      (It 1950)
The House on Telegraph Hill (20th 1951)
The Secret People (GFD 1952)
Lulù (It 1952)

La passeggiata (It 1953)
Donne proibite [Forbidden Women/Angels of Darkness] (It 1953)
Il matrimonio (It 1954)
Addio, mia bella signora! (It 1954)
The Barefoot Contessa [La contessa scalza] (UA 1954)
Avanzi di galera (It 1954)
Faccia da mascalzone (It 1955)
Il conte Aquila (It 1955)
Le amiche (It 1955)
Magic Fire (Rep 1956)
Dimentica il mio passato [Consuelo/Rio Gruadalquivir] (It-Sp
    1956)
Adriana Lecouvreur (It 1956)
Calabuch [Calabuig] (Sp-It 1956)
Amore è guai (It 1959)
Barabba [Barabbas] (It 1961)
Nasilje na trgu [Square of Violence] (Yug 1961)
La ragazza che sapeva troppo [The Evil Eye] (It 1962)
Axel Munthe, der Arzt von San Michell [La storia di San
    Michele](W Ger-It 1962)
La vendetta della signora [Au Besuch/The Visit/La Rancune]
    (It-W Ger-Fr-USA 1964)
Giulietta degli spiriti [Juliet of the Spirits] (It 1965)
La donna del lago (It 1965)
Le Soleil Noir [Black Sun/Dark Sunlight] (Fr 1966)
The Legend of Lylah Clare (MGM 1968)
Scusi, facciamo l'amore [Listen, Let's Make Love] (It 1968)
The Secret of Santa Vittoria (UA 1969)
Toh, è morta la nonna! [Well, Grandma's Dead!] (It 1968)
Les Caprices de Marie (Fr 1969)
Erste Liebe [First Love/Premier Amour] (Swi 1970)
Madly (Fr 1970)
Le Bateau sur l'herbe (Fr 1971)
Fratello Sole, Sorella Luna [Brother Sun, Sister Moon] (It 1971)
Imputazione di omicidio per uno studente (It 1971)
The Assassination of Trotsky [L'assassiano di Trotsky/L'Assas-
    sinat de Trotsky] (Fr-It-GB 1972)
L'iguana dalla lingua di fuoco (It 1972)
La Nuit américaine [Effetto notte/Day for Night] (Fr-It 1973)
Il bacio (It 1973)
Appassionata (It 1974)
Amore mio non farmi male (It 1974)

COSTA, BEATRIZ, b. Dec. 14, 1907, Charneca, Portugal
    O Diabo em Lisboa (Por 1925)
    Fátima Milagrosa (Por 1928)
    Lisboa, crónica anedotica (Por 1930)
    A minha noite de núpcias (Por 1931) [Por version of Merry
        Wedding Night]
    Beatriz Costa Memorealista (Por 1932)
    A canção de Lisboa (Por 1933)
    O trevo das quatro folhas (Por 1936)
    A aldeia da roupa branca (Por 1938)

Costinha

COSTINHA (Ernestino Augusto da Costa), b. Feb. 24, 1891, Santarêm, Portugal
Lisboa, crónica anedótica (Por 1930)
A severa (Por 1931)
As pupilas do Senhor Reitor (Por 1935)
O trevo das quatro folhas (Por 1936)
A rosa do adro (Por 1938)
A varanda dos rouxinóis (Por 1939)
João Ratão (Por 1940)
Os lobos da serra (Por 1942)
Camões (Por 1946)
Um homem do ribatejo (Por 1946)
Cais sodrê (Por 1946)
Os vizinjos do rês-do-chão (Por 1947)
Um vida para dois (Por 1948)
A morgadinha dos canaviais (Por 1949)
Sol e toiros (Por 1949)
Cantiga da rua (Por 1949)
Madragoa (Por 1951)
Rosa de Alfama (Por 1953)
O costa de Africa (Por 1954)
O noivo das caldas (Por 1956)
Perdeu-se um marido (Por 1956)
Dois dias no paraiso (Por 1957)
O homem do dia (Por 1958)
A costureirinha da sé (Por 1959)

COURTENAY, TOM, b. Feb. 25, 1937, Hull, England
    The Loneliness of the Long Distance Runner (Bry 1962)
    Private Potter (MGM 1962)
    Billy Liar! (AA 1963)
    King and Country (WPD 1964)
    Operation Crossbow [The Great Spy Mission] (MGM 1965)
    King Rat (Col 1965)
    Dr. Zhivago (MGM 1967)
    The Night of the Generals (Col 1966)
    The Day the Fish Came Out (20th 1967)
    A Dandy in Aspic (Col 1968)
    Otley (Col 1968)
    Catch Me a Spy (GB-Fr-USA 1971)
    One Day in the Life of Ivan Denisovitch (GB-Nor 1972)

COURTNEIDGE, CICELY, b. April 1, 1893, Sydney, Australia
    Elstree Calling (Wardour 1930)
    The Ghost Train (W & F 1931)
    Jack's the Boy [Night and Day] (W & F 1932)
    Happy Ever After (W & F 1932)
    Soldiers of the King [The Woman in Command] (W & F 1933)
    Falling for You (W & F 1933)
    Aunt Sally [Along Came Sally] (Gaumont 1933)
    Things Are Looking Up (Gaumont 1935)
    Me and Marlborough (Gaumont 1935)
    Everybody Dance (Gaumont 1936)
    Take My Tip (GFD 1937)
    Under Your Hat (BL 1940)
    The Spider's Web (UA 1960)
    The L-Shaped Room (BL 1962)
    Those Magnificent Men in Their Flying Machines: or, How I
       Flew from London to Paris in 25 Hrs. and 11 Minutes (20th
       1965)
    The Wrong Box (Col 1966)
    Not Now, Darling (LMG 1973)

COWARD, NOËL (Noël Pierce Coward), b. Dec. 16, 1899, Tedding-
    ton, Middlesex; d. March 26, 1973
    Hearts of the World (Artcraft 1917)
    The Scoundrel (Par 1935)
    In Which We Serve (BL 1942)
    Around the World in 80 Days (UA 1956)
    Our Man in Havana (Col 1959)
    Surprise Package (Col 1960)
    Paris When It Sizzles (Par 1964)
    Bunny Lake Is Missing (Col 1965)
    Boom! (Univ 1968)
    The Italian Job (Par 1968)

CRAIG, MICHAEL, b. Jan. 27, 1928, India
    Malta Story (GFD 1953)
    The Love Lottery (GFD 1954)

Svengali (Renown 1954)
Passage Home (GFD 1955)
The Black Tent (RFD 1956)
Eyewitness (RFD 1956)
Yield to the Night [Blonde Sinner] (ABP 1956)
House of Secrets [Triple Deception] (RFD 1956)
High Tide at Noon (RFD 1957)
Campbell's Kingdom (RFD 1957)
The Silent Enemy (IFD 1958)
Nor the Moon by Night [Elephant Gun] (RFD 1958)
Sea of Sand (RFD 1958)
Life in Emergency Ward 10 (Eros 1959)
Sapphire (RFD 1959)
Upstairs and Downstairs (RFD 1959)
The Angry Silence (BL 1960)
Cone of Silence [Trouble in the Sky] (Bry 1960)
Doctor in Love (RFD 1960)
Payroll (AA 1961)
No My Darling Daughter (RFD 1961)
A Pair of Briefs (RFD 1962)
The Mysterious Island (Col 1962)
Life for Ruth [Walk in the Shadow] (RFD 1962)

Michael Craig (right) with Anne Heywood (left), Raymond Massey, and Mylene Demongeot in Upstairs and Downstairs (1959).

The Iron Maiden (AA 1962)
Stolen Hours (UA 1963)
Life at the Top (Col 1965)
Modesty Blaise (20th 1966)
Star! [Those Were the Days] (20th 1968)
La Cena (Sp 1968)
Twinky [Lola] (RFD 1969)
The Royal Hunt of the Sun (RFD 1969)
Country Dance [Brotherly Love] (MGM-EMI 1969)
A Town Called Bastard (GB-Sp 1971)
La ultima senora Anderson (Sp-It 1972)
Historia de una chica sola (Sp-It 1972) [made in 1969]
Vault of Horror (Fox-Rank 1973)

Michael Crawford

CRAWFORD, MICHAEL, b. Jan. 19, 1942
    Soap Box Derby (CFF 1958)
    Blow Your Own Trumpet (CFF 1958)
    Two Living, One Dead (BL 1961)
    The War Lover (Col 1962)
    Two Left Feet (BL 1963)
    The Knack...and How to Get It (UA 1965)

A Funny Thing Happened on the Way to the Forum (UA 1966)
The Jokers (RFD 1966)
How I Won the War (UA 1967)
Hello, Dolly! (20th 1969)
The Games (20th 1969)
Hello--Goodbye (20th 1970)
Alice's Adventures in Wonderland (Fox-Rank 1972)

CURRIE, FINLAY, b. Jan. 20, 1878, Edinburgh; d. May 9, 1968
The War in the Air (GB 1908)
The Old Man (BL 1931)
The Frightened Lady [Criminal at Large] (Ideal 1932)
Rome Express (Gaumont 1932)
Excess Baggage (Radio 1933)
The Good Companions (Gaumont-Welsh-Pearson 1933)
Orders Is Orders (Ideal 1933)
Princess Charming (Gaumont 1934)
Little Friend (Gaumont 1934)
Gay Love (BL 1934)
Mister Cinders (Wardour 1934)
My Old Dutch (Gaumont 1934)
The Big Splash (MGM Br 1935)
The Improper Duchess (GFD 1936)
The Gay Adventure (Pathé 1936)
Wanted (SC 1937)
Glamorous Night (ABPC 1937)
Catch As Catch Can [Atlantic Episode] (20th Br 1937)
The Edge of the World (BIED 1937)
Command Performance (GFD 1937)
Paradise for Two [The Gaiety Girls] (UA 1937)
The Claydon Treasure Mystery (20th Br 1938)
Around the Town (BL 1938)
Follow Your Star (GFD 1938)
49th Parallel [The Invaders] (GFD 1941)
The Day Will Dawn [The Avengers] (GFD 1942)
Thunder Rock (MGM Br 1942)
The Bells Go Down (UA 1943)
Theatre Royal (Anglo 1943)
Undercover [Undercover Guerillas] (UA 1943)
Warn That Man (Pathé 1943)
They Met in the Dark (GFD 1943)
The Shipbuilders (Anglo 1943)
Don Chicago (Anglo 1945)
I Know Where I'm Going (GFD 1945)
The Trojan Brothers [Murder in the Footlights] (Anglo 1946)
Spring Song [Springtime] (Anglo 1946)
Woman to Woman (Anglo 1946)
School for Secrets [The Secret Flight] (GFD 1946)
Great Expectations (GFD 1946)
The Brothers (GFD 1947)
My Brother Jonathan (Pathé 1948)
So Evil My Love (Par Br 1948)
Mr. Perrin and Mr. Traill (GFD 1948)

Sleeping Car to Trieste (GFD 1948)
Bonnie Prince Charlie (BL 1948)
The History of Mr. Polly (GFD 1949)
Treasure Island (RKO 1950)
My Daughter Joy [Operation X] (BL 1950)
Trio (ep "Sanatorium") (GFD 1950)
The Black Rose (20th 1950)
The Mudlark (20th Br 1950)
People Will Talk (20th 1951)
Quo Vadis (MGM 1951)
Kangaroo (20th 1952)
Walk East on Beacon (Col 1952)
Ivanhoe (MGM Br 1952)
Stars and Stripes Forever [Marching Along] (20th 1952)
Treasure of the Golden Condor (20th 1953)
Rob Roy the Highland Rogue (RKO 1953)
The End of the Road (BL 1954)
Beau Brummell (MGM 1954)
Make Me an Offer (BL 1954)
Captain Lightfoot (Univ 1955)
Third Party Risk [The Deadly Game] (Ex 1955)
Footsteps in the Fog (Col 1955)
King's Rhapsody (BL 1955)
Around the World in 80 Days (UA 1956)
Zarak (Col 1957)
Abandon Ship! [Seven Waves Away] (Col 1957)
Saint Joan (UA 1957)
The Little Hut (MGM 1957)
Campbell's Kingdom (RFD 1957)
Dangerous Exile (RFD 1957)
The Naked Earth (20th 1958)
La tempesta [Tempest] (It 1958)
Corridors of Blood (MGM Br 1958)
Ben-Hur (MGM 1959)
Solomon and Sheba (UA 1959)
The Adventures of Huckleberry Finn (MGM 1960)
Kidnapped (BV 1960)
Giuseppe venduto dai fratelli [Joseph and His Brothers] (It 1960)
The Angel Wore Red (MGM 1960)
Hand in Hand (WPD 1960)
Five Golden Hours (Col 1961)
Clue of the Silver Key (AA 1961)
Francis of Assisi (20th 1961)
Go to Blazes (WPD 1962)
The Inspector [Lisa] (20th 1962)
The Amorous Prawn (BL 1962)
Billy Liar! (AA 1963)
The Cracksman (WPD 1963)
West 11 (WPD 1963)
The Three Lives of Thomasina (BV 1964)
Who Was Maddox? (AA 1964)
The Fall of the Roman Empire (Par 1964)
The Battle of the Villa Fiorita (WB 1965)
Bunny Lake Is Missing (Col 1965)

CUSACK, CYRIL, b. Nov. 10, 1910, Durban, South Africa
Knockagow (Film Co of Ireland 1918)
The Man Without a Face (Radio Br 1935) [billed as Cyril
Chosack]
Servants All (Fox Br 1936) [billed as Cyril Chosack]
Once a Crook (20th Br 1941)
Odd Man Out (GFD 1947)
Escape (20th Br 1948)
Esther Waters (GFD 1948)
Once a Jolly Swagman [Maniacs on Wheels] (GFD 1948)
The Small Back Room [Hour of Glory] (BL 1949)
All Over the Town (GFD 1949)
The Blue Lagoon (GFD 1949)
Gone to Earth [The Wild Heart] (BL 1950)
The Elusive Pimpernel (BL 1950)
Soldiers Three (MGM 1951)
The Secret of Convict Lake (20th 1951)
The Blue Veil (RKO 1951)
Saadia (MGM 1954)
Passage Home (GFD 1955)
The Man Who Never Was (20th 1956)
The Man in the Road (GN 1956)
The March Hare (BL 1956)
Jacqueline (RFD 1956)
The Spanish Gardener (RFD 1956)
Ill Met by Moonlight [Night Ambush] (RFD 1957)
Miracle in Soho (RFD 1957)
The Rising of the Moon (WB 1957)
Gideon's Day [Gideon of Scotland Yard] (Col Br 1958)
A Night to Remember (RFD 1958)
Floods of Fear (RFD 1958)
Shake Hands with the Devil (UA 1959)
A Terrible Beauty [The Night Fighters] (UA 1960)
Johnny Nobody (Col 1961)
The Power and the Glory (Par 1961)
Waltz of the Toreadors (RFD 1962)
I Thank a Fool (MGM Br 1962)
80,000 Suspects (RFD 1963)
Where the Spies Are (MGM Br 1965)
The Spy Who Came In from the Cold (Par 1965)
I Was Happy Here [Time Lost and Time Remembered] (RFD
1965)
Fahrenheit 451 (RFD 1966)
Oedipus the King (RFD 1967)
The Taming of the Shrew (It-GB 1968)
Galileo (It 1968)
David Copperfield (20th 1969)
Country Dance [Brotherly Love] (MGM-EMI 1971) [shot in 1969]
Trog (WB 1970)
King Lear (Col 1970)
Harold and Maude (Par 1971)
Sacco e Vanzetti (It-Fr 1971)
The Devil's Widow (AIP 1972) [started in 1969]

... Più forte, ragazzi [All the Way Boys] (It 1972)
La polizia ringrazia [The Law Enforcer] (It 1972)
La "mala" ordina [Manhunt in Milan] (It-W Ger 1972)
La mano spietata della legge [The Bloody Hands of the Law]
   (It 1973)
The Day of the Jackal (GB-Fr 1973)
The Homecoming (AFT 1973)
Joe e Margherita [Run, Joe, Run] (It 1974)
Juggernaut (UA 1974)
The Abdication (WB 1974)

CUSHING, PETER, b. May 26, 1913, Kenley, Surrey, England
   A Chump at Oxford (UA 1940)
   Vigil in the Night (RKO 1940)
   Laddie (RKO 1940)
   The Howards of Virginia (Col 1940)
   Hamlet (GFD 1948)
   Moulin Rouge (IFD 1953)
   The Black Knight (Col 1954)
   The End of the Affair (Col 1955)
   Time Without Pity (Eros 1957)
   The Curse of Frankenstein (WB 1957)
   The Abominable Snowman (WB 1957)
   Violent Playground (RFD 1958)
   Dracula [The Horror of Dracula] (Univ 1958)
   The Revenge of Frankenstein (Col 1958)
   Hound of the Baskervilles (UA 1959)
   The Mummy (Univ 1959)
   Cone of Silence [Trouble in the Sky] (Bry 1960)
   The Flesh and the Fiends [Mania] (RFI 1960)
   The Brides of Dracula (RFI 1960)
   The Sword of Sherwood Forest (Col 1960)
   Suspect (BL 1960)
   The Hellfire Club (RFI 1961)
   Fury at Smugglers Bay (RFI 1961)
   The Naked Edge (UA 1961)
   Cash on Demand (Col 1961)
   Captain Clegg [Night Creatures] (Univ 1962)
   The Man Who Finally Died (Magna 1962)
   The Evil of Frankenstein (Univ 1964)
   The Gorgon (Col 1964)
   Dr. Terror's House of Horrors (RFI 1964)
   She (WPD 1965)
   Dr. Who and the Daleks (RFI 1965)
   The Skull (Par 1965)
   Island of Terror (Planet 1966)
   Daleks: Invasion Earth A. D. 2150 (BL 1966)
   Frankenstein Created Woman (WPD 1967)
   Night of the Big Heat (Planet 1967)
   Torture Garden (Col 1967)
   Some May Live [In Saigon, Some May Live] (Butcher 1967)
   The Blood Beast Terror (Tigon 1968)
   Corruption (Col 1968)

Frankenstein Must Be Destroyed (WPD 1969)
The Vampire Lovers (MGM-EMI 1970)
The House That Dripped Blood (Cin 1970)
One More Time (UA 1970)
Incense for the Damned (GN 1971)
Twins of Evil (RFD 1971)
I, Monster (BL 1971)
Tales from the Crypt (Cin 1972)
Asylum (CIC 1972)
Dracula A. D. 1972 (Col-Warner 1972)
Dr. Phibes Rises Again (MGM-EMI 1972)
Nothing but the Night (Fox-Rank 1972)
The Creeping Flesh (Tigon 1972)
The Satanic Rites of Dracula (Col-Warner 1973)
Frankenstein and the Monster from Hell (Avco-Emb 1973)
Panico en el Transiberiano [Horror Express] (Sp-GB 1973)
From Beyond the Grave (Col-Warner 1974)
The Beast Must Die (BL 1974)
The Legend of the Seven Golden Vampires (GB-Hong Kong 1974)
... And Now the Screaming Starts! (Fox-Rank 1974)
Madhouse (EMI 1974)

DA COSTA, JOAQUIM see ALVES DA COSTA, JOAQUIM

DA CUNHA, JOSE MARIA see ALVES DA CUNHA, JOSE MARIA

DAGOVER, LIL (Maria Antonia Sieglinde Martha Senbert), b. Sept.
     30, 1897, Java, Indonesia
Harakiri (Ger 1919)
Das Kabinett des Dr. Caligari (Ger 1919)
Die Spinnen (Ger 1919)
Kabale und Liebe (Ger 1920)
Das Geheimnis von Bombay (Ger 1920)
Der Richter von Zalamea (Ger 1920)
Der weisse Pfau (Ger 1920)
Spiritismus (Ger 1920)
Die Totensel (Ger 1920)
Die Jagd nach dem Tod (Ger 1921)
Das Medium (Ger 1921)
Der müde Tod (Ger 1921)
Dr. Mabuse der Spieler (Ger 1922)
Luise Millerin (Ger 1922)
Macht der Versuchung (Ger 1922)
Phantom (Ger 1922)
Tiefland (Ger 1922)
Die Prinzessin Sawarin (Ger 1923)
Seine Frau, die Unbekannte (Ger 1923)
Komödie des Herzens (Ger 1924)
Der Demütige und die Sängerin (Ger 1925)
Liebe macht blind (Ger 1925)
Tartüff (Ger 1925)
Zur Chronik von Grieshuus (Ger 1925)
Die Brüder Schellenberg (Ger 1925)
Nur eine Tänzerin [Bara en danserska] (Ger-Swe 1926)

Der Veilchenfresser (Ger 1926)
Der Anwalt des Herzens (Ger 1926)
Orientexpress (Ger 1927)
Hans engelska Fru [Die Lady ohne Schleier] (Swe-Ger 1927)
Der geheime Kurier (Ger 1928)
Ungarische Rhapsodie (Ger 1928)
Tourbillon de Paris (Fr 1928)
Die Ehe (Ger 1928)
Es flüstert die Nacht... (Ger 1929)
Spielereien einer Kaisern (Ger 1929)
Der Günstling von Schönbrunn (Ger 1929)
Va banque (Ger 1930)
Das alte Lied (Ger 1930)
Der weisse Teufel (Ger 1930)
Boykott (Ger 1930)
Es gibt eine Frau, die Dich niemals vergisst (Ger 1930)
Die grosse Sehnsuch (Ger 1930)
Der Kongress tanzt (Ger 1931) [also Fr and Br versions]
Der Fall des Generalstabs-Oberst Redl (Ger 1931)
Woman from Monte Carlo (FN 1932)
Die Tänzerin von Sanssouci (Ger 1932)
Das Abenteuer der Thea Roland (Ger 1932)
Johannisnacht (Ger 1933)
Ich heirate meine Frau (Ger 1934)
Eine Frau, die weiss was sie will (Ger 1934)
Der Flüchtling von Chicago (Ger 1934)
Lady Windermeres Fächer (Ger 1935)
Der Vogelhändler (Ger 1935)
Der höhere Befehl (Ger 1935)
Schlussakkord (Ger 1936)
Fridericus (Ger 1936)
August der Starke (Ger 1936)
Das Mädchen Irene (Ger 1936)
Das Schönheitspflästerchen (Ger 1936)
Streit um den Knaben Jo (Ger 1937)
Die Kreutzersonate (Ger 1937)
Maja zwischen swei Ehen (Ger 1938)
Dreiklang (Ger 1938)
Rätsel um Beate (Ger 1938)
Unwege zum Glück (Ger 1939)
Friedrich Schiller (Ger 1940)
Bismarck (Ger 1940)
Wien 1910 (Aus 1942)
Kleine Residenz (Ger 1942)
Musik in Salzburg (Ger 1944)
Die Söhne des Herrn Gaspary (W Ger 1948)
Man spielt nicht mit der Liebe (W Ger 1949)
Vom Teufel gejagt W Ger 1950)
Es kommt ein Tag (W Ger 1950)
Rote Rosen, rote Lippen, roter Wein (W Ger 1953)
Könighliche Hoheit (W Ger 1953)
Schloss Hubertus (W Ger 1954)
Ich weiss, wofür ich lebe (W Ger 1955)

Die Barrings (W Ger 1955)
Der Fischer vom Heiligensee (W Ger 1955)
Rosen im Herbst [Effi Briest] (W Ger 1955)
Meine sechzehn Sohne (W Ger 1956)
Kronprinz Rudolfs letzte Liebe (W Ger 1956)
Die Bekenntnisse des Hochstaplers Felix Krull (W Ger 1957)
Unter Palmen am blauen Meer (W Ger 1957)
Die Buddenbrooks (W Ger 1959)
Die seltsame Grafin (W Ger 1961)
Der Fussgänger [The Pedestrian] (W Ger 1973)
Karl May (W Ger 1975)

DALIO, MARCEL, b. July 17, 1915, Paris
Mon chapeau (Fr 1933)
Turnandot (Fr 1934)
Cargaison blanche (Fr 1936)
Pepe le Moko (Fr 1936)
Quand minuit sonnera (Fr 1936)
Un Grand Amour de Beethoven (Fr 1936)
L'Or (Fr 1936)
La Grande Illusion [Grand Illusion] (Fr 1937)
Sarati le Terrible (Fr 1937)
Les Pirates du Rail (Fr 1937)
Les Perles de la Couronne (Fr 1937)
Alibi (Fr 1937)
Gribouille (Fr 1937)
L'Homme à abattre (Fr 1937)
Marthe Richard (Fr 1937)
Naples au Baiser de Feu (Fr 1937)
Miarka, la fille à l'ours (Fr 1937)
Troika (Fr 1937)
Chéri-Bibi (Fr 1938)
Mollenard (Fr 1938)
Lumières des Paris (Fr 1938)
Entrée des artistes (Fr 1938)
La Maison du Maltais (Fr 1938)
Conflit (Fr 1938)
La Tradition du minuit (Fr 1939)
La Regle du jeu [The Rules of the Game] (Fr 1939)
L'Esclave blanche (Fr 1939)
Le Bois sacre (Fr 1939)
Tempête sur Paris (Fr 1939)
The Shanghai Gesture (UA 1941)
Unholy Partners (MGM 1941)
Joan of Paris (RKO 1942)
Paris After Dark [The Night Is Ending] (20th 1943)
Casablanca (WB 1943)
Tonight We Raid Calais (20th 1943)
The Song of Bernadette (20th 1943)
The Constant Nymph (WB 1943)
The Desert Song (WB 1943)
Action in Arabia (20th 1944)
The Conspirators (WB 1944)

Pin-Up Girl (20th 1944)
To Have and Have Not (WB 1944)
Wilson (20th 1944)
A Bell for Adano (20th 1945)
Son dernier role (Fr 1945)
Pétrus (Fr 1946)
Bataillon du ciel (Fr 1946)
Les Maudits (Fr 1946)
Temptation Harbour (Pathé 1947)
Dedée d'Anvers (Fr 1947)
Erreur judicaire (Fr 1947)
Les Amants de Vérona (Fr 1948)
Sombre Dimanche (Fr 1948)
Hans le marin (Fr 1949)
Portrait d'un assassin (Fr 1949)
Aventure à Pigalle (Fr 1949)
Maya (Fr 1949)
Blackjack [Captain Blackjack] (Fr 1950)
Porte d'Orient (Fr 1950)
On the Riviera (20th 1951)
Nous irons à Monte-Carlo [Monte Carlo Baby] (Fr 1951)
Rich, Young and Pretty (MGM 1951)
The Merry Widow (MGM 1952)
The Happy Time (Col 1952)
The Snows of Kilimanjaro (20th 1952)
Lovely to Look At (MGM 1952)
Flight to Tangier (Par 1953)
Monsieur Scrupule, Gangster (Fr 1953)
Razzia sur la Chnouf [Chnouf] (Fr 1954)
Les Amants du Tage [Lovers of Lisbon] (Fr 1954)
Sabrina (Par 1954)
La Patrouille du sables (Fr 1954)
Jump into Hell (WB 1955)
Miracle in the Rain (WB 1956)
The Sun Also Rises (20th 1957)
Lafayette Escadrille (WB 1958)
Contrabande à Caire (Fr 1958)
The Perfect Furlough [Strictly for Pleasure] (Univ 1958)
The Man Who Understood Women (20th 1959)
Pillow Talk (Univ 1959)
Song Without End (Col 1960)
Can-Can (20th 1960)
Classe tous risques [The Big Risk] (Fr-It 1960)
Cartouche [Swords of Blood] (Fr-It 1961)
Le Petit Garçon et l'ascenseur (Fr 1962)
Jessica (UA 1962)
Le Diable et les Dix Commandements [The Devil and the 10 Com-
    mandments] (Fr-It 1962)
Le Loi des hommes (Fr 1962)
Donovan's Reef (Par 1963)
L'Abominable Homme des douanes (Fr 1963)
Un Monsieur de compagne [Male Companion] (Fr-It 1964)
Le Monocle rit jaune (Fr-It 1964)

Lady L (Fr-It 1965)
How to Steal a Million (20th 1966)
Le Plus Vieux Métier du monde (ep "Aujourd'hui") (Fr-W Ger-
It 1967)
How Sweet It Is! (National General 1963)
Mazel Tof; ou Le Mariage [Marry Me! Marry Me!] (Fr 1968)
Justine (20th 1969)
Catch 22 (Par 1970)
The Great White Hope (20th 1970)
Papa les petits bateaux (Fr 1971)
Les Aventures de Rabbi Jacob (Fr-It-Sp 1973)
Ursule et Grelu (Fr-It 1973)
La Bête (Fr 1975)
Le Faux-cul (Fr 1975)

DANOVA, CESARE (Cesare Deitinger), b. March, 1926, Rome
La figlia del capitano (It 1947)
Monaca santa (It 1948)
Cavalcata d'eroi (It 1949)
Final de una legenda (Sp 1950)
El correo del rey [Il messaggero del re] (Sp-It 1950)
Maschera nera (It 1952)
I tre corsari (It 1952)
Il maestro di Don Giovanni [Crossed Swords] (It 1952)
Processo contro ignoti (It 1952)
Pentimento (It 1952)
Balocchi e profumi (It 1953)
Jolanda la figlia del Corsaro nero (It 1953)
I cavalieri dell'illusione (It 1953)
L'ultima notte di Don Giovanni [Don Juan] (Aus-It 1955)
Questea maledette vacanza [Ces sacrêes vacanes] (It-Fr 1955)
Non scherzare con le donne (It 1955)
La cavallina storna (It 1956) [made in 1953]
Incatenata dal destino (It 1956)
The Man Who Understood Women (20th 1959)
Tarzan the Ape Man (MGM 1959)
King of Kings (MGM 1961)
Tender Is the Night (20th 1962)
Valley of the Dragons (Col 1962)
Cleopatra (20th 1963)
Gidget Goes to Rome (Col 1963)
Viva Las Vegas (MGM 1964)
Boy Did I Get a Wrong Number (UA 1966)
Chamber of Horrors (WB-7 Arts 1966)
Che! (20th 1967)
Mean Streets (WB 1973)

DARC, MIREILLE, b. May 15, 1938, Toulon (Vas), France
Les Distractions [Trapped by Fear] (Fr-It 1960)
Du côté de l'enfer (Fr 1960)
La Mort a les yeux bleus (Fr 1960)
La Bride sur le cou (Fr-It 1961)
Les Nouveaux Aristocrates (Fr 1961)
Virginie (Fr 1962)

Les Veinards (Fr 1962)
Des pissenlits par la racine [Have Another Bier] (W Ger 1963)
La Chasse à l'homme [Male Hunt] (Fr-It 1964)
Les Durs à cuire [Hardboiled] (Fr 1964)
Les Barbouzes [Undercover Men] (Fr 1964)
Monsieur (Fr-It-W Ger 1964)
Comment supprimer son prochain (Fr 1964)
Du Rififi à Paname [Rififi in Paris] (Fr-W Ger-It 1965)
Ne nous fâchons pas (Fr 1965)
Les Bons Vivants (Fr-It 1965)
Galia (Fr-It 1966)
À belles dents (Fr-It 1966)
La Blonde de Pekin (Fr-It-W Ger 1967)
Fleur d'épine (Fr 1967)
La Grande Sauterelle (Fr 1967)
Week-end (Fr-It 1968)
Summit (Fr-It 1968)
Quei temerari sulle loro pazze, scatenate, scalcinate carriole
    [Monte Carlo or Bust] (It-Fr 1969)
Jeff (Fr-It 1969)
La Main au feu (Fr 1969)
Un Corps une nuit (Fr 1969)
Andromac (Fr 1969?)
Madly (Fr-It 1970)
Fantasia chez les ploucs [Diamond Bikini] (Fr 1971)
Laisse aller, c'est une valse (Fr 1971)
Il était une fois un flic (Fr-It 1972)
Le Grand Blond avec une chaussure noire (Fr 1972)
La Valise (Fr 1973)
Dis-moi qui tu aimes (Fr 1974)
Le Retour du grand blond (Fr-It 1974)
Les Seins de glace (Fr-It 1974)
Le Telephone rose (Fr 1975)

DARRIEUX, DANIELLE, b. May 1, 1917, Bordeaux
    Le Bal (Fr 1931)
    Coquecigrolle (Fr 1931)
    Panurge (Fr 1931)
    Le Coffret de laque (Fr 1932)
    Le Château de rêve (Fr-Ger 1933)
    Mauvaise Graine (Fr 1933)
    Volga en flammes (Fr-Czech 1934)
    La Crise est finie (Fr 1934)
    Dédé (Fr 1934)
    Mon coeur t'appelle [Fr version of Mein Herz ruft nach dir]
        (Fr 1934)
    L'Or dans la rue (Fr 1935)
    Le Contrôleur des wagon-lits (Fr 1935)
    Quelle drôle de gosse (Fr 1935)
    J'aime toutes les femmes [Fr version of Ich liebe alle Frauen]
        (Fr 1935)
    Le Domino vert (Fr 1935)
    Mademoiselle Mozart (Fr 1935)
    Mon coeur t'appelle (Fr 1936)

Mayerling (Fr 1936)
Tarass Boulba (Fr
Club des Femmes (Fr 1936)
Port-Arthur (Fr 1936)
Un Mauvais Garçon (Fr 1936)
Abus de confiance (Fr 1937)
Mademoiselle ma mère (Fr 1937)
Katia (Hun 1938)
Retour à l'Aube (Fr 1938)
The Rage of Paris (Univ 1938)
Battements de Coeur [Fr version of Batticuore] (Fr 1939)
Premier Rendezvous (Fr 1941)
Caprices (Fr 1941)
La Fausse Maîtresse (Fr 1942)
Adieu Chérie (Fr 1945)
Au petit bonheur (Fr 1945)
Bethsabée (Fr 1947)
Ruy Blas (Fr 1947)
Jean de la Lune (Fr 1948)
Occupe-toi d'Amélie [Keep an Eye on Amelia] (Fr 1949)
La Ronde [Circle of Love] (Fr 1950)
Toselli (It 1950)
Rich, Young and Pretty (MGM 1950)
La Maison Bonnadieu (Fr 1951)
La Vérité sur Bébé Donge [The Truth About Our Marriage] (Fr
    1951)
Le Plaisir (Fr 1951)
Five Fingers (20th 1952)
Adorables Créatures (Fr 1952)
Le Bon Dieu sans confession (Fr 1953)
Madame de... (Fr-It 1953)
Châteaux en Espagne (Fr-Sp 1953)
Escalier de service (Fr 1954)
Napoléon (Fr 1954)
Bonnes à tuer [One Step to Eternity] (Fr 1954)
Le Rouge et le noir [Scarlet and Black] (Fr-It 1954)
L'Affaire des poisons (Fr-It 1955)
L'Amant de Lady Chatterley [Lady Chatterley's Lover] (Fr 1955)
Si Paris nour était conté (Fr 1955)
Alexander the Great (UA 1956)
Typhon sur Nagasaki [Typhoon Over Nagasaki] (Fr-Jap 1956)
Le salaire du péché (Fr 1956)
Pot-bouille [The Noise of Lovers] (Fr-It 1957)
Le Septième Ciel (Fr-It 1957)
La Vie à deux (Fr 1958)
Le Désordre et la nuit (Fr 1958)
Marie-Octobre (Fr 1958)
Un Drôle de dimanche (Fr 1958)
Meurtre en 45 tours (Fr 1959)
Les Yeux de l'amour (Fr 1959)
L'Homme à femmes (Fr 1960)
Vive Henri IV, vive l'amour (Fr-It 1960)
Les Lions sont lâchés (Fr-It 1961)
Les Bras de la nuit (Fr 1962)

The Greengage Summer [Loss of Innocence] (Col 1962)
Le Crime ne paie pas (Fr 1962)
Le Diable et le Dix Commandements (Fr-It 1962)
Landru (Fr-It 1962)
Méfiez-vous, Mesdames! (Fr-It 1963)
Du Grabuge chez les veuves (Fr-It 1963)
Patate [Friend of the Family] (Fr-It 1964)
Coup de grace (Fr-Canada 1965)
L'Or du duc (Fr-It 1965)
Le Dimanche de la vie [Sunday of Life] (Fr-W Ger-It 1966)
Les Demoiselles de Rochefort [The Young Girls of Rochefort]
    (Fr 1967)
L'Homme à la Buick (Fr 1967)
Les Oiseaux vont mourir au Pérou [The Birds Come to Die in
    Peru] (Fr 1968)
24 Heures de la vie d'une femme [24 Hours in a Woman's Life]
    (Fr 1968)
Divine (Fr 1975)

DA SILVA, ANTÔNIO, b. Aug. 15, 1886, Lisbon; d. March 2, 1971
    A canção de Lisboa (Por 1933)
    As pupilas do Senhor Reitor (Por 1935)
    Bocage (Por 1936)
    Maria Papoila (Por 1937)
    A varanda das rouxinois (Por 1939)
    João ratão (Por 1940)
    O feitiço do império (Por 1940)
    Os lobos da serra (Por 1942)
    O pátio das cantigas (Por 1942)
    O costa do castelo (Por 1943)
    O amor de perdição (Por 1943)
    A menina da rádio (Por 1944)
    A vizinhos do rés-do-chão (Por 1947)
    Três espelhos (Por 1947)
    O leão da estrela (Por 1947)
    Fado, a história de uma cantadeira (Por 1947)
    Heróis do mar (Por 1949)
    O grande Eliaś (Por 1950)
    Sonhar é fácil (Por 1951)
    O comissário da policia (Por 1952)
    Os três da vida airada (Por 1952)
    O dinheiro dos pobres (Por 1956)
    O noivo das caldas (Por 1956)
    Perdeu-se um marido (Por 1956)
    Dois dias no Paraiso (Por 1957)
    O passarinho da Ribeira (Por 1959)
    As pupilas do Sehnor Reitor (Por 1960) [remake]
    Aqui há fantasmas (Por 1963)
    Sarilho de fraldas (Por 1966)

DE CARVALHO, RAUL (Raúl de Carvalho Soares), b. Feb. 15, 1901
    Salvaterra do Extreme, Portugal
    O primo basilio (Por 1922)

Fado (Por 1923)
A canção do Berçe (Por 1931) [Por version of Sarah and Son]
A mulher que ri (Por 1931) [Por version of The Laughing Lady]
Gado bravo (Por 1934)
Bocage (Por 1936)
Inês de Castro (Sp 1945)
Três espelhos (Por 1947)
Bola ao centro (Por 1947)
Fado, a história de uma cantadeira (Por 1947)
Não há rapazes maus (Por 1948)
Uma vida para dois (Por 1948)
Heróis do mar (Por 1949)
A morgadinha dos canaviais (Por 1949)
Vendaval maravilhoso (Por 1949)
Fogo (Sp 1949)
Frei Luis de Sousa (Por 1950)
A Garcia e a Serpente (Por 1952)
Rosa de Alfama (Por 1953)
O cerre dos enforcados (Por 1954)
O Tarzan do 5º Esquerdo (Por 1958)
As pupilas do Senhor Reitor (Por 1960)

DE CARVALHO, RUI (Rui Alberto Rebelo Pires de Carvalho), b.
    March 1, 1926, Lisbon
Eram Duzentos Irmãos (Por 1951)
Raça (Por 1961)
Ribeira da Saudade (Por 1961)
Frute preibido (Por 1962) [unfinished]
Pássaros de asas cortadas (Por 1963)
Domingo à tarde (Por 1965)
O cerco (Por 1969)

DECLEIR, JAN, b. Belgium
Erasmus--Civis totius mundi (Bel 1969)
Maurice Maeterlinck (Bel 1969)
Mira (Bel-Dut 1970)
Rolande met de bles (Bel 1970)
Keromar (Bel 1971)
De Loteling (Bel 1973)
Verloren Maandag (Bel-Dut 1973)
Saluyt en de kost (Bel 1974)
Verbrande brug (Bel-Dut 1974)

DE CONYNCK, ROMEIN, b. Dec. 7, 1925, Ghent, Belgium
De Klucht van de Brave Moordenaan (Bel 1955)
Het Geluk Komt Morgen (Bel 1958)
Vrijgezel met 40 Kinderen (Bel 1958)
Het Dwaalicht (Bel-Dut 1971)
Salut en de Kost (Bel 1973)
Angela (Bel-Dut 1973)
Wondershop (Bel 1974)

DE CURTIS, ANTONIO ("Totò") (Antonio de Curtis Ducas Comnuno di Bisanzio), b. Feb. 15, 1898; d. April 15, 1967
Fermo con le mani (It 1936)
Animali Pazzi (It 1939)
San Giovanni Decollato (It 1940)
L'allegro fantasma (It 1941)
Due cuori fra le belve (It 1941)
Nella fossa dei leoni (It 1943)
Il ratto delle sabine (It 1945)
I due orfanelli (It 1947)
Totò al giro d'Italia (It 1948)
Fifa e arena (It 1948)
Yvonne la nuit (Fr 1949)
Totò cerca casa (It 1949)
I pompieri di Viggiù (It 1949)
Totò le Mokò (It 1949)
L'imperatore di Capri (It 1949)
Napoli milionaria (It 1949)
Totò cerca moglie (It 1950)
Totò Tarzan (It 1950)
Figaro qua, Figaro là (It 1950)
Le sei mogli di Barbablù (It 1950)
Totò sceicco (It 1950)
47, morto che parla (It 1950)
Totò terzo uomo (It 1951)
Guardie e ladri (It 1951)
Totò e i re di Roma (It 1951)
Sette ore di guai (It 1951)
Dov'è la liberta? (It 1952)
Una di quelle (It 1952)
Totò a colori (It 1952)
Totò e le donne (It 1952)
Un turco napoletano (It 1953)
Il più comico spettacolo del mondo (It 1953)
L'uomo la bestia e la virtù (It 1953)
Questa e la vita (ep "La patente") (It 1954)
Miseria e nobilità (It 1954)
Totò cerca pace (It 1954)
Tempi nostri (ep "La macchina fotografica") (It 1954)
L'oro di Napoli (ep "Il guappo")
I tre ladri (It 1954)
Il medico dei pazzi (It 1954)
Totò all'inferno (It 1954)
Carosello di varieta (It 1955)
Totò e Carolina (It 1955)
Racconti romani (It 1955)
Siamo uomini o caporali? (It 1955)
Destinazione Piovarolo (It 1955)
Il coraggio (It 1955)
La banda degli onesti (It 1956)
Totò, lascia o raddoppia? (It 1956)
Totò, Peppino e la... malafemmina (It 1956)
Totò, Peppino e i fuorilegge (It 1956)

Totò, Vittorio e la dottoressa [Mi mujer es doctor] (It-Sp 1957)
La Loi est la loi [La legge è legge] (Fr-It 1957)
I soliti ignoti (It 1958)
Gambe d'oro (It 1958)
Totò e Marcellino (It 1958)
Totò, Peppino e le fanatiche (It 1958)
Totò a Parigi (It-Fr 1958)
Totò nella luna (It 1958)
I tartassati (It 1959)
Totò, Eva e il pennello proibito [Madrid de noche/Un Coup Fumant] (It-Sp-Fr 1959)
Vacanze d'inverno (It 1959)
I ladri (It 1959)
La cambiale (It 1959)
Arrangiatevi! (It 1959)
Noi duri (It 1960)
Signori si nasce (It 1960)
Totò, Fabrizi e i giovani d'oggi (It 1960)
Letto a tre piazze (It 1960)
Risate di gioia (It 1960)
Chi si ferma è perduto (It 1961)
Sua eccelenza si fermò a mangiare (It 1961)
Totò, Peppino e la dolce vita (It 1961)
Totòtruffa '62 (It 1961)
I due marescialli (It 1961)
Totò contro Maciste (It 1962)
Totò diabolicus (It 1962)
Totò e Peppino divisi a Berlino (It 1962)
Totò di notte n.I (It 1963)
Lo smemorato di Collegno (It 1963)
I due colonnelli (It 1963)
Il monaco di Monza (It 1963)
Totò contro i quattro (It 1963)
Totò e Cleopatra (It 1963)
Totò sexy (It 1963)
Le motorizzate (It 1963)
Gli onorevoli (It 1963)
Il comandante (It 1963)
Che fine ha fatto Totò baby? (It 1964)
Totò contro il pirata nero (It 1964)
Totò d'Arabia [Totò de Arabia] (Sp-It 1964)
Gli amanti latini (ep "Amore e morte") (It 1965)
Le belle famiglie (ep "Amare è un po'morire") (It 1965)
Rita, la figlia americana (It 1965)
La Mandragola (It 1965)
Operazione San Gennaro [Operation San Gennaro] (It 1966)
Uccellacci e uccellini (It 1966)
Le streghe [The Witches] (ep "La terra vista dalla luna") (It 1967)
Capriccio all'italiana (ep "Che cosa sono le nuvole?" and "Il maestro della Domenica") (It 1968)

DE FILIPPO, EDUARDO (Eduardo Passarelli), b. May 24, 1900, Naples
   Tre uomini in frack (It 1932)

Il cappello a tre punte (It 1934)
Quei due (It 1934)
Una commedia fra i pazzi (It 1937)
Sono stato io (It 1937)
Ma l'amor mio non muore (It 1938)
Il marchese di Ruvolito (It 1938)
In campagna è caduta una stella (It 1940)
Il sogno di tutti (It 1941)
A che servono questi quattrini (It 1941)
Non ti pago! (It 1942)
Casanova farebbe così (It 1942)
Non mi muovo (It 1943)
Ti conosco, mascherina (It 1943)
La vita ricomencia (It 1945)
Uno tra la folla (It 1946)
Assunta Spina (It 1949)
Campane a martello (It 1949)
Napoli milionaria (It 1950)
Filomena Marturano (It 1951)
Le ragazze di Piazza di Spagna (It 1951)
Un ladro in paradiso (It 1952)
Cinque poveri in automobile (It 1952)
I sette peccati capitali (It 1952)
Marito e moglie (It 1952)
Ragazze da marito (It 1952)
Traviata '53 (It 1953)
Villa Borghese (It 1953)
Napoletani a Milano (It 1953)
Cento anni d'amore (It 1954)
Tempi nostri (It 1954)
L'oro di Napoli (ep "Don Ersilio") (It 1954)
Cortile (It 1956)
Fortunella (It 1958)
Cameriera bella presenza offresi (It 1959)
L'amore più bello [L'uomo dai calzoni corti/Talvez mañana] (It-Sp 1959)
Il sogno di una notte di mezza sbornia (It 1959)
Ferdinando I, re di Napoli (It 1959)
Tutti a casa [La Grande Pagaille] (It-Fr 1960)
Fantasmi a Roma [Ghosts of Rome] (It 1960)
Spara forte, più forte... non capisco [Shoot Loud, Louder... I Don't Understand] (It 1966)

DE FILIPPO, PEPPINO (Giuseppe Passarelli), b. Aug. 24, 1903, Naples, Italy
Tre uomini in frak (It 1932)
Il cappello a tre punte (It 1934)
Quei due (It 1934)
Sono stato io! (It 1937)
L'Amor mio non muore (It 1938)
Il marchese di Ruvolito (It 1938)
In campagna è caduta una stella (It 1940)
Il sogno di tutti (It 1941)
L'ultimo combattimento (It 1941)

Le signorine della villa accanto (It 1941)
A che servono questi quattrini? (It 1942)
Non ti pago! (It 1942)
Casanova farebbe così (It 1942)
Campo de fiori (It 1943)
Non mi muovo (It 1943)
Io t'ho incontrata a Napoli (It 1946)
Natale a campo 119 (It 1948)
Biancaneve e i sette ladri (It 1949)
La bisarca (It 1950)
Vivere a sbafo (It 1950)
Luci del varietà (It 1951)
Cameriera bella presenza offresi (It 1951)
Signori in carrozza (It 1951)
Bellezze in bicicletta (It 1951)
La famiglia Passaguai (It 1951)
Non è vero ma ci credo (It 1952)
Ragazze da marito (It 1952)
Totò e le donne (It 1952)
Una di quelle (It 1953)
Siamo tutti inquilini (It 1953)
Un giorno in pretura (It 1954)
Via Padova, 46 [Lo scocciatore] (It 1954)
Martin Tocaferro (It 1954)
Le signorine dello 04 (It 1955)
Il segno di Venere (It 1955)
Piccola posta (It 1955)
I due compari (It 1955)
Gli ultimi cinque minuti (It 1955)
Accadde al penitenziario (It 1955)
Io piccio [La via del successo con le donne] (It 1955)
Un po' de cielo (It 1956)
I pappagalli (It 1956)
Il cortile (It 1956)
Guardia, guardia scelta, brigadiere, maresciallo (It 1956)
Totò, Peppino e la... malafemmina (It 1956)
La banda degli onesti (It 1956)
Totò, Peppino e i fuorilegge (It 1956)
Motivo in maschera (It 1956)
Peppino, le modelle e... chella llà (It 1957)
La nonna Sabella (It 1957)
Vacanze a Ischia (It 1957)
Anna di Brooklyn (It 1958)
Totò, Peppino e le fanatiche (It 1958)
E permesso maresciallo? [Tuppe, tuppe, marescià] (It 1958)
Peppino e la nobile dama (It 1959) [made in 1954]
Pane, amore e Andalusia [Pan, amor y Andalucía] (It-Sp 1959)
La nipote Sabella (It 1959)
Policarpo, ufficiale di scrittura [Policarpo de Tapetti] (It-Sp 1959)
Arrangiatevi (It 1959)
Ferdinando I, re di Napoli (It 1959)
Genitori in blue jeans (It 1960)
Signori si nasce (It 1960)
Letto a tre piazze (It 1960)

A noi piace freddo (It 1960)
Il mattadore [The Matador] (It 1960)
Chi si ferma è perduto (It 1961)
Gli incensurati (It 1961)
Totò, Peppino e la dolce vita (It 1961)
Il carabiniere a cavallo (It 1961)
Boccaccio '70 (ep "Le tentazioni del dottor Antonio") (It 1961)
Il mio amico Benito (It 1962)
Totò e Peppino divisi a Berlino (It 1962)
I quattro monaci (It 1962)
Adultero lui, adultera lei (It 1963)
Gli onorevoli (It 1963)
I quattro moschettieri (It 1963)
Totò contro i quattro (It 1963)
I quattro tassisti (ep "Un'opera buona") (It 1964)
La vedovella (It 1965)
Ischia, operazione amore (It 1966)
Rita la zanzara (It 1966)
Non stuzzicare la zanzara (It 1967)
Soldati e capelloni (It 1967)
Zum zum zum (It 1969)
Zum zum zum N. 2 (It 1969)
Gli infermieri della mutua (It 1969)
Lisa dagli occhi blù (It 1970)
Nini Tirabuscio, la donna che inventò la "mossa" (It 1972)

DE FILIPPO, TITINA, b. March 23, 1898, Naples, Italy; d. Dec.
    26, 1963
Sono stato io! (It 1937)
L'amor mio non muore (It 1938)
Frenesia (It 1939)
Assenza ingiustificata (It 1939)
San Giovanni decollato (It 1941)
Villa da vendere (It 1941)
Una volta alla settimana (It 1941)
Non ti pago! (It 1942)
Casanova farebbe così (It 1942)
Ti conosco, mascherina! (It 1943)
Non mi muovo! (It 1943)
Uno tra ta folla (It 1946)
Assunta spina (It 1949)
Napoli milionaria (It 1950)
Bellissima (It 1951)
Cameriera bella presenza offresi (It 1951)
Filumena Marturano (It 1951)
Cani e gatti (It 1952)
Cinque poveri in automobile (It 1952)
Marito e moglie (It 1952)
Non è vero ma ci credo (It 1952)
Ragazze da marito (It 1952)
Il tallone di Achille (It 1952)
I morti non pagano tasse (It 1953)
Cento anni d'amore (It 1954)
Martin Toccaferro (It 1954)

Il fuoco nelle vene (It 1955)
La vena d'oro (It 1955)
La fortuna di essere donna (It 1956)
Guaglione (It 1956)
I pappagalli (It 1956)
Totò, Peppino e i fuorilegge (It 1956)
I vagabondi delle stelle (It 1956)
Non cantare, baciami (It 1957)
Totò, Vittorio e la dottoressa (It 1957)
La canzone del destino (It 1958)
Napoli, sole mio! (It 1958)
Ferdinando I, re di Napoli (It 1959)
Noi siamo due evasi (It 1959)

DE FUNES, LOUIS, b. July 31, 1914, Courbevoie, France
La Tentation de Barbizon (Fr 1945)
Six Heures à perdre (Fr 1946)
Dernier Refuge (Fr 1946)
Antoine et Antoinette (Fr 1946)
Croisière pour l'inconnu (Fr 1947)
Du Guesclin (Fr 1948)
Millionaires d'un jour (Fr 1949)
Pas de week-end pour notre amour (Fr 1949)
Un Certain Monsieur (Fr 1949)
Je n'aime que toi (Fr 1949)
Rendez-vous avec la chance (Fr 1949)
Mission à Tanger (Fr 1949)
Le Roi du bla bla bla (Fr 1950)
Boniface Somnambule (Fr 1950)
L'Amant de paille (Fr 1950)
La Rue sans loi (Fr 1950)
La Rose rouge (Fr 1950)
Folie douce (Fr 1950)
Boîte à vendre (Fr 1951)
Pas de vacances pour Monsieur le Maire (Fr 1951)
Ma Femme formidable (Fr 1951)
Ils étaient cinq (Fr 1951)
La Poison (Fr 1951)
Monsieur Leguignon Lampiste (Fr 1951)
Les Sept Péchés Capitaux [Seven Capital Sins] (Fr 1951)
Le Dindon (Fr 1951)
Un Amour de parapluie (Fr 1951?)
L'Amour n'est pas un péché (Fr 1952)
Monsieur Taxi (Fr 1952)
Je l'ai été trois fois (Fr 1952)
Moineaux de Paris (Fr 1952)
La Fugue de Monsieur Perle (Fr 1952)
Le Huitième Art...et la manière (Fr 1952)
Légère et court vêtue (Fr 1952)
Elle et moi (Fr 1952)
Au Diable la vertu (Fr 1952)
La Vie d'un honnête homme (Fr 1952)
La Dortoir des grandes [Girls' Dormitory] (Fr 1953)

Mon frangin du Sénégal (Fr 1953)
Capitaine Pantaufle (Fr 1953)
L'Etrange désir de Monsieur Bard (Fr 1953)
Le Blé en herbe (Fr-It 1953)
Le Chevalier de la nuit (Fr 1953)
Mam'zelle Nitouche [Oh No, Mam'zelle!] (Fr-It 1953)
Tourments (Fr 1953)
Week-end à Paris (Fr 1953)
Le Secret de Hélène Marimon (Fr 1953)
Faites-moi confiance (Fr 1953)
Les Compagnes de la nuit (Fr 1953)
Les Corsaires du Bois de Boulogne (Fr 1953)
Les Hommes ne pensent qu'à ça (Fr 1953)
Les Pépées font la loi (Fr 1954)
Les Intrigantes [The Plotters] (Fr 1954)
Huis-clos [Vicious Circle] (Fr 1954)
Napoléon (Fr 1954)
Frou-frou (Fr-It 1954)
Poisson d'Avril (Fr 1954)
La Reine Margot (Fr-It 1954)
Scènes de ménage (Fr 1954)
Le Mouton a cinq pattes [The Sheep Has Five Legs] (Fr 1954)
Ah! Les Belles Bacchantes (Fr 1954)
Escalier de service (Fr 1954)
Papa, Maman la bonne et moi (Fr 1954)
Les Impures (Fr 1955)
L'Impossible Monsieur Pipelet (Fr 1955)
Geschichte eines Fotomodels (W Ger 1955)
Sourire aux lèvres (Fr 1955)
Papa, Maman, ma femme et Moi (Fr 1955)
La Bande à Papa (Fr 1955)
Les Hussards (Fr 1955)
Bébés à Gogo (Fr 1956)
Courte-Tête (Fr 1956)
La Loi des rues (Fr 1956)
La Traversée de Paris [A Pig Across Paris] (Fr-It 1956)
Comme un cheveu sur la Soupe (Fr 1957)
Ni vu... ni connu (Fr 1957)
Taxi, roulette et corrida (Fr 1958)
La Vie à deux (Fr 1958)
Les Tourmentes (It-Fr 1959)
Fripouillard et Cie (Fr-It 1959)
Mon pote le Gitan (Fr 1959)
Certains l'aiment froide (Fr 1959)
Candide; ou L'Optimisme au XXe siecle (Fr 1960)
Les Tortillards (Fr 1960)
Dans l'eau... qui fait des bulles! (Fr 1960)
Le Capitaine Fracasse (Fr 1960)
Le Diable et les Dix Commandements (Fr-It 1961)
La Belle Américaine (Fr 1961)
Le Gentleman d'Epsom (Fr-It 1962)
La Vendetta (Fr-It 1962)
Nous irons à Deauville (Fr 1962)

Les Veinards (Fr 1962)
Un Clair de lune à Mauberge (Fr 1962)
Carambologes (Fr 1963)
Pouic Pouic (Fr 1963)
Faites sauter la banque (Fr 1963)
Des Pissenlits par la racine [Have Another Bier] (Fr-It 1963)
Fantômas (Fr-It 1964)
Le Gendarme de Saint-Tropez (Fr-It 1964)
Une Souris chez les hommes (Fr 1964)
Fantômas se dechaîne (Fr-It 1965)
Le Corniaud [The Sucker] (Fr-It 1965)
Le Gendarme à New York (Fr-It 1965)
Les Bons Vivants (Fr-It 1965)
La Grande Vadrouille (Fr 1966)
Le Grand Restaurant (Fr 1966)
Fantômas contre Scotland Yard (Fr-It 1967)
Oscar (Fr 1967)
Les Grandes Vacances (Fr-It 1967)
Le Tatoué (Fr-It 1968)
Le Petit Baigneur (Fr-It 1968)
Le Gendarme se marie (Fr-It 1968)
Hibernatus (Fr-It 1969)
Le Gendarme en balade (Fr-It 1970)
Jo (Fr 1971)
La Folie des grandeurs (Fr-It-Sp-W Ger 1971)
Les Aventures de Rabbi Jacob [The Mad Adventure of Rabbi Jacobs]

DE GOOYER, RIJK, b. Dec. 17, 1925, Utrecht
Het Wonderlijke Leven van Willem Parel (Dut 1955)
Kieren Maken de Man (Dut 1957)
Schachovelle (W Ger 1960)
Rififi in Amsterdam (Dut 1962)
De Blanke Slavin (Dut 1969)
De Inbreker (Dut 1972)
Geen Paniek (Dut 1972)
Naakt over de Schutting (Dut 1973)
Zwaarmoedige Verhalen voor bij de Centrale Verwarming (ep
    "Een Winkelier Keert Niet Weerom") (Dut 1975)
The Wilby Conspiracy (USA-GB 1975)
Rufus (Dut 1975)

DE LIGUORO, RINA (Elene Caterina Catardi De Liguoro), b. July
    24, 1892, Florence, Italy; d. April 7, 1966
La principessa Bebè (It 1920)
Saracinesca (It 1921)
Messalina (It 1923)
Il trittico (It 1923)
Maremma (It 1924)
Quo Vadis? (It 1924)
Bufera (It 1924)
Savitri Satyvan (It 1924)
La via del peccato (It 1924)
Il focolare spento [Il più grande amore] (It 1925)

Quello che non muore (It 1925)
Gli ultimi giorni di Pompei (It 1926)
Gallone (It 1926)
Garibaldi, l'eroe dei due mondi (It 1926)
La bella corsara (It 1927)
Il vetturale del Moncenisio (It 1927)
Casanova [Le avventure di Casanova] (Fr-It 1927)
Cagliostro (Fr 1928)
Der geheimnisvolle Spiegel (Ger 1928)
Femmina e madre [Certe donne!] (Aus 1928)
Mese Mariano (It 1929)
Assunta Spina (It 1929)
Madam Satan (MGM 1930)
Romance (MGM 1930)
Undercover Woman (MGM 1930)
Bachelor Father (MGM 1931) [Sp version only]
Angelita (Fox 1935)
Luisa Sanfelice (It 1942)
Ritrovarsi (It 1947)
Caterina da Siena (It 1947)
Buffalo Bill a Roma (It 1949)
Domani è un altro giorno (It 1950)
Il gattopardo [The Leopard] (It-Fr 1962)

DELON, ALAIN, b. Nov. 8, 1935, Sceaux, Paris
Quand la femme s'en mêlê (Fr-It-W Ger 1957)
Sois Belle et Tais-Toi [Blonde for Danger] (Fr 1957)
Christine (Fr-It 1958)
Faibles Femmes [Women Are Weak] (Fr 1958)
Le Chemin des ecoliers (Fr 1959)
Plein soleil [Purple Noon] (Fr-It 1959)
Rocco e i suoi fratelli [Rocco and His Brothers] (It-Fr 1960)
Che gioia vivere (It-Fr 1961)
Les Amours célèbres (ep "Agnes Bernauer") (Fr-It 1961)
L'Eclisse [The Eclipse] (Fr-It 1961)
Le Diable et les Dix Commandements (ep "L'Inceste") (Fr-It 1962)
Mélodie en sous-sol [The Big Snatch] (Fr-It 1962)
Il Gattopardo [The Leopard] (It-Fr 1962)
La Tulipe noire [The Black Tulip] (Fr-It-Sp 1962)
Les Felins [The Love Cage] (Fr 1963)
L'Insoumis (Fr-It 1964)
The Yellow Rolls-Royce (MGM 1964)
Once a Thief (MGM 1965)
Lost Command (Col 1966)
Paris brûle-t-il? [Is Paris Burning?] (Fr 1966)
Texas Across the River (Univ 1966)
Les Aventuriers [The Last Adventure] (Fr-It 1967)
Histoires extraordinaires [Spirits of the Dead] (ep "William
    Wilson") (Fr-It 1967)
Le Samourai [The Samurai] (Fr-It 1967)
Diaboliquement votre (Fr-It-W Ger 1967)
Girl on a Motorcycle (BL 1968)
Adieu l'ami [So Long, Pal] (Fr-It 1969)
La Piscine [The Swimming Pool] (Fr-It 1969)

Alain Delon (rear) and Jean Saudray in Jeff (1969).

Jeff (Fr-It 1969)
Le Clan des Siciliens [The Sicilian Clan] (Fr 1969) [2 versions;
    one in English]
Borsalino (Fr-It 1970)
Le Cercle rouge (Fr-It 1970)
Madly (Fr 1970)
Doucement les basses (Fr 1971)
Soleil rouge [Red Sun] (Fr-It-Sp 1971)
La Veuve Couderc (Fr-It 1971)
L'Assassinat de Trotsky (Fr-It-GB 1972)
Un Flic [Dirty Money] (Fr-It 1972)
Le Professeur (Fr-It 1972)
Scorpio (UA 1972)
Les Grandes Brulées (Fr 1973)

Tony Arzenta [Big Guns] (It-Fr 1973)
Deux hommes dans la ville (Fr-It 1973)
La Race des "seigneurs" [The "Elite" Group] (Fr 1974)
Les Seins de glace (Fr 1974)
Borsalino et Cie (Fr-It-W Ger 1974)
Flic Story (Fr-It 1975)
Zorro (Fr-It 1975)
Le Gitan (Fr-It 1975)
Docteur Justice (Fr 1975)

DELON, NATHALIE
  Le Samourai [The Samurai] (Fr-It 1967)
  La Leçon particulière [The Private Lesson] (Fr 1968)
  Les Sorelles (It-Fr 1969)
  La Main [The Hand] (Fr 1969)
  When Eight Bells Toll (RFD 1971)
  Doucement les basses (Fr-It 1971)
  Absencees répétées (Fr 1972)
  Sex Shop (Fr-It-W Ger 1972)
  Barbe-bleue [Bluebeard] (Fr-It-W Ger 1972)
  Le Moine [The Monk] (Fr-It-W Ger 1972)
  Profession: Aventuriers (?Fr-It 1972)
  L'Histoire très bonne et très joyeuse de Colinot Trousse-
    Chemise [The Skirt Puller-Upper] (Fr 1973)
  Vous intéressez-vous à la chose [First Time with Feeling] (Fr-
    W Ger 1973)
  Hold-up instantaneo di una rapina (Fr-It-W Ger 1974)
  Dream Time (?Fr 1974)
  The Romantic Englishwoman (GB-Fr 1975)
  Docteur Justice (Fr 1975)

DELORME, DANIELE (Danièle Girard), b. Oct. 9, 1926, Levallois-
    Perret, France
  Félicie Nanteuil (Fr 1942)
  La Belle Aventure (Fr 1942)
  Les Petites du Quai aux Fleurs (Fr 1943)
  Le Capitan (Fr 1945)
  Les Jeux sont faits (Fr 1947)
  L'Impasse des deux anges (Fr 1948)
  Gigi (Fr 1948)
  La Cage aux filles (Fr 1949)
  Rendez-vous avec la chance (Fr 1949)
  Miquette et sa Mère (Fr 1950)
  Agnès de rien (Fr 1950)
  Minne; ou l'Ingénue Libertine (Fr 1950)
  Souvenirs perdus [Lost Property] (Fr 1950)
  Sans laisser d'adressé (Fr 1951)
  La Jeune Folle (Fr 1952)
  Les Dents longues (Fr 1952)
  Le Guérisseur (Fr 1953)
  Tempi nostri (ep "Mara") (It-Fr 1953)
  Si Versailles m'était conté (Fr 1953)
  Casa Ricordi (It-Fr 1954)

Huis clos (Fr 1954)
Le Dossier noir (Fr-It 1955)
Voici le temps des assassins [Deadlier Than the Male] (Fr 1955)
Mitsou (Fr 1956)
Les Misérables (Fr-E Ger-It 1957)
Chaque jour a son secret (Fr 1958)
Prisons de Femmes (Fr 1958)
Cléo de 5 à 7 [Cleo from 5 to 7] (Fr-It 1961)
Le Septième Juré [The Seventh Juror] (Fr 1962)
Marie-Soleil (Fr 1964)
Des Christs par milliers (Fr 1969)
Le Voyou (Fr 1970)
Absences répétées (Fr 1972)
Passeport rouge (Fr 1975)
Une personne ne peut pas s'empecher de grandir et de vieillir
   (Fr 1975)

DENEUVE, CATHERINE (Catherine Dorleac), b. Oct. 20, 1943
Les Collégiennes (Fr 1956)
Les Petits Chats (Fr 1959)
Ce soir au jamais [Tonight or Never] (Fr 1960)
L'Homme à femmes (Fr 1960)
Les Portes claquent (Fr 1960)
Le Vice et la vertu [Vice and Virtue] (Fr-It 1962)
Les Parisiennes (ep "Sophie") (Fr-It 1962)
...Et Satan conduit le bal (Fr 1962)
Les Vacances portugaises (Fr 1963)
Les Plus Belles Escroqueries du monde (ep "L'homme qui vendit
   la tour Eiffel") (Fr-It 1963)
La costanza della ragione (It-Fr 1964)
La Chasse à l'homme [Male Hunt] (Fr-It 1964)
Un Monsieur de compagnie (Fr-It 1964)
Les Parapluies de Cherbourg [The Umbrellas of Cherbourg] (Fr-
   W Ger 1964)
Repulsion (Compton 1965)
Das Liebeskarussell [Belles d'un soir/Who Wants to Sleep?]
   (Aus 1965)
Le Chant du monde (Fr 1965)
Les Créatures (Fr-Swe 1966)
La Vie de château (Fr 1966)
Les Demoiselles de Rochefort [Those Young Girls from Roche-
   fort] (Fr 1967)
Benjamin (Fr 1967)
Belle de Jour (Fr-It 1967)
Manon 70 (Fr-It-W Ger 1968)
Mayerling (Fr-GB 1968)
La Chamade (Fr-It 1968)
The April Fools (WB 1969)
Le Sirene du Mississippi [Mississippi Mermaid] (Fr-It 1969)
Tout peut arriver [Don't Be Blue] (Fr 1969)
Henri Langlois (Fr 1970) [documentary] (cameo)
Tristana (It-Fr-Sp 1970)
Peau d'âne [The Magic Donkey/Donkey Skin] (Fr 1970)

Catherine Deneuve (right), Iska Khan, and Genevieve Page in Belle de jour (1967).

Ça n'arrive qu'aux autres (Fr-It 1971)
Liza (Fr-It 1972)
Un Flic [Dirty Money] (Fr-It 1972)
L'Evênement le plus important depuis que l'homme a marche
    sur la lune [The Slightly Pregnant Man] (Fr 1973)
Touche pas la femme blanche (Fr 1973)
La Femme aux boites rouges (Fr 1974)
Zig Zig (Fr 1974)
L'Affaire Morri (It-Fr 1974)
La Grande Bourgeoisie [Fatti di gente perbene] (Fr-It 1975)
L'Agression [Act of Aggression] (Fr 1975)
Hustle (Por 1975)
Le Sauvage (Fr 1975)

DENNER, CHARLES, b. May 29, 1926, Tarnow, Poland
    La Meilleure Part (Fr-It 1956)
    Ascenseur pour l'êchafaud [Lift to the Scaffold] (Fr 1957)
    Landru (Fr-It 1962)
    Les Plus Belles Escroqueries du monde (Fr-It-Jap 1963)

Les Pieds Nickelés (Fr 1964)
La Vie à l'envers [Life Upside Down] (Fr 1964)
Compartiment tueurs (Fr 1964)
Marie Chantal contre le Dr. Kha (Fr-Sp-It-Mor 1965)
Le Vieil Homme et l'enfant (Fr 1966)
Le Voleur [The Thief of Paris] (Fr-It 1966)
La Mariée était en noir [The Bride Wore Black] (Fr-It 1968)
Z (Fr-Alg 1969)
La Trêve (Fr 1969)
Le Corps de Diane (Fr-Czech 1969)
Le Voyou (Fr 1970)
Où est passé Tom? (Fr 1971)
L'Aventure c'est l'Aventure [Money, Money, Money] (Fr 1972)
Une Belle Fille comme moi (Fr 1972)
Defense de savoir (Fr-It 1973)
Les Gaspards (Fr-Bel 1973)
Toute une vie (Fr-It 1973)
Quand on-est mort c'est pour la vie (Fr 1974)
Peur sur la ville (Fr 1975)

DEPARDIEU, GERARD, b. Dec. 27, 1948, Château-roux, France
Nathalie Grangier (Fr 1971)
Le Cri du Cormoran le soir au-dessus des jongues (Fr 1971)
Le Tueur (Fr 1971)
Un peu de soleil dans l'eau froide (Fr 1972)
L'Affaire Dominici (Fr 1972)
Au rendez-vous de la mort joyeuse (Fr 1972)
Lune Coquelune (Fr 1972)
La Scoumoune (Fr 1972)
Deux Hommes dans la ville (Fr 1972)
Le Viager (Fr 1972)
Rude Journée pour la Reine (Fr 1973)
Les Gaspards (Fr 1973)
Les Valseuses (Fr 1973)
Stavisky (Fr 1973)
Vincent, François, Paul et les autres [Vincent, François, Paul
   and the Others] (Fr 1974)
Pasi si mechant que ça (Fr 1974)
Maîtresse (Fr 1975)
L'ultima donna [La Dernière Femme] (Fr 1975)

DESAILLY, JEAN, b. Aug. 24, 1920, Paris
Le Voyageur de la Toussaint (Fr 1942)
Le Père Goriot (Fr 1943)
Sylvie et le fantôme (Fr 1945)
Le Jugement dernier (Fr 1945)
Patrie (Fr 1945)
La Symphonie pastorale (Fr 1946)
Amour, délices et orgues (Fr 1946)
La Revanche de Roger-la-Honte (Fr 1946)
Carré de valets (Fr 1947)
Une Grande Fille toute simple (Fr 1947)
L'Echafaud peut attendre (Fr 1948)

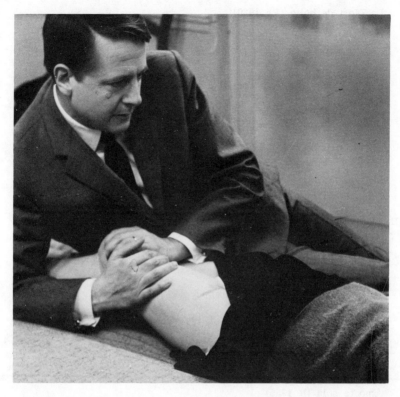

Jean Desailly (and the legs of Françoise Dorléac) in <u>La Peau douce</u> (1964).

Le Point du jour (Fr 1948)
La Veuve et l'innocent (Fr 1949)
Occupe-toi d'Amélie [Keep an Eye on Amelia] (Fr 1949)
Véronique (Fr 1949)
Chéri (Fr 1950)
Demain, nous divorçons (Fr 1950)
Jocelyn (Fr 1951)
Si Versailles m'était conté (Fr 1953)
Les Grandes Manoeuvres [Summer Maneuvres] (Fr-It 1955)
Maigret tend un piège [Maigret Sets a Trap] (Fr-It 1957)
Les Grandes Familles (Fr 1958)
Le Secret du Chevalier d'Eon (Fr-It 1959)
125, rue Montmartre (Fr 1959)
Le Saint mène la danse (Fr 1960)
Le Baron de l'Ecluse (Fr-It 1960)
Préméditation? (Fr 1960)
Un Soir sur la plage (Fr 1960)

La Mort de belle (Fr 1960)
Legge della Guerra (It-Fr 1961)
Les Sept Péchés Capitaux [Seven Capital Sins] (ep "La Luxure")
   (Fr-It 1961)
Les Amours célèbres (ep "Les Comédiennes") (Fr-It 1961)
Le Doulos (Fr 1962)
L'Année du bac (Fr-It 1963)
La Peau douce [Silken Skin] (Fr 1964)
Les Deux Orphélines (Fr-It 1965)
De Dans van de Reiger [The Dance of the Heron] (Holl-W Ger
   1965)
The 25th Hour (Fr-It-Yug 1966)
Le Franciscan de Bourges (Fr 1968)
L'Ardoise (Fr-It 1969)
Comptes à rebours [Countdown] (Fr 1970)
L'Ironie du sort (Fr 1974)

DE SICA, VITTORIO, b. July 7, 1901, Sera, Italy; d. Nov. 13,
   1974
L'affare Clémenceau (It 1918)
La bellezza del mondo (It 1926)
La compagnia dei matti (It 1928)
La vecchia signora (It 1931)
La segretaria per tutti (It 1931)
Due cuori felici (It 1932)
Gli uomini, che mascalzoni! (It 1932)
Passa l'amore (It 1933)
Un cattivo soggetto (It 1933)
Il signore desidera? (It 1933)
La canzone del sole (It 1934)
Lisetta (It 1934)
Amo te sola (It 1935)
Darò un milione (It 1936)
Tempo massimo (It 1936)
Ma non è una cosa seria (It 1936)
Lohengrim (It 1936)
Non ti conosco più (It 1936)
L'uomo che sorride (It 1936)
Napoli d'altri tempi (It 1937)
Il signor Max (It 1937)
Questi ragazzi (It 1937)
L'orologio a cucu (It 1938)
Partire (It 1938)
La mazurka di papà (It 1938)
Hanno rapito un uomo (It 1938)
Le due madri (It 1938)
Ai vostri ordini, signora! (It 1938)
Castelli in aria (It 1939) [also German version]
Grandi magazzini (It 1939)
Finisce sempre così (It 1939)
La peccatrice (It 1939)
Manon Lescaut (It 1939)

Pazzi di gioia (It 1939)
Rose scarlatte (It 1940)
Maddalona, zero in condotta (It 1940)
L'avventuriera del piano di spora (It 1940)
Teresa Venerdi (It 1941)
Un garibaldino al convento (It 1942)
Se io fossi onesto (It 1942)
La guardia del corpo (It 1942)
I nostri sogni (It 1943)
Nessuno torna indietro (It 1943)
Non sons superstizioso, ma... (It 1943)
L'ippocampo (It 1943)
Dieci minuti di vita (It 1943) [unreleased]
Lo sbaglio di essere vivo (It 1945)
Il mondo vuole così (It 1946)
Abbasso la ricchezza! (It 1946)
Roma, città libera [Open City (It 1946)
Lo sconosciuto di San Marino (It 1947)
Sperduti nel buio (It 1947)
Natale al campo 119 (It 1948)
Cuore (It 1948)
Domani è troppo tardi (It 1950)
Cameriera bella presenza offresi (It 1951)
Buongiorno, elefante! (It 1952)
Altri tempi (ep "Il processo di Frine") (It 1952)
Madame de... (Fr 1953)
Pane, amore e fantasia [Bread, Love, and Dreams] (It 1953)
Villa Borghese (It 1953)
Tempi nostri [Quelques Pas dans la vie] (It-Fr 1953)
Cento anni d'amore (It 1953)
Il matrimonio (It 1953)
Secrets d'alcôve (ep "Il divorzio") (Fr-It 1954)
Gran varietà (ep "Il fine dicitore") (It 1954)
Vergine moderna (It 1954)
L'allegro squadrone [Les gaîtês del'escadron] (It-Fr 1954)
Peccato che sia una canaglia (It 1954)
Pane, amore e gelosia (It 1954)
L'oro di Napoli (It 1954)
Il segno di Venere (It 1955)
La bella mugnaia (It 1955)
Gli ultimi cinque minuti (It 1955)
Pano, amore e... (It 1955)
Racconti romani (It 1955)
Cinema d'altri tempi (It-Fr 1955)
Il bigamo (It 1956)
Mio figlio Nerone (It 1956)
Tempo di villeggiatura (It 1956)
I giorni più belli (It 1956)
Montecarlo [The Monte Carlo Story] (It 1956)
Noi siamo le colonne (It 1956)
Padri e figli (It 1957)
I colpevoli [Responsabilitê limitêe] (It-Fr 1957)
Souvenir d'Italie [It Happened in Rome] (It 1957)

La donna che venne dal mare (It 1957)
Amore e chiacchiere [Hablemos de amor] (It-Sp 1957)
Il conte Max [El conde Max] (It-Sp 1957)
Casino de Paris (Fr-It 1957)
A Farewell to Arms (20th 1957)
Vacanze ad Ischia (It-Fr-W Ger 1957)
Il medico e lo stregone (It 1957)
Totò, Vittorio e la dottoressa (It-Fr-Sp 1957)
Anna di Brooklyn (It 1958)
Ballerina e Buon Dio (It 1958)
Domenica è sempre domenica (It 1958)
La ragazza di piazza San Pietro (It-Sp 1958)
Gli zitelloni (It 1958)
Pezzo, capopezzo e capitano [Kanonen serenade] (It-W Ger 1958)
Pane, amore e Andalusia [Pan, amor y Andalucía] (It-Sp 1959)
La prima notte (It-Fr 1959)
Uomini e nobiluomini (It 1959)
Vacanze d'inverno (It 1959)
Il medico di mia moglie (It 1959)
Il moralista (It 1959)
Il mondo dei miracoli (It 1959)
Il generale Della Rovere (It-Fr 1959)
Ferdinando I, re di Napoli (It 1959)
Gastone (It 1959)
Austerlitz (Fr-It 1960)
Fontana di Trevi (It 1960)
Le tre eccetera del colonnello (It 1960)
La sposa bella [The Angel Wore Red] (It 1960)
Il vigile (It 1960)
Le pillole d'Ercole (It 1960)
Un amore a Roma (It 1960)
It Started in Naples (Par 1960)
Vive Henri IV, vive l'amour! (Fr 1960)
The Millionairess (20th 1961)
Gli incensurati (It 1961)
L'onorata società (It 1961)
Il giudizio universale [Le Jugement dernier] (It-Fr 1961)
Gli attendenti (It 1961)
I due marescialli (It 1961)
Le meraviglie di Aladino [The Wonders of Aladdin] (It-USA 1962)
La Fayette [La Fayette, una spada per due bandiere] (Fr-It
   1962)
La pappa reale (It 1964)
The Amorous Adventures of Moll Flanders (Par 1965)
Caccià alla volpe [After the Fox] (It 1965)
Io, io, io... e gli altri (It 1966)
Un italiano in America (It 1967)
Caroline Chérie (Fr-It 1968)
Colpo grosso alla napoletana [The Biggest Bundle of Them All]
   (It 1968)
The Shoes of the Fisherman (MGM 1968)
Una su 13 (It 1969)
If It's Tuesday, This Must Be Belgium (UA 1969)
Cose di "Cosa nostra" (It 1970)

Snow Job [The Ski Raiders] (WB 1971)
L'Odeur des fauves (Fr 1971)
Siamo tutti in libertà provvisoria (It 1971)
Io non vedo, tu non parli, lui non sente (It 1972)
Ettore lo fusto (It 1972)
Trastevere (It 1972)
Storià de fratelli e de cortelli (It 1973)
Il delitto Matteotti (It 1973)
Dracula vuole vivere [Cerca sangue di vergine/Blood for Dracula] (It 1973)
C'iravams tanto amati (It 1975)

DEVÈRE, ARTHUR (Arthur Opdeweerdt), b. June 24, 1894, Brussels;
    d. 1961
Saïda enlève le Manneken Pis (Bel 1913)
Arthur fait du film (Bel 1922)
Occupe toi-d'Amêlie (Fr 1932)
Le Mariage de Melle Beulemans (Fr 1932)
L'Ange Gardien (Fr 1933)
La Kermesse heroïque [Carnival in Flanders] (Fr 1935)
Marie des angoisses (Fr 1935)
Martha (Ger 1936)
L'île des veuves (Fr 1936)
Les Amants terribles (Fr 1936)
Un de la Légion (Fr 1936)
Barnabe (Fr 1936)
L'Homme du jour (Fr 1936)
Les Loups entre eux (Fr 1936)
Miarka la fille à l'ourse (Fr 1937)
Les Hommes sans nom (Fr 1937)
Mollenard (Fr 1937)
Ernest le rebelle (Fr 1937)
Le Petit Chose (Fr 1938)
La Piste du Sud (Fr 1938)
La Goualeuse (Fr 1938)
Cafe de Paris (Fr 1938)
L'entraîneuse (Fr 1938)
La fin du jour (Fr 1938)
Fort Dolorès (Fr 1938)
Grisou (Fr 1938)
Bifur II (Fr 1939) [unreleased]
Bach en correctionnelle (Fr 1939)
Le Club des fadas (Fr 1939)
Jeunes Filles en détresse (Fr 1939)
Le Jour se lève (Fr 1939)
Documents secrets (Fr 1940)
L'Empreinte du Dieu (Fr 1940)
Caprices (Fr 1941)
Ici l'on pèche (Fr 1941)
L'Assassinat du Père Noël (Fr 1941)
Goupi mains rouges (Fr 1942)
Dernier Mêtro (Fr 1945)
Le Destin s'amuse (Fr 1946)

La Figure de proue (Fr 1947)
La Ferme des sept péchés (Fr 1948)
Le Mystère de la chambre jaune (Fr 1948)
Véronique (Fr 1949)
Au petit zouave (Fr 1949)
Occupe-toi d'Amélie (Fr 1949) [remake]
Rome-Express (Fr 1949)
Le Parfum de la dame en noir (Fr 1949)
Juliette, ou la clé des songes (Fr 1950)
Paris chante toujours (Fr 1951)
La Maison dans la dune (Fr 1951)
Le Plaisir (Fr 1951)
Ma femme, ma vache et moi (Fr 1951)
Le Banquet des fraudeurs (Fr-Bel 1951)
Suivez cet homme (Fr 1952)
Le Défroqué (Fr 1953)
Leur dernière nuit (Fr 1953)
Le Circuit de minuit (Bel 1956)

DIETRICH, MARLENE, b. Dec. 27, 1901, Berlin
Der kleine Napoleon (Ger 1923)
Tragödie der Liebe (Ger 1923)
Der Mensch am Wege (Ger 1923)
Der Sprung ins Leben (Ger 1924)
Die freudlose Gasse (Ger 1925)
Manon Lescaut (Ger 1926)
Eine Du Barry von Heute (Ger 1927)
Madame wünscht keine Kinder (Ger 1927)
Kopf hoch, Charly! (Ger 1927)
Der Juxbaron (Ger 1927)
Sein grösster Bluff (Ger 1927)
Cafe Electric (Ger 1927)
Prinzessin Olala (Ger 1928)
Ich küsse ihre Hand, Madame (Ger 1929)
Die Frau, nach der Man sich sehnt (Ger 1929)
Das Schiff der verlorenen Menschen (Ger 1929)
Gefahren der Brautzeit (Ger 1929)
Der Blaue Engel [The Blue Angel] (Ger 1930)
Morocco (Par 1930)
Dishonored (Par 1931)
Shanghai Express (Par 1932)
Blonde Venus (Par 1932)
Song of Songs (Par 1933)
The Scarlet Empress (Par 1934)
The Devil Is a Woman (Par 1935)
Desire (Par 1936)
The Garden of Allah (UA 1936)
Knight Without Armour (UA 1937)
Angel (Par 1937)
Destry Rides Again (Univ 1939)
Seven Sinners (Univ 1940)
The Flame of New Orleans (Univ 1941)
Manpower (WB 1941)

The Lady Is Willing (Col 1942)
The Spoilers (Univ 1942)
Pittsburgh (Univ 1942)
Follow the Boys (Univ 1944)
Kismet (MGM 1944)
Martin Roumagnac [The Room Upstairs] (Fr 1946)
Golden Earrings (Par 1948)
Foreign Affair (Par 1948)
Jigsaw (UA 1949) (cameo)
Stage Fright (WB 1950)
No Highway [in the Sky] (20th Br 1951)
Rancho Notorious (RKO 1952)
Around the World in 80 Days (UA 1956)
The Monte Carlo Story (UA Br 1957)
Witness for the Prosecution (UA Br 1958)
Touch of Evil (Univ 1958)
Judgment at Nuremberg (UA 1961)
Black Fox (Hermitage 1962) (narrator)
Paris When It Sizzles (Par 1964) (cameo)

DOLORES, CARMEN (Carmen Dolores Cohen Sarmento Vêres), b.
    April 22, 1924, Lisbon
    O amor de perdição (Por 1943)
    Um homem às direitas (Por 1944)
    A vizinha do lado (Por 1945)
    Camões (Por 1946)
    Três espelhos (Por 1947)
    A garça e a serpente (Por 1952)

DOMMELEN, JAN VAN   see   VAN DOMMELEN, JAN

DONAT, ROBERT, b. March 18, 1905, Withington, England; d. June
    9, 1958
    Men of Tomorrow (Par Br 1933)
    That Night in London [Overnight] (Par Br 1933)
    Cash [For Love or Money] (Par Br 1933)
    The Private Life of Henry VIII (UA 1933)
    The Count of Monte Cristo (UA 1934)
    The Thirty-Nine Steps (Gaumont 1935)
    The Ghost Goes West (UA 1935)
    Knight Without Armour (UA 1936)
    The Citadel (MGM Br 1938)
    Goodbye Mr. Chips (MGM Br 1939)
    Young Mr. Pitt (20th Br 1942)
    The Adventures of Tartu [Tartu] (MGM Br 1943)
    Perfect Strangers [Vacation from Marriage] (MGM Br 1945)
    Captain Boycott (GFD 1947)
    The Winslow Boy (BL 1948)
    The Cure for Love (BL 1949)
    The Magic Box (BL 1951)
    Lease of Life (GFD 1954)
    The Inn of the Sixth Happiness (20th 1958)

DOR, KARIN (Kathe Rose Derr), b. Feb. 22, 1936, Wiesbaden,
    Germany
  Rosen-Resli (W Ger 1954)
  Der schweigende Engel (W Ger 1954)
  Ihre grosse Prüfung (W Ger 1954)
  Solange du lebst (W Ger 1955)
  Santa Lucia (W Ger 1956)

Karin Dor and Maurice Ronet in Seul le vent connait la reponse
(1974).

  Kleiner Mann--ganz gross (W Ger 1957)
  Die Zwillinge vom Zillertal (W Ger 1957)
  Almenrausch und Edelweiss (Aus 1957)
  13 alte Esel und der Sonnenhof (W Ger 1958)
  Mit Eva fing die Sünde an [The Playgirls and the Bellboy] (W
    Ger 1958)
  Skandal um Dodo (W Ger 1959)
  Worüber man nicht spricht [False Shame] (W Ger 1959)
  So angelt man keinen Mann (W Ger 1959)
  Das blaue Meer und du (W Ger 1959)
  Ein Sommer, den man nicht vergisst (W Ger 1959)

Der Frosch mit der Maske [Froen med Masken] (W Ger-Dan
  1959)
Im weissen Rössl (W Ger 1960)
Die Bande des Schreckens (W Ger 1960)
Bei Pichler stimmt die Kasse nicht (W Ger 1961)
Der grüne Bogenschütze (W Ger 1961)
Der Fälscher von London (W Ger 1961)
Am Sonntag will mein Süsser mit mir Segeln gehn (W Ger 1961)
Ohne Krimi geht die Mimi nie ins Bett (W Ger 1962)
Teppich des Grauens [Il terrore di notte/Terror en la noche]
  (W Ger-It-Sp 1962)
Die unsichtbaren Krallen des Dr. Mabuse (W Ger 1962)
Der Schatz im Silbersee [Le Tresor du lac d'Argent/Blago u
  srebrnom jezeru/Treasure of Silver Lake] (W Ger-Fr-Yug 1963)
Das Geheimnis der schwarzen Witwe [Araña negra] (W Ger-Sp
  1963)
Die weisse Spinne (W Ger 1963)
Der Würger von Schloss Blackmoor (W Ger 1963)
Zimmer 13 (W Ger 1964)
Der letzte Mohikaner [El ultimo Mohicans] (W Ger-It-Sp 1965)
Winnetou II [Giorni di fusco/Le Tresor des montagnes bleues/
  Last of the Renegades] (W Ger-Yug-It-Fr 1964)
Hotel der toten Gäste [El extraño caso de Lucy Cornell] (W Ger-
  Sp 1965)
Io la conoscevo bene (It 1965)
The Face of Fu Manchu (WPD 1965)
Das Geheimnis der gelben Mönche (W Ger 1965)
Der unheimliche Mönch (W Ger 1965)
Upperseven, l'uomo da uccidere [Der Mann mit den tausend
  Masken] (It-W Ger 1966)
Gern hab' ich die Frauen gekillt [Spie contro il mondo/Le
  Carneval des barbouzes] (Aus-It-Fr 1966)
Caroline Cherie (W Ger-It-Fr 1967)
Die Nibelungen I & II (W Ger-Yug 1967)
Tiro a segno per uccidere (It-W Ger 1967)
Die Schlangengrube und das Pendel [The Blood Demon] (W Ger
  1967)
You Only Live Twice (UA 1967)
Winnetou und Shatterhand im Tal des Todes [L'uomo dal lungo
  Fucile] (W Ger-It-Yug 1968)
Topaz (Univ 1969)
Dracula Jagt Frankstein [Los monstruos del terror/El hombre
  que veno de Ummo] (W Ger-It-Sp 1970)
Freddy--Die Fahrt ins Abenteuer (W Ger 1971)
Seul le vent connait la reponse [Die Antwort kennt nur der wind]
  (Fr-W Ger 1974)

DORLEAC, FRANÇOISE, b. March 21, 1942, Paris; d. June 26,
  1967
  Les Loups dans la Bergèrie (Fr 1960)
  Ce soir ou jamais [Tonight or Never] (Fr 1960)
  Les Portes claquent (Fr 1960)
  Le Jeu de la vérité (Fr-It 1961)

A d'autres amours (Fr 1961)
La Gamberge (Fr 1961)
Tout l'or du monde (Fr-It 1961)
La Fille aux yeux d'or (Fr-It 1961)
Arsène Lupin contre Arsène Lupin (Fr-It 1962)
L'Homme de Rio [That Man from Rio] (Fr-It 1964)
La Chasse à l'homme [Male Hunt] (Fr-It 1964)
La Peau douce [Silken Skin] (Fr 1964)
Genghis Kahn (USA-W Ger-Yug 1965)
Where the Spies Are (MGM 1965)
Cul-de-Sac (Compton-Cameo 1966)
Les Demoiselles de Rochefort [Those Young Girls of Rochefort]
    (Fr 1967)
Billion Dollar Brain (UA 1967)

DORS, DIANA (Diana Fluck), b. Oct. 23, 1931, Swindon, England
The Shop at Sly Corner [The Code of Scotland Yard] (BL 1947)
Dancing with Crime (Par 1947)
Holiday Camp (GFD 1947)
Good Time Girl (GFD 1948)
Penny and the Pownall Case (GFD 1948)
The Calendar (GFD 1948)
My Sister and I (GFD 1948)
Oliver Twist (GFD 1948)
Here Come the Huggetts (GFD 1948)
Vote for Huggett (GFD 1949)
It's Not Cricket (GFD 1949)
A Boy, a Girl and a Bike (GFD 1949)
Diamond City (GFD 1949)
Dance Hall (GFD 1950)
Worm's Eye View (ABFD 1951)
Lady Godiva Rides Again (BL 1951)
The Last Page [Manbait] (Ex 1952)
My Wife's Lodger (Adelphi 1952)
The Great Game (Adelphi 1953)
Is Your Honeymoon Really Necessary? (Adelphi 1953)
The Saint's Return [The Saint's Girl Friday] (Ex 1953)
It's a Grand Life (Mancunian 1953)
The Weak and the Wicked (ABP 1954)
As Long As They're Happy (ABP 1955)
A Kid for Two Farthings (IFD 1955)
Miss Tulip Stays the Night (Adelphi 1955)
Value for Money (RFD 1955)
An Alligator Named Daisy (RFD 1955)
Yield to the Night [Blonde Sinner] (APB 1956)
I Married a Woman (RKO 1956)
Love Specialist [La Ragazza del Palio] (It 1957)
The Long Haul (Col Br 1957)
The Unholy Wife (Univ Br 1957)
Tread Softly Stranger (Renown 1958)
Passport to Shame [Room 43] (BL 1959)
Scent of Mystery (Todd Enterprises 1960)
On the Double (Par 1961)

The Big Bankroll [King of the Roaring Twenties--The Story of
    Arnold Rothstein] (AA 1961)
Mrs. Gibbon's Boys (BL 1962)
West 11 (WPD 1963)
Allez France [The Counterfeit Constable] (GB-Fr 1964)
The Sandwich Man (RFD 1966)
Berserk (Col 1967)
Danger Route (UA 1967)
Hammerhead (Col 1968)
Baby Love (Avco Embassy 1968)
Deep End (W Ger-USA 1970)
There's a Girl in My Soup (Col 1970)
Hannie Caulder (Tigon 1971)
The Pied Piper (Scotia-Barber 1972)
The Amazing Mr. Blunden (Hemdale 1972)
Nothing But the Night (Fox-Rank 1972)
Theatre of Blood (UA 1973)
Steptoe and Son Ride Again (MGM-EMI 1973)
From Beyond the Grave (ep "An Act of Kindness") (Col-Warner 1974)
Craze (EMI 1974)
Swedish Wildcats (USA-Swe 1974)
The Amorous Milkman (Variety 1974)
Bedtime with Rosie (London International 1975)
Three for All (Fox-Rank 1975)

DUBOIS, MARIE (Claudine Huzê), b. Jan. 12, 1937, Paris
    Le Signe du Lion (Fr 1959)
    Tirez sur le pianiste [Shoot the Piano Player] (Fr 1959)
    Une Femme est une femme (Fr 1960)

Marie Dubois

La Croix des vivants (Fr 1960)
Jules et Jim [Jules and Jim] (Fr 1961)
Le Monocle noir (Fr 1961)
Jusqu'au bout du monde (Fr 1962)
La Ronde (Fr 1964)
La Chasse à l'homme [Man Hunt] (Fr 1964)
L'Age ingrat (Fr 1964)
Week-end à Zuydcoote (Fr 1964)
Mata-Hari, agent H-21 (Fr 1964)
Les Grandes Gueules (Fr 1965)
Les Fêtes galantes (Fr 1965)
Le 17e Ciel (Fr 1965)
La Grande Vadrouille (Fr 1966)
Le Voleur (Fr 1966)
Ce sacré grand-père (Fr 1967)
Rublo de dos caras [Le Rouble à deux faces] (Sp-Fr 1967)
Stuntman [Le Cascadeur] (It-Fr 1968)
Monte Carlo or Bust! [Quei temperarai sulle loro pazze, scate-
nate, scalcinate carricole/Those Daring Young Men in Their
Jaunty Jalopies/Gonflés à bloc] (Par 1969)
La Maison des Bories (Fr 1970)
Bof... l'Anatomie d'un livreur (Fr 1970)
L'oeuf (Fr 1971)
Les Arpenteurs (Swi 1971)
Le Serpent (Fr 1972)
L'Escapade (Swi 1973)
Antoine et Sébastien (Fr 1973)
Vincent, François, Paul et les autres (Fr 1974)
Du bout des levres (Bel 1975)

DUCHAUSSOY, MICHEL, b. Nov. 29, 1938, Valenciennes, France
Jeu de Massacre (Fr 1967)
La Louve solitaire (Fr 1967)
La Femme infidèle (Fr 1968)
Bye Bye Barbara (Fr 1968)
Que la bête meure (Fr 1969)
La Main (Fr 1969)
Ils (Fr 1970)
Aussi loin que l'amour (Fr 1970)
La Rupture (Fr 1970)
Les Stances à Sophie (Fr 1970)
Juste avant la nuit (Fr 1971)
L'Homme au cerveau greffe (Fr 1971)
Traitement de choc (Fr 1972)
Le Complot (Fr 1973)
Nada (Fr 1973)
Femmes-femmes (Fr 1974)
Le Lion et la vierge (Fr-Swe 1974)
La Jeune Fille assassinée (Fr 1974)
Le Retour du Grand Blond (Fr 1974)

DULCE, MARIA (Maria Dulce Andrade Ferreira Alves), b. Oct. 11,
1936, Lisbon
Frei Luis de Sousa (Por 1950)

Michel Duchaussoy

Senhora de Fátima (Sp 1951)
Sor intrépida (Sp 1951)
Yo elijo el inferno (Sp 1952)
Carmen Porto (Sp 1953)
Um dia perdido (Sp 1954)
Enfim, sós e pedras vivas (Sp 1955)
O homen do dia (Por 1958)
A luz vem do alto (Por 1959)
Encontro con a vida (Por 1960)
Fruto proibido (Sp-USA 1962) [unreleased]

EATON, SHIRLEY, b. 1937, Middlesex
You Know What Sailors Are (GFD 1954)
Doctor in the House (GFD 1954)
The Love Match (BL 1955)
Charley Moon (BL 1956)
Sailor Beware! [Panic in the Parlour] (IFD 1956)
Three Men in a Boat (IFD 1956)
Doctor at Large (RFD 1957)
Date with Disaster (Eros 1957)
The Naked Truth [Your Past Is Showing] (RFD 1957)
Carry On, Sergeant (AA 1958)
Further Up the Creek (Col Br 1958)
Life Is a Circus (BL 1958)
Carry On, Nurse (AA 1959)
In the Wake of a Stranger (Butcher 1959)
Carry On, Constable (AA 1960)
A Weekend with Lulu (Col Br 1961)
Nearly a Nasty Accident (Britannia 1961)

Dentist on the Job [Get On with It] (AA 1961)
What a Carve Up! (RFI 1961)
The Girl Hunters (20th 1963)
Goldfinger (UA 1964)
Ten Little Indians (WPD 1965)
Sumuru [The 1,000,000 Eyes of Sumuru] (AA 1967)

EDWARDS, HENRY (Arthur Harold Ethelbert Edwards), b. Sept. 18,
    1883, Weston-super-Mare, England; d. Nov. 2, 1952
Alone in London (Ideal 1915)
My Old Dutch (Ideal 1915)
The Man Who Stayed at Home (Ideal 1915)
Lost and Won (Ideal 1915)
Far from the Madding Crowd (Ideal 1915)
A Welsh Singer (Butcher 1915)
Doorsteps (Hepworth 1916)
Grim Justice (Butcher 1916)
East Is East (Butcher 1916)
The Cobweb (Harma 1917)
Merely Mrs. Stubbs (Butcher 1917)
Dick Carson Wins Through (Butcher 1917)
Nearer My God to Thee (Moss 1917)
Broken Threads (Butcher 1917)
The Touch of a Child (Moss 1918)
The Hanging Judge (Moss 1918)
Towards the Light (Moss 1918)
His Dearest Possession (Hepworth 1919)
The Kinsman (Butcher 1919)
Possession (Butcher 1919)
The City of Beautiful Nonsense (Butcher 1919)
A Temporary Vagabond (Butcher 1920)
Aylwin (Hepworth 1920)
The Amazing Quest of Ernest Bliss   * (Imperial 1920)
John Forrest Finds Himself (Hepworth 1920)
The Lunatic at Large (Hepworth 1921)
The Bargain (Hepworth 1921)
Simple Simon (Hepworth 1922)
Tit for Tat (Hepworth 1922)
Lily of the Alley (Hepworth 1923)
Boden's Boy (Hepworth 1923)
The Naked Man (Ideal 1923)
The World of Wonderful Reality (Hepworth 1924)
The Flag Lieutenant (Astra-National 1926)
The Fake (WP 1927)
The Further Adventures of the Flag Lieutenant (WP 1927)
The Three Kings (British Foreign Films 1929)
Ringing the Changes (Argosy 1929)
The Call of the Sea (WB Br 1930)
The Girl in the Night (Wardour 1931)
Stranglehold (WB Br 1931)
The Flag Lieutenant (W & F 1932)
Captain's Orders (Liberty Films 1937)
East of Piccadilly [The Strangler] (Pathé 1942)

Spring Meeting (Pathé 1941)
The Magic Bow (GFD 1946)
Green for Danger (GFD 1946)
Take My Life (GFD 1947)
Oliver Twist (GFD 1948)
London Belongs to Me [Dulcimer Street] (GFD 1948)
Woman Hater (GFD 1948)
Quartet (ep "The Colonel's Lady") (GFD 1948)
Lucky Mascot (UA 1948)
All Over the Town (GFD 1949)
Dear Mr. Prohack (GFD 1949)
Madeleine [Strange Case of Madeleine] (GFD 1950)
Double Confession (ABP 1950)
Trio (ep "The Verger") (GFD 1950)
The Rossiter Case (Ex 1951)
White Corridors (GFD 1951)
The Magic Box (BL 1951)
The Lady with the Lamp (BL 1951)
Never Look Back (Ex 1952)
Something Money Can't Buy (GFD 1952)
Trent's Last Case (BL 1952)
The Long Memory (GFD 1953)

EGGAR, SAMANTHA, b. March 5, 1939, London
The Wild and the Willing (RFD 1962)
Dr. Crippen (WPD 1962)
Doctor in Distress (RFD 1963)
Psyche '59 (Col 1964)
The Collector (Col 1965)
Return from the Ashes (UA 1966)
Walk, Don't Run (Col 1966)
Dr. Dolittle (20th 1967)
The Molly Maguires (Par 1969)
The Walking Stick (MGM 1970)
La Dame dans l'auto avec des lunettes et un fusil [The Lady in
  the Car with Glasses and a Gun] (Fr 1970)
The Light at the End of the World (USA-Sp-Lich 1971)
Double Indemnity (ABC-TV 1974)
Man of Destiny (GB 1974)
All the Kind Strangers (ABC-TV 1974)

EGGERTH, MARTA, b. April 17, 1912, Budapest
Der Draufgänger (Ger 1931)
Trara um Liebe (Ger 1931)
Eine Nacht im Grandhotel (Ger 1931)
Die Bräutigamswitwe (Ger 1931)
Bridegroom for Two (Ger 1931) [Eng lang version of Die Brauti-
  gamswitwe]
Der Frauendiplomat (Ger 1932)
Kaiserwalzer (Ger 1932)
Das Blaue vom Himmel (Ger 1932)
Es war einmal ein Walzer (Ger 1932)
Ein Lied, ein Kuss, ein Mädel (Ger 1932)

Traum von Schönbrunn (Ger 1932)
Moderne Mitgift (Ger 1932)
Where Is This Lady? (BL 1932)
Leise flehen meine lieder [Schuberts unvollendete Symphonie]
   (Ger-Aus 1933)
The Unfinished Symphony (Ger-Aus 1933) [Eng lang version of
   Leise flehen meine lieder]
Der Zarewitsch (Ger 1933)
Die Blume von Hawaii (Ger 1933)
Mein Herz ruf nacht dir (Ger 1934)
My Heart Is Calling (Ger 1934) [Eng lang version of Mein Herz
   ruf nacht dir]
Die Czardasfürstin (Ger 1934)
Ihr grösster Erfolg (Ger 1934)
Die ganze Welt dreht sich um Liebe (Ger 1935)
Die blonde Carmen (Ger 1935)
Casta Diva (It 1935)
The Divine Spark (It 1935) [Eng lang version of Casta Diva]
Das Hofkonzert (Ger 1936)
La chanson du souvenir (Fr 1936) [Fr version of Das Hofkonzert]
Wo die Lerche singt (Ger-Hun-Swi 1936)
Das Schloss in Flandern (Ger 1936)
Zauber der Boheme (Aus 1937)
Immer, wenn ich glücklich bin (Aus 1938)
For Me and My Gal (MGM 1942)
Presenting Lily Mars (MGM 1943)
Addio Mimi [Her Wonderful Life] (It 1947)
Valse brillante (Fr 1949)
Das Land des Lächelns (W Ger 1952)
Frühling in Berlin (W Ger 1957)

EKLAND, BRITT (Britt-Marie Ekland), b. Oct. 6, 1942, Stockholm,
   Sweden
Kort Är Sommaren [Pan] (Swe 1963)
Det Är hos Mie Han Här Varit (Swe 1963)
Il diavolo [To Bed or Not to Bed] (It 1963)
Il comandante (It 1963)
Caccia alla Volpe [After the Fox] (It-USA 1966)
Too Many Thieves (MGM 1966)
The Double Man (WPD 1967)
The Bobo (WB-7 Arts 1967)
The Night They Raided Minsky's (UA 1968)
Gli intoccabili [At Any Price/Machine Gun McCain] (It 1969)
Nell'anno del signore (It-Fr 1969)
I cannibali [The Cannibals] (It 1969)
Stiletto (Avco Emb 1969)
Tinto Mara (Den 1970)
Percy (MGM-EMI 1971)
Get Carter (MGM-EMI 1971)
Time for Loving [A Room in Paris] (Hemdale 1972)
Asylum (CIC 1972)
Endless Night (BL 1972)

Night Hair Child (RFD 1973) [made in 1971]
Baxter! (MGM-EMI 1973)
The Wicker Man (BL 1973)
The Man with the Golden Gun (UA 1974)
Royal Flash (Fox-Rank 1975)
The Ultimate Thrill (1975--unreleased)
High Velocity (1975--unreleased)

ELLIOTT, DENHOLM, b. May 31, 1922, London
    Dear Mr. Prohack (GFD 1949)
    The Sound Barrier [Breaking the Sound Barrier] (BL 1952)
    The Holly and the Ivy (BL 1952)
    The Ringer (BL 1952)
    The Cruel Sea (GFD 1953)
    The Heart of the Matter (BL 1953)
    They Who Dare (BL 1954)
    Lease of Life (GFD 1954)
    The Man Who Loved Redheads (BL 1955)
    The Night My Number Came Up (GFD 1955)
    Pacific Destiny (BL 1956)
    Scent of Mystery (Todd Enterprises 1960)
    Station Six Sahara (BL 1962)
    Nothing But the Best (AA 1963)
    The High Bright Sun [McGuire Go Home!] (RFD 1964)
    You Must Be Joking! (Col 1965)
    King Rat (Col 1965)
    Alfie (Par 1966)
    The Spy with a Cold Nose (Par 1966)
    Maroc 7 (RFD 1966)
    Here We Go Round the Mulberry Bush (UA 1967)
    The Night They Raided Minsky's (UA 1968)
    The Seagull (WPD 1969)
    Too Late the Hero (Cin 1970)
    The Rise and Rise of Michael Rimmer (WB 1970)
    Percy (MGM-EMI 1970)
    The House That Dripped Blood (Cin 1970)
    Quest for Love (RFD 1971)
    Madame Sin (Scotia-Barber 1972)
    Vault of Horror (Fox-Rank 1973)
    A Doll's House (MGM-EMI 1973)
    The Apprenticeship of Duddy Kravitz (Can 1974)
    Percy's Progress (EMI 1974)
    Russian Roulette (Avco Emb 1975)

ETAIX, PIERRE, b. Nov. 23, 1928, Roanne (Loire), France
    Pickpocket (Fr 1959)
    Une Grosse Tête (Fr 1962)
    Le Soupirant (Fr 1962)
    Yoyo (Fr 1965)
    Tant qu'on a la santé (Fr 1966)
    Le Grand Amour (Fr 1969)
    Je serai serieux comme le plaisir (Fr 1974)

Dame Edith Evans and David Niven in Prudence and the Pill (1968).

EVANS, EDITH, b. Feb. 8, 1888, London; d. Oct. 14, 1976
    A Honeymoon for Three (KTC 1915)
    A Welsh Singer (Butcher 1915)
    East Is East (Butcher 1916)
    The Queen of Spades (ABP 1949)
    The Last Days of Dolwyn [Woman of Dolwyn] (BL 1949)
    The Importance of Being Earnest (RFD 1952)
    Look Back in Anger (ABP 1959)
    Tom Jones (UA 1963)
    The Chalk Garden (Univ 1964)
    Young Cassidy (MGM 1965)
    The Whisperers (UA 1967)
    Prudence and the Pill (20th 1968)
    Upon This Rock (Marstan 1970)
    Craze (EMI 1973)
    A Doll's House (GB-Fr 1973)

EYCK, PETER VAN see VAN EYCK, PETER

FABIAN, FRANÇOISE (Michele Cortes de Leone y Fabianera), b.
    May 10, 1932, Hussein Dey, Algeria
    Memoires d'un flic (Fr 1955)

Ce sacrée Amedée (Fr 1955)
Cette sacrée gamine [Mam'zelle Pigalle] (Fr 1955)
L'Aventurière des Champs-Elysees (Fr 1955)
Le Couturier de ces dames [Fernandel the Dressmaker] (Fr
   1956)
Les Aventures de Till l'Espiegle (Fr-Dut 1956)
La Belle et le corsaire (Fr-It 1956)
Le Feu aux poudres (Fr-It 1956)
Michel Strogoff (Fr-It-Yug 1956)

Françoise Fabian and Jean Vilar in Raphaël (1971).

Les Fanatiques [A Bomb for the Dictator] (Fr 1957)
Les Violents [The Coffin Came by Post] (Fr 1957)
Chaque jour a son secret (Fr 1958)
La Brune que voilà (Fr 1960)
Una domenica d'estate (It 1961)
Il magnifico avventuriero [The Magnificent Adventurer] (It-Fr-Sp
   1963)
Maigret voit rouge (Fr-It 1963)
Le Voleur [The Thief of Paris] (Fr-It 1966)
Belle de Jour (Fr-It 1967)
Ma nuit chez Maud [My Night with Maud] (Fr 1969)
L'Américain (Fr 1969)
Le Specialiste [Drop Them or I'll Shoot] (Fr-W Ger-It-Sp 1969)
Etes-vous fiancée à un marin grec ou à un pilote de ligne?
   (Fr 1970)

Un Conde [The Cop] (Fr-It 1970)
Raphaël; ou Le Débauché (Fr 1971)
Die Weibchen (W Ger-Fr-It 1971)
Les Voraces (Fr-It 1973)
La Bonne Année (Fr-It 1973)
Projection privée (Fr 1974)
Salut l'artiste [Salute the Artist] (Fr-It 1974)
Chi dice donna dice... donna (It 1975)
Par amare Ofelia (Fr-It 1975)
Out One [Spectre] (Fr 1975)
Perche si uccidi un magistrato (It-Fr 1975)
Per le antiche scale [Down the Ancient Stairs] (It-Fr 1975)

FABRIZI, ALDO, b. 1906, Rome
Avanti c'è posto (It 1942)
Campo de' Fiori (It 1943)
L'ultima carrozzella (It 1943)
Circo equestre Za-Bum (It 1944)
Roma, città aperta [Open City] (It 1946)
Mio figlio professore (It 1946)
Il delitto di Giovanni Episcopo (It 1947)
Tombolo, paradiso nero (It 1947)
Vivere in pace (It 1947)
Natale al campo 119 (It 1947)
Emigrantes (Arg-It 1948)
Benvenuto reverendo! (It 1949)
Antonio de Padova (It 1949)
Francesco, giullare di Dio (It 1950)
Prima comunione (It 1950)
Vita da cani (It 1950)
Tre passi a nord (It 1950)
Guardie e ladri (It 1951)
Parigi è sempre Parigi (It 1951)
Signori in carrozza! (It 1951)
Cameriera bella presenza offresi (It 1951)
Altri tempi (ep "Il carrettino dei libri vecchi") (It 1951)
La famiglia Passaguai fa fortuna (It 1951)
Cinque poveri in automobile (It 1952)
Una di quelle (It 1952)
La voce del silenzio (It 1952)
Papà diventa mamma (It 1952)
L'età dell'amore (It 1953)
Siamo tutti inquilini (It 1953)
Questa è la vita (ep "Marsina stretta") (It 1953)
Cose da pazzi [Närriscohe geschichten] (It-W Ger 1954)
Cento anni d'amore (ep "Garibaldina") (It 1954)
Hanno rubato un tram (It 1954)
Accadde al penitenziario (It 1955)
Carosello di varietà (It 1955)
Un po' di cielo (It 1955)
I due compari (It 1955)
Io piaccio [La vie del successo... con le donne] (It 1955)
Donatella (It 1956)

Guardia, guardia scelta, brigadiere e maresciallo (It 1956)
Mi permette, babbo? (It 1956)
I pappagalli (It 1956)
Il maestro [El maestro] (It-Sp 1957)
Festa di maggio (It 1958)
I prepotenti (It 1958)
Cameriera bella presenza offresi... (It 1959)
Ferdinando I, re di Napoli (It 1959)
Prepotenti più di prima (It 1959)
I tartassati [Fripouillard et Cie] (It-Fr 1959)
Un militare e mezzo (It 1960)
La sposa bella [The Angel Wore Red] (It 1960)
Totò, Fabrizi e i giovani d'oggi (It 1960)
Gerarchi si muore (It 1962)
Le meraviglie di Aladino [The Wonders of Aladdin] (It-USA 1962)
Orazi e Curiazi (It 1962)
I quattro monaci (It 1962)
Twist, lolite e vitelloni (It 1962)
I quattro moschettieri (It 1963)
Totò contro i quattro (It 1963)
Frà Manisco cerca guai (It 1964)
I quattro tassisti (It 1964)
La donna è una cosa meravigliosa (It 1966) [made in 1964]
Sette monaci d'oro (It 1966)
Tre morsi nella mela (It 1966)
Made in Italy (It 1966)
Cose di cosa Nostri (It 1970)
La Tosca (It 1972)
C'eravamo tanto amati (It 1974)

FALCONETTI, RENEE, b. 1901, Paris; d. 1946
La Passion de Jeanne d'Arc (Fr 1928)

FARRAR, DAVID, b. Aug. 21, 1908, Forest Gate, Essex, England
Return of a Stranger [The Face Behind the Scar] (Radio 1937)
Silver Top (Par 1938)
Sexton Blake and the Hooded Terror (MGM Br 1938)
A Royal Divorce (Par Br 1938)
Danny Boy (Butcher 1941)
Penn of Pennsylvania [The Courageous Mr. Penn] (Anglo 1941)
Sheepdog of the Hills (Butcher 1941)
Suspected Person (Pathé 1942)
Went the Day Well? [48 Hours] (UA 1942)
The Night Invader (WB-FN Br 1943)
The Dark Tower (WB-FN Br 1943)
They Met in the Dark (GFD 1943)
Headline (Ealing 1943)
The Hundred Pound Window (WB-FN Br 1943)
For Those in Peril (Ealing 1944)
Meet Sexton Blake (Anglo 1944)
The World Owes Me a Living (Anglo 1945)
The Echo Murders (Anglo 1945)
The Trojan Brothers* [Murder in the Footlights] (Anglo 1946)

Lisbon Story (Anglo 1946)
Black Narcissus (GFD 1947)
Frieda (GFD 1947)
Mr. Perrin and Mr. Traill (GFD 1948)
The Small Back Room [Hour of Glory] (BL 1949)
Diamond City (GFD 1949)
Gone to Earth [The Wild Heart] (BL 1950)
Cage of Gold (GFD 1950)
The Late Edwina Black [Obsessed] (IFD 1951)
Night Without Stars (GFD 1951)
The Golden Horde (Univ 1951)
Duel in the Jungle (ABP 1954)
The Black Shield of Falworth (Univ 1954)
Lilacs in the Spring [Let's Make Up] (Rep 1954)
Escape to Burma (RKO 1955)
The Sea Chase (WB 1955)
Pearl of the South Pacific (RKO 1955)
Lost [Tears for Simon] (RFD 1956)
Triangle on Safari [The Woman and the Hunter] (Kenya 1957)
I Accuse! (MGM 1958)
Son of Robin Hood (20th 1958)
Watusi (MGM 1959)
John Paul Jones (WB 1959)
Solomon and Sheba (UA 1959)
Beat Girl [Wild for Kicks] (Renown 1960)
The 300 Spartans (20th 1962)
The Webster Boy (RFI 1962)

FELMY, HANSJÖRG, b. 1931, Berlin
Der Stern von Afrika (W Ger 1957)
Haie und kleine Fische (W Ger 1957)
Das Herz von St. Pauli (W Ger 1957)
Der Greifer (W Ger 1958)
Herz ohne Gnade (W Ger 1958)
Wir Wunderkinder (W Ger 1958)
Der Maulkorb (W Ger 1958)
Unruhige Nacht (W Ger 1958)
Menschen im Netz (W Ger 1959)
Und ewig singen die Wälder (Aus 1959)
Buddenbrooks (W Ger 1959)
Ein Tag, der nie zu Ende geht (W Ger 1959)
Der Mann, der sich verkaufte (W Ger 1959)
An hehgen Wassern (W Ger-Swi 1960)
Die Botschafterin (W Ger 1960)
Schachnovelle (W Ger 1960)
Die zornigen jungen Männer (W Ger 1961)
Endstation 13 Sahara (W Ger 1962)
Die Ehe des Herrn Mississippi (W Ger-Swi 1961)
Die Flusspiraten vom Mississippi (W Ger 1962)
Der Henker von London (W Ger 1963)
Nebelmörder (W Ger 1964)
Das siebente Opfer (W Ger 1964)
Das Ungeheuer von London City (W Ger 1964)

An der Donau, wenn der Wein blüht (W Ger-Aus 1965)
Torn Curtain (Univ 1966)
Die tote aus der Themse (W Ger 1971)

FERNANDEL (Fernand-Joseph Désiré Contandin), b. May 8, 1903,
    Marseilles; d. Feb. 27, 1971
    Le Blanc et le noir (Fr 1930)
    Le Meilleure Bobonne (Fr 1931)
    La Veine d'Anatole (Fr 1931)
    Bric à Brac et Cie (Fr 1931)
    Paris-béguin (Fr 1931)
    On purge bébé (Fr 1931)
    Coeur de Lilas (Fr 1931)
    La Fine Combine (Fr 1931)
    Le Jugement de minuit (Fr 1932)
    Les Gâités de l'escadron (Fr 1932)
    La Porteuse de pain (Fr 1932)
    Le Rosier de Madame Husson (Fr 1932)
    L'Homme sans nou (Fr-Ger 1932)
    Lidoire (Fr 1932)
    Le Coq du régiment (Fr 1933)
    L'Ordonnance (Fr 1933)
    Ademai Aviateur (Fr 1934)
    D'Amour et d'eau fraîche (Fr 1934)
    La Garnison amoureux (Fr 1934)
    La Chéri de sa concierge (Fr 1934)
    Nuit de folies (Fr 1934)
    L'Hôtel du libre échange (Fr 1934)
    Angèle (Fr 1934)
    Les Bleus de la marine (Fr 1934)
    Le Train de 8h. 47 (Fr 1935)
    Le Cavalier Lafleur (Fr 1935)
    Ferdinand le noceur (Fr 1935)
    Jim le houlette (Fr 1935)
    Les Gâités de la finance (Fr 1935)
    Un de la légion (Fr 1936)
    Josette (Fr 1936)
    François Ier (Fr 1936)
    Les Dégourdis de la Orizième (Fr 1936)
    Les Rois du sport (Fr 1936)
    Un Carnet du bal [Christine] (Fr 1937)
    Ignace (Fr 1937)
    Regain (Fr 1937)
    Hercule (Fr 1937)
    Ernest le Rebelle (Fr 1937)
    La Schpountz (Fr 1938)
    Barnabé (Fr 1938)
    Tricoche et Cacolet (Fr 1938)
    Raphael le Tatoué (Fr 1938)
    Les Cinq Sous de lavarède (Fr 1938)
    Berlingot et Compagnie (Fr 1939)
    C'était moi (Fr 1939)
    Fric-Frac (Fr 1939)

Fernandel (center) with Heinz Rühmann (left) and Jean Carmet in
La Bourse et la vie (1965).

L'Héritier des mon désir (Fr-Ger 1939)
La Fille du puisatier (Fr 1940)
Monsieur Hector, l'acrobate (Fr 1940)
Un Chapeau de paille (Fr 1940)
La Nuit merveilleuse (Fr 1940)
L'Âge d'or (Fr 1940)
Les Petits Riens (Fr 1941)
Une Vie de chien (Fr 1941)
Le Club des soupirants (Fr 1941)
Ne le criez pas sur les toits (Fr 1942)
La Bonne Etoile (Fr 1942)
Simplet (Fr 1942)
Adrien (Fr 1943)
La Cavalcade des heures (Fr 1943)
Le Mystère Saint-Val (Fr 1944)
Naïs (Fr 1945)
Les Gueux au paradis (Fr 1945)
L'Aventure de Cabassou (Fr 1945)
Pétrus (Fr 1946)
Coeur-de-coq (Fr 1946)
Emile l'africain (Fr 1947)
Si ça peut vous faire plaisir (Fr 1948)
L'Armoire volante (Fr 1948)
On demande un assassin (Fr 1949)

L'Héroïque Monsieur Boniface (Fr 1950)
Botta e Risposta (It 1950)
Casimir (Fr 1950)
Tu m'as sauvé la vie (Fr 1950)
Topaze (Fr 1950)
Meutres (Fr 1950)
Uniformes et grandes manoeuvres (Fr 1950)
Boniface somnambule (Fr 1950)
L'Auberge rouge [The Red Inn] (Fr 1951)
La Table aux crévés [The Village Feud] (Fr 1951)
Adhémar; ou Le Jouet de la fatalité (Fr 1951)
Il piccolo mondo di Don Camillo (It-Fr 1951)
Coiffeurs par dames (Fr 1952)
Le Fruit défendu [Forbidden Fruit] (Fr 1952)
Le Boulanger de Valorgue [The Baker of Valorgue] (Fr-It 1952)
Le Retour de Don Camillo (Fr-It 1952)
Mam'zelle Nitouche [Oh No, Mam'zelle] (Fr-It 1953)
Carnaval (Fr 1953)
L'ennemi public no. 1 [Public Enemy No. 1] (Fr-It 1953)
Le Mouton a cinq pattes [The Sheep Has Five Legs] (Fr 1954)
Ali-Baba et les quarante voleurs [Ali Baba] (Fr 1954)
Le Printemps, l'automne et l'amour (Fr-It 1954)
La Grande Bagarre de Don Camillo (It 1955)
Don Juan (Sp 1955)
Le Coutourier de ces dames [Fernandel the Dressmaker] (Fr
  1956)
Around the World in 80 Days (UA 1956)
Quatres pas dans les nuages (Fr-It 1956)
Honoré de Marseille (Fr 1956)
L'Homme à l'imperméable [The Man in the Raincoat] (Fr-It 1956)
Le Chômeur de Clochmerle (Fr 1957)
Sénéchal le magnifique (Fr-It 1957)
A Paris tous les deux [Paris Holiday] (Fr-It 1957)
La Vie à deux (Fr 1958)
La Loi... c'est la loi (Fr-It 1958)
Le Grand Chef [The Big Chief] (Fr-It 1958)
Le Confident de ces dames (Fr 1959)
La Vache et le prisonnier [The Cow and I] (Fr 1959)
Crésus (Fr 1960)
Le Caïd (Fr 1960)
Cocagne (Fr-It 1960)
Le Jugement dernier [Il guidizio universale] (Fr-It 1961)
Dynamite Jack (Fr 1961)
L'assassin est dans l'annuaire (Fr 1961)
Cet imbécile de Rimoldi (Fr-It 1961)
Monseigneur Don Camillo (It-Fr 1961)
Avanti la musica (It-Fr 1962)
Le Diable et le Dix Commandements (Fr-It 1962)
Le Voyage à Biarritz (Fr-It 1962)
Blaque dans le coin (Fr 1963)
Le bon roi Dagobert (Fr-It 1963)
Le Complex de Philémon (Fr 1964)
Relaxe-toi chérie (Fr-It 1964)

L'Âge ingrat (Fr-It 1964)
La Cuisine au beurre (Fr-It 1964)
Il compagno Don Camillo (It-Fr 1965)
La Bourse et la vie [Money or Your Life] (Fr-W Ger-It 1966)
Le Voyage du père (Fr-It 1966)
L'Homme à la Buick (Fr 1967)

FERNANDES, NASCIMENTO (Manuel Fernandes do Nascimento), b.
    Nov. 6, 1886, Faro, Portugal; d. Aug. 15, 1955
Rapto duma actriz (Por 1907)
Os crimes do Diego Alves (Por 1909)
Vida nova (Por 1919)
Nascimento sapateiro (Por 1919)
Nascimento musico (Por 1919)
Nascimento detective (Por 1919)
Lisboa, crênica anedôtica (Por 1930)
Der weisse Dämon (Ger 1932)
O trevo de quatro folhas (Por 1936)
Anikibobó (Por 1942)
A vizinha do lado (Por 1945)

FERZETTI, GABRIELE (Pasquale Ferzetti), b. March 17, 1925,
    Rome
Via delle cinque lune (It 1942)
I miserabili (It 1947)
Fabiola (It 1947)
Guglielmo Tell [William Tell] (It 1948) [unreleased]
Vertigine d'amore (It 1948)
Barriera a settentrione (It 1949)
Benvenuto, reverendo! (It 1949)
Rondini in volo (It 1949)
Lo zappatore (It 1950)
Gli amanti di Ravello (It 1950)
I falsari (It 1950)
Core'ngrato (It 1951)
Tre storie proibite (It 1951)
Inganno (It 1952)
La provinciale (It 1952)
Puccini (It 1953)
Il sole negli occhi [Celestina] (It 1953)
Cento anni d'amore (It 1953)
Vestire gli ignudi (It 1953)
Vergine moderna (It 1954)
Casa Ricordi (It 1954)
Camilla (It 1954)
Le avventure di Giacomo Casanova (It 1954)
Le amiche (It 1955)
Adriana Lecouvreur (It 1955)
Un po' di cielo (It 1955)
Il prezzo della gloria (It 1956)
Donatella (It 1956)
Difendo il mio amore (It 1956)
Parola di ladro (It 1957)

Souvenir d'Italie (It 1957)
Nata di marzo (It 1958)
Racconti d'estate (It 1958)
Ballerina e Buon Dio (It 1958)
Storie d'amore proibite [Le Suret du chevalier d'Eon] (It-Fr 1959)
Le insaziabili [Tant d'amour perdu] (It-Fr 1959)
Tutti innamorati (It 1959)
Annibale (It 1959)
L'avventura (It 1960)
La lunga notte del '43 (It 1960)
Labbra rosse (It 1960)
Il carro armato dell'8 settembre (It 1960)
Femmine di lusso (It 1960)
La Croix des vivants (Fr 1961)
Rencontres (Fr 1961)
Jessica (It-USA 1962)
Le Crime ne fai pas [Il dilitto non paga] (Fr-It 1962)
Congo vivo (It 1962)
La monaca di Monza (It 1962)
Venus imperiale [Venere imperiale] (Fr-It 1962)
Mort, où est ta victoire? (Fr 1963)
I dongiovanni della Costa azzura (It 1963)
Un tentativo sentimentale (It 1963)
Il giorno più corto (It 1963)
Crucers de Verano (Sp 1963)
Finché dura la tempesta [Beta Som] (It 1964)
La calda vita (It 1964)
Desideri d'estate (It 1964)
Par un beau matin d'été [Rapina al sole] (Fr-It 1965)
Trois chambres à Manhattan (Fr 1965)
La Bibbia [The Bible] (20th 1966)
L'arcidiavolo [The Devil in Love] (It 1966)
Lo scippo (It 1966)
A ciascuno il suo (It 1967)
Escalation (It 1968)
Grazie zia (It 1968)
I protagonisti (It 1968)
C'erà una volta il West [Once Upon a Time in the West] (It 1968)
L'età del malessere (It 1968)
Meglio vedova [Better a Widow] (It 1968)
Roma come Chicago [Banditi a Roma] (It 1968)
Un diablo bajo la almohada [La Diable sous l'oveiller] (Sp-Fr-It 1969)
Un bellissimo novembre (It 1969)
L'amica (It 1969)
Gli intoccabili (It 1969)
On Her Majesty's Secret Service (UA 1969)
L'aveu (Fr 1969)
Sacco alla Ugina (It 1969)
Par un beau matin d'été [Rapina al sole/Secuestro bajo el sol] (Fr-It-Sp 1969)
Cuori solitari (It 1970)

Cannabis (Fr 1970)
Divorce (Br 1972)
Mendiants et orgrieteaux (Fr 1972)
Trois sans ascensuer (Fr-It 1972)
Basturi la mapa bianca (It 1973)
Proasso per direttissima (It 1974)
Appassionata (It 1974)
Doppia coppia con regina (It 1974)
Portiere di notte [The Night Porter] (It 1974)
Corruzione al palazzo di giustizia (It 1975)

FEUILLERE, EDWIGE (Edwige Caroline Cunati), b. Oct. 29, 1907,
      Vesoul, France
Le Cordon bleu (Fr 1931)
Le Perle (Fr 1931)
La Fine Combine (Fr 1931)
Topaze (Fr 1932)
Monsieur Albert (Fr 1932)
Une Petite Femme dans la train (Fr 1932)
Maquillage (Fr 1932)
Les Aventures du Roi Pausole (Fr 1933)
T'oi que j'adore (Fr 1933)
Matricule 33 (Fr-Ger 1933)
Ces messieurs de la santé (Fr 1934)
Le Miroir aux alouettes (Fr 1934)
L'Appel de la nuit (Fr 1934)
Lucrèce Borgia (Fr 1935)
Golgotha (Fr 1935)
Barcarolle (Ger 1935)
Stradivarius (Fr 1935)
La Route heureuse (Fr 1936)
Mister Flow (Fr 1936)
Marthe Richard (Fr 1937)
Feu (Fr 1937)
La Dame de Malacca (Fr 1937)
J'étais une aventurière (Fr 1938)
L'Emigrante (Fr 1939)
De Mayerling à Sarajevo (Fr 1939)
Sans landemain (Fr 1940)
Mam'zelle Bonaparte (Fr 1941)
La Duchesse de Langeais (Fr 1942)
L'Honourable Catherine (Fr 1942)
Lucrèce (Fr 1943)
La Part de l'ombre (Fr 1945)
Tant que je vivrai (Fr 1945)
L'Idiot (Fr 1946)
Il Suffit d'une fois (Fr 1946)
L'Aigle a deux têtes (Fr 1947)
Womanhater (GFD 1948)
Julie de Carneilhan (Fr 1949)
Olivia (Fr 1950)
Souvenirs perdus (Fr 1950)
Le Cap de l'Espérance (Fr 1951)

Adorable créatures (Fr 1952)
Le Blé en herbe (Fr-It 1953)
Les Fruits de l'été (Fr 1954)
Le Septième Commandement (Fr 1956)
Quand la femme s'en mêle (Fr-It-W Ger 1957)
En cas de malheur [Love Is My Profession] (Fr-It 1958)
La Vie à deux (Fr 1958)
La Princesse de Clèves (Fr 1960)
Les Amours célèbres (ep "Les Comédiennes") (Fr-It 1961)
Le Crime ne paie pas [Crime Does Not Pay] (Fr-It 1962)
Claire de terre (Fr 1970)

FIELDS, GRACIE (Gracie Stansfield), b. Jan. 9, 1898, Rochdale,
      Lancashire, England
Sally in Our Alley (Radio 1931)
Looking on the Bright Side (Radio 1932)
This Week of Grace (Radio 1933)
Love, Life and Laughter (ABFD 1934)
Sing As We Go (ABFD 1934)
Look Up and Laugh (ABFD 1935)
Queen of Hearts (ABFD 1936)
The Show Goes On (ABFD 1937)
We're Going to Be Rich (20th Br 1938)
Keep Smiling [Smiling Along] 20th Br 1938)
Shipyard Sally (20th Br 1939)
Molly and Me (20th 1945)
Madame Pimpernel [Paris Underground] (UA 1945)

FINCH, JON, b. 1942, London
The Horror of Frankenstein (MGM-EMI 1970)
The Vampire Lovers (MGM-EMI 1970)
Sunday, Bloody Sunday (UA 1971)
L'Affaire Martine Desclos (Fr 1972)
Macbeth (Col-Warner 1972)
Frenzy (Univ 1972)
Lady Caroline Lamb (GB-It 1972)
The Final Programme [Last Days of Man on Earth] (AIP Br
      1973)
Diagnosis: Murder (CIC 1975)

FINCH, PETER, b. Sept. 28, 1916, London, d. Jan. 14, 1977
Mr. Chedworth Steps Out (Aust 1938)
The Rudd Family Goes to Town (Aust 1938)
The Power and the Glory (Aust 1942)
The Rats of Tobruk (Aust 1944)
A Son Is Born (Aust 1946)
Eureka Stockade (GFD 1949)
Train of Events (GFD 1949)
The Wooden Horse (BL 1950)
The Miniver Story (MGM Br 1950)
The Story of Robin Hood and His Merrie Men (RKO 1952)
The Story of Gilbert and Sullivan [The Great Gilbert and Sullivan]
      (BL 1953)

The Heart of the Matter (BL 1953)
Father Brown [The Detective] (Col 1954)
Elephant Walk (Par 1954)
Make Me an Offer (BL 1954)
Passage Home (GFD 1955)
The Dark Avenger [The Warriors] (20th 1955)
Simon and Laura (RFD 1955)
Josephine and Men (BL 1955)
A Town Like Alice [Rape of Malaya] (RFD 1956)
The Battle of the River Plate [Pursuit of the Graf Spee] (RFD
    1956)
The Shiralee (MGM 1957)
Robbery Under Arms (RFD 1957)
Windom's Way (RFD 1957)
Operation Amsterdam (RFD 1959)
The Nun's Story (WB 1959)
Kidnapped (BV 1960)
The Trials of Oscar Wilde [The Man with the Green Carnation]
    (Eros 1960)
No Love for Johnnie (RFD 1961)
The Sins of Rachel Cade (WB 1961)
I Thank a Fool (MGM 1962)
In the Cool of the Day (MGM 1963)
Girl with Green Eyes (UA 1964)
First Man in the Moon (Col 1964)
The Pumpkin Eater (Col 1964)
The Flight of the Phoenix (20th 1965)
Judith (Par 1965)
10. 30 P. M. Summer (Loppert 1966)
Come Spy with Me (20th 1967) (unbilled cameo)
Far From the Madding Crowd (WPD 1967)
The Legend of Lylah Clare (MGM 1968)
The Red Tent [La tenda rossa] (It-USSR 1969)
Sunday, Bloody Sunday (UA 1971)
Lost Horizon (Col 1972)
Bequest to the Nation [The Nelson Affair] (CIC 1972)
England Made Me (Hemdale 1973)
Something to Hide (Avco Emb 1973) [made in 1971]
The Abdication (WB 1974)

FINNEY, ALBERT, b. May 9, 1936, Salford, Lancashire,
        England
The Entertainer (Bry 1960)
Saturday Night and Sunday Morning (Bry 1960)
Tom Jones (UA 1963)
Night Must Fall (MGM 1964)
Two for the Road (20th 1967)
Charlie Bubbles (RFD 1967)
Scrooge (20th 1970)
Gumshoe (Col 1971)
Picasso Summer (Br TV 1972) [begun as feature 1967, com-
    pleted 1969 but first seen on TV]
Murder on the Orient Express (Par 1974)

Albert Finney in Tom Jones (1963).

FIORE, MARIA (Jolanda Di Fiore), b. Oct. 1, 1935, Rome
    Due soldi di speranza (It 1952)
    Canzone di mezzo secolo (It 1952)
    Città canora (It 1952)
    Bellezze in motorscooter (It 1953)
    Canzone d'amore (It 1954)
    Carosello napoletano [Neopolitan Carousel] (It 1954)
    Cento serenate (It 1954)
    La domenica della buona gente (It 1954)
    Gran varietà (It 1954)
    L'oro di Napoli (It 1954)
    Scampolo [Les Femmes vienent le jeu] (It-Fr 1954)
    Tempi nostri [Quelques pas dans la vie] (It-Fr 1955)
    Bella non piangere (It 1955)
    Graziella (It 1955)
    I pappagalli (It 1955)
    Napoli terra d'amore (It 1956)
    Il principe dalla maschera rossa (It 1956)
    Quando tramonta il sole (It 1956)
    Malafemmina (It 1957)

Serenata a Maria (It 1957)
Terrore sulla citta [Terreur sur Rome] (It-Fr 1957)
Carosello di canzoni (It 1958)
È arrivata la parigina (It 1958)
Il romanzo di un giovane povero (It 1958)
Sorrisi e canzoni (It 1958)
Arriva la banda (It 1959)
La Garçonnière (It 1960)
Quanto, sei bella Roma [Que bella eres, Roma!] (It-Sp 1960)
Le gladiatrici (It 1963)
Se permettete, parliamo di donne [Let's Talk about Women]
    It 1964)
Prostituzione (It 1974)

FISCHER, OTTO WILHELM (O. W. Fischer), b. April 1, 1915,
    Klosterneuberg, Austria
Burgtheater (Aus 1936)
Anton der Letzte (Ger 1939)
Meine Tochter lebt in Wien (Ger 1940)
Der Meineidbauer (Ger 1941)
Wien 1910 (Ger 1942)

O. W. Fischer (center), Juliette Greco and William Sylvester in
Whirlpool (1959).

Sommerliebe (Ger 1942)
Die beiden Schwestern (Ger 1943)
Sieben Briefe (Ger 1944)
Glück unterwegs (Ger 1944)
Spiel (Ger 1944)
Shiva und die Galgenblume (Ger 1945)
Triumph der Liebe (Aus 1947)
Leuchtende Schatten (W Ger 1947)
Sag' endlich ja (W Ger 1947)
Das unsterbliche Antlitz (Aus 1947)
Das verlorene Rennen (Aus 1948)
Hin und her (Aus 1948)
Liebling der Welt [Rosender liebe/Hoheit darf nichtküssen]
   (Aus 1950)
Erzherzog Johanns grosse Liebe (Aus 1950)
Märchen vom Glück (Aus 1950)
Verträumte Tage (W Ger-Fr 1951)
Heidelberger Romanze (W Ger 1951)
A Tale of Five Women [A Tale of Five Cities] (GN 1951)
Das letzte Rezept (W Ger 1952)
Tausend röte Rosen blühn (W Ger 1952)
Ich hab' mich so an Dich gewöhnt [Geschiedenes Fräulein] (Aus
   1952)
Bis wir uns Wiedersehen (W Ger 1952)
Cuba Cabana (W Ger 1952)
Der träumende Mund (W Ger 1953)
Ein Herz spielt falsch (W Ger 1953)
Solange Du da bist (W Ger 1953)
Tagebuch einer Verliebten (W Ger 1953)
Eine Liebesgeschichte (W Ger 1954)
Napoléon (Fr 1954)
Bildnis einer Unbekannten (W Ger 1954)
Ludwig II (W Ger 1955)
Hanussen (W Ger 1955)
Ich suche Dich (W Ger 1956)
Mein Vater, der Schauspieler (W Ger 1956)
Herrscher ohne Krone (W Ger 1957)
Skandal in Ischl (Aus 1957)
El Hakim (W Ger 1957)
Don Vesuvio und das Haus der Strolche (W Ger-It 1958)
Das gab's mir einmal (W Ger 1958) [compilation of old clips]
...und nichts als die Wahrheit (W Ger 1958)
Helden (W Ger 1958)
Peter Voss, der Millionendieb (W Ger 1958)
Menschen im Hotel (W Ger-Fr 1959)
Und das am Montagmorgen (W Ger 1959)
Whirlpool (RFD 1959)
Abschied von den Wolken (W Ger 1959)
Peter Voss, der Held des Tages (W Ger 1959)
Scheidungsgrund Liebe (W Ger 1960)
Mit Himbeergeist geht alles besser (Aus 1960)
Das Riesenrad (W Ger 1961)
Es muss nicht immer Kaviar sein (W Ger 1961)

Diesmal muss es Kaviar sein (W Ger-Fr 1961)
Axel Munthe, der Arzt von San Michele (W Ger-It-Fr 1962)
Früstück in Doppelbett (W Ger 1963)
La reina de la noche (Sp 1963)
Das Geheimnis der schwarzen Witwe [Araña negra] (W Ger-Sp 1963)
Heisses Pflaster Casablanca (W Ger 1963)
Onkel Toms Hütte (W Ger-It 1965)
No hago la guerra...prefiero el amor [Non faccio la guerra, faccio l'amore] (It-Sp 1966)
El margués (Sp-Dan 1967)
Liebesvögel (W Ger-It 1969)
Das weite Land (Aus 1973)

FLICKENSCHILDT, ELISABETH, b. 1905, Hamburg-Blankenese, Germany
Grossreinemachen (Ger 1935)
Du kannst nicht treu sein (Ger 1936)
Der ahnungslose Engel (Ger 1936)
Streit um den Knaben Jo (Ger 1937)
Der zerbrochene Krug (Ger 1937)
Tango Notturno (Ger 1937)
Starke Herzen (Ger 1937)
Heiratsschwindler (Ger 1937)
Der Maulkorb (Ger 1938)
Jugend (Ger 1938)
Ein Mädchen geht an Land (Ger 1938)
Der Schritt vom Wege (Ger 1939)
Robert Koch (Ger 1939)
Die barmherzige Lüge (Ger 1939)
Die unheimlichen Wünsche (Ger 1939)
Der Fuchs von Glenarvon (Ger 1940)
Ohm Krüger (Ger 1941)
Treck, der Pandur (Ger 1941)
Der grösse Konig (Ger 1942)
Zwischen Himmel und Erde (Ger 1942)
Ewiger Rembrandt (Ger 1942)
Altes Herz wird wieder jung (Ger 1943)
Liebesgeschichten (Ger 1943)
Romanze in Moll (Ger 1943)
Die beiden Schwestern (Ger 1943)
Philharmoniker (Ger 1943)
Familie Buchholz (Ger 1944)
Neigungsehe (Ger 1944)
Seiner zeit zu meiner Zeit (Ger 1944)
Meine Herren Söhne (Ger 1945)
Der Mann, dem man den Namen stahl (Ger 1945)
Ein toller Tag (Ger 1945)
Shiva und die Galgenblume (Ger 1945)
Eine grosse Liebe (W Ger 1949)
Madonna in Ketten (W Ger 1949)
König für eine Nacht (W Ger 1950)
Pikanterie (W Ger 1951)

Toxi (W Ger 1952)
Der Tag vor der Hochzeit (W Ger 1952)
Hokuspokus (W Ger 1952)
Die Nacht ohne Moral (W Ger 1953)
Hochzeitsglocken (W Ger 1954)
Das ideale Brautpaar (W Ger 1954)
Rittmeister Wronski (W Ger 1954)
Die spanische Fliege (W Ger 1955)
Sohn ohne Heimat (W Ger 1955)
Herrscher ohne Krone (W Ger 1957)
Robinson soll nicht sterben (W Ger 1957)
Stefanie (W Ger 1958)
Auferstehung (W Ger 1958)
Wir Wunderkinder (W Ger 1958)
Labyrinth (W Ger 1958)
Agatha, lass das Morden sein (W Ger 1960)
Die Bande des Schreckens (W Ger 1960)
Brucke des Schicksals (W Ger 1960)
Faust (W Ger 1960)
Eheinstitut Aurora (W Ger 1962)
Frauenarzt Dr. Sibelius (W Ger 1962)
Das Gasthaus an der Themse (W Ger 1962)
Das schwarz-weiss-röte Himmelbett (W Ger 1962)
Ferien vom Ich (W Ger 1962)
Das indische Tuch (W Ger 1963)
Das grosse Liebesspiel (W Ger-Aus 1963)
DM Killer (Aus 1964)
Einer frisst den an deren [La mortevestita di dollari/Dog Eat
    Dog/When Strangers Meet] (W Ger-It 1964)
Lausbubengeschichten (W Ger 1964)
Das Phantom von Soho (W Ger 1964)
Un Milliard dans un billard [Diamantenbillard] (W Ger-Fr-It
    1965)
Tante Frieda--neue Lausbubengeschichten (W Ger 1965)
Onkel Filser--Allerneueste Lausbubengeschichten (W Ger 1966)
Der Lügner und die Nonne (Aus 1967)
Wenn Ludwig ins Manover zieht (W Ger 1967)
Dr. med. Fabian--Lachen ist die beste Medizin (W Ger 1969)
Ludwig auf FreiersFüssen (W Ger 1969)
Käpt'n Rauhbein aus St. Pauli (W Ger 1971)
Als Mutter streikte (W Ger 1974)
Undine 74 (Aus 1974)
Mitgift (W Ger 1975)

FORMBY, GEORGE, b. May 26, 1904, Wigan, Lancashire, England;
    d. March 22, 1961
    By the Shortest of Heads (LIFT 1915)
    Boots! Boots! (Butcher 1934)
    Off the Dole (Mancunian 1935)
    No Limit (ABFD 1935)
    Keep Your Seats Please (ABFD 1936)
    Feather Your Nest (ABFD 1937)
    Keep Fit (ABFD 1937)

I See Ice (ABFD 1938)
It's in the Air [George Takes the Air] (ABFD 1938)
Trouble Brewing (ABFD 1939)
Come On, George (ABFD 1939)
Spare a Copper (ABFD 1940)
Let George Do It (ABFD 1940)
Turned Out Nice Again (UA 1941)
South American George (Col Br 1941)
Much Too Shy (Col Br 1942)
Get Cracking (Col Br 1943)
Bell Bottom George (Col Br 1943
He Snoops to Conquer (Col Br 1944)
I Didn't Do It (Col Br 1945)
George in Civvy Street (Col Br 1946)

FORST, WILLI, b. March 7, 1903, Vienna
Der Wegweiser (Aus 1920)
Oh du lieber Augustin (Aus 1922)
Strandgut (Aus 1924)
Café Electric (Aus 1927)
Die Drei Niemandskinder (Ger 1927)
Die Elf Teufel (Ger 1927)
Amor auf Ski (Ger 1928)
Ein besserer Herr (Ger 1928)
Die blaue Maus (Ger 1928)
Liebfräumilch (Ger 1928)
Die lustigen Vagabunden (Ger 1928)
Unfug der Liebe (Ger 1928)
Fräulein Fahnrich (Ger 1929)
Die Frau, die jeder liebt, bist du! (Ger 1929)
Katherina Knie (Ger 1929)
Gefahren der Brautzeit (Ger 1929)
Der Sträfling aus Stambul (Ger 1929)
Die weissen Rosen von Ravensburg (Ger 1929)
Atlantik (Ger 1930)
Ein Tango für dich (Ger 1930)
Der Herr auf Bestellung (Ger 1930)
Das Lied ist Aus (Ger 1930)
Zwei Herzen im 3/4-Takt (Ger 1930)
Ein Burschenlied aus Heidelberg (Ger 1930)
Die lustigen Weiber von Wien (Ger 1931)
Der Raub der Mona Lisa (Ger 1931)
Peter Voss, der Millionendieb (Ger 1931)
So ein Madel vergisst man nicht (Ger 1932)
Der Prinz von Arkadien (Ger-Aus 1932)
Ein blonder Traum (Ger 1932)
Ihre Durchlaucht, die Verkäuferin (Ger 1932)
Brennendes Gehemnis (Ger 1933)
So endete eine Liebe (Ger 1934)
Ich kenn' dich nicht und liebe dich (Ger 1934)
Ich bin Sebastian Otto (Ger 1939)
Bel Ami (Ger 1939)
Operette (Ger 1940)

Wiener Blut (Ger 1942) (also director)
Wiener Madeln (Ger 1945) (also script, director)
Es geschehen noch Wunder (W Ger 1951) (also co-script, director)
Bei Dir war es immer so schön (W Ger 1954)
Ein Mann vergisst die Liebe (W Ger 1954)
Der Weg in die Vergangenheit (W Ger 1954)

FORSTER, RUDOLF, b. Oct. 30, 1884, Gröbming, Germany; d. Oct. 28, 1968
Fahrt ins Bläue (Ger 1919)
Das Geheimnis der Gladiatorenwerke (Ger 1920)
Glanz und Elend der Kurtisanen (Ger 1920)
Die Jagd nach der Wahrheit (Ger 1920)
Kurfürstendamm (Ger 1920)
Manolescus Memoiren (Ger 1920)
Der Schädel der Pharaonentochter (Ger 1920)
Zehn milliarden Volt (Ger 1920)
Die Abenteuer (Ger 1920)
Die röte Hexe (Ger 1921)
Frau Sünde (Ger 1922)
Das Licht um Mitternacht (Ger 1922)
Die Mäusefalle (Ger 1922)
Die Schuhe einer schönen Frau (Ger 1922)
Der stärkste Trieb (Ger 1922)
Adam und Eva (Ger 1923)
Fridericus Rex [Ein Königsschicksal] (Ger 1923)
Auferstehung (Ger 1923)
Das Erbe (Ger 1923)
Fröken Fob (Swe 1923)
Erdgeist (Ger 1923)
Die Marionetten der Fürstin (Ger 1923)
SOS (Ger 1923)
Der Insel der Tränen (Ger 1923)
Ssanin (Ger 1924)
Tragödie der Liebe (Ger 1924)
Horrido (Ger 1924)
Zur Chronik von Grieshuus (Ger 1924)
Sein grosser Fall (Ger 1926)
Fame (Ger 1926)
Die Hose (Ger 1927)
Pique Dame (Ger 1927)
Die Dreigroschenoper (Ger 1931)
Yorck (Ger 1931)
Ariane (Ger 1931)
Die Gräfin von Monte Christo (Ger 1932)
Der träumende Mund (Ger 1932)
Morgenrot (Ger 1933)
Hohe Schule das Geheimnis des Carlo Cavelli (Ger 1934)
Nur ein Komodiant (Ger 1935)
Die ganz grossen Torheiten (Ger 1935)
Wien 1910 (Ger 1942)
Ein Blick zurück (Ger 1944)

Am Vorabend [Ein Blick zuruck] (Ger 1944)
Der gebieterische Ruf (Ger 1944)
Fahrt ins Glück (Ger 1945)
Der Mann, der zweimal leben wollte (W Ger 1950)
Liebestraum [Die todlichen Traume] (W Ger 1951)
Unvergängliches Licht (W Ger 1951)
Im weissen Rössl (W Ger 1952)
Wiktoria und ihr Husar (W Ger 1954)
Rittmeister Wronski (W Ger 1954)
Eine Frau genügt nicht? (W Ger 1955)
Der letzte Mann (W Ger 1955)
Regine (W Ger 1956)
Spionage (Aus 1956)
Waldwinter (W Ger 1956)
Kaiserjäger (W Ger 1956)
Liane, das Mädchen aus dem Urwald (W Ger 1956)
Und führe uns nicht in Versuchung (W Ger 1957)
Skandal in Ischl (W Ger 1957)
Spielbankaffäre (W Ger 1957)
Die unentschuldigte Stunde (W Ger 1957)
Kleines Herz in grosser Nor (Aus 1958)
Der Rest ist Schweigen (W Ger 1958)
Die Halbzarte (Aus 1959)
Man musste nochmal zwazig sein (Aus 1959)
Lass mich am Sonntag night allein (W Ger 1959)
Der liebe Augustin (W Ger 1959)
Morgen wirst Du um mich weinen (W Ger 1959)
Das Glass Wasser (W Ger 1960)
Im Stahlnetz Des Dr. Mabuse (W Ger 1961)
Das Riesenrad (W Ger 1961)
Der Teufel spielte Balaleika (W Ger 1961)
Er kann's nicht lassen (W Ger 1962)
Lulu (W Ger 1962)
Der Henker von London (W Ger 1963)
Die Gruft mit dem Ratsel schloss (W Ger 1964)
Tonio Kröger (W Ger 1964)
Der Turm der verbotenen Liebe [La Tour de Nesle] (W Ger-It-
   Fr 1968)
Von Haut zu Haut (W Ger 1968)

FOX, JAMES, b. May 19, 1939, London
As William Fox:
   The Miniver Story (MGM Br 1950)
   The Magnet (GFD 1950)
As James Fox:
   The Loneliness of the Long Distance Runner (Bry 1960)
   Tamahine (WPD 1963)
   The Servant (Elstree 1963)
   Those Magnificent Men in Their Flying Machines; or, How I
      Flew from London to Paris in 25 Hrs and 11 Minutes (20th
      1965)
   King Rat (Col 1965)
   The Chase (Col 1965)

Thoroughly Modern Millie (Univ 1967)
Duffy (Col 1968)
Arabella (It 1969)
Isadora [The Loves of Isadora] (RFD 1969)
Performance (WB 1970)

FRANCEN, VICTOR, b. Aug. 6, 1888, Tirlemont, Belgium
Crespuscule d'épouvante (Fr 1922)
La Niege sur les pas (Fr 1923)
Le Doute (Fr 1924)
La Fin du monde (Fr 1930)
Après l'amour (Fr 1931)
L'Aiglon (Fr 1931)
Les Ailes brisées (Fr 1932)
Mélo (Fr 1933)
L'Aventurier (Fr 1934)
Ariane, jeune fille russe (Fr 1934)
Le Voleur (Fr 1934)
Le Chemineau (Fr 1935)
Veille d'armes (Fr 1935)
La Porte du large (Fr 1936)
Nuits de feu (Fr 1936)
L'Appel de la vie (Fr 1936)
Le Roi (Fr 1936)
Tamara le complaisante (Fr 1937)
Feu (Fr 1937)
Forfaiture (Fr 1937)
J'accuse! (Fr 1938)
La Vierge folle (Fr 1938)
Double Crime sur la Ligne Maginot (Fr 1938)
Entente Cordiale (Fr 1939)
La Fin du jour (Fr 1939)
Hold Back the Dawn (Par 1941)
The Tuttles of Tahiti (RKO 1942)
Ten Gentlemen from West Point (20th 1942)
Tales of Manhattan (20th 1942)
The Desert Song (WB 1943)
Madame Curie (MGM 1943)
Mission to Moscow (WB 1943)
Hollywood Canteen (WB 1944)
The Conspirators (WB 1944)
The Mask of Dimitrios (WB 1944)
Passage to Marseille (WB 1944)
In Our Time (WB 1944)
Confidential Agent (WB 1945)
San Antonio (WB 1945)
Devotion (WB 1946) [made in 1943]
The Beast with Five Fingers (WB 1946)
Night and Day (WB 1946)
The Beginning or the End (MGM 1947)
La Revoltée (It 1947)
To the Victor (WB 1948)
La Nuit s'acheve (Fr 1949)

The Adventures of Captain Fabian (Rep 1951)
Hell and High Water (20th 1954)
A Farewell to Arms (20th 1957)
Der Tiger von Eschnapur (W Ger-Fr-It 1959)
Fanny (WB 1961)
Top Crack (Br 1966)

FRANCHI, FRANCO, b. Aug. 5, 1922, Palermo, Italy
With Ciccio Ingrassia--see latter entry
Without Ciccio Ingrassia:
    Il figlioccio del padrino (It 1973)
    Il gatto di Brooklin, aspirante detective (It 1973)
    Ku-Fu dalla Sicilia con furore (It 1973)
    Il sergente Rompiglioni (It 1973)
    Ultimo tango a Zagarol (It 1973)
    Paolo il freddo (It 1974)
    Piedino il questurino (It 1974)
    L'eredità dello zio buonanima (It 1975)
    Il giustiziere di mezzogiorno (It 1975)
    Il sergenti Rompiglioni diventa... caperale (It 1975)

FRANK, HORST, b. May 28, 1929, Lübeck, Germany
Haie und kleine Fische (W Ger 1957)
Der Stern von Afrika (W Ger 1957)
Der Greifer (W Ger 1958)
Blitzmädels an die Front (W Ger 1958)
Das Mädchen Rosemarie (W Ger 1958)
Das Mädchen vom Moorhof [The Girl of the Moors] (W Ger 1958)
Meine 99 Bräute (W Ger 1958)
Schwarze Nylons, heisse Nächte [Indecent] (W Ger 1958)
Die Nackte und der Satan [The Head] (W Ger 1958)
Hunde wollt ihr ewig leben (W Ger 1959)
Abschied von den Wolken (W Ger 1959)
Bumerang [Cry Double Cross] (W Ger 1960)
La Chatte sort ses griffes (Fr 1960)
Fabrik der Offiziere (W Ger 1960)
Le Bois des amants (Fr 1960)
Kein Engel ist so rein (W Ger 1960)
Die zornigen jungen Männer (W Ger 1960)
Treibjagd auf ein Leben (W Ger 1960)
Unser Haus in Kamerun (W Ger 1961)
Cariño mio (Sp 1961)
Hass ohne Gnade (W Ger 1962)
Zwischen Shanghai und St. Pauli [I rinnegati di Capitan Kidd]
    (W Ger-It 1962)
Heissen Hafen Hongkong (W Ger-It 1962)
Die Flusspiraten vom Mississippi (W Ger-It-Fr 1962)
Les Tontons flingueurs [Mein Onkel, der Gangster] (Fr-W Ger
    1963)
Der schwarze Panther von Ratana (W Ger-It 1963)
Tu ne tueras point (Fr 1963)
Die weisse Spinne (W Ger 1963)
Die Diamantenhölle am Meking (W Ger-It 1964)

Das Geheimnis der chinesischen Nelke [F. B. I. contre l'oeillet
    chinois] (W Ger-It-Fr 1964)
Die Goldsucher von Arkansas [Les Chercheurs d'or de l'Arkan-
    sas] (W. Ger-It-Fr 1964)
Die letzten Zwei von Rio [Le pistole no discutono/Las pistolas
    no discuten] (W Ger-It-Sp 1964)
Die Tote von Beverly Hills [The Corpse of Beverly Hills] (W
    Ger 1964)
Weisse Fracht für Hongkong [Le Mystère de la jongue rouge]
    (W Ger-It-Fr 1964)
Der Fluch des schwarzen Rubins [Espionnage à Bangkok] (W Ger-
    Fr-It 1965)
Die letzten Drei der Albatros [L'Aventure vient de Manille/La
    morte vieneda Manila] (W Ger-Fr-It 1965)
Die schwarzen Adler von Santa Fe [Les Aigles noirs de Santa
    Fe] (W Ger-Fr-It 1965)
Das Geheimnis der drei Dschunken [A-009 Missione Hong Kong/
    Red Dragon] (W Ger-It 1965)
Der Spion, der in die Hölle ging [Corrida pour unespion] (W Ger-
    It-Fr 1965)
Fünf vor zwölf in Caracas (W Ger-Fr 1965)
I Deal in Danger (20th 1966)
Fur eine Handvöll Diamanten (W Ger-Fr 1966)
Um null Uhr schnappt die Falle zu (W Ger 1966)
Fünf gegen Casablanca [Les Chiens verts du desert/Attentato ai
    tre grandi] (W Ger-It-Fr 1966)
Geheimnisse in goldenen Nylons [Deux Billets pour Mexico/
    Segreti che scottano/Dead Run] (W Ger-It-Fr 1966)
Die letzte Kompanie [Eine Handroll Helden/Per un pugno di eroi]
    (W Ger-It 1967)
Die Rache des Dr. Fu Man Chu [The Vengeance of Fu Manchu]
    (W Ger-GB 1967)
Django--Die Totengräber warten schon [Quella sporea storia del
    West/Johnny Hamlet] (W Ger-It 1968)
Django--Ein Sarg voll Blut (W Ger-It 1968)
Marquis de Sade [Justine ovvero le disavventure della virtù]
    (W Ger-It-Fr 1968)
Le Paria [Jaque mate] (Fr-Sp 1968)
Così dolce... così perverse (W Ger-It 1968)
Catherine--Ein Leben für die Liebe [Catherine, il suffit d'un
    amour] (W Ger-Fr-It 1968)
Die Engel von St. Pauli (W Ger 1970)
Die neunschwanzige Katze [Il gatto a nove code/The Cat o' Nine
    Tails] (W Ger-It-Fr 1971)
Fluchtweg St. Pauli [Heisse spur St. Pauli] (W Ger 1971)
Der scharfe Heinrich--die bumsfidelen Abenteuer einer zimzen
    Ehe (W Ger 1971)
Und Jimmy ging zum Regenbogen (W Ger 1971)
L'occhio nel labirinto (It-W Ger 1972)
L'etrusco uccide ancora [The Dead Are Alive] (It 1972)
Il grande duello [Le grand duel] (It-W Ger-Fr 1972)
Das Amulett des Todes (W Ger 1975)
Anch Mimosen wollen blühen (W Ger 1975)
Der flüsternde Tod (W Ger 1975)

Pamela Franklin and Fred in a BBC television series, Quick Before They Catch Us.

FRANKLIN, PAMELA, b. Feb. 4, 1949, Japan
    The Innocents (20th 1961)
    The Lion (20th 1962)
    The Horse Without a Head (BV 1963)
    A Tiger Walks (BV 1963)
    The Third Secret (20th 1964)
    Flipper and the Pirates [Flipper's New Adventure] (MGM 1964)
    See How They Run (NBC-TV 1964)
    The Nanny (WPD 1965)
    Our Mother's House (MGM 1967)
    The Night of the Following Day (Univ 1968)
    The Prime of Miss Jean Brodie (20th 1969)
    Sinful Davey (UA 1969)
    David Copperfield (20th 1969)
    And Soon the Darkness (WPD 1970)
    The Legend of Hell House (Fox-Rank 1973)
    Ace Eli and Rodger of the Sky (20th 1973) [shot ca. 1971]
    The Letters (ABC-TV 1973)
    Satan's School for Girls (ABC-TV 1973)
    Crossfire (ABC-TV 1975)

FRENCH, EDWIGE, b. Dec. 24, 1948, Bône, Algeria
Toutes folles de lui (Fr 1967)
Frau Wirtin hat auch einen Grafen [Susanna ed i suoi dolci vizi alla corte del re] (W Ger-It 1968)
Il figlio di Aquila Nera (It 1968)
Samoa, regina della giungla (It 1968)
Alle Kätzchen naschen gern (W Ger 1969)
Die tolldreisten Geschichten des Honoré de Balzac [Komm, liebe Maid, und mache...] (W Ger 1969)
Frau Wirtin hat auch eine Nichte (W Ger-Aus-It 1969)
Der Mann mit dem goldenen Pinsel [L'uomo dal pennello d'oro] (W Ger-It 1969)
Madame und ihre Nichte (W Ger 1969)
Die nackte Bovary [I peccati di Madame Bovary] (W Ger-It 1969)
Top Sensation [The Seducers] (It 1969)
Testa o croce (It 1969)
L'Année de la contestation (Fr 1969)
Cinque bambole per la luna d'agosto (It 1970)
Satiricosissimo (It 1970)
Swinging Young Seductress, Part III (It 1970)
Le Mans, scorciatoia per l'inferno (It 1970)
Lo strano vizio della signora Ward [Uno strano fiore con cinque gocce di sangue/La perversa Señora Ward] (It-Sp 1970)
Deserto di fuoco (It 1971)
Le calde notti di Don Giovanni [Le avventure e gli amori di Don Giovanni/Los amores de Don Juan] (It-Sp 1971)
Perche quelle strane gocce di sangue sul corpo di Jennifer? (It 1972)
Il tuo vizio è una stanza chiusa e solo io ne ho le chiavi (It 1972)
La bella Antonia, prima monaca e poi dimonia (It 1972)
Quando le donne si chiamavano madonne (It 1972)
Quel gran pezzo dell'Ubalda tutta nuda e tuta calda [Due bellissime donzelle] (It 1972)
Tutti i colori del buio [Todas los colores de la oscurided] (It-Sp 1972)
Anna, quel particolare piacere (It 1973)
Giovannona coscialunga disonorata con onore (It 1973)
La vedova inconsolabile ringrazia quanti la consolarono (It 1973)
Fuori uno, sotto un altro, arriva "il passatore" (It-Sp 1973)
Il suo nome faceva tremare... Interpol in allarme [Dio, sei proprio un padreterno/L'Homme aux nerfs d'acier] (It-Fr 1973)
La signora gioca bene a scopa? (It 1974)
Innocenza e turbamento (It 1974)
Grazie, nonna (It 1975)
La moglie vergine (It 1975)
Il vizio di famiglia (It 1975)
40 gradi all'ombra del lenzuolo (It 1975)

FRESNAY, PIERRE (Pierre Laudenbach), b. April 4, 1897, Paris; d. Jan. 9, 1975
France d'abord (Fr 1915)
Baillonnée (Fr 1921)

L'Esson (Fr 1921)
Les Mystères de Paris (Fr 1922)
Le Diamant noir (Fr 1923)
Rocambole (Fr 1924)
La Vierge folle (Fr 1928)
Ça aussi c'est Paris (Fr 1931)
Marius (Fr 1931)
Fanny (Fr 1932)
La Dame aux camélias (Fr 1934)
Aime de clown (Fr 1934)
Le Roman d'un jeune homme pauvre (Fr 1935)
Königsmark (Ger 1935)
The Man Who Knew Too Much (Gaumont 1935)
Sous les yeux d'Occident (Fr 1936)
César (Fr 1936)
Mademoiselle Docteur (Fr 1937)
La Grande Illusion (Fr 1937)
La Bataille silencieuse (Fr 1937)
La Puritan (Fr 1937)
Chéri-bibi (Fr 1938)
Alerte en Méditerranée (Fr 1938)
Adrienne Lecouvreur (Fr 1938)
Trois Valses (Fr 1938)
Le Duel (Fr 1939)
La Charrette fantôme (Fr 1939)
Le Dernier des six (Fr 1941)
Le Briseur de chaîne Mamouret (Fr 1941)
Le Journal tombe à cinq heures (Fr 1942)
L'Assassin habite au 21 (Fr 1942)
La Main du diable (Fr 1942)
Le Voyageur sans bagages (Fr 1943)
Le Corbeau (Fr 1943)
Je suis avec toi (Fr 1943)
L'Escalier sans fin (Fr 1943)
La Fille du diable (Fr 1945)
Le Visiteur (Fr 1946)
Monsieur Vincent (Fr 1947)
Les Condamnés (Fr 1948)
Barry (Fr 1949)
Au grand balcon (Fr 1949)
La Valse de Paris (Fr 1949)
Vient de paraître (Fr 1949)
Dieu a besoin des hommes [Isle of Sinners] (Fr 1950)
Un Grand Patron (Fr 1951)
Monsieur Fabre (Fr 1951)
Le Voyage en Amérique (Fr 1951)
Il est minuit Docteur Schweitzer (Fr 1952)
La Défroqué (Fr 1954)
Les Evadés (Fr 1955)
Les Aristocrates (Fr 1955)
L'Homme aux clefs d'or (Fr 1956)
Les Fanatiques [A Bomb for the Dictator] (Fr 1957)
Les Oeufs de l'autruche [The Ostrich Has Two Eggs] (Fr 1957)

Et ta soeur? (Fr 1958)
Tant d'amour perdu (Fr-It 1958)
Les Affreux (Fr 1959)
La Millième Fenêtre (Fr 1959)
Les Vieux de le vieille [The Old Guard] (Fr-It 1960)

FREY, SAMI (Samuel Frei), b. Oct. 13, 1937, Paris
Pardonnez nos offenses [Forgive Us Our Tresspasses] (Fr 1956)
Jeux dangereux (Fr-It 1958)
La Nuit des traqués [Men Without Morals] (Fr-Bel 1959)
Le Travail, c'est la liberté (Fr 1959)

Sami Frey

La Vérité [The Truth] (Fr 1960)
Cleo de 5 à 7 [Cleo from 5 to 7] (Fr-It 1961)
Gioventu di notte [Jeunesse de Nuit] (It-Fr 1961)
Les Sept Péchés Capitaux [Seven Capital Sins] (ep "L'Orgueil")
    (Fr-It 1961)
Il disordine [Le désordre] (It-Fr 1962)
Thérèse Desqueyroux (Fr 1962)
L'Appartement des filles (Fr-It-W Ger 1963)
El juego de la verdad [Le Couple Interdit] (Sp-Fr 1963)
Bande à part (Fr 1964)
La Constanza de la ragione [Avec amour et avec rage] (It-Fr
    1964)
Une Balle au coeur (Fr 1965)
Angélique et le roy (Fr-W Ger-It 1965)
Qui êtes-vous, Polly Magoo? (Fr 1966)
Manon 70 (Fr-It-W Ger 1968)

L'Ecume des jours [The Froth of Time] (Fr 1968)
Mister Freedom (Fr 1968)
La Chasse royale (Fr-Czech 1969)
"M" comme Mathieu (Fr 1970)
Les Mariés de l'an deux [The Scoundrel] (Fr-It-Rum 1970)
Rak (Fr 1971)
Paulina 1880 (Fr 1972)
Le Journal d'un Suicide (Fr 1972)
César et Rosalie [Cesar and Rosalie] (Fr 1972)
Sweet Movie (Fr 1975)
Le Jardin qui bascule (Fr 1975)

FRITSCH, WILLY, b. Jan. 27, 1899, Kattowitz, Germany; d. July
    13, 1973
Razzia (Ger 1921)
Die Fahrt ins Glück (Ger 1923)
Seine Frau, die Unbekannte (Ger 1923)
Guillotine (Ger 1924)
Mutter und Kind (Ger 1924)
Blitzzug der Liebe (Ger 1925)
Der Farmer aus Texas (Ger 1925)
Das Mädchen mit der Protektion (Ger 1925)
Der Tänzer meiner Frau (Ger 1925)
Ein Walzertraum (Ger 1925)
Die Boxerbraut (Ger 1926)
Die Fahrt ins Abenteuer (Ger 1926)
Die keusche Susanne (Ger 1926)
Der Prinz und die Tänzerin (Ger 1926)
Die Frau im Schrank (Ger 1927)
Der letzte Walzer (Ger 1927)
Schuldig (Ger 1927)
Die selige Exzellenz (Ger 1927)
Die sieben Töchter der Frau Gyurkovics [Flickorna Gyurkovics]
    (Ger-Swe 1926)
Die Carmen von St. Pauli (Ger 1927)
Ihr dunkler Punkt (Ger 1928)
Spione (Ger 1928)
Der Tanzstudent (Ger 1928)
Ungarische Rhapsodie (Ger 1928)
Die Frau im Mond (Ger 1929)
Melodie des Herzens (Ger 1929)
Die drei von der Tankstelle (Ger 1930)
Liebeswalzer (Ger 1930)
Einbrecher (Ger 1930)
Hokuspokus (Ger 1930)
Ronny (Ger 1931)
Im Geheimdienst (Ger 1931)
Ihre Hoheit befielt (Ger 1931)
Der Kongress tanzt (Ger 1931)
Ich bei Tag und du bei Nacht (Ger 1932)
Ein blonder Traum (Ger 1932)
Frechdachs (Ger 1932)

Ein toller Einfall (Ger 1932)
Saison in Kairo (Ger 1933)
Des jungen Dessauers grosse Liebe (Ger 1933)
Walzerkrieg (Ger 1933)
Prinzessin Turandot (Ger 1934)
Die Töchter Ihrer Exzellenz (Ger 1934)
Die Insel (Ger 1934)
Schwarze Rosen (Ger 1935)
Amphitryon [Aus den Wolken kommt das glück] (Ger 1935)
Glückskinder (Ger 1935)
Boccaccio (Ger 1936)
Streit um den Knaben Jo (Ger 1937)
Menschen ohne Vaterland (Ger 1937)
Gewitterflug zu Claudia (Ger 1937)
Sieben Ohrfeigen (Ger 1937)
Preussische Liebesgeschichte (Ger 1938)
Am seidenen Faden (Ger 1938)
Zwischen den Eltern (Ger 1938)
Das Mädchen von gestern Nacht (Ger 1938)
Frau am Steuer (Ger 1939)
Die Geliebte (Ger 1939)
Die keusche Geliebte (Ger 1940)
Die unvollkommene Liebe (Ger 1940)
Das leichte Mädchen (Ger 1940)
Leichte Muse (Ger 1941)
Dreimal Hochzeit (Ger 1941)
Frauen sind doch bessere Diplomaten (Ger 1941)
Wiener Blut (Ger 1942)
Anschlag auf Baku (Ger 1942)
Geliebte Welt (Ger 1942)
Die Gattin (Ger 1943)
Der kleine Grenzverkehr (Ger 1943)
Liebesgeschichten (Ger 1943)
Junge Adler (Ger 1944)
Die tolle Susanne (Ger 1945)
Das leben geht weiter (Ger 1945) [unfinished]
Die Fledermaus (Ger 1945)
Finale (W Ger 1948)
Film ohne Titel (W Ger 1948)
Hallo--Sie haben Ihre Frau vergessen (W Ger 1949)
Derby (W Ger 1949)
Kätchen für alles (W Ger 1949)
Zwölf Herzen für Charly (W Ger 1949)
König für eine Nacht (W Ger 1949)
Die wunderschöne Galathee (W Ger 1950)
Herrliche Zeiten (W Ger 1950)
Schatten der Nacht (W Ger 1950)
Mädchen mit Beziehungen (W Ger 1950)
Schön muss man sein (W Ger 1951)
Die verschleierte Maja (W Ger 1951)
Grün ist die Heide (W Ger 1951)
Die Dubarry (W Ger 1951)
Mikosch rückt ein (W Ger 1952)

Ferien vom Ich (W Ger 1952)
Am Brunnen von dem Tore (W Ger 1952)
Von Liebe reden wir später (W Ger 1953)
Damenwahl (W Ger 1953)
Wenn der weisse Flieder wieder blüht (W Ger 1953)
Ungarische Rhapsodie (W Ger 1954)
Weg in die Vergangeheit (Aus 1954)
Maxie (Aus 1954)
Stern von Rio (W Ger 1955)
Drei Tage Mittelarrest (W Ger 1955)
Der fröhliche Wanderer (W Ger 1955)
Liebe ist ja nur ein Märchen [Amour, tango et mandolme] (W Ger-Fr 1955)
Die drei van der Tankstelle [Le chemin du paradis] (W Ger-Fr 1955)
Solange noch die Rosen blühn (W Ger 1956)
Das Donkosakenlied (W Ger 1956)
Schwarzwaldmelodie (W Ger 1956)
Wo die alten Wälder rauschen (W Ger 1956)
Der schräge Otto (W Ger 1957)
Die Beine von Dolores (W Ger 1957)
Zwei Herzen im Mai (W Ger 1958)
Schwarzwälder Kirsch (W Ger 1958)
Mit Eva fing die Sünde an (W Ger 1958)
Liebling der Götter (W Ger 1959)
Hubertusjagd (W Ger 1959)
Was macht Papa denn in Italien? (W Ger 1961)
Das hab' ich von Papar gelernt (W Ger-Hun 1964)
Verliebt in Heidelberg (W Ger 1964)

FROBE, GERT, b. Dec. 25, 1912, Planitz, Germany
Berliner Ballade [The Berliner] (W Ger 1948)
Nach Regen scheint Sonne (W Ger 1949)
Der Tag vor der Hochzeit (W Ger 1952)
Salto mortale (W Ger 1953)
Die vertagte Hochzeitsnacht (W Ger 1953)
Ein Herz Spielt Falsch (W Ger 1953)
Arlette erobert Paris (W Ger 1953)
Man on a Tightrope (20th 1953)
Hochzeit auf Reisen (W Ger 1953)
Die Kleine Stadt will schlafen gehn [Sieben Sünder] (W Ger 1954)
Les Héros sont fatigués [Heroes and Sinners] (Fr 1954)
Morgengrauen (W Ger 1954)
Das Kreuz am Jagersteig (W Ger 1954)
Mannequins für Rio (W Ger 1954)
Das zweite Leben [Double Destiny] (W Ger-Fr 1954)
Ewiger Walzer [The Eternal Waltz] (W Ger 1954)
Von Himmel gefallen [Special Delivery] (W Ger 1955)
Der dunkle Stern (W Ger 1955)
Ich Weiss, wofür ich lebe (W Ger 1955)
Das Forsthaus in Tirol (W Ger 1955)
Ein Mädchen aus Flandern (W Ger 1956)

Ein Herz schlägt für Erika (W Ger 1956)
Waldwinter (W Ger 1956)
Typhon sur Nagasaki [Wasure-enu bojo] (Fr-Jap 1956)
Celui qui doit mourir [Le Christ Recrucifie/He Who Must Die]
   (Fr 1956)
Robinson soll nicht sterben (W Ger 1957)
Charmants Garçons (Fr 1957)
Echec au porteur (Fr 1957)
El Hakim (W Ger 1957)
Der tolle Bomberg (W Ger 1957)
Das Herz von St. Pauli (W Ger 1957)
Nasser Adpahlt (W Ger 1958)
Es geschah am hellichten Tag [It Happened in Broad Daylight]
   (W Ger-Swi 1958)
It Happened in Broad Daylight (GB 1958) [Eng lang version of
   preceding film]
Grabenplatz 17 (W Ger 1958)
Das Mädchen Rosemarie [Rosemary/The Girl Rosemarie] (W
   Ger 1958)
Der Pauker (W Ger 1958)
Das Mädchen mit den Katzenaugen (W Ger 1958)
Il Batteliere del Volga [Prisoner of the Volga/The Boatmen]
   It 1958)
Nick Knattertons Abenteuer (W Ger 1959)
Menschen im Hotel (W Ger 1959)
Jons und Erdme (W Ger 1959)
Und ewig singen die Wälder [Vengeance in Timber Valley] (Aus
   1959)
Alt-Heidelberg (W Ger 1959)
Am Tag, als der Regen Kam (W Ger 1959)
Der Schatz vo in Töplitzsa [Schüss im Morgengrauen] (W Ger
   1959)
Bis dass das Geld euch scheidet (W Ger 1960)
Das kunstseidene Mädchen [La Grande Vie/La gran via] (W Ger-
   Fr-It 1960)
Der Gauner und der Liebe Gott [Le Bois des amants/Il bosco
   degli amanti] (W Ger-Fr-It 1960)
Soldatensender Calais (W Ger 1960)
12 Stunden Angst [Douze Heures d'horloge] (W Ger-Fr 1960)
Die tausend Augen des Dr. Mabuse [It diabolico dottor Mabuse/
   Le Diabolique Docteur Mabuse/The Thousand Eyes of Dr.
   Mabuse] (W Ger-It-Fr 1960)
Auch tote zahlen den vollen Preis (W Ger 1960)
Im Stahlnetz des Dr. Mabuse [F.B.I. contro Dottor Mabuse/Le
   Retour du docteur Mabuse/The Return of Dr. Mabuse] (W Ger-
   It-Fr 1961)
Es muss nicht immer Kaviar sein (W Ger 1961)
Der grüne Bogenschütze (W Ger 1961)
Via Mala (W Ger 1961)
Mein Mann, das Wirtschaftswunder (W Ger 1961)
Auf Wiedersehen [Auf wiedersehen in Arizona] (W Ger 1962)
Die Rote [La rossa/The Redhead] (W Ger-It 1962)

Heute Kundigt mir mein Mann (W Ger 1962)
Das Testament des Dr. Mabuse [The Testament of Dr. Mabuse]
  (W Ger 1962)
The Longest Day (20th 1962)
Die Dreigroschenoper (W Ger 1963)
Peau de banane [Lelle di banana/Buccia di banana/Banana Peel]
  (Fr-It 1963)
Erotikon--Karussell der Leidenschaften (W Ger 1963)
Der Mörder [Le Meurtrier/Enough Rope] (W Ger-Fr-It 1963)
Tonio Kröger (W Ger 1964)
Cent Mille Dollars au soleil [Cento mille dollari al sole/Greed
  in the Sun] (Fr-It 1964)
Goldfinger (UA 1964)
A High Wind in Jamaica (20th 1965)
Those Magnificent Men in Their Flying Machines, or How I Flew
  from London to Paris in 25 Hours and 11 Minutes (20th 1965)
Eschappement libre [Escape libre/Scappamento aperto/Backfire]
  (Fr-Sp-It 1965)
Das Liebeskarussell [Who Wants to Sleep] (ep "Angela") (Aus
  1965)
Du Rififi à Paname [The Upper Hand/Rififi internazionale] (Fr-
  W Ger-It 1966)
Paris, brûle-t-il? [Is Paris Burning?] (Par 1966)
Ganovenchre (W Ger 1966)
Triple Cross [La Fantastique Histoire vrai d'Eddie Chapman]
  (GB-Fr 1966)
Jules Verne's Rocket to the Moon [Those Fantastic Flying Fools/
  Blast-Off] (AIP 1967)
J'ai tué Raspoutine [I Killed Rasputin] (Fr 1967)
Caroline Cherie (Fr 1967)
Chitty Chitty Bang Bang (UA 1968)
Monte Carlo or Bust! [Quei temerari sulle loro pazze, scate-
  nate, scalcinate carricole/Those Daring Young Men in Their
  Jaunty Jalopies] (Par 1969)
"$" [The Heist] (Col 1971)
Ludwig [Ludwig II] (W Ger-It-Fr 1972)
Der Räuber Hotzenplotz (W Ger 1974)
Les Nuits rouges (Fr 1974)
And Then There Were None [Epoi non remase nessuno] (EMI
  1974)
Les Magiciens (Fr-It-Tunisian 1975)
Mein Onkel Theodor [Oder wie man viel Geld in Schlat verdient]
  (W Ger 1975)

FUCHSBERGER, JOACHIM, b. 1927, Stuttgart, Germany
  08/15 I (W Ger 1954)
  Wenn ich einmal der Herrgott wär' (W Ger 1954)
  Das Lied von Kaprun (W Ger 1955)
  08/15 II (W Ger 1955)
  Der letzte Mann (W Ger 1955)
  08/15 in der Heimat (W Ger 1956)
  Symphonie in Gold (W Ger 1956)
  Lumpazivagabundus (W Ger 1956)

Joachim Fuchsberger in The Face of Fu Manchu (1965).

Wenn Poldi ins Manöver zieht (W Ger 1956)
Vater macht Karriere (W Ger-Aus 1957)
Eva küsst nur Direktoren (W Ger 1957)
Keine Zeit für schwache Stunden (Aus 1958)
Kleine Mann--ganz gross (W Ger 1958)
Die Zwillinge vom Zillertal (W Ger 1958)
Die grünen Teufel von Monte Cassino (W Ger 1958)
Liebe kann wie Gift sein (W Ger 1958)
U 47--Kapitänleutnant Prien (W Ger 1958)
Mein Schatz ist aus Tirol (W Ger 1958)
Das Mädchen mit den Katzenaugen (W Ger 1958)
Die feuerröte Baronesse (W Ger 1959)
Zwischen Glück und Krone (W Ger 1959)
Der Frosch mit der Maske [Froen med Masken] (W Ger-Dan 1959)
Mein Schatz, komm mit ans blaue Meer (W Ger 1959)
Die Bande des Schreckens (W Ger 1960)

Endstation "Röte Laterne" (W Ger 1960)
Die toten Augen von London [Dead Eyes of London] (W Ger 1960)
Die zornigen jungen Männer (W Ger 1960)
Das Geheimnis der gelben Narzissen (W Ger 1961)
Die seltsame Gräfin (W Ger 1961)
Auf Wiedersehen (W Ger 1962)
Das Gasthaus an der Themse (W Ger 1962)
Teppich des Grauens [Il terrore di notte/Terror en la noche]
    (W Ger-It-Sp 1962)
Mystery Submarine (Britannia 1963)
Der Fluch der gelben Schlange (W Ger 1963)
Der schwarze Abt (W Ger 1963)
Die weisse Spinne (W Ger 1963)
Der Hexer (W Ger 1964)
Zimmer 13 (W Ger 1964)
Hotel der toten Gäste [El extraño caso de Lucy Cornell] (W Ger-
    Sp 1965)
The Face of Fu Manchu (WPD 1965)
Der letzte Mohikaner (W Ger 1965)
Bel Ami 2000; oder Wie verführt man einen Playboy? [100
    ragazze per un playboy/How to Seduce a Playboy] (Aus-It
    1966)
5000 Dollar für den Kopf von Jonny R [La balada de Johnny
    Ringo] (W Ger-Sp 1966)
Ich habe sie gut gekannt [Io la conoscevo bene] (W Ger-It-Fr 1966)
Lange Beiner, lange Finger (W Ger 1966)
Siebzehn Jahr, blondes Haar [La battaglia dei Mods/The Battle
    of the Mods] (W Ger-It 1966)
Feuer frei auf Frankie [Per 50.000 maledetti dollari/Misión en
    Ginebra] (W Ger-It-Sp 1967)
Der Mönch mit der Peitsche (W Ger 1967)
Commandos [Himmel Fahrts Kommando] (It-W Ger 1968)
Im Banne des Unheimlichen (W Ger 1968)
The Unnatural (It 1969)
Kashba (W Ger 1969)
Schreie in der Nacht (W Ger 1969)
Sieben Tage Frist (W Ger 1969)
Cosa avete fatto a Solanzi (It 1971)
Ein Käfer gibt Vollgas (W Ger-Swi 1972)
Das Geheimnis der grünen Stecknadel (W Ger 1972)
Das fliegende Klassenzimmer (W Ger 1973)
Das Mädchen from Hongkong [Une Chinoise aux nerfs d'acier]
    (W Ger-Fr 1973)

FYFFE, WILL, b. 1885, Dundee, Scotland; d. Dec. 14, 1947
Elstree Calling (Wardour 1930)
Happy (Wardour 1934)
Rolling Home (AP & D 1935)
King of Hearts* [Little Gel] (Butcher 1936)
Debt of Honour (GFD 1936)
Love in Exile (GFD 1936)
Men of Yesterday (AP & D 1936)
Annie Laurie (Butcher 1936)

Well Done, Henry (Butcher 1937)
Spring Handicap (ABPC 1937)
Cotton Queen* [Crying Out Loud] (BIED 1937)
Said O'Reilly to McNab [Sez O'Reilly to McNab] (GFD 1937)
Owd Bob [To the Victor] (GFD 1938)
The Mind of Mr Reeder [The Mysterious Mr. Reeder] (GN 1939)
Rulers of the Sea (Par 1939)
The Missing People (GN 1939)
They Came by Night (20th 1940)
For Freedom (GFD 1940)
Neutral Port (GFD 1940)
The Prime Minister (WB Br 1941)
Heaven Is Round the Corner (Anglo 1944)
Give Me the Stars (Anglo 1944)
The Brothers (GFD 1947)

Jean Gabin

GABIN, JEAN (Jean-Alexis Moncorgé), b. May 17, 1904, Paris; d. Nov. 15, 1976
    Chacun sa chance (Fr 1931)
    Coeur de lilas (Fr 1931)
    Paris béguin (Fr 1931)
    Méphisto (Fr 1931)
    Tout ça ne vaut pas l'amour (Fr 1931)
    Les Gaîtés de l'escadron (Fr 1932)
    La Belle Marinière (Fr 1932)

Gloria (Fr 1932)
La Foule hurle (Fr 1933) [Fr version of The Crowd Roars]
L'Etoile de Valencia (Fr 1933)
Adieu les beaux jours (Fr 1933)
Le tunnel [Tunnel] (Ger 1933) [Fr version of Der Tunnel]
Du haut en bas (Fr 1933)
Zouzou (Fr 1934)
Maria Chapdeleine (Fr 1934)
Au bout du monde (Fr 1934)
Golgotha (Fr 1935)
La Bandera (Fr 1935)
Variétés (Fr 1935)
La Belle Equipe (Fr 1936)
Les Bas-fonds (Fr 1936)
Pépé-le-Moko (Fr 1936)
La Grande Illusion [Grand Illusion] (Fr 1937)
Le Messager (Fr 1937)
Gueule d'amour (Fr 1937)
Quai des brumes (Fr 1938)
La Bête humaine (Fr 1938)
Le Recif de corail (Fr 1939)
Le Jour se lève [The End of the Day] (Fr 1939)
Remorques (Fr 1939)
Moontide (20th 1942)
The Imposter/Strange Confession (Univ 1943)
Martin Roumagnac [The Room Upstairs] (Fr 1946)
Miroir (Fr 1947)
Au-delà des grilles [Le mura di Malapaga] (Fr-It 1948)
La Marié du port (Fr 1949)
Pour l'amour du ciel [E più facile che un cammello...] (Fr-It
    1950)
Victor (Fr 1951)
Le Plaisir (Fr 1951)
La Nuit est mon royaume (Fr 1951)
La Vérité sur Bébé Donge [The Truth of Our Marriage] (Fr
    1951)
Fille dangereuse [BuFere] (Fr-It 1952)
La Minute de vérité [The Moment of Truth] (Fr-It 1952)
Leur Dernière Nuit (Fr 1953)
La Vierge du Rhin [Rhine Virgin] (Fr 1953)
Touchez pas au grisbi [Honour Among Thieves] (Fr 1954)
L'Air de Paris (Fr-It 1954)
French Can-Can (Fr-It 1954)
Le Port du désir (Fr 1954)
Razzia sur la chnouf [Chnouf] (Fr 1954)
Napoléon (Fr 1954)
Chiens perdus sans collier (Fr-It 1955)
Voici le temps des assassin [Deadlier Than the Male] (Fr 1955)
Gas-oil (Fr 1955)
Des gens sans importance (Fr 1955)
Le Cas du Docteur Laurent (Fr 1956)
Le Sang à la tête (Fr 1956)
Le Traversée de Paris [A Pig Across Paris] (Fr-It 1956)

Crime et châtiment [Crime and Punishment] (Fr 1956)
Le Rouge est mis [Speaking of Murder] (Fr 1957)
Le Désordre et la nuit (Fr-It 1957)
Maigret tend un piège [Maigret Sets a Trap] (Fr-It 1957)
Les Misérables (Fr-It-E Ger 1957)
En cas de malheur [Love Is My Profession] (Fr-It 1958)
Archimède le clochard (Fr 1958)
Les Grandes Familles (Fr 1958)
Maigret et l'affaire Saint Fiacre (Fr-It 1959)
Rue des Prairies (Fr-It 1959)
Le Baron de l'écluse (Fr-It 1960)
Les Vieux de la vieille (Fr 1960)
Le Président (Fr-It 1961)
Le Cave se rebiffe (Fr-It 1961)
Un Singe en hiver (Fr 1962)
Le Gentleman d'Epsom (Fr-It 1962)
Maigret voit rouge [Maigret Sees Red] (Fr-It 1963)
Mélodie en sous-sol [The Big Snatch] (Fr-It 1963)
Monsieur (Fr-W Ger-It 1964)
L'Âge ingrat (Fr 1964)
Le Tonnerre de Dieu (Fr-W Ger-It 1965)
Du Rififi à Paname [Rififi in Paris] (Fr-It-W Ger 1965)
Le Jardinier d'Argenteuil (Fr-W Ger 1966)
Le Soleil des voyous [Action Man] (Fr-It 1967)
La Pacha [Showdown] (Fr-It 1968)
Le Tatoué (Fr-It-W Ger 1968)
La Horse (Fr-It-W Ger 1969)
Le Clan des Siciliens (Fr 1969)
The Sicilian Clan (20th 1969) [Eng lang version of Le Clan des
    Siciliens]
Le Petit Navire (Fr 1969)
Sous le signe du taureau (Fr 1969)
Le Patriarche (Fr 1970)
Le Chat (Fr-It 1970)
Le Drapeau noir flotte sur la marmite (Fr 1971)
L'Affaire Dominici (Fr 1973)
Deux Hommes dans la ville (Fr-It 1973)
Verdict (Fr-It 1974)

GARCIN, HENRI, b. April 11, 1929, Antwerp
Mademoiselle et son gang (Fr 1957)
Le Grand Bluff (Fr 1957)
Arsène Lupin, contre Arsène Lupin (Fr 1962)
Les Amoureux du France (Fr 1963)
Mata Hari, Agent H 21 (Fr 1964)
Moi et les hommes de 40 ans (Fr 1964)
La Vie de château (Fr 1965)
La Bonne Occase (Fr 1965)
Le Judoka agent secret (Fr 1966)
Fleur d'Oseille (Fr 1967)
Les Gauloises bleues (Fr 1968)
Détruire, dit-elle (Fr 1969)
La Nuit bulgare (Fr 1969)

Henri Garcin

Un Conde (Fr 1970)
Quelqu'un derrière la porte (Fr 1971)
La Cavale (Fr 1971)
Pic et Pic et Colegram (Fr 1971)
Un Cave (Fr 1971)
Kill! [Kill Kill Kill] (Fr-Sp 1972)
Le Mouton Enragé (Fr 1973)
Ursule et Grelu (Fr 1973)
Verdict (Fr-It 1974)
Les Guichets du Louvre (Fr 1974)
Dupont Lajoie (Fr 1974)
Catherine et Cie (Fr 1975)

GASSMAN, VITTORIO, b. Sept. 1, 1922, Genoa
Preludio d'amore (It 1946)
Daniele Cortis (It 1946)
La figlia del capitano (It 1947)
Le avventure di Pinocchio (It 1947)
L'ebreo errante (It 1947)
Il cavaliere misterioso (It 1949)
Riso amaro [Bitter Rice] (It 1949)
Il lupo della Sila (It 1949)
Una voce nel tuo cuore (It 1949)
Ho sognato il paradiso (It 1949)
Lo sparviero del Nilo (It 1949)
I fuorilegge (It 1950)
Il leone di Amalfi (It 1950)
Il tradimento (It 1951)

La corona negra (Sp 1951)
Anna (It 1951)
Il sogno di Zorro (It 1951)
La tratta delle bianche (It 1952)
Cry of the Hunted (MGM 1953)
The Glass Wall (Col 1953)
Sombrero (MGM 1953)
Rhapsody (MGM 1954)
Mambo (Par 1955)
La donna più bella del mondo (It 1955)
War and Peace (Par 1956)
Difendo il mio amore (It 1956)
Kean (It 1956)
Giovanni dalle bande nere (It 1956)
La ragazza del palio (It 1957)
I soliti ignoti (It 1957)
La tempesta [The Tempest] (It-USA 1958)
The Miracle (WB 1959)
Le sorprese dell'amore (It 1959)
La grande guerra (It 1959)
Audace colpo dei soliti ignoti (It 1959)
La cambiale (It 1959)
Il mattatore [The Matadore] (It 1959)
Crimen (It 1959)
Fantasmi a Roma [Ghosts of Rome] (It 1961)

Vittorio Gassman (right) and Adolfo Celi in L'arcangelo (1969).

Barabba [Barabbas] (It 1961)
Una vita difficile (It 1961)
Il giudizio universale (It 1961)
I briganti italiani (It 1961)
Anima nera (It 1962)
La marcia su Roma (It 1962)
Il sorpasso (It 1962)
L'amore difficile (ep "L'avaro") (It 1962)
La smania addosso (It 1963)
Il successo (It 1963)
I mostri (It 1963)
Frenesia dell'estate (It 1964)
Se permettete, parliamo di donne (It 1964)
Il gaucho (It 1964)
La congiuntura (It 1965)
Slalom (It 1965)
La guerra segreta [Guerre secrete/The Dirty Game] (It-Fr
    1965)
Una vergine per il principe (It 1965)
L'arcidiavolo [Il diavolo innamorato/The Devil in Love] (It 1965)
L'armata Brancaleone (It 1966)
Le piacevoli notti (It 1966)
Questi fantasmi (It 1967)
Lo scatenato (It 1967)
Woman Times Seven (Emb 1967)
Il tigre [The Tiger and the Pussycat] (It 1967)
Il profeta (It 1968)
La pecora nera (It 1968)
L'alibi (It 1968)
Dove vai tutta nuda? (It 1969)
L'arcangelo (It 1969)
Una an 13 (It 1969)
Contestazione generale (It 1969)
Il divozzio (It 1970)
Scipione, detta anche "l'Africano" (It 1970)
Brancaleone (It 1971)
In nome del popolo italiano (It 1972)
Senza famiglie, nullatenenti, cercano affeto (It 1972)
L'udienza (It 1972)
Che c'entriamo noi con la rivoluzione? (It 1972)
La Tosca (It 1972)
C'eravamo tanto amati (It 1974)
Profumo di doma (It 1974)
A mezzamotte va la ronda del pracere (It 1975)
Telefoni bianchi (It 1975)
Come una rosa al naso (It 1975)

GASTONI, LISA ("Jane Fate"), b. July 28, 1935, Alassio, Italy
You Know What Sailors Are (GFD 1954)
The Runaway Bus (Eros 1954)
They Who Dare (BL 1954)
Beautiful Stranger [Twist of Fate] (Br 1954)
Doctor in the House (GFD 1954)

Dance Little Lady (Renown 1955)
Man of the Moment (RFD 1955)
Josephine and Men (BL 1955)
Three Men in a Boat (IFD 1956)
Face in the Night [Menace in the Night] (GN 1957)
The Baby and the Battleship (BL 1957)
Man from Tangier [Thunder over Tangier] (Butcher's 1957)
The Strange Awakening (AA 1958)
Blue Murder at St. Trinian's (BL 1958)
Family Doctor [RX Murder] (Templar 1958)
The Truth about Women (BL 1958)
Intent to Kill (Zonic 1959)
Visa to Canton [Passport to China] (Col Br 1960)
The Breaking Point [The Great Armored Car Swindle] (Butcher's
   1961)
Le avventure di Mary Read (It 1961)
Duello nella Sila (It 1962)
Le roi du village (Fr-It 1962)
Tharus, figlio di Attila (It 1962)
Eva (It 1962)
Diciottenni al sole (It 1962)
Gidget Goes to Rome (Col 1963)
Rogopag (ep "Il pollo ruspante") (It 1963)
I piombi di Venezia (It 1963)
Il mito (It 1963)
I quattro moschettieri (It 1963)
Il monaco di Monza (It 1963)
I maniaci (It 1963)
Il vendicatore mascherato (It 1964)
L'ultimo gladiatore (It 1964)
Crimine a due (It 1965)
Gli invincibili tre (It 1965)
Le sette vipere (It 1965)
I tre centurioni (It 1965)
I criminali della galassia (It 1966)
I diafanoidi vengono da Marte (It 1966)
Le notti della violenza (It 1966)
L'uomo che ride (It 1966)
Svegliati e uccidi (It-Fr 1966)
Grazie, zia (It 1968)
I sette fratelli cervi (It 1968)
La pecora nera (It 1968)
L'amica (It 1969)
Invasione (It 1970)
Maddalena (It 1972)
La seduzione (It 1973)
Amore amaro (It 1974)
Mussolini ultimo atte (It 1974)

GEESON, JUDY, b. Sept. 10, 1948, England
   To Sir, with Love (Col 1966)
   Berserk [Circus of Blood] (Col 1967)
   Here We Go Round the Mulberry Bush (UA 1967)

Prudence and the Pill (20th 1968)
Hammerhead (Col 1968)
Two Gentlemen Sharing (AIP 1969) [unreleased in GB]
Three Into Two Won't Go (RFD 1969)
Goodbye Gemini (CIRO 1970)
The Executioner (Col 1970)
10 Rillington Place (Col 1970)
Doomwatch (Tigon 1972)
Fear in the Night (MGM-EMI 1972)
Una Vela para el Diablo [A Candle for the Devil] (Tigon 1973)
    [GB release in Jan. 1975]
Percy's Progress (EMI 1974)
Brannigan (UA 1975)
Diagnosis: Murder (CIC 1975)

GELIN, DANIEL, b. May 19, 1921, Angers (Brittany), France
Premier Rendezvous (Fr 1941)
Les Cadets de l'ocean (Fr 1942)
Les Petites du zuai aux fleurs (Fr 1943)
La Tentation de Barbizon (Fr 1945)
Un Ami viendra ce soir (Fr 1945)
La Nuit de Sybille (Fr 1946)
Martin Roumagnac [The Room Upstairs] (Fr 1946)
La Femme en rouge (Fr 1946)
Miroir (Fr 1947)
Le Mannequin assassiné (Fr 1947)
Le Paradis des pilotes perdus (Fr 1948)
Rendez-vous de Juillet (Fr 1948)
La Ronde [Circle of Love] (Fr 1950)
Dieu à Besoin des hommes [Isle of Sinners] (Fr 1950)
Edouard et Caroline (Fr 1951)
Les Mains sales (Fr 1951)
Une Histoire d'amour (Sp-Fr 1951)
Le Plaisir (Fr 1951)
Adorable Créatures (Fr 1952)
La Minute de vérité [The Moment of Truth] (Fr-It 1952)
La Maison du silence (It-Fr 1952)
Les Dents longues (Fr 1952)
La Neige était sale (Fr 1952)
Rue de l'Estrapade [Françoise Steps Out] (Fr 1953)
Sang et lumières (Sp-Fr 1953)
L'Esclave (Fr-It 1953)
Si Versailles m'était conté (Fr 1953)
L'Affaire Maurizius [On Trial] (Fr-It 1953)
Rumeur publique (Fr-It 1953)
Les Amants du Tage [Lovers of Lisbon] (Fr 1954)
Napoléon (Fr 1954)
Les Gaîtés de l'escadron (Fr-It 1954)
La Belle Romaine (Fr-It 1954)
The Man Who Knew Too Much (Par 1956)
Je reviendrai à Kandara (Fr 1956)
En effeuillant la Marguerite (Fr 1956)
Bonsoir Paris...bonjour l'amour (Fr-W Ger 1956)

Daniel Gelin

Mort en fraude [Fugitive in Saigon] (Fr 1956)
Retour de Manivelle [There's Always a Price Tag] (Fr 1957)
Trois Jours à vivre (Fr 1957)
Charmants Garçons (Fr 1957)
La Fille de Hambourg (Fr 1958)
Suivez-moi jeune homme (Fr 1958)
Ce corps tant désiré [Way of the Wicked] (Fr 1958)
Julie la rousse (Fr 1959)
Le Testament d'Orphée (Fr 1960)
Les Trois Etc...du Colonel (Fr 1960)
Cartagine in Fiamme [Carthage in Flames] (It-Fr 1960)
Austerlitz (Fr-It-Liech-Yug 1960)
La Morte Saison des amours [The Season for Love] (Fr 1960)
La Proie pour l'ombre (Fr 1960)
Réveille-toi Chérie (Fr 1960)
Les Petits Matins [Girl on the Road] (Fr 1961)
Règlements de Compte (Fr 1962)

Climats [Climates of Love] (Fr 1962)
Les Egarements (Fr 1962)
Vacances portugaises (Fr 1963)
Three Girls in Paris (Dan 1963)
La Bonne Soupe (Fr-It 1964)
El Nino y el Muro (Sp-Mex 1964)
L'Heure de la vérité (Fr 1964)
Die Zeugin aus der Hölle (W Ger-Yug 1965)
Paris-brûle-t-il? [Is Paris Burning?] (Fr 1966)
La Ligne de démarcation (Fr 1966)
A belles dents (Fr-It 1966)
Les Sultans (Fr 1966)
Zwei Girls vom roten Stern (W Ger-Fr-Aus 1966)
Soleil noir (Fr-It 1966)
Avec Claude Monet (Fr 1966) [narrator]
Le Mois le plus beau (Fr 1968)
La Trêve (Fr 1969)
Slogan (Fr 1969)
Détruie, dit-elle [Destroy She Says] (Fr 1969)
Christa [Swedish Fly Girls] (USA-Den 1970)
Le Souffle au coeur [Dearest Love] (Fr-It-W Ger 1971)

GEMMA, GIULIANO (Montgomery Wood), b. Sept. 2, 1938,
    Rome
Ben-Hur (MGM 1959)
I Titani (It 1961)
Il gattopardo [Le Guepard/The Leopard] (It-Fr 1962)
Shéhérazade (Fr-It-Sp 1962)
Maciste, l'eroei più grande del mondo (It 1963)

Giuliano Gemma [Montgomery Wood]

Il pianeta degli uomini spenti (It 1963)
Angélique, Marquise des Anges (Fr 1964)
La rivolta dei pretoriani (It 1964)
I due gladiatori (It 1965)
Un pistola per Ringo [Un Pistolel pour Ringo] (It-Fr 1965)
Merveilleuse Angélique (Fr 1965)
Ercole contre i figli del sole [Hercule contre les fils du dieu
    soleil] (It-Fr 1965)
Il ritorno di Ringo (It 1965)
Un dollaro buccato (It 1965)
Adios gringo (It 1965)
Erik, il vichingo (It 1965)
La ragazzola (It 1965)
Kiss Kiss Bang Bang (It 1966)
Arizona Colt (It 1966)
I lunghi giorni della vendetta (It 1966)
Per pochi dollari ancora (It-Fr 1966)
Wanted (It 1967)
I giorni dell'ira (It 1967)
E per tetto un cielo di stelle (It 1967)
I Gatti [I bastardi/Le Batard] (It-Fr 1968)
Un estate in quattro [Violenza al sole] (It 1969)
Vivi o preferibilmente morti (It 1969)
Il prezzo del potere [Texas] (It 1969)
Quando le donne avevano la coda (It 1970)
L'arciere di fuoco (It 1970)
Corbari (It 1970)
La betia (It 1970)
Amico stammi lontano almeno un palmo (It 1971)
L'amante dell'Orsa Maggiore (It 1971)
Un uomo da rispettare (It 1972)
Il maschio ruspante (It 1972)
Anche gli angeli mangiano fagioli (It 1973)
Troppo rischio per un uomo solo (It 1973)
Delitto d'amore (It 1974)
Il bianco, il giallo, il nero (It 1974)
Anche gli angeli tirano di destro (It 1974)
Africa Express (It 1975)

GEORGE, HEINRICH, b. 1893, Stettin, Germany; d. Sept. 26, 1946
    Kean (Ger 1921)
    Lady Hamilton (Ger 1921)
    Der Roman der Christine von Herre (Ger 1921)
    Das fränkische Lied (Ger 1922)
    Lukrezia Borgia (Ger 1922)
    Erdgeist (Ger 1922)
    Die Sonne von St. Moritz (Ger 1923)
    Steuerlos (Ger 1923)
    Soll und Haben (Ger 1924)
    Zwischen Morgen und Morgen (Ger 1924)
    Metropolis (Ger 1925)
    Das Panzergewolbe (Ger 1926)
    Überflüssige Menschen (Ger-Rus 1926)

Die versunkene Flotte [Die Schlacht am Skagerak] (Ger 1926)
Bigamie (Ger 1927)
Die Ausgestossenen (Ger 1927)
Die Leibeigenen (Ger 1927)
Das Meer (Ger 1927)
Orientexpress (Ger 1927)
Die Dame mit der Maske (Ger 1928)
Kinder der Strasse (Ger 1928)
Das letzte Fort (Ger 1928)
Das letzte Souper [Der schuss in der grossen Oper] (Ger 1928)
Der Mann mit dem Laubfrosch [Verbrechen] (Ger 1928)
Rutschbahn [Schicksalskämpfe einer Sechzehn jährigen] (Ger 1928)
Song (Ger 1928)
Manolescu [Der König der Hochstapler] (Ger 1929)
Sprengbagger 1010 (Ger 1929)
Der Sträfling aus Stambul [Die zwei Frauen des Thomas Zezi]
    (Ger 1929)
Der Andere (Ger 1930)
Dreyfus (Ger 1930)
Menschen im Käfig (Ger 1930) [Ger version of Cape Forlorn]
Der Mann, der den Mord Begin [Nächte am Bosporus] (Ger 1930)
Wir Schalten um auf Hollywood (Ger 1931) [Ger version of Holly-
    wood Revue of 1929]
Berlin - Alexanderplatz (Ger 1931)
Goethe lebt! (Ger 1932)
Reifende Jugend (Ger 1933)
Das Meer ruft (Ger 1933)
Schleppzug M 17 (Ger 1933)
Hitlerjunge Quex (Ger 1935)
Stützen der Gesellschaft (Ger 1935)
Das Mädchen Johanna (Ger 1935)
Die grosse und die kleine Welt (Ger 1935)
Stjenka Rasin (Ger 1936)
Wenn der Hahn kräht (Ger 1936)
Hermine und die sieben Aufrechten (Ger 1936)
Nacht der Verwandlung [Demaskierung] (Ger 1936)
Ball im Metropol (Ger 1937)
Der Biberpelz (Ger 1937)
Unternehmen Michael (Ger 1937)
Ein Volksfeind (Ger 1937)
Versprich mir nichts (Ger 1937)
Frau Sylvelin (Ger 1937)
Heimat (Ger 1938)
Das unsterbliche Herz (Ger 1938)
Sensationsplozess Casilla (Ger 1939)
Der Postmeister (Ger 1940)
Friedrich Schiller [Der Triumph eines Gemes] (Ger 1940)
Jud Süss (Ger 1940)
Pedro soll hangen (Ger 1941)
Der grosse Schatten (Ger 1942)
Wien 1910 (Ger 1942)
Schicksal (Ger 1942)
Hochzeit auf Bärenhof (Ger 1942)

Andreas Schlüter (Ger 1942)
Der Verteidiger hat das Wort (Ger 1944)
Die Degenhardts (Ger 1944)
Dr. phil. Döderlein (Ger 1944) [uncompleted]
Kolberg (Ger 1945)
Das leben geht weiter (Ger 1945)
Frau über Bord [Kabine 1927] [uncompleted--released in 1952 in
  a modified, newly-directed version under the title Das
  Mädchen Juanita]

GEORGE, SUSAN, b. July 26, 1950, Surbiton (Surrey), England
Cup Fever (CFF 1965)
Davy Jones' Locker (CFF 1966)
The Sorcerors (Tigon 1967)
Up the Junction (Par 1967)
Billion Dollar Brain (UA 1967)

Susan George

The Strange Affair (Par 1968)
All Neat in Black Stockings (AA 1968)
The Looking Glass War (Col 1969)
Twinky [Lola] (RFD 1969)
Spring and Port Wine (WPD 1970)
Eyewitness (MGM-EMI 1970)
Die Screaming, Marianne (London Screen 1970)
Fright (BL 1971)
Straw Dogs (Cin 1971)
J & S [Jed & Sonny] (It 1973) [unreleased]
Dr. Jekyll and Mr. Hyde (NBC-TV 1973)

Dirty Mary, Crazy Larry (20th 1974)
Mandingo (Par 1975)
Out of Season (EMI 1975)

GEORGES-PICOT, OLGA, b. Jan. 6, 1944, China
Je t'aime, je t'aime (Fr 1968)
Adieu, l'ami [So Long, Pal] (Fr-It 1968)
Un Corps, une nuit (Fr-It 1968)
Summit (Fr-It 1968)
Catherine: Il suffit d'un amour (Fr-W Ger-It 1968)
Connecting Rooms (London Screen 1969)
The Man Who Haunted Himself (WPD 1970)
La Révélation [Sex Is Beautiful] (Fr 1971)
La Cavale (Fr 1971)
Feminin, Feminin (Fr-Bel 1972)
Deplacements progressifs du plaisir (Fr 1973)
Les Mesaventures d'un lit trop accueillant (Fr 1973)

GHIONE, EMILIO, b. 1879, Torino, Italy; d. Jan. 7, 1930
San Francisco [Il Poverello di Assisi] (It 1911)
Il pellegrino (It 1912)
Idillio tragico (It 1912)
Lagrime e sorrisi (It 1912)
Il pappagello della zia Berta (It 1912)
L'anima del demi-monde (It 1913)
La maestrina (It 1913)
Tramonto (It 1913)
L'arma dei vigliacchi (It 1913)
In faccio al destino (It 1913)
Terra promessa (It 1913)
La Gloria (It 1913)
L'arrivista (It 1913)
L'ultima carta (It 1913)
La cricca dorata (It 1913)
Idolo infranto (It 1913)
Histoire d'un pierrot (Fr-It 1914)
L'amazzone mascherata (It 1914)
Nelly la gigolette (It 1914)
Anime buie (It 1915)
La banda delle cifre (It 1915)
Ciceruacchio (It 1915)
Guglielmo Oberdan (It 1915)
Il naufragatore (It 1915)
Tresa (It 1915)
La sposa della morte (It 1915)
Don Pietro Caruso (It 1916)
La rosa di Granata (It 1916)
Za la mort (It 1916)
L'imboscata (It 1916)
Tormento gentile (It 1916)
Ananke (It 1916)
Un dramma ignorato (It 1916)
Il numero 121 (It 1917)

L'ultima impresa (It 1917)
Il triangolo giallo (It 1917)
I Topi Grigi (It 1918)
Nel gorgo (It 1918)
Dollari e fraks (It 1919)
L'ultima livrea (It 1920)
Un frak ed un apache (It 1920)
Za la Mort (It 1921)
Il quadrante d'oro (It 1921)
Ultimissime di notte (It 1922)
I quattro tramonti (It 1922)
Il sogno di Za la Vie (It 1921)
L'incubo di Za la Vie (It 1923)
Za la Mort e Za la Vie (It 1923)
L'ergastolano innocente (It 1924)
La via del peccato (It 1924)
La cavalcata ardente (It 1925)
Gli ultimi giorni di Pompei (It 1926)

GIACHETTI, FOSCO, b. March 28, 1904, Livorno, Italy; d. Dec.
1974
Il trattota scomparso (It 1933)
Luci sommerse (It 1934)
Fiordalisi d'oro (It 1935)
L'ultimo dei Bergerac (It 1935)
Tredici uomini e un cannone (It 1936)
Cuor di vagabondo (It 1936)
Squadrone bianco [White Squadron] (It 1936)
L'ultima nemica (It 1937)
Sentinelle di bronzo (It 1937)
Orgoglio (It 1937)
Scipione l'Africano (It 1937)
Giuseppe Verdi (It 1938)
La signora di Montecarlo (It 1938)
Napoli che non muore (It 1938)
Il sogno di Butterfly (It 1939)
Uragano ai tropici (It 1939)
Carmen fra i rossi (It 1939)
Luce nelle tenebre (It 1940)
La figlia del Corsaro Verdi (It 1940)
L'assedio dell'Alcazar (It 1940)
La peccatrice (It 1940)
Senza Cielo (It 1940)
L'amante segrata (It 1941)
Fari nella nebera (It 1941)
Ridi, pagliaccio! (It 1941)
Nozze di sangue (It 1942)
Inferno giallo (It 1942)
Labbra serrate (It 1942)
Noi vivi-Addio, Kira (It 1942)
Bengasi (It 1942)
La statua vivente (It 1942)
Un colpo di pistola (It 1942)

Una piccola moglie (It 1943)
L'abito nero da sposa (It 1943)
Il sole di Montecassino (It 1945)
La vita ricomincia (It 1945)
Notte di tempesta (It 1945)
Addio, mia bella Napoli! (It 1946)
L'altra (It 1947)
I fratelli Karamazoff (It 1948)
Voragine (It 1948)
Una lettera all'alba (It 1949)
Carrefour des passions [Gli uomini sono nemici] (Fr-It 1950)
Voragine (It 1950)
L'amante di una notte [La Chateua de Verre] (It-Fr 1950)
I falsari (It 1950)
Romanticismo (It 1951)
Quattro rose rosse (It 1951)
Gli uomini non guardano il cielo (It 1952)
Carne de horca [Il terrore dell'Andalusia] (Sp-It 1954)
Casa Ricordi [La Maison du souvenir] (It-Fr 1954)
Sous le ciel de Provence (Fr 1956)
Erà di venerdi 17 (Fr-It 1956)
Un uomo facile (It 1959)
Il mattatore [L'Homme aux cent visages] (It-Fr 1960)
Il conquistatore d'oriente (It 1961)
Il relitto [The Wastrel] (It 1961)
La monaca di Monza (It 1962)
L'ira di Achille (It 1962)
Giacobbe ed Esaú (It 1963)
Le Fils de Tarass Boulba (Fr-It 1964)
Sambo (Sp 1965)
La mujer de otro (Sp 1968)
Il conformista [Le Conformiste] (It-Fr 1970)
Scipione detto anche l'africano (It 1972)
L'Héritier [L'erede] (Fr-It 1973)

GIEHSE, THERESE, b. June 3, 1898, Munich; d. March 3, 1975
    Der Lietesexpress Acht Tage Gluck (Ger 1931)
    Die verkaufte Braut (Ger 1932)
    Peter Voss, der Millionendieb (Ger 1932)
    Die zwei vom Südexpress (Ger 1932)
    Die Nacht der Versuchung (Ger 1932)
    Rund um eine Million (Ger 1933)
    Der Meisterdetektiv (Ger 1933)
    Die missbrauchten Liebebriefe (Swi 1940)
    Menschen, die vorubenziehen (Swi 1942)
    Das Gespensterhaus (Swi 1942)
    Die letzte Chance (Swi 1945)
    The Mark of Cain (GFD 1948)
    Anna Karenina (BL 1948)
    König für eine Nacht (W Ger 1950)
    Herz der Weit (W Ger 1951)
    Vater braucht eine Frau (W Ger 1952)
    Miss man sich gleich scheiden lassen? (W Ger 1953)

Roman einer Siebzehnjahrigen (W Ger 1955)
Ferien im Tirol/Zärtliches Geheimnis (W Ger 1955)
Kinder, Mutter und ein General (W Ger 1955)
Der 10. Mai/Angst vor der Gewalt (Swi 1957)
Mädchen in Uniform (W Ger 1958)
Petersburger Nachte (W Ger 1958)
Sturm im Wasserglas (W Ger 1960)
Lacombe Lucien (Fr 1973)
Black Moon (Fr 1975)

GIELGUD, JOHN, b. April 14, 1904, London
Who Is the Man (Napoleon 1924)
The Clue of the New Pin (PDC 1929)
Insult (Par Br 1932)
The Good Companions (Gaumont-Welsh-Pearson 1933)
The Secret Agent (Gaumont 1936)
The Prime Minister (WB Br 1941)
Julius Caesar (MGM 1953)
Romeo and Juliet (GFD 1954)
Richard III (IFD 1955)
Around the World in 80 Days (UA 1956)
The Barretts of Wimpole Street (MGM 1957)
Saint Joan (UA 1957)
The Immortal Land (RFD 1958) [documentary] (part narrator)
Hamlet (WB 1964) (voice only)
Becket (Par 1964)
The Loved One (MGM 1965)
Chimes at Midnight [Falstaff] (Sp-Swi 1966)
Sebastian (Par 1967)
The Charge of the Light Brigade (UA 1968)
The Shoes of the Fisherman (MGM 1968)
Oh! What a Lovely War (Par 1969)
Assignment to Kill (WB-7 Arts 1969)
Julius Caesar (CUE 1970)
Eagle in a Cage (Cin 1970)
Lost Horizon (Col 1972)
QB VII (ABC 1974)
11 Harrowhouse (Fox-Rank 1974)
Gold (Hemdale 1974)
Frankenstein: The True Story (CIC 1974)
Murder on the Orient Express (Par 1974)
Galileo (AFT 1974)
QB VII (ABC-TV 1974)

GILLER, WALTER, b. Aug. 23, 1927, Recklinghausen,
    Germany
Artistenblut (W Ger 1949)
Kein Engel ist so rein (W Ger 1950)
Das Mädchen aus der Südsee (W Ger 1950)
Insel ohne Moral (W Ger 1950)
Die Frauen des Herrn S. (W Ger 1950)
Sensation in San Remo (W Ger 1951)
Wildwest in Oberbayern (W Ger 1951)

Walter Giller in Grimms Märchen von lüsternen Pärchen (1969).

Primanerinnen (W Ger 1951)
Falschmünzer am Werk (W Ger 1951)
Der bunte Traum (W Ger 1952)
Die Diebin von Bagdad (W Ger 1952)
Liebe im Finanzamt (W Ger 1952)
Der Tag vor der Hochzeit (W Ger 1952)
Skandal im Mädchenpensionat (W Ger 1953)
Südliche Nächte (W Ger 1953)
Heimlich, still und leiser (W Ger 1953)
Fräulein Casanova (Aus 1953)
Irene in Noten (Aus-Yug 1953)
Schlagerparade (W Ger 1953)
Die tolle Lola (W Ger 1953)
An jedem Finger zehn (W Ger 1954)
Sie (W Ger 1954)
Musik, Musik--und nur Musik (W Ger 1955)
Schwedenmädel [Sommar Flickan] (W Ger-Swe 1955)
Charleys Tante (W Ger 1955)
Die Drei von der Tankstelle (W Ger 1955)
Das Bad auf der Tenne (Aus 1956)
Ich und meine Schwiegersöhne (W Ger 1956)

Spion für Deutschland (W Ger 1956)
Nichts als Ärger mist der Liebe (Aus 1956)
Was die Schwalbe sang (W Ger 1956)
Der Hauptmann von Köpenick (W Ger 1956)
Das Sonntagskind (W Ger 1956)
Schwarzwald-Melodie (W Ger 1956)
Drei Mann auf einem Pferd (W Ger 1957)
Der schräge Otto (W Ger 1957)
Das Glück liegt auf der Strasse (W Ger 1957)
Blaue Jungs (W Ger 1957)
Die grosse Chance (W Ger 1957)
Frühling in Berlin (W Ger 1957)
Italienreise--Liebe inbegriffen (W Ger 1958)
Zwei Herzen im Mai (W Ger 1958)
Peter Voss, der Millionendieb (W Ger 1958)
Geliebte Bestie [Hippodrome] (Aus 1959)
So angelt man keinen Mann (W Ger 1959)
Rosen für den Staatsanwalt [Roses for the Prosecutor] (W Ger
    1959)
Liebe auf krummen Beinen (W Ger 1959)
Bobby Dodd greift ein (W Ger 1959)
Peter Voss, der Held des Tages (W Ger 1960)
Ingeborg (W Ger 1960)
Heldinnen (W Ger 1960)
Geliebte Hochstaplerin (W Ger 1961)
Affäre Nina B (W Ger-Fr 1961)
Drei Mann in einem Boot (W Ger-Aus 1961)
Zwei unter Millionen (W Ger 1961)
La Chambre ardente [The Burning Court] (Fr 1962)
Liebling, ich muss Dich erschiessen (W Ger 1962)
Schneewittchen und die sieben Gaukler (W Ger-Swi 1962)
Ape regina [Le Lit conjugal/The Conjugal Bed] (It-Fr 1963)
Die Dreigroschenoper [Threepenny Opera] (W Ger 1963)
Schloss Gripsholm (W Ger 1963)
Das grosse Liebesspiel [And So to Bed] (W Ger-Aus 1963)
Der Würger von Schloss Blackmoor (W Ger 1963)
Die Tote von Beverly Hills [The Corpse of Beverly Hills] (W
    Ger 1964)
Der letzte Ritt nach Santa Cruz (W Ger-Aus 1964)
Begegnung in Salzburg (W Ger-Fr 1964)
Tonio Kröger (W Ger-Fr 1964)
Fanny Hill--Memoirs of a Woman of Pleasure (W Ger-GB 1964)
Heiss weht der Wind (W Ger-Aus 1964)
DM Killer (Aus 1964)
Pfeifen, Betten, Turteltauben (Aus-Czech 1966)
Le Carnaval des barbouzes [Gern hab'ich die Frauen gekillt/
    Spie contro il mondo] (Fr-W Ger-Aus-It 1966)
Ich suche einen Mann (W Ger 1966)
Jonny Banco--geliebter tangenichts [Johnny Banco] (W Ger-Fr-
    It 1967)
Le Soleil des voyous [Il più grande colpo del secolo/Action Man]
    (Fr-It 1967)
Vergiss nicht deine Frau zu kussen (W Ger-Dan 1968)

El ultimo rey de los Incas (Sp-W Ger-It 1968)
A Fine Pair [Ruba al prossimo tuo] (USA-It 1968)
Klassenkeile [Pauker werden ist nicht schwer/Schüler sein
  dagegensehr] (W Ger 1969)
Grimms Märchen von lüsternen Pärchen [Grimm's Fairy Tales
  for Adults Only] (W Ger 1969)
Die Feuerzgangenbowle (W Ger 1970)
Der Herren mit der weissen Weste (W Ger 1970)
Ein Käfer auf Extratour (W Ger 1973)
Das verrückteste Auto der Welt (W Ger 1975)

GIOI, VIVI (Vivien Trumphy), b. Jan. 2, 1917, Livorno, Italy; d.
  July 12, 1975
Ma non è una cosa seria (It 1936)
Bionda sotto chiave (It 1939)
Alessandro sei grande! (It 1939)
Rose scarlatta (It 1939)
Frenesia (It 1939)
Vento di milioni (It 1939)
Mille chilometri al minuto (It 1939)
Dopo divorzieremo (It 1940)
Cento lettere d'amore (It 1940)
La canzone rubala (It 1940)
Il pozzo dei miracoli (It 1940)
L'amante segreta (It 1941)
Primo amore (It 1941)
L'attore scomparso (It 1941)
Giungla (It 1941)
Bengasi (It 1941)
Sette anni di felicità (It 1941)
Cortocircuito (It 1942)
Harlem (It 1942)
Lascia cantare il cuore (It 1942)
Serira de nuit (It-Fr 1943)
Turno di notte (It 1943)
La casa senza tempo (It 1943)
Tutta la città canta (It 1943)
Piazza San Sepolcro (It 1943)
Il marito povero (It 1945)
Caccia tragica (It 1948)
Il grido della terra (It 1949)
Donne senza nome (It 1949)
Gente così (It 1949)
La portatrice di pane (It-Fr 1950)
Senza bandiera (It 1951)
La risaia (It 1955)
Il processo di Verona (It 1963)
Dio non paga il sabato (It 1963)

GIRARDOT, ANNIE, b. Oct. 25, 1931, Paris
Treize à table (Fr 1955)
L'Homme aux clefs d'or (Fr 1955)
Reproduction interdite (Fr 1956)

Le Rouge est mis [Speaking of Murder] (Fr 1957)
L'Amour est en jeu/Ma femme, mon gosse et moi (Fr-It 1957)
Le Désert de Pigalle (Fr-It 1957)
Maigret tend un piège [Maigret Sets a Trap] (Fr-It 1957)
La Corde raide (Fr 1959)
Recours en grâce (Fr-It 1959)
La Française et l'amour (ep "Le Divorce") (Fr 1960)
Rocco e i suoi fratelli [Rocco and His Brothers] (It-Fr 1960)
La Proie pour l'ombre [Shadow of Adultery] (Fr 1960)
Le Rendez-vous (Fr-It 1961)
Les Amours célèbres (ep "Les Comediennes") (Fr-It 1961)
Le Bateau d'Emile (Fr-It 1961)
Le Crime ne paie pas (ep "L'Affaire Fenayrou") (Fr-It 1961)
Smog Brouillard (It 1961)
Pourquoi Paris? (Fr-It 1962)
Le Vice et la vertu [Vice and Virtue] (Fr-It 1962)
I compagni [The Organiser] (It-Fr 1963)
I fuorilegge del matrimonio (It 1964)
La Bonne Soupe (Fr-It 1964)
La donna scimmia [The Ape Woman] (It-Fr 1964)
L'Autre Femme [The Other Woman] (Fr-Sp-It 1964)
Un Monsieur de compagnie [Male Companion] (Fr-It 1964)
Le belle famiglie (It-Fr 1965)
L'Or du duc (Fr-It 1965) (uncredited cameo)
Déclic et des claques (Fr 1965)
La ragazza in prestito (It 1965)
Una voglia da morire (It-Fr 1965)
La guerra segreta [The Dirty Game] (It-Fr-W Ger 1965)
Trois Chambres à Manhattan (Fr 1965)
Le streghe [The Witches] (ep "La strega bruciata viva") (It-Fr 1967)
Zhurnalist [Journalist] (USSR 1967) (cameo)
Vivre pour vivre [Live for Life] (Fr-It 1967)
Les Gauloises bleues (Fr 1968)
Les Anarchistes [La bande à Bonnot] (Fr-It 1968)
Dillinger è morto [Dillinger Is Dead] (It 1968)
Metti una sera a cena [The Love Circle] (It 1969)
Bice skoro propast sveta [It Rains in My Village] (Yug-Fr 1969)
Erotissimo (Fr-It 1969)
Un Homme qui me plaît [Again a Love Story] (Fr 1969)
Il seme dell'uomo (It 1969)
Storia di una donna [Story of a Woman] (It-USA 1970)
Elle boit pas, elle fume pas, elle drague pas, mais...elle cause!
    (Fr 1970)
Les Novices (Fr-It 1970)
Mourir d'aimer (Fr 1971)
Fantasia chez les plouces [Diamond Bikini] (Fr-It 1971)
La Vieille Fille [The Old Maid] (Fr-It 1971)
La Mandarine (Fr 1971)
Les Feux de la chandeleur [Hearth Fires] (Fr-It 1971)
Elle cause plus, elle flingue (Fr-It 1972)
Traitement de choc [The Doctor in the Nude] (Fr-It 1972)
Il n'y a pas de fumée sans feu [There Is No Smoke Without

Fire] (Fr-It 1973)
Juliette et Juliette (Fr-It 1973)
La Gifle [The Slap] (Fr-It 1974)
Il pleut sur Santiago (Fr-Bul 1975)
Il faut vivre dangereusement (Fr 1975)
Docteur François Gailland (Fr 1975)
Le Gitan (Fr-It 1975)

GIROTTI, MARIO (Terence Hill), b. March 23, 1939,
    Venice
As Mario Girotti:
    Vacanze col gangster (It 1951)
    La voca del silencio [La Maison du silence] (It-Fr 1952)
    Villa Borghese [Les Amants de la Villa Borghese] (It-Fr 1953)
    Divisione Folgore (It 1954)
    La vena d'oro (It 1955)
    Bambino (It 1956)
    La lunga strada azzura [Un Dénommé squarcio] (It-Fr 1957)
    Lazzarella (It 1958)
    Anna di Brooklyn (It 1958)
    Cartagine in fiamme [Carthage en Flammes] (It-Fr 1958)
    Primo amore (It 1958)
    Annibale (It 1959)
    Il padrone delle ferriere [La Maitre de Forges] (It-Fr-Sp 1959)
    Giuseppe, venduto dai fratelli (It 1961)
    Pecado de amor [Magdalena/Ave Maria] (Sp-It-Fr 1961)
    Sir Francis Drake, il dominatore dei sette mari [Le Corsaire de la
        Reine] (It-Fr 1961)
    Le meraviglie di Aladino [Les Mille et Une Nuits/The Wonders
        of Aladdin] (It-Fr 1961)
    Il gattopardo [Le Guepard/The Leopard] (It-Fr 1962)
    Winnetou II (W Ger-Yug-It 1964)
    Schusse in 3/4 Takt [Du Suif dans l'Orient-Express] (W Ger-
        Fr 1965)
    Der Ölprins (W Ger 1965)
    Ruf der Wälder (W Ger 1965)
    Duell vor Sonnenuntergang (W Ger 1965)
    Old Surehand 1 [Flaming Frontier] (W Ger-Yug 1965)
    Die Nibelungen [Part I] (W Ger-It 1966)
    Die Nibelungen [Part II] (W Ger-It 1966)
    La feldmarescialla [La Grosse pagaille] (It-Fr 1966)
    El misterioso señor Van Eyck (Sp 1966)
    Io non protesto, io amo (It 1967)
As Terence Hill:
    Little Rita nel West (It 1967)
    Preparati la bara (It 1968)
    I quattro dell'Ave Maria (It 1968)
    Barbagia, la società del malessere (It 1969)
    Dio perdona... io no (It 1969)
    La Collina degli Stivali (It 1969)
    Lo chiamavano Trinità [They Call Me Trinity] (Sp-It-Fr 1970)
    La collera del vento (It 1970)
    Continuavano a chiamarlo Trinità [They Still Call Me Trinity]

Mario Girotti [Terence Hill]

(Sp-It-Fr 1971)
Il vero e il falso (It 1971)
Baron Blood (It 1972)
Più forte, ragazzi (It 1972)
La colera del viento [La Colère du vent] (It-Fr 1972)
... e poi lo chiamavano il Magnifico [El Magnifico] (It-Sp 1972)
El corsario nero [Il corsaro nero] (Sp-It 1972)
Il mio nome è Nessuno [Mon nom est Personne] (It-Fr 1973)
Altrimenti ci arrabbiamo (It 1973)
Porgi l'altra guancia (It 1974)

GIROTTI, MASSIMO, b. May 18, 1918, Mogliano, Italy
Dora Nelson (It 1939)
Una romantica avventura (It 1940)
La corona di ferro (It 1940)
Tosca (It 1940)
La famiglia Brambilla in vacanza (It 1941)
I pirati della Malesia (It 1941)
Le due tigri (It 1941)
La cena delle beffe (It 1941)
Un pilota ritorna (It 1941)
Ossessione (It 1942)
Harlem (It 1942)
Apparizione (It 1943)
Appassionata (It 1943)
La carne e l'anima (It 1943)
I dieci comandamenti (It 1945)
La porta del cielo (It 1945)

Desiderio (It 1946) [made in 1943]
Un giorno nella vita (It 1946)
Preludio d'amore (It 1946)
Fatalità (It 1946)
Caccia tragica (It 1947)
Natale al campo 119 (It 1947)
Desiderio (It 1948)
Gioventù perduta (It 1948)
Anni difficili (It 1948)
Molti sogni per le strade (It 1948)
Fabiola (It 1949)
In nome della legge (It 1949)
Cronaca di un amore (It 1950)
Benvenuto reverendo! (It 1950)
Duello senza onore (It 1950)
Altura (It 1950)
Persiane chiuse (It 1950)
Roma, ore 11 (It 1951)
Clandestino a Trieste (It 1951)
Nez de cuir [Naso di cuoio-Gentiluomo d'onore] (Fr-It 1951)
Il tenente Giorgio (It 1952)
Il segreto delle tre punte (It 1952)
Spartaco (It 1952)
Ai margini della metropoli (It 1952)
Sul ponte dei sospiri (It 1953)
Un marito per Anna Zaccheo (It 1953)
Senso (It 1953)
Vortice (It 1953)
L'Amour d'une femme [L'amore di una donna] (Fr-It 1954)
I quattro del getto tonante (It 1955)
La vena di oro (It 1955)
La tua donna (It 1956)
I vagabondi delle stelle (It 1956)
Disperato addio (It 1956)
Marguerite de la nuit [Margherita della notte] (Fr-It 1956)
Lazzarella [Lazzarella, petite canaille] (It-Fr 1957)
Dimentica il mio passato Consuelo [Rio Guadalginvir] (It-Sp 1957)
Saranno uomini (It 1957)
Souvenir d'Italie (It 1957)
La Venere di Cheronea [Aphrodite, déesse de l'amour] (It-Fr 1957)
Asphalte (Fr 1958)
La trovatella di Pompei (It 1958)
Erode il grande [Le roi cruel] (It-Fr 1958)
La strada lunga un anno [Cesta duga godinu dana] (It-Yug 1959)
Giuditta e Oloferne (It 1959)
Lupi nell'abisso (It 1959)
La cento chilometri (It 1959)
Juke-box, urli d'amore (It 1959)
I cosacchi [Les cosaques] (It-Fr 1960)
Le legioni di Cleopatra [Les Legions de Cleopatre/Las Legiones de Cleopatra] (It-Fr-Sp 1960)
Cavalcata selvaggia (It 1960)

Le notte dei teddy boys (It 1960)
Lettere di una novizia [La Novice/Rita] (It-Fr 1960)
I giganti della Tessaglia [Le Géant de Thessalie] (It-Fr 1960)
Romolo e Remo [Romulus et Remus/Duel of the Titans] (It-Fr 1960)
Venere imperiale [Vénus imperiale] (It-Fr 1962)
Oro per i Cesari [L'Or des Cesars/Gold for the Cesars] (Fr-It 1963)
Mafia alla sbarra (It 1963)
Le meravigliose avventure di Marco Polo [Marco the Magnificent] (It 1965)
El misterioso senor Van Eych (Sp-It 1966)
Idoli controluce (It 1966)
Le streghe [The Witches] (ep "La strega bruciata viva") (It 1967)
Scusi, facciamo l'amore [Et si on fai soit l'amour/Let's Make Love] (It-Fr 1968)
Teorema (It 1968)
Le sorelle (It 1969)
Medea (It-W Ger 1969)
Il mio corpo con rabbia (It 1970)
Gli orrori del castellodi Norimberga [Baron Blood] (It 1972)
Ultimo tango a Parigi [Dernier tango à Paris/Last Tango in Paris] (It-Fr 1972)
Beau Masque (Fr-It 1972)
L'ultima chance (It 1973)

GOOYER, RIJK DE   see   DE GOOYER, RIJK

GOTTSCHALK, JOACHIM, b. 1904, Calau/Niederlausitz, Germany; d. Nov. 16, 1941
Du und Ich (Ger 1938)
Flucht ins Dunkel (Ger 1939)
Aufruhr in Damaskus (Ger 1939)
Eine Frau wie Due (Ger 1939)
Das Mädchen von Fanö (Ger 1940)
Ein Leben lang (Ger 1940)
Die schwedische Nachtigall (Ger 1941)

GOUDSMIT, LEX, b. March 15, 1913, Brussels
Het Wonderlijke Levan van Willem Parel (Dut 1955)
Strading (Dut 1957)
Operation Amsterdam (GB-USA 1959)
De Vergeten Medeminnaar (Dut 1963)
Fietsen Naar de Maan (Dut 1963)
10. 32 (Dut 1966)
Frank en Eva (Dut 1973)
Alicia (Dut 1974)
Oom Ferdinand en de Toverdrank (Dut 1974)
Zwaarmoedige Verhalen Voor biu de Centrale Verwarming (ep "De Smalle Oude Man") (Dut 1975)
De Laatste Trein (Dut 1975)

GRANGER, STEWART (James Stewart), b. May 6, 1913, London
A Southern Maid (Wardour 1933)

Evergreen (Gaumont 1934)
Over the Garden Wall (Wardour 1934)
Give Her a Ring (Pathe 1934)
So This Is London (20th Br 1939)
Convoy (ABFD 1940)
Secret Mission (GFD 1942)
Thursday's Child (Pathe 1943)
The Man in Grey (GFD 1943)
The Lamp Still Burns (GFD 1943)
Fanny by Gaslight [Man of Evil] (GFD 1944)
Love Story [A Lady Surrenders] (EL 1944)
Madonna of the Seven Moons (EL 1944)
Waterloo Road (GFD 1945)
Caesar and Cleopatra (EL 1946)
Caravan (GFD 1946)
The Magic Bow (GFD 1946)
Captain Boycott (GFD 1947)
Blanche Fury (GFD 1948)
Saraband for Dead Lovers (GFD 1948)
Woman Hater (GFD 1948)
Adam and Evelyne [Adam and Evalyn] (GFD 1949)
King Solomon's Mines (MGM 1950)
Soldiers Three (MGM 1951)
The Light Touch (MGM 1951)
The Wild North (MGM 1952)
Scaramouche (MGM 1952)
The Prisoner of Zenda (MGM 1952)
Young Bess (MGM 1953)
Salome (Col 1953)
All the Brothers Were Valiant (MGM 1953)
Beau Brummel (MGM 1954)
Green Fire (MGM 1955)
Moonfleet (MGM 1955)
Footsteps in the Fog (Col 1955)
The Last Hunt (MGM 1956)
The Little Hut (MGM 1957)
Gun Glory (MGM 1957)
The Whole Truth (Col 1958)
Harry Black [Harry Black and the Tiger] (20th 1958)
North to Alaska (20th 1960)
The Secret Partner (MGM 1961)
Sodoma e Gommorra [Sodom and Gomorrah] (It-USA 1962)
Swordsman of Siena [La Spadaccino di Siena] (It-Fr 1962)
Marcia o Crepa [The Legion's Last Patrol] (It-Sp-W Ger 1963)
I giorno più corto [The Shortest Day] (It 1963)
Unter Geiern [Among Vultures/Frontier Hellcat] (W Ger-Fr-It-
    Yug 1964)
The Secret Invasion (20th 1964)
The Crooked Road (Tigon 1964)
Das Geheimnis der drei Dschunken [Red Dragon] (W Ger-It 1965)
Der Olprinz [Rampage at Apache Wells] (W Ger-Yug 1965)
Old Surehand [Flaming Frontier] (W Ger-Yug 1965)
Killers Carnival (W Ger-It-GB 1965)

Das Geheimnis der Gelben Monche [Target for Killing/How to
  Kill a Lady] (W Ger-Aust-It 1966)
The Trygon Factor (RFD 1967)
The Last Safari (Par 1967)
Requiem per un Agente Segreto [Gern hab' ich die Frauen
  Gekillt/Requiem for a Secret Agent] (Fr-W Ger-Sp 1968)
Any Second Now (NBC-TV 1969)
Sherlock Holmes: The Hound of the Baskervilles (ABC-TV 1972)

GRAY, SALLY (Constance Vera Stevens), b. Feb. 14, 1916, Hollo-
  way, London
The School for Scandal (Par Br 1930)
Radio Pirates* [Big Ben Calling] (AP & D 1935)
Marry the Girl (BL 1935)
Cross Currents (B & D - Par 1935)
Lucky Days (B & D - Par 1935)
Checkmate (B & D - Par 1935)
Cheer Up! (ABFD 1936)
Calling the Tune (ABFD 1936)
Honeymoon Merrygoround (RKO Br 1936)
Cafe Colette [Danger in Paris] (ABFD 1937)
Over She Goes (ABPC 1937)
Saturday Night Revue (Pathe 1937)
Mr. Reeder in Room 13 [Mystery of Room 13] (ABPC 1938)
Hold My Hand (ABPC 1938)
Lightning Conductor (GFD 1938)
The Lambeth Walk (MGM Br 1939)
Sword of Honour (Butcher 1939)
The Saint in London (RKO-Radio 1939)
A Window in London [Lady in Distress] (GFD 1939)
The Saint's Vacation (RKO-Radio 1941)
Dangerous Moonlight [Suicide Squadron] (RKO-Radio 1941)
Carnival (GFD 1946)
Green for Danger (GFD 1946)
They Made Me a Fugitive [I Became a Criminal] (WB Br 1947)
The Mark of Cain (GFD 1948)
Silent Dust (ABP 1949)
Obsession [The Hidden Room] (GFD 1949)
Escape Route [I'll Get You] (Eros 1953)

GRECO, COSETTA (Cesarina Rossi), b. Oct. 8, 1930, Trento, Italy
La città si difende (It 1951)
Le Cap de l'espérance (Fr 1951)
La nostra pelle (It 1951)
Le ragazze di piazza di Spagna (It 1951)
Il brigante di Tacca del Lupo (It 1951)
Art...519 Codice penale [Violence charnelle] (It-Fr 1952)
La nemica (It 1952)
Gli eroi della domenica (It 1952)
Canzoni di mezzo secolo (It 1952)
Viale della speranza (It 1952)
La Maison du silence [La voce del silenzio] (Fr-It 1953)
Canzoni, canzoni, canzoni (It 1953)

In amore si pecca in due (It 1953)
Musoduro (It 1953)
Scampolo (It-Fr 1954)
Opinione pubblica (It 1954)
Cronache di poveri amanti (It 1954)
Terroristi a Madrid (Sp-It 1954)
Foglio di via (It 1954)
La nostra pelle (It 1954)
Je suis un sentimental [Io sono un sentimentale] (Fr-It 1955)
Napoléon (Fr 1955)
Gli innamorati (It 1956)
I pappagalli (It 1956)
I sogni nel cassetto (It 1957)
Cronache del '22 (It 1962)
Plagio (It 1969)
Lo sceriffo di Rochspring (It 1971)

GREENWOOD, JOAN, b. March 4, 1921, Chelsea, London
John Smith Wakes Up (BL 1940)
My Wife's Family (Pathe 1941)
He Found a Star (GFD 1941)
The Gentle Sex (GFD 1943)
They Knew Mr. Knight (GFD 1945)
Latin Quarter (Anglo 1945)
Girl in a Million (BL 1946)
The Man Within [The Smugglers] (GFD 1947)
The October Man (GFD 1947)
The White Unicorn [Bad Sister] (GFD 1947)
Saraband for Dead Lovers (GFD 1948)
The Bad Lord Byron (GFD 1949)
Whisky Galore! [Tight Little Island] (GFD 1949)
Kind Hearts and Coronets (GFD 1949)
Flesh and Blood (BL 1951)
Young Wives' Tale (ABP 1951)
The Man in the White Suit (GFD 1951)
La Passe muraille [Mr. Peek-a-Boo] (Fr 1951)
The Importance of Being Earnest (GFD 1952)
Knave of Hearts [Lovers, Happy Lovers/Lover Boy] (ABP 1954)
Father Brown [The Detective] (Col 1954)
Moonfleet (MGM 1955)
Stage Struck (BV 1958)
The Mysterious Island (Col 1962)
The Amorous Prawn (BL 1962)
Tom Jones (UA 1963)
The Moon-Spinners (BV 1964)
Girl Stroke Boy (London Screen Distributors 1971)

GREGSON, JOHN, b. March 15, 1919, Liverpool; d. Jan. 9, 1975
Saraband for Dead Lovers (GFD 1948)
Scott of the Antarctic (GFD 1948)
Whisky Galore! [Tight Little Island] (GFD 1949)
Train of Events (GFD 1949)
Treasure Island (RKO 1950)

Cairo Road (ABP 1950)
The Lavendar Hill Mob (GFD 1951)
Angels One Five (ABP 1952)
The Brave Don't Cry (ABFD 1952)
The Holly and the Ivy (BL 1952)
Venetian Bird [The Assassin] (GFD 1952)
The Titfield Thunderbolt (GFD 1953)
Genevieve (GFD 1953)
The Weak and the Wicked (ABP 1954)
Conflict of Wings [Fuss Over Feathers] (BL 1954)
The Crowded Day [Shop Soiled] (Adelphi 1954)
To Dorothy a Son [Cash on Delivery] (IFD 1954)
Above Us the Waves (GFD 1955)
Three Cases of Murder (ep "You Killed Elizabeth") (BL 1955)
Value for Money (RFD 1955)
Jacqueline (RFD 1956)
The Battle of the River Plate [Pursuit of the Graf Spee] (RFD
    1956)
True As a Turtle (RFD 1957)
Miracle in Soho (RFD 1957)
Rooney (RFD 1958)
Sea of Sand (RFD 1958)
The Captain's Table (RFD 1959)
S. O. S. Pacific (RFD 1959)
Faces in the Dark (RFD 1960)
Hand in Hand (WPD 1960)
The Treasure of Monte Cristo [The Secret of Monte Cristo]
    (RFI 1961)
The Frightened City (AA 1961)
The Longest Day (20th 1962)
Live Now--Pay Later (RFI 1962)
Tomorrow at Ten (Planet 1962)
The Night of the Generals (Col 1966)
Fright (BL 1971)

GRETLER, HEINRICH, b. Oct. 1, 1897, Zurich
    Die Entstehung der Eidgenossenschaft (Swi 1921)
    Der geheimnisvolle Spiegel (Ger 1928)
    Menschen am Sonntag (Ger 1929)
    Deruga (Ger 1929)
    Die letzte Kompanie (Ger 1930)
    Das Flotenkonzert von Sans-Souci (Ger 1930)
    Berlin-Alexanderplatz (Ger 1931)
    Voruntersuchung (Ger 1931)
    Fünf von der Jazzband (Ger 1932)
    Ich und die Kaiserin (Ger 1933)
    Das Testament des Dr. Mabuse (Ger 1933)
    Zyt isch Gald (Swi 1933)
    Wie d'Warret würkt (Swi 1933)
    Jä-soo! (Swi 1935)
    Füsilier Wipf (Swi 1938)
    Farinet; ou, L'Or dans la Montagne (Swi 1938)
    Wachtmeister Studer (Swi 1939)

Euseri Schwyz (Swi 1939)
Die missbrauchten Liebesbriefe (Swi 1940)
Gilberte de Courgenay (Swi 1941)
Landammann Stauffacher (Swi 1941)
Steibruch [Gottesmühlen] (Swi 1942)
Marie-Louise (Swi 1944)
Matto regiert (Swi 1947)
Das weisse Gold [Angela] (Aus 1949)
Piccolo Bandito (Swi 1949)
Swiss Tour (Swi 1949)
Vom Teufel gejagt (W Ger 1950)
Der Seelenbräu (Aus 1950)
Fohn [Drei Menschen am Piz Palü] (Swi-W Ger 1950)
Der fidele Bauer (Aus 1951)
Herz der Welt (W Ger 1951)
Gefangene Seele (W Ger 1951)
Nachts auf den Strassen (W Ger 1951)
Heidi (Swi 1952)
Der letzte Schuss (W Ger 1952)
Die grosse Versuchung (W Ger 1952)
The Devil Makes Three (MGM 1952)
Die Venus von Tivoli [Zwiespalt des Herzens] (Swi-W Ger 1952)
Der Haflinger Sepp [Junges Herz voll Liebe] (W Ger 1953)
Mit 17 beginnt das Leben (W Ger 1953)
Das Dorf unterm Himmel [Las mich nie mehr allein] (W Ger
    1953)
Dein Herz ist meine Heimat (W Ger 1953)
Weibertausch (W Ger 1954)
Uli der Knecht (Swi 1954)
Die Sonne von Sankt-Moritz (W Ger 1954)
Frühlingslied [S'Vreneli am Guggisberg] (Swi 1954)
Rosenresli (W Ger 1954)
Heidi und Peter (Swi 1955)
Uli der Pachter [Und ewig ruf die Heimat] (Swi 1955)
Oberarzt Dr. Solm (W Ger 1955)
Sohn ohne Heimat (W Ger 1955)
Die Försterbuben (Aus 1955)
Das Erbe vom Pruggerhof (W Ger 1955)
Zwischen uns die Berge [Das Lied der Heimat] (Swi 1956)
Ein Mann vergisst die Liebe (W Ger 1956)
Der Pfarrer von Kirchfeld (W Ger 1956)
Der Fischer vom Heiligensee (W Ger 1956)
Rosenmontag (W Ger 1956)
Kleines Zelt und grosse Liebe (W Ger 1956)
Der Glockengiesser vom Tirol (W Ger 1956)
Es geschah am hellichten Tage (Swi 1957)
Der 10. Mai [Angst vor der Gewalt] (Swi 1957)
Der Schandfleck (W Ger 1957)
Robinson soll nicht sterben (W Ger 1957)
Der König der Bernina (W Ger 1957)
Jungfrauenkrieg (W Ger 1957)
Die Heilige und ihr Narr (W Ger 1957)
Der Pfarrer von St. Michael (W Ger 1958)

Ein wunderbarer Sommer [Ludmilla die Kuh] (Swi-Aus 1958)
Der schwarze Elitz (W Ger 1958)
...und nichts als die Wahrheit (W Ger 1958)
Die Käserei in der Vehfreude (Swi 1958)
Die ideale Frau (W Ger 1959)
Alt-Heidelberg (W Ger 1959)
Hast noch der Sohne ja (Swi 1959)
Kinder der Berge (W Ger 1959)
La Vache et le prisonnier (Fr 1959)
Anne Bäbi Jowäger (Swi 1960)
Scheidungsgrund Liebe (W Ger 1960)
Himmel, Amor und Zwirn (W Ger 1960)
Immer will ich Dir gehoren (W Ger 1960)
Sabine und die hundert Manner (W Ger 1960)
Liebling der Götter (W Ger 1960)
Via Mala (W Ger 1961)
Die Gejagten (Swi 1961)
Der 42. Himmel (Swi 1961)
Le Cave se rebiffe (Fr 1961)
Es Dach überem Chopf (Swi 1962)
Freddy und das Lied der Sudsee (W Ger 1962)
Wildwasser (W Ger 1962)
Rauberhauptmann Tinderle (W Ger 1962)
Kohlliesels Töchter (W Ger 1962)
Der Unsichtbare (W Ger 1963)

GRIFFITH, HUGH, b. May 30, 1912, Marian Glas, Anglesey, Eng-
   land
   Neutral Port (GFD 1940)
   The Silver Darlings (Pathe 1947)
   The First Gentleman [Affairs of a Rogue] (Col Br 1948)
   The Three Weird Sisters (Pathe 1948)
   So Evil My Love (Par Br 1948)
   London Belongs to Me [Dulcimer Street] (GFD 1948)
   The Last Days of Dolwyn [Woman of Dolwyn] (BL 1949)
   Dr. Morelle--The Case of the Missing Heiress (Ex 1949)
   Kind Hearts and Coronets (GFD 1949)
   A Run for Your Money (GFD 1949)
   Gone to Earth [The Wild Heart] (BL 1950)
   The Galloping Major (IFD 1951)
   Laughter in Paradise (ABP 1951)
   The Titfield Thunderbolt (GFD 1953)
   The Beggar's Opera (BL 1953)
   The Sleeping Tiger (AA 1954)
   Passage Home (GFD 1955)
   The Good Companions (ABPC 1957)
   Lucky Jim (BL 1957)
   The Story on Page One (20th 1959)
   Ben-Hur (MGM 1959)
   The Day They Robbed the Bank of England (MGM 1960)
   Key Witness (MGM 1960)
   Exodus (UA 1960)
   The Counterfeit Traitor (Par 1961)

Mutiny on the Bounty (MGM 1962)
The Inspector [Lisa] (20th 1962)
Term of Trial (WPD 1962)
Hide and Seek (Albion 1963)
Tom Jones (UA 1963)
The Bargee (WPD 1964)
The Amorous Adventures of Moll Flanders (Par 1965)
How to Steal a Million (20th 1966)
Oh, Dad, Poor Dad, Mamma's Hung You in the Closet and I'm
   Feelin' So Sad (Par 1967)
Sailor from Gibraltar (UA 1967)
The Chastity Belt [La cintura di castita] (It 1967)
Start the Revolution Without Me (WB 1969)
Lock Up Your Daughters! (Col 1969)
Cry of the Banshee (AIP 1970)
Wuthering Heights (Anglo-EMI 1970)
I racconti di Canterbury [The Canterbury Tales] (It-Fr 1971)
The Abominable Dr. Phibes (AIP 1971)
Che? [What!] (It-Fr-W Ger 1972)
Who Slew Auntie Roo? (AIP 1971)
Dr. Phibes Rises Again (AIP 1972)
Luther (AFT 1973)
The Final Programme (MGM-EMI 1973)
Crescete e moltiplicatevi (It 1973)
Take Me High (MGM-EMI 1974)
Cugini carnali [The Visitor] (It 1974)
Craze (EMI 1974)
Frankenstein: The True Story (CIC 1974)
Legend of the Werewolf (Fox-Rank 1975)

GROEN, DORA VAN DER see VAN DER GROEN, DORA

GRUNDGENS, GUSTAF, b. Dec. 12, 1899, Dusseldorf, Germany;
   d. Dec. 7, 1963
Das Erbe in Pretoria (Ger 1929)
Va banque (Ger 1930)
Barcarole (Ger 1930)
Der Brand in der Oper (Ger 1930)
Danton (Ger 1931)
M (Ger 1931)
Luise, Königin von Preussen (Ger 1931)
Yorck (Ger 1931)
Der Raub der Mona Lisa (Ger 1931)
Teilnehmer antwortet nicht (Ger 1932)
Die Gräfin von Monte Christo (Ger 1932)
Eine stadt steht kopf (Ger 1932) (director only)
Liebelei (Ger 1933)
Ich glaub nie mehr an eine Frau (Ger 1933)
Hokuspokus (Ger 1933)
Der Tunnel (Ger 1933)
Die schönen Tage von Aranjuez (Ger 1933)
Die Finanzen des Grossherzogs (Ger 1934) (director only)
Schwarzer Jäger Johanna (Ger 1934)

So endete eine Liebe (Ger 1934)
Pygmalion (Ger 1935)
Hundert Tage (Ger 1935)
Das Mädchen Johanna (Ger 1935)
Eine Frau ohne Bedeutung (Ger 1936)
Capriolen (Ger 1937)
Tanz auf dem Vulkan (Ger 1938)
Ein Schritt vom Wege (Ger 1939) (director only)
Swei welten (Ger 1940) (director only)
Friedemann Bach (Ger 1941)
Ohm Krüger (Ger 1941)
Das Glas Wasser (W Ger 1960)
Faust (W Ger 1960)

GUINNESS, ALEC, b. April 2, 1914, London
Evensong (Gaumont 1934) (extra)
Great Expectations (GFD 1946)
Oliver Twist (GFD 1948)
Kind Hearts and Coronets (GFD 1949)
A Run for Your Money (GFD 1949)
Last Holiday (ABP 1950)
The Mudlark (20th 1950)
The Lavender Hill Mob (GFD 1951)
The Man in the White Suit (GFD 1951)
The Card [The Promoter] (GFD 1952)
Malta Story (GFD 1953)
The Captain's Paradise (BL 1953)
Father Brown [The Detective] (Col 1954)
To Paris with Love (GFD 1955)
The Prisoner (Col 1955)
The Ladykillers (RFD 1955)
The Swan (MGM 1956)
The Bridge on the River Kwai (Col 1957)
Barnacle Bill [All at Sea] (MGM 1957)
The Horse's Mouth (UA 1959)
The Scapegoat (MGM 1959)
Our Man in Havana (Col 1960)
Tunes of Glory (UA 1961)
HMS Defiant [Damn the Defiant!] (Col 1962)
A Majority of One (WB 1962)
Lawrence of Arabia (Col 1962)
The Fall of the Roman Empire (Par 1964)
Situation Hopeless, But Not Serious (Par 1965)
Doctor Zhivago (MGM 1966)
Hotel Paradise (MGM 1966)
The Quiller Memorandum (RFD 1967)
The Comedians (MGM 1967)
Cromwell (Col 1970)
Scrooge (20th 1971)
Fratello Sole, Sorella Luna [Brother Sun, Sister Moon] (It 1972)
Hitler: The Last Ten Days (GB-It 1973)

GUITRY, SACHA, b. Feb. 21, 1885, St. Petersburg, Russia; d.
July 24, 1957
Pasteur (Fr 1935)
Bonne Chance (Fr 1935)
Le Nouveau Testament (Fr 1936)
Le Roman d'un tricheur (Fr 1936)
Mon Père avait Raison (Fr 1936)
Faisons un rêve (Fr 1936)
Le Mot de Cambronne (Fr 1936)
Les Perles de la Couronne (Fr 1937)
Desire (Fr 1937)
Quadrille (Fr 1937)
Remontons les Champs-Elysees (Fr 1938)
Ils étaient neuf célibataires (Fr 1939)
Le Destin fableux de Désirée Clary (Fr 1941)
Donne-moi tes yeux (Fr 1943)
Le Malibran (Fr 1944)
Le Comedien (Fr 1948)
Le Diable boiteux (Fr 1948)
Aux deux colombes (Fr 1949)
Toa (Fr 1949)
Le Tresor de Cantenac (Fr 1950)
Tu m'as sauve la vie (Fr 1950)
Deburau (Fr 1951)
Adhemar; ou, Le Jouet de la fatalité (Fr 1951)
La Poison (Fr 1951)
Je l'ai été trois fois (Fr 1952)
La Vie d'un honnête homme (Fr 1953)
Si Versailles m'était conté (Fr 1953)
Napoléon (Fr 1954)
Si Paris nous était conté (Fr 1955)
Assassins et voleurs (Fr 1956)

GWENN, EDMUND, b. Sept. 26, 1875, London; d. July 7, 1959
The Real Thing at Last (British Actors 1916)
Unmarried (Granger's Exclusives 1920)
The Skin Game (Granger-Binger 1920)
The Skin Game (Wardour 1931)
How He Lied to Her Husband (Wardour 1931)
Hindle Wakes (Gaumont 1931)
Frail Women (Radio 1932)
Money for Nothing (Pathe 1932)
Condemned to Death (W & F 1932)
Love on Wheels (W & F 1932)
Tell Me Tonight [Be Mine Tonight] (W & F 1932)
The Good Companions (Gaumont-Welsh-Pearson 1933)
Cash [For Love or Money] (Par Br 1933)
I Was a Spy (W & F 1933)
Smithy (WB 1933)
Channel Crossing (W & F 1933)
Early to Bed (W & F 1933)
Marooned (Fox Br 1933)
Friday the Thirteenth (ep "Wakefield the City Man") (Gaumont 1933)

Waltzes from Vienna [Strauss's Great Waltz] (Gaumont 1934)
The Admiral's Secret (Radio 1934)
Passing Shadows (Fox Br 1934)
Warn London (BL 1934)
Java Head (ABFD 1934)
Father and Son (WB 1934)
Spring in the Air (Pathe 1934)
The Bishop Misbehaves [The Bishop's Misadventures] (MGM
    1935)
Sylvia Scarlett (RKO 1935)
The Walking Dead (WB 1936)
Anthony Adverse (WB 1936)
All American Chump [Country Bumpkin] (MGM 1936)
Laburnum Grove (ABFD 1936)
Mad Holiday (MGM 1936)
Parnell (MGM 1937)
South Riding (UA 1938)
A Yank at Oxford (MGM Br 1938)
Penny Paradise (ABFD 1938)
Cheer Boys Cheer (ABFD 1939)
Madmen of Europe [An Englishman's Home] (UA 1939)
Earl of Chicago (MGM 1940)
Pride and Prejudice (MGM 1940)
Foreign Correspondent (UA 1940)
Cheers for Miss Bishop (UA 1941)
The Devil and Miss Jones (RKO 1941)
One Night in Lisbon (Par 1941)
Scotland Yard (20th 1941)
Charley's Aunt [Charley's American Aunt] (20th 1941)
A Yank at Eton (MGM 1942)
The Meanest Man in the World (20th 1943)
Forever and a Day (RKO 1943)
Lassie Come Home (MGM 1943)
Between Two Worlds (WB 1944)
The Keys of the Kingdom (20th 1944)
Bewitched (MGM 1945)
Dangerous Partners (MGM 1945)
She Went to the Races (MGM 1946)
Undercurrent (MGM 1946)
Of Human Bondage (WB 1947)
Miracle on 34th Street [The Big Heart] (20th 1947)
Green Dolphin Street (MGM 1947)
Thunder in the Valley [Bob, Son of Battle] (20th 1947)
Life with Father (WB 1948)
Apartment for Peggy (20th 1948)
Hills of Home [Master of Lassie] (MGM 1949)
Challenge to Lassie (MGM 1949)
A Woman of Distinction (Col 1950)
Louisa (Univ 1950?)
Mr. 880 (20th 1950)
For Heaven's Sake (20th 1950)
Pretty Baby (WB 1951)
Peking Express (Par 1951)

Sally and Saint Anne (Univ 1952)
Les Miserables (20th 1952)
Bonzo Goes to College (Univ 1952)
Something for the Birds (20th 1952)
Mister Scoutmaster (20th 1952)
The Bigamist (Filmakers 1953)
Them! (WB 1954)
The Student Prince (MGM 1954)
It's a Dog's Life (MGM 1955)
The Trouble with Harry (Par 1956)
Calabuch (Sp 1956)

GYNT, GRETA (Greta Woxholt), b. 1916, Oslo
Boys Will Be Boys (BIED 1937) (as Greta Woxholt)
The Last Curtain (B & D-Par Br 1937)
Second Best Bed (GFD 1938)
Sexton Blake and the Hooded Terror (MGM 1938)
The Last Barricade (Fox Br 1938)
Too Dangerous to Live (WB-FN Br 1939)
Dark Eyes of London [The Human Monster] (Pathe 1939)
The Arsenal Stadium Mystery (GFD 1939)
She Couldn't Say No (ABPC 1939)
The Middle Watch (ABPC 1939)
Two for Danger (WB Br 1940)
Bulldog Sees It Through (ABPC 1940)
Room for Two (GN 1940)
Crook's Tour (Anglo 1940)
The Common Touch (Anglo 1941)
Tomorrow We Live [At Dawn We Die] (BL 1942)
It's That Man Again (GFD 1943)
Mr. Emmanuel (EL 1944)
London Town [My Heart Goes Crazy] (EL 1946)
Take My Life (GFD 1947)
Dear Murderer (GFD 1947)
Easy Money (GFD 1948)
The Calendar (GFD 1948)
Mr. Perrin and Mr. Traill (GFD 1948)
Shadow of the Eagle (IFD 1950)
I'll Get You for This [Lucky Nick Cain] (IFD 1951)
Whispering Smith Hits London [Whispering Smith vs. Scotland
    Yard] (Ex 1952)
I'm a Stranger (Apex 1952)
The Ringer (BL 1952)
Three Steps in the Dark (ABP 1953)
Forbidden Cargo (GFD 1954)
Devil's Point [Devil's Harbour] (Monarch 1954)
See How They Run (BL 1955)
The Blue Peter [Navy Heroes] (BL 1955)
My Wife's Family (ABP 1956)
Fortune Is a Woman [She Played with Fire] (Col 1957)
Morning Call (Astral 1958)
The Witness (AA 1959)
Bluebeard's Ten Honeymoons (WPD 1960)

GYS, LEDA (Giselda Lombardi), b. March 10, 1892, Rome; d. Oct. 2, 1957

Sfumatura (It 1913)
Dopo la morte (It 1913)
Sua cognata [Lussuria] (It 1913)
Il gomitolo nero (It 1913)
Amore bendato (It 1913)
La tutela (It 1913)
La dama di picche (It 1913)
Histoire d'un pierrot (It 1913)
L'amazzone mascherata (It 1914)
Rose e spine (It 1914)
Il piccolo cerinaio (It 1914)
I cavalieri moderni (It 1915)
Per non morire (It 1915)
Leda innamorata (It 1915)
Sempre nel cuor la patria (It 1915)
La divetta del reggimento (It 1915)
Cuore di neve (It 1915)
Un giuramento (It 1915)
Marcia nuziale (It 1915)
L'amor tuo mi redime (It 1915)
La pantomima della morte (It 1915)
Come in quel giorno (It 1916)
Fiore d'autunno (It 1916)
Amore che uccide [Chi mi darà l'oblio senza morire?] (It 1916)
Passano gli unni (It 1916)
La vita e la morte (It 1916)
La matrigna (It 1916)
Christus (It 1916)
Dopo la raffica (It 1916)
Fra gli artigli del veleno (It 1916)
Maschera di mistero (It 1916)
L'amica (It 1916)
Ananke [Fatalità] (It 1916)
La principessa (It 1917)
Fernanda (It 1917)
Quando si ama (It 1917)
Le rose del miracolo (It 1917)
La Bohème (It 1917)
Treno di lusso (It 1917)
La Leda senza cigno (It 1917)
Il naso rosso (It 1917)
La donna che inventò l'amore (It 1918)
Sole! (It 1918)
Una peccatrice (It 1918)
Il rifugio (It 1918)
Io ti uccido! (It 1918)
Più che l'amore (It 1919)
Quando l'amore è vero (It 1919)
Il miracolo (It 1919)
Friquet (It 1919)
I figli di nessuno (It 1920)

Scrollina (It 1920)
Un cuore nel mondo (It 1920)
La donna e i bruti (It 1921)
La cingallegra (It 1921)
L'arte di farsi amare (It 1922)
Leoparda ferita (It 1922)
La trappola (It 1922)
Lily Lolette (It 1922)
Mia moglie si e fidanzata (It 1922)
Santarellina (It 1923)
Coiffeur pour dames (Fr 1923)
Sole mio (It 1923)
La schiava (It 1923)
La pianista di Haines (It 1924)
La fanciulla di Pompei [La madonna del rosario] (It 1924)
Saitra la ribelle (It 1924)
Profanazione (It 1924)
Vide Napule, e po'... mori (It 1924)
Grand Hôtel Paradis (It 1925)
La cieca di Sorrento (It 1925)
Napoli è una canzone (It 1926)
Nina non fare la stupida (It 1926)
La madonnina dei marinai (It 1927)
I 28 giorni di Claretta (It 1927)
La regina del varietà (It 1928)
Napule... e niente cchiù (It 1928)
Mam'zelle Kikiriki (It 1928)
Rondine (It 1929)

HAACK, KATHE, b. Aug. 11, 1892, Berlin, Germany
Die Stricknadeln (Ger 1916)
Die Hochzeit im Excentricclub (Ger 1917)
Baccarat (Ger 1919)
Der Weg der in die Verdammnis führt (Ger 1920)
Föhn (Ger 1920)
Der Spieler (Ger 1920)
Am Webstuhl der Zeit (Ger 1921)
Arme kleine Eva (Ger 1921)
Die Diktatur der Liebe (Ger 1921)
Die Dame und der Landstreicher (Ger 1922)
Freund Ripp (Ger 1922)
Jugend (Ger 1922)
Das Liebesnest (Ger 1922)
Die Schuhe einer schönen Frau (Ger 1922)
Die brennende Kugel (Ger 1923)
Das Kind des Andern (Ger 1923)
Wilhelm Tell (Ger 1923)
Hedda Gabler (Ger 1924)
Lebende Buddhas (Ger 1924)
Mein Leopold (Ger 1924)
Heiratsschwindler (Ger 1924)
Kubinke der Barbier und die drei Dienstmädchen (Ger 1926)
Menschen untereinander (Ger 1926)

Schwester Veronika (Ger 1926)
Die Unehelichen (Ger 1926)
Die versunkene Flotte (Ger 1926)
Der alte Fritz (Ger 1927)
Der Katzensteg (Ger 1927)
Bennos Stehkragen (Ger 1927)
Irrwege der Liebe (Ger 1927)
Unter der Laterne (Ger 1928)
Detektiv des Kaisers (Ger 1930)
Skandal um Eva (Ger 1930)
Alraune (Ger 1930)
Der Hauptmann von Köpernick (Ger 1931)
Emil und die Detektive (Ger 1931)
Nachtkolonne (Ger 1931)
Dann schon lieber Lebertran (Ger 1931)
Berlin--Alexanderplatz (Ger 1931)
Quick (Ger 1932)
Das schöne Abenteuer (Ger 1932)
Tannenberg (Ger 1932)
Die Herren vom Maxim (Ger 1932)
Liebe muss verstanden sein (Ger 1933)
Der Traum vom Rhein (Ger 1933)
Zwei glücklich Tage (Ger 1933)
Hanneles Himmelfahrt (Ger 1934)
Wilhelm Tell (Ger 1934)
Konjunkturritter (Ger 1934)
Der Meisterboxer (Ger 1934)
Der schwarze Walfisch (Ger 1934)
Ich heirate meine Frau (Ger 1934)
Herz ist Trumpf (Ger 1934)
Die vier Musketiere (Ger 1934)
Der Polizeibericht meldet (Ger 1934)
Hermine und die sieben Aufrechten (Ger 1934)
Die törichte Jungfrau (Ger 1935)
Wunder des Fliegens (Ger 1935)
Ein falscher Fuffziger (Ger 1935)
Pygmalion (Ger 1935)
Familie Schimek (Ger 1935)
Hans im Glück (Ger 1936)
Donner, Blitz und Sonnenschein (Ger 1936)
Geheimnis eines alten Hauses (Ger 1936)
Fridericus (Ger 1936)
Eine Frau ohne Bedeutung (Ger 1936)
Familienparade (Ger 1936)
Schloss Vogelöd (Ger 1936)
Der Herrscher (Ger 1937)
Urlaub auf Ehrenwort (Ger 1937)
Krach und Glück bei Künnemann (Ger 1937)
Rätsel um Beate (Ger 1938)
Steputat & Co. (Ger 1938)
Das Ehesanatorium (Ger 1938)
Kleiner Mann, ganz gross (Ger 1938)
Der Tag nach der Scheidung (Ger 1938)

Der Fall Deruga (Ger 1938)
Der Schritt vom Wege (Ger 1939)
Verdacht auf Ursula (Ger 1939)
Dein Leben gehört mir (Ger 1939)
Der Stammbaum des Dr. Pistorius (Ger 1939)
Die gute Sieben (Ger 1940)
Bismarck (Ger 1940)
Bal pare (Ger 1940)
Heimaterde (Ger 1941)
Sechs Tage Heimaturlaub (Ger 1941)
Das himmelblaue Abendkleid (Ger 1941)
Annelie (Ger 1941)
Zwei in einer grossen Stadt (Ger 1942)
Liebesbriefe (Ger 1943)
Wildvogel (Ger 1943)
Münchausen (Ger 1943)
Sophienlund (Ger 1943)
Seinerzeit zu meiner Zeit (Ger 1944)
Das Konzert (Ger 1944)
Meine vier Jungens (Ger 1944)
Eine alltägliche Geschichte (Ger 1945)
Dr. phil. Döderlein (Ger 1945)
Ruf an das Gewissen (Ger 1945)
Und finden dereinst wir uns wieder (W Ger 1947)
Der grosse Mandarin (W Ger 1949)
Anonyme Briefe (W Ger 1949)
Der Biberpelz (W Ger 1949)
Nachtwache (W Ger 1949)
Gefährliche Gäste (W Ger 1949)
Absender unbekannt (W Ger 1950)
Gabriela (W Ger 1950)
Das Mädchen aus der Südsee (W Ger 1950)
Opfer des Herzens (W Ger 1950)
Die verschleierte Maja (W Ger 1951)
Königin einer Nacht (W Ger 1951)
Wenn die Abendglocken läuten (W Ger 1951)
Mein Freund der Dieb (W Ger 1951)
Herz der Welt (W Ger 1952)
Das Bankett der Schmuggler [Le banquet des Fraudeurs] (W Ger-
    Fr-Bel 1952)
Der Fürst von Pappenheim (W Ger 1952)
Heimweh nach Dir (W Ger 1952)
Der Tag vor der Hochzeit (W Ger 1952)
Lockende Sterne (W Ger 1952)
Ich warte auf Dich (W Ger 1952)
Von der Liebe reden wir spater (W Ger 1953)
Die vertagte Hochzeitsnacht (W Ger 1953)
Alles für Papa (W Ger 1953)
Die tolle Lola (W Ger 1953)
Sie (W Ger 1954)
Rosen-Resli (W Ger 1954)
Heimweh nach Deutschland (W Ger 1954)
Die 7 Kleider der Katrin (W Ger 1954)

Feuerwerk (W Ger 1954)
Die Mücke (W Ger 1954)
Schützenliesl (W Ger 1954)
Der letzte Sommer (W Ger 1954)
Heideschulmeister Uwe Karsten (W Ger 1954)
Der Himmel ist nie ausverkauft (W Ger 1955)
Eine Frau genügt nicht? (W Ger 1955)
Das Schweigen im Walde (W Ger 1955)
Studentin Helen Willfüer (W Ger 1955)
Auf Wiedersehen am Bodensee (W Ger 1956)
Die Stimme der Sehnsucht (W Ger 1956)
...wie einst Lili Marleen (W Ger 1956)
Jede Nacht in einem andern Bett (W Ger 1957)
Die grosse Chance (W Ger 1957)
Das Leben geht weiter (W Ger 1957)
Schwarze Nylons--heisse Nächte (W Ger 1958)
Ist Mama nicht Fabelhaft? (W Ger 1958)
Liebe, Luft und lauter Lugen (W Ger 1959)
Bezaubernde Arabelle (W Ger 1959)
Zarte Haut in schwarzer Seide (W Ger-Fr 1961)

HAID, LIANE, b. Aug. 16, 1895, Vienna
Mit Herz und Hand für Vaterland (Aus 1915)
Auf der Höhe (Aus 1916)
Die Landstreicher (Aus 1916)
Mit Gott für Kaiser and Reich (Ger 1916)
Sommeridylle (Aus 1916)
Die Tragödie auf Schloss Rottersheim (Aus 1916)
Lebenswogen (Aus 1917)
Mir Kommt keiner aus (Aus 1917)
Der Schandfleck (Aus 1917)
Der Verschwender (Aus 1917)
Der Doppelselbstmord (Aus 1918)
Der König amüsiert sich (Aus 1918)
So fallen die Lose des Lebens (Aus 1918)
Die Ahnfrau (Aus 1919)
Doktor Ruhland (Aus 1920)
Durch Wahrheit zum Narren (Aus 1920)
Eva, die Sunde (Aus 1920)
Freut euch des Lebens (Aus 1920)
Der Herr des Lebens (Aus 1920)
Der Laiermann (Aus 1920)
Lasset die Kleinen zu mir kommen (Aus 1920)
Die Stimme des Gewissens (Aus 1920)
Der tanzende Tod (Aus 1920)
Verschneit (Aus 1920)
Die Filme der Prinzessin Fantoche (Aus 1921)
Die Frau in Weiss (Aus 1921)
Das Geheimnis Lord Percivals (Aus 1921)
Der Roman eines Dienstmädchens (Aus 1922)
Sein Lebenslicht (Aus 1922)
Das Geld auf der Strasse (Ger 1922)
Lady Hamilton (Ger 1922)

Lukrezia Borgia (Ger 1922)
Der Pantoffelheld (Aus 1922)
Die Tochter des Brigadiers (Aus 1922)
Schlagende Wetter (Ger 1923)
Ich liebe Dich (Ger 1925)
Die Insel der Träume (Ger 1925)
Liebesfeuer (Ger 1925)
Als ich wiederkam (Ger 1926)
Die Brüder Schellenberg (Ger 1926)
Der fesche Erzherzog (Ger 1926)
Im weissen Rössl (Ger 1926)
Der Provinzonkel (Ger 1926)
Der Sohn des Hannibal (Ger 1926)
Die Czardasfürstin (Ger 1926)
Die Dollarprinzessin und ihre sechs Freier (Ger 1927)
Der goldene Abgrund (Ger 1927)
Der letzte Walzer (Ger 1927)
Die weisse Sklavin (Ger 1927)
Die Dame in Schwarz (Ger 1928)
Die Königin seines Herzens (Ger 1928)
Marquis d'Eon, der Spion der Pompadour (Ger 1928)
Schiff in Not SOS (Ger 1928)
Der Weiberkrieg (Ger 1928)
Zwei röte Rosen (Ger 1928)
Schwarzwaldmädel (Ger 1929)
Spiel um den Mann (Ger 1929)
Die grosse Sehnsucht (Ger 1930)
Das Lied ist Aus (Ger 1930)
Der unsterbliche Lump (Ger 1930)
Zweimal Hochzeit (Ger 1930)
Madame hat Ausgang (Ger 1931)
Die Manner um Lucie (Ger 1931)
Schatten der Manege (Ger 1931)
Meine Cousine aus Warschau (Ger 1931)
Grock (Ger 1931)
Kaiserliebchen (Ger 1931)
Opernredoute (Ger 1931)
Der Prinz von Arkadien (Aus 1932)
Der Diamant des Zaren (Ger 1932)
Ich will nicht wissen, wer Du bist (Ger 1932)
Stern von Valencia (Ger 1933)
Eine Frau wie Du (Ger 1933)
Sag' mir wer Du bist (Ger 1933)
Ihre Durchlaucht, die Verkäuferin (Ger 1933)
Madame wünscht keine Kinder (Ger-Aus 1933)
Roman einer Nacht (Ger 1933)
Keine Angst vor Liebe (Ger 1933)
Das Schloss im Süden (Ger 1933)
Besuch am Abend (Ger 1934)
Polizeiakte 909 (Ger 1934)
Bei der blondern Kathrein (Ger 1934)
Die Fahrt in die Jugend (Aus 1935)
Tanzmusik (Ger 1935)

Ungeküsst soll man nicht schlafen gehn (Aus 1936)
Peter im Schnee (Ger 1937)
Die unvollkommene Liebe (Ger 1940)
Die fuñf Karnickel (Aus 1953)

HAMPSHIRE, SUSAN, b. May 12, 1941, London
The Woman in the Hall (GFD 1947)
Upstairs and Downstairs (RFD 1959)
During One Night (Gala 1961)
The Long Shadow (RFD 1961)
The Three Lives of Thomasina (BV 1964)
Night Must Fall (MGM Br 1964)
Wonderful Life (Elstree 1964)
Paris au Mois d'Aout [Paris in August] (Fr 1966)
The Fighting Prince of Donegal (BV 1966)
The Trygon Factor (RFD 1967)
Quei temerari sulle loro Pazze, Scatenate, Scalcinate Carriole
    [Monte Carlo or Bust] (It-Fr 1969)
The Violent Enemy (Monarch 1969)
David Copperfield (20th 1969)
Living Free (Col 1972)
A Time for Loving [A Room in Paris] (Hemdale 1972)
Malpertius (Bel-Fr 1972)
Baffled! (Scotia-Barber 1972)
Neither the Sea nor the Sand (Tigon 1972)
Dr. Jekyll and Mr. Hyde (NBC-TV 1973)

HANIN, ROGER (Roger Levy), b. Oct. 20, 1925, Alger
La Môme vert-de-gris (Fr 1952)
Le Chemin de damas (Fr 1952)
Série noire (Fr 1954)
Gas-Oil (Fr 1955)
Les Hussards (Fr-It 1955)
Vous pigez? (Fr 1955)
Celui qui doit mourir (Fr 1957)
Escapade (Fr 1957)
Tamango (Fr 1957)
Sois belle et tais-toi (Fr 1958)
La Chatte (Fr 1958)
Le Désordre et la nuit (Fr 1958)
Une Balle dans le canon (Fr 1958)
Drôle de dimanche (Fr 1958)
Ramuntcho (Fr 1958)
Du rififi chez les femmes (Fr 1959)
A bout de souffle (Fr 1959)
Le Fric (Fr 1959)
La Valse du gorille (Fr 1959)
La Sentence (Fr 1959)
L'Affaire d'une Nuit (Fr 1960)
L'Ennemi dans l'ombre (Fr 1960)
Rocco e i suoi fratelli [Rocco et ses freres/Rocco and His
    Brothers] (It-Fr 1960)
Vive Henri IV, vive l'amour (Fr-It 1961)

Roger Hanin

Le Miracle des loups (Fr 1961)
Les Ennemis (Fr 1961)
Les Bras de la nuit (Fr 1961)
Carillons sans joie (Fr 1961)
La Loi des hommes (Fr 1961)
Le Gorille a mordu l'Archevêque (Fr 1962)
La marcia su Roma [La Marche sur Rome] (It-Fr 1962)
Vacances Portugaises (Fr 1962)
Un Mari à prix fixe (Fr 1963)
Le Tigre aime la chair fraîche [The Tiger Likes Fresh Blood]
    (Fr 1964)
Passeport diplomatique, Agent K 8 (Fr 1965)
Corrida pour un espion (Fr 1965)
Marie-Chantal contre le Dr. Kha (Fr 1965)
Le Tigre se parfume à la dynamite [An Orchid for the Tiger]
    (Fr 1965)
Le Hibou chasse la nuit (Fr 1965)
Le Feu aux poudres (Fr 1965)
Via Macao (Fr 1966)
Carré de dames pour un as (Fr 1966)
Le Solitaire passe à l'attaque (Fr-Sp 1966)
Il gioco delle spie [Bagarre a Bagdad pour x. 27] (It-Fr 1966)
Da Berlino l'apocalisse [Le Tigre sort sans sa mere] (It-Fr 1966)
The Brides of Fu Manchu [Les 13 Fiancées de Fu Manchu] (GB-
    Fr 1966)
Le Canard en fer blanc (Fr-Sp 1967)
Le chacal traque les filles (Fr 1967)
Las Vegas 500 milliones [Les Hommes de Las Vegas] (Sp-Fr-
    It 1967)

Bruno, l'enfant du dimanche (Fr 1968)
Les Deux Marseillaises (Fr 1969)
Plus jamais seul (Fr 1969)
La Main (Fr 1969)
Clair de Terre (Fr 1970)
Une Fille libre (Fr 1970)
Senza via d'uscita (It-Sp 1970)
Les Aveux les plus doux (Fr-Alg 1971)
The Revengers (National General 1973)
La raison du plus fou (Fr 1973)
Tony Arzenta [Les Grands Fusils/Big Guns] (It-Fr 1973)
Le Protecteur (Fr 1973)
Le Concierge (Fr 1973)
L'Intrépide (Fr 1975)
Le Faux cul (Fr 1975)

HARE, ROBERTSON, b. Dec. 17, 1891, Barnesbury, London
Rookery Nook [One Embarrassing Night] (W & F 1930)
On Approval (W & F 1930)
Tons of Money (W & F 1931)
Plunder (W & F 1931)
A Night Like This (W & F 1932)
Thark (W & F 1932)
Just My Luck (W & F 1933)
It's a Boy (W & F 1933)
A Cuckoo in the Nest (W & F 1933)
Friday the Thirteenth (ep "Mr. Lightfoot in the Park") (Gaumont 1933)
Turkey Time (Gaumont 1933)
A Cup of Kindness (Gaumont 1934)
Are You a Mason? (Univ Br 1934)
Dirty Work (Gaumont 1934)
Oh Daddy (Gaumont 1935)
Fighting Stock (Gaumont 1935)
Stormy Weather (Gaumont 1935)
Car of Dreams (Gaumont 1935)
Foreign Affairs (Gaumont 1935)
Jack of All Trades [The Two of Us] (Gaumont 1936)
Pot Luck (Gaumont 1936)
You Must Get Married (GFD 1936)
Aren't Men Beasts (ABPC 1937)
A Spot of Bother (GFD 1938)
So This Is London (20th Br 1939)
Banana Ridge (Pathe 1941)
Women Aren't Angels (Pathe 1942)
He Snoops to Conquer (Col Br 1944)
Things Happen at Night (Renown 1948)
One Wild Oat (Eros 1951)
The Magic Box (BL 1951)
Our Girl Friday [The Adventures of Sadie] (Renown 1954)
My Wife's Family (ABP 1956)
Three Men in a Boat (IFD 1956)
The Night We Got the Bird (BL 1960)

Out of the Shadow (NR 1961)
The Young Ones (WPD 1961)
Seven Keys (AA 1962)
Crooks Anonymous (AA 1962)
Hotel Paradiso (MGM 1966)
Salt and Pepper (UA 1968)
Raising the Roof (CFF 1972)

HARELL, MARTE, b. Jan. 4, 1909, Vienna
Opernball (Ger 1939)
Wiener Gschichten (Ger 1940)
Traummusik (Ger 1940)
Rosen in Tirol (Ger 1940)
Dreimal Hochzeit (Ger 1941)
Bruederlein fein (Ger 1942)
Die heimliche Graefin (Ger 1942)
Der dunkle Tag (Ger 1943)
Frauen sind keine Engel (Ger 1943)
Tolle Nacht (Ger 1943)
Schrammeln (Ger 1944)
Romantische Brautfahrt (Ger 1944)
Die tolle Susanne (Ger 1945) [unfinished]
Die Fledermaus (Ger 1945) [not shown until 1946]
Umwege zu Dir (Ger 1945) [not shown until 1947]
Glaube an mich! (Aus 1946)
Nach dem Sturm (Swi 1949)
Erzherzog Johanns grosse Liebe (Aus 1950)
Wien tanzt (Aus-Liechtenstein 1951)
Du bist die Rose vom Woerthersee (W Ger 1952)
Liebeskrieg nach Noten (W Ger 1953)
Spionage (Aus 1955)
Der Kongress tanzt (Aus 1955)
Im Prater bluehn wieder die Baeume (Aus 1958)
Die grosse Kuer (Aus-W Ger 1964)
Begegnung in Salzburg (W Ger-Fr 1964)
Otto ist auf Frauen scharf (Aus-W Ger 1968)
Was geschah auf Schloss Wildberg? [Sie nannten ihn Krambam-
    buli] (Aus-W Ger 1972)
Abenteuer eines Sommers (Aus 1974)

HARKER, GORDON, b. Aug. 7, 1885, London; d. March 2, 1967
The Ring (Wardour 1927)
The Farmer's Wife (Wardour 1928)
Champagne (Wardour 1928)
The Wrecker (W & F 1928)
Return of the Rat (W & F 1929)
The Crooked Billet (W & F 1929)
Taxi for Two (W & F 1929)
The Cockney Spirit in War (Butcher 1930) [three shorts; two com-
    bined as feature]
Elstree Calling (Wardour 1930)
The W Plan (Wardour 1930)
The Squeaker (BL 1930)

Escape (Radio 1930)
Third Time Lucky (W & F 1931)
The Stronger Sex (Ideal 1931)
The Sport of Kings (Ideal 1931)
Shadows (FN-P 1931)
The Ringer (Ideal 1931)
The Man They Could Not Arrest (W & F 1931)
The Calendar [Bachelor's Folly] (W & F 1931)
The Professional Guest (Fox Br 1931)
Condemned to Death (W & F 1932)
The Frightened Lady [Criminal at Large] (Ideal 1932)
Whiteface (W & F 1932)
Love on Wheels (W & F 1932)
Rome Express (Gaumont 1932)
The Lucky Number (Ideal 1933)
Britannia of Billingsgate (Ideal 1933)
This Is the Life (BL 1933)
Friday the Thirteenth (ep "Wakefield, the City Man") (Gaumont
    1933)
My Old Dutch (Gaumont 1934)
Road House (Gaumont 1934)
Dirty Work (Gaumont 1934)
The Phantom Light (Gaumont 1935)
The Lad (Univ Br 1935)
Admirals All (Radio 1935)
Squibs (Gaumont 1935)
Boys Will Be Boys (Gaumont 1935)
Hyde Park Corner (Pathe 1935)
The Amateur Gentleman (UA Br 1936)
Wolf's Clothing (Univ Br 1936)
Two's Company (UA Br 1936)
Millions (GFD 1936)
Beauty and the Barge (Wardour 1937)
The Frog (GFD 1937)
Blondes for Danger (BL 1938)
No Parking (BL 1938)
Lightning Conductor (GFD 1938)
The Return of the Frog (BL 1938)
Inspector Hornleigh (20th Br 1939)
Inspector Hornleigh on Holiday (20th Br 1939)
Saloon Bar (ABFD 1940)
Inspector Hornleigh Goes to It [Mail Train] (20th Br 1941)
Once a Crook (20th Br 1941)
Warn That Man (Pathe 1943)
29 Acacia Avenue [The Facts of Love] (Col Br 1945)
Things Happen at Night (Renown 1948)
Her Favourite Husband [The Taming of Dorothy] (Renown 1950)
The Second Mate (ABFD 1951)
Derby Day [Four Against Fate] (BL 1952)
Bang! You're Dead [Game of Danger] (BL 1954)
Out of the Clouds (GFD 1955)
A Touch of the Sun (Eros 1956)
Small Hotel (ABP 1957)
Left, Right and Centre (BL 1959)

HARRIS, RICHARD, b. Oct. 31, 1921, Limerick, Ireland
Alive and Kicking (ABF 1958)
Shake Hands with the Devil (UA 1959)
The Wreck of the Mary Deare (MGM 1959)
A Terrible Beauty [The Nightfighters] (UA 1960)
The Long and the Short and the Tall (WPD 1961)
The Guns of Navarone (Col 1961)
Mutiny on the Bounty (MGM 1962)
This Sporting Life (RFD 1963)
Il deserto rosso [The Red Desert] (It-Fr 1964)
I tre volti [Three Faces of a Woman] (ep "Gli amanti celebri"
    ["Famous Lovers"]) (It-Fr 1964)
Major Dundee (Col 1965)
The Heroes of Telemark (Col 1965)
The Bible... in the Beginning [La Bibbia] (20th 1966)
Hawaii (UA 1966)
Caprice (20th 1967)
Camelot (WB-7 Arts 1967)
The Molly Maguires (Par 1970)
A Man Called Horse (National General 1970)
Cromwell (Col 1970)
Bloomfield [The Hero] (20th 1971) [made in 1969]
Man in the Wilderness (Col 1971)
The Snow Goose (GB TV 1971)
The Deadly Trackers (WB 1973)
Gulliver's Travels (USA TV 1973)
Juggernaut (UA 1974)
99 and 44/100% Dead [Call Harry Crown] (20th 1974)
The Last Castle (20th 1975)

HARRISON, REX, b. March 5, 1908, Huyton, Lancashire
The Great Game (Gaumont 1930)
The School for Scandal (Par Br 1930)
Get Your Man (BD/Par 1934)
Leave It to Blanche (FN Br 1934)
All at Sea (Fox Br 1935)
Men Are Not Gods (UA 1936)
Storm in a Teacup (UA 1937)
School for Husbands (GFD 1937)
Over the Moon (UA 1937)
St. Martin's Lane [Sidewalks of London] (ABPC 1938)
The Citadel (MGM Br 1938)
The Silent Battle [Continental Express] (Par Br 1939)
Ten Days in Paris [Missing Ten Days] (Col Br 1939)
Night Train to Munich [Night Train/Gestapo] (MGM Br 1940)
Major Barbara (GFD 1941)
Journey Together (RKO 1944) (role cut from most prints)
I Live in Grosvenor Square [A Yank in London] (Pathe 1945)
Blithe Spirit (GFD 1945)
The Rake's Progress [Notorious Gentleman] (EL 1945)
Anna and the King of Siam (20th 1946)
The Ghost and Mrs Muir (20th 1947)
The Foxes of Harrow (20th 1947)

Escape (20th 1948)
Unfaithfully Yours (20th 1948)
The Long Dark Hall (BL 1951)
The Fourposter (Col 1952)
Main Street to Broadway (MGM 1953)
King Richard and the Crusaders (WB 1954)
The Constant Husband (BL 1955)
The Reluctant Debutante (MGM 1958)
Midnight Lace (Univ 1960)
The Happy Thieves (UA 1962)
Cleopatra (20th 1963)
My Fair Lady (WB 1964)
The Yellow Rolls Royce (MGM 1965)
The Agony and the Ecstasy (20th 1965)
The Honey Pot (UA 1967)
Doctor Dolittle (20th 1967)
A Flea in Her Ear (20th 1968)
Battle of Britain (UA 1969)
Staircase (20th 1969)

HARVEY, LAURENCE (Larry Skikne), b. Oct. 1, 1928, Yonishkis;
    d. Nov. 26, 1973
House of Darkness (BL 1948)
Man on the Run (ABP 1949)
Landfall (Renown 1949)
Man from Yesterday (ABP 1949)
Cairo Road (ABP 1950)
The Black Rose (20th 1950)
There Is Another Sun [Wall of Death] (Butcher 1951)
Scarlet Thread (Butcher 1951)
I Believe in You (GFD 1952)
A Killer Walks (GN 1952)
Women of Twilight [Twilight Women] (IFD 1952)
Innocents in Paris (IFD 1953)
The Good Die Young (IFD 1954)
Romeo and Juliet (GFD 1954)
I Am a Camera (IFD 1955)
Storm Over the Nile (IFD 1955)
Three Men in a Boat (IFD 1956)
After the Ball (IFD 1957)
The Truth About Women (BL 1958)
The Silent Enemy (IFD 1958)
Room at the Top (IFD 1959)
Expresso Bongo (Britannia 1959)
The Alamo (UA 1960)
Butterfield 8 (MGM 1960)
The Long and the Short and the Tall (WPD 1961)
Two Loves [The Spinster] (MGM 1961)
Summer and Smoke (Par 1961)
Walk on the Wild Side (Col 1962)
The Wonderful World of the Brothers Grimm (MGM 1962)
A Girl Named Tamiko [Tamiko] (Par 1962)
The Manchurian Candidate (UA 1962)

Laurence Harvey

The Running Man (Col Br 1963)
The Ceremony (UA 1963) [also director]
Of Human Bondage (MGM Br 1964)
The Outrage (MGM 1964)
Darling... (AA 1965)
Life at the Top (Col Br 1965)
The Spy with a Cold Nose (Par 1966)
The Winter's Tale (WPD 1968)
A Dandy in Aspic (Col Br 1968)
Heisses Spiel fur harte Manner (W Ger-It-Sp 1968)
Rebus (It 1968)
She and He [L'assoluto naturale] (It 1969)
Der Kampf un Rom [The Battle for Rome] (W Ger-It 1968/1969)
   [shown in two parts]
Tchaikovsky (USA-USSR 1970) (narrator)
WUSA (Par 1970)
Habricha El Hashemesh [Escape to the Sun] (Isr-W Ger-Fr 1972)
Night Watch (Avco Emb 1973)
Welcome to Arrow Beach (Brut 1973)

HARVEY, LILIAN, b. Jan. 19, 1906, London; d. July 27, 1968
    Der Fluch (Aus 1925)
    Leidenschaft [Die liebschaften der Hella von Gilsa] (Ger 1925)
    Liebe und Trompetenblasen (Ger 1925)
    Die kleine von Bummel (Ger 1925)
    Die Keusche Susanne (Ger 1926)
    Prinzessin Trulala (Ger 1926)
    Vater werden ist nicht schwer (Ger 1926)
    Die tolle Lola (Ger 1927)
    A Knight in London [Eine Nacht in London] (Br-Ger 1927)
    Eheferien (Ger 1927)
    Du sollst nicht stehlen (Ger 1928)
    Ihr dunkler Punkt (Ger 1929)
    Adieu Mascotte [Die Modell von Montparnasse] (Ger 1929)
    Wenn du einmal dein Herz verschenkst (Ger 1930)
    Liebeswalzer (Ger 1930)
    Love Waltz [Eng lang version of Liebeswalzer] (Ger 1930)
    Hokuspokus (Ger 1930)
    The Temporary Widow [Eng lang version of Hokuspokus] (Ger
        1930)
    Die drei von der Tankstelle (Ger 1930)
    Le Chemin du Paradis [Fr version of Die drei von der Tank-
        stelle] (Ger 1930)
    Einbrecher (Ger 1930)
    Princesse a vos ordes [Fr version of Ihre Hoheit Befiehlt] (Ger
        1931)
    Nie wieder Liebe (Ger 1931)
    Calais-Douvres [Fr version of Nie wieder Liebe] (Ger 1931)
    Der Kongress Tanzt (Ger 1931)
    Le Congres s'amuse [Fr version of Der Kongress Tanzt] (Ger
        1931)
    The Congress Dance [Eng lang version of Der Kongress Tanzt]
        (Ger 1931)
    Zwei Herzen und ein Schlag (Ger 1932)
    La Fille et le Garçon [Fr version of Zwei Herzen und ein
        Schlag] (Ger 1932)
    Quick (Ger 1932)
    Quick [Fr version of Quick] (Ger 1932)
    Ein blonder Traum (Ger 1932)
    Un Rêve blond [Fr version of Ein blonder Traum] (Ger 1932)
    Happy Ever After [Eng lang version of Ein blonder Traum] (Ger
        1932)
    Ich und die Kaiserin (Ger 1933)
    Moi et l'imperatrice [Fr version of Ich und die Kaiserin] (Ger
        1933)
    The Only Girl [Heart Song] (Eng lang version of Ich und die
        Kaiserin) (Ger 1933)
    My Weakness (Fox 1933)
    My Lips Betray (Fox 1933)
    I Am Suzanne (Fox 1934)
    Let's Live Tonight (Col 1935)
    Schwarze Rosen (Ger 1935)
    Roses Noires [Fr version of Schwarze Rosen] (Ger 1935)

Invitation to the Waltz (Wardour 1935)
Glückskinder (Ger 1936)
Les Gais Lurons [Fr version of Glückskinder] (Ger 1936)
Did I Betray? [Black Roses] [Eng lang version of Schwarze
 Rosen] (Ger 1936)
Sieben Ohrfeigen (Ger 1937)
Fanny Elssler (Ger 1937)
Capriccio (Ger 1938)
Ins blaue Leben (Ger 1939)
Castelli in Aria (It version of Ins blaue Leben) (Ger 1939)
Frau am Steuer (Ger 1939)
Sérénade [Sérénade éternelle] (Fr 1940)
Miquette [Miquette et sa mere] (Fr 1940)

HASSE, OTTO EDUARD, b. July 11, 1903, Obersitzka, Germany
Peter Voss, der Millionendieb (Ger 1932)
Muss mann sich gleich scheiden lassen? (Ger 1933)
Kreuzer Emden (Ger 1933)
Fräulein Hoffmanns Erzahlungen (Ger 1933)
Die vertauschte Braut (Ger 1934)
Peer Gynt (Ger 1934)
Ein ganzer Kerl (Ger 1935)
Die Gefangene des Königs (Ger 1935)
Der Schüchterne Casanova (Ger 1936)
Diener lassen bitten (Ger 1936)
Der ahnungslose Engel (Ger 1936)
Die grosse und die kleine Welt (Ger 1936)
So weit geht die Liebe nicht (Ger 1937)
Drei wunderschöne Tage (Ger 1939)
Illusion (Ger 1941)
Stukas (Ger 1941)
Alles für Gloria (Ger 1941)
Dr. Crippen an Bord (Ger 1942)
Die Entlassung (Ger 1942)
Rembrandt (Ger 1943)
Gefährtin meines Sommers (Ger 1943)
Geliebter Schatz (Ger 1943)
Der ewige Klang (Ger 1943)
Philharmoniker (Ger 1944)
Aufruhr der Herzen (Ger 1944)
Der Täter ist unter uns (Ger 1944)
Der grosse Preis (Ger 1944)
Komm zu mir zurück (Ger 1944)
Berliner Ballade (W Ger 1948)
Anonyme Briefe (W Ger 1949)
The Big Lift (20th 1950)
Epilog (W Ger 1950)
Decision Before Dawn (20th 1952)
Der grosse Zapfenstreich (W Ger 1952)
Der letzte Walzer (W Ger 1952)
I Confess (WB 1952)
Wenn am Sonntagabend die Dorfmusik spielt (W Ger 1953)
Lachkabinett (W Ger 1953)

Canaris (W Ger 1954)
Betrayed (MGM 1954)
Alibi (W Ger 1955)
08/15 in der Heimat (W Ger 1955)
08/15 II (W Ger 1955)
Above Us the Waves (GFD 1955)
Kitty und die grosse Welt (W Ger 1956)
Les Aventures d'Arséne Lupin (Fr 1957)
Sait-on jamais (Fr-It 1957)
Les Espions (Fr 1957)
Die Letzten werden, die Ersten zein (W Ger 1957)
Der gläserne Turm (W Ger 1957)
De Arzt von Stalingrad (W Ger 1958)
Der Maulkorb (W Ger 1958)
Solange das Herz schlägt (W Ger 1958)
Frau Warrens Gewerbe (W Ger 1960)
Au voleur [Affäre Nabob] (Fr-W Ger 1962)
Die Ehe des Herrn Mississippi (W Ger 1962)
Das Leben beginnt um acht (W Ger 1962)
Lulu (W Ger 1962)
Le Caporal épinglé (Fr 1962)
Le Vice et la vertu (Fr 1963)
Die Todesstrahlen des Dr. Mabuse [I raggi mortali del dottor
    Mabuse] (W Ger-It 1964)
Trois Chambres à Manhattan (Fr 1965)
Etat de Siège [L'Amerikano] (Fr-It 1972)
L'età della pace (It 1975)
Eisqert (W Ger 1975)

HAUFLER, MAX, b. June 4, 1910, Basel; d. June 25, 1965
    Farinet; ou, L'Or dans la Montagne (Swi 1939) (director and
        script only)
    Emil, me muess halt rede mitenand (Swi 1941) (director and co-
        script only)
    Gotthard-Express '41 (Swi 1942) (director and co-script only)
    Menschen, die vorüberziehen (Swi 1942) (director and co-script
        only)
    Steibruch (Swi 1942)
    Matto regiert (Swi 1947)
    Nach dem Sturm (Swi-W Ger 1948)
    Der Geist von Allenwyl (Swi 1951) (director and co-script
        only)
    Heidi (Swi 1952)
    Uli der Knecht (Swi 1954)
    Zwischen uns die Berge (Swi 1956)
    Bäckerei Zurrer (Swi 1957)
    Der 10. Mai (Swi 1957)
    Es geschah am hellichten Tage (Swi 1958)
    Die Käserei von der Vehfreude (Swi 1958)
    Ein wunderbarer Sommer/Ludmilla die Kuh (Swi-Aus 1958)
    Hinter den sieben Gleisen (Swi 1959)
    Ein Mann geht durch die Want (W Ger 1959)
    Der Mustergatte (Swi 1959)

Anne Babi Jowäger (Swi 1960)
Jakobli und Meyli (Swi 1960)
Der Teufel hat gut lachen (Swi 1960)
Town without Pity (UA 1961)
Chikita (Swi 1961)
Geld und Geist (Swi 1961)
Die Schatten werden länger (Swi 1961) (assistant director only)
Morituri (20th 1962)
The Miracle of the White Stallions (BV 1962)
Le Procès [The Trial] (Fr 1963)

HAWKINS, JACK, b. Sept. 14, 1910, London; d. July 18, 1973
Birds of Prey [The Perfect Alibi] (Radio 1930)
The Lodger [The Phantom Fiend] (W & F 1932)
The Good Companions (Gaumont-Welsh-Pearson 1933)
The Lost Chord (AP & D 1933)
I Lived with You (W & F 1933)
The Jewel (Par Br 1933)
A Shot in the Dark (Radio 1933)
Autumn Crocus (ABFD 1934)
Death at Broadcasting House (ABFD 1934)

Jack Hawkins struggles with Cecile Aubry in The Black Rose (1950).

Peg of Old Drury (UA 1935)
Beauty and the Barge (Wardour 1937)
The Frog (GFD 1937)
Who Goes Next? (20th Br 1938)
A Royal Divorce (Par Br 1938)
Murder Will Out (WB 1939)
The Flying Squad (ABPC 1940)
Next of Kin (UA 1942)
The Fallen Idol (BL 1948)
Bonnie Prince Charlie (BL 1948)
The Small Back Room [Hour of Glory] (BL 1949)
State Secret [The Great Manhunt] (BL 1950)
The Black Rose (20th 1950)
The Elusive Pimpernel (BL 1950)
The Adventurers [The Great Adventure/South African Story]
    (GFD 1951)
No Highway [No Highway in the Sky] (20th Br 1951)
Home at Seven [Murder on Monday] (BL 1952)
Angels One Five (ABP 1952)
Mandy [Crash of Silence] (GFD 1952)
The Planter's Wife [Outpost in Malaya] (GFD 1952)
The Cruel Sea (GFD 1953)
Twice Upon a Time (BL 1953)
Malta Story (GFD 1953)
The Intruder (BL 1953)
Front Page Story (BL 1954)
The Seekers [Land of Fury] (GFD 1954)
The Prisoner (Col Br 1955)
Land of the Pharoahs (WB 1955)
Touch and Go [The Light Touch] (RFD 1955)
The Long Arm [The Third Key] (RFD 1956)
The Man in the Sky [Decision Against Time] (MGM 1957)
Fortune Is a Woman [She Played with Fire] (Col 1957)
The Bridge on the River Kwai (Col 1957)
Gideon's Day [Gideon of Scotland Yard] (Col 1958)
The Two-Headed Spy (Col 1958)
Ben-Hur (MGM 1959)
The League of Gentlemen (RFD 1960)
The Spinster [Two Loves] (MGM 1961)
Five Finger Exercise (Col 1962)
Lawrence of Arabia (Col 1962)
Rampage (WB 1963)
Lafayette (Fr 1963)
Zulu (Par 1963)
The Third Secret (20th 1964)
Guns at Batasi (20th 1964)
Masquerade (UA 1964)
Lord Jim (Col 1965)
Judith (Par 1965)
Great Catherine (WPD 1967)
Shalako (WPD 1968)
Monte Carlo or Bust [Quei temerari sulle loro Pazze, Scatenate,
    Scalcinate Carriole] (It-Fr 1969)

Oh! What a Lovely War (Par 1969)
Twinky [Lola] (RFD 1969)
Waterloo (It-USSR 1970)
The Adventures of Gerard (GB-It-Swi 1970)
Jane Eyre (BL 1971)
When Eight Bells Toll (RFD 1971)
Nicholas and Alexandra (Col 1971)
Kidnapped (RFD 1971)
Young Winston (Col Br 1972)
Habricha El Hashemesh [Escape to the Sun] (Israel-W Ger-Fr 1972)
Theatre of Blood (UA 1973)
Tales That Witness Murder (Par 1973)
QB VII (ABC-TV 1974)

HAY, WILL (William Thompson Hay), b. Dec. 6, 1888, Aberdeen, Scotland; d. April 19, 1949
Those Were the Days (Wardour 1934)
Radio Parade of 1935 [Radio Follies] (Wardour 1934)
Dandy Dick (Wardour 1935)
Boys Will Be Boys (Gaumont 1935)
Where There's a Will (Gaumont 1936)
Windbag the Sailor (Gaumont 1936)
Good Morning Boys [Where There's a Will] (Gaumont 1937)
Oh, Mr. Porter! (GFD 1937)
Convict 99 (GFD 1938)
Hey! Hey! U.S.A.! (GFD 1938)
Old Bones of the River (GFD 1938)
Ask a Policeman (MGM Br 1939)
Where's That Fire? (20th Br 1939)
The Ghost of St. Michaels (ABFD 1941)
The Black Sheep of Whitehall (UA 1941)
The Big Blockade (UA 1942)
The Goose Steps Out (UA 1942)
My Learned Friend (Ealing 1943)

HELD, MARTIN, b. Nov. 11, 1908, Berlin
Schwarze Augen (W Ger 1951)
Heimweh nach dir (W Ger 1952)
Canaris (W Ger 1953)
Alibi (W Ger 1955)
Vor Sonnenuntergang (W Ger 1956)
Spion für Deutschland (W Ger 1956)
Der Hauptmann von Köpenick (W Ger 1956)
Friederike von Barring (W Ger 1956)
Der Fuchs von Paris (W Ger 1957)
Banktresor 713 (W Ger 1957)
Nasser Asphalt (W Ger 1958)
Meine Tochter Patricia (W Ger 1959)
Rosen für den Staatsanwalt (W Ger 1959)
Bumerang (W Ger 1960)
Der letzte Zeuge (W Ger 1960)
Die Ehe des Herrn Mississippi (W Ger-Swi 1961)

Frau Cheney's Ende (W Ger-Swi 1961)
Der Traum von Liebschen Müller (W Ger 1961)
90 Minuten nach Mitternacht (W Ger 1962)
Das schwarz-weiss-rote Himmelbett (W Ger 1962)
Das grosse Liebesspiel [And So to Bed] (W Ger-Aus 1963)
Ein fast anständiges Mädchen [Una chica casi formal] (W Ger-
    Sp 1963)
Liebe will gelernt sein (W Ger 1963)
Verdammt zur Sünde (W Ger 1964)
Das älteste Gewerbe der Welt [Le Plus Vieux Métier au monde/
    L'amore attraverso i secoli] (W Ger-Fr-It 1966)
Lange Beine, lange Finger (W Ger 1966)
Der Kommandant von Molinette (W Ger 1967)
Fast ein Held (W Ger-Yug 1967)
Dr. Fabian--Lachen ist die beste Medizin (W Ger 1969)
Die Herren Mit der Weissen Weste (W Ger 1970)
Le Serpent (Fr 1973)

HELM, BRIGITTE (Gisele Eve Schittenhelm), b. March 17, 1906,
    Berlin
Metropolis (Ger 1926)
Alraune (Ger 1927)
Am Rande der Welt (Ger 1927)
Die Liebe der Jeanne Ney (Ger 1927)
Abwege [Begierde] (Ger 1928)
Die Jacht der sieben Sünden [Yoshiwara] (Ger 1928)
Skandal in Baden-Baden (Ger 1928)
Manolescu (Ger 1929)
Die wunderbare Lüge der Nina Petrowna (Ger 1929)
L'Argent (Fr 1929)
Die singende Stadt (Ger 1930)
Alraune (Ger 1930)
Gloria [also Fr version] (Ger 1931)
Im Geheimdienst (Ger 1931)
Die Herrin von Atlantis (Ger 1932)
L'Atlantide [Fr version of Die Herrin von Atlantis] (Ger 1932)
Eine von uns (Ger 1932)
Die Gräfin von Monte Cristo (Ger 1932)
The Blue Danube (Ger 1932)
Hochzeitsreise zu Dritt [Wenn ich einmal eine Dummheit mache]
    (Aus 1932)
Voyage de noces [Fr version of Hochzeitsreise zu Dritt] (Aus
    1932)
Der Läufer von Marathon (Ger 1933)
L'Etoile de Valencia (Fr 1933)
Inge und die Millionen (Ger 1933)
Spione am Werk (Ger 1933)
Die schönen Tage von Aranjuez (Ger 1933)
Adieu les beaux joms [Fr version of Die schönen Tage von
    Aranjuez] (Ger 1933)
Die Insel (Ger 1934)
Vers l'abime [Fr version of Die Insel] (Ger 1934)
Gold (Ger 1934)

L'Or [Fr version of Gold] (Ger 1934)
Fürst Woronzeff (Ger 1934)
Le Suret des Woronzelf [Fr version of Fürst Woronzeff] (Ger 1934)
Ein idealer Gatte (Ger 1935)

David Hemmings and Samantha Eggar in The Walking Stick (1970).

HEMMINGS, DAVID, b. Nov. 18, 1941, Guildford, Surrey, England
    The Rainbow Jacket (GFD 1954) (extra)
    Five Clues to Fortune [The Treasure of Woburn Abbey] (BL-CFF 1957)
    The Heart Within (RFD 1957)
    St. Joan (UA 1957)
    No Trees in the Street (ABP 1959)
    Men of Tomorrow (NR 1959)
    In the Wake of a Stranger (Butcher 1959)
    The Wind of Change (Bry 1961)
    The Painted Smile (Planet 1962)

Some People (AA 1962)
Live It Up [Sing and Swing] (RFD 1963)
The System [The Girl Getters] (Bry 1964)
Two Left Feet (BL 1965) [made in 1963]
Be My Guest (RFD 1965)
Blow-Up (MGM 1967)
Camelot (WB-7 Arts 1967)
Eye of the Devil [13] (MGM 1968) [made in 1966]
Barbarella (Fr-It 1968)
The Charge of the Light Brigade (UA 1968)
Only When I Larf (Par 1968)
The Long Day's Dying (Par 1968)
Alfred the Great (MGM 1969)
The Best House in London (MGM 1969)
The Walking Stick (MGM 1970)
Fragment of Fear (Col 1970)
Unman, Wittering & Zigo (Par 1971)
The Love Machine (Col 1971)
Voices (Hemdale 1973)
Juggernaut (UA 1974)
Mr. Quilp [The Old Curiosity Shop] (EMI 1975)

HEYWOOD, ANNE (Violet Pretty), b. 1932, Handsworth, Birmingham
Find the Lady (RFD 1956)
Checkpoint (RFD 1956)
Doctor at Large (RFD 1957)
The Depraved (UA 1957)
Dangerous Exile (RFD 1957)
Violent Playground (RFD 1958)
Floods of Fear (RFD 1958)
The Heart of a Man (RFD 1959)
Upstairs and Downstairs (RFD 1959)
Cartagine in Fiamme [Carthage in Flames] (It-Fr 1959)
A Terrible Beauty [The Night Fighters] (UA 1960)
Petticoat Pirates (WPD 1961)
Stork Talk (Unifilms 1962)
Vengeance (Garrick 1962)
The Very Edge (Garrick 1963)
Tricetjedna Ve Stinu [90⁰ in the Shade] (Czech-GB 1965)
The Fox (WB-7 Arts 1968)
La monaca di Monza [Una storia Lombarda/The Awful Story of
    the Nun of Monza] (It 1968)
A Run on Gold [The Midas Run] (CIRO 1969)
The Most Dangerous Man in the World [The Chairman] (20th
    1969)
Assassina è al telefono [The Killer Is on the Phone] (It 1972)
I Want What I Want (Cin 1972)
Le monache di Sant'Arcangelo [The Nun and the Devil] (It-Fr
    1973)
All'aperto [Dance Under the Elms] (It 1975)

HILL, TERENCE see GIROTTI, MARIO

HILLER, WENDY, b. Aug. 15, 1912, Bramhall, Cheshire, England
  Lancashire Luck (B & D-Par 1937)
  Pygmalion (GFD 1938)
  Major Barbara (GFD 1941)
  I Know Where I'm Going (GFD 1945)
  Outcast of the Islands (BL 1951)
  Sailor of the King [Singlehanded] (20th Br 1953)
  How to Murder a Rich Uncle (Col Br 1957)
  Something of Value (MGM 1957)
  Separate Tables (UA 1958)
  Sons and Lovers (20th 1959)
  Toys in the Attic (UA 1963)
  A Man for All Seasons (Col 1966)
  David Copperfield (20th 1969)
  Murder on the Orient Express (EMI 1974)

HOERBIGER, PAUL, b. April 29, 1894, Budapest
  Spione (Ger 1928)
  Sechs Mädchen suchen Nachtquartier (Ger 1928)
  Song (Ger 1928)
  Der fesche Husar (Ger 1928)
  Die Dame mit der Maske (Ger 1928)
  Die grosse Abenteurin (Ger 1928)
  Heut spielt der Strauss (Ger 1928)
  Das letzte Souper (Ger 1928)
  Die Räuberbande (Ger 1928)
  Die Wochenendbraut (Ger 1928)
  Die tolle Komtesse (Ger 1928)
  Geschichten aus dem Wienerwald (Ger 1928)
  Asphalt (Ger 1929)
  Möblierte Zimmer (Ger 1929)
  Die Frau, die jeder liebt, bist Du (Ger 1929)
  Ein kleiner Vorschuss auf die Seligkeit (Ger 1929)
  Der Sträfling aus Stambul (Ger 1929)
  Das grüne Monokel (Ger 1929)
  Frauen am Abgrund (Ger 1929)
  Die 3 um Edith (Ger 1929)
  Wer wird denn weinen, wenn man auseinandergeht (Ger 1929)
  Der unsterbliche Lump (Ger 1930)
  Ich glaub nie mehr an eine Frau (Ger 1930)
  Zwei Herzen im 3/4 Takt (Ger 1930)
  Delikatessen (Ger 1930)
  Nur Du (Ger 1930)
  Wie werde ich reich und glücklich? (Ger 1930)
  Das alte Lied (Ger 1930)
  Drei Tage Mittelarrest (Ger 1930)
  Der Herr auf Bestellung (Ger 1930)
  Die Försterchristl (Ger 1931)
  Grock (Ger 1931)
  Ihre Hoheit befiehlt (Ger 1931)
  Die lustigen Weiber von Wien (Ger 1931)
  Walzerparadies (Ger 1931)
  Der Zinker (Ger 1931)

Kyritz-Pyritz (Ger 1931)
Mein Herz sehnt sich nach Liebe (Ger 1931)
Der ungetreue Eckehart (Ger 1931)
Sein Scheidungsgrund (Ger 1931)
Reserve hat Ruh (Ger 1931)
Der Kongress Tanzt (Ger 1931)
Arm wie eine Kirchenmaus (Ger 1931)
Der verjüngte Adolar (Ger 1931)
Lügen auf Rügen (Ger 1932)
Ein steinreicher Mann (Ger 1932)
Peter Voss, der Millionendieb (Ger 1932)
Es war einmal ein Walzer (Ger 1932)
Ein toller Einfall (Ger 1932)
Quick (Ger 1932)
Johann Strauss, K und K. Hofballmusikdirector (Ger 1932)
Zwei glückliche Tage (Ger 1932)
Drei von der Kavallerie (Ger 1932)
Ein blonder Traum (Ger 1932)
Scampolo, ein Kind der Strasse (Aus-Ger 1932)
Annemarie, die Braut der Kompanie (Ger 1932)
Trenck (Ger 1932)
Friederike (Ger 1932)
Paprika (Ger 1932)
Das Geheimnis um Johann Orth (Ger 1932)
Die unsichtbare Front (Ger 1932)
So ein Mädel vergisst man nicht (Aus-Ger 1933)
Audienz in Ischl/Kaiserwalzer (Ger 1933)
Der Grosse Bluff (Ger 1933)
Zwei gute Kameraden (Ger 1933)
Keinen Tag ohne Dich (Ger 1933)
Liebelei (Ger 1933)
Ein Lied für Dich (Ger 1933)
Heimkehr ins Glück (Ger 1933)
Gruss und Kuss, Veronika (Ger 1933)
Walzerkrieg (Ger 1933)
Skandal in Budapest (Ger-Hun 1933)
Des jungen Dessauers grosse Liebe (Ger 1933)
Fräulein Frau (Ger 1934)
Mein Herz ruft nach Dir (Ger 1934)
...heute abend bei mir (Ger 1934)
Die Csardasfürstin (Ger 1934)
Rosen aus dem Süden (Ger 1934)
Spiel mit dem Feuer (Ger 1934)
Frühjahrsparade (Aus-Ger-Hun 1934)
Ich heirate meine Frau (Ger 1934)
Besuch am Abend (Ger 1934)
Der Herr ohne Wohnung (Aus 1934)
Herz ist Trumpf (Ger 1934)
Petersburger Nächte (Ger 1935)
Frischer Wind aus Kanada (Ger 1935)
Endstation (Ger 1935)
Das Einmaleins der Liebe (Ger 1935)
Köningswalzer (Ger 1935)

Wenn die Musik nacht waer (Ger 1935)
Liebeslied (Ger 1935)
Die Puppenfee (Aus 1936)
Drei Mäderl um Schubert (Ger 1936)
Seine Tochter ist der Peter (Aus 1936)
Fiakerlied (Ger 1936)
Lumpazivagabundus (Aus 1936)
Kinderarzt Dr. Engel (Ger 1936)
Peter im Schnee (Aus 1937)
Der Scheidungsgrund (Ger-Czech 1937)
Die Landstreicher (Ger 1937)
Florentine (Aus 1937)
Immer, wenn ich glücklich bin (Aus 1938)
Einmal werd' ich Dir gefallen (Ger 1938)
Heiraten--aber wen? (Aus-Ger-Czech 1938)
Heimat (Ger 1938)
Liebelei und Liebe (Ger 1938)
Der Blaufuchs (Ger 1938)
Drunter und drueber (Ger 1939)
Prinzessin Sissy (Ger 1939)
Männer müssen so sein (Ger 1939)
Salonwagen E 4 1 7 (Ger 1939)
Ich bin Sebastian Ott (Ger 1939)
Unsterblicher Walzer (Ger 1939)
Kitty und der Weltkonferenz (Ger 1939)
Hochzeitsreise zu Dritt (Ger 1939)
Maria Ilona (Ger 1939)
Mutterliebe (Ger 1939)
Opernball (Ger 1939)
Wiener Geschichten (Ger 1940)
Falstaff in Wien (Ger 1940)
Der liebe Augustin (Ger 1940)
Operette (Ger 1940)
Herzensfreud--Herzenslied (Ger 1940)
Wunschkonzert (Ger 1940)
Oh diese Männer! (Ger 1941)
Wir bitten zum Tanz (Ger 1941)
Brüderlein fein (Ger 1942)
Die grosse Liebe (Ger 1942)
So ein Früchtchen (Ger 1942)
Die heimliche Gräfin (Ger 1942)
Wen die Götter lieben (Ger 1942)
Lache Bajazzo (Ger 1943)
Schwarz auf weiss (Ger 1943)
Schrammeln (Ger 1944)
Romantische Brautfahrt (Ger 1944)
Die Zaubergeige (Ger 1944)
Der Hofrat Geiger (Aus 1947)
Der Engel mit der Posaune (Aus 1948)
Kleine Melodie aus Wien (Aus 1948)
The Third Man (BL 1949)
Der Bagnostraefling (W Ger 1949)
Der Seelenbraeu (Aus 1950)

Eine Nacht im Separee (W Ger 1950)
Epilog (W Ger 1950)
Schwarzwaldmädel (W Ger 1950)
Dämonische Liebe (Aus-W Ger 1951)
Der alte Sünder (Aus 1951)
Die Frauen der Herrn S (W Ger 1951)
Verklungenes Wien (Aus 1951)
Was das Herz befiehlt (W Ger 1951)
Der fidele Bauer (Aus 1951)
Wenn die Abendglocken läuten (W Ger 1951)
Hallo, Dienstmann! (Aus 1952)
Frühlingsstimmen (Aus 1952)
Ich heisse Niki (W Ger 1952)
Mein Herz darfst Du nicht fragen (W Ger 1952)
Das Land das Lächelns (W Ger 1952)
Mikosch rückt ein (W Ger 1952)
Ich hab' mein Herz in Heidelberg verloren
   (W Ger 1952)
1 April 2000 (Aus 1952)
Man lebt nur einmal (W Ger 1952)
Hannerl (Aus 1952)
Die Fiakermilli (Aus 1953)
Von Liebe reden wir später (W Ger 1953)
Die Rose von Stambul (W Ger 1953)
Glück muss man haben (Aus 1953)
Junges Herz voll Liebe (W Ger 1953)
Der Feldherrnhügel (Aus 1953)
Das tanzende Herz (W Ger 1953)
Mit 17 beginnt das Leben (W Ger 1953)
Die Privatsekretärin (W Ger 1953)
Die Perle von Tokay (Aus 1954)
Der Raub der Sabinerinnen (W Ger 1954)
Der treue Husar (W Ger 1954)
Meine Schwester und ich (W Ger 1954)
Der Zigeunerbaron (W Ger-Fr 1954)
Die schöne Müllerin (W Ger 1954)
Bruder Martin (W Ger 1954)
Schützenliesel (W Ger 1954)
Begegnung in Rom (W Ger 1954)
Mädchenjahre einer Königin (Aus 1954)
Die Stadt ist voller Geheimnisse (W Ger 1955)
An der schönen blauen Donau (Aus 1955)
Ehesanatorium (Aus 1955)
Eine Frau genügt nicht? (W Ger 1955)
Die Deutschmeister (Aus 1955)
Banditen der Autobahn (W Ger 1955)
Sarajevo--Um Thron und Liebe (Aus 1955)
Du mein stilles Tal (W Ger 1955)
Der fröhliche Wanderer (W Ger 1955)
Ein Herz bleibt allein (W Ger 1955)
Die Försterbuben (W Ger 1955)
Ja, ja die Liebe in Tirol (W Ger 1955)
Charleys Tante (W Ger 1956)

Bademeister Spargel (Aus 1956)
Ein Herz und eine Seele (Aus 1956)
Hilfe-sie liebt mich! (Ger 1956)
Lügen haben hübsche Beine (Aus 1956)
Lumpazivagabundus (W Ger 1956)
Ihr Korporal (Aus-W Ger 1956)
Was die Schwalbe sang (W Ger 1956)
Das Donkosakenlied (W Ger 1956)
Manöverball (W Ger 1956)
Die Christel von der Post (W Ger 1956)
Der schräge Otto (W Ger 1957)
...und die Liebe lacht dazu (W Ger 1957)
Ober, zahlen! (Aus 1957)
Lemkes selige Witwe (W Ger 1957)
Hoch droben auf dem Berg (W Ger 1957)
Der schönste Tag meines Lebens (Aus 1957)
Heimweh..dort, wo die Blumen blueh'n (Aus 1957)
Die Winzerin von Langerlois (Aus 1957)
Wien, Du Stadt meiner Träume (Aus 1957)
Heiratskandidaten (Aus-W Ger 1958)
Hallo, Taxi (Aus 1958)
Hoch klingt der Radetzkymarsch (Aus 1958)
Sebastian Kneipp--der Wasserdoktor (Aus 1958)
Heimat--Deine Lieder (W Ger 1959)
Sabine und die 100 Männer (W Ger 1960)
Kauf Dir einen bunten Luftballon (Aus 1961)
...und Du, mein Schatz, bleibst hier (Aus 1961)
Der Orgelbauer von St. Marien (Aus 1961)
Tanze mit mir in den Morgen (Aus 1962)
...und ewig knallen die Räuber (Aus 1962)
Drei Liebesbriefe aus Tirol (Aus 1962)
Die lustigen Vagabunden (Aus 1963)
Unsere tollen Nichten (Aus 1963)
Sing, aber spiel nicht mit mir (Aus 1963)
Ferien vom Ich (W Ger 1963)
Im singenden Rössl am Königssee (Aus 1963)
Die ganze Welt ist himmelblau (Aus 1964)
Die grosse Kuer (Aus-W Ger 1964)
Das hab' ich von Papa gelernt (Aus-W Ger 1964)
Happy-end am Attersee (Aus-W Ger 1964)
Das ist mein Wien (Aus 1965)
Ruf der Wälder (Aus 1965)
Der Alpenkönig und der Menschenfeind (Aus 1965)
Was geschah auf Schloss Wildberg? (Aus-W Ger 1972)

HOFFMAN, ROBERT, b. Aug. 30, 1939, Salzburg,
    Austria
Vie privée [A Very Private Affair] (Fr-It 1961)
Angélique, marquise des anges (Fr-W Ger-It 1964)
Neues vom Hexer (W Ger 1965)
Up from the Beach (20th 1965)
Trois Chambres à Manhattan (Fr 1965)
Io la conoscevo bene (It-W Ger-Fr 1965)

Lutring, réveille-toi et meurs [Wake Up and Kill] (Fr-It 1966)
Come imparai ad amare le donne (It-W Ger-Fr 1966)
Domani non siamo più qui (It 1967)
Mille e non più mille (It-Fr 1967)
Ad ogni costo [Grand Slam] (It-Sp-W Ger 1967)
Assignment K (Col 1967)
Der Lügner und die Nonne (Aus 1968)
24 Heures de la vie d'une femme [24 Hours in a Woman's Life]
    (Fr 1968)
Tuvia Vesheva Benotar (Isr-W Ger 1968)
Exhibition (It-Fr 1969)
La morte non ha sesso [A Black Veil for Lisa] (It-W Ger 1969)
Certo, certissimo, anzi probabile (It 1969)
Avventure ed amori di Don Giovanni (It-Fr 1970)

HOLLOWAY, STANLEY, b. Oct. 1, 1890, London
    The Rotters (Ideal 1921)
    The Co-Optimists (New Era 1929)
    Sleeping Car (Gaumont 1933)
    The Girl from Maxim's (UA 1933)
    Lily of Killarney [Bride of the Lake] (AP & D 1934)
    Love at Second Sight [The Girl Thief] (Wardour 1934)
    Sing As We Go (ABFD 1934)
    Road House (Gaumont 1934)
    D'Ye Ken John Peel [Captain Moonlight] (AP & D 1935)
    In Town Tonight (BL 1935)
    Squibs (Gaumont 1935)
    Play Up the Band (ABFD 1935)
    Song of the Forge [The Village Blacksmith] (Butcher 1937)
    The Vicar of Bray (ABPC 1937)
    Cotton Queen [Crying Out Love] (BIED 1937)
    Sam Small Leaves Town [It's Sam Small Again] (British Screen
        Services 1937)
    Our Island Nation (Br 1937)
    Major Barbara (GFD 1941)
    Salute John Citizen (Anglo 1942)
    This Happy Breed (EL 1944)
    The Way Ahead [The Immortal Batallion] (EL 1944)
    Champagne Charlie (Ealing 1944)
    The Way to the Stars [Johnny in the Clouds] (UA 1945)
    Brief Encounter (GFD 1946)
    Caesar and Cleopatra (EL 1946)
    Wanted for Murder [Voice in the Night] (20th 1946)
    Carnival (GFD 1946)
    Meet Me at Dawn [The Gay Duellist] (20th 1947)
    Nicholas Nickleby (GFD 1947)
    One Night with You (GFD 1948)
    Hamlet (GFD 1948)
    Noose [The Silk Noose] (Pathe 1948)
    Saraband for Dead Lovers (GFD 1948)
    The Winslow Boy (BL 1948)
    Another Shore (GFD 1948)
    Passport to Pimlico (GFD 1949)

The Perfect Woman (GFD 1949)
Midnight Episode (Col 1950)
One Wild Oat (Eros 1950)
The Lavender Hill Mob (GFD 1951)
The Magic Box (BL 1951)
Lady Godiva Rides Again (BL 1951)
The Happy Family [Mr. Lord Says No] (Apex 1952)
Meet Me Tonight (ep "Fumed Oak") (GFD 1952)
The Titfield Thunderbolt (GFD 1953)
The Beggar's Opera (BL 1953)
A Day to Remember (GFD 1953)
Meet Mr. Lucifer (GFD 1953)
Fast and Loose (GFD 1954)
An Alligator Named Daisy (RFD 1955)
Jumping for Joy (RFD 1956)
Alive and Kicking (ABF 1958)
Hello London (RFI 1958)
No Trees in the Street (ABP 1959)
No Love for Johnnie (RFD 1961)
On the Fiddle [Operation Snafu/Operation Warhead] (AA 1961)
My Fair Lady (WB 1964)
Ten Little Indians (WPD 1965)
The Sandwich Man (RFD 1966)
Mrs. Brown, You've Got a Lovely Daughter (MGM 1968)
What's in It for Harry [How to Make It] [unreleased 1968]
The Private Life of Sherlock Holmes (UA 1970)
Flight of the Doves (Col 1971)

HOOL, ROGER VAN see VAN HOOL, ROGER

HOPPE, MARIANNE, b. April 26, 1911, Rostock, Germany
Heideschulmeiser Uwe Karsten (Ger 1933)
Der Judas von Tirol (Ger 1933)
Der Schimmelreiter (Ger 1934)
Krach um Jolanthe (Ger 1934)
Schwarzer Jäger Johanna (Ger 1934)
Alles hört auf mein Kommando (Ger 1934)
Oberwachtmeister Schwenke (Ger 1935)
Anschlag auf Schweda (Ger 1935)
Die Werft zum grauen Hecht (Ger 1935)
Wenn der Hahn Kräht (Ger 1936)
Eine Frau ohne Bedeutung (Ger 1936)
Gabriele eins, zwei, drei (Ger 1937)
Capriolen (Ger 1937)
Der Herrscher (Ger 1937)
Der Schritt vom Wege (Ger 1937)
Kongo-Express (Ger 1939)
Auf Wiedersehen, Franziska (Ger 1941)
Stimme des Herzens (Ger 1942)
Romanze in Moll (Ger 1943)
Ich brauche Dich (Ger 1944)
Das Leben geht weiter (Ger 1945)
Das verlorene Geschit (W Ger 1948)

Schicksal aus Zweiter Hand (W Ger 1949)
Nur eine Nacht (W Ger 1950)
Der Mann meines Lebens (W Ger 1954)
13 Kleine Esel und der Sonnenhof (W Ger 1958)
Die seltsame Gräfin (W Ger 1961)
Der Schatz im Silbersee (W Ger-Yug 1962)
Die Goldsucher von Arkansas (W Ger-It-Fr 1964)
Falsche Bewegung (W Ger 1975)

HORDERN, MICHAEL, b. Oct. 4, 1911, Berkhamsted, England
The Girl in the News (MGM Br 1940)
School for Secrets [Secret Flight] (GFD 1946)
Good Time Girl (GFD 1948)
Portrait from Life [The Girl in the Painting] (GFD 1948)
The Astonished Heart (GFD 1950)
Trio (ep "The Verger") (GFD 1950)
Highly Dangerous (GFD 1950)
The Magic Box (BL 1951)
The Hour of 13 (MGM Br 1952)
Street Corner [Both Sides of the Law] (GFD 1953)
Grand National Night [Wicked Wife] (Renown 1953)
Personal Affair (GFD 1953)
The Heart of the Matter (BL 1953)
You Know What Sailors Are (GFD 1954)
Forbidden Cargo (GFD 1954)
The Beachcomber (GFD 1954)
The Night My Number Came Up (GFD 1955)
The Constant Husband (BL 1955)
The Dark Avenger [The Warriors] (20th 1955)
Storm over the Nile (IFD 1955)
The Man Who Never Was (20th 1956)
Alexander the Great (UA 1956)
Pacific Destiny (BL 1956)
The Baby and the Battleship (BL 1956)
The Spanish Gardener (RFD 1956)
No Time for Tears (ABPC 1957)
Windom's Way (RFD 1957)
I Accuse! (MGM Br 1958)
The Spaniard's Curse (IFD 1958)
I Was Monty's Double [Hell, Heaven and Hoboken] (ABPC 1958)
Girls at Sea (ABPC 1958)
Sink the Bismarck! (20th 1960)
Moment of Danger [Malaga] (WPD 1960)
Man in the Moon (RFD 1960)
Macbeth (BL 1961)
El Cid (AA 1961)
Cleopatra (20th 1962)
The V.I.P.s (MGM 1963)
Dr. Syn-Alias the Scarecrow (BV 1963)
The Yellow Rolls Royce (MGM 1964)
The Spy Who Came in from the Cold (Par 1965)
Cast a Giant Shadow (UA 1966)
Khartoum (UA 1966)

A Funny Thing Happened on the Way to the Forum (UA 1966)
The Jokers (RFD 1966)
How I Won the War (UA 1967)
I'll Never Forget What's 'is Name (RFD 1967)
Where Eagles Dare (MGM 1968)
The Taming of the Shrew (It-GB 1968)
The Bed Sitting Room (UA 1969)
Futtocks End (BL 1970)
Anne of the Thousand Days (RFD 1970)
Some Will, Some Won't (WPD 1970)
Up Pompeii (MGM-EMI 1971)
Girl Stroke Boy (London Screen Distributors 1971)
Demons of the Mind (MGM-EMI 1972)
The Pied Piper (Scotia-Barber 1972)
Alice's Adventures in Wonderland (Fox-Rank 1972)
The Mackintosh Man (WB 1973)
Juggernaut (UA 1974)
Royal Flash (Fox-Rank 1975)
Mr. Quilp [The Old Curiosity Shop] (EMI 1975)
Lucky Lady (20th 1975)
The Slipper and the Rose (CIC 1976)

HORNEY, BRIGITTE, b. March 29, 1921, Berlin
Abschied (Ger 1930)
Fra Diavolo (Ger-It-Fr 1931)
Rasputin (Ger 1932)
Heideschulmeister Uwe Karsten (Ger 1933)
Der ewige Traum (Ger 1934)
Liebe Tod und Teufel (Ger 1934)
Ein Mann will nach Deutschland (Ger 1934)
Der grüne Domino (Ger 1935)
Blütsbruder (Ger 1935)
Stadt Anatol (Ger 1936)
Savoy-Hotel 217 (Ger 1936)
Der Katzensteg (Ger 1937)
Revolutions Hochzeit (Ger 1937)
Verklungene Melodie (Ger 1938)
Du und Ich (Ger 1938)
Anna Varetti (Ger 1938)
Zwei in den Wolken (Ger 1938)
Der Gouverneur (Ger 1939)
Das Mädchen von Fanö (Ger 1940)
Illusion (Ger 1941)
Geliebte Welt (Ger 1942)
Am Ende der Welt (Ger 1943)
Münchhausen (Ger 1943)
Die Frau am Wege (W Ger 1948)
Verspieltes Leben (W Ger 1949)
Melodie des Schicksals (W Ger 1950)
Solange Du da Bist (W Ger 1953)
Gefangene der Liebe (W Ger 1954)
Der letzte Sommer (W Ger 1954)
Der gläserne Turm (W Ger 1957)

Nacht fiel über Gotenhafen (W Ger 1960)
Das Erbe von Björndal (W Ger 1960)
Der Ruf der Wildgänse (Aus 1961)
Neues vom Hexer (W Ger 1965)
Ich suche einen Mann (W Ger 1966)

HOSSEIN, ROBERT (Robert Hosseinoff), b. Dec. 30, 1927, Paris
Quai des Blondes (Fr 1953)
Du Rififi chez les hommes (Fr 1954)
Série noire (Fr 1955)
Les Salauds vont en enfer [The Wicked Go to Hell] (Fr 1955)
Crime et châtiment (Fr 1956)
Sait on jamais [Tonight or Never] (Fr 1956)
Méfiez-vous fillettes [Young Girls Beware] (Fr 1957)
Liberté surveillée (Fr-Czech 1957)
Des femmes disparaissent (Fr 1958)
Toi le venin [Nude in a White Car] (Fr 1958)
La Nuit des espions (Fr 1959)
La Sentence (Fr 1959)
Les Canailles [Take Me As I Am] (Fr-It 1959)
Les Scélérats [Torment] (Fr 1960)
La Menace (Fr-It 1960)
Le Gout de la violence (Fr-W Ger-It 1960)
Le Jeu de la vérité (Fr 1961)
Madame Sans-Gène (Fr-It-Sp 1961)
Les Petits Matins [Girl on the Road] (Fr 1961)
Le Monte-Charge (Fr-It 1961)
Le Repos du guerrier [Love on a Pillow] (Fr-It 1962)
Le Vice et la vertu (Fr-It 1962)
Pourquoi Paris? (Fr-It 1962)
Les Grands Chemins (Fr-It 1963)
Le Meurtrier [Enough Rope] (Fr-It-W Ger 1963)
Le Mort d'un tueur (Fr-It 1963)
Chaire de poule (Fr 1964)
Les yeux cernés (Fr-It 1964)
L'Echiqueur de Dieu (Fr-It 1964)
Le Vampire de Düsseldorf (Fr 1964)
Angélique, marquise des anges (Fr-W Ger-It 1964)
Pour OSS II7 Banco à Bangkok (Fr-It 1964)
Le Commissaire mène l'enquête (Fr 1964) (cameo)
Madamigella de Maupin (It-Fr-Sp-Yug 1965)
Guerra segreta [The Dirty Game] (It-Fr-W Ger 1965)
La Fabuleuse Aventure de Marco Polo (Fr-It-Yug-Eg-Afghani-
    stan 1965)
Le Tonnere de dieu [God's Thunder] (Fr-W Ger-It 1965)
Pour un regard si doux (Fr 1965)
La Seconde Vérité (Fr-It 1966)
La Musica (Fr 1966)
Angélique et le roy (Fr-W Ger-It 1966)
Brigade anti-gangs (Fr-It 1966)
La Longue Marche (Fr 1966)
L'Homme qui trahit la mafia (Fr-It 1967)
Lamiel (Fr-It 1967)

Angélique indomptable (Fr-W Ger-It 1967)
Angélique et la sultan (Fr-W Ger-It 1967)
J'ai tué Raspoutine (Fr-It 1967)
Niente rose per OSS II7 (It-Fr 1967)
La Petite Vertu (Fr 1968)
La Leçon particulière [The Private Lesson] (Fr 1968)
Le Voleur de crimes (Fr-It 1968)
Une Corde...un colt (Fr-It 1968)
Les Noces de Carla (Fr 1968)
C'erà una volta il West [Once Upon a Time in the West] (It 1968)
La battaglia di El Alamein [Desert Tanks] (It-Fr 1969)
Le Temps des loups [Carbon Copy] (Fr-It 1969)
Nell'anno del signore (It-Fr 1969)
Maldonne (Fr-It 1969)
Les Libertines [Versatile Lovers] (Fr-It 1969)
La femme écarlate (Fr-It 1969)
Point de chute (Fr 1970)
La Part des Lions (Fr-It 1971)
Le Casse (Fr 1971)
Helle (Fr 1971)
Un Meutre est un meutre (Fr-It 1972)
Prêtés interdites (Fr 1973)
Le Protecteur (Fr 1974)

HOWARD, TREVOR, b. Sept. 29, 1916, Cliftonville, England
The Way Ahead [The Immortal Battalion] (EL 1944)
The Way to the Stars [Johnny in the Clouds] (UA 1945)
Brief Encounter (GFD 1945)
I See a Dark Stranger [The Adventuress] (GFD 1946)
Green for Danger (GFD 1946)
So Well Remembered (RKO Br 1947)
They Made Me a Fugitive [I Became a Criminal] (WB 1947)
The Passionate Friends [One Woman's Story] (GFD 1949)
The Third Man (BL 1949)
Golden Salamander (GFD 1950)
Odette (BL 1950)
The Clouded Yellow (GFD 1950)
Outcast of the Islands (BL 1951)
The Gift Horse [Glory at Sea] (IFD 1952)
The Heart of the Matter (BL 1953)
Les Amants du Tage [Lovers of Lisbon] (Fr 1953)
The Stranger's Hand (BL 1954)
Cockleshell Heroes (Col 1955)
Run for the Sun (UA 1956)
Around the World in 80 Days (UA 1956)
Interpol [Pickup Alley] (Col 1957)
Fire Down Below (Col 1957)
Manuela [Stowaway Girl] (RFD 1957)
The Key (Col 1958)
The Roots of Heaven (20th 1958)
Moment of Danger [Malaga] (WPD 1960)
Sons and Lovers (20th 1960)
Mutiny on the Bounty (MGM 1962)

The Lion (20th 1962)
The Man in the Middle (20th 1963)
Father Goose (Univ 1964)
Von Ryan's Express (20th 1965)
Operation Crossbow [The Great Spy Mission] (MGM 1965)
The Saboteur: Code Name Morituri [Morituri] (20th 1965)
Danger Grows Wild [The Poppy Is Also a Flower] (UN 1966)
Pretty Dolly [A Matter of Innocence] (RFD 1967)
The Long Duel (RFD 1967)
The Charge of the Light Brigade (UA 1968)
Battle of Britain (UA 1969)
Twinky [Lola] (RFD 1969)
Ryan's Daughter (MGM-EMI 1970)
The Night Visitor (UMC 1971)
Catch Me a Spy (GB-Fr-USA 1971)
Mary, Queen of Scots (RFD 1972)
Pope Joan [The Devil's Imposter] (Col-Warner 1972)
The Offence (UA 1972)
A Doll's House (GB-Fr 1973)
Ludwig II [Le Crepuscule des dieux/Ludwig] (W Ger-Fr-It 1973)
Craze (EMI 1974)
11 Harrowhouse (Fox-Rank 1974)
Persecution (Doverton 1974)
Hennessey [The 5th of November] (CIC 1975)
Conduct Unbecoming (BL 1975)

HUBSCHMID, PAUL (Paul Christian), b. July 20, 1917, Aarau,
    Switzerland
Füsilier Wipf (Swi 1938)
Maria Ilona (Ger 1939)
Der letzte Appell (Ger 1939) [uncompleted]
My Dream (Swi 1940)
Mir lönd nud lugg (Swi 1940)
Die missbrauchten Liebesbriefe (Swi 1940)
Der Fall Rainer [Ich warte auf dich] (Ger 1942)
Meine Freundin Josephine (Ger 1942)
Altes Herz wird wieder jung (Ger 1943)
Liebesbriefe (Ger 1943)
Wilder Urlaub (Swi 1943)
Der gebieterische Ruf (Ger 1944)
Dar Gesetz der Liebe (Ger 1944)
Das seltsame Fräulein Sylvia (Ger 1945)
Gottes Engel sind uberall (Aus 1948)
Arlberg-Express (Aus 1948)
Der himmlische Walzer (Aus 1948)
Geheimnisvolle Tiefe (Aus 1949)
Bagdad (Univ 1949)
The Thief of Venice (It 1950)
No Time for Flowers (20th 1952)
The Beast from 20,000 Fathoms (WB 1953)
Maske in Blau (W Ger 1953)
Musik bei Nacht (W Ger 1953)
Mit siebzehn beginnt das Leben (W Ger 1953)

Die Venus von Tivoli [Zwiepalt des Herzene] (Swi-W Ger 1953)
Les Cloches n'ont pas sonne [Ungarische Rhapsodie (Fr-W Ger
   1953)
Glückliche Reise (W Ger 1954)
Schule für Ehegluck (W Ger 1954)
Il Tesoro di Rommel (It 1955)
Die Frau des Botschafters (W Ger 1955)
Ingrid, die Geschichte eines Fotomodells (W Ger 1955)
Liebe die den Kopf verliert (W Ger 1956)
Die goldene Brucke (W Ger 1956)
Heute heiratet mein Mann (W Ger 1956)
Du bist Musik (W Ger 1956)
Glücksritter (W Ger 1957)
Salzburger Geschichten (W Ger 1957)
Die Zurcher Verlobung (W Ger 1957)
Scampolo (W Ger 1957)
La morte viene dallo spazio (It 1958)
Ihr 106. Geburtstag (W Ger 1958)
Italienreisse--Liebe inbegriffen (W Ger 1958)
Meine schöne Mama [Kleines Biest mit langen Haaren] (W Ger
   1958)
Der Tiger von Eschnapur (W Ger 1958)
Das indische Grabmal (W Ger 1958)
Zwei Gitarren (W Ger 1959)
Auskunft im Cockpit (Swi 1959)
Alle Tage ist kein Sonntag (W Ger 1959)
Liebe, Luft und lauter Lugen (W Ger 1959)
Marili (W Ger 1959)
Heldinnen (W Ger 1960)
Festival [Schwarze Rose/Rosemarie] (Sp-W Ger 1960)
Die rote Hand (W Ger 1960)
Die junge Sunderin (W Ger 1960)
Ich bin auch nur eine Frau (W Ger 1962)
Elf Jahre und ein Tag (W Ger 1963)
Das grosse Liebesbed [And So to Bed] (W Ger 1963)
Die Diamantenhölle am Mekong (W Ger 1964)
Heirate mich, Chéri! (W Ger 1964)
Die Lady (W Ger 1964)
Le Grain de sable (Fr 1964)
Die Herren (W Ger 1965)
Playgirl (W Ger 1965)
Ruf der Walder (W Ger 1965)
Die schwedische Jungfrau (W Ger 1965)
Moi et les hommes de guarante ans (Fr 1966)
Ich suche einen Mann (W Ger 1966)
Karriere [A belles dents] (W Ger-Fr 1966)
Upperseven, l'uomo da uccidere (It 1966)
Funeral in Berlin (Par 1966)
Mozambique (Fr 1966)
Ein gewissen Verlangen (W Ger 1966)
Hemmungslose Manon [Manon 70] (W Ger-Fr 1967)
In Enemy Country (Univ 1967)
Negresco (W Ger 1967)

A Taste of Excitement (Crispin 1969)
Skullduggery (Univ 1970)
Versuschung im Sommerwind (W Ger 1973)

HUNT, MARTITA, b. Jan. 30, 1900, Argentine Republic; d. June 13, 1969
A Rank Outsider (Walturdaw 1920)
Service for Ladies [Reserved for Ladies] (Par Br 1932)
Love on Wheels (W & F 1932)
I Was a Spy (W & F 1933)
Friday the Thirteenth (ep "Mr. Lightfoot in the Park") (Gaumont 1933)
Too Many Millions (WB Br 1934)
Mr. What's His Name (FN Br 1935)
The Case of Gabriel Perry (BL 1935)
First a Girl (Gaumont 1935)
When Knights Were Bold (GFD 1936)
Pot Luck (Gaumont 1936)
Tudor Rose [Nine Days a Queen] (Gaumont 1936)
The Interrupted Honeymoon (BL 1936)
Sabotage [A Woman Alone] (Gaumont 1936)
The Mill on the Floss (NPFD 1937)
Good Morning Boys [Where There's a Will] (Gaumont 1937)
Farewell Again [Troopship] (UA 1937)
Second Best Bed (GFD 1938)
Strange Boarders (GFD 1938)
Prison Without Bars (UA 1938)
The Nursemaid Who Disappeared (WB Br 1939)
Trouble Brewing (ABFD 1939)
A Girl Must Live (20th Br 1939)
The Good Old Days (FN Br 1939)
Young Man's Fancy (ABFD 1939)
At the Villa Rose [House of Mystery] (ABPC 1939)
Old Mother Riley Joins Up (Anglo 1939)
The Middle Watch (ABPC 1939)
Tilly of Bloomsbury (RKO Br 1940)
East of Piccadilly [The Strangler] (Pathe 1941)
Freedom Radio [A Voice in the Night] (Col Br 1941)
Quiet Wedding (Par Br 1941)
Once a Crook (20th Br 1941)
They Flew Alone [Wings and the Woman] (RKO Br 1942)
Sabotage at Sea (Anglo 1942)
Lady from Lisbon (Anglo 1942)
The Man in Grey (GFD 1943)
Welcome Mr. Washington (Anglo 1944)
The Wicked Lady (EL 1945)
Great Expectations (GFD 1946)
The Little Ballerina (GFD 1947)
The Ghosts of Berkeley Square (Pathe 1947)
So Evil My Love (BL 1948)
Anna Karenina (BL 1948)
My Sister and I (GFD 1948)
Lady Windemere's Fan [The Fan] (20th 1949)

The Story of Robin Hood and His Merrie Men (RKO 1952)
Treasure Hunt (IFD 1952)
Meet Me Tonight (ep "Red Peppers") (GFD 1952)
It Started in Paradise (GFD 1952)
Folly to Be Wise (BL 1952)
Melba (UA 1953)
King's Rhapsody (BL 1955)
The March Hare (BL 1956)
Three Men in a Boat (IFD 1956)
Anastasia (20th 1956)
The Admirable Crichton [Paradise Lagoon] (Modern Screenplays
    1957)
Les Espions (Fr-It 1957)
Dangerous Exile (RFD 1957)
Bonjour Tristesse (Col 1958)
Me and the Colonel (Col 1958)
Bottoms Up! (WPD 1960)
The Brides of Dracula (Univ 1960)
Song Without End (Col 1960)
Mr. Topaze [I Like Money] (20th 1961)
The Wonderful World of the Brothers Grimm (MGM 1962)
Becket (Par 1964)
The Unsinkable Molly Brown (MGM 1964)
Bunny Lake Is Missing (Col 1965)
The Long Day's Dying (Par 1968)
The Best House in London (MGM 1969)

HUNTLEY, RAYMOND, b. April 23, 1904, Birmingham
Can You Hear Me, Mother? (PDC 1935)
Whom the Gods Love [Mozart] (ABFD 1936)
Rembrandt (UA 1936)
Knight without Armour (UA 1937)
Dinner at the Ritz (20th Br 1937)
The Lion Has Wings (UA 1939)
Night Train to Munich [Night Train] (MGM Br 1940)
The Ghost of St. Michael's (ABFD 1941)
Freedom Radio [A Voice in the Night] (Col Br 1941)
The Ghost Train (GFD 1941)
Inspector Hornleigh Goes To It [Mail Train] (20th Br 1941)
Pimpernel Smith [Mister V] (Anglo 1941)
When We Are Married (Anglo 1943)
The Way Ahead (EL 1944)
They Came to a City (Ealing 1944)
I See a Dark Stranger [The Adventuress] (GFD 1946)
School for Secrets [Secret Flight] (GFD 1946)
So Evil My Love (Par Br 1948)
Broken Journey (GFD 1948)
Mr. Perrin and Mr. Traill (GFD 1948)
It's Hard to Be Good (GFD 1948)
Passport to Pimlico (GFD 1949)
Trio (ep "Sanatorium") (GFD 1950)
The Long Dark Hall (BL 1951)
I'll Never Forget You [The House in the Square] (20th 1951)

Mr. Denning Drives North (BL 1951)
The Last Page [Manbait] (Ex 1952)
Laxdale Hall [Scotch on the Rocks] (ABFD 1953)
Glad Tidings (Eros 1953)
Meet Mr. Lucifer (GFD 1953)
Hobson's Choice (BL 1954)
Orders Are Orders (BL 1954)
Aunt Clara (BL 1954)
The Teckman Mystery (BL 1954)
The Constant Husband (BL 1955)
The Prisoner (Col Br 1955)
The Dam Busters (ABPC 1955)
Doctor at Sea (RFD 1955)
Geordie [Wee Geordie] (BL 1955)
The Last Man to Hang? (Col 1956)
The Green Man (BL 1956)
Town on Trial (Col Br 1957)
Brothers in Law (BL 1957)
Next to No Time (BL 1958)
Room at the Top (IFD 1959)
Carlton-Browne of the F.O. [Man in a Cocked Hat] (BL 1959)
Innocent Meeting (UA 1959)
The Mummy (Univ 1959)
I'm All Right Jack (BL 1959)
Our Man in Havana (Col 1960)
Bottoms Up! (WPD 1960)
Make Mine Mink (RFD 1960)
Follow That Horse! (WPD 1960)
Sands of the Desert (WPD 1960)
A French Mistress (BL 1960)
Suspect [The Risk] (BL 1960)
Pure Hell of St. Trinian's (BL 1960)
Only Two Can Play (BL 1962)
Waltz of the Toreadors (RFD 1962)
Crooks Anonymous (AA 1962)
On the Beat (RFD 1962)
Nurse on Wheels (AA 1963)
The Yellow Teddybears (Compton 1963)
Father Came Too (RFD 1963)
The Black Torment (Compton 1964)
Rotten to the Core (BL 1965)
The Great St. Trinian's Train Robbery (BL 1966)
Hostile Witness (UA 1968)
The Adding Machine (RFD 1969)
Arthur, Arthur (Gallu 1969) [unreleased]
Destiny of a Spy [The Gaunt Woman] (NBC-TV 1970)
Young Winston (Col-Warner 1972)
That's Your Funeral (Fox-Rank 1973)
When the Bough Breaks (GB 1973) [unreleased]

HURT, JOHN, b. 1940, Cleethorpe, Lincs, England
    The Wild and the Willing (RFD 1962)
    A Man for All Seasons (Col 1967)

Sinful Davey (UA 1969)
Before Winter Comes (Col 1969)
In Search of Gregory (RFD 1969)
Mr. Forbush and the Penguins (BL 1971)
10 Rillington Place (20th 1971)
The Ghoul (Fox-Rank 1975)
Little Malcolm and His Struggle Against the Eunuchs (Multicetera
    Investments 1974)

HYDE WHITE, WILFRID, b. May 12, 1903, Bowton-on-the-Water,
    Gloucestershire, England
Josser on the Farm (Fox Br 1934)
Night Mail (MGM 1935)
Admirals All (Radio 1935)
Alibi Inn (MGM 1935)
Murder by Rope (B & D-Par Br 1936)
Rembrandt (UA 1936)
The Scarab Murder Case (B & D-Par Br 1936)
Elephant Boy (UA 1937)
Bulldog Drummond at Bay (Wardour 1937)
Change for a Sovereign (FN Br 1937)
Meet Mr. Penny (ABPC 1938)
I've Got a Horse (BL 1938)
The Lambeth Walk (MGM Br 1939)
Poison Pen (ABPC 1939)
Turned Out Nice Again (UA 1941)
Lady from Lisbon (Anglo 1942)
Asking for Trouble (Anglo 1942)
The Demi-Paradise [Adventure for Two] (GFD 1943)
Appointment with Crime (Anglo 1946)
While the Sun Shines (Pathe 1947)
Meet Me at Dawn (20th Br 1947)
The Ghosts of Berkeley Square (Pathe 1947)
My Brother Jonathan (Pathe 1948)
My Brother's Keeper (GFD 1948)
The Winslow Boy (BL 1948)
Quartet (ep "The Colonel's Lady") (GFD 1948)
The Passionate Friends [One Woman's Story] (GFD 1949)
The Bad Lord Byron (GFD 1949)
Britannia Mews [Forbidden Street] (20th Br 1949)
Adam and Evelyne [Adam and Evalyn] (GFD 1949)
That Dangerous Age [If This Be Sin] (BL 1949)
Helter Skelter (GFD 1949)
Conspirator (MGM 1949)
The Third Man (BL 1949)
Golden Salamander (GFD 1950)
The Angel with the Trumpet (BL 1950)
Last Holiday (ABP 1950)
Trio (ep "Mr. Knowall") (GFD 1950)
The Mudlark (20th 1950)
Highly Dangerous (GFD 1950)
Midnight Episode (Col 1950)
Blackmailed [Mr. Christopher] (GFD 1951)

Mr. Drake's Duck (Eros 1951)
The Browning Version (GFD 1951)
No Highway [No Highway in the Sky] (20th 1951)
Mr. Denning Drives North (BL 1951)
Outcast of the Islands (BL 1951)
Top Secret [Mr. Potts Goes to Moscow] (ABP 1952)
The Story of Gilbert and Sullivan [The Great Gilbert and Sulli-
    van] (BL 1953)
The Triangle (ep "Priceless Packet") (BL 1953)
The Million Pound Note [Man with a Million] (GFD 1954)
The Rainbow Jacket (GFD 1954)
Duel in the Jungle (ABP 1954)
Betrayed (MGM 1954)
To Dorothy a Son [Cash on Delivery] (IFD 1954)
See How They Run (BL 1955)
John and Julie (BL 1955)
The Adventures of Quentin Durward (MGM 1956)
The March Hare (BL 1956)
My Teenage Daughter [Teenage Bad Girl] (BL 1956)
The Silken Affair (RKO 1956)
That Woman Opposite [City After Midnight] (Monarch 1957)
The Vicious Circle [The Circle] (IFD 1957)
Tarzan and the Lost Safari (MGM 1957)
Up the Creek (WB 1958)
Wonderful Things (ABP 1958)
The Lady Is a Square (ABP 1959)
Carry on Nurse (AA 1959)
Life in Emergency Ward 10 (Eros 1959)
Libel (MGM 1959)
North West Frontier [Flame over India] (RFD 1959)
Two-Way Stretch (BL 1960)
Let's Make Love (20th 1960)
His and Hers (Eros 1961)
On the Double (Par 1961)
On the Fiddle (AA 1961)
Ada (MGM 1961)
Crooks Anonymous (AA 1962)
In Search of the Castaways (BV 1962)
My Fair Lady (WB 1964)
You Must Be Joking! (Col 1965)
Ten Little Indians (WPD 1965)
John Goldfarb, Please Come Home (20th 1965)
The Liquidator (MGM 1965)
Our Man in Marrakesh [Bang Bang You're Dead] (AA 1966)
The Sandwich Man (RFD 1966)
Hotel (WB 1967)
Sumuru [The 1,000,000 Eyes of Sumuru] (AA 1967)
P J [New Face in Hell] (Univ 1967)
Gaily, Gaily [Chicago Chicago] (UA 1969)
Skullduggery (Univ 1969)
Fragment of Fear (Col 1970)
The Cherry Picker (Fox-Rank 1974) [made in 1972]

INGRASSIA, CICCIO, b. Oct. 5, 1923, Palermo, Italy
With Franco Franchi:
Appuntamento a Ischia (It 1960)
L'onorata società (It 1961)
Pugni, pupe e marinai (It 1961)
Il guidizio universale [Le Jugement dernier] (It-Fr 1961)
Gerarchi si muore (It 1962)
I tre nemici (It 1962)
Il due della legione (It 1962)
Il mio amico Benito (It 1962)
I motorizzati (It 1962)
Il giorno più corto (It 1963)
La donna degli altri è sempre più bella (ep "I promessi sposi")
   (It 1963)
Avventura al motel (It 1963)
Le massaggiatrici (It 1963)
Tutto è musica (It 1963)
Due samurai per cento geishe (It 1963)
Vino, whisky e acqua salata (It 1963)
Gli imbroglioni (It 1963)
Obiettivo ragazze (It 1963)
I due mafiosi (It 1964)
Due mafiosi nel Far-West [Dos pistoleros] (It-Sp 1964)
I due evasi di Sing Sing (It 1964)
002 agenti segretissimi (It 1964)
Sedotti e bedonati (It 1964)
I due toreri [Dos toreros de Aupa] (It-Sp 1964)
Due mattachioni al Moulin Rouge (It 1964)
Le tardoni (ep "Un delitto quasi perfetto") (It 1964)
Scandali...nudi (It 1964)
I maniaci (It 1964)
Canzoni, bulli e pupe (It 1964)
Queste pazze, pazze donne (It 1964)
I marziane hanno dodici mani (It 1964)
L'amore primitivo (It 1964)
Cadavere per signora (It 1964)
Amore facile (ep "Un uomo corretto") (It 1964)
Due marinos e un generale (It 1965)
Due mafiosi contro Goldfinger (It 1965)
Un monstro e mezzo (It 1965)
Le sette vipere (It 1965)
I due percoli pubblici (It 1965)
Soldati e caporali (It 1965)
Veneri al sole (It 1965)
Per un pugno nell'occhio [Por un puñado de golpes] (It-Sp 1965)
I figli del leopardo (It 1965)
Io uccido, tu uccidi (ep "Cavalleria rusticana") (It 1965)
Letti sbagliati (ep "La seconda moglie") (It 1965)
Come inguaiammo l'esercito (It 1965)
Veneri in collegio (It 1965)
I due sergenti del generale Custer [Dos vivales en fuerte Alamo]
   (It-Sp 1965)
Gli amanti latini (ep "Amanti latini") (It 1965)

002 operazione Luna [Dos cosmonautas a la fuerza] (It-Sp 1965)
Los mangantes [Imbroglioni] (Sp-It 1965)
Dos de la maffia (Sp-It 1965)
Las otoñales [Le tardone] (Sp-It 1965)
Dos cosmaonautas a la fuerza (Sp-It 1965)
Dos pistoleros [Due mafiosi nel Far West] (Sp-It 1966)
Dos toreros de Aupa [I due toreri] (Sp-It 1966)
Come svaligiammo la Banca d'Italia (It 1966)
I due pari (It 1966)
Due mafiosi contro Al Capone [Dos contra Al Capone] (It-Sp 1966)
I due sanculotti (It 1966)
Le spie vengono dal semi-freddo [Dr. Goldfoot and the Girl
    Bombs] (It 1966)
Il lungo, il corto, il gatto (It 1967)
Due Rrringos nel Texas (It 1967)
Come rubammo la bomba atomica (It 1967)
Il bello, il bruto, il cretino (It 1967)
I due figli di Ringo (It 1967)
Il barbiere di Sicilia (It 1967)
I due vigili (It 1967)
Nel sole (It 1967)
Stasera mi butto (It 1967)
Brutti di notte (It 1968)
L'oro del mondo [I due salumieri] (It 1968)
Franco, Ciccio e le vedove allegre (It 1968)
Capriccio all'italiana (ep "Che cosa sono le nuvole?") (It 1968)
I due crociati (It 1968)
Ciccio perdona...io no! (It 1968)
Don Chisciotte e Sancio Panza (It 1968)
I due pompieri (It 1968)
I nipoti di Zorro (It 1968)
I due deputati (It 1969)
Franco e Ciccio...ladro e guardia (It 1969)
Indovina chi viene a merenda (It 1969)
Franco e Ciccio e il pirata Barbarera (It 1969)
Don Franco e Don Ciccio nell'anno della contestazione (It 1970)
I due maghi del pallone (It 1970)
Due bianchi nell'Africa nera (It 1970)
Franco, Ciccio sul sentiero di guerra (It 1970)
Ma chi ti ha dato la patente? (It 1970)
Principe coronato cercasi per ricca ereditiera (It 1970)
Satiricosissimo (It 1971)
Mazzabubu...Quante coma stanno quaggiù? (It 1971)
Viva le done (It 1971)
Armiamoci e partite (It-Fr 1971)
I due assi del guantone (It 1971)
Il clan dei due Borsalini (It 1971)
I due della formula 1 alla corsa più pazza, pazza del mondo (It
    1971)
Ma che musica, maestro! (It 1971)
I due pezzi da (It 1971)
Riuscira l'avvacate Franco Benenato a sconfiggere il suo acer-
    rimo nemico il pretore Ciccio de Ingras? (It 1972)

Scusi, ma lei le paga le tasse? (It 1972)
Venga a fare il soldato da noi (It 1972)
L'avventura di Pinocchio (It 1972)
Continuavano a chiamarli i due piloti più matti del mondo (It 1972)
Continuavano a chiamerti...è più ex meno (It 1972)
I due figli di Trinità (It 1972)
Due gattoni a nove code...e mezza ad Amsterdam (It 1972)
Storia di fifa e di coltello (It 1972)
Farfallon (It 1974)
Without Franco Franchi:
    La violenza quinto potere (It 1973)
    Amarcord (It 1973)
    l'esoriccio (It 1975)

JACKSON, GLENDA, b. 1937, Birkenhead, England
    The Persecution and Assassination of Jean-Paul Marat as per-
        formed by the Inmates of the Asylum of Charenton under the
        direction of the Marquis De Sade (UA 1967)
    Tell Me Lies (Condon Continental 1968)
    Women in Love (UA 1969)
    Negatives (Crispin 1970) [made in 1968]
    The Music Lovers (UA 1971)
    Sunday, Bloody Sunday (UA 1971)
    The Boy Friend (MGM-EMI 1972)
    Mary, Queen of Scots (RFI 1972)
    The Triple Echo (Hemdale 1972)
    A Touch of Class (Avco Emb 1973)
    Bequest to the Nation [The Nelson Affair] (CIC 1973)
    The Tempter (GB-It 1974)
    The Maids (AFT 1974)
    The Romantic Englishwoman (GB-Fr 1975)

JACKSON, GORDON, b. Dec. 19, 1923, Glasgow
    The Foreman Went to France [Somewhere in France] (UA 1942)
    Nine Men (UA 1943)
    Millions Like Us (GFD 1943)
    San Demetrio--London (Ealing 1943)
    Pink Strings and Sealing Wax (EL 1945)
    The Captive Heart (GFD 1946)
    Against the Wind (GFD 1948)
    Eureka Stockade (GFD 1949)
    Floodtide (GFD 1949)
    Stop Press Girl (GFD 1949)
    Whisky Galore! [Tight Little Island] (GFD 1949)
    Bitter Springs (GFD 1950)
    Happy Go Lovely (ABP 1951)
    The Lady with a Lamp (BL 1951)
    Castle in the Air (ABP 1952)
    Death Goes to School (Eros 1953)
    Malta Story (GFD 1953)
    Meet Mr. Lucifer (GFD 1953)
    The Love Lottery (GFD 1954)
    The Delavine Affair (Monarch 1954)

As Long As They're Happy (GFD 1955)
Passage Home (GFD 1955)
Windfall (Eros 1955)
The Quatermass Experiment [The Creeping Unknown] (Ex 1955)
Pacific Destiny (BL 1956)
Women Without Men [Blonde Bait] (Ex 1956)
The Baby and the Battleship (BL 1956)
Sailor Beware! [Panic in the Parlour] (IFD 1956)
Seven Waves Away [Abandon Ship!] (Col 1957)
Hell Drivers (RFD 1957)
The Black Ice (Archway 1957)
Blind Spot (Butcher 1958)
Three Crooked Men (Par 1958)
Rockets Galore (RFD 1958)
Yesterday's Enemy (Col 1959)
The Bridal Path (BL 1959)
Blind Date [Chance Meeting] (RFD 1959)
The Navy Lark (20th 1959)
Devil's Bait (RFD 1959)
The Price of Silence (GN 1960)
Cone of Silence [Trouble in the Sky] (Bry 1960)
Snowball (RFD 1960)
Tunes of Glory (UA 1960)
Greyfriars Bobby (BV 1961)
Two Wives at One Wedding (Par 1961)
Mutiny on the Bounty (MGM 1962)
The Great Escape (UA 1963)
The Long Ships (Col 1964)
The Ipcress File (RFD 1965)
Operation Crossbow [The Great Spy Mission] (MGM 1965)
Those Magnificent Men in Their Flying Machines; or, How I
    Flew from London to Paris in 25 Hrs. and 11 Minutes (20th
    1965)
Cast a Giant Shadow (UA 1966)
The Fighting Prince of Donegal (BV 1966)
The Night of the Generals (Col 1967)
Triple Cross (GB-Fr 1967)
Danger Route (UA 1967)
The Prime of Miss Jean Brodie (20th 1969)
On the Run (CFF 1969)
Run Wild, Run Free (Col 1969)
Hamlet (Col 1969)
Scrooge (20th 1970)
Kidnapped (RFD 1972)
Madame Sin (Scotia-Barber 1972)
Russian Roulette (Avco Emb 1975)

JACOBINI, MARIA, b. Feb. 17, 1890, Rome; d. Nov. 20, 1944
    Lucrezia Borgia (It 1910)
    Beatrice Cenci (It 1910)
    L'ultimo amplesso (It 1911)
    La fuggitiva (It 1912)
    Il figlio della plaude (It 1912)

L'onta nascosta (It 1912)
Vampe di gelosia (It 1912)
Il cadavere vivente (It 1913)
Il focolare domestico (It 1913)
L'erede di Jago (It 1913)
Giovanna d'Arco (It 1913)
In Hoc Signo Vinces (It 1913)
Sulla falsa strada (It 1913)
Il vel d'Iside (It 1913)
Gli abitatori delle fogne (It 1914)
Capriccio di gran signore (It 1914)
Il film rivelatore (It 1914)
L'esplosione del Forte B (It 1914)
La busta nera (It 1914)
I cavalieri moderni (It 1915)
Per non morire (It 1915)
Quando la primavera roitrnò (It 1915)
La raffica (It 1915)
Il segreto della camera chiusa (It 1915)
Sotto l'ala della morte (It 1915)
Ananke [Fatalità] (It 1916)
La corsara (It 1916)
Eroismo d'amore (It 1916)
Tragico convegno (It 1916)
L'eredità di Gabriella (It 1916)
Articolo IVº (It 1916)
Come le foglie (It 1916)
Il quanto bianco (It 1917)
La meschera dell'amore (It 1917)
Resurrezione (It 1917)
Sfinge (It 1917)
La via più lunga (It 1917)
La signora Arlecchino (It 1917)
Il filo della vita (It 1918)
La regina del carbone (It 1918)
Quando tramonta il sole (It 1918)
Addio, giovinezza! (It 1918)
L'emigrata (It 1918)
Onesta del peccato (It 1918)
Anima tormentata (It 1919)
La vergine folle (It 1919)
Cainà (It 1920)
La casa di vetro (It 1920)
Il richiamo (It 1921)
Amore rosso (It 1921)
La casa sotto la neve (It 1921)
Il viaggio (It 1921)
La preda (It 1921)
L'incognita (It 1922)
Glauco (It 1922)
Orient (Ger 1922)
Zauber des Bohème [La Bohème] (Ger 1923)
"XXX" [Una moglie e...due mariti] (Ger 1924)

Schreckliche Stunden (Ger 1924)
La bocca chiusa (It 1924)
Transatlantisches (Ger 1925)
Beatrice Cenci (It 1926)
Il carnevale di Venezia (It 1927)
Villa Falconieri (Ger 1928)
Fünf bange Tage (Ger 1928)
Die Frauengasse in Algier (Ger 1928)
"X" [Bigamia/Naufraghi] (Ger 1928)
Unfug der Liebe (Ger 1928)
Ariadne Hoppegarten (Ger 1928)
Vera Mirzew [Vera Mirzewa/L'ultimo convegno] (Ger-It 1929)
Der lebende Leichnam (Ger 1929)
Maman Colbri (Fr 1929)
Perchè no? (Fr 1930)
La scala (It 1931)
Patatrac (It 1931)
La stella de cinema (It 1931)
Paraninfo (It 1934)
Come le foglie (It 1934)
Gli uomini non sono ingrati (It 1937)
Chi è più felice di me? (It 1938)
Giuseppe Verdi (It 1938)
Le educande di Saint Cyr (It 1939)
Melodie eterne (It 1940)
Cento lettere d'amore (It 1940)
L'attore scomparso (It 1941)
La danza del fuoco (It 1942)
La signorina (It 1942)
Signorinette (It 1942)
Tempesta sud golfo (It 1943)
La donna della montagna (It 1943)

JAGGER, MICK (Michael Philip Jagger), b. July 26, 1944, Dartford,
    Kent, England
    The T.A.M.I. Show [Gather No Moss] (Electronovision 1964)
        [documentary]
    Sympathy for the Devil [filmed as One Plus One] (Conn 1968)
    Rock and Roll Circus (US 1969) [documentary]
    Ned Kelly (UA 1970)
    Performance (WB 1970)
    Gimme Shelter (20th 1970) [documentary]
    Jimi Hendrix (WB 1973) [documentary]
    Cocksucker Blues (GB 1974) [unreleased]
    Ladies and Gentlemen, the Rolling Stones (Dragon Air 1974)
        [documentary]

JAMES, SIDNEY, b. May 8, 1913, Johannesburg, South Africa; d.
    April 26, 1976
    Black Memory (Ambassador 1947)
    Night Beat (BL 1948)
    No Orchids for Miss Blandish (Renown 1948)
    Once a Jolly Swagman [Maniac on Wheels] (GFD 1948)

The Small Back Room [Hour of Glory] (BL 1949)
Paper Orchid (Col 1949)
Give Us This Day [Salt to the Devil] (GFD 1949)
The Man Is Black (Ex 1950)
Last Holiday (ABP 1950)
The Lady Craved Excitement (Ex 1950)
Talk of a Million [You Can't Beat the Irish] (ABP 1951)
The Galloping Major (IFD 1951)
The Lavendar Hill Mob (GFD 1951)
The Magic Box (BL 1951)
Lady Godiva Rides Again (BL 1951)
The Gift Horse [Glory at Sea] (IFD 1952)
Time Gentlemen Please! (ABFD 1952)
Father's Doing Fine (ABP 1952)
Venetian Bird [The Assassin] (GFD 1952)
The Yellow Balloon (ABP 1952)
Miss Robin Hood (ABFD 1952)
Cosh Boy [The Slasher] (IFD 1953)
The Titfield Thunderbolt (GFD 1953)
The Wedding of Lilli Marlene (Monarch 1953)
Will Any Gentleman? (ABP 1953)
The Square Ring (GFD 1953)
The Flanagan Boy [Bad Blonde] (Ex 1953)
Is Your Honeymoon Really Necessary? (Adelphi 1953)
Park Plaza 605 [Norman Conquest] (Eros 1953)
Escape by Night (Eros 1954)
The Weak and the Wicked (ABP 1954)
The House Across the Lake [Heatwave] (ABP 1954)
The Rainbow Jacket (GFD 1954)
Father Brown [The Detective] (Col 1954)
Seagulls over Sorrento [Crest of the Wave] (MGM Br 1954)
The Belles of St. Trinian's (BL 1954)
The Crowded Day (Adelphi 1954)
Orders Are Orders (BL 1954)
For Better-For Worse [Cocktails in the Kitchen] (ABP 1954)
Aunt Clara (BL 1954)
Out of the Clouds (GFD 1955)
A Kid for Two Farthings (IFD 1955)
John and Julie (BL 1955)
The Glass Cage [The Glass Tomb] (Ex 1955)
The Deep Blue Sea (20th 1955)
Joe MacBeth (Col 1955)
A Yank in Ermine (Monarch 1955)
It's a Great Day (Butcher 1956)
The Extra Day (BL 1956)
Trapeze (UA 1956)
Ramsbottom Rides Again (BL 1956)
Wicked As They Come (Col 1956)
The Iron Petticoat (IFD 1956)
Dry Rot (IFD 1956)
Quatermass II [Enemy from Space] (UA 1957)
The Smallest Show on Earth (BL 1957)
Interpol [Pickup Alley] (Col 1957)

The Shiralee (MGM 1957)
Hell Drivers (RFD 1957)
The Story of Esther Costello [Golden Virgin] (Col 1957)
Campbell's Kingdom (RFD 1957)
A King in New York (Archway 1957)
The Silent Enemy (IFD 1958)
Another Time, Another Place (Par 1958)
Next to No Time (BL 1958)
The Man Inside (Col 1958)
I Was Monty's Double (ABP 1958)
The Sheriff of Fractured Jaw (20th 1958)
Too Many Crooks (RFD 1959)
Make Mine a Million (BL 1959)
The 39 Steps (RFD 1959)
Idle on Parade (Col 1959)
Upstairs and Downstairs (RFD 1959)
Tommy the Toreador (WPD 1959)
Desert Mice (RFD 1959)
And the Same to You (Eros 1960)
Carry On, Constable (AA 1960)
Watch Your Stern (AA 1960)
The Pure Hell of St. Trinian's (BL 1960)
Double Bunk (Bry 1961)
Carry On, Regardless (AA 1961)
A Weekend with Lulu (Col 1961)
The Green Helmet (MGM Br 1961)
What a Carve Up! (RFI 1961)
Raising the Wind (AA 1962)
What a Whopper! (RFI 1962)
Carry On, Cruising (AA 1962)
We Joined the Navy (WPD 1962)
Carry On, Cabby (AA 1963)
The Beauty Jungle [Contest Girl] (RFD 1964)
Carry On, Cleo (AA 1964)
Three Hats For Lisa (AA 1965)
The Big Job (AA 1965)
Carry On, Cowboy (AA 1965)
Where the Bullets Fly (GEF 1966)
Don't Lose Your Head (RFD 1966)
Carry On, Doctor (RFD 1967)
Carry On...Up the Khyber (RFD 1968)
Carry On Camping (RFD 1969)
Carry On Again, Doctor (RFD 1969)
Carry On Up the Jungle (RFD 1970)
Carry On Loving (RFD 1970)
Carry On, Henry (RFD 1971)
Carry On at Your Convenience (RFD 1972)
Carry On, Matron (RFD 1972)
Carry On Abroad (Fox-Rank 1972)
Bless This House (Fox-Rank 1973)
Carry On, Girls (Fox-Ranx 1973)
Carry On, Dick (Fox-Rank 1974)

JANNINGS, EMIL (Theodor Friedrich Emil Janenz), b. July 23,
    1884, Rorschach, Switzerland; d. Jan. 2, 1950
  Im Schützengraben (Ger 1914)
  Frau Eva [Fromont jeune et Risler ainé] (Ger 1916)
  Nächte des Grauens (Ger 1916)
  Passionelles Tagebuch (Ger 1916)
  Stein unter Steinen (Ger 1916)
  Unheilbar (Ger 1917)
  Die Ehe der Luise Rohrbach (Ger 1917)
  Das Leben ein Traum (Ger 1917)
  Ein Fideles Gefängnis [Das Fidele Gefängnis] (Ger 1917)
  Lulu (Ger 1917)
  Wenn vier Dasselbe machen (Ger 1917)
  Die Augen der Mumie Ma [The Eyes of the Mummy] (Ger 1918)
  Fuhrmann Henschel (Ger 1918)
  Keimendes Leben (Ger 1919) [In 3 parts; Jannings not in part 3,
    Moral und Sinnlichkeit]
  Der Mann der Tat (Ger 1919)
  Die Tochter des Mehamed (Ger 1919)
  Madame DuBarry [Passion] (Ger 1919)
  Rose Bernd (Ger 1919)
  Vendetta [Blutrache] (Ger 1919)
  Kohlhiesels Tochter (Ger 1920)
  Das grosse Licht (Ger 1920)
  Die gebrüder Karamasoff (Ger 1920)
  Algol [Power] (Ger 1920)
  Colombine [Die Braut des Apachen] (Ger 1920)
  Der Schädel der Pharaonentochter (Ger 1920)
  Anna Boleyn [Deception] (Ger 1920)
  Der Stier von Olivera (Ger 1921)
  Der Schwur des Peter Hergatz (Ger 1921)
  Danton [All for a Woman] (Ger 1921)
  Die Ratten (Ger 1921)
  Das Weib des Pharaohs [The Loves of Pharaoh] (Ger 1921)
  Othello [The Moor] (Ger 1922)
  Peter der Grosse [Peter the Great] (Ger 1922)
  Die Tragödie der Liebe (Ger 1923) [in 4 parts]
  Alles für Geld [Fortune's Fool] (Ger 1923)
  Quo Vadis? (It 1923)
  Das Wachsfigurenkabinett [The Three Waxworks/Waxworks]
    (Ger 1924)
  Nju [Eine unverstandene Frau/Husbands or Lovers?] (Ger 1924)
  Der Letzte Mann [The Last Laugh] (Ger 1924)
  Tartüff [Herr Tartüff/Tartuffe, the Hypocrite] (Ger 1925)
  Liebe Macht Blind [Love Makes Us Blind] (Ger 1925)
  Varieté [Variety] (Ger 1925)
  Faust, Eine Deutsche Volkssage [Faust] (Ger 1926)
  The Way of All Flesh (Par 1927)
  The Last Command (Par 1928)
  Sins of the Father (Par 1928)
  The Patriot (Par 1928)
  The Street of Sin (Par 1928)
  Betrayal (Par 1929)

Der Blaue Engel (Ger 1930)
The Blue Angel (Par 1930 [Eng lang version of preceding film]
Liebling der Götter [Der Grosse Tenor] (Ger 1930)
Sturme der Leidenschaft [Storms of Passion/The Tempest] (Ger 1931)
König Pausolé [Die Abenteuer des König Pausolé] (Aus 1938)
The Merry Monarch (GB 1933) [Eng lang version of preceding film]
Der schwarze Walfisch (Ger 1934)
Der Alte und der Junge König [The Making of a King] (Ger 1934)
Tramulus (Ger 1935)
Der Herrscher [The Ruler] (Ger 1937)
Der zerbrochene Krug [The Broken Jug] (Ger 1937)
Robert Koch, der Bekämpfer des Todes (Ger 1939)
Ohm Krüger (Ger 1941)
Die Entlassung (Ger 1942)
Altes Herz Wird Wieder Jung (Ger 1943)
Wo Ist Herr Belling? (Ger 1944) [unfinished]

JANSSENS, CHARLES, b. June 8, 1906, Borgenhout, Belgium
Janssens Tegen Peters (Bel 1938)
Een Engel van en Man (Bel 1939)
Jansseens en Peters Dikke Vrienden (Bel 1940)
Antoon de Flierefluiter (Bel 1942)
Een Aardig Geval (Bel 1942)
Het Schipperskwartier (Bel 1952)
De Moedige Bruidegom (Bel 1952)
Uit Hetzelfde Nest (Bel 1952)
Sinjorenbloed (Bel 1953)
De Spotvogel (Bel 1953)
De Hemel op Aarde (Bel 1954)
Min of Meer (Bel 1954)
De Klucht van de Brave Moordenaar (Bel 1955)
Vuur, Liefde en Vitaminen (Bel 1956)
Wat Doen We Met de Liefde (Bel 1957)
Het Geluk Komt Morgen (Bel 1958)
Vrijgezel met 40 Kinderen (Bel 1958)
Vive le Duc (Bel 1960)
Mira (Bel-Dut 1971)
Malpertuis (Bel-Fr-W Ger 1972)
Verbrande Brug (Bel-Dut 1975)

JEANS, ISABEL, b. Sept. 16, 1891, London
The Prolifigate (Walturdaw 1917)
Tilly of Bloomsbury (Moss 1921)
The Rat (W & F 1925)
The Triumph of the Rat (W & F 1926)
Downhill [When Boys Leave Home] (W & F 1927)
Easy Virtue (W & F 1927)
The Further Adventures of the Flag Lieutenant (WP 1927)
Power over Men (Par Br 1929)
The Return of the Rat (W & F 1929)

Sally Bishop (BL 1932)
Rolling in Money (Fox Br 1934)
The Love Affair of the Dictator [The Loves of a Dictator/For
    Love of a Queen] (Gaumont 1935)
The Crouching Beast (Gaumont 1935)
Tovarich (WB 1937)
Fools for Scandal (WB 1938)
Secrets of an Actress (WB 1938)
Youth Takes a Fling (Univ 1938)
Hard to Get (WB 1938)
Garden of the Moon (WB 1938)
Good Girls Go to Paris (Col 1939)
Man About Town (Par 1939)
Banana Ridge (Pathe 1941)
Suspicion (RKO 1941)
Great Day (RKO 1945)
Souvenir d'Italie (It 1957)
Gigi (MGM 1958)
A Breath of Scandal [Olympia] (Par 1960)
Heavens Above! (BL-Romulus 1963)
The Magic Christian (CUE 1969)

JOBERT, MARLENE, b. Nov. 4, 1943, Algiers
Masculin Feminin [Masculine Feminine] (Fr-Swed 1966)
Martin Soldat (Fr 1966)
Le Voleur [The Thief of Paris] (Fr-It 1966)
Alexandere le Bonheur (Fr 1967)
L'Astragale (Fr-W Ger 1968)
Faut pas prendre les enfants du bon dieu pour des canards
    sauvages (Fr 1969)
Le Passager de la pluie (Fr-It 1969)

Marlene Jobert

Dernier Domicile connu (Fr-It 1969)
Les Mariés de l'an 11 [The Scoundrel] (Fr-It-Rum 1970)
La Poudre d'escampette (Fr 1971)
La Decade prodigeuse [Ten Days Wonder] (Fr-It 1971)
Catch Me a Spy [Les Doigts croisés] (GB-Fr-USA 1971)
Nous ne vieillirons pas ensemble [We Will Not Grow Old To-
    gether] (Fr-It 1972)
Rappresaglia [Represailles] (Fr 1972)
Juliette et Juliette (Fr-It 1973)
Le Secret (Fr 1974)
Trop ce trop (Fr 1975)
Folle à tuer (Fr-It 1975)
Les Bons et les merchants (Fr 1975)
Pas si mechant que ça (Fr-Swi 1975)

JOHN, ROSAMUND (Nora Rosamund Jones), b. Oct. 19, 1913, Tot-
    tenham, London
The Secret of the Loch (ABFD 1934)
The First of the Few [Spitfire] (GFD 1942)
The Gentle Sex (GFD 1943)
The Lamp Still Burns (GFD 1943)
Tawny Pipit (GFD 1944)
The Way to the Stars [Johnny in the Clouds] (UA 1945)
Green for Danger (GFD 1946)
The Upturned Glass (GFD 1947)
Fame Is the Spur (GFD 1947)
When the Bough Breaks (GFD 1947)
No Place for Jennifer (ABP 1950)
She Shall Have Murder (IFD 1950)
Never Look Back (Ex 1952)
Street Corner [Both Sides of the Law] (GFD 1953)
Operation Murder (ABP 1957)

JOHNS, GLYNIS, b. Oct. 5, 1923, Durban, South Africa
South Riding (UA 1938)
Murder in the Family (Fox 1938)
Prison Without Bars (UA 1938)
On the Night of the Fire [The Fugitive] (GFD 1939)
Mr. Briggs' Family [The Briggs Family] (WB 1940)
Under Your Hat (BL 1941)
The Prime Minister (WB 1941)
49th Parallel [The Invaders] (GFD 1941)
Adventures of Tartu [Tartu] (MGM Br 1943)
The Halfway House (Ealing 1944)
Perfect Strangers [Vacation from Marriage] (MGM-London 1945)
This Man Is Mine (Col 1946)
Frieda (GFD 1947)
An Ideal Husband (BL 1947)
Miranda (GFD 1948)
Third Time Lucky (GFD 1949)
Helter Skelter (GFD 1949)
Dear Mr. Prohack (GFD 1949)
State Secret [The Great Manhunt] (BL 1950)

Flesh and Blood (BL 1951)
No Highway [No Highway in the Sky] (20th 1951)
The Magic Box (BL 1951)
Appointment with Venus [Island Rescue] (GFD 1951)
Encore--Gigolo and Gigolette (GFD 1951)
The Card [The Promoter] (GFD 1952)
The Sword and the Rose (RKO 1953)
Personal Affair (GFD 1953)
Rob Roy the Highland Rogue (RKO 1953)
The Weak and the Wicked (ABP 1954)
The Seekers [Land of Fury] (GFD 1954)
The Beachcomber (GFD 1954)
Mad About Men (GFD 1954)
Josephine and Men (BL 1955)
The Court Jester (Par 1956)
Loser Takes All (BL 1956)
Around the World in 80 Days (UA 1956)
All Mine to Give [The Day They Gave Babies Away] (Univ 1957)
Another Time, Another Place (Par 1958)
Shake Hands with the Devil (UA 1959)
The Spider's Web (UA 1960)
The Sundowners (WPD 1961)
The Cabinet of Dr. Caligari (20th 1962)
The Chapman Report (WB 1962)
Mary Poppins (BV 1964)
Dear Brigitte (20th 1965)
Don't Just Stand There! (Univ 1967)
Lock Up Your Daughters (Col 1969)
Under Milk Wood (RFD 1972)
Vault of Horror [ep "The Neat Job"] (Fox-Rank 1973)

JOHNSON, CELIA, b. Dec. 18, 1908, Richmond, Surrey, England
In Which We Serve (BL 1942)
Dear Octopus [The Randolph Family] (GFD 1943)
This Happy Breed (EL 1944)
Brief Encounter (GFD 1945)
The Astonished Heart (GFD 1950)
I Believe in You (GFD 1952)
The Holly and the Ivy (BL 1952)
The Captain's Paradise (BL 1953)
A Kid for Two Farthings (IFD 1955)
The Good Companions (ABPC 1957)
The Prime of Miss Jean Brodie (20th 1969)

JOHNSON, RICHARD, b. July 30, 1927, Upminster, Essex, England
Never So Few (MGM 1959)
Cairo (MGM 1963)
The Haunting (MGM 1963)
80,000 Suspects (RFD 1963)
L'Autre Femme [La otra mujer/The Other Woman] (Fr-Sp-It 1964)
The Pumpkin Eater (Col 1964)
The Amorous Adventures of Moll Flanders (Par 1965)
Operation Crossbow [The Great Spy Mission] (MGM 1965)
Khartoum (UA 1966)

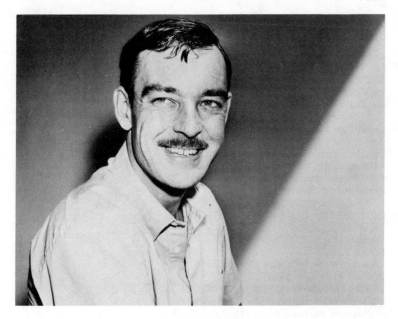

Richard Johnson

Deadlier Than the Male (RFD 1966)
La strega in amore [Strange Obsession/The Witch in Love] (It 1966)
L'avventuriere [The Rover] (It 1967)
Danger Route (UA 1967)
A Twist of Sand (UA 1967)
Oedipus the King (RFD 1967)
Columna [Column] (Rum-W Ger-Fr 1968)
Lady Hamilton--Zwischen Schmach und Liebe [Emma Hamilton] (W Ger-It-Fr 1969)
Some Girls Do (RFD 1969)
Julius Caesar (CUE 1970)
Gott mit Uns [The Deserters] (It-Yug 1970)
The Beloved (MGM-EMI 1971)
Chi sei? [Beyond the Door] (It 1974)
Hennessey [The 5th of November] (CIC 1975)
Moses [Moses, the Law Giver] (It-GB 1975) (narrator)

JOSZ, MARCEL, b. May 9, 1899, Molenbeek (Brussels)
Les maisons de la misère (Bel 1937)
Soldats sans uniforme (Bel 1944)
Terroristes (Bel 1945)
Forçats d'honneur (Bel 1945)
Thanasse et Casimir (Bel 1945)
Les Atouts de M. Wens (Bel 1946)
En êtes-vous bien sûr (Bel 1946)

Le Cocu magnifique (Bel 1946)
On ne triche pas avec la vie (Fr 1949)
M. Leguignon, lampiste (Fr 1951)
Le Plus Heureux des hommes (Fr 1952)
Le Témoin de minuit (Fr 1952)
Seuls au monde (Fr 1952)
Le Guérisseur (Fr 1953)
La Belle Otero (Fr 1954)
Nuit blanche et rouge à lèvres [quelle sacreé soirée] (Fr 1957)
Quelqu'un frappe à la porte (Bel 1958)
Université catholique de Louvains (Bel 1960)
Une Industrie dans un parc (Bel 1960)
L'Homme de Mykonos (Fr 1966)
Pleins feux sur Nick Jordan (Fr-Bel 1969)
Home Sweet Home (Bel-Fr 1974)

JOUVET, LOUIS, b. Dec. 24, 1887, Crozon, France; d. Aug. 16,
    1951
Topaze (Fr 1932)
Knock (Fr 1933)
La Kermesse heroique (Fr 1935)
Mister Flow (Fr 1936)
Les Bas-fonds (Fr 1936)
Mademoiselle docteur (Fr 1937)
Un Carnet du bal (Fr 1937)
Drôle de drame (Fr 1937)
Alibi (FR 1937)
La Marseillaise (Fr 1937)
Ramuntcho (FR 1937)
La Maison du maltais (FR 1938)
Entrée des artistes (Fr 1938)
Education du Prince (Fr 1938)
Le Drame à Shanghai (Fr 1938)
Hôtel du nord (Fr 1938)
La Fin du jour (Fr 1939)
La Charrette fantôme (Fr 1939)
Volpone (Fr 1939)
Un Tel père et fils [Heart of a Nation] (USA-Fr 1940)
Sérénade (Fr 1940)
Un Revenant (Fr 1946)
Copie conforme (Fr 1946)
Quai des Orfevres (Fr 1947)
Les Amoureux sont seuls au monde (Fr 1948)
Entre onze heure et minuit (Fr 1949)
Retour à la vie [Return to Life] (Fr-It 1949)
Miquette et sa mère (Fr 1949)
Lady Paname (Fr 1949)
Knock (Fr 1950)
Une Histoire d'amour (Fr 1951)

JUDICE, BRUNILDE (Brunilde Judice Carusou), b. May 11, 1902,
    Milan
Amor de perdição (Por 1921)

Mulheres da beira (Por 1921)
Tempestade da vida (Por 1922)
Voz de operárie (Por 1931)
Catedral do Bem (Por 1931)
Ladrão, precisa-se (Por 1946)
Amanhã como hoje (Sp 1947)
Ribatejo (Por 1949)
O cerre dos enforcados (Por 1954)
Quando o mar galgou a terra (Por 1954)
Traicao inveresimil (Por 1972)

JUGO, JENNY, b. June 14, 1905, Mürzzuschlag/Steiermark, Austria
Die Puppe vom Lunapark (Ger 1924)
Blitzzug der Liebe (Ger 1925)
Friedenblut (Ger 1925)
Die gefundene Braut (Ger 1925)
Liebe macht blind (Ger 1925)
Schiff in Not (Ger 1925)
Wenn die Liebe nicht wär! (Ger 1925)
Ledige Töchter (Ger 1926)
Die Hose (Ger 1926)
Die indiskrete Frau (Ger 1927)
Pique Dame (Ger 1927)
Prinz Louis Ferdinand (Ger 1927)
Die blaue Maus (Ger 1928)
Die Carmen von St. Pauli (Ger 1928)
Looping the Loop (Ger 1928)
Sechs Mädchen suchen Nachtquartier (Ger 1928)
Der Bund der Drei (Ger 1929)
Die Flucht von der Liebe (Ger 1929)
Die Schmugglerbraut von Malorca (Ger 1929)
Heute Nacht--eventuell (Ger 1930)
Ich bleib' bei Dir (Ger 1931)
Kopfüber ins Gluck (Ger 1931)
Die nackte Wahrheit (Ger 1931) [Ger version of Nothing But the
    Truth]
We nimmt die Liebe ernst (Ger 1931)
Fünf von der Jazzband (Ger 1932)
Eine Stadt steht Kopf (Ger 1932)
Zigeuner der Nacht (Ger 1932)
Es gibt nur eine Liebe (Ger 1933)
Ein Lied für Dich (Ger 1933)
Herz ist Trumpf (Ger 1934)
Pechmarie (Ger 1934)
Fräulein Frau (Ger 1934)
Heute Abend (Ger 1934)
Pygmalion (Ger 1935)
Die Nacht mit dem Kaiser (Ger 1936)
Mädchenjahre einer Königin (Ger 1936)
Allotria (Ger 1936)
Gefährliches Spiel (Ger 1937)
Die kleine und die grosse Liebe (Ger 1938)
Ein hoffnungsloser Fall (Ger 1938)

Nanette (Ger 1938)
Unser Fräulein Doktor (Ger 1940)
Viel Lärm um Nixi (Ger 1942)
Non mi sposo più! (It 1942)
Die Gattin (Ger 1943)
Sag' endlich ja (Ger 1945)
Traum' nicht Annette (W Ger 1949)
Königskinder (W Ger 1950)

JULLIEN, SANDRA (Sandra Calaputti), b. Feb. 14, 1950, Toulon,
    France
L'Etrangleur (Fr 1970)
Le Frisson des vampires (Fr 1970)
Atout sexe (Fr 1971)
Je suis une nymphomane (Fr 1971)
Comment le désir vient aux filles [Je suis frigide, pourquoi?]
    (Fr 1972)
Dany la ravageuse (Fr 1972)
Gentai Porunoden Sentensei Inpu [The Insatiable] (Jap 1972)
Tokugawa Sex Kinohirai, Skijo Daimyo [The Shogunate's Harem]
    (Jap 1972)
Les Gourmandines (Fr 1973)
Nada (Fr 1973)
Le Permis de conduire (Fr 1973)
Les Murs ont des oreilles (Fr 1974) (as: Sandra Barry)
La Maison des filles perdues [La casa delle bambole crudeli]
    (Fr-It 1974)
Les Filles du Golden Saloon (Fr 1975)

JURGENS, CURT, b. Dec. 13, 1912, Munich
Hundert Tage (Ger-It 1935)
Königswalzer [The Royal Waltz] (Ger 1935)
Familienparade (Ger 1936)
Die Unbekannte (Ger 1936)
Liebe kann Lügen (Ger 1937)
Zu neuen Ufern (Ger 1937)
Salonwagen # E 417 (Ger 1939)
Weltrekord im Seitensprung (Ger 1939)
Herz ohne Heimat (Ger 1940)
Operette [Operetta] (Aus 1940)
Stimme des Herzens (Ger 1942)
Wen die Götter lieben [Mozart/The Mozart Story] (Aus 1942)
Frauen sind Keine Engel (Aus 1943)
Ein glücklicher Mensch Schule des Lebens] (Ger 1943)
Ein Blick zurück [Am Vorabend] (Aus 1944)
Eine Kleine Sommermelodie (Ger 1944)
Wiener Mädeln (W Ger 1949) [made in 1945]
Das singende Haus (Aug 1947)
Hin und her (Aus 1948)
Leckerbissen (W Ger 1948) [compilation feature; scenes from
    Operette]
Der Engel mit der Pasaune (Aus 1948)
Der himmlich Walzer (Aus 1948)

An Klingenden Ufern (Aus 1948)
Das verlorene Rennen (Aus 1948)
Das Kuckucksei (Aus 1948)
Lambert fuhlt sich Gedroht (Aus 1949)
Hexen (Aus 1949)
Der Schuss durchs Fenster (Aus 1949)
Die Gestörte Hochzeitsnacht (Aus 1950)
Prämien auf den Tod (Aus 1950)
Küssen ist keine Sünd (W Ger 1950)
Pikanterie (Aus 1950)
Das Geheimnis einer Ehe (Aus 1951)
Gangsterpremiere (Aus 1951)
Der Schweigende Mund (Aus 1951)
Hans des Lebens (Aus 1952)
Knall und Fall als Hochstapler (W Ger-Aus 1952)
1. April 2000 (Aus 1952)
Du bist die Rose vom Wörthersee (Aus 1952)
Man nennt es Liebe (Aus 1953)
Musik bei Nacht (Aus 1953)
Der letzte Walzer (Aus 1953)
Alles für Papa (Aus 1953)
Meines Vaters Pferde (Aus 1953) (only in part 1 of a 2-part
    film)
Les Héros sont fatigués [Heroes and Sinners] (Fr 1954)
Praterherzen [Tingel-Tangel] (Aus 1954)
Eine Frau von Heute (W Ger 1954)
Rummelplatz der Liebe [Circus of Love] (W Ger-USA 1954)
Gefangene der Liebe (W Ger 1954)
Das Bekenntnis der Ina Kahr [The Confession of Ina Kahr] (W
    Ger 1954)
Du bist die Richtige (W Ger-Aus 1954)
Des Teufels General [The Devil's General] (W Ger 1955)
Liebe ohne Illusion (W Ger 1955)
Die Ratten (W Ger 1955)
Due mein stilles Tal (W Ger 1955)
Orientexpress (W Ger-Fr-It 1955)
Teufel in Seide (W Ger 1955)
Et dieu créa la femme [And God Created Woman] (Fr 1956)
Die goldene Brücke (W Ger 1956)
Ohne Dich wird es Nacht (W Ger 1956)
Michel Strogoff [Michele Strogoff/Mihailo Strogov] (Fr-It-Yug
    1956)
Amère Victoire [Bitter Victory] (Fr-GB 1957)
Les Espions (Fr 1957)
Oeil pour Oeil [Occhio per occhio/An Eye for an Eye] (Fr-It
    1957)
Londra chiama Polo Nord [The House of Intrigue] (It 1957)
Tamango (Fr-It 1957)
The Enemy Below (20th 1957)
This Happy Feeling (Univ 1958)
Me and the Colonel (Col 1958)
The Inn of the Sixth Happiness (20th 1958)
Der Schinderhannes (W Ger 1958)

Le Vent se lève [Il vento si alza/Time Bomb] (Fr-It 1958)
Ferry to Hong Kong (RFD 1959)
The Blue Angel (20th 1959)
Katia [The Magnificent Sinner] (Fr 1959)
Die Schachnovelle [Brainwashed] (W Ger 1960)
I Aim at the Stars (Col 1960)
Gustav Adolfs Page (Aus 1960)
Operette aus Wien [100 Jahre Wiener Operette] (Aus 1961) [compilation feature containing footage from Operette]
Bankraub in der rue Latour (W Ger 1961)
Le Triomphe de Michel Strogoff [The Triumph of Michael Strogoff] (Fr-It 1961)
I don Giovanni della Costa azzurra (It 1962)
The Longest Day (20th 1962)
Le Desordre (Il disordine/Disorder] (Fr-It 62)
The Miracle of the White Stallions (BV 1963)
Die Dreigroschenoper (L'Opéra de quat' sous] (W Ger-Fr 1963)
Begegnung in Salzburg [Deux Jours à vivre] (W Ger-Fr 1963)
Of Love and Desire (20th 1963)
Château en Suede [Il castello di Svegia/Nutty, Naughty Chateau] (Fr-It 1963)
Psyche 59 (Col 1963)
Los parias de la gloria [Les Parias de la gloire/I disperati della gloria] (Sp-Fr-It 1963)
Hide and Seek (Albion 1963)
DM-Killer (Aus 1964)
Tokyo Olympiad (Japanese 1964)
Lord Jim (Col 1965)
Das Liebeskarussel (Aus 1965)
Zwei Girls vom roten Stern [Duel à la vodka] (W Ger-Aus-Fr 1965)
Der Kongress amüsiert sich [Le Congrès s'amuse] (W Ger-Aus-Fr 1966)
Le Jardinier d'argenteuil [Blüten, Gauner, und die Nacht von Nizza (Fr-W Ger 1966)
Wie tötet man eine Dame! [Das Geheimnis der gelbe Monche/Target for Killing] (Aus 1966)
The Karate Killers (MGM 1967)
Der Lugner und die Nonne (Aus 1967)
The Karate Killers (MGM 1967)
Dalle Ardenne all'inferno [La Gloire des canailles/...und Morgen fahrt ihr zur Hölle/The Dirty Heroes] (It-Fr-W Ger 1968)
Die Artisten in der Zirkuskuppel: ratlos (W Ger 1968)
La brigada de los condenados [La legione dei donnati] (W Ger-It-Sp 1968)
Der Arzt von St. Paule (W Ger 1968)
Pas de roses pour OSS 117 [Niente rose per OSS 17/OSS 117 Murder for Sale] (Fr-It 1968)
La battaglia della Neretva [Die Schlacht an dei Neretva/Bitka na Neretvi/Battle of Neretva] (It-W Ger-Yug 1969)
Cannabis [The Mafia Wants Your Blood] (Fr 1969)
The Assassination Bureau (Par 1969)
The Battle of Britain (UA 1969)

Auf der Reeperbahn nachts um halb eins (W Ger 1969)
The Invisible Six (USA-Iranian 1969)
Ohrfeigen (W Ger 1970)
Der Pfarrer von St. Pauli (W Ger 1970)
Des Studentenhotel von St. Pauli (W Ger 1970)
Hello-Goodbye (20th 1970)
The Mephisto Waltz (20th 1971)
Kapt'n Rauhbein aus St. Pauli (W Ger 1971)
Kill! [Kill Kill Kill] (Fr-It-Sp 1971)
Nicholas and Alexandria (Col Br 1971)
Fieras sin jaula [Due maschi per Alexia] (Sp-It 1972)
Profession: Aventuriers (Fr 1972)
A la guerre comme à la guerre [Le eccitanti guerre di Ade-
    leine] (Fr-It 1972)
The Vault of Horror (Cin 1973)
Soft Beds, Hard Battles (20th-Rank 1974)
Cagliostro (It 1975)
Der Sweite Frŭling (W Ger 1975)
Auch Mimosen wollen blühen (W Ger 1975)

JUSTICE, JAMES ROBERTSON, b. June 15, 1906, Scotland; d. July
    2, 1975
For Those in Peril (Ealing 1944)
Champagne Charlie (Ealing 1944)
Fiddlers Three (Ealing 1944)
Vice Versa (GFD 1947)
My Brother Jonathan (Pathe 1947)
Against the Wind (GFD 1947)
Quartet [ep "The Facts of Life"] (GFD 1948)
Stop Press Girl (GFD 1949)
Christopher Columbus (GFD 1949)
Whisky Galore! [Tight Little Island] (GFD 1949)
Poet's Pub (GFD 1949)
Private Angelo (ABP 1949)
Prelude to Fame (GFD 1950)
My Daughter Joy [Operation X] (BL 1950)
The Black Rose (20th 1950)
Blackmailed [Mr. Christopher] (GFD 1951)
Pool of London (GFD 1951)
Anne of the Indies (20th 1951)
Captain Horatio Hornblower, RN (WB-FN 1951)
The Story of Robin Hood and His Merrie Men (RKO 1952)
David and Bathsheba (20th 1952)
The Voice of Merrill [Murder Will Out] (Eros 1952)
Miss Robin Hood (ABFD 1952)
Les Miserables (20th 1952)
The Sword and the Rose (RKO 1953)
Rob Roy the Highland Rogue (RKO 1953)
Doctor in the House (GFD 1954)
Out of the Clouds (GFD 1955)
Above Us the Waves (GFD 1955)
Doctor at Sea (RFD 1955)
Storm over the Nile (IFD 1955)

Land of the Pharoahs (WB 1955)
An Alligator Named Daisy (RFD 1955)
The Iron Petticoat (MGM 1956)
Moby Dick (WB 1956)
Checkpoint (RFD 1956)
Seven Thunders [Beasts of Marseilles] (RFD 1957)
Doctor at Large (RFD 1957)
Campbell's Kingdom (RFD 1957)
Living Idol (MGM 1957)
Thérèse Etienne (FR 1957)
Orders to Kill (BL 1958)
Upstairs and Downstairs (RFD 1959)
Doctor in Love (RFD 1960)
A French Mistress (BL 1960)
Foxhole in Cairo (Britannia 1960)
Very Important Person (RFD 1961)
The Guns of Navarone (Col 1961)
Raising the Wind (AA 1961)
Murder She Said (MGM 1961)
A Pair of Briefs (RFD 1962)
Crooks Anonymous (AA 1962)
Guns of Darkness (WPD 1962)
Dr. Crippen (WPD 1962)
Warrior's Rest [Le Repos du guerrier] (Fr-It 1962)
The Fast Lady (RFD 1962)
Mystery Submarine (Britannia 1963)
Das Feuershiff (W Ger 1963)
Doctor in Distress (RFD 1963)
Father Came Too (RFD 1963)
You Must Be Joking! (Col 1965)
The Face of Fu Manchu (WPD 1965)
Doctor in Clover (RFD 1965)
Up from the Beach (20th 1965)
The Trygon Factor (RFD 1967)
Two Weeks in September (RFD 1967)
Hell Is Empty (RFD 1967)
Histoires Extraordinaires [Spirits of the Dead] [ep "Metzenger-
     stein"] (Fr-It 1967)
Mayerling (MGM 1968)
Chitty Chitty Bang Bang (VA 1968)
Zeta One (Tigon 1969)
Some Will, Some Won't (WPD 1970)
Doctor in Trouble (RFD 1970)

KARINA, ANNA (Hanne Karin Bayer), b. Sept. 22, 1940, Copenhagen
     Le Petit Soldat (Fr 1960) [release delayed until 1963)
     Ce soir au jamais [Tonight or Never] (Fr 1961)
     Une Femme est une femme [A Woman Is a Woman] (Fr 1961)
     She'll Have to Go (AA 1962)
     Cleo de 5 à 7 [Cleo from 5 to 7] (Fr-It 1961)
     Le Soleil dans l'oeil (Fr 1962)
     Vivre sa vie (Fr 1962)
     Les Quatres Vérités (Fr-It-Sp 1963)

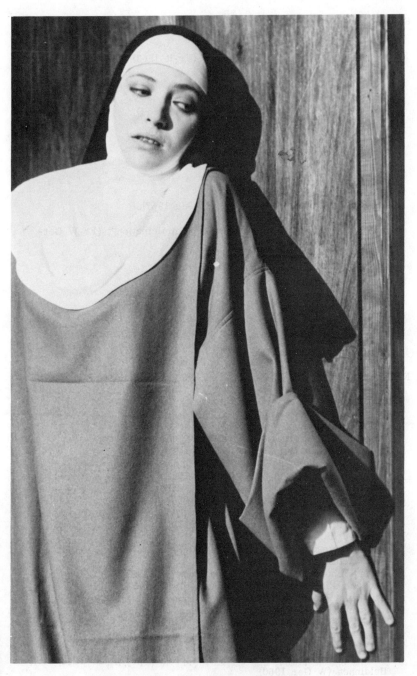

Anna Karina in <u>La Religieuse</u> (1966)

Shéhérazade (Fr-It-Sp 1963)
Dragées au poivre [Sweet & Sour] (Fr-It 1963)
Un Mari à prix fixe (Fr-It 1963)
Bande a part (Fr 1964)
La Ronde (Fr-It 1964)
Le Voleur de Tibidabo (Fr 1965)
De l'amour (Fr-It 1965)
Alphaville (Fr-It 1965)
Pierrot le fou (Fr-It 1965)
La Soldatesse (It-Fr-Yug 1965)
Made in USA (Fr 1966)
La Religeuse (Fr 1966)
Zärtliche Haie (W Ger-It 1967)
Lo Straniero [The Stranger] (It-Fr-Alg 1967)
Lamiel (Fr-It 1967)
Le Plus Vieux Métier du monde (ep "Anticipation") (Fr-W Ger-
    It 1967)
Before Winter Comes (Col 1969)
Michael Kolhaas, der Rebell (W Ger 1969)
The Magus (20th 1969)
Justine (20th 1969)
Laughter in the Dark (GB-Fr 1969)
Rendezvous a Bray (Fr-W Ger 1971)
L'Alliance (Fr 1971)
Vivre Ensemble (Fr 1973)
L'Assassin musicien (Fr 1975)

KAUFMANN, CHRISTINE, b. Jan. 14, 1945, Lengdorf/Steiermark,
    Austria
Im weissen Rössl (W Ger 1952)
Salto mortale (Ger 1953)
Der Klosterjäger (W Ger 1953)
Staatsanwältin Corda (W Ger 1954)
Rosen-Rösli (W Ger 1954)
Der schweigende Engel (W Ger 1954)
Wenn die Alpenrosen Glühn (W Ger 1955)
Ein Herz schlagt für Erika (W Ger 1956)
Die Stimme der Sehnsucht (W Ger 1956)
Witwer mit fünf Tochtern (W Ger 1957)
Die Winzerin von Langenlois (Aug 1957)
Mädchen in Uniform (W Ger 1958)
Der veruntreute Himmel [Embezzled Heaven] (W Ger 1958)
Alle Lieben Peter (W Ger 1959)
Primo Amore [Junge Leute--von Heute] (It 1959)
Vacanze d'Inverno [Brèves Amours] (It-Fr 1959)
Gli ultimi giorni di Pompei [Los ultimos/Les Derniers Jours de
    Pompei/Die letzten Tage von Pompei/The Last Days of Pom-
    peii] (It-Sp-Fr-W Ger 1959)
Ein Thron für Christine [Un trono para Cristy] (Sp-W Ger 1960)
Der letzte Fussgänger (W Ger 1960)
Labbra Rosse [Les Fausses ingenues/Red Lips] (It-Fr 1960)
Heldinnen (W Ger 1960)
Costantino il grande [Constantine and the Cross] (It 1961)

Un Nommé la Rocca (Fr 1961)
Toller Hecht auf Krummer Tour [The Phoney American] (W
    Ger 1961)
Via Mala (W Ger 1961)
Town Without Pity [Stadt ohne Mitleid] (USA-W Ger 1961)
Neunzig Minuten nach Mitternacht [Terror After Midnight] (W
    Ger 1962)
Tunnel 28 [Escape from East Berlin] (W Ger-USA 1962)
La congiura dei dieci [Lo spadaccino di Siena /Swordsman of
    Siena/Le Mercenaire] (It-Fr 1962)
Der Zigeunerbaron (W Ger 1962)
Taras Bulba (UA 1962)
Wild and Wonderful (Univ 1964)
Liebesvögel (W Ger 1969)
Der Tod der Maria Maltbran (W Ger 1971)
Murders in the Rue Morgue (AIP 1971)
Willow Spring (W Ger 1973)
Zum Abschied Chrysanthemum (W Ger 1974)

KELLER, MARTHE, b. Jan. 28, 1945, Basel, Switzerland
Funeral in Berlin (Par 1966)
Le Diable par la queue (Fr-It 1968)
Les Caprices de Marie [Les Figuarants du Nouveau-Monde] (Fr-
    It 1969)
Les Demoiselles d'Avignon (Fr TV 1970)
Arsène Lupin: Victor de la Brigade mondaine (Fr TV 1970)
Arsène Lupin contre Herlock Sholmes (Fr TV 1970)
L'Arrestation d'Arsène Lupin (Fr TV 1970)
La Vieille Fille (Fr-It 1971)
Un Cave (Fr 1971)
Elle court, elle court la banlieue (Fr-It 1972)
La Chute d'un corps (Fr 1973)
La Raison du plus fou (Fr 1973)
Toute une vie (Fr-It 1974)
Die Antwort kennt nur der Wind [Seul le vent connait la réponse
    (W Ger-Fr 1974)
L'Aigle a deux têtes (Fr TV 1974)
Le Guêpier (Fr 1975)
Per le antiche scale [Vertiges] (It-Fr 1975)

KENDALL, KAY (Justine McCarthy), b. May 21, 1927, Hull, England;
    d. Sept. 6, 1959
Champagne Charlie (Ealing 1944)
Fiddlers Three (Ealing 1944)
Dreaming (Ealing 1944)
Waltz Time (Anglo 1945)
London Town [My Heart Goes Crazy] (EL 1946)
Dance Hall (GFD 1950)
Happy-Go-Lovely (ABP 1951)
Lady Godiva Rides Again (BL 1951)
Wings of Danger [Dead on Course] (Ex 1952)
It Started in Paradise (GFD 1952)
Street of Shadows [Shadow Man] (AA 1953)

Genevieve (GFD 1953)
The Square Ring (GFD 1953)
Meet Mr. Lucifer (GFD 1953)
Fast and Loose (GFD 1954)
Doctor in the House (GFD 1954)
The Constant Husband (BL 1955)
Simon and Laura (RFD 1955)
The Adventures of Quentin Durward (MGM 1956)
Abdullah's Harem (20th 1956)
Les Girls (MGM 1957)
The Reluctant Debutante (MGM 1958)
Once More, With Feeling (Col 1960)

KENT, JEAN (Joan Summerfield), b. June 29, 1921, Brixton, London
Who's Your Father? (Col 1935)
The Rocks of Valpre [High Treason] (Radio 1935)
Hullo Fame! (British Films 1940) (as Jean Carr)
It's That Man Again (GFD 1943)
Miss London Ltd (GFD 1943)
Warn That Man (Pathe 1943)
Bees in Paradise (GFD 1944)
Fanny by Gaslight [Man of Evil] (GFD 1944)
Champagne Charlie (Ealing 1944)
2,000 Women (GFD 1944)
Madonna of the Seven Moons (EL 1944)
Waterloo Road (GFD 1945)
The Rake's Progress [Notorious Gentleman] (EL 1945)
Caravan (GFD 1946)
The Magic Bow (GFD 1946)
Carnival (GFD 1946)
The Man Within [The Smugglers] (GFD 1947)
The Loves of Joanna Godden (GFD 1947)
Bond Street (Pathe 1948)
Sleeping Car to Trieste (GFD 1948)
Trottie True [Gay Lady] (GFD 1949)
The Reluctant Widow (GFD 1950)
The Woman in Question [Five Angles on Murder] (GFD 1950)
Her Favourite Husband [The Taming of Dorothy] (Renown 1950)
The Browning Version (GFD 1951)
The Lost Hours [The Big Frame] (Eros 1952)
Before I Wake [Shadow of Fear] (GN 1955)
The Prince and the Showgirl (WB 1957)
Bonjour Tristesse (UA 1958)
Grip of the Strangler [The Haunted Strangler] (Eros 1958)
Beyond This Place [Web of Evidence] (Renown 1959)
Please Turn Over (AA 1959)
Bluebeard's Ten Honeymoons (WPD 1960)

KERR, DEBORAH (Deborah Kerr-Trimmer), b. Sept. 30, 1921,
Helensburgh, Scotland
Contraband [Blackout] (Anglo 1940) (role cut from release print)
Major Barbara (GFD 1941)
Love on the Dole (Anglo 1941)
Penn of Pennsylvania [The Courageous Mr. Penn] (Anglo 1961)

Deborah Kerr slaps Hayley Mills in The Chalk Garden (1963).

Hatter's Castle (Par Br 1941)
The Day Will Dawn [The Avengers] (GFD 1942)
The Life and Death of Colonel Blimp [Colonel Blimp] (GFD 1943)
Perfect Strangers [Vacation from Marriage] (MGM Br 1945)
I See a Dark Stranger [The Adventuress] (GFD 1946)
Black Narcissus (GFD 1947)
The Hucksters (MGM 1947)
If Winter Comes (MGM 1948)
Edward, My Son (MGM Br 1949)
Please Believe Me (MGM 1950)
King Solomon's Mines (MGM 1950)
Quo Vadis? (MGM 1951)
The Prisoner of Zenda (MGM 1952)
Thunder in the East (Par 1953) [made in 1950]
Young Bess (MGM 1953)
Dream Wife (MGM 1953)
Julius Caesar (MGM 1953)
From Here to Eternity (Col 1953)
The End of the Affair (Col 1955)
The King and I (20th 1956)
The Proud and Profane (Par 1956)
Tea and Sympathy (MGM 1956)
Heaven Knows, Mr. Allison (20th 1957)
An Affair to Remember (20th 1957)

Bonjour Tristesse (UA 1958)
Separate Tables (UA 1959)
The Journey (MGM 1959)
Count Your Blessings (MGM 1959)
Beloved Infidel (20th 1959)
The Sundowners (WB 1960)
The Grass Is Greener (Univ 1961)
The Naked Edge (UA 1961)
The Innocents (20th 1961)
The Chalk Garden (Univ 1963)
Night of the Iguana (MGM 1964)
Marriage on the Rocks (WB 1965)
Eye of the Devil [13] (MGM 1966)
Casino Royale (Col 1967)
Prudence and the Pill (20th 1968)
The Gypsy Moths (MGM 1969)
The Arrangement (WB 1969)

KIEPURA, JAN, b. March 18, 1902, Sosnowice, Poland; d. Aug. 15,
    1966
Die singende Stadt (Ger 1930)
City of Song [Farewell to Love] (Eng lang version of Die Singende
    Stadt) (Ger 1930)
Das Lied einer Nacht (Ger 1932)
Tell Me Tonight [Be Mine Tonight] (Eng lang version of Das Lied
    einer Nacht) (Ger 1932)
La Chanson d'une nuit (Fr version of Das Lied einer Nacht)
    (Ger 1932)
Ein Lied für Dich (Ger 1933)
My Song for You (Eng lang version of Ein Lied für Dich) (Ger
    1933)
Tout pour l'amour (Fr version of Ein Lied für Dich) (Ger 1933)
Mein Herz ruf nacht Dir (Ger 1934)
My Heart Is Calling (Eng lang version of Mein Herz ruf nacht
    Dir) (Ger 1934)
Mon coeur t'appelle (Fr version of Mein Herz ruf nacht Dir)
    (Ger 1934)
Ich liebe alle Frauen (Ger 1935)
J'aime tontes les femmes (Fr version of Ich liebe alle Frauen)
    (Ger 1935)
Im Sonnenschein [Opernring] (Aus 1936)
Give Us This Night (Par 1936)
Zauber der Boheme (Aus 1937)
Addio Mimi [Her Wonderful Life] (It 1946)
Valse brillante (Fr 1949)
Das Land des Lächelns (W Ger 1952)

KINSKI, KLAUS (Nikolaus Gunther Nakszynski), b. Oct. 18, 1926,
    Zoppot, Danzig
Morituri (W Ger 1948)
Um Thron und Liebe [Sarajevo] (W Ger 1955)
Ludwig II (W Ger 1955)
Hanussen (W Ger 1955)

Kinder, Mütter und ein General (W Ger 1955)
Waldwinter (W Ger 1956)
Geliebte Corinna (W Ger 1956)
A Time to Love and a Time to Die (Univ 1958)
Der Rächer (W Ger 1960)
Bankraub in der Rue Latour (W Ger 1961)
Die toten Augen von London [Dead Eyes of London] (W Ger 1961)
The Counterfeit Traitor (Par 1961)
Das Geheimnis der gelben Narzissen [The Devil's Daffodil] (W
    Ger-GB 1961)
Das Rätsel der roten Orchideen (W Ger 1961)
Die seltsame Gräfin (W Ger 1961)
Der rote Rausch (W Ger 1962)
Das Gasthaus an der Themse (W Ger 1962)
Die Tür mit den sieben Schlossern (W Ger 1962)
Das geheimnis der schwarzen Witwe [Araña negra] (W Ger-Sp 1963)
Das indische Tuch (W Ger 1963)
Piccadilly, null Uhr zwölf (W Ger 1963)
Der schwarze Abt (W Ger 1963)
Die schwarze Kobra (W Ger 1963)
Scotland Yard jagd Mabuse (W Ger 1963)
Der Zinker (W Ger 1963)
Das Geheimnis der chinesischen Nelke (W Ger 1964)
Die Gruft mit dem Rätselschloss (W Ger 1964)
Guerre secrète [Guerra secreta/Spione unter sich] (Fr-It-W Ger
    1964)
Wartezimmer zum Jenseits (W Ger 1964)
Kali-Yug, la dea della vendetta [Kali Yug I--Göttin der Rache/
    Kali-Yug, déesse de la vengeance] (It-W Ger-Fr 1964)
Il misterio del tempio indiano [Kali Yug II--Das Geheimnis des
    indischen Tempels/Le Mystère du temple hindou] (It-W Ger-
    Fr 1964)
Winnetou II [Giorni di fuoco/Le Trésor des montagnes bleues/
    Vinetu II/Last of the Renegades] (W Ger-It-Fr-Yug 1964)
Der letzte Ritt nach Santa Cruz (W Ger 1964)
A qualsiasi prezzo [Vatican Story] (It 1965)
The Pleasure Girls (Compton 1965)
L'enfer est vide (Fr-W Ger 1965)
The Traitor's Gate [Das Verratertor] (GB-W Ger 1965)
Operación Estambul [Colpo grosso a Galata Bridge/L'Homme
    d'Istamboul/That Man in Istanbul] (Sp-It-Fr-W Ger 1965)
Per qualche dollari in più [Für ein paar Dollar mehr/For a Few
    Dollars More] (It-W Ger 1965)
Our Man in Marrakesh [Bang Bang You're Dead] (AA 1965)
Circus of Fear [Psycho-Circus] (GB-W Ger 1966)
Das Rätsel des silbernen Dreiecks (Ger version of Circus of
    Fear) (W Ger 1966)
Doctor Zhivago (MGM 1966)
Neues vom Hexer (Ger 1966)
Gern hab' ich die Frauen gekillt [Spie contro il mondo/Le Car-
    naval des barbouzes] (W Ger-It-Fr 1966)
Das Geheimnis der gelben Mönche (W Ger 1966)
Quien sabe? [El Chuncho/A Bullet for the General] (It 1966)

Die blaue Hand (W Ger 1967)
Deux billets pour Mexico [Geheimnisse in goldenen Nylons] (Fr-
W Ger-It 1967)
Jules Verne's Rocket to the Moon [Those Fantastic Flying
Fools/Blast Off] (GB-W Ger 1967)
Sumuru [The 1,000,000 Eyes of Sumuru] (AA 1967)
Ad ogni costo [Diamantes a go-go/Grand Slam] (It-Sp 1967)
Coplan sauve sa peau (Fr 1967)
Five Golden Dragons (AA 1967)
Die Pagode zum fünften Schrecken [Ger version of Five Golden
Dragons] (W Ger 1967)
Kampf um Rom I & Kampf um Rom II: Der Verrat [La guerra
per Roma, prima parte & seconda parte/Lupta pentru Roma]
(W Ger-It-Rum 1968)
Se incontri Sartana, prega per la tua morte [Sartana--bete um
deinen Tod] (It-W Ger 1968)
L'uomo, l'orgoglio, la vendetta (It 1968)
Justine ovvero le disavventure della virtù (It 1968)
I bastardi [Der Bastard] (It-W Ger 1968)
Il grande silenzio [Le grand silence] (It-Fr 1968)
Ognuno per se [Das Gold von Sam Cooper/The Ruthless Four]
(It-W Ger 1968)
Sigpress contro Scotland Yard (It 1968)
Mister zehn Prozent [Miezen und Moneten] (W Ger 1968)
Cinque per l'inferno (It 1969)
Due volte Giuda [Dos veces Judas] (It-Sp 1969)
Paroxismus [Puo una morte rivivere per amore?/Venus in
Furs] (It-W Ger-GB 1969)
...E Dio disse a Caino (It 1969)
Wie kommt ein so reizendes Mädchen wie Sie zu diesem Ge-
werbe? (W Ger 1969)
La legge dei gangsters (It 1969)
Sono Sartana, il vostro becchino (It 1969)
Il dito nella piaga (It 1969)
A doppia faccia [Das Gesicht im Dunkeln] (It-W Ger 1969)
Una bara di dollari per una carogna (It 1969)
Count Dracula (Sp-It 1970)
Appuntamento col disonore (It-Yug-Monaco 1970)
Giù la testa, hombre! (It 1970)
La Peau de Torpédo [Der Mann mit der Torpedohaut] (Fr-W Ger-
It 1970)
Mir hat es immer Spass gemacht (W Ger 1970)
I leopardi di Churchill [Los leopardos de Churchill] (It-Sp 1970)
Nella stretta morsa del ragno [Dracula im Schloss des Schreckens]
(It-Fr-W Ger 1971)
Prega il morto e ammazza il vivo (It 1971)
La bestia uccide a sangue freddo [Das Schloss der blauen Vögel]
(It-W Ger 1971)
Per una bara piena di dollari (It 1971)
Lo chiamavano King (It 1971)
Il venditore di morte [La mano nascosta di Dio] (It 1971)
La belva (It 1971)
L'occhio del ragno [El ojo de la araña] (It-Sp 1971)

La vendetta è un piatto che si serve freddo (It 1971)
Ti attende una corda, Ringo [Il ritorno di Clint il solitario]
     (It-Sp 1972)
Black Killer (It 1972)
Aguirre, der Zorn Gottes (W Ger 1972)
La mano destra del diavolo (It 1972)
Il mio nome è Shangay Joe [Mezzogiorno di fuoco per Han-Hao]
     (It 1973)
La mano spietata della legge (It 1973)
Cinque pistole di violenza (It 1973)
Rivelazioni di uno psichiatra sul mondo perverso del sesso (It
     1973)
La morte sorride all'assassino (It 1973)
L'Important, c'est d'aimer (Fr 1974)
Le orme (It 1974)
Lifespan (Dut-It 1974)
La mano che nutre la morte (It 1974)
Un genio, due compari, un pollo (It 1975)
Das Netz (W Ger 1975)

KLEIN-ROGGE, RUDOLF, b. November 4, 1888, Cologne, Germany;
     d. 1955
Morphium (Ger 1919)
Das wandernde Bild (Ger 1920)
Kampfende Herzen (Ger 1921)
Perlen bedeuten Tränen (Ger 1921)
Zirkus des Lebens (Ger 1921)
Dr. Mabuse der Spieler (Ger 1922)
Die Prinzessin Suwarin (Ger 1923)
Der Steinerne Reiter (Ger 1923)
Die Nibelungen (Ger 1924)
Pietro, der Korsar (Ger 1924)
Der Mann seiner Frau (Ger 1925)
Der rosa Diamant (Ger 1925)
Der Herr der Nacht (Ger 1926)
Die lachende Grille (Ger 1926)
Mädchenhandel (Ger 1926)
Metropolis (Ger 1926)
Die letzte Nacht (Ger 1927)
Das Mädchen aus Frisco (Ger 1927)
Die raffinierteste Frau Berlins (Ger 1927)
Die Sandgräfin (Ger 1927)
Tingel-Tangel (Aus 1927)
Der Zigeunerbaron (Ger 1927)
Mädchenschicksale (Ger 1928)
Die schönste Frau von Paris (Ger 1928)
Spione (Ger 1928)
Wolga-Wolga (Ger 1928)
Meineid (Ger 1929)
Der weisse Gott (Ger 1931)
Der Judas von Tirol (Ger 1933)
Das Testament des Dr. Mabuse (Ger 1933)
Elisabeth und der Narr (Ger 1933)

Zwischen Himmel und Erde (Ger 1934)
Hanneles Himmelfahrt (Ger 1934)
Der Fall Brenken (Ger 1934)
Die Welt ohne Maske (Ger 1934)
Grenzfeuer (Ger 1934)
Gern hab' ich die Frauen geküsst (Ger 1934)
Die Frauen vom Tannhof (Ger 1934)
Der alte and der junge König (Ger 1935)
Das Einmaleins der Liebe (Ger 1935)
Der Kosak und die Nachtigall (Aus 1935)
Der Ammenkönig (Ger 1935)
Ein seltsamer Gast (Ger 1936)
Moral (Ger 1936)
Truxa (Ger 1936)
Das Hofkonzert (Ger 1936)
Der Kaiser von Kalifornien (Ger 1936)
Intermezzo (Ger 1936)
Die un-erhörte Frau (Ger 1936)
Madame Bovary (Ger 1937)
Die göttliche Jette (Ger 1937)
Der Herrscher (Ger 1937)
Die gelbe Flagge (Ger 1937)
Streit um den Knaben Jo (Ger 1937)
Der Katzensteg (Ger 1937)
Zwei Frauen (Ger 1938)
Ab Mitternacht (Ger-Fr 1938)
Abenteuer in Marokko (Ger 1939)
Kennwort Machin (Ger 1939)
Parkstrasse (Ger 1939)
Robert Koch (Ger 1939)
Schneider Wibbel (Ger 1939)
Rheinische Drautfahrt (Ger 1939)
Menschen vom Varieté (Ger-Hun 1939)
Die unvollkommene Liebe (Ger 1950)
Das Herz einer Königin (Ger 1940)
Hochzeit auf Bärenhof (Ger 1942)

KNEF, HILDEGARD (Hildegard Neff), b. Dec. 28, 1925, Ulm, Germany
Unter den Brücken (Ger 1945)
Traümerei (W Ger 1946)
Die Mörder sind unter uns [Murderers Among Us] (W Ger 1947)
Zwischen Gestern und Morgen (W Ger 1947)
Film ohne Titel [Film without a Name] (W Ger 1947)
Fahrt ins Glück (W Ger 1948) (made in 1945)
Die Sünderin (W Ger 1950)
Es Geschehen noch Wunder (W Ger 1951)
Nachts auf den Strassen (W Ger 1951)
Decision before Dawn (20th 1952)
Diplomatic Courier (20th 1952)
The Snows of Kilimanjaro (20th 1952)
Night Without Sleep (20th 1952)
Alraune (W Ger 1952)

Hildegard Knef in <u>Three Penny Opera</u> (1963).

Illusion in Moll (W Ger 1952)
La Fête à Henriette [Holiday for Henrietta] (Fr 1952)
The Man Between (BL/UA 1953)
Eine Liebesgeschichte [A Love Story] (W Ger 1954)
Geständnis unter vier Augen (W Ger 1954)
Svengali (W Ger 1954)
Madeleine und der Legionär (W Ger 1957)
La Fille de Hambourg [Port of Desire] (Fr 1958)
Subway in the Sky (Britannia 1958)
La strada dei giganti (It 1959)
Der Mann, der sich verkauft (It 1959)
Lulu [No Orchids for Lulu] (Aus 1962)
Caterina di Russia [Catherine de Russie] (It-Fr 1962)
Landru (Fr 1962)
Ballade pour un Voyou (Fr 1962)
Das grosse Liebesspiel [And So to Bed] (W Ger 1963)
Die Dreigroschenoper [L'opera de quat'sous] (W Ger-Fr 1963)
Gibraltar [Spionaggio a Gibilterra/Misión en el estrecho/The
    Spy] (Fr-It-Sp 1963)
Verdammt zur Sünde (W Ger 1964)
Wartezimmer zum Jenseits [Mark of the Tortoise] (W Ger 1964)
Mozambique (7 Arts 1964)

The Lost Continent (RFD 1968)
Jeder stirbt für sich allein (W Ger 1975)

KOCH, MARIANNE (Marianne Cook), b. Aug. 19, 1930,
   Munich
Der Mann, der zweimal leben wollte (W Ger 1950)
Dr. Holl (W Ger 1950)
Czardas der Herzen (W Ger 1951)
Das Geheimnis einer Ehe (W Ger 1951)
Mein Freund, der Dieb (W Ger 1951)
Der keusche Lebemann (W Ger 1952)
Wetterleuchten am Dachstein (Aus 1953)
Skandal im Mädchenpensionat (W Ger 1953)
Der Klösterjäger (W Ger 1953)
Die grosse Schuld (Aus 1953)
Liebe und Trompetenblasen (W Ger 1953)
Geh mach dein Fensterl auf (Aus 1954)
Schloss Hubertus (W Ger 1954)
Night People (20th 1954)
Ludwig II (W Ger 1955)
Des Teufels General [The Devil's General] (W Ger 1955)
Der Schmied von St. Bartholomä (W Ger 1955)
Königswalzer (W Ger 1955)
Solange du lebst (W Ger 1955)
Zwei blaue Augen (W Ger 1955)
Und der Himmel lacht dazu (Aus 1955)
Die Ehe des Dr. med. Danwitz (W Ger 1956)
Wenn wir alle Engel wären (W Ger 1956)
Salzburger Geschichten (W Ger 1957)
Vater sein dagegen sehr (W Ger 1957)
Der Stern von Afrika [La estrella de Africa] (W Ger-Sp 1957)
Four Girls in Town (Univ 1957)
Interlude (Univ 1957)
Der Fuchs von Paris (W Ger 1957)
...und nichts als die Wahrheit (W Ger 1958)
Die Landärztin (W Ger 1958)
Gli Italiani sono matti [Los Italianos estan locos] (It-Sp 1958)
Frau im besten Mannesalter (W Ger 1959)
Die Frau am dunkeln Fenster (W Ger 1960)
Heldinnen (W Ger 1960)
Mit Himbeergeist geht alles besser (W Ger 1960)
Pleins feux sur l'assassin (Fr 1961)
Unter Ausschluss der Öffentlichkeit (W Ger 1961)
Napoléon II, l'aiglon (Fr 1961)
Die Fledermaus (Aus 1962)
Heisser Hafen Hongkong (W Ger 1962)
Im Namen des Teufels [The Devil's Agent] (Ger-GB 1962)
Liebling, ich muss Dich erschiessen (W Ger 1962)
Der letzte Ritt nach Santa Cruz (W Ger-Aus 1963)
Der schwarze Panther von Ratana (W Ger-It 1963)
Für eine Handvoll Dollars [Per un pugno di dollari/Por un
   punado de dolares] (W Ger-It-Sp 1964)
Das Ungeheuer von London City (W Ger 1964)

Der Fall x 701 [Frozen Alive] (W Ger-GB 1964)
Coast of Skeletons (BL 1964)
Die Hölle von Manitoba [Un lugar llamado "Glory"/A Place Called Glory] (W Ger-Sp 1965)
Vergeltung in Catano [Terra de prego/Sunscorched] (Ger-Sp 1965)
Mivtza Kahir [Einer spielt falsch/Trunk to Cairo] (Israeli-W Ger 1966)
5000 Dollar für der Kopf von Jonny R [La balada de Johnny Ringo] (W Ger-Sp 1966)
Schreie in der Nacht (W Ger-It 1968)
Clint, el solitario [Clint, il solitario] (Sp-It-W Ger 1968)
España, otra vez (Sp 1969)

KOCZIAN, JOHANNA VON, b. Oct. 30, 1933, Berlin
Viktor und Viktoria (W Ger 1957)
Petersburger Nächte (W Ger 1958)
Serenade einer grossen Liebe [For the First Time] (USA-W Ger 1959)
Wir Wunderkinder (W Ger 1958)
Menschen im Netz (W Ger 1959)
Bezaubernde Arabella (W Ger 1959)
Jacqueline (W Ger 1959)
Lampenfieber (W Ger 1960)
Heldinnen (W Ger 1960)
Agatha, lass das Morden sein (W Ger 1960)
Die Ehe des Herrn Mississippi (W Ger 1961)
Unser Haus in Kamerun (W Ger 1961)
Strasse der Verheissung (W Ger 1962)
Das Liebeskarussel (Aus 1965)
Kapt'n Rauhbein aus St. Pauli (W Ger 1971)

KÖRBER, HILDE, b. July 3, 1906, Vienna; d. 1969
Fridericus (Ger 1936)
Maria, die Magd (Ger 1936)
Der Herrscher (Ger 1936)
Patrioten (Ger 1937)
Mein Sohn, der Herr Minister (Ger 1937)
Heiratsschwindler (Ger 1937)
Die Kreutzersonate (Ger 1937)
Brillanten (Ger 1937)
Der Spieler (Ger 1938)
Maja zwischen zwei Ehen (Ger 1938)
Eine Frau kommt in die Tropen (Ger 1938)
Grossalarm (Ger 1938)
Fasching (Ger 1939)
Der singende Tor (Ger 1939)
Salonwagen E 417 (Ger 1939)
Robert Koch (Ger 1939)
Leidenschaft (Ger 1939)
Der Sündenbock (Ger 1940)
Der Fuchs von Glenarvon (Ger 1940)
Ohm Krüger (Ger 1941)
Jakko (Ger 1941)

Der grosse König (Ger 1942)
Damals (Ger 1943)
Ein Blick zurück (Ger 1944)
Das Leben geht weiter (Ger 1944)
Wie sagen wir es unseren Kindern? (Ger 1944)
Via Mala (Ger 1944)
Morituri (W Ger 1948)
Verführte Jugend (W Ger 1950)
Wenn die Abendglocken läuten (W Ger 1951)
Das letzte Rezept (W Ger 1952)
Mein Herz darst Du nicht fragen (W Ger 1952)
Rosen blühen auf dem Heidegrab (W Ger 1952)
Ave Maria (W Ger 1953)
Mit Siebzehn beginnt das Leben (W Ger 1953)
Sauerbruch--Dar was mein Leben (W Ger 1953)
Das Bekenntnis der Ina Kahr (W Ger 1954)
Rittmeister Wronski (W Ger 1954
Die Toteninsel (W Ger 1954)
Mein Vater der Schauspieler (W Ger 1955)
Teufel in Seide (W Ger 1956)
Heisse Ente (W Ger 1956)
Anders als Du und ich (W Ger 1957)
Das Mädchen vom Moorhof (W Ger 1958)
Ich werde Dich auf Händen tragen (W Ger 1958)

KORTNER, FRITZ, b. March 12, 1892, Vienna; d. July 20, 1970
Sonnwendfeuer (Ger 1916)
Police 1111 (Ger 1916)
Das zweite Leben (Ger 1916)
Der Brief eines Toten (Aus 1917)
Das andere Ich (Ger 1918)
Frauenehre (Aus 1918)
Der Märtyrer seines Herzens (Aus 1918)
Sonnwendhof (Aus 1918)
Der Starkere (Aus 1918)
Das Auge des Buddha (Ger 1919)
Else von Erlenhof (Aus 1919)
Gerechtigkeit (Ger 1919)
Ohne Zeugen (Aus 1919)
Prinz Kuckuck (Ger 1919)
Satanas (Ger 1919)
Die Brüder Karamasoff (Ger 1920)
Das Haus zum Mond (Ger 1920)
Die Jagd nach der Wahrheit (Ger 1920)
Katherina die Grosse (Ger 1920)
Die Lieblingsfrau des Maharadscha (Ger 1920)
Die Nacht der Königin Isabeau (Ger 1920)
Der Schädel der Pharaonentochter (Ger 1920)
Va Banque (Ger 1920)
Die Verschwörung zu Genua (Ger 1920)
Weltbrand (Ger 1920)
Am roten Kliff (Ger 1921)
Christian Wahnschaffe (Ger-Dan 1921)

Danton (Ger 1921)
Der Eisenbahnkönig (Ger 1921)
Die Hintertreppe (Ger 1921)
Die Finsternis ist ihr Eigentum (Ger 1922)
Flammende Völker (Ger 1922)
Der Graf von Essex (Ger 1922)
Das Haus der Qualen (Ger 1922)
Luise Millerin (Ger 1922)
Landstrasse und Grosstadt (Ger 1922)
Die Mausefalle (Ger 1922)
Peter der Grosse (Ger 1922)
Ein Puppenheim (Ger 1922)
Ruf des Schicksals (Ger 1922)
Der stärkste Trieb (Ger 1922)
Sterbende Völker (Ger 1922)
Arme Sünderin (Ger 1923)
Nora (Ger 1923)
Schatten (Ger 1923)
Ein Weib, ein Tier, ein Diamant (Ger 1923)
Armes kleines Mädchen (Ger 1924)
Dr. Wislizenus (Ger 1924)
Moderne Ehe (Ger 1924)
Orleans Hände (Ger 1925)
Dürfen wir schweigen? (Ger 1926)
Alpentragödie (Ger 1927)
Die Ausgestossenen (Ger 1927)
Beethoven (Aus 1927)
Die Geliebe des Gouverneurs (Ger 1927)
Maria Stuart (Ger 1927)
Mata Hari (Ger 1927)
Mein Leben für das Deine (Ger 1927)
Primanerliebe (Ger 1927)
Frau Sorge (Ger 1928)
Marquis d'Eon, der Spion der Pompadour (Ger 1928)
Revolutionshochzeit (Ger 1928)
Die Büchse der Pandora (Ger 1929)
Die Frau im Talar (Ger 1929)
Die Frau nach der man sich sehnt (Ger 1929)
Giftgas (Ger 1929)
Die stärkere Macht (Ger 1929)
Das Schiff der verlorenen Menschen (Ger 1929)
Somnambul (Ger 1929)
Atlantic (Ger 1929)
Dreyfus (Ger 1930)
Menschen im Käfig (Ger 1930)
Der Andere (Ger 1930)
Die grosse Sehnsucht (Ger 1930)
Der Mörder Dimitri Karamasoff (Ger 1931)
Danton (Ger 1931)
Chu Chin Chow (Gaumont (1933)
Evensong (Gaumont 1933)
Abdul the Damned (Wardour 1935)
The Crouching Beast (Radio 1935)

The Strange Death of Adolph Hitler (Univ 1943)
The Hitler Gang (Par 1943)
Wife of Monte Cristo (PRC 1946)
Somewhere in the Night (20th 1946)
The Razor's Edge (20th 1946)
The Brasher Doubloon (20th 1947)
Berlin Express (RKO 1948)
Vicious Circle (UA 1948)
Der Ruf (W Ger 1949)
Epilog (W Ger 1950)
Blaubart [Ger version of Barbe-Bleune] (W Ger 1951)

KOSCINA, SYLVA, b. Aug. 22, 1933, Zagreb
Il ferroviere (It 1956)
Michele Strogoff (It-Yug 1956)
Guendalina (It 1957)
I fidanzati della morte (It-W Ger 1957)
La nonna Sabella (It 1957)
Femmine tre volte [Operación Popoff] (It-Sp 1957)
Gerusalemme liberata (It 1957)
Le Naïf aux guarante infants (Fr 1957)
Le fatiche di Ercoe [Hercules] (It 1958)
Ladro lui, ladra lei (It 1958)
Racconti d'estate (It 1958)
Giovani mariti (It 1958)
Totò a Parigi (It 1958)
Non sono più guaglione (It 1958)
Quande gli angeli piangono (It 1958)
Totò nella luna (It 1958)
Poveri milionari (It-Sp 1959)
Ercole e la regina di Lidia [Hercules Unchained] (It 1959)
La nipote Sabella (It 1959)
Psicanalista per signora [Le confident de ces dames] (It-Fr
    1959)
La cambiale (It 1959)
Tempi duri per i vampiri (It 1959)
Le sorprese dell'amore (It 1959)
L'assedio di Siracusa [The Siege of Syracuse] (It 1960)
Genitori in blue jeans (It 1960)
I piaceri dello scapolo (It 1960)
Il vigile (It 1960)
Femmine di lusso (It 1960)
Le pillole di Ercole (It 1960)
Mariti in pericolo (It 1961)
Les Distractions [Le distrazioni] (Fr-It 1961)
Rairssante [Le mogli degli altri] (Fr-It 1961)
Il sicario (It 1961)
Mani in alto [En pleine bagarre] (It-Fr 1961)
Jessica (UA 1961)
Copacabana palace (It 1962)
Le massaggiatrici [Les Faux Jetons] (It-Fr 1962)
La congiura dei dieci [Lo spadacino di Siena/Swordsman of
    Sienna] (It 1962)

Les quatre vérités [Le quatro verite] (ep "La Leprée la tar-
   taruga") (Fr-It 1963)
Cyrano et d'Artagnan [Cyrano e d'Aratagnan] (Fr-It 1963)
Il fornaretto d'Venezia [Le proces des doges] (It-Fr 1963)
Le monachine (It 1963)
Hot Enough for June [Agent 8 3/4] (Rank 1963)
Judex [L'uomo in nero] (Fr-It 1963)
Le Masque de fer [L'uomo dalla maschera di ferra] (Fr-It 1963)
L'Appartement des filles [L'appartamento delle ragazze] (Fr-It
   1964)
Se permette parliamo di donne (It 1964)
Amore in quattro dimensioni (It 1964)
Cadavere per signora (It 1964)
L'idea fissa (ep "Sabato 18 luglio") (It 1964)
Il triangolo circolare (It 1965)
Colpo grosso a Galata Bridge [Operación Estambul/L'Homme
   d'Istamboul/That Man in Istanbul] (It-Sp-Fr 1965)
Thrilling (ep "L'autostrada del sole") (It 1965)
Giulietta degli spiriti [Juliet of the Spirits] (It 1965)
Corpo a corpo [L'Arme à gauche] (It-Fr 1965)
Le Grain de sable (Fr 1965)
I soldi (It 1965)
Io, io, io...e gli altri (It 1966)
Monnari de sinzi [I sette falsari] (Fr-It 1965)
Made in Italy (It 1965)
Carré de dames pour un as [Layton...karate e bambole/De-
   masiadas mujeres para Layton] (Fr-It-Sp 1966)
Agente X-77, ordine di uccidere [Operación silencio/Baraka sur
   X-13] (It-Sp-Fr 1966)
Una storia di notte (It 1966)
Il morbidone (It 1966)
Racconti a due piazze [Le Lit à deux places] (It-Fr 1966)
Das Gemüsse etwas der Frauen [Come imparai ad amare le
   donne] (W Ger-It 1967)
Deadlier than the Male (Univ 1967)
Three Bites of the Apple (MGM 1967)
I protagonisti (It 1968)
Johnny Banco [Johnny Banco, geliebter Taugenichts] (It-W Ger
   1968)
Vedo Nudo (It 1968)
The Secret War of Harry Frigg (Univ 1968)
A Lovely Way to Die (Univ 1968)
Kampf un Rom (It-W Ger 1968)
Kampf un Rom I und Kampf un Rom II: der Verrat [La guerra
   per Roma, prima parte e seconda parte/Lupta pentru Roma]
   (W Ger-It-Rum 1968)
Justine ovvero le disavventure della virtù (It 1969)
L'assoluto naturale (It 1969)
Bitka na Neretvi (Yug 1969)
La Modification [La moglie nuova] (Fr-It 1969)
Hornet's Nest [Il vespaio/I lupi attaccano in branco] (USA-It
   1970)
La colomba non deve volare (It 1970)

Vergite pour un tueur [Vertigine per un assassino] (Fr-It 1970)
Les Jambes en l'air [Week-end proibito di una famiglia quasi per
    bene] (Fr-It 1970)
Nini Tirabuscio, la donna che invento la mossa (It 1970)
Il sesso del diavolo (It 1971)
Mazzabubu, quante corna stanno quaggiù (It 1971)
Uccidere in Silenzio (It 1971)
Boccaccio (It 1972)
Homo eroticus (It 1972)
Sette scialli di seta gialla (It 1972)
Historia de una traición [African Story] (Sp-It 1972)
La "mala" ordina [Der Mafia-Boss--sie töteten wie Schackale]
    (It-W Ger 1972)
Rivelazioni di un maniaco sessuale al capo della squadra mobile
    (It 1972)
La strana legge del Dr. Menga (It-Sp 1972)
Lisa e il diavolo (It 1972)
Beati i ricchi (It 1972)
No desearas la mujer del vacino (Sp 1972)
Qualcuno ha visto uccidere (It-Sp 1973)
Il tuo piacere e il mio (It 1973)
So Sweet, So Dead (It-Sp 1974)
Delitto d'autore (It 1974)
Dracula in Brianza [Il cav. Costante Nicosia demoniaco ovvero
    Dracula in Brianza] (It 1975)
Un par de zapatos del 39 (Sp 1975)
Las correrias del Visconde Arnau (Sp 1975)

KRAHL, HILDE, b. Dec. 15, 1915, Brod [on Sava], Yugoslavia
Die Puppenfee (Aus 1936)
Mädchenpensionat (Aus 1936)
Lumpazivagabundus (Aus 1937)
Serenade (Ger 1937)
Der Hampelmann (Ger 1938)
Gastspiel im Paradies (Ger 1938)
Die barmherzige Lüge (Ger 1939)
Der Weg zu Isabell (Ger 1939)
Herz modern möbliert (Ger 1940)
Donauschiffer (Ger 1940)
Der Postmeister (Ger 1940)
Komödianten (Ger 1941)
Das andere Ich (Ger 1941)
Meine Freundin Josefine (Ger 1942)
Anuschka (Ger 1942)
Grossstadtmelodie (Ger 1943)
Träumerei (Ger 1944)
Das Leben geht weiter (Ger 1945)
Das Gesetz der Liebe (Ger 1945)
Liebe 47 (W Ger 1947)
Wenn eine Frau liebt (W Ger 1950)
Meine nichte Susanne (W Ger 1950)
Schatten der Nacht (W Ger 1950)
Weisse Schatten (W Ger 1951)

Herz der Welt (W Ger 1952)
Der Weibsteufel (Aus 1952)
Das Tor zum Frieden (Aus 1952)
1. April 2000 (W Ger 1952)
Die Mücke (W Ger 1953)
Hochstaplerin der Liebe (W Ger 1954)
Ewiger Walzer (W Ger 1954)
Kinder, Mutter und ein General (W Ger 1955)
Eine Frau genügt nicht? (W Ger 1955)
Geheimnis einer Ärztin (W Ger 1955)
Mein Vater, der Schauspieler (W Ger 1956)
Nacht der Entscheidung (W Ger 1956)
Das Glas Wasser (W Ger 1960)
Heute kundigt mir mein Mann (W Ger 1962)
90 Minuten nach Mitternacht (W Ger 1962)

KRAUSS, WERNER, b. July 8, 1884, Koburg, Germany; d. July 23,
   1959
Die Pagode (Ger 1941)
Hoffmanns Erzählungen (Ger 1916)
Nacht des Grauens (Ger 1916)
Zirkusblug (Ger 1916)
Die Rache der Toten (Ger 1917)
Die Seeschlacht (Ger 1917)
Wenn Frauen lieben und hassen (Ger 1917)
Es werde Licht (Ger 1917)
Opium (Ger 1918)
Die Frau mit den Orchideen (Ger 1919)
Das Kabinett des Dr. Caligari (Ger 1919)
Rose Bernd (Ger 1919)
Totentanz (Ger-Aus 1919)
Die Beichte einer Toten (Ger 1920)
Die Brüder Karamasoff (Ger 1920)
Der Bucklige und die Tänzerin (Ger 1920)
Hölle und Verfall (Ger 1920)
Johannes Goth (Ger 1920)
Das lachende Grauen (Ger 1920)
Die Beute der Erinnyen (Ger 1921)
Christian Wahnschaffe (Ger 1921)
Danton (Ger 1921)
Die Frau ohne Seele (Ger 1921)
Grausige Nächte (Ger 1921)
Der Mann ohne Namen (Ger 1921)
Das Medium (Ger 1921)
Der Roman der Christine von Herre (Ger 1921)
Scherben (Ger 1921)
Der Tanz um Liebe und Glück (Ger 1921)
Sappho (Ger 1921)
Zirkus des Lebens (Ger 1921)
Der brennende Acker (Ger 1922)
Der Graf von Essex (Ger 1922)
Josef und seine Brüder (Ger 1922)
Luise Millerin [Kebale und Liebe] (Ger 1922)

Lady Hamilton (Ger 1922)
Die Marquise von Pompadour (Ger 1922)
Die Nacht der Medici (Ger 1922)
Nathan der Weise (Ger 1922)
Othello (Ger 1922)
Tragikomödie (Ger 1922)
Adam und Eva (Ger 1923)
Das alte Gesetz (Ger 1923)
Alt-Heidelberg (Ger 1923)
Fräulein Raffke (Ger 1923)
Fridericus Rex (Ger 1923)
I. N. R. I. (Ger 1923)
Der Kaufmann von Venedig (Ger 1924)
Der Menschenfeind (Ger 1924)
Der Puppenmacher von Kiang-Ning (Ger 1924)
Der Schatz (Ger 1924)
Das unbekannte Morgen (Ger 1924)
Zwischen Abend und Morgen (Ger 1924)
Dekameron Nächte (Ger 1924)
Ein Sommernachtstraum (Ger 1924)
Das Wachsfigurenkabinett (Ger 1925)
Die Dame aus Berlin (Ger 1925)
Die Moral der Grasse (Ger 1925)
Eifersucht (Ger 1925)
Die freudlose Gasse (Ger 1925)
Das Haus der Lüge (Ger 1925)
Die Moral der Gasse (Ger 1925)
Reveille, das grosse Wecken (Ger 1925)
Tartüff (Ger 1925)
Der Trodler von Amsterdam (Ger 1925)
Geheimnisse einer Seele (Ger 1926)
Das graue Haus (Ger 1926)
Kreuzzug des Weibes (Ger 1926)
Man spielt nicht mit der Liebe! (Ger 1926)
Nana (Ger 1926)
Der Student von Prag (Ger 1926)
Überflüssige Menschen (Ger 1926)
Da hält die Welt den Atem an (Ger 1926)
Der fidele Bauer (Ger 1927)
Funkzaubet (Ger 1927)
Die Hölle der Jungfrauen (Ger 1927)
Die Hose (Ger 1927)
Laster der Menschheit (Ger 1927)
Unter Ausschluss der Öffentlichkeit (Ger 1927)
Looping the Loop (Ger 1928)
Napoleon auf St. Helena (Ger 1928)
Yorck (Ger 1931)
Mench ohne Namen (Ger 1932)
Hundert Tage (Ger 1935)
Burgtheater (Ger 1936)
Robert Koch (Ger 1936)
Jud Süss (Ger 1940)
Annelie (Ger 1941)

Die Entlassung (Ger 1942)
Zwischen Himmel und Erde (Ger 1942)
Paracelsus (Ger 1943)
Prämien auf den Tod (W Ger 1950)
Der fallende Stern (W Ger 1950)
Sohn ohne Heimat (W Ger 1955)

KRISTEL, SYLVIA, b. Sept. 28, 1952, Utrecht
Niet voor de poesjes [Because of the Cats] (Dut-Bel 1973)
Frank en Eva (Dut 1973
Naakt over de Schutting (Dut 1973)
Emmanuelle (Fr 1974)
Es war nicht die Nachtigall (W Ger 1974)
Un Linceul n'a pas de poches (Fr 1974)
Le Jeu avec le feu [Giochi di fuoco] (Fr-It 1974)
Emmanuelle II [Emmanuelle l'anti-vierge] (Fr 1975)

KRÜGER, HARDY (Ebenhard Krüger), b. April 12, 1928, Berlin
Junge Adler (Ger 1944)
Das Fräulein und der Vagabund (W Ger 1949)
Diese Nacht vergess' ich nie (W Ger 1949)
Kätchen für alles (W Ger 1949)
Das Mädchen aus der Südsee (W Ger 1950)
Insel ohne Moral (W Ger 1950)
Schön muss man sein (W Ger 1951)
Mein Freund der Dieb (W Ger 1951)
Ich heisse Niki (W Ger 1952)
Alle Kann ich nicht Heiraten (W Ger 1952)
Illusion in Moll (W Ger 1952)
The Moon Is Blue (UA 1953)
Die Jungfrau auf dem Dach [Ger version of The Moon Is Blue]
    (UA 1953)
Solange Du da bist (W Ger 1953)
Muss man sich gleich scheiden lassen? (W Ger 1953)
Ich und Du (W Ger 1953)
Der letzte Sommer (W Ger 1954)
An der schönen Blauen Donau (Aus 1955)
Der Himmel ist nie ausverkauft (W Ger 1955)
Alibi (W Ger 1955)
Liane, das Mädchen, aus dem Urwald [Liane, Young Goddess]
    (W Ger 1956)
Die Christl von der Post (W Ger 1956)
The One That Got Away (RFD 1957)
Banktresor 713 (W Ger 1957)
Der Fuchs von Paris [Mission Diabolique] (W Ger-Fr 1957)
Gestehen Sie, Dr. Corda! [Confess, Dr. Corda] (W Ger 1958)
Bachelor of Hearts (RFD 1958)
Die Nackte und der Satan (W Ger 1959)
Der Rest ist Schweigen [The Rest Is Silence] (W Ger 1959)
Chance Meeting [Blind Date] (RFD 1959)
Die Gans von Sedan [Sans tambour ni trompette] (W Ger-Fr
    1959)
Bumerang [Cry Double Cross] (W Ger 1960)

Un Taxi pour Tobrouk [Un Taxi para Tobrouk/Taxi for Tobruk]
  (Fr-Sp 1960)
Zwei unter Millionen (W Ger 1961)
Les Dimanches de Ville-d'Avray [Sundays and Cybele/Cybelle]
  (Fr 1961)
Hatari! (Par 1962)
Les Quatre Vérités [Las cuatros Verdades/Le quattro verita]
  (ep "La Mort et le bûcheron") (Fr-Sp-It 1962)
Le Gros Coup [Il triangolo del delitto] (Fr-It 1964)
Le Chant du monde (Fr-It-W Ger 1964)
Les Pianos mécaniques [Los pianos mecanicos/The Uninhibited]
  (Fr-Sp-It 1965)
The Flight of the Phoenix (20th 1965)
Lautlose Waffen [L'Espion/The Defector] (W Ger-Fr 1966)
La Grande Sauterelle [Ein Mädchen wie das Meer/Femmina]
  (Fr-W Ger-It 1966)
Le Franciscain de Bourges (Fr 1968)
La monaca di Monza [Una storia lombarda/The Awful Story of
  the Nun of Monza] (It 1968)
La tenda rossa [Krasnaya Palatka/The Red Tent] (It-USSR 1969)
The Secret of Santa Vittoria (UA 1969)
La battaglia della Neretva [Bitka na Neretvi/Die Schlacht au der
  Neretva/The Battle of Neretva] (Yug-W Ger-It 1969)
Tod eines Fremden [The Execution] (W Ger-Israel 1972)
Le Solitaire (Fr 1972)
Night Hair Child (RFD 1973) [made in 1971]
Paper Tiger (Fox-Rank 1975)
Barry Lyndon (WB Br 1975)

LAFONT, BERNADETTE, b. Oct. 28, 1938, Nimes, France
Le Beau Serge (Fr 1958)
Bal de nuit (Fr 1959)
A Double Tour [Leda] (Fr 1959)
L'Eau à la bouche (Fr 1959)
Les Bonnes Femmes (Fr 1959)
Les Mordus (Fr 1960)
Les Godelureaux (Fr 1961)
Me faire ça à moi (Fr 1961)
Tiré au flanc (Fr 1961)
Jusqu' à plus soif (Fr 1961)
Et Satan conduit le bal (Fr 1962)
Une Grosse Tête (Fr 1962)
Un Clair de lune à Mauberge (Fr 1963)
Les Femmes d'abord (Fr-It 1963)
La Chasse à l'homme [Male Hunt] (Fr-It 1964)
Tout les enfants du monde (Fr 1964)
Les Bons Vivants (Fr-It 1965)
Pleins feux sur Stanislas (Fr 1965)
Le Voleur [The Thief of Paris] (Fr-It 1966)
Lamiel (Fr-It 1967)
Un Idiot à Paris [An Idiot in Paris] (Fr 1967)
La Piège [The Trap] (Fr-It 1968)
Falak [Walls] (Hun 1968)

Les Idoles (Fr 1968)
Paul (Fr 1969)
Le Voleur de crimes (Fr-It 1969)
L'Amour, c'est gai, c'est triste (Fr 1969)
La Fiancée du pirate [A Very Curious Girl] (Fr 1969)
La Décharge (Fr 1970)
Valparaiso, Valparaiso (Fr 1971)
Les Stances à Sophie (Fr-Canada 1971)
Une Belle Fille comme moi (Fr 1972)
Trop Jolies pour être honnêtes (Fr-It-Sp 1972)
Le Maman et le putain (Fr 1973)
Defense de savoir (Fr-It 1973)
L'Histoire très bonne et très joyeuse de Colinot Trousse-Che-
    mise (Fr-It 1973)
Une Baleine qui avait mal aux dents (Fr 1973)
Zig Zag (Fr 1974)
Vincent mit l'âne dans un Fre (Fr 1975)

LALANDE, MARIA (Maria Adelaide Lalande), b. Nov. 7, 1913,
    Salgueiro do Campo, Portugal; d. March 21, 1968
Lisboa, crônica anedótica (Por 1930)
Campinos (Por 1932)
A rosa do Adro (Por 1938)
Fátima, terra de fé (Por 1943)
Não há rapazes maus (Por 1948)

Maria Lalande

LAMARR, HEDY (Hedwig Kiesler), b. Nov. 9, 1913, Vienna
  Das Geld liegt auf der Strasse (Aus 1930)
  Die Blumenfrau von Lindenau (Aus 1931)
  Die Koffer des Herrn O. F. (Ger 1931)
  Man braucht kein Geld (Ger 1931)
  Symphonie der Liebe [Ekstase/Ecstasy] (Ger 1932)
  Algiers (UA 1938)
  Lady of the Tropics (MGM 1939)
  I Take This Woman (MGM 1940)
  Boom Town (MGM 1940)
  Comrade X (MGM 1940)
  Come Live with Me (MGM 1941)
  Ziegfeld Girl (MGM 1941)
  H. M. Pulham, Esq. (MGM 1941)
  Tortilla Flat (MGM 1942)
  Crossroads (MGM 1942)
  White Cargo (MGM 1942)
  The Heavenly Body (MGM 1942)
  The Conspirators (WB 1944)
  Experiment Perilous (RKO 1944)
  Her Highness and the Bellboy (MGM 1945)
  The Strange Woman (UA 1940)
  Dishonored Lady (UA 1947)
  Let's Live a Little (EL 1948)
  Samson and Delilah (Par 1949)
  A Lady without Passport (MGM 1950)
  Copper Canyon (Par 1950)
  My Favorite Spy (Par 1951)
  L'amate de Paride [The Face that Launched a Thousand Ships]
    (It 1954)
  Femmina (It 1954)
  The Story of Mankind (WB 1957)
  The Female Animal (Univ 1957)

LANCHESTER, ELSA (Elizabeth Sullivan), b. Oct. 28, 1902, London
  One of the Best (W & F 1927)
  The Constant Nymph (W & F 1928)
  Comets (JMG 1930)
  The Love Habit (Wardour 1931)
  The Stronger Sex (Ideal 1931)
  Potiphar's Wife [Her Strange Desire] (FN Br 1931)
  The Officer's Mess (Par Br 1931)
  The Private Life of Henry VIII (UA 1933)
  David Copperfield (MGM 1935)
  Naughty Marietta (MGM 1935)
  The Bride of Frankenstein (Univ 1935)
  The Ghost Goes West (UA 1936)
  Rembrandt (UA 1936)
  Vessel of Wrath [The Beachcomber] (ABPC 1938)
  Ladies in Retirement (Col 1941)
  Son of Fury (20th 1942)
  Tales of Manhattan (20th 1942)
  Forever and a Day (RKO 1943)

Thumbs Up (Rep 1943)
Lassie Come Home (MGM 1943)
Passport to Destiny [Passport to Adventure] (RKO 1944)
Son of Lassie (MGM 1945)
The Spiral Staircase (RKO 1946)
The Razor's Edge (20th 1947)
Northwest Outpost (Rep 1947)
The Bishop's Wife (RKO 1947)
The Big Clock (Par 1948)
The Secret Garden (MGM 1949)
Come to the Stable (29th 1949)
The Inspector General (WB 1949)
Buccaneer's Girl (Univ 1950)
Mystery Street (MGM 1950)
The Petty Girl [Girl of the Year] (Col 1950)
Frenchie (Univ 1950)
Les Miserables (20th 1952)
Androcles and the Lion (RKO 1952)
Dreamboat (20th 1952)
Girls of Pleasure Island (Par 1953)
Hell's Half Acre (Rep 1954)
Three-Ring Circus (Par 1954)
The Glass Slipper (MGM 1955)
Witness for the Prosecution (UA 1957)
Bell, Book and Candle (Col 1958)
Honeymoon Hotel (MGM 1964)
Mary Poppins (BV 1964)
Pajama Party (AIP 1964)
That Darn Cat (BV 1965)
Easy Come, Easy Go (Par 1967)
Blackbeard's Ghost (BV 1968)
Rascal (BV 1969)
Me, Natalie (Nat Gen 1969)
My Dog, the Thief (BV 1969)
Willard (Cin 1971)
Arnold (Cin 1973)
Terror in the Wax Museum (Cin 1973)

LASSANDER, DAGMAR, b. Prague
Andrea, wie ein Blatt auf nackter Haut (W Ger 1968)
Femina ridens (It 1969)
Il rosso segno della follia [Un hacha para la luna de miel]
    (It-Sp 1970)
Von Haut zu Haut (W Ger 1970)
Un caso di coscienza (It 1970)
Le foto proibite di una signora per bene (It 1970)
L'iguana dalla lingua di fucco (It 1971)
Guardami nuda (It 1972)
Dias de angustia (Sp-It 1972)
Il consigliori (It 1973)
Basta con la guerra, facciamo l'amore (It 1974)
Verginità (It 1975)

LAUGHTON, CHARLES, b. July 1, 1899, Scarborough, Yorkshire,
       England; d. Dec. 15, 1962
    Piccadilly (Wardour 1929)
    Comets (JMG 1930)
    Wolves [Wanted Men] (W & F 1930)
    Down River (Gaumont 1931)
    The Old Dark House (Univ 1932)
    The Devil and the Deep (Par 1932)
    Payment Deferred (MGM 1932)
    The Sign of the Cross (Par 1932)
    If I Had a Million (Par 1932)
    Island of Lost Ships (Par 1933)
    The Private Life of Henry VIII (UA 1933)
    White Woman (Par 1933)
    The Barretts of Wimpole Street [Forbidden Alliance] (MGM 1934)
    Ruggles of Red Gap (Par 1935)
    Les Miserables (UA 1935)
    Mutiny on the Bounty (MGM 1935)
    Rembrandt (UA 1936)
    I, Claudius (1937) [unfinished]
    Vessel of Wrath [The Beachcomber] (ABPC 1938)
    St. Martin's Lane [Sidewalks of London] (ABPC 1938)
    Jamaica Inn (ABPC 1939)
    The Hunchback of Notre Dame (RKO 1939)
    They Knew What They Wanted (RKO 1939)
    It Started with Eve (Univ 1941)
    The Tuttles of Tahiti (RKO 1942)
    Tales of Manhattan (20th 1942)
    Stand By for Action (MGM 1942)
    Forever and a Day (RKO 1943)
    This Land Is Mine (RKO 1943)
    The Man from Down Under (MGM 1943)
    The Canterville Ghost (MGM 1944)
    The Suspect (Univ 1944)
    Captain Kidd (UA 1945)
    Because of Him (Univ 1946)
    The Paradine Case (Selznick 1948)
    A Miracle Can Happen [On Our Merry Way] (UA 1948)
    The Big Clock (Par 1948)
    Arch of Triumph (UA 1948)
    The Girl from Manhattan (UA 1948)
    The Bribe (MGM 1949)
    The Man on the Eiffel Tower (RKO 1949)
    The Blue Veil (RKO 1951)
    The Strange Door (Univ 1951)
    O'Henry's Full House (ep "The Cop and the Anthem") (20th 1952)
    Abbott and Costello Meet Captain Kidd (WB 1952)
    Salome (Col 1953)
    Young Bess (MGM 1953)
    Hobson's Choice (BL 1954)
    Witness for the Prosecution (UA 1957)
    Under Ten Flags (USA-It 1960)
    Spartacus (Univ 1960)

Advise and Consent (Col 1962)

LAWFORD, PETER (Peter Sydney Ernest Lawford), b. Sept. 7,
    1923, London
  Poor Old Bill (Wardour 1931)
  A Gentleman of Paris (Gaumont 1931)
  Lord Jeff [The Boy from Barnado's] (MGM 1938)
  A Yank at Eton (MGM (1942)
  Eagle Squadron (Univ 1942)
  Mrs. Miniver (MGM 1942)
  Thunder Birds (20th 1942)
  The Purple V (Rep 1943)
  Paris after Dark (20th 1943)
  Someone to Remember (Rep 1943)
  The Man from Down Under (MGM 1943)
  The White Cliffs of Dover (MGM 1944)
  The Canterville Ghost (MGM 1944)
  Mrs. Parkington (MGM 1944)
  Son of Lassie (MGM 1945)
  The Picture of Dorian Gray (MGM 1945)
  Two Sisters from Boston (MGM 1946)
  Cluny Brown (20th 1946)
  My Brother Talks to Horses (MGM 1946)
  It Happened in Brooklyn (MGM 1947)
  Good News (MGM 1947)
  On an Island with You (MGM 1948)
  Big Town Scandal (Par 1948)
  Julia Misbehaves (MGM 1948)
  Little Women (MGM 1949)
  The Red Danube (MGM 1949)
  Please Believe Me (MGM 1950)
  Just This Once (MGM 1952)
  Kangaroo (20th 1952)
  You for Me (MGM 1952)
  The Hour of Thirteen (MGM 1952)
  Rogue's March (MGM 1953)
  It Should Happen to You (Col 1954)
  Never So Few (MGM 1959)
  Ocean's Eleven (WB 1960)
  Exodus (UA 1960)
  Sergeants Three (UA 1962)
  Advise and Consent (Col 1962)
  The Longest Day (20th 1962)
  Johnny Cool (UA 1963)
  Dead Ringer (WB 1964)
  Sylvia (Par 1965)
  Harlow (Par 1965)
  The Oscar (Emb 1966)
  A Man Called Adam (Emb 1966)
  How I Spend My Summer Vacation [Deadly Roulette] (NBC-TV
    1967)
  Qui veut tuer Carlos? [Dead Run] (Fr 1967)
  Deux Billets pour Mexico [Two Tickets for Mexico] (Fr 1967)

Salt and Pepper (UA 1968)
Skidoo (Par 1968)
Buona Sera, Mrs. Campbell (UA 1968)
Hook, Line and Sinker (Col 1969)
The April Fools (Nat Gen 1969)
One More Time (UA 1970)
A Step Out of Time (CBS TV 1971)
The Deadly Hunt (CBS TV 1971)
The Clay Pigeon [Trip to Kill] (MGM 1971)
They Only Kill Their Masters (MGM 1972)
That's Entertainment! (MGM 1974) (co-narrator/host)
Rosebud (UA 1974)

LAWSON, WILFRID (Wilfrid Worsnop), b. Jan. 14, 1900, Bradford,
    England; d. Oct. 10, 1966
East Lynne on the Western Front (Gaumont 1931)
Strike It Rich (BL 1933)
Turn of the Tide (Gaumont 1935)
Ladies in Love (20th 1936)
White Hunter (20th 1936)
The Man Who Made Diamonds (Par Br 1937)
Bank Holiday [Three on a Weekend] (GFD 1938)
The Terror (ABPC 1938)
Yellow Sands (ABPC 1938)
The Gaunt Stranger [The Phantom Strikes] (ABFD 1938)
Pygmalion (GFD 1938)
Stolen Life (Par Br 1939)
Dead Man's Shoes (ABPC 1939)
Allegheny Uprising [The First Rebel] (RKO 1939)
Pastor Hall (GN 1940)
Gentlemen of Venture [It Happened to One Man] (RKO 1940)
The Long Voyage Home (UA 1940)
The Farmer's Wife (Pathe 1941)
The Man at the Gate [Men of the Sea] (GFD 1941)
Danny Boy (Butcher 1941)
Jeannie (GFD 1941)
The Tower of Terror (Pathe 1941)
Hard Steel [What Shall It Profit?] (GFD 1942)
The Night Has Eyes [Terror House] (Pathe 1942)
The Great Mr. Handel (GFD 1942)
Thursday's Child (Pathe 1943)
Fanny by Gaslight [Man of Evil] (GFD 1944)
The Turners of Prospect Road (AA 1947)
Make Me an Offer (BL 1954)
The Prisoner (Col 1955)
An Alligator Named Daisy (RFD 1955)
Now and Forever (ABP 1956)
War and Peace (Par 1956)
Hell Drivers (RFD 1957)
The Naked Truth [Your Past Is Showing] (RFD 1957)
Room at the Top (IFD 1958)
Tread Softly Stranger (Renown 1958)
Expresso Bongo (Britannia 1959)

The Naked Edge (UA 1961)
Nothing Barred (BL 1961)
Over the Odds (RFD 1961)
Go to Blazes (WPD 1962)
Postman's Knock (MGM Br 1962)
Tom Jones (UA 1963)
Becket (Par 1964)
The Wrong Box (Col 1966)
The Viking Queen (WPD 1967)

LAWTON, FRANK, b. Sept. 30, 1904, London; d. June 10, 1969
Young Woodley (Wardour 1930)
Birds of Prey [The Perfect Alibi] (Radio 1930)
The Skin Game (Wardour 1931)
The Outsider (MGM 1931)
Michael and Mary (Ideal 1931)
After Office Hours (Wardour 1932)
Cavalcade (Fox 1933)
Heads We Go [The Charming Deceiver] (Wardour 1933)
Friday the Thirteenth (ep "Blake, the Gentleman of Fortune")
    (Gaumont 1933)
Over the River [One More River] (Univ 1934)
David Copperfield (MGM 1935)
The Invisible Ray (Univ 1936)
The Devil-Doll (MGM 1936)
The Mill on the Floss (NPFD 1937)
The Four Just Men [The Secret Four] (ABFD 1939)
Went the Day Well? [48 Hours] (UA 1942)
The Winslow Boy (BL 1948)
Rough Shoot [Shoot First] (UA 1953)
Doublecross (BL 1956)
The Rising of the Moon (ep "1921") (WB 57)
Gideon's Day [Gideon of Scotland Yard] (Col 1958)
A Night to Remember (RFD 1958)
The Queen's Guards (20th 1961)

LEANDER, ZARAH (Zarah Hedberg), b. March 15, 1900, Karlstadt,
    Sweden
Dantes mysterier (Swe 1930)
Dante's mysteries [Eng lang version of Dantes mysterier] (Swe
    1930)
Falska millionären (Swe 1931)
Äktenskapsleken (Swe 1935)
Premiere (Aus 1937)
Zu neuen Ufern (Ger 1937)
La Habanera (Ger 1937)
Der Blaufuchs (Ger 1938)
Es war eine rauschende Ballnacht (Ger 1939)
Heimat (Ger 1939)
Das Lied der Wüste (Ger 1939)
Das Herz einer Königin (Ger 1940)
Der Weg ins Freie (Ger 1941)
Die grosse Liebe (Ger 1942)

Damals (Ger 1943)
Gabriela (W Ger 1950)
Cuba Cabana (W Ger 1952)
Ave Maria (W Ger 1953)
Bei Dir war es immer so schön (W Ger 1954)
Der blaue Nachtfalter (W Ger 1959)
Come imparai ad amare le donne [Das gewisse Etwas der Franen] (It-W Ger 1966)

LEAUD, JEAN-PIERRE, b. May 5, 1944, Paris
Les 400 Coups (Fr 1959)
Boulevard (Fr 1960)
Le Testament d'Orphée (Fr 1960)
L'Amour à 20 ans [Love at Twenty] (Fr-It-W Ger-Jap-Pol 1961)
Masculin-Féminin (Fr-Swe 1966)
Made in USA (Fr 1966)
La Père Nöel a les yeux bleues [Father Christmas Has Blue Eyes] (Fr 1966)
Le Plus Vieux Métier du monde (ep "Anticipation") (Fr-W Ger-It 1967)
La Chinoise (Fr 1967)
Le Départ (Bel 1967)
Week-end (Fr-It 1967)
Baisers volés [Stolen Kisses] (Fr 1968)
Le Gai Savoir (Fr-W Ger 1968)
Dialog (Czech 1968)
Porcile [Pitsty] (It-Fr 1969)
Paul (Fr 1969)
Os herdeiros (Brazil 1969)
Le Lion a sept têtes (Brazil 1970)
Domicile conjugale [Bed & Board] (Fr-It 1970)
Une Nouvelle Aventure de Billy the Kid (Fr 1971)
Les Deux Anglaises et le continent [Anne and Muriel] (Fr 1971)
Out One (Fr 1971)
L'ultimo tango a Parigi [Last Tango in Paris] (It-Fr 1972)
La Nuit américaine [Day for Night] (Fr-It 1973)
La Maman et la putain [The Mother and the Whore] (Fr 1973)
Out Spectre 1 (Fr 1974) [shortened version of 1970 film Out One which was only shown once commercially in a full version]
Le Lolos de Lola (Fr 1975)

LEE, CHRISTOPHER (Christopher Frank Carandini Lee), b. May 27, 1922, London
One Night with You (GFD 1948)
Penny and the Pownall Case (GFD 1948)
Corridor of Mirrors (GFD 1948)
Hamlet (GFD 1948)
A Song for Tomorrow (GFD 1948)
My Brother's Keeper (GFD 1948)
Saraband for Dead Lovers (GFD 1948)
Scott of the Antarctic (GFD 1948)
Trottie True [The Gay Lady] (GFD 1949)
They Were Not Divided (GFD 1950)

Prelude to Fame (GFD 1950)
Captain Horatio Hornblower (WB 1951)
Valley of the Eagles (GFD 1951)
Paul Temple Returns (Butcher 1952)
Babes in Bagdad (UA 1952)
The Crimson Pirate (WB 1952)
Moulin Rouge (IFD 1953)
Innocents in Paris (IFD 1953)
The Triangle (ep "An American Duel") (BL 1953)
Destination Milan (BL 54)
The Death of Michael Turbin (BL 1955)
That Lady (20th 1955)
The Dark Avenger [The Warriors] (20th 1955)
Storm over the Nile (IFD 1955)
Cockleshell Heroes (Col 1955)
Private's Progress (BL 1956)
Port Afrique (Col 1956)
Alias John Preston (BL 1956)
Beyond Mombasa (Col 1956)
The Battle of the River Plate [The Pursuit of the Graf Spee]
    (RFD 1956)
Ill Met by Moonlight [Night Ambush] (RFD 1957)
Fortune Is a Woman [She Played with Fire] (Col 1957)
The Curse of Frankenstein (WB 1957)
The Traitor [The Accursed] (AA 1957)
Bitter Victory (Col 1958)
A Tale of Two Cities (RFD 1958)
The Truth About Women (BL 1958)
Dracula [Horror of Dracula] (Univ 1958)
Battle of the V.1. [Unseen Heroes] (Eros 1958)
Corridors of Blood (MGM 1958)
The Hound of the Baskervilles (UA 1959)
The Man Who Could Cheat Death (Par 1959)
The Mummy (Univ 1959)
Treasure of San Teresa [Long Distance/Hot Money Girl] (Britan-
    nia 1959)
Tempi duri per i vampiri [Uncle Was a Vampire] (It 1959)
The City of the Dead [Horror Hotel] (Britannia 1960)
The Hands of Orlac (Britannia 1960)
Beat Girl [Wild for Kicks] (Renown 1960)
The Two Faces of Dr. Jekyll [House of Fright] (Col 1960)
Too Hot to Handle (WPD 1960)
Taste of Fear [Scream of Fear] (Col 1961)
The Terror of the Tongs (Col 1961)
Das Ratsel der roten Orchidee (W Ger 1961)
The Devil's Daffodil [Secret of the Devil's Daffodil/The Daffodil
    Killer] (Britannia 1961) [Eng lang version of preceding film]
Ercole al centro della terra [Hercules in the Haunted World]
    (It 1961)
The Longest Day (20th 1962) (stuntman only)
The Pirates of Blood River (Col 1962)
Sherlock Holmes und das Halsband des Todes [Sherlock Holmes
    and the Deadly Necklace] (W Ger-Fr-It 1962)

The Devil's Agent [In Names des Teufels] (W Ger-GB 1962)
Katarsis (It 1963)
La vergine de Norimberga [The Castle of Terror] (It-Fr 1963)
La frustra e il corpo [Night Is the Phantom/What!] (It-Fr 1963)
La cripta e l'incubo [Crypt of Horror/Terror in the Crypt] (It-Sp 1963)
The Devil-Ship Pirates (WPD 1964)
The Gorgon (Col 1964)
Dr. Terror's House of Horrors (RFI 1964)
Il castello dei morti vivi [Castle of the Living Dead] (It-Fr 1964)
She (WPD 1965)
The Face of Fu Manchu (WPD 1965)
The Skull (Par 1965)
Dracula--Prince of Darkness (WPD 1965)
Rasputin the Mad Monk (WPD 1965)
Circus of Fear [Psycho-Circus] (AA 1966)
Das Ratsel des silbernen Dreiecks (W Ger 1966) [Ger version of Circus of Fear]
Theatre of Death [Blood Fiend] (LIP 1966)
The Brides of Fu Manchu (AA 1966)
Five Golden Dragons (AA 1967)
Night of the Big Heat [Island of the Burning Damned] (Planet 1967)
Vengeance of Fu Manchu (AA 1967)
Die Schlangengrube und das Pendel [Torture Room/Bloos Demon] (W Ger 1967)
The Devil Rides Out [The Devil's Bride] (WPD 1968)
Curse of the Crimson Altar [Crimson Cult] (Tigon 1968)
The Face of Eve [Eve] (WPD 1968)
Fu Manchu y el beso de la muerte [The Blood of Fu Manchu/Kiss and Kill] (Sp-GB 1968)
Dracula Has Risen from the Grave (WPD 1968)
El castillo de Fu Manchu (Sp-It-W Ger 1968)
Assignment Istanbul (Dec 1969) (narrator)
The Oblong Box (WPD 1969)
Philosophy in the Boudoir [Eugenie--The Story of Her Journey into Perversion] (GB 1970)
The Magic Christian (CUE 1969)
Scream and Scream Again (WPD 1969)
El Conde Dracula [Bram Stoker's Count Dracula] (Sp-W Ger-It-Lich 1969)
Vampir (Sp 1969) [documentary]
El proceso de las brujas (Sp-It-W Ger 1970)
Julius Caesar (CUE 1970)
One More Time (UA 1970)
El Umbracle (Sp 1970)
The Private Life of Sherlock Holmes (UA 1970)
The Scars of Dracula (MGM-EMI 1970)
The House That Dripped Blood (Cin 1971)
Hannie Caulder (Tigon 1971)
I, Monster (BL 1971)
Panico en el Transiberio [Horror Express] (Sp-GB 1972)

Dracula A.D. 1972 (Col-Warner 1972)
The Creeping Flesh (Tigon 1972)
Death Line (RFD 1972)
Nothing but the Night (Fox-Rank 1972)
The Wicker Man (BL 1973)
Poor Devil (NBC-TV 1973)
The Three Musketeers [The Queen's Diamonds] (20th 1973)
The Four Musketeers The Revenge of Milady (20th 1974)
The Diamond Mercenaries (Switz 1975)
Diagnosis: Murder (CIC 1975)

LEE, MARGARET, b. 1943, London
Maciste contro i mostri (It 1962)
Sansone contro i pirati (It 1963)
La vedovella (It 1963)
Un mostro e messo (It 1964)
In ginocchio da te (It 1964)
I maniaci (It 1964)
I Marziani hanno dodici mani (It 1964)
Questo pazzo, pazzo mondo della canzone (It 1964)
Casanova '70 (It-Fr 1964)
Le Lit à deux places [Racconti a due piazze] (Fr-It 1965)
La ragazzola (It 1965)
Agente 077: dall'Oriente con furore [Fureur sur le Bosphore]
    (It-Fr-Sp 1965)
Arrivaderci, a domani (It 1965)
I soldi (It 1965)
Mondo pazzo, gente pazza (It 1965)
Traffico proibito: Operazione violenza (It 1965)
I due sergenti del Generale Custer (It 1965)
Il morbidone (It 1964)
I quattro tassisti (It 1965)
Quattro assi e una pistola (It 1965)
On a volé la Joconde [Il ladro della Gioconda] (Fr-It 1965)
Le Tigre se parfume à la dynamite [La tigre profumata alla
    dinamite] (Fr-It 1966)
Kiss the Girls and Make Them Die [Se tutte le donne del mon-
    do/Operazione Paradiso] (USA-It 1966)
New York ciama Superdrago [Hollenjagd auf heisse Ware/New
    York appelle Super Dragon/Secret Agent Super Drago] (It-
    W Ger-Fr 1966)
Gern hab'ich die Frauen gekillt [Le Carnaval des barbouzes/Spie
    contro il mondo] (W Ger-Fr-It 1966)
Our Man in Marrakesh [Bang Bang You're Dead] (AA 1966)
Circus of Fear [Psycho-Circus] (AA 1966)
Le Soleil des voyous [Il più grande colpo del secolo/Action Man]
    (Fr-It 1966)
Matchless (It 1967)
Dick Smart 2007 (It 1967)
Questi fantasmi [Ghosts--Italian Style] (It 1967)
Da Berlino l'apocalisse [Le Tigre sort sans sa mère] (It-Fr
    1967)
Arriva Dorellik (It 1967)

Coplan sauve sa peau [Horror: l'assassino ha le ore contate]
(Fr-It 1967)
Colpo maestro al servizio di Sua Maestà Britannica [Gran golpe
al servicio de Su Majesdad Britanica] (It-Sp 1967)
El Djurado (It-Sp 1968)
Franco e Ciccio e le vedove allegre (It 1968)
Banditi a Milano [The Violent Four] (It 1968)
Niente rose per OSS 117 [Pas de roses pour OSS 117] (It-Fr
1968)
Jim Golden Poker (Sp 1968)
Frau Wirtin hat auch eine Nichte (W Ger-Aus-It 1969)
Sai cosa faceva Stalin alle donne? (It 1969)
I bastardi I gatti [Sons of Satan] (It 1969)
A doppia faccia [Das Gesicht im Dunkeln] (It-W Ger 1969)
La vera storia dei fratelli Mannata [Viva America!] (It-Sp 1969)
Il dio chiamato Dorian [Das Bildnis des Dorian Gray/Dorian
Gray] (It-W Ger-Liechtenstein 1969)
Cinque per l'inferno (It 1969)
Paroxismus [Puo una morte riviere per amore?/Venus in Furs/
Venus im Pelz] (It-GB-W Ger 1969)
Un sudario a la medida (Sp-It 1969)
Appuntamento col disonore (It-Sp 1970)
Le belve (It 1970)
Il trono di fuoco [El juez sangriente/Der Hexentöter von Black-
moor/Night of the Blood Monster] (It-Sp-W Ger 1970)
La bestia uccide a sangue freddo (It 1971)
Knock-Out (It 1971)
Five Nights in a Neighbor's House (It 1972)
Gli assassini sono nostri ospiti (It 1974)
Mitra sulla follia (It 1974)
La sensualità: è un attimo di vita (It 1975)

LEIGH, VIVIEN (Vivien Mary Hartley), b. Nov. 5, 1913, Darjeeling,
India; d. July 8, 1967
Things Are Looking Up (Gaumont 1935)
The Village Squire (B & D-Par Br 1935)
Gentleman's Agreement (B & D-Par Br 1935)
Look Up and Laugh (ABFD 1935)
Fire Over England (UA 1937)
Dark Journey [The Anxious Years] (UA 1937)
Storm in a Teacup (UA 1937)
21 Days [21 Days Together] (Col 1937)
A Yank at Oxford [MGM Br 1938)
St. Martin's Lane [Sidewalks of London] (ABPC 1938)
Gone with the Wind (MGM 1939)
Waterloo Bridge (MGM 1939)
Lady Hamilton [That Hamilton Woman] (UA 1941)
Caesar and Cleopatra (EL 1946)
Anna Karenina (BL 1948)
A Streetcar Named Desire (WB 1951)
The Deep Blue Sea (20th 1955)
The Roman Spring of Mrs. Stone (WB 1961)
Ship of Fools (Col 1965)

Vivien Leigh and Kenneth More in The Deep Blue Sea (1955)

LEIGHTON, MARGARET, b. Feb. 26, 1922, Barnt Green, Worcestershire, England; d. Jan. 13, 1976
 The Winslow Boy (BL 1948)
 Bonnie Prince Charlie (BL 1948)
 Under Capricorn (WB 1949)
 The Astonished Heart (GFD 1950)
 The Elusive Pimpernel (BL 1950)
 Calling Bulldog Drummond (MGM Br 1951)
 Home at Seven [Murder on Monday] (BL 1952)
 The Holly and the Ivy (BL 1952)
 The Good Die Young (IFD 1954)
 The Teckman Mystery (BL 1954)
 Carrington V. C. [Court-Martial] (IFD 1954)
 The Constant Husband (BL 1955)
 The Passionate Stranger [A Novel Affair] (BL 1956)
 The Sound and the Fury (20th 1959)
 Waltz of the Toreadors (RFD 1962)
 The Best Man (UA 1964)
 The Loved One (MGM 1965)
 Seven Women (MGM 1965)
 The Madwoman of Chaillot (WPD 1969)

The Go-Between (MGM-EMI 1970)
Zee & Co [X, Y & Zee] (Col-Warner 1972)
Lady Caroline Lamb (GB-It 1972)
Bequest to the Nation [The Nelson Affair] (CIC 1973)
From Beyond the Grave (Col-Warner 1973)
Frankenstein: The True Story (CIC 1974)
Galileo (AFT 1974)

LESTER, MARK, b. July 11, 1958, Richmond, Surrey, England
Allez France! [The Counterfeit Constable] (Gala 1964)
Spaceflight IC-1 (20th 1965)
Cuckoo Patrol (GN 1965)
Fahrenheit 451 (RFD 1966)
The Witches [The Devil's Own] (WPD 1966)
Drop Dead Darling [Arrivederci Baby] (Par 1966)
The Bells of Hell Go Ting-a-Ling-a-Ling (Br 1966) [unfinished]
Our Mother's House (MGM 1967)
Oliver! (Col 1968)
Run Wild, Run Free (Col 1969)
Eyewitness [Sudden Terror] (MGM-EMI 1970)
S.W.A.L.K. (BL 1971) [Filmed as Melody]
Who Slew Auntie Roo? [Whoever Slew Auntie Roo?] (AIP
1972)

Mark Lester (right) and John Mills in Run Wild, Run Free (1969).

Senza ragione [Redneck] (It-GB 1972) [Not shown in GB until 1976]
Night Hair Child (RFD 1973) [made in 1971]
Scalawag (USA-It 1973)
The Dream Time (Br 1973) [unfinished]
All' Aperto [Dance Under the Elms] (It 1975)
Mañana seras hombre [Seen Dimly before Dawn] (It 1975)

LEUWERIK, RUTH, b. April 23, 1926, Essen, Germany
13 unter einem Hut (W Ger 1950)
Vater braucht eine Frau (W Ger 1952)
Die grosse Versuchung (W Ger 1952)
Ein Herz spielt falsch (W Ger 1952)
Muss man sich gleich scheiden lassen? (W Ger 1953)
Geliebtes Leben (W Ger 1953)
Königliche Hoheit (W Ger 1953)
Bildnis einer Unbekannten (W Ger 1954)
Ludwig II (W Ger 1955)
Geliebte Feindin (W Ger 1955)
Rosen im Herbst (W Ger 1955)
Die goldene Brücke (W Ger 1956)
Die Trapp-Familie (W Ger 1956)
Königin Luise (W Ger 1957)
Auf Wiedersehen, Franziska (W Ger 1957)
Immer wenn der Tag beginnt (W Ger 1957)
Taiga (W Ger 1958)
Die Trapp-Familie in Amerika (W Ger 1958)
Dorothea Angermann (W Ger 1959)
Die ideale Frau (W Ger 1959)
Ein Tag, der nie zu Ende geht (W Ger 1959)
Liebling der Götter (W Ger 1960)
Eine Frau fürs ganze Leben (W Ger 1960)
Auf Engel schiesst man nicht (W Ger 1960)
Die Stunde, die Du glücklich bist (W Ger 1961)
Die Rote (W Ger-It 1962)
Ein Alibi zerbricht (Aus 1963)
Elf Jahr und ein Tag (W Ger 1963)
Das Haus in Montevideo (W Ger 1963)
Und Jimmy ging zum Regenbogen (W Ger 1971)

LIBEAU, GUSTAVE, b. Nov. 8, 1877, Brussels; d. 1957
500,000 Francs (Bel 1922)
Le mariage de Mademoiselle Beulemans (Fr 1925)
Direct au coeur (Fr 1932)
Le Coucher de la mariée (Fr 1933)
En avant la musique (Bel 1935)
Avec le sourire (Fr 1936)
C'était le bon temps (Bel 1936)
Gardons le sourire (Bel 1937)
Mon père et mon papa (Bel 1938)
Bossemans et Coppenolle (Bel 1938)
Carillons et dentelles (Bel 1938)

Ils étaient neuf celibataires (Fr 1939)
Le Gang des tractions arrière (Fr 1950)
Scandale à la Belgique joyeuse (Bel 1959)

LIEVEN, ALBERT, b. June 23, 1904, Hohenstein, Germany; d.
Dec. 23, 1971
Ich bei Tag und Du bei Nacht (Ger 1932)
Annemarie, die Braut der Kompanie (Ger 1932)
Kampf um Blond (Ger 1932)
Reifende Jugend (Ger 1933)
Die vom Niederrhein (Ger 1933)
Eine Siebzehnjährige (Ger 1934)
Charleys Tante (Ger 1934)
Gluckspilze (Ger 1934)
Es tut sich was um Mitternacht (Ger 1934)
Fräulein Liselott (Ger 1934)
Krach um Jolanthe (Ger 1934)
Die klugen Frauen (Ger Fr 1935)
Mach' mich glücklich (Ger 1935)
Hermine und die sieben Aufrechten (Ger 1935)
Kater Lampe (Ger 1936)
Eine Frau ohne Bedeutung (Ger 1936)
Victoria the Great (Radio 1937)
Night Train to Munich [Night Train/Gestapo] (MGM Br 1940)
Jeannie (GFD 1940)
The Life and Death of Colonel Blimp [Colonel Blimp] (GFD 1943)
The Seventh Veil (GFD 1945)
Beware of Pity (EL 1946)
Frieda (GFD 1947)
Sleeping Car to Trieste (GFD 1948)
Hotel Sahara (GFD 1951)
Die Dubarry (W Ger 1951)
Fritz und Friederike (W Ger 1952)
Klettermaxe (W Ger 1952)
Die Rose von Estambul (W Ger 1953)
Geliebtes Leben (W Ger 1953)
Desperate Moment (GFD 1953)
Heimweh nach Deutschland (W Ger 1954)
Das Bekenntnis der Ina Kahr (W Ger 1954)
Frühlingslied (W Ger 1954)
Das Lied von Kaprun (W Ger 1955)
Des Teufels General [The Devil's General] (W Ger 1955)
Der Fischer vom Heilingensee (W Ger 1955)
Reifende Jugend (W Ger 1955)
El Batallon de las sombras (Sp 1956)
Nacht der Entscheidung (W Ger 1956)
Lindra chiama Polo Nord (It 1957)
Alle sünden dieser Erde (W Ger 1958)
...und abends in die Scala (W Ger 1958)
Subway in the Sky (Britannia 1959)
Schachnovelle (W Ger 1960)
Rommel ruft Kairo (W Ger 1960)
Foxhole in Cairo (W Ger 1960) [Eng lang version of Rommel ruft
Kairo]

Conspiracy of Hearts (RFD 1960)
Das Geheimnis der gelben Narzissen (W Ger 1960)
The Devil's Daffodil (W Ger 1960) [Eng lang version of Das
   Geheimnis der gelben Narzissen]
The Guns of Navarone (Col 1961)
Freddy und das Lied der Südsee (W Ger 1962)
Im Namen des Teufels (W Ger 1962)
The Devil's Agent (W Ger 1962) [Eng lang version of Im Namen
   des Teufels]
The Victors (Col 1963)
Mystery Submarine (Britannia 1963)
Traitor's Gate (Col Br 1964)
Der Gorilla von Soho (W Ger 1968)

LISI, VIRNA (Virna Pieralisi), b. Aug. 11, 1937, Ancona, Italy
...e Napoli canta (It 1953)
La corda d'acciao (It 1953)
Desiderio è sole (It 1954)
Lettera napoletana (It 1954)
Ripudiata (It 1954)
Piccola santa (It 1954)
Violenza sul lago (It 1954)
Il cardinale Lambertini (It 1954)
Il vetturale del Moncenisio (It 1954)

Nino Manfredi and Virna Lisi in Le Bambole (1964).

Les Hussards (Fr 1955)
Luna nova (It 1955)
La rossa (It 1955)
Vendicata (It 1955)
Lo scapolo (It 1955)
Le diciottenni (It 1955)
La donna del giorno (It 1956)
Il conte di Matera (It 1957)
Caterina Sforza, leonessa de Romagna (It 1958)
Totò, Peppino e le fanatiche (It 1958)
Un Seul Survivra [Vita perduta] (Fr-It 1958)
Il padrone delle ferriere (It 1958)
Un militare e mezzo (It 1960)
Romolo e Remo (It 1961)
Cinque marine per cento raggazze (It 1961)
Sua Eccelenza si fremo a mangiare (It 1961)
Eva (It 1962)
Les Bonnes Causes (Fr 1963)
La Tulipe noire (Fr 1963)
Il giorno più corto (It 1963)
Coplan prend des risques (Fr 1963)
How to Murder Your Wife (UA 1964)
Casanova 70 (It 1964)
I complessi (It 1964)
La donna del lago (It 1964)
Le bambole [Four Kinds of Love] (ep "La telefonata") (It 1964)
Oggi, domani e doppo domani (It 1964)
Una vergina per il principe (It 1965)
Made in Italy (It 1965)
Signore e signori (It 1965)
La volta vuona (It 1965)
Not with My Wife, You Don't (WB-7 Arts 1966)
La 25e Heure [The 25th Hour] (Fr 1966)
La ragazza e il generale [The Girl and the General] (It 1966)
Arabella (It 1967)
Le dolci signore (It-Fr 1967)
Tenderly (It 1968)
Meglio vedova [Better a Widow] (It 1968)
The Secret of Santa Vittoria (UA 1969)
L'Arbre de Noël [The Christmas Tree] (Fr-It 1969)
Lo smemsrato [Kiss the Other Sheik] (It 1969)
Le Temps des loups (Fr 1969)
If It's Tuesday, This Must Be Belgium (UA 1969)
Trigon (It 1969)
Un Beau Monstre [Il bel mostro] (Fr-It 1970)
Giochi particolari (It 1970)
Roma bene (It 1971)
The Statue (Cin 1971)
Les Galets d'Etretat [Improvvisamonte una sera, un amore] (Fr-It 1972)
Barbablu (It 1972)
Le Sergent (Fr-It 1972)
Fanna bianca (It 1973)

LISTER, MOIRA, b. Aug. 6, 1923, Cape Town, South Africa
  The Shipbuilders (Anglo 1943)
  Love Story [A Lady Surrenders] (EL 1944)
  My Ain Folk (Butcher 1944)
  The Agitator (Anglo 1945)
  Don Chicago (Anglo 1945)
  Wanted for Murder [A Voice in the Night] (20th 1946)
  Mrs. Fitzherbert (Pathe 1947)
  So Evil My Love (Par Br 1948)
  Uneasy Terms (Pathe 1948)
  Another Shore (GFD 1948)
  Once a Jolly Swagman [Maniac on Wheels] (GFD 1948)
  A Run for Your Money (GFD 1949)
  Pool of London (GFD 1951)
  Files from Scotland Yard (IFD 1951)
  White Corridors (GFD 1951)
  Something Money Can't Buy (GFD 1952)
  The Cruel Sea (GFD 1953)
  Grand National Night [Wicked Wife] (Renown 1953)
  The Limping Man (Eros 1954)
  Trouble in Store (GFD 1954)
  John and Julie (BL 1955)
  The Deep Blue Sea (20th 1955)
  Mon Phoque (Fr 1956)
  Seven Waves Away [Abandon Ship!] (Col 1957)
  The Yellow Rolls-Royce (MGM 1964)
  The Double Man (WPD 1967)
  Stranger in the House (RFD 1967)
  Not Now, Darling (LMG 1973)

LIVESEY, ROGER, b. June 25, 1906, Barry, South Wales
  Where the Rainbow Ends (Pioneer 1921)
  The Four Feathers (Stoll 1921)
  Maisie's Marriage (Napoleon 1923)
  East Lynne on the Western Front (Gaumont 1931)
  The Veteran of Waterloo (Par Br 1933)
  A Cuckoo in the Nest (W & F 1933)
  Blind Justice (Real Art 1934)
  Lorna Doone (ABFD 1935)
  The Price of Wisdom (B & D-Par Br 1935)
  Midshipman Easy [Men of the Sea] (ABFD 1935)
  Rembrandt (UA 1936)
  The Drum [Drums] (UA 1938)
  Keep Smiling [Smiling Along] (20th Br 1938)
  The Rebel Son (GB-Fr 1939)
  Spies of the Air (ABPC 1939)
  The Girl in the News (MGM Br 1940)
  The Life and Death of Colonel Blimp [Colonel Blimp] (GFD
    1943)
  I Know Where I'm Going (GFD 1945)
  A Matter of Life and Death [Stairway to Heaven] (GFD 1946)
  Vice Versa (GFD 1948)
  That Dangerous Age [If This Be Sin] (BL 1949)

Green Grow the Rushes [Brandy Ashore] (BL 1951)
The Master of Ballantrae (WB 1953)
The Intimate Stranger [Finger of Guilt] (AA 1956)
Es Geschah am Hellichten Tag [Assault in Broad Daylight]
   (Swit 1958)
The League of Gentlemen (RFD 1959)
The Entertainer (Bry 1960)
No, My Darling Daughter (RFD 1961)
Of Human Bondage (MGM Br 1964)
The Amorous Adventures of Moll Flanders (Par 1965)
Oedipus the King (RFD 1967)
Futtock's End (BL 1970)

LOCKWOOD, MARGARET (Margaret Day), b. Sept. 15, 1916, Kara-
   chi, India
*Lorna Doone (ABFD 1935)
The Case of Gabriel Perry (BL 1935)
Some Day (WB 1935)
Honours Easy (Wardour 1935)
Man of the Moment (FN 1935)
Midshipman Easy [Men of the Sea] (ABFD 1935)
Jury's Evidence (BL 1936)
The Amateur Gentleman (UA 1936)
The Beloved Vagabond (ABFD 1936)
Irish for Luck (FN Br 1936)
The Street Singer (ABPC 1937)
Who's Your Lady Friend? (ABFD 1937)
Dr. Syn (GFD 1937)
Melody and Romance (BL 1937)
Owd Bob [To the Victor] (GFD 1938)
Bank Holiday [Three on a Weekend] (GFD 1938)
The Lady Vanishes (MGM Br 1938)
A Girl Must Live (20th Br 1939)
The Stars Look Down (GN 1939)
Night Train to Munich [Night Train] (MGM Br 1940)
The Girl in the News (MGM Br 1940)
Quiet Wedding (Par Br 1941)
Alibi (BL 1942)
The Man in Grey (GFD 1943)
Dear Octopus [The Randolph Family] (GFD 1943)
Give Us the Moon (GFD 1944)
Love Story [A Lady Surrenders] (EL 1944)
A Place of One's Own (EL 1945)
I'll Be Your Sweetheart (GFD 1945)
The Wicked Lady (EL 1945)
Bedelia (GFD 1946)
Hungry Hill (GFD 1947)
Jassy (GFD 1947)
The White Unicorn [Bad Sister] (GFD 1947)
Look Before You Love (GFD 1948)
Cardboard Cavalier (GFD 1949)
Madness of the Heart (GFD 1949)
Highly Dangerous (GFD 1950)

Trent's Last Case (BL 1952)
Laughing Anne (Rep Br 1953)
Trouble in the Glen (Rep Br 1954)
Cast a Dark Shadow (Eros 1955)
The Slipper and the Rose (CIC 1976)

LOLLOBRIGIDA, GINA (Luigina Lollobrigida), b. July 4, 1927,
    Subiaco, Rome
Aquila nera (It 1946)
L'elisir d'amore (It 1947)
Il segreto di don Giovanni (It 1947)
Il delitto di Giovanni Episcopo (It 1947)
Lucia di Lammermoor (It 1948)
Follie per l'opera (It 1948)
Vendetta nel sole (It 1949)
I pagliacci [Love of a Clown/Amore tragico] (It 1949)
Campane a martello (It 1949)
La sposa non puo attendere [Anselmo ha fretta] (It 1950)
Cuori senza frontiere (It 1950)
Vita de cani (It 1950)
Alina (It 1950)
Miss Italia (It 1951)
La città si defende [The City Defends Itself] (It 1951)
Enrico Caruso, leggenda di una voce [The Young Caruso) (It
    1951)
Achtung banditi! (It 1951)
Amor non ho, pero, pero... (It 1951)
Passaporto per l'Oriente [Storie de cinque città/A Tale of Five
    Cities] (ep "Cinque mamme ed una culla") (It-GB-W Ger
    1952)
Fanfan la tulipe [Fanfan the Tulip] (Fr 1952)
Altri tempi [Time Gone By] (ep "Il processo di Frine") (It 1952)
Belles de nuit (Fr 1952)
Moglie per una notte (It 1952)
Il maestro di don Giovanni [Crossed Swords] (It 1952)
Pane, amore e fantasia [Bread, Love and Dreams] (It 1953)
La provinciale (It 1953)
Le infideli [Wayward Wife] (It 1953)
Il tesoro dell'Africa [Beat the Devil] (It-USA 1953)
La romana [Woman of Rome/La Belle Romaine] (It 1954)
Le Grand Jeu [The Grand Game] (Fr 1954)
Pan, amore e gelosia [Bread, Love and Jealousy] (It 1954)
La donna più bella del mondo [The World's Most Beautiful
    Woman] (It 1955)
Trapeze (UA 1956)
Notre-Dame de Paris (Fr 1956)
Anna di Brooklyn (It 1958)
La Loi [La legge/Where the Hot Wind Blows] (Fr-It 1959)
Never So Few (MGM 1959)
Solomon and Sheba (UA 1959)
Go Naked in the World (MGM 1960)
Come September (Univ 1961)
Vénus imperiale [Venere imperiale/Imperial Venus] (Fr-It 1962)

David Niven, Gina Lollobrigida, and John Moulder Brown in King, Queen and Joker (1972).

La bellezza d'Ippolita (It 1962)
Mare matto (It 1963)
Strange Bedfellows (Univ 1964)
Woman of Straw (UA 1964)
La bambole [Four Kinds of Love] (ep "Mr. Cupid") (It 1965)
Hotel Paradiso (MGM 1965)
Le piacevoli notti (It 1966)
Io, io, io...e gli altri (It 1966)
Cervantes (AIP 1966)
Les Sultans (Fr 1966)
The Private Navy of Sgt. O'Farrell (UA 1967)
La morte ha fatto l'uovo (It 1968)
Un bellissimo novembre (It 1968)
Buena sera, Mrs. Campbell (UA 1969)
Le Cascadeur [Stuntman] (It-Fr 1969)
E continuavano a frezaroi il rustione di dollari [Bad Man's River] (It-Sp 1971)
König, Dame, Brige [King, Queen and Joker] (W Ger 1972)
Peccato mortale [No encontie roses para mi madre] (It-Sp 1972)
L'avventura di Pinocchio (It 1972)

LOM, HERBERT (Herbert Schluderpacheru), b. 1917, Prague
Mein Kampf--My Crimes (ABPC 1940)
The Young Mr. Pitt (20th Br 1942)
Secret Mission (GFD 1942)

Tomorrow We Live [At Dawn We Die] (BL 1942)
The Dark Tower (WB-FN Br 1943)
Hotel Reserve (RKO-Radio 1944)
The Seventh Veil (GFD 1945)
Night Boat to Dublin (Pathe 1946)
Appointment with Crime (Anglo 1946)
Dual Alibi (Pathe 1947)
Snowbound (RKO 1948)
Good Time Girl (GFD 1948)
Portrait from Life [The Girl in the Painting] (GFD 1948)
Lucky Mascot (UA 1948)
Golden Salamander (GFD 1950)
Night and the City (20th 1950)
State Secret [The Great Manhunt] (BL 1950)
The Black Rose (20th 1950)
Cage of Gold (GFD 1950)
Hell Is Sold Out (Eros 1951)
Two on the Tiles (GN 1951)
Mr. Denning Drives North (BL 1951)
Whispering Smith Hits London [Whispering Smith versus Scotland
    Yard] (Ex 1952)
The Ringer (BL 1952)
The Man Who Watched Trains Go By [Paris Express] (Eros 1953)
The Net [Project M 7] (GFD 1953)
Rough Shoot [Shoot First] (UA 1953)
The Love Lottery (GFD 1954)
Star of India (Eros 1954)
Beautiful Stranger [Twist of Fate] (BL 1954)
The Ladykillers (RFD 1955)
War and Peace (Par 1956)
Fire Down Below (Col 1957)
Hell Drivers (RFD 1957)
Action of the Tiger (MGM 1957)
Chase a Crooked Shadow (ABP 1958)
I Accuse! (MGM Br 1958)
Intent to Kill (20th 1958)
Roots of Heaven (20th 1958)
Passport to Shame [Room 43] (BL 1959)
No Trees in the Street (ABP 1959)
The Big Fisherman (BV 1959)
North West Frontier [Flame Over India] (RFD 1959)
Third Man on the Mountain (BV 1959)
I Aim at the Stars (Col 1960)
Spartacus (Univ 1960)
Mr. Topaze [I Like Money] (20th 1961)
The Frightened City (AA 1961)
El Cid (AA 1961)
The Phantom of the Opera (Univ 1962)
Tiara Tahiti (RFD 1962)
Mysterious Island (Col 1962)
Der Schatz im Silbersee [The Treasure of Silver Lake] (W Ger-
    Yug 1962)
The Horse without a Head (BV 1963)

A Shot in the Dark (UA 1964)
Onkel Tom's Hutte [Uncle Tom's Cabin] (W Ger-It-Yug-Fr 1965)
Return from the Ashes (UA 1965)
Our Man in Marrakesh [Bang, Bang, You're Dead] (AA 1966)
Gambit (Univ 1966)
Die Nibelungen [Whom the Gods Wish to Destroy] (W Ger-Yug
    1967) [released in two parts]
Villa Rides (Par 1968)
The Face of Eva [Eva] (GB-Sp 1968)
Assignment to Kill (WB-7 Arts 1969)
99 Mujeres [99 Women] (Sp-W Ger-GB-It 1969)
Mister Jerico (RFD 1969)
Doppelganger [Journey to the Far Side of the Sun] (Univ 1970)
Das Bildnis des Dorian Gray [Dorian Gray] (W Ger-It-Licht
    1970)
El conde Dracula [Count Dracula] (Sp-W Ger-It-Licht 1970)
Murders in the Rue Morgue (AIP 1971)
Asylum (Cinema International 1972)
...And Now the Screaming Starts (Fox-Rank 1974)
Ein unbekannter rechnet ab [Death in Persepolis] (W Ger-Fr-Sp-
    It 1975)
Dark Places (Bruton 1975)
The Return of the Pink Panther (UA 1975)

LONSDALE, MICHEL, b. May 24, 1931, Paris
C'est arrivé à Aden (Fr 1956)
La Main chaude (Fr 1957)
Une Balle dans le canon (Fr 1958)
Les Portes claquent (Fr 1960)
Adorable Menteuse (Fr 1961)
Les Snobs (Fr 1961)
La Denonciation (Fr 1961)
Le Procès [The Trial] (Fr 1962)
Behold a Pale Horse (Col 1963)
Jaloux comme un tigre (Fr 1964)
Tous les enfants du monde (Fr 1964) (unfinished)
Les Copains (Fr 1964)
Je vous salue, Mafia (Fr 1965)
La Bourse et la Vie (Fr 1965)
Les Compagnons de la Marguerite (Fr 1966)
Le Judoka Agent Secret (Fr 1966)
L'Homme à la Buick (Fr 1967)
L'Authentique Procès de Carl Emmanuel Jung (Fr 1967)
La Mariée etait en noir (Fr 1967)
La Grande Lessive (Fr 1968)
Baisers volés (Fr 1968)
Hibernatus (Fr 1969)
Détruire, dit-elle (Fr 1969)
L'Hiver (Fr 1969)
L'Etalon (Fr 1970)
Out One (Fr 1970)
Le Printemps (Fr 1970)
Le Souffle au coeur [Soffio al cuore] (Fr-It 1970)

Michel Lonsdale

La Rose et le revolver (Fr 1970)
Les assassins de l'ordre (Fr 1971)
Jaune le soleil (Fr 1971)
La Vieille Fille (Fr 1971)
Papa, les petit bateaux (Fr 1971)
L'Automne (Fr 1971)
Il était une fois un flic (Fr 1971)
La Grande Paulette (Fr 1972)
Chut (Fr 1972)
La Raison du plus fou (Fr 1972)
The Day of the Jackal (Univ 1973)
La Fille au violoncelle (Fr-Swi 1973)
Les Grands Sentiments font les bons gueuletons (Fr 1973)
Glissements progressifs du plaisir (Fr 1973)
Stavisky (Fr 1974)
Une Baleine qui avait mal aux dents (Fr 1974)
Le Fantôme de la liberté [Phantom of Liberty] (Fr 1974)
Un Linceul n'a pas de poches (Fr 1974)
Out One Spectre (Fr 1974)
Aloïse (Fr 1974)
Caravan to Vaccares [Le Passager] (GB-Fr 1974)
Galileo (AFT 1974)
Les Suspects (Fr 1974)
Sérieux comme le plaisir (Fr 1974)
Section Spéciale (Fr 1974)
The Romantic Englishwoman (GB-Fr 1975)
India Song (Fr 1975)
Le Télephone rose (Fr 1975)
La Traque (Fr 1975)
Folle à tuer (Fr 1975)

LOREN, SOPHIA (Sofia Villani Scicolone) (a. k. a. Sofia Lazzaro), b.
    Sept. 20, 1932, Rome
  Quo Vadis (MGM 1950)
  Cuori sul mare [Hearts at Sea] (It-Fr 1950)
  Il voto [The Vote] (It 1950)
  Le sei moglie di Barbarbù [Bluebeard's Seven Wives] (It 1950)
  Io sono il capataz (It 1950)
  Milana miliardaria (It 1951)
  Anna (It 1951)
  Il mago per forza (It 1951)
  Il sogno di Zorro [Zorro's Dream] (It 1951)
  È arrivato l'accordatore [The Tuner Has Arrived] (It 1951)
  Erà Lui... Si, Si [It's Him--Yes, Yes!] (It 1951)
  La favorita (It 1952)
  Africa sotto i mari [Africa under the Seas/Woman of the Red
    Seas] (It 1952)
  La tratta delle bianche [Girls Marked for Danger/The White
    Slave Trade] (It 1952)
  Aida (It 1953)
  Carosello Napoletano [Napolitan Fantasy] (It 1953)
  Ci troviamo in galleria [We'll Meet in the Gallery] (It 1953)
  Tempi nostri [Our Times/Anatomy of Love] (It-Fr 1953)
  La domenica della buona genti [Good Folks' Sunday] (It 1953)
  Il paese dei campanelli (It 1953)
  Un giorno in pretura [A Day in Court] (It 1953)
  Due notti con Cleopatra [Two Nights with Cleopatra] (It 1953)
  Pellegrini d'amore [Pilgrim of Love] (It 1953)
  Attila, flagello di Dio [Attila, Fléau de dieu/Attila the Hun]
    (It-Fr 1953)
  Miseria e Nobilità [Poverty and Nobility] (It 1954)
  L'oro di Napoli [Gold of Naples/Every Day's a Holiday] (It 1954)
  La donna del fiume [Woman of the River] (It 1954)
  Peccato che sia una canaglia [Too Bad She's Bad] (It 1954)
  Il segno di Venere [The Sign of Venus] (It 1955)
  La bella mugnaia [The Miller's Wife] (It 1955)
  Pane, amore e... [Scandal in Sorrento] (It-Fr 1955)
  La fortuna di essere donna [Lucky to be a Woman] (It-Fr 1955)
  The Pride and the Passion (UA 1957)
  Boy on a Dolphin (20th 1957)
  Legend of the Lost (UA 1957)
  Desire under the Elm (Par 1958)
  Houseboat (Par 1958)
  The Key (Col 1958)
  Black Orchid (Par 1959)
  That Kind of Woman (Par 1959)
  Heller in Pink Tights (Par 1960)
  It Started in Naples (Par 1960)
  A Breath of Scandal [Olympia] (Par 1960)
  The Millionairess (20th 1960)
  La ciociara [Two Women] (It-Fr 1961)
  El Cid (AA 1961)
  Madame Sans-Gene [Madame] (It-Fr-Sp 1961)
  Boccaccio '70 (ep "The Raffle") (It-Fr 1961)

Sophia Loren (right) and Margaret Lee in Questi fantasmi (1967).

La Couteau dans la plaie [Il Coltrello nella piaga/Five Miles to
    Midnight] (Fr-It 1962)
I sequestrati di Altona [The Condemned of Altona] (20th 1962)
Ieri, oggi e domani [Yesterday, Today and Tomorrow] (It 1963)
The Fall of the Roman Empire (Par 1964)
Matrimonio all'italiana [Marriage, Italian Style] (It-Fr 1964)
Operation Crossbow [The Great Spy Mission] (MGM 1965)
Lady L (MGM 1965)
Judith (Par 1965)
Arabesque (Univ 1966)
A Countess from Hong Kong (Univ 1966)
C'erà una volta [More than a Miracle/Happily Ever After/Cin-
    derella, Italian Style] (MGM 1967)
Questi fantasmi [Ghosts, Italian Style/Three Ghosts] (It-Fr 1967)
I girasoli [Sunflowers] (It-USSR 1969)
La moglie del prete [The Priest's Wife] (It 1970)
Mortadella [Lady Liberty] (It-Fr 1971)
Bianco, Rosso e [White Sister/The Sin] (It-Fr-Sp 1971)
Man of La Mancha (UA 1972)
The Voyage (UA 1973)
Le Verdict (Fr-It 1974)
La pupa del gangster [Gun Moll] (It 1975)

LORRE, PETER, b. June 26, 1904, Rosenberg, Hungary; d. March
   23, 1964
  Die Koffer des Herrn O. F. (Ger 1931)
  M (Ger 1931)
  Bomben auf Monte Carlo (Ger 1931)
  F. P. I. antwortet nicht (Ger 1932)
  Schuss im Morgengrauen (Ger 1932)
  Der weisse Dämon [Rauschgift] (Ger 1932)
  Unsichtbare Gegner (Aus 1933)
  Les reguins du petrole [Fr version of Unsichtbare Gegner] (Fr
   1933)
  Funf von der Jazzband (Ger 1932)
  Was Fraüen traumen (Ger 1933)
  De haut en bas (Fr 1934)
  The Man Who Knew Too Much (Gaumont 1934)
  Mad Love (MGM 1935)
  Crime and Punishment (Col 1935)
  The Secret Agent (Gaumong 1936)
  Crack Up (20th 1936)
  Lancer Spy (20th 1937)
  Think Fast, Mr. Moto (20th 1937)
  Thank You, Mr. Moto (20th 1937)
  Mr. Moto's Gamble (20th 1938)
  I'll Give a Million (20th 1938)
  Mr. Moto Takes a Chance (20th 1938)
  Mysterious Mr. Moto (20th 1938)
  Mr. Moto on Danger Island (20th 1939)
  Mr. Moto Takes a Vacation (20th 1939)
  Mr. Moto's Last Warning (20th 1939)
  Strange Cargo (MGM 1940)
  I Was an Adventuress (20th 1940)
  Island of Doomed Men (Col 1940)
  Stranger on the Third Floor (RKO 1940)
  You'll Find Out (RKO 1940)
  Mr. District Attorney (Rep 1941)
  The Face Behind the Mask (Col 1941)
  They Met in Bombay (MGM 1941)
  The Maltese Falcon (WB 1941)
  All Through the Night (WB 1942)
  Invisible Agent (Univ 1942)
  The Boogie Man Will Get You (Col 1942)
  Background to Danger (WB 1942)
  Casablanca (WB 1942)
  Cross of Lorraine (MGM 1943)
  Passage to Marseilles (WB 1944)
  Mask of Dimitrious (WB 1944)
  Arsenic and Old Lace (WB 1944)
  The Conspirators (WB 1944)
  Hollywood Canteen (WB 1944)
  Hotel Berlin (WB 1945)
  Confidential Agent (WB 1945)
  Three Strangers (WB 1946)
  Black Angel (Univ 1946)
  The Chase (Univ 1946)

The Verdict (WB 1946)
The Beast with Five Fingers (WB 1946)
My Favorite Brunette (Par 1947)
Casbah (Univ 1948)
Rope of Sand (Par 1949)
Quicksand (UA 1950)
Double Confession (ABD 1950)
Der Verlorene (W Ger 1950)
Beat the Devil (UA 1953)
20,000 Leagues under the Sea (BV 1954)
Congo Crossing (Univ 1956)
Around the World in 80 Days (UA 1956)
The Buster Keaton Story (Par 1956)
Silk Stockings (MGM 1957)
The Story of Mankind (War 1957)
Hell Ship Mutiny (Rep 1957)
Sad Sack (Par 1958)
The Big Circus (AA 1959)
Scent of Mystery (Mike Todd Jr. 1959)
Voyage to the Bottom of the Sea (20th 1961)
The Raven (AIP 1963)
Comedy of Terrors (AIP 1963)
The Patsy (Par 1964)

LUPI, ROLDANO (Roldano Squassoni-Lupi), b. Feb. 8, 1909, Milan
Sissignora (It 1941)
Giacomo l'idealista (It 1942)
Gelosia (It 1942)
Addio, amore! (It 1942)
Nessuno torna indietro (It 1943)
Sogno d'amore (It 1943)
Appassionata (It 1943)
Il cappello da prete (It 1943)
La freccia nel fianco (It 1943)
Circo equestre Za-Bum (It 1944)
I dieci comandamenti (It 1944)
L'adultera (It 1944)
Malià (It 1945)
Il testimone (It 1946)
La porta del cielo (It 1946) [made in 1943]
Umanità (It 1946)
Tempesta d'anime (It 1946)
Pian delle stelle (It 1947)
Il delitto di Giovanni Episcopo (It 1947)
L'urio (It 1947)
Amanti senza amore (It 1948)
Il diavolo bianco (It 1948)
Giudicatemi (It 1948)
Il fiacre n. 13 (It 1948)
L'uomo dal guanto grigio (It 1948)
Duello senza onore (It 1949)
Vespro siciliano (It 1949)
Altura (It 1949)

L'isola di Montecristo (It 1950)
L'edera (It 1950)
Gli ultimi giorni di Pompei (It 1950)
Altri tempi (ep "La morsa") (It 1951)
Les Loups chassent la nuit (Fr 1951)
La fiammata (It 1952)
Königsmark (Fr 1952)
Il maestro di don Giovanni [Crossed Swords] (It-USA 1952)
Il segreto delle tre punte (It 1952)
La ragazza di Trieste (It 1953)
Frine, cortigiana d'Oriente (It 1953)
La camagna di San Giusto (It 1954)
I moschettieri della regina (It 1954)
Casa Ricordi [La Maison du souvenir] (It-Fr 1954)
La contessa di Castiglione [La Castiglione] (It-Fr 1955)
I cavalieri della regina (It 1955)
La cortigiana di Babilonia (It 1955)
L'Affaire des poisons [Il processo dei veleni] (Fr-It 1955)
Il vetturale del Moncenisio (It 1956)
L'angelo del peccato (It 1959)
Il gigante di Metropolis [The Giant of Metropolis] (It 1961)
Le sette sfide [The Seven Revenges] (It 1961)
I mongoli [Les Mongols/The Mongols] (It-Fr 1961)
Il giustizieri dei mari [Le Boucainer des îles] (It-Fr 1962)
Il conte di Montecristo [Le Comte de Monte-Cristo] (It-Fr 1962)
Le prigioniere dell'isola del diavolo (It 1962)
Kali Yug, la dea della vendetta [Kali Yug (I): Göttin der Rachel/
    Kali Yug, déesse de la vengeance] (It-W Ger-Fr 1963)
Il mistero del tempio indiano [Kali Yug, das Geheimnis des in-
    dischen Tempels (2)/Le Mystère du temple hindou] (It-W Ger-
    Fr 1964)
Maciste nell'inferno di Gengis Khan (It-Fr 1964)
Buffalo Bill l'eroe del Far West [Buffalo Bill, le héros du Far
    West/Das war Buffalo Bill] (It-Fr-W Ger 1965)
La vendetta dei gladiatori (It 1965)

McDOWALL MALCOLM, b. June 13, 1943, Leeds, Yorkshire,
    England
If... (Par 1968)
Figures in a Landscape (20th 1970)
The Raging Moon [Long Ago, Tomorrow] (MGM-EMI 1970)
A Clockwork Orange (WB 1971)
O Lucky Man! (WB 1973)
Royal Flash (Fox-Rank 1975)

McDOWALL, RODDY, b. Sept. 17, 1928, London
Scruffy (BIED 1938)
Murder in the Family (20th 1938)
I See Ice (ABFD 1938)
Convict 99 (GFD 1938)
Hey, Hey, U.S.A.! (GFD 1938)
Yellow Sands (ABPC 1938)
John Halifax, Gentleman (MGM 1938)

The Outsider (ABPC 1939)
Poison Pen (ABPC 1939)
Dead Man's Shoes (ABPC 1939)
His Brother's Keeper (WB 1939)
Just William (ABPC 1939)
Saloon Bar (ABFD 1940)
You Will Remember (BL 1940)
This England [Our Heritage] (Anglo 1941)
Man Hunt (20th 1941)
Confirm or Deny (20th 1941)
How Green Was My Valley (20th 1941)
Son of Fury (20th 1942)
The Pied Piper (20th 1942)
On the Sunny Side (20th 1942)
My Friend Flicka (20th 1943)
Lassie Come Home (MGM 1943)
The White Cliffs of Dover (MGM 1944)
The Keys of the Kingdom (20th 1945)
Hangover Square (20th 1945)
Thunderhead, Son of Flicka (20th 1945)
Molly and Me (20th 1945)
Holiday in Mexico (MGM 1946)
Rocky (Mon 1948)
Macbeth (Rep 1948)
Kidnapped (Mon 1948)
Tuna Clipper (Mon 1949)
Killer Shark (Mon 1950)
Everybody's Dancin' (Lip 1950)
Big Timber (Mon 1950)
The Steel Fist (Mon 1952)
The Subterraneans (MGM 1960)
Midnight Lace (Univ 1960)
The Longest Day (20th 1962)
Cleopatra (20th 1963)
Shock Treatment (20th 1964)
The Greatest Story Ever Told (UA 1965)
The Third Day (WB 1965)
The Loved One (MGM 1965)
That Darn Cat! (BV 1965)
Inside Daisy Clover (WB 1965)
The Adventures of Bullwhip Griffin (BV 1965)
Lord Love a Duck (UA 1965)
L'Espion [The Defector] (Fr-W Ger 1966)
It! (WB 1966)
The Cool Ones (WB 1967)
Planet of the Apes (20th 1967)
5 Card Stud (Par 1968)
Hello Down There (Par 1968)
The Midas Run [A Run on Gold] (Cin 1969)
Pretty Maids All in a Row (MGM 1971)
Escape from the Planet of the Apes (20th 1971)
Bedknobs and Broomsticks (BV 1971)
Tam Lin [The Devil's Widow] (CUE 1971) [made in 1969] [only
    director]

Angel, Angel, Down We Go [Cult of the Damned] (AIP 1972)
[made in 1969]
Corky [Going All Out] (MGM 1972)
The Life and Times of Judge Roy Bean (Nat Gen 1972)
Conquest of the Planet of the Apes (20th 1972)
The Poseidon Adventure (20th 1972)
The Legend of Hell House (Fox-Rank 1973)
Battle for the Planet of the Apes (20th 1973)
Arnold (Avco Emb 1973)
Dirty Mary, Crazy Larry (20th 1974)
Funny Lady (Col 1975)
*

McGOOHAN, PATRICK, b. March 19, 1928, New York
The Dambusters (ABPC 1955)
Passage Home (GFD 1955)
I Am a Camera (IFD 1955)
Zarak (Col 1957)
High Tide at Noon (RFD 1957)
Hell Drivers (RFD 1957)
The Gypsy and the Gentleman (RFD 1958)
Nor the Moon by Night [Elephant Gun] (RFD 1958)
Two Living, One Dead (BL 1961)
All Night Long (RFD 1962)
The Quare Fellow (Bry 1962)
Life for Ruth [Walk in the Shadow] (RFD 1962)
Dr Syn--Alias the Scarecrow (BV 1963)
The Three Lives of Thomasina (BV 1964)
Koroshi (USA-TV 1968)
Ice Station Zebra (MGM 1968)
The Moonshine War (MGM 1970)

MACISTE see PAGANO, BARTOLOMEO

McKENNA, VIRGINIA, b. June 7, 1931, London
Father's Doing Fine (ABPC 1952)
The Second Mrs. Tanqueray (ABFD 1952)
The Oracle [The Horse's Mouth] (ABFD 1953)
The Cruel Sea (GFD 1953)
Simba (GFD 1955)
The Ship That Died of Shame [PT Raiders] (GFD 1955)
A Town Like Alice [Rape of Malaya] (RFD 1956)
The Barretts of Wimpole Street (MGM Br 1957)
The Smallest Show on Earth (BL 1957)
Carve Her Name with Pride (RFD 1958)
Passionate Summer (RFD 1958)
The Wreck of the Mary Deare (MGM 1959)
Two Living One Dead (BL 1961)
Born Free (Col 1965)
Ring of Bright Water (RFD 1969)
An Elephant Called Slowly (BL 1969)
Waterloo (It-USSR 1970)
The Lion at World's End (EMI 1974) [made in 1971]
Swallows and Amazons (EMI 1974)
*Also appeared in several TV movies

MAGNANI, ANNA, b. April 11, 1908, Alexandria, Egypt; d. Sept.
26, 1973
La cieca di Sorrento (It 1934)
Tempo massimo (It 1934)
Cavalleria (It 1936)
Trenta secondi d'amore (It 1936)
La principessa Tarakanova (It 1938)
Una lampade alla finestra (It 1940)
Finalmente soli (It 1941)
La fuggitiva (It 1941)
Teresa Venerdì (It 1941)
La fortuna viene dal cielo (It 1942)
L'avventura di annabella (It 1942)
La vita è bella (It 1943)
Campo dei fiori (It 1946)
Il fiore sotto gli occhi (It 1943)
L'ultima carrozzella (It 1943)
Quartletto pazzo (It 1945)
Roma, città aperta (It 1945)
Abbasso la miseria (It 1945)
Un uomo ritorna (It 1946)
Avanti a lui tremava tutta Roma (It 1946)
Il bandito (It 1946)
Abbasso la ricchezza! (It 1946)
Lo sconosciuto di San Marino (It 1947)
L'onorevole Angelina (It 1947)
Molti sogni per le strade (It 1948)
Amore (It 1948)
Assunta Spina (It 1948)
La voce umona e Il miracolo (It 1948)
Vulcano (It 1949)
Bellissima (It 1951)
Camicie rosse (It 1952)
La corrozza d'oro (It 1952)
Siamo donne (ep "Anna Magnani") (It 1953)
Carosello di varientà! (It 1955)
The Rose Tattoo (Par 1955)
Suor Letizia [The Awakening] (It 1956)
Wild Is the Wind (Par 1957)
Nella città l'inferno [...And the Wild Wild Woman] (It 1958)
The Fugitive Kind (UA 1960)
Risate di gioia [The Passionate Thief] (It 1960)
Mamma Rosa (It 1962)
Le magot de Josefa [La pila della Peppa] (Fr-It 1964)
Made in Italy (It 1965)
The Secret of Santa Vittoria (United Artists 1969)
Correva l'anno di grazia 187 (It 1971)
Felini's Roma (It-Fr 1972)

MAIA, LEONOR (Maria da Conceição Vasconcelos), b. Dec. 8, 1921,
Lourençe Marques, Mozambique
O pai tirano (Por 1941)
A ave de arribação (Por 1943)

Madalena, zero em compartamento (Sp 1945)
Ladrao, precisa-se (Por 1946)
Camões (Por 1946)
Amanhã come hoje (Sp 1947)
Serra brava (Por 1948)
Uma vida para dois (Por 1948)
Sol e toires (Por 1949)
A volta do José do Telhado (Por 1949)
Amor e desespero (Por-It 1950)
Chikwembo (Por 1952)
Matar para não morrer (Sp 1953)

MANGANO, SILVANA, b. April 21, 1930, Rome
L'elisir d'amore [Elixir of Love] (It 1946)
Il delitto di Giovanni Episcopo (It 1947)
Gli uomini sono nemici [Le Carrefour des Passions] (It-Fr 1948)
Black Magic [Cagliostro] (It-USA 1949)
Riso amaro [Bitter Rise] (It 1949)
Il lupo della Sila [The Wolf of Sila/Lure of the Sila] (It 1950)
Il brigante Musolino [Fugitive/Musolino, the Briand] (It 1950)
Anna (It 1951)
Mambo (It 1954)
Ulisse [Ulysses] (It 1954)
L'oro di Napoli [Gold of Naples] (It 1955)
Uomini e lupi [Hommes et loups] (It-Fr 1956)
La diga sul Pacifico [The Sea Wall/This Angry Age] (It-Fr 1958)
La tempesta [Tempest] (It 1959)
La grande guerra [The Great War] (It 1959)
Jovanka e le Altre [Five Branded Women] (It-USA 1960)
Una vita difficile (It 1961)
Il giudizio universale [The Last Judgment] (It 1961)
Crimen [...And Suddenly It's Murder] (It 1961)
Barabba [Barabbas] (It-USA 1962)
Il processo di Verona (It 1963)
La mia signora (It 1964)
Il disco volante [The Flying Saucer] (It 1965)
Io, io, io...e gli altri [I, I, I,...and the Others] (It 1966)
Scusi, lei è favorevole o contrario? [Excuse Me, Are You for
  or Against?] (It 1967)
Le streghe [The Witches] (It 1967)
Edipo re [Oedipus Rex] (It 1967)
Capriccio all'italiana (It 1968)
Teorema (It 1968)
Morte a Venezia [Death in Venice] (It 1971)
Scipione detto anche l'Africano (It 1971)
Il decamerone [The Decameron] (It 1971)
D'amor si muore (It 1973)
Ludwig II [Le Crepuscule des dieux/Ludwig] (W Ger-Fr-It 1973)
Lo scopone scientifico (It 1973)
Gruppo di famiglia in un interno [Conversation Piece] (It 1975)

MANNHEIM, LUCIE, b. April 30, 1899, Berlin
Die Austreibung (Ger 1923)

Die Prinzessin Suwarin (Ger 1923)
Der Puppenmacher von Kiang-Ning (Ger 1923)
Der Schatz (Ger 1923)
Der steinerne Reiter (Ger 1923)
Atlantik (Ger 1930)
Der Ball (Ger 1930)
Danton (Ger 1931)
Madame wünscht keine Kinder (Ger 1933)
The Thirty-Nine Steps (GB 1935)
East Meets West (Gaumont 1936)
The High Command (ABFD 1937)
Yellow Canary (RKO 1943)
Hotel Reserve (Radio)
Tawny Pipit (GFD 1944)
Nachts auf der Strassen (W Ger 1952)
So Little Time (ABP 1952)
Ich und Du (W Ger 1953)
Das ideale Brautpaar (W Ger 1954)
Die Stadt ist voller Geheimnisse (W Ger 1955)
Du darft nicht länger schweigen (W Ger 1955)
Erauenartz Dr. Betram (W Ger 1957)
Gestehen Sie, Dr. Corda (W Ger 1958)
Ihr 106. Geburtstag (W Ger 1958)
Der eiserne Gustav (W Ger 1958)
Arzt aus Leidenschaft (W Ger 1959)
Der letzte Zeuge (W Ger 1960)
Erste Liebe (W Ger 1960)
Beyond the Curtain (RFD 1960)
Bunny Lake Is Missing (Col Br 1965)

MAR, FIEN DE LA (Josephina Johanna de la Mar), b. Feb. 2, 1898,
    Amsterdam; d. April 23, 1965
Bleeke Bet (Dut 1934)
De Jantjes (Dut 1934)
De Big van het Regiment (Dut 1935)
Het Leven Is Niet Zo Kwaad (Dut 1935)
Op Stap (Dut 1935)
Klokslag Twaalf (Dut 1936)
De Spooktrein (Dut 1939)
Ergens in Nederland (Dut 1940)

MARAIS, JEAN (Jean Vilain-Marais), b. Dec. 11, 1913, Cherbourg,
    France
L'Epervier (Fr 1933)
Dans les rues (Fr 1933)
L'Aventurier (Fr 1934)
Le Bonheur (Fr 1934)
Nuits de feu (Fr 1936)
Les Hommes nouveaux (Fr 1936)
Le Pavillon brûle (Fr 1941)
Le Lit à Colonnes (Fr 1942)
Carmen (It 1943)
L'Eternel Retour (Fr 1943)

Jean Marais and Sylvie Vartan in <u>Patate</u> (1964).

Voyage sans espoir (Fr 1943)
La Belle et la bête [Beauty and the Beast] (Fr 1945)
Les Chouans (Fr 1946)
Ruy Blas (Fr 1947)
L'Aigle à deux têtes (Fr 1947)
Aux yeux du souvenir (Fr 1948)
Les Parents terribles (Fr 1948)
Le Secret de Mayerling (Fr 1949)
Orphée (Fr 1950)
Le Château de verre (Fr 1951)
Les Miracles n'ont lieu qu'une fois (Fr 1951)
Nez de cuir (Fr 1952)
La Maison du silence (Fr-It 1952)
L'Appel du destin (Fr 1952)
Les Amants de minuit [Lovers at Midnight] (Fr 1953)
Julietta (Fr 1953)
Dortoir des grandes [Girls' Dormitory] (Fr 1953)
Le Guérisseur (Fr 1953)
Le Comte de Monte-Cristo (Fr-It 1953)
Futures vedettes [Sweet Sixteen] (Fr 1954)
Si Versailles m'était conté (Fr 1954)
Napoléon (Fr 1954)

Goubbiah [Kiss of Fire] (Fr-It 1955)
Si Paris nous était conté (Fr 1955)
Toute la ville accuse (Fr 1956)
Elena et les hommes [Paris Does Strange Things] (Fr-It 1956)
Typhon sur Nagasaki [Typhoon Over Nagasaki] (Fr-Jap 1956)
S. O. S. Noronha (Fr-It-W Ger 1957)
Notti bianche [White Nights] (It-Fr 1957)
Un Amour de poche (Fr 1957)
La Tour, prends garde (Fr-It-Yug 1957)
Chaque jour a son secret (Fr 1958)
La Vie à deux (Fr 1958)
Le Bossu (Fr-It 1959)
Le Testament d'Orphée (Fr 1960)
Austerlitz (Fr-It-Yug 1960)
Le Capitan [Captain Blood] (Fr-It 1960)
La Princesse de clèves (Fr 1960)
Le Capitaine Fracasse (Fr 1961)
Le Miracle des loups [Blood on His Sword] (Fr-It 1961)
Napoléon 11, l'aiglon (Fr 1961)
Ponzio Pilato (It 1961)
Il ratto delle Sabine [The Rape of the Sabine Women] (It-Fr 1961)
Les Mystères de Paris [The Mysteries of Paris] (Fr-It 1962)
Le Masque de fer (Fr-It 1962)
L'Honorable Stanislas, agent secret [Reluctant Spy] (Fr-It 1963)
Fantômas (Fr-It 1964)
Patate [Friend of the Family] (Fr-It 1964)
Le Gentleman de Cocody [Ivory Coast Adventure] (Fr-It 1965)
Pleins feux sur Stanislas (Fr-W Ger 1965)
Train d'enfer (Fr-Sp 1965)
Fantômas se déchaine [The Phantom] (Fr-It 1965)
Le Saint prend l'affût [The Saint Lies in Wait] (Fr-It 1966)
Sept Hommes et une garce [Seven Guys and a Gal] (Fr-It-Rum
    1966)
Fantômas contre Scotland Yard (Fr-It 1967)
Le Paria (Fr-Sp 1968)
La Provocation (Fr 1970)
Peau d'âne [The Magic Donkey] (Fr 1970)

MARIAN, FERDIAND, b. Aug. 14, 1902, Vienna; d. Aug. 7, 1946
Der Tunnel (Ger 1933)
Ein Hochzeitstraum (Ger 1936)
Madame Bovary (Ger 1937)
Die Stimme des Herzens (Ger 1937)
La Habanera (Ger 1937)
Nordlicht (Ger 1938)
Morgen werde ich verhaftet (Ger 1938)
Der Vierte kommt nicht (Ger 1939)
Dein Leben gehört mir (Ger 1939)
Der Fuchs von Glenarvon (Ger 1940)
Aus erster Ehe (Ger 1940)
Jud Süss (Ger 1940)
Ohm Kruger (Ger 1941)
Ein Zug fährt ab (Ger 1942)

Die Reise in die Vergangenheit (Ger 1943)
Tonelli (Ger 1943)
Romanze in Moll (Ger 1943)
Münchhausen (Ger 1943)
Freunde (Ger 1944)
In flagranti (Ger 1944)
Dreimal Komödie (Ger 1944)
Das Gesetz der Liebe (Ger 1945)
Die Nacht der Zwölf (Ger 1945)

MARSHALL, HERBERT (Herbert Brough Falcon Marshall), b. May
    23, 1890, London; d. Jan. 22, 1969
Mumsie (W & F 1927)
Dawn (W & F 1928)
The Letter (Par 1929)
Murder (Wardour 1930)
Secrets of a Secretary (Par 1931)
Michael and Mary (Ideal 1931)
The Calendar [Bachelor's Folly] (W & F 1931)
The Faithful Heart [Faithful Hearts] (Ideal 1932)
Blonde Venus (Par 1932)
Trouble in Paradise (Par 1932)
Evenings for Sale (Par 1932)
Solitaire Man (MGM 1933)
I Was a Spy (W & F 1933)
Riptide (MGM 1934)
Four Frightened People (Par 1934)
Outcast Lady (MGM 1934)
The Painted Veil (MGM 1934)
The Good Fairy (Univ 1935)
The Flame Within (MGM 1935)
Accent on Youth (Par 1935)
The Dark Angel (UA 1935)
If You Could Only Cook (Col 1935)
The Lady Consents [The Lady Confesses] (RKO 1936)
Forgotten Faces (Par 1936)
'Til We Meet Again (Par 1936)
Girls' Dormitory (20th 1936)
A Woman Rebels (RKO 1936)
Make Way for a Lady (RKO 1936)
Breakfast for Two (RKO 1937)
Angel (Par 1937)
Mad About Music (Univ 1938)
Always Goodbye (20th 1938)
Woman Against Woman (MGM 1938)
Zaza (Par 1939)
A Bill of Divorcement (RKO 1940)
Foreign Correspondent (UA 1940)
The Letter (WB 1940)
Adventures in Washington (Col 1941)
The Little Foxes (RKO 1941)
When Ladies Meet (MGM 1941)
Kathleen (MGM 1941)

The Moon and Sixpence (UA 1942)
Forever and a Day (RKO 1943)
Flight for Freedom (RKO 1943)
Young Ideas (MGM 1943)
Andy Hardy's Blonde Trouble (MGM 1944)
The Unseen (Par 1945)
The Enchanted Cottage (RKO 1945)
The Razor's Edge (20th 1946)
Crack-Up (RKO 1946)
Duel in the Sun (Selznick Releasing 1946)
Ivy (Univ 1947)
The High Wall (MGM 1947)
The Secret Garden (MGM 1949)
The Whipped [Underworld Story] (UA 1950)
Black Jack [Captain Black Jack] (Fr-USA 1950)
Anne of the Indies (20th 1951)
Angel Face (RKO 1952)
Riders to the Stars (UA 1954)
The Black Shield of Falworth (Univ 1954)
Gog (UA 1954)
The Virgin Queen (20th 1955)
Wicked As They Come (Col 1956)
The Weapon (Eros 1956)
The Fly (20th 1958)
Stage Struck (BV 1958)
College Confidential (Univ 1960)
Midnight Lace (Univ 1960)
A Fever in the Blood (WB 1961)
Five Weeks in a Balloon (20th 1962)
The Caretakers [Borderlines] (UA 1963)
The List of Adrian Messenger (Univ 1963)
The Third Day (WB 1965)

MARTINELLI, ELSA, b. Jan. 13, 1935, Grosseto, Italy
The Indian Fighter (UA 1955)
La risaia (It 1956)
Donatella (It 1956)
Four Girls in Town (Univ 1956)
Manuela (It 1956)
La mina (It 1958)
I battellieri del Volga [Les Bateliers de la Volga] (It-Fr 1958)
Ciao, ciao, bambina (It 1959)
Costa azzura (It 1959)
Tunisi top secret (It 1959)
La notte brava (It 1959)
Et mourir de plaisir [Il sangue e la rose/Blood and Roses]
    (Fr-It 1960)
I piaceri del sabato notte (It 1960)
Un amore a Roma (It 1960)
Il carro armato dell'8 settembre (It 1960)
Le Capitan [Il capitano del re] (Fr-It 1960)
La Menace [La minaccia] (Fr-It 1961)
Hatari! (Par 1962)

The Trial (Gibralter Films 1962)
The Pigeon That Took Rome (Par 1962)
The V. I. P. s (MGM 1963)
Rampage (WB 1963)
Pelle viva (It 1963)
De l'amour [La calda pelle] (Fr-It 1965)
La decima vittima [The Tenth Victim] (It 1965)
La Fabuleuse Aventure de Marco Polo [Le meravigliose avventure di Marco Polo/Marco de Magnificent] (Fr-It 1965)
L'Or du duc (Fr 1965)
Un Milliard dans un billard [Diamanten billard] (Fr-W Ger 1965)
Je vous salue, mafia [Da New York: mafia uccide!] (Fr-It 1965)
Come imparai ad amare le donne [Das gewisse Etwas der Frauen] (It-W Ger 1966)
Le Plus Vieux Métier du monde [L'amore attraverso i secoli] (Fr-It 1967)
Qualcuno ha tradito [Requiem pour une canaille] (It-Fr 1967)
Maroc 7 (RFD 1967)
Sette volte donne [Woman Times Seven] (ep "La super Simone") (It-USA 1967)
Manon '70 (Fr-It 1968)
Belle Starr Story [Il mio corpo per un poker] (It 1968)
Maldonne (Fr-It 1968)
Un dollaro per setti vigliacchi [Madigan's Millions/El millón de Madigan] (It-USA-Sp 1968)
Candy (It-USA 1968)
If It's Tuesday, This Must Be Belgium (UA 1969)
Les Chemins de Catmandou (Fr-It 1969)
L'amica (It 1969)
OSS, 117, prend des vacances (Fr-Braz 1969)
Una sull'altra [Una historia perversa/Perversion Story] (It-Sp-Fr 1969)
La Araucana [L'aracuano massacro degli dei] (Sp-It 1972)

MASINA, GIULIETTA (Giulia Anna Masina), b. Feb. 22, 1920, Bologna
Paisà (It 1946)
Senza pietà (It 1948)
Luci del varietà [Variety Lights] (It 1951)
Persiane chiuse (It 1950)
Cameriera bella presenza offresi (It 1951)
Sette ore di guai (It 1951)
Europa '51 (It 1951)
Lo sciecco blanco [The White Shiek] (It 1952)
Wanda la peccatrice (It 1952)
Il romanzo della mia vita (It 1952)
Ai margini della metropoli (It 1952)
Donne proibite (It 1953)
Via Padova 46 [Lo scocciatore] (It 1954)
Cento anni d'amore (It 1953)
La Strada (It 1954)
Buonanotte, avvocato! [Lo scocciatore] (It 1955)
Il bidone (It 1955)

Giulietta Masina in <u>Juliet of the Spirits</u> (1965).

Le notti di Cabiria [Night of Cabiria] (It 1957)
Fortunella (It 1958)
Nella città l'inferno [...And the Wild Wild Women] (It 1958)
Jons und Erdme (W Ger 1959)
Das kunstseidene mädchen [La gran vita] (W Ger-It-Fr 1959)
Giulietta degli spiriti [Juliet of the Spirits] (It 1965)
Scusi, lei è favorevolo o contrario? (It 1966)
Non stuzzicare la zanzara (It 1967)
The Madwoman of Chaillot (WB-7 Arts 1969)

MASON, JAMES, b. May 15, 1909, Huddersfield, England
Late Extra (20th Br 1936)
Twice Branded [Father and Son] (Radio 1936)
Troubled Waters (20th Br 1936)
Prison Breaker (Col Br 1936)
Blind Man's Bluff (Fox 1936)
Secret of Stamboul [The Spy in White] (GFD 1937)
The Mill on the Floss (NPFD 1937)
The High Command (ABFD 1937)
Fire Over England (UA 1937)
Catch As Catch Can [Atlantic Episode] (20th Br 1937)
The Return of the Scarlet Pimpernel (UA 1938)
I Met a Murderer (GN 1939)
This Man Is Dangerous [The Patient Vanishes] (Pathe 1941)
Hatter's Castle (Par Br 1941)
The Night Has Eyes [Terror House] (Pathe 1942)
Alibi (BL 1942)

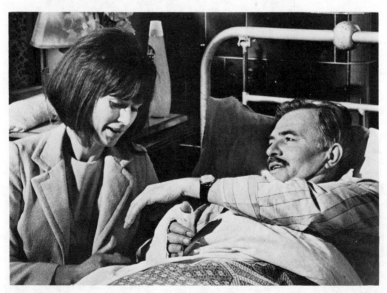

James Mason and Harriet Andersson in The Deadly Affair (1967).

Secret Mission (GFD 1942)
Thunder Rock (MGM Br 1942)
The Bells Go Down (UA 1943)
The Man in Grey (GFD 1943)
They Met in the Dark (GFD 1943)
Candlelight in Algeria (BL 1944)
Fanny by Gaslight [Man of Evil] (GFD 1944)
Hotel Reserve (RKO Br 1944)
A Place of One's Own (EL 1945)
They Were Sisters (GFD 1945)
The Seventh Veil (GFD 1945)
The Wicked Lady (EL 1946)
Odd Man Out (GFD 1947)
The Upturned Glass (GFD 1947)
Caught (MGM 1949)
Madame Bovary (MGM 1949)
The Reckless Moment (Col 1949)
East Side, West Side (MGM 1949)
One Way Street (Univ 1950)
Pandora and the Flying Dutchman (MGM 1951)
The Desert Fox [Rommel--Desert Fox] (20th 1951)
Lady Possessed (Rep 1952)
Five Fingers (20th 1952)
The Prisoner of Zenda (MGM 1952)
Face to Face (ep "The Secret Sharer") (RKO 1952)
The Desert Rats (20th 1953)
Julius Caesar (MGM 1953)
The Story of Three Loves (ep "The Jealous Lover") (MGM 1953)
Botany Bay (Par 1953)
The Man Between (BL 1953)
Charade (Monarch 1953)
Prince Valiant (20th 1954)
20,000 Leagues Under the Sea (BV 1954)
A Star Is Born (WB 1954)
Forever Darling (MGM 1956)
Bigger Than Life (20th 1956)
Island in the Sun (20th 1957)
Cry Terror! (MGM 1958)
The Decks Ran Red (MGM 1958)
North by Northwest (MGM 1959)
Journey to the Center of the Earth (20th 1959)
A Touch of Larceny (Par 1960)
The Trials of Oscar Wilde [The Man with the Green Carnation]
    (Eros 1960)
The Marriage-Go-Round (20th 1961)
Hero's Island [The Land We Love] (UA 1962)
Escape from Zahrain (Par 1962)
Tiara Tahiti (RFD 1962)
Lolita (MGM 1962)
The Fall of the Roman Empire (Par 1964)
Torpedo Bay [Beta Som/Finche dura la tempesta] (It 1964)
The Pumpkin Eater (BL 1964)
Lord Jim (Col 1965)

Les Pianos Mecaniques [The Player Pianos] (Fr-Swe 1965)
Genghis Khan (Col 1965)
The Blue Max (20th 1966)
Georgy Girl (Col 1966)
The Deadly Affair (Col 1967)
Stranger in the House (RFD 1967)
Duffy (Col 1968)
Mayerling (MGM 1968)
The London Nobody Knows (BL 1969) [documentary made in 1967]
   (guide/narrator)
Age of Consent (Col 1969)
The Sea Gull (WPD 1969)
Spring and Port Wine (WPD 1970)
Cold Sweat [De la part des copains] (Fr-It 1970)
Bad Man's River (Sp-Fr-It 1971)
Tam Lin [The Devil's Widow] (CUE 1971) [made in 1969]
The Last of Sheila (WB 1973)
Kill! [Kill Kill Kill] (Fr-Sp 1972)
Child's Play (Par 1972)
The Mackintosh Man (WB 1973)
11 Harrowhouse (Fox-Rank 1974)
The Marseille Contract (GB-Fr 1974)
Frankenstein: The True Story (CIC 1974)
Mandingo (CIC 1975)
Inside Out (Col-Warner 1975)
Autobiography of a Princess (Cont 1975)
Gente di rispetto (It 1975)

MASSEY, RAYMOND, b. Aug. 30, 1896, Toronto
The Speckled Band (W & F 1931)
The Old Dark House (Univ 1932)
The Face at the Window (Radio 1932)
The Scarlet Pimpernel (UA 1935)
Things to Come (UA 1936)
Fire Over England (UA 1937)
Dreaming Lips (UA 1937)
Under the Red Robe (20th Br 1937)
The Prisoner of Zenda (UA 1937)
The Hurricane (UA 1937)
The Drum [Drums] (UA 1938)
Black Limelight (ABPC 1939)
Abe Lincoln in Illinois [Spirit of the People] (RKO 1940)
The Santa Fe Trail (WB 1940)
Dangerously They Live (WB 1941)
49th Parallel [The Invaders] (GFD 1941)
Desperate Journey (WB 1942)
Reap the Wild Wind (Par 1942)
Action in the North Atlantic (WB 1943)
Arsenic and Old Lace (WB 1944)
Woman in the Window (RKO 1944)
Hotel Berlin (WB 1945)
God Is My Co-Pilot (WB 1945)
A Matter of Life and Death [Stairway to Heaven] (GFD 1946)

Possessed (WB 1947)
Mourning Becomes Electra (RKO 1947)
The Fountainhead (WB 1949)
Roseanna McCoy (RKO 1949)
Chain Lightning (WB 1950)
Barricade (WB 1950)
Challenge--Science Against Cancer (WB 1950) [documentary] (narrator)
Dallas (WB 1950)
Sugarfoot [Swirl of Glory] (WB 1951)
Come Fill the Cup (WB 1951)
David and Bathsheba (20th 1952)
Carson City (WB 1952)
The Desert Song (WB 1953)
Prince of Players (20th 1955)
Battle Cry (WB 1955)
Seven Angry Men (AA 1955)
East of Eden (WB 1955)
The True Story of the Civil War (Camera Eye 1956) [documentary] (narrator)
Omar Khayyam (Par 1957)
The Naked Eye (Stoumen Film Reps Inc 1957) [documentary] (narrator)
The Great Impostor (Univ 1961)
The Fiercest Heart (20th 1961)
The Queen's Guards (20th 1961)
Jacqueline Kennedy's Asian Journey (United States Information Service 1962) [documentary] (narrator)
How the West Was Won (MGM 1963)
McKenna's Gold (Col 1969)

MASTROIANNI, MARCELLO, b. Sept. 28, 1923, Fontana Liri, Italy
I miserabili (It 1947)
Vent'anni (It 1949)
Passaporto per l'Oriente (It 1949)
Una domenica d'agosto (It 1949)
Cuori sul mare (It 1949)
Atto d'accusa (It 1950)
Contro la legge (It 1950)
Vita da cani (It 1950)
Parigi è sempre Parigi (It 1951)
L'eterna catena (It 1951)
La ragazze di Piazza di Spagna (It 1951)
Tragico Ritorno (It 1952)
Sensualità (It 1952)
Passaporto per l'Oriente [A Tale of Five Cities] (It 1952)
Gli eroi della domenica (It 1952)
Penne nere (It 1953)
Febbre di vivere (It 1953)
Lulù (It 1953)
Il viale della speranza (It 1953)
Non è mai troppo tardi (It 1953)
Tempi nostri (ep "Il pupo") (It-Fr 1953)

Marcello Mastroianni and Virna Lisi in <u>Lo smemorato</u> (1968).

La valigia dei sogni (It 1953)
Schiava del peccato (It 1954)
Cronache di poveri amanti (It 1954)
Casa Ricordi (It 1954)
La muta di Portici (It 1954)
Giorni d'amore (It 1954)
Peccato che sia una canaglia (It 1954)
La principessa delle Canarie (Sp-It 1955)
Tam tam Mayumbe (It 1955)
La bella mugnaia (It 1955)
La fortuna di essere donna (It 1955)
L'eterna catena (It 1956)
Il bigamo [The Bigamist] (It 1956)
Padri e figli (It 1956)
Harte Männer Heisse Liebe [Salz und Brot/La ragazza della salina] (W Ger-It 1957)
Il momento più bello (It 1957)
Le notti bianche [White Nights] (It 1957)
Il medico e lo stregone (It 1957)
I soliti ignoti (It 1958)
Racconti d'estate [Femmes d'un été] (It-Fr 1958)
La Loi [La legge] (Fr-It 1958)
Amore e guai (It 1958)

Un ettaro di cielo (It 1959)
Il meaico di mia moglie [Il marito bello] (It 1959)
Tutti innamorati (It 1959)
Ferdinando I, re di Napoli (It 1959)
La dolce vita (It 1959)
Adua e le compagne (It 1960)
Il bell'Antonio (It 1960)
Fantasmi a Roma [Ghosts of Rome] (It 1961)
La notte (It 1961)
L'assassino (It 1961)
Divorzio all'italiana [Divorce, Italian Style] (It 1961)
Vie privée [Vita privata/A Very Private Affair] (Fr-It 1962)
Cronaca familiare [Journal intime] (It-Fr 1962)
Otto e mezza [$8\frac{1}{2}$] (It 1963)
I compagni [Les Camarades] (It-Fr 1963)
Ieri, oggi, domani [Yesterday, Today, and Tomorrow] (It 1963)
Matrimonio all'italiana [Marriage, Italian Style] (It 1964)
Casanova '70 (It 1965)
Oggi, domani e dopo domani (It 1965)
La decima vittima [The Tenth Victim] (It 1965)
Io, io, io...e gli altri (It 1966)
La volta buona (It 1966)
Spara forte, più forte...non capisco [Shoot Loud, Louder...I
    Don't Understand] (It 1966)
The Poppy Is Also a Flower (Comet 1966)
L'Etranger [Lo straniero/The Stranger] (Fr-It 1967)
Diamonds for Breakfast (Par 1968)
Gli amanti (It 1968)
Lo smemorato (It 1968)
Break-Up (It 1969)
I girasoli [Sunflower] (It-USSR 1969)
Leo the Last (UA 1969)
Dramma della gelosia tutti i particolari in cronaca (It 1970)
Giochi particolari (It 1971)
Fellini's Roma (It 1971)
La moglie del prete [The Priest's Wife] (It 1971)
Scipione, detto anche "l'Africano" (It 1971)
La cagna [Liza] (It-Fr 1972)
Permette? Rocco Papaleo (It 1972)
Che? [What?] (It 1972)
Ça n'arrive qu'aux autres [Tempo d'amore] (Fr-It 1972)
Mordi e fuggi (It 1973)
L'Evénement le plus important depuis que l'homme a marche sur
    la lune [Niente di grave...suo uiarito è incinto] (Fr-It 1973)
Rappresaglia [Massacre in Rome] (It 1973)
La Grande Bouffe [La grande abbriffata] (Fr-It 1973)
Allonsanfan (It 1974)
Salut l'artiste (Fr-It 1974)
Touche pas à la femme blanche [Non toccare la donna bianca]
    (Fr-It 1974)
C'eravamo tanto amati (It 1974)
La pupa del gangster [Gun Moll] (It 1975)
Per le antiche scale [Down the Ancient Staircase] (It 1975)

La donna della domenica [La Femme du dimanche] (It-Fr 1975)
La divina creatura (It 1975)

MATOS, MARIA (Maria da Conceição de Matos e Silva), b. Sept. 29,
    1891, Silva; d. Sept. 18, 1952
    As pupilas do Senhor Reitor (Por 1935)
    A varanda dos rouxinois (Por 1939)
    O costa do castelo (Por 1943)
    A menina da rádio (Por 1944)
    Um homem às direitas (Por 1944)
    Não há rapazes maus (Por 1948)
    Heróis do mar (Por 1949)
    Morgadinha dos canaviais (Por 1949)

Maria Matos

MATTHEWS, JESSIE (Jessie Margaret Matthews), b. March 11,
    1907, London
    The Beloved Vagabond (Astra-National 1923)
    Straws in the Wind (Gaumont 1924)
    Out of the Blue (Pathe 1931)
    There Goes the Bride (Ideal 1932)
    The Midshipmaid (W & F 1932)
    The Man from Toronto (Ideal 1933)
    The Good Companions (Gaumont-Welsh-Pearson 1933)
    Friday the Thirteenth (ep "Millie the Non-Stop Variety Girl")
    (Gaumont 1933)
    Waltzes from Vienna [Strauss's Great Waltz] (Gaumont 1934)
    Evergreen (Gaumont 1934)

First a Girl (Gaumont 1935)
It's Love Again (Gaumont 1936)
Head Over Heels [Head Over Heels in Love] (Gaumont 1937)
Gangway (GFD 1937)
Sailing Along (GFD 1938)
Climbing High (MGM Br 1939)
Forever and a Day (RKO 1943)
Candles at Nine (Anglo 1944)
Tom Thumb (MGM 1958)

MATZ, JOHANNA, b. Oct. 5, 1932, Vienna
Der alte Sünder (W Ger 1951)
Asphalt (W Ger 1951)
Maria Theresia (Aus 1951)
Du bist die Schönste für mich (W Ger 1951)
Zwei in einem Auto (Aus 1951)
Die Försterchristl (W Ger 1952)
Saison in Salzburg (Aus 1952)
Der grosse Zapfenstreich (W Ger 1952)
Im weissen Rössl (W Ger 1952)
Hannerl (Aus 1952)
Arlette erobert Paris (W Ger 1953)
The Moon Is Blue (UA 1953)
Die Jung Frau auf dem Dach [Ger version of the Moon Is Blue]
    (UA 1953)
Alles für Papa (W Ger 1953)
Die Perle von Tokay (Aus 1954)
Mannequins für Rio (W Ger 1955)
Ingrid--Die Geschichte eines Fotomodells (W Ger 1955)
Der Kongress tanzt (Aus 1955)
Reich mir die Hand, mein Leben (Aus 1955)
Regine (W Ger 1956)
...und führe uns nicht in Versuchung (W Ger 1957)
Es wird alles wieder gut (Aus 1957)
Im Prater blüh'n wieder die Bäume (W Ger 1958)
Hoch klingt der Radetzky-marsch (Aus 1958)
Man müsste nochmal zwanzig sein (Aus 1958)
Das Dreimäderlhaus (Aus 1958)
Die unvollkommene Ehe (Aus 1959)
Frau Warrens Gewerbe (W Ger-Swi 1960)
Die glückichen Jahre der Thorwalds (W Ger 1962)
Das Leben beginnt um acht (W Ger 1962)
Die ganze Welt ist himmelblau (Aus 1964)
Ruf der Wälder (Aus 1965)
Gern hab'ich die Frauen gekillt [Le Carnaval des barbouzes/Spie
    contro il mondo] (Aus-W Ger-It-Fr 1966)
Der Kapitän (W Ger 1971)
Als Mutterstreikte (W Ger 1974)

MENICHELLI, PINA (Giuseppina Menichelli), b. 1893, Sicily
Il lettino vuoto (It 1913)
Scuola di eroi (It 1913)
Il romanzo (It 1913)

I contrabbandieri di Bell'Orrido (It 1913)
Checco è sfortunato in amore (It 1913)
Il grido dell'innocenza (It 1914)
Retaggio d'odio (It 1914)
Il getto d'acqua (It 1914)
Il degreto del castello di Monroe (It 1914)
Alma mater (It 1915)
Alla deriva (It 1915)
La morta del lago (It 1915)
Papà (It 1915)
Il sottomarino no 27 (It 1915)
La casa di nessuno (It 1915)
Lulù (It 1915)
Vincolo segreto (It 1915)
La contessa di San Germano (It 1915)
Il fuoco (It 1915)
Tigre reale (It 1916)
Angoscia suprema (It 1916)
Più forte dell'odio e dell'amore (It 1916)
La colpa (It 1916)
La fidanzata dell'aviatore (It 1916)
Ninna nanna (It 1916)
Mèche d'or (It 1916)
A sipario calato (It 1917)
La trilogia di Dorina (It 1917)
Una sventatella (It 1917)
La passeggiera (It 1917)
La moglie di Claudio (It 1917)
Gemma di S. Erasmo (It 1918)
Il giardino della voluttà (It 1918)
Olocausto (It 1918)
Il padrone delle ferriere (It 1918)
Visi e maschere (It 1918)
Le tre illusioni (It 1918)
La disfatta delle Erinni (It 1919)
Noris (It 1919)
L'ospite sconosciuta (It 1919)
Malafemmina (It 1920)
La storia di una donna (It 1920)
Il romanzo di un giovane povero (It 1920)
La verità nuda (It 1921)
Una pagina d'amore (It 1921) [made in 1919]
L'età critica (It 1921)
L'uomo e la donna (It 1922)
La seconda moglie (It 1922)
La vagabonda del deserto (It 1922)
La dama di chez-Maxim's (It 1923)
La biondina (It 1923) [made in 1919]
Occupati d'Amelia (It 1924)

MERCIER, MICHÈLE (Jocelyne Mercier), b. Jan. 1, 1939, Nice
    Retour de Manivelle [There's Always a Price Tag] (Fr-It 1957)
    Donnez-moi ma chance (Fr 1957)

Le notti di Lucrezia (It-Fr 1959)
La Ligne de Mire (Fr 1959)
Ein Engel auf Erden (W Ger-Fr 1959)
Tirez sur le pianiste [Shoot the Pianist] (Fr 1959)
La Brune que voilà (Fr 1960)
Le Saint mene la danse (Fr 1960)
Goodbye Again [Aimez-vous Brahms?] (UA 1961)
Fury at Smugglers Bay (RFI 1961)
The Wonders of Aladdin (USA-It 1961)
I giustiziere del mari (It-Fr 1961)
Le prigioniere dell'isola del diavolo (It-Fr 1961)
Anni Ruggenti [Roaring Years] (It 1962)
Symphonie pour un massacre [The Corrupt] (It-Fr 1963)
I tre volti della paura [Black Sabbath] (It-USA 1963)
L'Ainé des Ferchaux [Magnet of Doom] (Fr-It 1963)
La Pupa [Every Night of the Week] (It 1963)
Via Veneto (It 1963)
Frenesia dell'estate (It-Fr 1963)
I giovedi (It 1963)
I mostri [Fifteen from Rome] (It 1963)
Alta Infedeltà (ep "Les Gens moderns") (It-Fr 1963)
A Global Affair (MGM 1964)
Angélique, marquise des anges (Fr-W Ger-It 1964)
Amore in quattro dimensione (It-Fr 1964)
Merveilleuse Angélique [The Road to Versailles] (Fr-W Ger-It
    1964)
Casanova '70 (It-Fr 1965)
I complessi (It 1965)
Le Tonnerre de Dieu [God's Thunder] (Fr-It-W Ger 1965)
Angélique et le roy (Fr-It-W Ger 1965)
La Seconde Vérité (Fr-It 1966)
I nostri mariti (It-Fr 1966)
Come imparai ad amare le donne [How I Learned to Love Women]
    (W Ger-Fr-It 1966)
Le Soleil noir [Black Sun] (Fr-It 1966)
Le Plus Vieux Métier du monde (ep "L'Amore nei Secoli") (Fr-
    W Ger-It 1967)
Indomptable Angélique (Fr-W Ger-It 1967)
Une Corde, un Colt (Fr-It 1968)
Angélique et le sultan (Fr-It-W Ger 1968)
Lady Hamilton (Fr-It-W Ger 1968)
Une Veuve en or (Fr-W Ger-It 1969)
You Can't Win 'em All (Col 1970)

MERIL, MACHA (Macha Gagarin), b. Sept. 3, 1940, Rabat, Morocco
    La Main chaude (Fr-It 1960)
    Adorable menteuse (Fr 1961)
    Le Repos du guerrier [Love on a Pillow] (Fr-It 1962)
    La Vie conjugale: Françoise (Fr-It 1963)
    La Vie conjugale: Jean-Marc (Fr-It 1963)
    Who's Been Sleeping in My Bed? (Par 1963)
    Une Femme mariée (Fr 1964)
    Der Ölprinz [Rampage at Apache Wells] (W Ger-Yug 1965)
    L'Espion [Lautlose Waffen/The Defector] (Fr-W Ger 1967)

Belle de jour (Fr-It 1967)
L'Horizon (Fr 1967)
Au pan coupé (Fr 1967)
Ne jouez pas avec les martians (Fr 1968)
La Chaise longue (Fr 1969)
La notte dei fiori [Night of the Flowers] (It 1972)
Nous ne vieillirons pas ensemble [We Will Not Grow Old To-
gether] (Fr-It 1972)

MESSEMER, HANNES, b. March 17, 1924, Dillingen, Germany
Rose Bernd (W Ger 1957)
Nachts wenn der Teufel kam (W Ger 1957)
Der gläserne Turm (W Ger 1957)
Madeleine und der Legionär (W Ger 1957)
Taiga (W Ger 1958)
Der Arzt von Stalingrad (W Ger 1958)
Menschen im Netz (W Ger 1958)
Das kunstseidene Mädchen [La Grande Vie/La gran via] (W Ger-
Fr-It 1959)
Ein Tag, der nie zu Ende geht (W Ger 1959)
Il generale della Rovere [Le Général de la Rovere] (It-Fr 1959)
Lampenfieber (W Ger 1960)
Die rote Hand (W Ger 1960)
Brücke des Schicksals (W Ger 1960)
Auf Engel schiesst man nicht (W Ger 1960)
12 stunden Angst [Douze Heures d'horloge] (W Ger-Fr 1960)
Era notte a Roma [Les Avades de la nuit] (It-Fr 1961)
Der Transport (W Ger 1961)
The Great Escape (UA 1963)
Mord am Canale Grande (W Ger 1964)
Grieche sucht Griechin (W Ger 1966)
Der Kongress amüsiert sich [Le Congrès s'amuse] (W Ger-Aus-
Fr 1966)
L'Espion [Lautlose Waffen/The Defector] (Fr-W Ger 1967)
Wir stirbt schon gerne unter Palmen (W Ger-Sri Lanka 1974)
The Odessa File (Col 1975)

METSERS, HUGO, b. April 1, 1943, Hulst
Blue Movie (Dut-W Ger 1971)
Louisa, een Woord van Liefde (Bel 1972)
V.D. (Dut 1972)
Frank en Eva (Dut 1973)
Alicia (Dut 1974)
Mens Ergen Je Niet (Dut 1975)
Zwaarmoedige Verhalen voor bij de Centrale Verwarming (ep
"Mijnheer Frits en Juffrouw Lenie") (Dut 1975)

MEURISSE, PAUL, b. Dec. 21, 1912, Dunkirk, France
Ne bougez plus (Fr 1941)
Montmartre-sur-Seine (Fr 1941)
Defense d'amour (Fr 1942)
Mariage d'amour (Fr 1942)
La Ferme aux Loups (Fr 1943)

L'Insaissable Frédéric (Fr 1945)
Marie le misère (Fr 1945)
Monsieur Chasse (Fr 1946)
Inspecteur Sergil (Fr 1946)
Macadam (Fr 1946)
Bethsabée (Fr 1947)
La Dame d'Onze Heures (Fr 1947)
Le Dessous des Cartes (Fr 1947)
La Fleur de l'âge (unfinished 1947)
Scandale (Fr 1948)
Le Colonel Durand (Fr 1948)
Sergil et le dictateur (Fr 1948)
L'Impasse des deux anges (Fr 1948)
Agnes de rien (Fr 1949)
Dernière Heure... edition spéciale (Fr 1949)
Sérénade au bourreau (Fr 1950)
Maria du bout du monde (Fr 1950)
Sergil chez les filles (Fr 1951)
Je suis un mouchard (Fr 1952)
La Castiglione (Fr-It 1954)
Fortune carrée (Fr-It 1954)
Les Diaboliques [The Fiends] (Fr 1955)
Affaire des poisons (Fr-It 1955)
L'Inspecteur aime la bagarre (Fr 1956)
Jusqu'au dernier (Fr 1956)
Echec au porteur (Fr 1957)
Le Septième Ciel (Fr 1957)
Les Violents [The Coffin Came by Post] (Fr 1957)
La Tête contre les murs [The Keepers] (Fr 1958)
Guingette (Fr-It 1958)
Marie-Octobre (Fr 1958)
Le Déjeuner sur l'herbe (Fr 1959)
La Française et l'amour [Love and the Frenchwoman] (Fr 1960)
La Vérité (Fr 1960)
Le Jeu de la vérité (Fr 1961)
Le Monocle noir (Fr 1961)
Les Nouveaux Aristocrates (Fr 1961)
Carillons sans joie (Fr-It 1961)
L'Oeil du monocle (Fr 1962)
Du Mouron pour les petits oiseaux (Fr-It 1963)
Méfiez-vous, mesdames! (Fr-It 1963)
Le Monocle rit jaune (Fr-It 1964)
Le Majordome (Fr 1964)
Moi et les hommes de 40 ans (Fr-It-W Ger 1965)
La Grosse Caisse (Fr 1965)
Le Deuxième Souffle (Fr 1966)
Der Kongress amüsient sich (W Ger-Aus-Fr 1966)
Quand passent les faisans (Fr 1966)
L'Armée des ombres (Fr-It 1969)
Le Cercle rouge (Fr-It 1969)
Le Cri du cormoran le soir au-dessus des jonques (Fr 1971)
Doucement les basses (Fr 1971)
Les Voraces (Fr-It 1973)

L'Education amoureuse de Valentin (Fr 1974)
La Pieuvre (Fr-It 1974)
Le Gitan (Fr-It 1975)

MICHELL, KEITH, b. Dec. 1, 1926, Adelaide, South Australia
True as a Turtle (RFD 1957)
Dangerous Exile (RFD 1957)
The Gypsy and the Gentleman (RFD 1958)
The Hellfire Club (RFI 1961)
All Night Long (RFD 1962)
Seven Seas to Calais (USA-It 1963)
Prudence and the Pill (20th 1968)
House of Cards (Univ 1969)
The Executioner (Col 1970)
Henry VIII and His Six Wives (MGM-EMI 1972)
Moments (Col 1974)

MIDROLET, ROGER, b. Oct. 2, 1926, Belgium
En êtes-vous bien sûr? (Bel 1946)
Le Cocu magnifique (Bel 1946)
Les Atouts de Monsieur Wens (Bel 1946)
Tire-au-flanc (Fr 1949)
Le Pélerin de l'enfer (Bel 1949)
Le Chéri de sa concierge (Fr 1951)
Le banquet des fraudeurs (Bel-Fr 1952)
Un Soir de joie (Bel 1954)
L'Amour est quelque part (Bel 1955)
Expo en avant! (Bel 1958)

MILES, BERNARD, b. Sept. 27, 1907, Hillingdon, Middlesex, England
Channel Crossing (W & F 1933)
The Love Test (Fox Br 1935)
Twelve Good Men (WB Br 1936)
Midnight at Madame Tussaud's [Midnight at the Wax Museum]
    (Par Br 1936)
The Challenge (UA 1938)
13 Men and a Gun (GB-It 1938)
The Citadel (MGM Br 1938)
Rebel Son (GB-Fr 1939)
The Spy in Black [U-Boat 29] (Col 1939)
The Lion Has Wings (UA 1939)
Pastor Hall (GN 1940)
Freedom Radio [A Voice in the Night] (Col Br 1941)
Quiet Wedding (Par 1941)
The Common Touch (Anglo 1941)
The Big Blockade (UA Br 1942)
This Was Paris (WB Br 1942)
One of Our Aircraft Is Missing (Anglo 1942)
The Day Will Dawn [The Avengers] (GFD 1942)
The First of the Few [Spitfire] (GFD 1942)
In Which We Serve (BL 1942)
Tawny Pipit (GFD 1944)

Tunisian Victory (Butcher 1944) (voice only)
Carnival (GFD 1946)
Great Expectations (GFD 1946)
Nicholas Nickleby (GFD 1947)
Fame Is the Spur (GFD 1947)
The Guinea Pig (Pathe 1948)
Chance of a Lifetime (BL 1950)
The Magic Box (BL 1951)
Never Let Me Go (MGM Br 1953)
Moby Dick (WB 1956)
Tiger in the Smoke (RFD 1956)
Zarak (Col 1957)
Fortune Is a Woman [She Played with Fire] (Col 1957)
The Smallest Show on Earth (BL 1957)
Saint Joan (UA 1957)
Tom Thumb (MGM 1958)
Sapphire (RFD 1959)
Heavens Above! (BL-Romulus 1963)

MILES, SARAH, b. 1941, London
Term of Trial (WPD 1962)
The Ceremony (USA-Sp 1963)
The Servant (Elstree 1963)
Those Magnificent Men in Their Flying Machines; or, How I
    Flew from London to Paris in 25 Hrs and 11 Minutes (20th
    1965)

Sarah Miles in The Ceremony (1963).

I Was Happy Here [Time Lost and Time Remembered] (RFD
    1965)
Blow-Up (MGM 1967)
Ryan's Daughter (MGM-EMI 1970)
Lady Caroline Lamb (GB-It 1972)
The Hireling (Col Br 1973)
The Man Who Loved Cat Dancing (CIC 1973)
Pepita Jimenez (Sp 1975)

MILLS, HAYLEY, b. April 18, 1946, Denham, London
    Tiger Bay (RFD 1959)
    Pollyanna (BV 1960)
    The Parent Trap (BV 1961)
    Whistle Down the Wind (RFD 1961)
    In Search of the Castaways (BV 1962)
    Summer Magic (BV 1962)
    The Chalk Garden (Univ 1964)
    The Moon-Spinners (BV 1964)
    The Truth about Spring (Univ 1964)
    That Darn Cat (BV 1965)
    Sky West and Crooked [Gipsy Girl] (RFD 1965)
    The Trouble with Angels (Col 1966)
    The Family Way (BL 1966)
    Pretty Polly [A Matter of Innocence] (RFD 1967)
    Twisted Nerve (BL 1968)
    Take a Girl Like You (Col 1971) [made in 1969]
    Mr. Forbush and the Penguins (BL 1971)
    Endless Night (BL 1972)
    Deadly Strangers (Fox-Rank 1975)
    What Changed Charley Farthing? (Fox-Rank 1975)

MILLS, JOHN, b. Feb. 22, 1908, Felixstowe, East Suffolk, England
    The Midshipmaid (W & F 1932)
    Britannia of Billingsgate (Ideal 1933)
    The Ghost Camera (Radio 1933)
    A Political Party (Pathe 1934)
    The River Wolves (Radio 1934)
    Those Were the Days (Wardour 1934)
    The Lash (Radio 1934)
    Blind Justice (Real Art 1934)
    Doctor's Orders (Wardour 1934)
    Royal Cavalcade [Regal Cavalcade] (Wardour 1935)
    Forever England [Born for Glory] (Gaumont 1935)
    Charing Cross Road (BL 1935)
    Car of Dreams (Gaumont 1935)
    First Offence (Gaumont 1936)
    Tudor Rose [Nine Days a Queen] (Gaumont 1936)
    O. H. M. S. [You're in the Army Now] (Gaumont 1937)
    Goodbye, Mr. Chips (MGM Br 1939)
    The Green Cockatoo [Race Gang] (20th Br 1940) [made in 1937]
    Old Bill and Son (GFD 1940)
    Cottage to Let [Bombsight Stolen] (GFD 1941)
    The Black Sheep of Whitehall (UA 1941)

Hayley Mills and John Mills

The Big Blockade (UA 1942)
The Young Mr. Pitt (20th Br 1942)
In Which We Serve (BL 1942)
We Dive at Dawn (GFD 1943)
This Happy Breed (EL 1944)
Total Warfare in Britain (Film Facts 1945) [documentary] (narrator)
Waterloo Road (GFD 1945)
The Way to the Stars [Johnny in the Clouds] (UA 1945)
Land of Promise (Films of Fact 1945) [documentary]
Great Expectations (GFD 1946)
So Well Remembered (RKO Br 1947)
The October Man (GFD 1947)
Scott of the Antarctic (GFD 1948)
The History of Mr. Polly (GFD 1949)
The Rocking Horse Winner (GFD 1949)
Morning Departure [Operation Disaster] (GFD 1950)
Mr. Denning Drives North (BL 1951)
The Gentle Gunman (GFD 1952)
The Long Memory (GFD 1953)
Hobson's Choice (BL 1954)
The Colditz Story (BL 1955)
The End of the Affair (Col 1955)

Above Us the Waves (GFD 1955)
Escapade (Eros 1955)
War and Peace (Par 1956)
It's Great to Be Young (ABP 1956)
The Baby and the Battleship (BL 1956)
Around the World in 80 Days (UA 1956)
Town on Trial (Col 1957)
The Vicious Circle [The Circle] (IFD 1957)
Dunkirk (MGM 1958)
Ice Cold in Alex [Desert Attack] (ABPC 1958)
I Was Monty's Double [Hell, Heaven or Hoboken] (ABPC 1958)
Tiger Bay (RFD 1959)
Summer of the Seventeenth Doll [Season of Passion] (UA 1960)
Tunes of Glory (UA 1960)
Swiss Family Robinson (BV 1961)
The Singer Not the Song (RFD 1961)
Flame in the Streets (RFD 1961)
The Valiant (GB-It 1962)
Tiara Tahiti (RFD 1962)
The Chalk Garden (Univ 1964)
The Truth About Spring (Univ 1964)
King Rat (Col 1965)
Operation Crossbow [The Great Spy Mission] (MGM 1965)
The Wrong Box (Col 1966)
The Family Way (BL 1966)
Chuka (Par 1967)
Africa-Texas Style (Par 1967)
Oh! What a Lovely War (Par 1969)
Run Wild, Run Free (Col 1969)
Zwischen Schmach und Liebe, Lady Hamilton [Emma Hamilton/
    Lady Hamilton] (W Ger-It-Fr 1969)
La morte non ha sesso [A Black Veil for Lisa] (It-W Ger 1969)
Adam's Woman (WB-7 Arts 1970)
Ryan's Daughter (MGM 1970)
Dulcima (MGM-EMI 1971)
Young Winston (Col 1972)
Lady Caroline Lamb (GB-It 1972)
Oklahoma Crude (Col 1973)

MILU (Maria de Lurdes de Almeida Lemos), b. April 24, 1926,
    Lisbon
A aldeia da roupa branca (Por 1938)
O Porto de Abrigo (Por 1941) (dubbed Graca Maria in song)
O costa do castelo (Por 1943)
As doze luas de mel (Sp 1944)
E perigoso debruçar-se (Por 1946) (appeared in musical number)
El barrio (Sp 1947)
Viela, a rua sem sol [Por version of El barrio] (Sp 1947)
O leão da estrela (Por 1947)
A volta do José do telhado (Por 1949)
O grande elias (Por 1950)
Os três da vida airada (Por 1952)
Agora é que são elas (Por 1953)

Vidas sem rumo (Por 1956)
Dois dias no paraiso (Por 1957)
O diabo era outre (Por 1969)

MIRANDA, ISA (Ines Isabella Sampietro), b. July 5, 1909, Milan
Gli uomini, che mascalzoni (It 1932)
Il caso Haller (It 1933)
Il cardinale Lambertini (It 1934)
Creature della notte (It 1934)
Tenebre (It 1934)
La signora di tutti (It 1934)
Come le foglie (It 1935)
Passaporto rosso (It 1935)
Dopo una notte d'amore (It 1935)
Maria Baschkirtzeff (Aus 1936)
Du bist mein Glück (Ger 1937)
Una donne fra due mondi (It 1937)
L'Homme de nulle part [Il fu Mattia Pascal] (Fr-It 1937)
La mensonge de Nina Petrovna (Fr 1937)
Scipione l'Africano (It 1937)
Come le foglie (It 1938)
Hotel Imperial (Par 1939)
Adventure in Diamonds (Par 1940)
Senza cielo (It 1940)
È caduta una donna (It 1941)
Documento Z 3 (It 1941)
Malombra (It 1942)
Zazà (It 1943)
La carne e l'anima (It 1943)
Lo sbaglio di essere vivo (It 1945)
L'aventure commence demain [L'avventura comincia domani]
    (Fr-It 1947)
Au delà des grilles [Le mura di Malapaga] (Fr-It 1949)
Patto col diavolo (It 1949)
La Ronde (Fr 1950)
Cameriera bella presenza offresi (It 1951)
Gli uomini non guardano il cielo (It 1952)
Les Sept Péchés capitaux [I setti peccati capitali] (Fr-It 1952)
Siamo donne (ep "Isa Miranda") (It 1953)
Avant le déluge [Prima del dilvio] (Fr-It 1954)
Gli sbandati (It 1954)
Le Secret d'Hélène [Il tradimento di Elena Marimon] (Fr-It 1954)
Tempo d'estate (It 1955)
Raspoutine [Rasputin] (Fr-It 1955)
Summertime (UA 1955)
Il tesoro di Rommel [Rommel's Treasure] (It 1955)
I pinguini ci guardano (It 1956)
I colpevoli (It 1956)
Arrivano i dollari! (It 1957)
Une Manche et la belle [La febbre del possesso] (Fr-It 1957)
Le Secret du Chevalier d'Eon [Storie d'amore proibito] (Fr-It
    1958)
La noia (It 1963)

La corruzione (It 1963)
Hardi, Pardaillan! [Le armi della vendetta] (Fr-It 1963)
The Yellow Rolls Royce (MGM 1964)
Un mondo nuovo [Un Monde nouveau] (It-Fr 1965)
Dog Eat Dog [Einer frisst deu anderen/La morte vestita di dollari] (USA-W Ger-It 1965)
Die gentlemen bitten zur Vasse (W Ger 1966)
Una storia di notte (It 1966)
Caroline Cherie (Fr-It 1968)
The Shoes of the Fisherman (MGM 1968)
Colpo rovente (It 1969)
La marcusiana (It 1969)
La donna ad una dimensione (It 1969)
L'assoluto naturale (It 1969)
Il dio chiamato Dorian/Das Bildnis des Dorian Gray] (It-W Ger 1970)
Roy Colt e Winchester Jack (It 1970)
Un' estate con sentimento (It 1970)
L'artefalto [Ecologia del delitto] (It 1971)
Dopo di che uccide il maschio e lo divora [Marta] (It-Sp 1971)
Portiere di notte [The Night Porter] (It 1971)
Marta (Sp 1972)
Le farò da padre (It 1974)

MISTRAL, JORGE (Modesto Llosas Rosell), b. 1920, Aldama, Valencia, Spain
La llamada del mar (Sp 1944)
Mision blanca (Sp 1945)
Boton de ancla (Sp 1947)
Locura de amor (Sp 1948)
La duquesa de Benameji (Sp 1948)
Deseada (Sp 1950)
La trinca del aire (Sp 1951)
El derecho de nocer (Sp 1952)
La hermana San Sulpicio (Sp 1952)
Abisimos de pasion (Mex 1953)
Un caballero andaluz (Sp 1954)
Expreso de Andalucia (Sp 1956)
La legion del silencio (Sp 1956)
La gata (Sp 1956)
Boy on a Dolphin (20th 1957)
La venganza (Sp 1958)
Carmen de la Ronda (Sp 1959)
El amor des los amores (Sp 1961)
Historia de una noche (Sp 1961)
Ventolera (Sp 1961)
Shéhérazade (Fr-It-Sp 1962)
Los pistoleros de Casa Grande (Sp-USA 1963)

MITCHELL, YVONNE, b. 1925, Cricklewood, London
The Queen of Spades (ABPC 1949)
Children of Chance (BL 1949) [not generally shown until 1951]
Turn the Key Softly (GFD 1953)

The Divided Heart (GFD 1954)
Escapade (Eros 1955)
Yield to the Night [Blonde Sinner] (ABPC 1956)
Woman in a Dressing Gown (ABPC 1957)
Passionate Summer (RFD 1958)
Tiger Bay (RFD 1959)
Sapphire (RFD 1959)
Conspiracy of Hearts (RFD 1960)
The Trials of Oscar Wilde [The Man with the Green Carnation]
   (Eros 1960)
Johnny Nobody (Col 1961)
The Main Attraction (MGM 1962)
The Corpse (GN 1972) [made in 1969]
Demons of the Mind (MGM-EMI 1972)
The Great Waltz (MGM-EMI 1972)

Yvonne Mitchell and Theodore Bikel in The Divided Heart (1954).

MODOT, GASTON, b. Dec. 31, 1887, Paris; d. Feb. 19, 1970
   Onésime ___ * (Fr 1909)
   Les Papas de Francine (Fr 1909)
   Cent Dollars mort ou vit (Fr 1909)
   Le Collier vivant (Fr 1909)
   Sur le sentier de la guerre (Fr 1909)
   Coeur de Tzigane (Fr 1909)
   Sous la griffe (Fr 1909)
   Fauves et bandits (Fr 1909)
   Les Poilus de la 9e (Fr 1910)

La Zone de la mort (Fr 1911)
Nernrod et Compagnie (Fr 1911)
Ame de pierre (Fr 1912)
Le Comte de Monte-Cristo (Fr 1914)
Mater Dolorosa (Fr 1914)
La Danseuse voilée (Fr 1916)
Un Ours (Fr 1916)
Le Chevalier de Gaby (Fr 1916)
Elle (Fr 1918)
La Sultane de l'amour (Fr 1919)
La Fête espagnole (Fr 1920)
Fièvre (Fr 1920)
Mathias Sandorff (Fr 1920)
La Terre du diable (Fr 1921)
Le Sang d'Allah (Fr 1921)
Le Mystères de Paris (Fr 1922)
Au delà de la mort (Fr 1922)
Au Senils du harem (Fr 1922)
La Bouquetière des innocents (Fr 1922)
Petit Hôtel à louer (Fr 1923)
La Mendiante de St. Sulpice (Fr 1923)
Nène (Fr 1924)
Le Cousin Pons (Fr 1924)
Le Miracle des loups (Fr 1924)
A l'horizon du sud (Fr 1924)
Les Elus de la mer (Fr 1925)
Veille d'armes (Fr 1925)
Naples au baiser de feu (Fr 1925)
La Châtelaine du Liban (Fr 1926)
Carmen (Fr 1926)
Sous la ciel d'Orient (Fr 1927)
La Ville des mille joies (Fr 1928)
Shéhérazade (Fr 1928)
Monte-Cristo (Fr 1928)
La Mervieilleuse Vie de Jeanne d'Arc (Fr 1928)
La Navire des hommes perdus (Fr 1929)
Liberté enchaînée (Fr 1929)
Le Fantôme du bonheur (Fr 1929)
Le Monocle vert (Fr 1929)
Sous les toits de Paris [On the Rooftops of Paris] (Fr 1930)
L'Age d'or (Fr 1930)
L'Opéra de quat' sous (Fr 1931)
Autour d'une enquête (Fr 1931)
Fantômas (Fr 1931)
Coups de feu à l'aube (Fr 1932)
La Mille et deuxième nuit (Fr 1932)
Les Chaînes (Fr 1933)
Le Taxi de minuit (Fr 1933)
Sous le casque de cuir (Fr 1933)
Quatorze juillet (Fr 1933)
Quelque'un à tué (Fr 1933)
Le Billet de mille (Fr 1933)
Colomba (Fr 1933)

L'Auberge du Petit Dragon (Fr 1934)
Le Mystère Imberger (Fr 1934)
Crainquebille (Fr 1935)
Le Clown Bux (Fr 1935)
Lucrèce Borgia (Fr 1935)
La Bandéra (Fr 1935)
Pépé-le-Moko (Fr 1936)
Les Réprouvés (Fr 1936)
Mademoiselle docteur (Fr 1937)
La Grande Illusion [Grand Illusion] (Fr 1937)
La Vie est à nous (Fr 1937)
Le Temps des cérises (Fr 1938)
La Marseillaise (Fr 1938)
Le Joueur d'échecs (Fr 1938)
La Règle du jour [The Rules of the Game] (Fr 1939)
La Fin du jour (Fr 1939)
Plein aux as (Fr 1939)
L'Irrésistible Rebelle (Fr 1939)
Dernier atout (Fr 1942)
Le Brigand gentilhomme (Fr 1942)
L'Homme des Londres (Fr 1943)
Les Enfants du paradis [Children of Paradise] (Fr 1945)
Le Bossu (Fr 1944)
Dernier Refuge (Fr 1946)
Antoine et Antoinette (Fr 1946)
Le Silence est d'or [Man About Town] (Fr 1947)
Eternel Conflit (Fr 1947)
L'Armoire volante (Fr 1947)
Le Pont du jour (Fr 1947)
L'Ecole buissonnière (Fr 1947)
Le Mystère de la chambre jaune (Fr 1947)
Le Parfum de la dame en noir (Fr 1949)
La Beauté du diable (It-Fr 1949)
Rendez-vous de juillet (Fr 1949)
Casque d'or [Golden Helmet] (Fr 1950)
Ce coquin d'Anatole (Fr 1951)
Monsieur Octave (Fr 1951)
La Môme Vert-de-Gris [Gun Moll] (Fr 1952)
French Can-Can (Fr 1954)
Cela s'appelle l'aurore (Fr 1955)
Les Truands (Fr 1955)
Eléna et les hommes [Paris Does Strange Things] (Fr 1956)
La Belle et le tzigane (Hun-Fr 1957)
Les Amants (Fr 1958)
Les Testaments du Docteur Cordelier (Fr 1959)

MONTAND, YVES (Ivo Livi), b. Oct. 13, 1921, Monsumagno, Italy
Etoile sans lumière (Fr 1944)
Les Portes de la nuit (Fr 1946)
L'Idole (Fr 1947)
Souvenirs perdus [Lost Property] (Fr 1950)
Paris chante toujours (Fr 1950)
Paris est toujours Paris (Fr-It 1951)

Le Salaire de la peur [Wages of Fear] (Fr-It 1952)
Tempi nostri (ep "Mara") (It-Fr 1953)
Napoléon (Fr 1954)
Les Héros sont fatigués (Fr 1955)
Marguerite de la nuit (Fr-It 1955)
Uomini e lupi (It-Fr 1956)
Les Sorcières de Salem [The Witches of Salem] (Fr-E Ger 1956)
La lunga strada azzurra (It-Fr 1957)
Premier Mal (Fr-It 1957)
La Loi [Where the Hot Wind Blows] (Fr-It 1958)
Let's Make Love (20th 1960)
Sanctuary (20th 1960)
Goodbye Again [Aimez-vous Brahms?] (UA 1961)
My Geisha (USA-Japan 1962)
Compartiment tueurs [The Sleeping Car Murders] (Fr-It 1965)
Paris brûle-t-il? [Is Paris Burning?] (Fr 1966)
La Guerre est finie [The War Is Over] (Fr 1966)
Grand Prix (MGM 1966)
Vivre pour vivre [Live for Life] (Fr-Swe 1967)
Un soir, un train (Fr-Bel 1967)
Mister Freedom (Fr 1968)
Z (Fr-Alg 1968)
Le Diable par la queue (Fr-It 1968)

Annie Girardot and Yves Montand in Live for Life (1967).

On a Clear Day You Can See Forever (Par 1970)
L'Aveu [The Confession] (Fr-It 1970)
Le Cercle rouge (Fr-It 1970)
La Folie des grandeurs (Fr-It-Sp-W Ger 1971)
Tout va bien (Fr-It 1972)
César et Rosalie (Fr-It 1972)
Le Hasard et la violence (Fr-It 1973)
Vincent, François, Paul et les autres (Fr-It 1974)
Le Sauvage (Fr 1975)

MOORE, KIERON (Kieron O'Hanrahan), b. Oct. 5, 1925, Skibbereen,
    Co. Cork, Ireland
  The Voice Within (GN 1945) (as Kieron O'Hanrahan)
  A Man About the House (BL 1947)
  Mine Own Executioner (BL 1947)
  Anna Karenina (BL 1948)
  Saints and Sinners (BL 1949)
  Maria Chapdelaine [The Naked Heart] (Fr 1950)
  Honeymoon Deferred (BL 1951)
  Ten Tall Men (Col 1951)
  David and Bathsheba (20th 1952)
  Mantrap [Woman in Hiding] (Hammer 1953)
  Recoil (Eros 1953)
  Conflict of Wings [Fuss Over Feathers] (BL 1954)
  The Green Scarf (BL 1954)
  The Blue Peter [Navy Heroes] (BL 1955)
  Satellite in the Sky (WB 1956)
  The Steel Bayonet (UA 1957)
  Three Sundays to Live (UA 1957)
  The Key (Col 1958)
  The Angry Hills (MGM 1958)
  Darby O'Gill and the Little People (BV 1959)
  League of Gentlemen (RFD 1960)
  The Day They Robbed the Bank of England (MGM 1960)
  The Siege of Sidney Street (RFI 1960)
  Dr. Blood's Coffin (UA 1961)
  The Day of the Triffids (RFD 1962)
  The 300 Spartans (20th 1962)
  I Thank a Fool (MGM 1962)
  The Main Attraction (MGM 1962)
  Hide and Seek (Albion 1963)
  Girl in the Headlines (Bry 1963)
  Bikini Paradise (AA 1964) [Br release delayed until 1970]
  Crack in the World (Par 1965)
  Arabesque (RFD 1966)
  Custer of the West (Cin 1967)
  Robe de Diamantes [Run Like a Thief] (Sp-USA 1967)
  The Progress of People (Con 1975)

MOORE, ROGER, b. Oct. 14, 1928, London
  Perfect Strangers [Vacation from Marriage] (MGM Br 1945)
    (extra)
  Caesar and Cleopatra (EL 1946) (extra)

Trottie True [Gay Lady] (GFD 1949) (extra)
The Paper Orchid (Col 1949) (extra
Stars and Stripes Forever [Marching Along] (20th 1952)
Pickup on South Street (20th 1953)
The Last Time I Saw Paris (MGM 1954)
Interrupted Melody (MGM 1955)
The King's Thief (MGM 1955)
Diane (MGM 1956)
The Miracle (WB 1959)
Gold of the Seven Saints (WB 1961)
The Sins of Rachel Cade (WB 1961)
Il ratto dei Sabine [Rape of the Sabine Women] (It-Fr 1962)
Un branco di vigliaceli [No Man's Land] (It-Fr 1962)
Crossplot (UA 1969)
The Man Who Haunted Himself (WPD 1970)
Live and Let Die (UA 1973)
Gold (Hemdale 1974)
The Man with the Golden Gun (UA 1974)
That Lucky Touch (Fox-Rank 1975)

MORE, KENNETH, b. Sept. 20, 1914, Gerrards Cross, Bucking-
     hamshire, England
Windmill Revels (Ace 1937)
Carry On London (Ace 1937)
School for Secrets [Secret Flight] (GFD 1946)
Scott of the Antarctic (GFD 1948)
For Them That Trespass (ABP 1949)
Man on the Run (ABP 1949)
Stop Press Girl (GFD 1949)
Now Barabbas Was a Robber (WB 1949)
Morning Departure [Operation Disaster] (GFD 1950)
Chance of a Lifetime (BL 1950)
The Clouded Yellow (GFD 1950)
The Franchise Affair (ABP 1951)
No Highway [No Highway in the Sky] (20th 1951)
Appointment with Venus [Island Rescue] (GFD 1951)
Brandy for the Parson (ABFD 1952)
The Yellow Balloon (ABP 1952)
Never Let Me Go (MGM Br 1953)
Genevieve (GFD 1953)
Our Girl Friday [The Adventures of Sadie] (Renown 1954)
Doctor in the House (GFD 1954)
Raising a Riot (BL 1955)
The Deep Blue Sea (20th 1955)
Reach for the Sky (RFD 1956)
The Admirable Crichton [Paradise Lagoon] (Modern Screenplays
     1957)
A Night to Remember (RFD 1958)
Next to No Time (BL 1958)
The Sheriff of Fractured Jaw (20th 1958)
The Thirty-Nine Steps (RFD 1959)
North West Frontier [Flame Over India] (RFD 1959)
Sink the Bismarck! (20th 1960)

Kenneth More (right) and Taina Elg check in--<u>The Thirty-Nine Steps</u>
(1959).

Man in the Moon (RFD 1960)
The Greengage Summer [Loss of Innocence] (Col 1961)
The Longest Day (20th 1962)
Some People (AA 1962)
We Joined the Navy (WPD 1962)
The Comedy Man (BL 1963)
Dark of the Sun [The Mercenaries] (MGM 1968)
Oh! What a Lovely War (Par 1969)
Fraulein Doktor (Yug-It 1969)
Battle of Britain (UA 1969)
Scrooge (20th 1970)

MOREAU, JEANNE, b. Jan. 23, 1928, Paris
Dernier Amour (Fr 1948)
Meutres (Fr 1950)
Pigalle-Saint-Germain-des Prés (Fr 1950)
L'uomo della una vite [The Man in My Life] (It-Fr 1951)
Il est minuit, Dr. Schweitzer (Fr 1952)
Dortoir des grandes [Girls' Dormitory] (Fr 1953)
Julietta (Fr 1953)
Secrets d'alcove [The Bed] (ep "Le Billet de logement") (Fr-It
    1953)
Touchez pas au Grisbi [Honor Among Thieves] (Fr 1955)

Les Intrigantes [The Plotters] (Fr 1955)
Le Reine Margot [Woman of Evil] (Fr-It 1955)
Les Hommes en blanc [Men in White] (Fr 1956)
M'Sieur la caille [The Parasites] (Fr 1956)
Gas-Oil (Fr 1956)
Le Salaire du péché (Fr 1957)
Jusqu'au dernier (Fr 1957)
Les Louves [The She-Wolves] (Fr 1957)
L'Etrange Monsieur Stève (Fr 1957)
Trois Jours a vivre (Fr 1957)
Ascenseur pour l'echafaud [Lift to the Scaffold] (Fr 1957)
Echec au porteur (Fr 1958)
Les Dos au mur [Evidence in Concrete] (Fr 1958)
Les Amants [The Lovers] (Fr 1958)
Les Quatre Cents Coups [The 400 Blows] (Fr 1959) (cameo)
Les Liasons dangereuses 1960 (Fr-It 1959)
Jovanka e le altre [Five Branded Women] (It-USA 1960)
Le Dialogue des Carmélites (Fr-It 1960)
Moderato cantabile [Seven Days...Seven Nights] (Fr 1960)
La Notte (It-Fr 1961)
Une Femme est une femme [A Woman Is a Woman] (Fr 1961)
Jules et Jim [Jules and Jim] (Fr 1962)
Eve [Eva] (Fr-It 1962)
La Baie des anges [Bay of Angels] (Fr 1963)
Le Feu follet [Will o' the Wisp] (Fr-It 1963)
Le Procès [The Trial] (Fr-It-W Ger 1963)

Jeanne Moreau

The Victors (Col 1963)
Peau de banane [Banana Peel] (Fr-It 1963)
Le Journal d'une femme de chambre [Diary of a Chambermaid]
  (Fr-It 1963)
The Yellow Rolls Royce (MGM 1964)
Mata Hari--agent H 21 (Fr-It 1964)
The Train (Fr-It-USA 1964)
Viva Maria! (Fr-It 1965)
Campanadas a medianoche [Falstaff] (Sp-Swi 1966)
Mademoiselle (GB-Fr 1966)
The Sailor from Gibraltar (UA 1967)
Lamiel (Fr-It 1967)
Le Plus Vieux metier du monde (ep "Mademoiselle Mimi") (Fr-
  W Ger-It 1967)
La Mariée était en noir [The Bride Wore Black] (Fr-It 1968)
Great Catherine (WPD 1968)
Histoire immortelle [The Immortal Story] (Fr 1968)
Le Corps de Diane (Fr-Czech 1969)
Le Petit Théatre de Jean Renoir (ep "Quand l'amour se meurt")
  (Fr-It-W Ger TV 1969)
Monte Walsh (20th 1970)
Alex in Wonderland (MGM 1970)
Compte a rebours [Countdown] (Fr 1970)
Mille Baisers de Florence (Fr 1971)
L'Humeur vagabonde (Fr 1971)
Chère Louise [Louise] (Fr-It 1972)
Nathalie Granger (Fr 1972)
Joanna Francesa [Joan, the Frenchwoman] (Brazil 1973)
Je t'aime (Canada 1974)
Les Valseuses [Making It] (Fr 1974)
La Race des "seigneurs" [The Race of "Elites"] (Fr 1974)
Pleurs (Fr 1975)
Le Jardin qui bascule (Fr 1975)
Souvenirs d'en France (Fr 1975)

MORGAN, MICHELE (Simone Roussel), b. Feb. 29, 1920, Neuilly-
  sur-Seine, France
Le Mioche (Fr 1936)
Gribouille (Fr 1937)
Orage (Fr 1937)
Quai des Brumes (Fr 1938)
L'Entraîneuse (Fr 1938)
Le Récif de Corail (Fr 1939)
La Loi du nord (Fr 1939)
Remorques (Fr 1939)
Untel Père et fils [Heart of a Nation] (Fr-USA 1940) [completed
  in USA]
Joan of Paris (RKO 1942)
Two Tickets to London (Univ Br 1943)
Higher and Higher (RKO 1944)
Passage to Marseilles (WB 1944)
Symphonie Pastorale (Fr 1946)
The Chase (UA 1946)

The Fallen Idol (BL 1948)
Fabiola (Fr 1948)
Aux yeux du souvenir (Fr 1948)
The Naked Heart [Maria Chapdeleine] (Fr-GB 1950)
Le Chateau de verre (Fr-It 1950)
L'Etrange Madame X (Fr 1951)
Les Sept Péchés capitaux [Seven Capital Sins] (Fr 1951)
La Minute dé vérité [The Moment of Truth] (Fr-It 1952)
Destinées (ep "Jeanne d'Arc") (Fr-It 1952)
L'Orgueilleux [The Proud Ones] (Fr-Mex 1953)
Obsession (Fr-It 1954)
Napoléon (Fr 1954)
Oasis (Fr-W Ger 1954)
Les Grandes Manoeuvres [Summer Manouvres] (Fr-It 1955)
Marguerite de la nuit (Fr-It 1955)
Si Paris nous était conté (Fr 1955)
Marie-Antoinette [Shadow of the Guillotine] (Fr 1955)
The Vintage (MGM 1957)
Retour à Manivelle [There's Always a Price Tag] (Fr-It 1957)
Le Miroir a deux faces [The Mirror Has Two Faces] (Fr-It
    1958)
Femmes d'un été [Racconti d'un été] (It-Fr 1958)
Maxime (Fr 1958)
Pourquoi viens-tu si tard? (Fr 1958)
Brèves Amours (It 1959)
Grand Hotel (W Ger 1959)
Les Scélérats [Tormented] (Fr 1960)
Fortunat (Fr-It 1960)
La Puits aux trois vérités (Fr-It 1961)
Les Lions sont lâchés (Fr-It 1961)
Rencontres (Fr-It 1962)
Le Crime ne paie pas [Crime Does Not Pay] (Fr-It 1962)
Landru (Fr-It 1962)
Il fornaretto di Venezia (It-Fr 1963)
Méfiez-vous, mesdames! (Fr-It 1963)
Constance aux enfers [Web of Fear] (Fr-It-Sp 1963)
Un balcon sobre el infierno (Fr-Sp 1964)
Les Pas perdus (Fr 1964)
Les Yeux cernés (Fr-It 1964)
Dis moi qui tuer (Fr 1965)
Lost Command (Col 1966)
Benjamin (Fr 1968)
Le Chat et le souris (Fr 1975)

MORLEY, ROBERT, b. May 26, 1908, Semley, Wiltshire, England
    Marie Antoinette (MGM 1938)
    You Will Remember (BL 1940)
    Major Barbara (GFD 1941)
    This Was Paris (WB Br 1942)
    The Big Blockade (UA 1942)
    The Foreman Went to France [Somewhere in France] (UA 1942)
    The Young Mr. Pitt (20th Br 1942)
    I Live in Grosvenor Square [A Yank in London] (Pathe 1945)

Ghosts of Berkeley Square (Pathe 1947)
The Small Back Room [Hour of Glory] (BL 1949)
Edward, My Son (MGM Br 1949)
Outcast of the Islands (BL 1951)
The African Queen (IFD 1951)
Curtain Up (GFD 1952)
The Final Test (GFD 1953)
The Story of Gilbert and Sullivan [The Great Gilbert and Sulli-
    van] (BL 1953)
Melba (UA 1953)
Beat the Devil (IFD 1954)
The Good Die Young (IFD 1954)
The Rainbow Jacket (GFD 1954)
Beau Brummell (MGM Br 1954)
The Adventures of Quentin Durward (MGM Br 1956)
Loser Takes All (BL 1956)
Around the World in 80 Days (UA 1956)
Law and Disorder (BL 1958)
The Sheriff of Fractured Jaw (20th 1958)
The Journey (MGM 1959)
The Doctor's Dilemma (MGM 1959)
Libel (MGM 1959)
The Battle of the Sexes (Bry 1959)
Oscar Wilde (20th 1960)
Giuseppe venduto dai fratelli [Joseph and His Brethren] (It 1961)
The Young Ones (WPD 1961)
Go to Blazes (WPD 1962)
The Boys (Gala 1962)
The Road to Hong Kong (UA 1962)
Nine Hours to Rama (20th 1963)
Murder at the Gallop (MGM 1963)
Take Her, She's Mine (20th 1963)
The Old Dark House (Col 1963)
Ladies Who Do (Bry 1963)
Hot Enough for June [Agent 8-3/4] (RFD 1963)
Of Human Bondage (MGM 1964)
Topkapi (UA 1964)
Genghis Khan (Col 1965)
Those Magnificent Men in Their Flying Machines; or, How I
    Flew from London to Paris in 25 Hrs and 11 Minutes (20th
    1965)
A Study in Terror [Fog] (Compton 1965)
The Alphabet Murders (MGM 1965)
Life at the Top (Col 1965)
The Loved One (MGM 1966)
Hotel Paradise (MGM 1966)
Finders Keepers (UA 1966)
The Trygon Factor (RFD 1967)
Hot Millions (MGM 1968)
Some Girls Do (RFD 1969)
Sinful Davey (UA 1969)
Twinky [Lola] (RFD 1969)
Cromwell (Col 1970)

Song of Norway (Cin 1970)
Doctor in Trouble (RFD 1970)
When Eight Bells Toll (RFD 1971)
Theatre of Blood (UA 1973)

MOSCHIN, GASTONE, b. June 8, 1929, Verona, Italy
Audace colpo dei soliti ignoti [Fiasco in Milan] (It 1959)
Tiro al piccione (It 1960)
Il mantenuto (It 1961)
Anni ruggenti (It 1962)
L'amore difficile [Erotica/Of Wayward Love] (ep "Il serpente")
  (It-W Ger 1962)
La visita (It 1963)
Il fornaretto di Venezia (It 1963)
Il successo (It 1963)
La rimpatriata (It 1963)
Il vendicatore mascherato (It 1964)
Amore in quattro dimensione [Love in Four Dimensions] (ep
  "Amore e vita") (It 1964)
Extraconjugale (ep "La doccia") (It 1965)
I cento cavalieri (It 1965)
Berlino, appuntamento per le spie [Spy in Your Eye] (It 1965)
Sette uomini d'oro [Seven Golden Men] (It 1965)
Le fate [The Queens] (It 1965)
Ray Master l'inafferrabile [Tilt à Bangkok] (It-Fr 1966)
Il grande colpo dei sette uomini do'oro (It 1966)
Du mou dans la gâchette [Due Killers in fuga] (Fr-It 1966)
Le stagioni del nostro amore (It 1966)
Signore e signori [The Birds, the Bees, and the Italians] (It
  1966)
Le Plus Vieux Métier du monde [L'amore attraverso i secoli/
  The Oldest Profession] (Fr-It 1967)
Top Crack (It 1967)
L'harem (It 1967)
La notte e fatta per... rubare (It 1967)
Italian Secret Service (It 1968)
Una moglie giapponese (It 1968)
Sissignore (It 1968)
Colpo di sole (It 1968)
Sette volte sette (It 1969)
Gli specialisti [Le Spécialiste] (It-Fr 1969)
Dove vai tutta nuda? (It 1969)
Concerto per pistola solista (It 1970)
Mio padre monsignore (It 1970)
Il conformista [Le Conformiste/The Conformist] (It-Fr 1970)
L'inefferrabile e invincibile Mr. Invisible (It 1970)
Nini Tirabusciò, la donna che invento la "mossa" (It 1970)
Causa di divorcio (It 1971)
Io non vedo, tu non parli, lui non sente (It 1971)
Roma bene [Liebe und Sex in Rom] (It-W Ger 1971)
Stanza 17-17, palazzo delle tasse, ufficio delle imposte (It 1971)
Don Camillo e i giovani d'oggi (It 1972)
Milano calibro 9 (It 1972)

La violenza: quinto potere (It 1972)
Fiorina la vacca (It 1973)
Paolo il caldo (It 1973)
Il delitto Mattcotti (It 1973)
...e cominciò il viaggio della vertigine (It 1974)
L'extomane (It 1974)
Squadra volante (It 1974)
The Godfather, Part II (Par 1974)

MOSER, HANS, b. Aug. 6, 1880, Vienna; d. June 18, 1964
Kleider machen Leute (Aus 1922)
Hofmanns Erzahlungen (Aus 1923)
Ssanin (Aus 1924)
Stadt ohne Juden (Aus 1924)
Das Spielzeug von Paris (Aus 1925)
Der Feldherrnhugel (Aus 1926)
Die Familie ohne Moral (Aus 1927)
Im Hotel zur süssen Nachtigall (Aus 1928)
Die Lampelgasse (Aus 1928)
Geld auf der Strasse (Aus 1930)
Liebling der Götter (Ger 1930)
Der verjüngte Adolar (Ger 1931)
Ehe mit beschränkter Haftung (Ger 1931)
Man braucht kein Geld (Ger 1931)
Dienstmann Nr 13 (Ger 1932)
Leise flehen meine Lieder (Aus 1933)
Liebelei (Ger 1933)
Madame wünscht keine Kinder (Aus 1933)
Frasquita (Aus 1934)
Frühjahrsparade (Aus-Hun 1934)
Hohe Schule (Aus 1934)
Der junge Baron Neuhaus (Ger 1934)
Karneval und Liebe (Aus 1934)
Maskerade (Aus 1934)
Polenblut (Ger-Czech 1934)
Endstation (Ger 1935)
Eva (Aus 1935)
Die Fahrt in die Jugend (Aus 1935)
Familie Schimek (Ger 1935)
Die ganze Welt dreht sich um Liebe (Aus 1935)
Der Himmel auf Erden (Aus 1935)
Ein junger Herr aus Oxford (Aus 1935)
Zirkus Saran (Aus 1935)
Nur ein Komödiant (Aus 1935)
Vostadtvarieté (Aus 1935)
Winternachtstraum (Ger 1935)
Alles für Veronika (Ger 1936)
Burgtheater (Aus 1936)
Hannerl und ihre Liebhaber (Aus 1936)
Das Gasschen zum Paradies (Aus-Czech 1936)
Confetti (Aus 1936)
Schabernack (Ger 1936)
Wer zu letzt küsst (Aus 1936)

Die Fledermaus (Ger 1937)
Die glücklichste Ehe von Wien (Aus 1937)
Der Mann, von dem man spricht (Aus 1937)
Mein Sohn, der Herr Minister (Ger 1937)
Mutterlied (Ger-It 1937)
Die unentschuldigte Stunde (Aus 1937)
Die verschwundene Frau (Aus 1937)
13 Stühle (Aus 1938)
Finale (Aus 1938)
Immer wenn ich glücklich bin (Aus 1938)
Es leuchten die Sterne (Ger 1938)
Kleines Bezirksgericht (Ger 1938)
Anton der Letzte (Ger 1939)
Das Ekel (Ger 1939)
Liebe streng verboten (Ger 1939)
Menschen vom Varieté (Ger 1939)
Opernball (Ger 1939)
Der Herr im Haus (Ger 1940)
Meine Tochter lebt in Wien (Ger 1940)
Rosen in Tirol (Ger 1940)
Sieben Jahre Pech (Ger 1940)
Der ungetreue Eckehard (Ger 1940)
Wiener Geschichten (Ger 1940)
Lieber ist zollfrei (Ger 1941)
Wir bitten zum Tanz (Ger 1941)
Wunschkonzert (Ger 1941)
Einmal der liebe Herrgott sein (Ger 1942)
Maske in Blau (Ger 1942)
Sieben Jahre Glück (Ger 1942)
Wiener Blut (Ger 1942)
Abenteuer im Grandhotel (Ger 1943)
Das Ferienkind (Ger 1943)
Karneval der Liebe (Ger 1943)
Reisebekanntschaft (Ger 1943)
Schwarz auf Weiss (Ger 1943)
Schrammeln (Ger 1944)
Der Millionär (W Ger 1947) [made in 1945]
Die Welt dreht sich verkehrt (Aus 1947)
Der Hofrat Geiger (Aus 1947)
Der Herr Kanzleirat (Aus 1948)
Das singende Haus (Aus 1948)
1-2-3- aus! (Aus 1949)
Wiener Mädeln (W Ger 1949) [made in 1945]
Um eine Nasenlänge (W Ger 1949)
Es liegt was in der Luft (W Ger 1950)
Es schlagt 13 (Aus 1950)
Küssen ist keine Suend (Aus 1950)
Der Theodor im Fussballtor (W Ger 1950)
Zwei in einem Auto (Aus 1951)
Du bist die Rose vom Wörthersee (W Ger 1952)
1 April 2000 (Aus 1952)
Hallo, Dienstmann! (Aus 1952)
Der Onkel aus Amerika (W Ger 1952)

Schäme Dich, Brigitte! (Aus 1952)
Hollandmädel (W Ger 1953)
Einen Jux will er sich machen (Aus 1953)
Kaisermanöver (Aus 1954)
Verliebte Leute (Aus 1954)
Die Deutschmeister (Aus 1955)
Die Drei von der Tankstelle (W Ger 1955)
Ehesanatorium (Aus 1955)
Ja, ja, die Liebe in Tirol (W Ger 1955)
Der Kongress tanzt (Aus 1955)
Ein Herz und eine Seele (Aus 1956)
Kaiserball (Aus 1956)
Lumpazivagabundus (W Ger 1956)
Meine Tante--deine Tante (W Ger 1956)
Opernball (Aus 1956)
Roter Mohn (Aus 1956)
Solange noch die Rosen blühn (W Ger 1956)
Symphonie in Gold (Aus 1956)
Heute blau und morgen blau (W Ger 1957)
Die Lindenwirtin vom Donaustrand (Aus 1957)
Ober, zahlen! (Aus 1957)
Die unentschuldigte Stunde (Aus 1957)
Vier Mädel aus der Wachau (Aus 1957)
Die Zwillinge vom Zillertal (W Ger 1957)
Gräfin Mariza (W Ger 1958)
Hallo, Taxi! (W Ger 1958)
Herrn Josefs letzte Liebe (W Ger 1958)
Ooh--diese Ferien (Aus 1958)
Der Sündenbock von Spatzenhausen (W Ger 1958)
Zirkuskinder (Aus 1958)
Die schöne Lügnerin (W Ger 1959)
Der Bauer als Millionär (Aus 1961)
Mariandl (Aus 1961)
Und Du, mein Schatz, bleibst hier (Aus 1961)
Drei Liebesbriefe aus Tirol (Aus 1962)
Die Fledermaus (Aus 1962)
Mariandls Heimkehr (Aus 1962)
Der verkaufte Grossvater (W Ger 1962)
Kaiser Joseph und die Bahnwärterstochter (Aus 1963)

MULLER, RENATE, b. April 26, 1907, Munich; d. Oct. 7, 1937
Peter, der Matrose (Ger 1929)
Revolte im Erziehungshaus (Ger 1929)
Drei machen ihr Glück (Ger 1929)
Liebe im Ring (Ger 1930)
Liebling der Götter (Ger 1930)
Der Sohn der weissen Berge (Ger 1930)
Das Flötenkonzert von Sanssouci (Ger 1930)
Die Blumenfrau von Lindenau (Ger 1931)
Liebeslied (Ger-It 1931)
Die Privatsekretärin (Ger 1931)
Sunshine Susie (Ideal 1931) [Eng lang version of Die Privatsekre-
    tärin)

Der kleine Seitensprung (Ger 1931)
Mädchen zum Heiraten (Ger 1932)
Wie sag ich's meinem Mann (Ger 1932)
Wenn die Liebe Mode macht (Ger 1932)
Walzerkrieg (Ger 1933)
Viktor und Viktoria (Ger 1933)
Die englische Heirat (Ger 1934)
Liselotte von der Pfalz (Ger 1935)
Liebesleute (Ger 1935)
Allotria (Ger 1936)
Eskapade (Ger 1936)
Togger (Ger 1937)

MUNCH, RICHARD, b. 1916, Giessen, Germany
Es geschehen noch Wunder (W Ger 1951)
Der Verlorene (W Ger 1951)
Zwei blaue Augen (W Ger 1955)
Dr. Crippen lebt (W Ger 1958)
Nasser Asphalt (W Ger 1958)
Unruhige Nacht (W Ger 1958)
Der Schinderhannes (W Ger 1958)
Frau im besten Mannesalter (W Ger 1959)
Verbrechen nach Schulschluss (W Ger 1959)
Hunde wollt ihr ewig leben (W Ger 1959)
Himmel, Amor und Zwirn (W Ger 1960)
Das Wunder des Malachias (W Ger 1961)
Das Gasthaus an der Themse (W Ger 1962)
Die Rote [La rossa] (W Ger-It 1962)
Der Besuch [La Rancune/La vendetta della signora/The Visit]
    (W Ger-Fr-It 1964)
Wartezimmer zum Jenseits (W Ger 1964)
Das Liebeskarussell (W Ger-Aus 1965)
Mordnacht in Manhattan (W Ger 1965)
Schüsse aus dem Geigenkasten (W Ger 1965)
Hokuspokus--oder wie lasse ich meinen Mann verschwinden (W
    Ger 1966)
In Frankfurt sind die Nächte heiss (W Ger 1966)
Pfeifen, betten, Turteltauben (Aus 1966)
La Carnaval des barbouzes [Gern hab'ich die Frauen gekillt/Spie
    contro il mondo] (Fr-W Ger-Aus-It 1966)
Um null Uhr schnappt die Falle Zu (W Ger 1966)
Die Rechnung--eiskalt serviert (W Ger-Fr 1966)
Heisses Pflaster Köln (W Ger 1967)
Der Mörderclub von Brooklyn (W Ger 1967)

MUÑOZ, EUNICE (Eunice Carmo Muñoz), b. July 30, 1928, Ama-
    releja, Portugal
Camões (Por 1946)
Um homem do ribatejo (Por 1946)
Os vizinhos do rés-do-chão (Por 1947)
Não há rapazes maus (Por 1948) [narrator]
A morgadinha dos canaviais (Por 1949)
Ribatejo (Por 1949)
Cantiga da rua (Por 1949)

O-trigo e o jóio (Por 1965)

MURRAY, Stephen, b. Sept. 6, 1912, Partney, Lincolnshire, England
Pygmalion (GFD 1938)
The Prime Minister (WB Br 1941)
Next of Kin (UA 1942)
Undercover [Underground Guerillas] (UA 1943)
Master of Bankdam (GFD 1947)
My Brother Jonathan (Pathe 1948)
London Belongs to Me [Dulcimer Street] (GFD 1948)
Silent Dust (ABP 1949)
For Them That Trespass (ABP 1949)
Now Barabbas Was a Robber (WB 1949)
The Magnet (GFD 1950)
24 Hours of a Woman's Life [Affair in Monte Carlo] (ABP 1952)
Four Sided Triangle (Ex 1953)
The Stranger's Hand (BL 1954)
The End of the Affair (Col 1955)
Guilty? (GN 1956)
At the Stroke of Nine (GN 1957)
A Tale of Two Cities (RFD 1958)
The Nun's Story (WB 1959)
Master Spy (GN 1963)

MUTI, ORNELLA, b. 1956
Un posto ideale per uccidere (It 1970)
La moglie più bella (It 1970)
Il sole nella pelle (It 1971)
La casa de las palomas (Sp 1972)
Un solo grande amore (It 1972)
Fiorina la vacca (It 1972)
Cronace di altri tempe (It 1973)
L'altra faccia del padrino (It 1973)
Amore a morte (It 1973)
Le monache di Sant'Arcangelo (It 1973)
Paolo il caldo (It 1973)
La seduzione (It 1973)
Tutti figli di mamma santissima [Italian Graffiti] (It 1973)
Appassionata (It 1974)
Romanzo popolare [Come Home and Meet My Wife] (It 1974)
La Jeune Mariée (Sp 1975)
Mio dio, come sono caduta in basso (It 1975)
Leonor (Fr-Sp 1975)

NAGY, KATHE VON (Ekaterina Nagy von Cziser) (a.k.a. Kate de
    Nagy), b. April 14, 1904, Germany; d. Dec. 1973
Das brennende Schiff (Ger 1927)
Gustav Mond...Du gehst so stille (Ger 1927)
Der Anwalt des Hazens (Ger 1927)
Männer vor der Ehe (Ger 1927)
Die Sandgräfin (Ger 1927)
Veronika (Ger 1927)
Hans Engelska Fru (Swe 1928)
Die Königin seines Herzens (Ger 1928)

Aufruhr im Junggesellenheim (Ger 1929)
Maskottchen (Ger 1929)
Unschuld (Ger 1929)
Der Weg durch die Nacht (Ger 1929)
Gaukler [Les Saltimbanques/I saltimbanchi] (Ger-Fr-It 1929)
Rotaie (It 1929)
Der Andere (Ger 1930)
Le capitaine Craddock (Fr 1931)
Ihre Majestät die Liebe (Ger 1931)
Meine Frau, die Hochstaplerin (Ger 1931)
Ronny [also Fr version] (Ger 1931)
Ihre Hoheit befiehlt (Ger 1931)
Das schöne Abenteuer (Ger 1932)
La belle aventure [Fr version of Das schöne Abenteuer] (Ger 1932)
Ich bei Tag und Du bei Nacht (Ger 1932)
A moi le jour, à toi la nuit (Ger 1932) [Fr version of Ich bei
    Tag und Du bei Nacht]
Der Sieger (Ger 1932)
Le Vainqueur [Fr version of Der Sieger] (Ger 1932)
Flüchtlinge (Ger 1933)
Au bout du monde (Ger 1933) [Fr version of Flüchtlinge]
Die Töchter ihrer Exzellenz (Ger 1934)
La Jeune Fille d'une nuit [Fr version of Die Töchter ihrer Ex-
    zellenz] (Ger 1934)
Einmal eine grosse Dame sein (Ger 1934)
Un jour viendra [Fr version of Einmal eine grosse Dame sein]
    (Ger 1934)
Liebe, Tod und Teufel (Ger 1934)
Le Diable en bouteille [Fr version of Liebe, Tod und Teufel]
    (Ger 1934)
Prinzessin Turandot (Ger 1934)
Turandot, princesse de chine [Fr version of Prinzessin Turan-
    dot] (Ger 1934)
Der junge Baron Neuhaus (Ger 1934)
Nuit de mai [Fr version of Der junge Baron Neuhaus] (Ger 1934)
Die Freundin eines grossen Mannes (Ger 1934)
La Ronte imperiale (Fr 1935)
Die Pompadour (Aus 1935)
Cargaison blanche [Le Chemin de Rio] (Fr 1936)
Ave Maria (Ger 1936)
La Bataille silencieuse (Fr 1937)
Nuits de princes (Fr 1937)
Unsere kleine Frau (Ger 1938)
Mia moglie si diverte [It version of Unsere kleine Frau] (Ger
    1938)
Accord final (Fr-Swi 1938)
Die unruhigen Mädchen (Ger 1938)
Am seidenen Faden (Ger 1939)
Salonwagen E 417 (Ger 1939)
Renate im Quartett (Ger 1939)
Mahlia la metisse (Fr 1942)
Cargaison clandestine (Fr 1947)
Die Försterchristl (W Ger 1952)

NAT, MARIE JOSE (Marie Benhalassa), b. April 20, 1940, Bonifaccio, Corsica
Crime et châtiment [Crime and Punishment] (Fr 1956)
Club de femmes (Fr-It 1956)
Donnez-moi ma chance (Fr 1957)
Les Arênes joyeuses (Fr 1957)
Secret professionel (Fr 1958)
Vous n'avez rien à declarer? (Fr 1958)
Rue des Prairies (Fr-It 1959)
La Française et l'amour [Love and the Frenchwoman] (ep "Le Mariage") (Fr 1959)
La Vérité [The Truth] (Fr-It 1960)
Le Amours de Paris (Fr 1960)
La Menace (Fr-It 1960)
Amélie ou le temps d'aimer (Fr 1961)
L'Education sentimentale (Fr-It 1961)
Les Sept Péchés capitau [Seven Capital Sins] (ep "La Colére") (Fr-It 1962)
La Vie conjugale: Françoise [Anatomy of a Marriage] (Fr-It 1963)
La Vie conjugale: Jean-Marc [Anatomy of a Marriage] (Fr-It 1963)
La Bonne Occase (Fr 1964)
Le Journal d'une femme blanc [Woman in White] (Fr-It 1964)
Safari diamant (Fr-W Ger 1966)
Le Paria [Diamond Rush] (Fr-Sp 1968)
Elise ou la vraie vie (Fr-Alg 1969)
Embassy (Hemdale 1972)
6 rue du Calvaire (Bel 1972)
Le Violons du bal [Violins of the Ball] (Fr 1974)
Dis-moi qui tu m'aimes (Fr 1975)

NAZZARI, AMEDEO (Salvatore Amedeo Buffa), b. Dec. 10, 1907, Cagliari, Italy
Ginerva degli Almieri (It 1935)
Cavalleria (It 1937)
La fossa degli angeli (It 1937)
I fratelli Castiglioni (It 1937)
Luciano Serra, pilota (It 1938)
Il conte di Bréchard (It 1938)
Montevergine (It 1938)
Fuochi d'artificio (It 1938)
La casa del peccato (It 1938)
Assenza ingiustificata (It 1939)
Esbarcato un marinaio (It 1939)
La notte delle beffe (It 1939)
Centomila dollari (It 1939)
Cose dell'altro monde (It 1939)
L'uomo del romanzo (It 1940)
Dopo divorzieremo (It 1940)
Caravaggio, il pittore maledetto (It 1940)
Scarpe grosse (It 1940)
Il cavaliero senza nome (It 1941)
Sancta Maria [also Ger version] (It 1941)

L'ultimo ballo (It 1941)
I mariti (It 1941)
Scampolo tempesta d'amore (It 1941)
La cena delle beffe (It 1941)
Fedora (It 1942)
La bisbetica domata (It 1942)
Bengasi (It 1942)
Villa da vendere (It 1942)
Giorni felici (It 1942)
Oltre l'amore (It 1942)
La bella addormentata (It 1942)
Ninna Nanna, pappa sta in guerra (It 1942)
Quelli della montagna (It 1942)
Il romanzo di un giovane povero (It 1942)
Harlem (It 1942)
L'invasore (It 1943)
La donna della montagna (It 1943)
Apparizione (It 1943)
Grazia (It 1943) [unfinished]
I dieci comandamenti (It 1945)
Un giorno nella vita (It 1946)
Il bandito (It 1946)
Il cavaliere del sogno [Donizetti] (It 1946)
Cuando los angeles duermen [Quando gli angeli dormono] (Sp-It
    1946)
Malacarne (It 1946)
Fatalità (It 1946)
La figlia del capitano (Sp 1947)
Conflicto inesperado (Sp 1947)
Don Juan de Serralonga [Il ribelle di Castiglia] (Sp-It 1948)
Il Lupo della Sila (It 1949)
Catene (It 1949)
Barriera e Settentrione (It 1949)
Amori e velene (It 1949)
Il vedovo allegro (It 1949)
Alina (It 1950)
Il brigante Musolino (It 1950)
I figli di nessuno (It 1950)
Donne e briganti (It 1950)
Tormento (It 1950)
Volver a la vida (It 1951)
Tradimento [Il Passato che uccide] (It 1951)
Lebbra bianca (It 1951)
Romanticismo (It 1951)
Ultimo incontro (It 1951)
Sensualità (It 1951)
Altri tempi (ep "La morsa") (It 1951)
Il brigante di tacca del lupo (It 1951)
Processo alla città (It 1952)
La fiammata (It 1952)
Siamo tutti assassini [Nous sommes tous des assassine] (It-Fr
    1952)
Il mondo le condanna (It 1952)

Chi è senza peccato (It 1952)
Un marito per Anna Zaccheo (It 1953)
Ti ho sempre amato (It 1953)
Torna! (It 1953)
Les révoltés de Lomanach [L'eroe della Vandea] (Fr-It 1954)
Pietà per chi cade (It 1954)
Appassionatamente (It 1954)
Proibito [Du sang dans le soleil] (It-Fr 1955)
L'angelo bianco (It 1955)
L'intrusa (It 1955)
L'ultimo amante (It 1956)
La puerta abierta [L'ultima notte d'amore] (Sp-It 1956)
Le notte di Cabiria [Nights of Cabiria] (It 1957)
La morte ha viaggiato con me (It 1957)
Il cielo brucia (It 1958)
Malinconico autumno [Cafe de puerto] (It-Sp 1958)
Anna di Brooklyn (It 1958)
The Naked Maja (It-USA 1958)
Il raccomandato di ferro (It 1959)
Policarpo ufficiale di scrittura [Policarpo de Tapetti (It-Sp 1959)
Carmen la de ronda [The Devil Made a Woman] (Sp 1959)
Labyrinth [Neurose] (W Ger-It 1959)
Il mondo dei miracoli (It 1959)
Cartagine in fiamme [Carthage en Flammes] (It-Fr 1959)
La contessa azzura (It 1960)
Antinea, l'amante della città sepolta [L'Atlantide/Journey Be-
    neath the Desert] (It-Fr 1961)
I due nemici [The Best of Enemies] (It 1961)
I fratelli Corsi (It 1961)
Nefertite, regina del Nilo [Queen of the Nile] (It 1962)
La leggenda di Fra' Diavolo (It 1962)
Odio mortale (It 1963)
Le monachine [The Little Nuns] (It 1963)
Frenesia dell'estate (It 1964)
Il Gaucho (It 1964)
Mister Dynamit--Morgen Küsst euch der Todd [Mister Dinamita,
    manana os besara la meurte] (W Ger-Sp-It 1966)
A bajo espera la muerte [Delitto d'amore] (Sp-It 1966)
The Poppy Is Also a Flower (Comet 1966)
Le Clan des siciliens [The Sicilian Clan] (Fr 1969)
Joe Valachi [I segreti di Cosa Nostra] (It 1972)

NEAGLE, ANNA (Marjorie Robertson), b. Oct. 20, 1904, Forest
    Gate, London
    The Chinese Bungalow (WP 1930)
    Should a Doctor Tell? (BL 1930)
    Goodnight Vienna [Magic Night] (W & F 1932)
    The Flag Lieutenant (W & F 1932)
    The Little Damozel (W & F 1933)
    Bitter Sweet (UA 1933)
    The Queen's Affair [Runaway Queen] (UA 1934)
    Nell Gwyn (UA 1934)
    Peg of Old Drury (UA 1935)

Limelight [Backstage] (GFD 1936)
The Three Maxims [The Show Goes On] (GFD 1936)
London Melody [Girls in the Street] (GFD 1937)
Victoria the Great (Radio 1937)
Sixty Glorious Years [Queen of Destiny/Queen Victoria] (RKO
   Br 1938)
Nurse Edith Cavell (RKO 1939)
Irene (RKO 1940)
No, No, Nanette (RKO 1941)
Sunny (RKO 1941)
They Flew Alone [Wings and the Woman] (RKO Br 1942)
Forever and a Day (RKO 1943)
Yellow Canary (RKO 1943)
I Live in Grosvenor Square [A Yank in London] (Pathe 1945)
Piccadilly Incident (Pathe 1946)
The Courtneys of Curzon Street [The Courtney Affair] (BL 1947)
Royal Wedding (GFD 1947) [documentary] (narrator)
Spring in Park Lane (BL 1948)
Elizabeth of Ladymead (BL 1949)
Maytime in Mayfair (BL 1949)
Odette (BL 1950)
Lady with the Lamp (BL 1951)
Derby Day [Four Against Fate] (BL 1952)
Lilacs in the Spring [Let's Make Up] (Rep 1954)
King's Rhapsody (BL 1955)
My Teenage Daughter [Teenage Bad Girl] (BL 1956)
No Time for Tears (ABPC 1957)
The Man Who Wouldn't Talk (BL 1958)
The Lady Is a Square (ABP 1959)

NEFF, HILDEGARD see HILDEGARD KNEF

NEGRI, POLA (Barbara Appolonia Chapulek), b. Dec. 31, 1894
   Niewolnica Zmyslow [Raba Straster/Raba Poroka/Slave of the
      Senses] (Rus-Pol 1914)
   Czarna ksiazeczka o zolty paszport (Pol-Rus 1915)
   Zona [Wife/I nse oplakano-osmeyano-razbito] (Pol-Rus 1915)
   Studenci [Students] (Pol 1916)
   Bestia [Beast] (Pol 1916)
   Tajemnica Alei Ujazdowskich [Mystery of Ujazlowsky Alley]
      (Pol 1917)
   Arabella (Pol 1917)
   Pokoj NR 13 [Room #13] (Pol 1917)
   Jego Ostatni Czyn [His Final Act] (Pol 1917)
   Rosen, die der Sturm entblättert (Ger 1917)
   Die toten Augen (Ger 1917)
   Nicht lange täuschte mich das Glück (Ger 1917)
   Zügelloses Blut (Ger 1917)
   Küsse, die Man stiehlt im Dunkeln (Ger 1917)
   Wenn das Herz in Hass erglüht (Ger 1918)
   Mania [Geschichte einer Zigarettenarbetterin] (Ger 1918)
   Der Gelbe Schein [The Devil's Paw] (Ger 1918)
   Die Augen, der Mumie Ma [Eyes of the Mummy] (Ger 1918)

Carmen [Gypsy Blood] (Ger 1918)
Karussell des Lebens [The Last Payment] (Ger 1919)
Vendetta [Blutrache] (Ger 1919)
Kreuziget Sie! [Die Frau am Scheidewege] (Ger 1919)
Madame DuBarry [Passion] (Ger 1919)
Comtesse Doddy (Ger 1920)
Die Marchesa d'Arminiani (Ger 1920)
Sumurun [One Arabian Night] (Ger 1920)
Das Martyrium (Ger 1920)
Die geschlossene Kette (Ger 1920)
Arme Violette [The Red Peacock] (Ger 1920)
Die Bergkatze (Ger 1921)
Sappho [Mad Love] (Ger 1921)
Die Flamme [Montmartre] (Ger 1922)
Bella Donna (Par 1923)
The Cheat (Par 1923)
Hollywood (Par 1923)
The Spanish Dancer (Par 1923)
Shadows of Paris (Par 1924)
Men (Par 1924)
Lily of the Dust (Par 1924)
Forbidden Paradise (Par 1924)
East of Suez (Par 1924)
The Charmer (Par 1925)
Flower of Night (Par 1925)
A Woman of the World (Par 1925)
The Crown of Lies (Par 1926)
Good and Naughty (Par 1926)
Hotel Imperial (Par 1926)
Barbed Wire (Par 1927)
The Woman on Trial (Par 1927)
The Secret Hour (Par 1928)
Three Sinners (Par 1928)
Lives of an Actress (Par 1928)
The Woman from Moscow (Par 1928)
The Woman He Scorned [Die Strasse der Verlorenen Seelen]
    (GB-Ger 1929)
A Woman Commands (RKO 1932)
Fanatisme (Fr 1934)
Mazurka (Ger 1935)
Moskau-Shanghai [Der Weg nach Shanghai] (Ger 1936)
Madame Bovary (Ger 1937)
Tango Notturno (Ger 1937)
Die Fromme Lüge (Ger 1938)
Die Nacht der Entscheidung (Ger 1938)
Hi Diddle Diddle (UA 1943)
The Moon Spinners (BV 1964)

NEGULESCO, JULIAN, b. Jan. 22, 1946, Ploiesti, Romania
    L'Apocalypse (Fr 1970)
    Bob--Anatomie d'un livreur (Fr 1971)
    Chère Louise [Louise] (Fr-It 1972)
    Un Officer de police adjoint sans importance (Fr 1973)

Une Fille à fenêtre (Fr 1973)
Le Mariage à la mort (Fr 1974)
La Soupe froide [The Cold Soup] (Fr 1975)

NERO, FRANCO (Franco Spartanero), b. Nov. 23, 1941, Parma,
    Italy
La celestina (It 1964)
Io la conoscevo bene [Ich hab' sie gut gehánnt] (It-W Ger 1965)
I criminali della galassia [The Wild, Wild Planet] (It 1965)
I diafanoidi vengono da morte (It 1965)
Gli uomini dal passo pesante [The Tramplers] (It 1965)
La bibbia [The Bible] (It-USA 1966)
Django (It 1966)
Il terzo occhio (It 1966)
Le colt cantarono la morte e fu temps di anazzacro [Tempo di
    massacro/The Brute and the Beast] (It 1966)
Tecnica di un omicidio [The Hired Killer] (It 1966)
Texas Addio (It 1966)
La morte viene dal Pianeta Aytin (It 1967)

Franco Nero

Camelot (WB-7 Arts 1967)
L'uomo, l'orgoglio, la vendetta (It 1967)
Il giorno della civettà [Mafia] (It 1967)
Un tranquillo posto di campagna [A Quiet Place in the Country]
    (It 1968)
Il mercenario [The Mercenary] (It 1968)
Die Schlacht an dei Neretva [La battaglia della Neretva/Bitka na
    Neretvi/Battle of Neretva] (W Ger-It-Yug 1969)
The Virgin and the Gypsy (AA 1969)
Gott mit uns (W Ger-It 1969)

Tristana (Sp-It-Fr 1969)
Un detective macchie di belletto [Detective Belli] (It 1969)
Dropout (It 1970)
Vamos a matar, compañeros (Sp 1970)
Giornata nera per l'Arieste (It 1971)
Confessione di un commissario di polizia al Procuratore della
    Republica (It 1971)
Pope Joan [The Devil's Imposter] (Col 1972)
L'Istruttoria è chiusa: dimentichi (It 1972)
Viva la muerta tua! (It 1972)
La vacanza (It 1972)
Le Moine [Il monaco] (Fr-It 1972)
Senza ragione [Redneck] (It 1972)
Il delitto Matteotti (It 1972)
Los Amigos (It 1973)
Zanna Bianca [White Fang] (It 1973)
La polizia incrimina, la legge assolve (It 1973)
Il ritorno di Zanna Bianca (It 1974)
I guappi (It 1974)
Il cittadino si ribella (It 1974)
Mussolini: ultimo atto (It 1974)
Perche si uccide un magistrato? (It 1975)
Corruzione al palazzo di giustizia (It 1975)
I quattro dell'apocalisse (It 1975)
Un attimo di vita (It 1975)
L'ispettore (It 1975)
Il cipollaro (It 1975)
Gente di rispetto (It 1975)
The Legend of Valentino (ABC-TV 1975)

NEWLEY, ANTHONY, b. Sept. 24, 1931, Clapton, England
    Dusty Bates (GFD 1947)
    The Little Ballerina (GFD 1947)
    Vice Versa (GFD 1948)
    Oliver Twist (GFD 1948)
    The Guinea Pig (Pathe 1948)
    Vote for Huggett (GFD 1949)
    A Boy, a Girl and a Bike (GFD 1949)
    Don't Ever Leave Me (GFD 1949)
    Highly Dangerous (GFD 1950)
    These People Next Door (Eros 1953)
    Top of the Form (GFD 1953)
    Up to His Neck (GFD 1954)
    Above Us the Waves (GFD 1955)
    The Blue Peter [Navy Heroes] (BL 1955)
    Cockleshell Heroes (Col 1955)
    Port Afrique (Col 1956)
    X the Unknown (Ex 1956)
    The Last Man to Hang? (Col 1956)
    The Battle of the River Plate [Pursuit of the Graf Spee] (RFD
        1956)
    The Good Companions (ABPC 1957)
    Fire Down Below (Col 1957)

How to Rob a Rich Uncle (Col 1957)
High Flight (Col 1957)
No Time to Die [Tank Force] (Col 1958)
The Man Inside (Col 1958)
The Lady Is a Square (ABP 1959)
Idle on Parade (Col 1959)
The Bandit of Zhobe (Col 1959)
The Heart of a Man (RFD 1959)
Killers of Kilimanjaro (Col 1959)
Jazzboat (Col 1960)
Let's Get Married (Eros 1960)
In the Nick (Col 1960)
The Small World of Sammy Lee (Bry-7 Arts 1963)
Stop the World I Want to Get Off (WPD 1966)
Doctor Dolittle (20th 1967)
Sweet November (WB-7 Arts 1968)
Can Hieronymus Merkin Ever Forget Mercy Humppe and Find
     True Happiness? (RFD 1969)

NEWTON, ROBERT, b. June 1, 1905, Shaftesbury, England; d.
     March 23, 1956
Reunion (MGM 1932)
Fire over England (UA 1937)
Dark Journey [The Anxious Years] (UA 1937)
Farewell Again [Troopship] (UA 1937)
The Squeaker [Murder on Diamond Row] (UA 1937)
I, Claudius (Br 1937) [unfinished]
Vessel of Wrath [The Beachcomber] (ABPC 1938)
Yellow Sands (ABPC 1938)
Dead Men Are Dangerous (Pathe 1939)
Jamaica Inn (ABPC 1939)
Poison Pen (ABPC 1939)
Hell's Cargo [Dangerous Cargo] (ABPC 1939)
21 Days [21 Days Together] (Col 1939) [made in 1937]
The Green Cockatoo [Race Gang] (20th 1940) [made in 1937]
Bulldog Sees It Through (ABPC 1940)
Gaslight [Angel Street] (Anglo 1940)
Busman's Honeymoon [Haunted Honeymoon] (MGM Br 1940)
Major Barbara (GFD 1941)
Hatter's Castle (Par Br 1941)
They Flew Alone [Wings and the Woman] (RKO Br 1942)
This Happy Breed (EL 1944)
Henry V (EL 1945)
Night Boat to Dublin (Pathe 1946)
Odd Man Out (GFD 1947)
Temptation Harbour (Pathe 1947)
Snowbound (RKO Br 1948)
Oliver Twist (GFD 1948)
Kiss the Blood Off My Hands (Univ 1948)
Obsession [The Hidden Room] (GFD 1949)
Treasure Island (RKO 1950)
Waterfront [Waterfront Women] (GFD 1950)
Soldiers Three (MGM 1951)

Robert Newton and Kay Walsh in <u>Oliver Twist</u> (1948).

Tom Brown's Schooldays (Renown 1951)
Les Miserables (20th 1952)
Androcles and the Lion (RKO 1952)
Blackbeard the Pirate (RKO 1952)
The Desert Rats (20th 1953)
The High and the Mighty (WB 1954)
The Beachcomber (GFD 1954)
Long John Silver (DCA 1954)
Around the World in 80 Days (UA 1956)

NOEL, MAGALI, b. June 27, 1932, Smirna, Turkey
Demain, nous divorçons (Fr 1950)
Seul dans Paris (Fr 1951)
Mourez...nous ferons le reste (Fr 1953)
Razzia sur la Chnouf (Fr 1954)
Le Fils de Caroline Chérie (Fr 1954)
Du Rififi chez les hommes (Fr 1954)
Les Grandes Manoeuvres [Summer Manouvres] (Fr-It 1955)
Chantage [The Lowest Crime] (Fr 1955)
Les Possédées (Fr-It 1955)

Elena et les hommes [Paris Does Strange Things] (Fr-It 1956)
C'est arrivé à Aden [It Happened in Aden] (Fr 1957)
Assassins et voleurs (Fr 1956)
OSS 117 n'est pas mort (Fr 1956)
Si le roi savait ça (Fr-It 1956)
Le Désir mène les hommes (Fr 1957)
La Piège [The Trap] (Fr 1958)
Des femmes disparaissent (Fr 1958)
L'Ile du bout du monde [Temptation Island] (Fr 1958)
Oh! Que Mambo (Fr-It 1958)
Marie des Isles [The Wild and the Wanton] (Fr 1959)
La dolce vita (It 1959)
La douceur de vivre (Fr 1960)
Boulevard (Fr 1960)
Le Sahara brûle (Fr 1960)
La Fille dans la vitrine (Fr-It 1960)
Dans la gueule du loup Gastone (It 1960)
Au boulets rouge (Fr 1961)
Jeunesse de nuit (Fr-It 1961)
Le Jeu de l'assassin (Fr-W Ger 1961)
La Loi de la guerre (It-Yug 1961)
L'Accident (Fr 1962)
Racconti proibiti...di niente vestiti (It 1973)
Amarcord (It 1973)
La braca di monate (It 1975)

NOIRET, PHILIPPE, b. Oct. 1, 1931, Lille, France
La Pointe courte (Fr 1955)
Zazie dans le metro (Fr 1960)
Ravissante (Fr-It 1960)
Le Capitaine Fracasse (Fr-It 1960)
Le Rendez-vous (Fr-It 1961)
Tout l'or du monde [All the Gold in the World] (Fr-It 1961)
Les Amours célèbres (ep "Lauzun") (Fr-It 1961)
La Crime ne paie pas [Crime Does Not Pay] (Fr-It 1962)
Comme un poisson dans l'eau (Fr 1962)
Cyrano et D'Artagnan (Sp-It-Fr 1962)
Thérèse Desqueyroux (Fr 1962)
Ballade pour un voyou (Fr 1962)
Les Masseuses (Fr 1962)
Clémentine chérie (Fr-It 1963)
La Porteuse de pain (Fr-It 1963)
Monsieur (Fr-W Ger-It 1964)
Les Copains (Fr 1964)
La Vie de château (Fr 1966)
Lady L (Fr-It 1966)
Tendre voyou (Fr-It 1966)
Les Sultans (Fr-It 1966)
Qui êtes-vous, Polly Magoo? (Fr 1966)
Le Voyage du père (Fr-It 1966)
The Night of the Generals (Col 1967)
Woman Times Seven (USA-Fr 1967)
Alexandre le bienheureux (Fr 1967)

Marc Porel (left), Philippe Noiret, and Roger Hanin in <u>Les Aveux</u>
<u>les plus doux</u> (1971).

L'Une et l'autre (Fr 1967)
Adolphe ou l'âge tendre (Fr 1968)
La Grand Lessive (Fr 1968)
Mister Freedom (Fr 1968)
The Assassination Bureau (Par 1969)
Topaz (Univ 1969)
Justine (20th 1969)
Mon oncle Benjamin (Fr-It 1969)
Clérambard (Fr 1969)
Andromac (Fr 1969)
Les Caprices de Marie [Give Her the Moon] (Fr-It 1969)
L'Etalon (Fr 1970)
Les Aveux les plus doux (Fr-Alg 1971)
La Vieille Fille [The Old Maid] (Fr-It 1971)
Le Trefle à cinq feuilles (Fr 1972)
L'Attenat [Plot] (Fr 1972)
Les Gaspards (Fr-Bel 1973)
La Grande Bouffe [The Big Blowout] (Fr-It 1973)
Touche pas la femme blanche (Fr 1973)
L'Horloger de Saint-Paul [The Watchmaker of Saint-Paul] (Fr
    1973)
Un Nuage entre les dents (Fr 1973)
Le Jeu avec le feu (Fr-It 1974)

Le Secret (Fr 1974)
Le Vieux Fusil (W Ger-Fr 1975)
Que la fête commence (Fr 1975)

NORIS, ASSIA (Anastasia Noris von Gerzfeld), b. Feb. 26, 1912,
    Petrograd, Russia
La signorina dell'autobus (It 1932)
Tre uomini in frak (It 1932)
Eve cherche un père (It 1933)
Et avec ça, papa... (Fr 1933)
La signorina dell'autobus (It 1933)
Giallo (It 1933)
Marcia nuziale (It 1934)
Quei due (It 1934)
Una donna fra due mondi (It 1935)
Darò un milione (It 1935)
Ma non è una cosa seria (It 1936)
Voglio vivere con Letizia! (It 1937)
Nina, non far la stupida (It 1937)
L'uomo che sorride (It 1937)
Il signor Max (It 1937)
Allegri masnadieri (It 1937)
La casa del peccato (It 1938)
Batticuore (It 1938)
Grandi magazzini (It 1939)
Dora Nelson (It 1939)
Centomila dollari (It 1939)
Una romantica avventura (It 1940)
Con le donne non si scherza (It 1941)
Luna di miele (It 1941)
Margherita fra i tre (It 1941)
Un colpo di pistola (It 1941)
Una storia d'amore (It 1942)
Le Voyageur de la Toussaint [Il viaggiatore di orgrissanti] (Fr-
    It 1942)
Le Capitaine Fracasse (Fr 1943)
Una piccola moglie (It 1943)
Che distinta famiglia! (It 1943)
Dieci minuti di vita (It 1943) [unreleased)
I dieci commandamenti (It 1945)
Amiena [La peccatria bianca] (Egyptian-It 1949)
La celestina (It 1965)

NOVELLI, AMLETO, b. Oct. 18, 1885, Bologna; d. April 16, 1924
Passione di Cristo (It 1909)
Gabrielle di Beaulieu (It 1909)
La nuova mammina (It 1909)
Il conte Ugolino (It 1909)
Calilena (It 1910)
Giovanni dalla bande nere (It 1910)
Giovanni la pallida (It 1910)
Il moro dell'Apuxarra (It 1911)
La rosa di Tebe (It 1912)

La spionatrice ambulante (It 1912)
Quo Vadis? (It 1912)
La Gerusalemme liberata (It 1913)
Marc' Antonio e Cleopatra (It 1913)
Scuolo di eroi (It 1913)
Cajus Julius Caesar (It 1914)

Amleto Novelli

Attenti alle spie! (It 1915)
Avatar (It 1915)
Fratelli d'Italia (It 1915)
L'Italia s'è desta (It 1915)
Ivan il terrible (It 1915)
Marcia nuziale (It 1915)
Christus (It 1916)
Madame Tallien (It 1916)
Malombra (It 1916)
La chiamavano cosetta (It 1916)
Fabiola (It 1917)
La maschera dell'amore (It 1917)
Uragano (It 1918)
Il voto (It 1918)
La piovra (It 1918)
Spiritesmo (It 1918)
Il padrone della ferriere (It 1918)

Beatrice (It 1919)
La figlia unica (It 1919)
L'onore della famiglia (It 1919)
L'ombra (It 1919)
Il mulino (It 1919)
Rabagas (It 1919)
La morte civile (It 1919)
Abbandono (It 1920)
Zingari (It 1920)
I tre amanti (It 1920)
La casa di vetro (It 1920)
La fugitiva (It 1920)
Fantasia bianca (It 1920)
Amore rosso (It 1921)
La preda (It 1921)
La fornace (It 1921)
Marthù che ha visto il diavolo (It 1922)
Dante nella vita dei tempi suoi (It 1922)
I dul foscari (It 1922)
Marco Visconti (It 1923)
L'ombra (It 1923)
La piccola parrocchia (It 1923)
Il povero fornaretto di Venezia (It 1923)
Il corsaro (It 1923)
La congiura di San Marco (It 1923)
Scuolo di eroi (It 1923)
La preda (It 1924)
La casa dei pulcini (It 1924)

OBERON, MERLE (Estelle Merle O'Brien-Thompson), b. Feb. 19,
    1911, Port Arthur, Tasmania
Alf's Button (Gaumont 1930)
Never Trouble Trouble (PDC 1931)
Fascination (Wardour 1931)
Service for Ladies [Reserved for Ladies] (Par Br 1932)
Ebb Tide (Par Br 1932)
Aren't We All? (Par Br 1932)
Wedding Rehearsal (Ideal 1932)
Men of Tomorrow (Par Br 1932)
For the Love of Mike (Wardour 1932)
The Private Life of Henry VIII (UA 1933)
The Battle [Thunder in the East/Hara-Kiri] (GB-Fr 1934)
The Broken Melody [Vagabond Violinist] (AP & D 1934)
The Private Life of Don Juan (UA 1934)
The Scarlet Pimpernel (UA 1935)
Folies Bergere (UA 1935)
The Dark Angel (UA 1935)
These Three (UA 1936)
Beloved Enemy (UA 1936)
I, Claudius (UA 1937) [unfinished]
Over the Moon (UA 1937)
The Divorce of Lady X (UA 1938)
The Cowboy and the Lady (UA 1938)

Wuthering Heights (UA 1939)
The Lion Has Wings (UA 1939)
'Til We Meet Again (WB 1940)
That Uncertain Feeling (UA 1941)
Affectionately Yours (WB 1941)
Lydia (UA 1941)
Forever and a Day (RKO 1943)
Stage Door Canteen (UA 1943)
First Comes Courage (UA 1943)
The Lodger (20th 1944)
Dark Waters (UA 1944)
A Song to Remember (Col 1945)
This Love of Ours (Univ 1945)
A Night in Paradise (Univ 1946)
Temptation (Univ 1946)
Night Song (RKO 1947)
Berlin Express (RKO 1948)
Pardon My French (UA 1951)
24 Hours of a Woman's Life [Affair in Monte Carlo] (ABP 1952)
Todo es possible en Granada (Sp 1954)
Desiree (20th 1954)
Deep in My Heart (MGM 1954)
The Price of Fear (Univ 1956)
Of Love and Desire (20th 1963)
The Oscar (Emb 1966)
Hotel (WB 1967)
Interval (Avco Emb 1973)

O'CONNOR, UNA, b. Oct. 23, 1893, Belfast; d. Feb. 4, 1959
    Dark Red Roses (BIFD 1929)
    Murder (Wardour 1930)
    To Oblige a Lady (BL 1931)
    Cavalcade (Fox 1933)
    Pleasure Cruise (Fox 1933)
    Mary Stevens M.D. (WB 1933)
    The Invisible Man (Univ 1933)
    Orient Express (Fox 1934)
    The Poor Rich (Univ 1934)
    All Men Are Enemies (Fox 1934)
    Stingaree (RKO 1934)
    The Barretts of Wimpole Street (MGM 1934)
    Chained (MGM 1934)
    Horseplay (Univ 1934)
    David Copperfield (MGM 1935)
    Father Brown--Detective (Par 1935)
    Bride of Frankenstein (Univ 1935)
    The Informer (RKO 1935)
    Thunder in the Night (Fox 1935)
    The Perfect Gentleman (MGM 1935)
    Little Lord Fauntleroy (UA 1936)
    Rose-Marie (MGM 1936)
    Suzy (MGM 1936)
    Lloyds of London (20th 1936)

The Plough and the Stars (RKO 1936)
Personal Property (MGM 1937)
Call It a Day (WB 1937)
The Adventures of Robin Hood (WB 1938)
We Are Not Alone (WB 1939)
His Brother's Keeper (FN Br 1939)
All Women Have Secrets (Par 1940)
It All Came True (WB 1940)
Lillian Russell (20th 1940)
The Sea Hawk (WB 1940)
He Stayed for Breakfast (Col 1940)
The Strawberry Blonde (WB 1941)
Her First Beau (Col 1941)
Three Girls About Town (Col 1941)
Always in My Heart (WB 1942)
My Favorite Spy (RKO 1942)
Random Harvest (MGM 1942)
This Land Is Mine (RKO 1943)
Forever and a Day (RKO 1943)
Holy Matrimony (20th 1943)
Government Girl (RKO 1943)
The Canterville Ghost (MGM 1944)
My Pal Wolf (RKO 1944)
Christmas in Connecticut [Indiscretion] (WB 1945)
The Bells of St. Mary's (RKO 1945)
Cluny Brown (20th 1946)
Of Human Bondage (WB 1946)
Child of Divorce (RKO 1946)
Unexpected Guest (UA 1946)
The Return of Monte Cristo (Col 1946)
Lost Honeymoon (EL 1947)
Banjo (RKO 1947)
Ivy (Univ 1947)
The Corpse Came C.O.D. (Col 1947)
Fighting Father Dunne (RKO 1948)
Adventures of Don Juan (WB 1949)
Witness for the Prosecution (UA 1957)

OGIER, BULLE, b. Aug. 9, 1939, Boulogne-Billancourt, France
Le Désordre a 20 ans (Fr 1965)
Les Idoles (Fr 1967)
L'Amour fou (Fr 1967)
48 Heures d'amour (Fr 1968)
Pierre et Paul (Fr 1968)
Prologue, suivi de piège (Fr 1968)
Paulina s'en va (Fr 1969)
M. comme Mathieu (Fr 1970)
Le Cinéma de Papa (Fr 1970)
Out One [after 1974 shortened version shown as Out 1: Spectre]
    (Fr 1970)
Stances à Sophie (Fr 1970)
La Salamandre (Swi 1970)
Rendez-vous à Bray (Fr-Bel 1971)

Bulle Ogier

La Vallée [The Valley Observed by Clouds] (Fr 1971)
Les Stances à Sophie (Fr-Canada 1971)
Georges qui? (Fr 1972)
Le Charme discret de la bourgeoisie [The Discreet Charm of
    the Bourgeoisie] (Fr 1972)
Le Gang des otages (Fr 1972)
Bel Ordure (Fr 1973)
Io e lui (It 1973)
Projection Privée (Fr 1973)
Un Ange au paradis (Fr 1973)
Flocons d'or [Goldflocken] (Fr-W Ger 1973)
Céline et Julie vont en bateau (Fr 1973)
La Paloma (Swi 1974)
Un Ange passe (Fr 1974)
Le Mariage (Fr 1974)
Un Divorce heureux (Fr-Dan 1975)
Les Filles du feu (I): Viva (Fr 1975)
Jamais plus toujours (Fr 1975)
La Doctoresse (Fr 1975)
Maîtresse (Fr 1975)

OLGUIM, MARIA (Maria Ciprinna Lobato Olguim), b. April 26, 1894,
    Castelo Branco, Portugal
Tinoco em Bolandas (Por 1922)
Ala-arriba (Por 1942)
O costa do castelo (Por 1943)
A menina da radio (Por 1944)
O hóspedo do quarto n.º 13 (Sp 1946)
Um homem do Ribatejo (Por 1946)
Os vizinhos do rés-do-chão (Por 1947)

Viela, a rua sem sol (Sp 1947)
O leão da estrela (Por 1947)
Não há rapazes maus (Por 1948)
Uma vida para dois (Por 1948)
Heróis do mar (Por 1949)
A morgadinha dos canaviais (Por 1949)
O vendaval maravilhoso (Por 1949)
A volta do José do telhado (Por 1949)
Sol e toiros (Por 1949)
Cantiga da rua (Por 1949)
Frei Luis de Sousa (Por 1950)
O grande elias (Por 1950)
Sonhar é fácil (Por 1951)
Saltimbancos (Por 1951)
Madragoa (Por 1951)
Nazaré (Por 1952)
Parabéns, Senhor Vicente (Sp 1954)
Vidas sem rumo (Por 1956)
O noivo das caldas (Por 1956)
O Tarzan do 5º esquerdo (Por 1958)
A costureirinha da sé (Por 1959)
O primo basilio (Por 1959)
Encontro com a vida (Por 1960)
A ribeira da saudade (Por 1961)
Retalhos da vida um de medico (Por 1962)
O crime de aldeia velha (Por 1964)
O trigo e o jóio (Por 1965)
Letagão esgotada (Por 1972)

Eduardo de Oliveira Martins

OLIVEIRA MARTINS, EDUARDO DE, b. June 13, 1911, Lisbon
   Lisboa, crónica anedótica (Por 1930)
   Maria do mar (Por 1930)
   A severa (Por 1931)
   As pupilas do Senhor Reitor (Por 1935)
   Bocage (Por 1936)
   A rosa do adro (Por 1938)
   A varanda dos rouxinois (Por 1939)
   Fátima, terra de fé (Por 1943)
   Viela, a rua sem sol (Por 1947)

OLIVIER, LAURENCE, b. May 22, 1907, Dorking, Surrey, England
   Too Many Crooks (Fox 1930)
   The Temporary Widow (Ger-GB 1930)
   Potiphar's Wife [Her Strange Desire] (FN-P 1931)
   The Yellow Ticket (Fox 1931)
   Friends and Lovers (RKO 1931)
   Westward Passage (RKO 1931)
   Perfect Understanding (UA 1933)
   No Funny Business (UA 1933)
   Moscow Nights [I Stand Condemned] (GFD 1935)
   As You Like It (20th Br 1936)
   Fire Over England (UA 1937)
   The Divorce of Lady X (UA 1938)
   Q Planes [Clouds Over Europe] (Col Br 1939)
   Wuthering Heights (UA 1939)
   21 Days [21 Days Together] (Col Br 1939) [made in 1937]
   Rebecca (UA 1940)
   Conquest of the Air (UA 1940) [started ca. 1936]
   Pride and Prejudice (MGM 1940)
   Lady Hamilton [That Hamilton Woman] (UA 1941)
   49th Parallel [The Invaders] (GFD 1941)
   The Demi-Paradise [Paradise for Two] (GFD 1943)
   Henry V (EL 1945)
   Hamlet (GFD 1948)
   The Magic Box (BL 1951)
   Carrie (Par 1952)
   A Queen Is Crowned (RFD 1953) [documentary] (part commenta-
      tor)
   The Beggar's Opera (BL 1953)
   Richard III (IFD 1955)
   The Prince and the Showgirl (WB 1957)
   The Devil's Disciple (UA 1959)
   The Entertainer (Bry 1960)
   Spartacus (Univ 1960)
   The Power and the Glory (Par 1962)
   Term of Trial (WPD 1962)
   Bunny Lake Is Missing (Col 1965)
   Othello (Eagle 1965)
   Khartoum (UA 1966)
   Romeo and Juliet (Par 1968) (voice only)
   The Shoes of the Fisherman (MGM 1968)
   Oh! What a Lovely War (Par 1969)

Sir Laurence Olivier (left), Anthony Nicholls and Maggie Smith in Othello (1965).

Battle of Britain (UA 1969)
The Dance of Death (Par 1969)
David Copperfield (20th 1969)
Three Sisters (BL 1970)
Nicholas and Alexandra (Col 1971)
Lady Caroline Lamb (GB-It 1972)
Sleuth (Fox-Rank 1973)

ONDRA, ANNY (Anny Ondrakova), b. March 15, 1903, Tarnow,
    Poland
Führe uns nicht in Versuchung (Aus 1922)
Hütet eure Töchter (Aus 1922)
Zigeunerliebe (Aus 1922)
Der Mann ohne Herz (Ger 1923)
Ich liebe Dich (Ger 1925)
Trude, die Sechzehnjährige (Ger 1926)
Pratermizzi (Aus 1927)
Seine Hoheit, der Eintänzer (Ger 1927)
Der erste Kuss (Ger 1928)
Evas Töchter (Ger 1928)
Saxophon-Susi (Ger 1928)
Die Kaviarprinzessin (Ger 1928)
Das Mädel mit der Peitsche (Ger 1929)
Sündig und süss (Ger 1929)
The Manxman (Wardour 1929)
Blackmail (Wardour 1929)
Das Mädel aus USA (Ger 1930)
Die grosse Sehnsucht (Ger 1930)
Eine Freudin so goldig wie Du (Ger 1930)
Die vom Rummelplatz (Ger 1930)
Er und seine Schwester (Ger 1930)
Mamsell Nitouche (Ger 1931)
Die Fledermaus (Ger 1931)
La Canse-souris [Fr version of Die Fledermaus] (Ger 1931)
Baby [also Fr version] (Ger-Fr 1932)
Kiki [also Fr version] (Ger 1932)
Die grausame Freudin (Ger 1932)
Faut-il les marier? [Fr version of Die grausame Freudin] (Ger
    1932)
Eine Nacht im Paradies (Ger 1932)
Une Nuit au paradis [Fr version of Eine Nacht im Paradies]
    (Ger 1932)
Die Tochter des Regiments (Ger-Aus 1933)
La Fille du regiment [Fr version of Die Tochter des Regiments]
    (Ger-Aus 1933)
Betragen ungenügend (Ger-Czech 1933)
Das verliebte Hotel (Ger 1933)
Fräulein Hoffmanns Erzählungen (Ger 1933)
Klein Dorrit (Ger 1934)
Polen blut (Ger 1934)
Die vertauschte Braut (Ger 1934)
L'Amour en cage [Fr version of Die vertauschte Braut] (Ger 1934)
Grossreinemachen (Ger 1934)

Der junge Graf (Ger 1935)
Knockout (Ger 1935)
Flitterwochen (Ger 1936)
Ein Mädel vom Ballett (Ger 1937)
Donogoo Tonka (Ger 1936)
Vor Liebe wird gewarnt (Ger 1937)
Der Unwiderstehliche (Ger 1937)
Der Scheidungsgrund (Ger 1937)
Narren im Schnee (Ger 1938)
Der Gasmann (Ger 1941)
Himmel, wir erben ein Schloss (Ger 1943)
Schön muss man sein (W Ger 1951)

OSWALDA, OSSI, b. Feb. 2, 1899, Berlin; d. Jan. 1, 1948
Der GmbH-Tenor (Ger 1916)
Nacht des Grauens (Ger 1916)
Schuhpalast Pinkus (Ger 1916)
Ein fideles Gefängnis (Ger 1917)
Osis Tagebuch (Ger 1917)
Prinz Sami (Ger 1917)
Wenn vier dasselbe tun (Ger 1917)
Der Fall Rosentopf (Ger 1917)
Das Mädchen vom Ballett (Ger 1917)
Meine Frau, die Filmschauspielerin (Ger 1918)
Der Rodelkavalier (Ger 1918)
Die Austernprinzessin (Ger 1919)
Die Puppe (Ger 1919)
Schwabemädle (Ger 1920)

Ossi Oswalda

Die Millionenerbschaft (Ger 1920)
Der blinde Passagier (Ger 1921)
Das Mädel mir der Maske (Ger 1922)
Das Milliardensouper (Ger 1923)
Colibri (Ger 1924)
Niniche (Ger 1924)
Blitzzug der Liebe (Ger 1925)
Herrn Filip Collins Abenteuer (Ger 1926)
Das Mädchen mit Protektion (Ger 1926)
De Fahrt ins Abenteuer (Ger 1926)
Gräfin Plättmamsell (Ger 1926)
Die Kleine vom Varieté (Ger 1926)
Das Mädchen auf der Schaukel (Ger 1926)
Schatz, mach' Kasse (Ger 1926)
Eine tolle Nacht (Ger 1926)
Es zogen dre Burschen (Ger 1926)
Frühere Verhältnissen (Ger 1927)
Ein schwerer Fall (Ger 1927)
Wochenendbraut (Ger 1927)
Eddy Polo mit Pferd und Lasso (Ger 1927)
Das Haus ohne Männer (Ger 1928)
Ossi hat die Hosen an (Ger 1928)
Die Vierte von rechts (Ger 1929)
Der Dieb im Schlafcoupe (Ger 1929)
Der keusche Joseph (Ger 1930)
Stern von Valencia (Ger 1933)

O'TOOLE, PETER, b. Aug. 2, 1932, Connemara, Co. Galway, Ireland
Kidnapped (BV 1960)
The Day They Robbed the Bank of England (MGM 1960)
The Savage Innocents (Par 1961)
Lawrence of Arabia (Col 1962)
Becket (Par 1964)
Lord Jim (Col 1965)
What's New, Pussycat? (USA-Fr 1965)
La Bibbia [The Bible...In the Beginning] (It-USA 1966)
How to Steal a Million (20th 1966)
The Night of the Generals (Col 1967)
Great Catherine (WPD 1968)
The Lion in Winter (Avco Emb 1969)
Goodbye, Mr. Chips (MGM 1969)
Murphy's War (London Screen 1970)
Country Dance [Brotherly Love] (MGM-EMI 1971) [made in 1969]
Under Milk Wood (RFD 1972)
The Ruling Class (UA 1972)
Man of La Mancha (It 1972)
Rosebud (UA 1975)
Man Friday (Avco Emb 1975)

PACHECO, ASSIS (Arnaldo da Silva Pacheco), b. Dec. 3, 1903, Lisbon
O amor de perdição (Por 1943)

Peter O'Toole and Katharine Hepburn in The Lion in Winter (1969).

A ave de arribação (Por 1944)
Um homem do Ribatejo (Por 1946)
Camoēs (Por 1946)
Não há rapazes maus (Por 1948)
Uma vida para dois (Por 1948)
Heróis do mar (Por 1949)
Madragoa (Por 1951)
Duas causas (Por 1952)

PAGANO, BARTOLOMEO (Maciste), b. Sept. 27, 1878, Genoa; d.
    July 24, 1947
Cabiria (It 1914)
Maciste (It 1915)
Maciste alpino (It 1916)
Maciste bersagliere (It 1916)
Maciste atleta (It 1917)
Maciste poliziotto (It 1917)
Maciste medium (It 1917)
Maciste sonnambulo (It 1918)
Maciste Iº (It 1919)
La rivincita di Maciste (It 1919)
La trilogia di Maciste (It 1919)
Il viaggio di Maciste e Il testamento di Maciste (It 1919)
Maciste innamorato (It 1919)
Maciste in vacanza (It 1920)

Assis Pacheco

Maciste salvato dalle acque (It 1920)
Maciste e la figlia de re della Plato (Ger-It 1922)
Maciste und die chinesische Truhe (Ger 1923)
Maciste contro Maciste (Ger 1923)
Maciste e il nipote d'America (It 1924)
Maciste imperatore (It 1924)
Maciste contro lo sceicco (It 1925)
Maciste all'inferno (It 1926)
Il gigante delle Dolomiti (It 1926)
Maciste nella gabbia dei leoni (It 1926)
Il vetturale del Moncenisio (It 1927)
Gli ultimi zar (It 1928)
  Giuditta e Oloferne (It 1928)

PAGLIERO, MARCELLO, b. Jan. 15, 1907, London
Roma, città aperta (It 1945)
L'altra (It 1947)
Les Jeux sont faits [The Chips Are Down] (Fr 1947)
Dédée d'Anvers [Dedee] (Fr 1948)
La Voix du rêve (Fr 1948)
Tourbillon (Fr 1953)
Vergine moderna (It 1954)
Seven Thunders [The Beats of Marseilles] (RFD 1957)
Les Mauvais Coups [Naked Autumn] (Fr 1961)
Ton ombre est la mienne [Your Shadow Is Mine] (Fr 1962)
Je vous salue, Maffia [Da New York: Mafia uccide] (Fr-It 1965)
Nick Carter et le trefle rouge [Nick Carter e il trifoglio rosso]
  (Fr-It 1965)

Les Gauboises bleues (Fr 1967)

PALMER, LILLI (Maria Lilli Peiser), b. March 12, 1914, Posen,
    Germany
    Bad Blood (Br 1935)
    Crime Unlimited (WB-Br 1935)
    First Offence (Gaumont 1936)
    Wolf's Clothing (Univ Br 1936)
    The Secret Agent (Gaumont 1936)
    Good Morning, Boys [Where There's a Will] (Gaumont 1937)
    The Great Barrier [Silent Barriers] (Gaumont 1937)
    Sunset in Vienna [Suicide Legion] (GFD 1937)
    Command Performance (GFD 1937)
    Crackerjack [The Man with a Hundred Faces] (GFD 1938)
    A Girl Must Live (20th Br 1939)
    Blind Folly (RKO Br 1939)
    The Door with Seven Locks [Chamber of Horrors] (Pathe 1940)
    Thunder Rock (MGM Br 1940)
    The Gentle Sex (GFD 1943)
    English without Tears [Her Man Gilbey] (GFD 1944)
    The Rake's Progress [A Notorious Gentleman] (EL 1945)
    Beware of Pity (EL 1946)
    Cloak and Dagger (WB 1946)
    Body and Soul (UA 1947)
    My Girl Tisa (WB 1947)
    No Minor Vices (MGM 1948)

Lilli Palmer and Herbert Lom in Murders in the Rue Morgue (1972).

Hans le marin [The Wicked City] (Fr 1949)
The Long Dark Hall (BL 1951)
Pictura, Adventures in Art (Pictura Pictures 52) (co-narrator)
The Four Poster (Col 1952)
Main Street to Broadway (MGM 1953)
Feuerwerk [Oh! My Pa-Pa] (W Ger 1954)
Teufel in Seide (W Ger 1955)
Anastasia, die letzten Zarentochter [Is Anna Anderson Anastasia?]
    (W Ger 1956)
Zwischen Zeit und Ewigkeit [Entre hoy y la eternidad/Between
    Time and Eternity] (W Ger-Sp 1956)
Wie ein Sturmwind [Tempestuous Love/The Night of the Storm]
    (W Ger 1957)
Der glaserne Turm [The Glass Tower] (W Ger 1957)
La Vie à deux [Life Together] (Fr 1957)
Eine Frau, die weiss, was sie will (W Ger 1958)
Mädchen in Uniform [Jeunes Filles en Uniforme] (W Ger-Fr
    1958)
Montparnasse 19 [Montparnasse/Modigliani of Montparnasse/The
    Lovers of Montparnasse] (Fr-It 1958)
But Not for Me (Par 1959)
Conspiracy of Hearts (RFD 1960)
Frau Warrens Gewerbe (W Ger 1960)
Frau Cheney's Ende [La Mystèrieuse Madame Cheney] (W Ger-
    Fr 1961)
The Pleasure of His Company (Par 1961)
Léviathan (Fr 1961)
Le Rendezvous de minuit [Rendezvous at Midnight] (Fr 1961)
Julia, Du bist zauberhaft [Adorable Julia/Seduction of Julia] (W
    Ger-Aus-Fr 1962)
The Counterfeit Traitor (Par 1962)
Finden Sie, dass Constanze sich richtig verhalt? (W Ger 1962)
Finchè dura la tempesta [Beta Som/Torpedo Bay] (It 1962)
Erotica [L'Amore difficle] (ep "Il Serpente") (W Ger-It 1963)
Das Grosse Liebesspiel [And So to Bed] (W Ger-Aus 1963)
The Miracle of the White Stallion (BV 1964)
Ein Frauenarzt Klagt an (W Ger 1964)
Die letzten Zwei von Rio Bravo (W Ger 1964)
Le Grain de sable [Die Unmoralischen/Il triangolo Circolare]
    (Fr-W Ger-It 1964)
The Amorous Adventures of Moll Flanders (Par 1965)
Operation Crossbow (The Great Spy Mission/Operazione Cross-
    bow] (MGM 1965)
Le Tonnerre de Dieu [Herr auf Schloss Brassac/Matrimonis alla
    francese] (Fr-W Ger-It 1965)
Zwei Girls vom roten Stern [Duel à la vodka] (W Ger-Aus 1966)
Der Kongress amüsiert sich [Le Congrès s'amuse] (W Ger-Aus-
    Fr 1966)
Le Voyage du père [Destinazione Marciaprede] (Fr-It 1966)
Paarungen (W Ger-Aus 1967)
Jack of Diamonds (W Ger-MGM 1967)
Sebastian (Par Br 1967)
Oedipus the King (RFD 1967)

Nobody Runs Forever [The High Commissioner] (RFD 1968)
Hard Contract (20th 1969)
DeSade (AIP 1969)
La Peau de torpedo [Der Mann mit der Torpedo hant] (Fr-W
   Ger 1969)
La residencia [The House that Screamed] (Sp 1970)
Hauser's Memory (NBC-TV 1970)
Murders in the Rue Morgue (AIP 1972)
Night Hair Child (RFD 1973) [made in 1971]
Lotte in Weimar (E Ger 1974)

PARLO, DITA, b. Sept. 4, 1906, Stettin, Germany; d. Dec. 1,
   1972
Die Dame mit der Maske (Ger 1928)
Geheimnisse des Orients (Ger 1928)
Heimkehr (Ger 1929)
Ungarische Rhapsodie (Ger 1929)
Manolescu (Ger 1929)
Melodie des Herzens (Ger 1929)
Au bonheur des dames (Fr 1929)
Menschen hinter Gittern [Ger version of The Big House] (Ger
   1930)
Kismet (Ger 1930)
Tropennächte (Ger 1931)
Wir schalten um auf Hollywood [Ger version of Hollywood Revue
   of 1929] (Ger 1931)
Die heilige Flamme (Ger 1931)
Tanzerinnen für Sud-Amerika gesucht (Ger 1931)
Honor of the Family [Mister Broadway] (WB 1933)
L'Atalante (Fr 1934)
Rapt (Fr-Swi 1934)
Mademoiselle docteur (Fr 1937)
La Grande Illusion (Fr 1937)
L'Affaire du courrier de Lyon [Courier of Lyons] (Fr 1937)
L'Inconnue de Monte-Carlo (Fr 1938)
Paix sur le Rhin (Fr 1938)
La Rue sans joie (Fr 1938)
Ultimatum (Fr 1938)
L'Or du Cristobal (Fr 1939)
Justice est faite (Fr 1950)
Quand le Soleil Montera (Fr 1956)
La Dame de pique (Fr 1965)

PATRICK, NIGEL (Nigel Wemyss), b. May 2, 1913, London
Mrs. Pym of Scotland Yard (GN 1939)
Spring in Park Lane (BL 1948)
Uneasy Terms (Pathe 1948)
Noose [The Silk Noose] (Pathe 1948)
Silent Dust (ABP 1949)
The Jack of Diamonds (Ex 1949)
The Perfect Woman (GFD 1949)
Morning Departure [Operation Disaster] (GFD 1950)
Trio (ep "Mr. Knowall") (GFD 1950)

Pandora and the Flying Dutchman (IFD 1951)
The Browning Version (GFD 1951)
Young Wives' Tale (ABP 1951)
Encore (ep "The Ant and the Grasshopper") (GFD 1951)
Who Goes There? [The Passionate Beauty] (BL 1952)
The Sound Barrier [Breaking the Sound Barrier] (BL 1952)
Meet Me Tonight (ep "Ways and Means") (GFD 1952)
The Pickwick Papers (Renown 1952)
Grand National Night [Wicked Wife] (Renown 1953)
Forbidden Cargo (GFD 1954)
The Sea Shall Not Have Them (Eros 1954)
A Prize of Gold (Col 1955)
All for Mary (RFD 1955)
How to Murder a Rich Uncle (Col 1957)
Count Five and Die (20th 1958)
The Man Inside (Col 1958)
Sapphire (RFD 1959)
The League of Gentlemen (RFD 1960)
The Trials of Oscar Wilde [The Man with the Green Carnation]
   (Eros 1960)
Johnny Nobody (Col 1961)
The Informers [Underworld Informers] (RFD 1963)
Battle of Britain (UA 1969)
The Virgin Soldiers (Col Br 1969)
The Executioner (Col 1970)
Tales from the Crypt (ep "Blind Alleys") (Cin 1972)
The Great Waltz (MGM 1972)
The Mackintosh Man (WB 1973)

PENELLA, EMMA (Ruiz Penella), b. 1930, Madrid
Barce, sin rumbe (Sp 1950)
Los ojos dejan huellas (Sp 1952)
Comicos (Sp 1952)
Los peces rojos (Sp 1955)
Fedra (Sp 1956)
Un marido de ida y vuelta (Sp 1956)
La guerra empieza en Cuba (Sp 1957)
De espaldas a la puerta (Sp 1959)
Un Angel tuvo la culpa (Sp 1959)
Sentencia contra una mujer (Sp 1960)
El amor de los amores (Sp 1961)
Carta a una mujer (Sp 1961)
La cuarta ventana (Sp 1961)
Alegre juventud (Sp 1962)
Scana Boa (Sp-It 1962)
El verduo (Sp-It 1963)
Dios Eligio sus viajeros (Sp 1963)
Duelo en al Amazonas (W Ger-Fr-Sp 1965)
Lola, espejo oscure (Sp 1965)
La muerte viaja demasiado (Fr-It-Sp 1965)
La busca (Sp 1966)
Fortunata y Jacinta (Sp 1969)
La primera entrega (It-Sp 1971)

PEREIRA, MARIO, b. May 12, 1934, Barreiro
  O homem do dia (Por 1958)
  A luz vem do alto (Por 1959)
  Um dia de vida (Por 1962)
  O crime de aldeia velha (Por 1964)
  O trigo e o joio (Por 1965)
  Uma vontade maior (Por 1966)
  Sarilho de fraldas (Por 1966)
  Gil Vicente e seu teatro (Por 1966)
  Traição inverosimil (Por 1971)

PETERS, WERNER, b. 1918, Werlitzsch, Germany; d. March 31,
  1971
  Affäre Blum (E Ger 1948)
  Der Biberpelz (W Ger 1948)
  Die Buntkarierten (W Ger 1948)
  Rotation (E Ger 1949)
  Der Kahn der fröhlichen Leute (W Ger 1949)
  Karriere in Paris (W Ger 1951)
  Modell Bianka (W Ger 1951)
  Der Untertan (E Ger 1952)
  Anna Susanna (W Ger 1952)
  Die Unbesiegbaren (W Ger 1952)
  Die Geschichte vom kleinen Muck (W Ger 1953)
  Ernst Thälmann--Sohn seiner Klasse (E Ger 1954)
  Der 20. Juli (W Ger 1955)
  Ernst Thalmann--Führer seiner Klasse (W Ger 1955)
  Sommerliebe (W Ger 1955)
  Der Teufel vom Mühlenberg (W Ger 1955)
  Ein Polterabend (W Ger 1955)
  Star mit fremden Federn (W Ger 1955)
  Hotel Adlon (W Ger 1955)
  Vor Gott und den Menschen (W Ger 1956)
  Anastasia, die letzte Zarentochter (W Ger 1956)
  Das Sonntagskind (W Ger 1956)
  Die Stimme der Sehnsucht (W Ger 1956)
  Spion für Deutschland (W Ger 1956)
  Ein Abenteuer aus 1001 Nacht (W Ger 1956)
  Nachts wenn der Teufel Kam (W Ger 1957)
  Das Herz von St. Pauli (W Ger 1957)
  Madeleine und der Legionär (W Ger 1958)
  Der Greifer (W Ger 1958)
  Lilli--Ein Mädchen aus der Grosstadt (W Ger 1958)
  Schmutziger Engel (W Ger 1958)
  Grabenplatz 17 (W Ger 1958)
  Liebe kann wie Gift Sein (W Ger 1958)
  Blitzmädels an die Front (W Ger 1958)
  Das Mädchen Rosemarie (W Ger 1958)
  Unruhige Nacht (W Ger 1958)
  13 kleine Esel und der Sonnenhof (W Ger 1958)
  Meine 99 Bräute (W Ger 1958)
  Romarei--Das Mädchen mit den grünen Augen (W Ger 1959)
  Die feuerrote Baronesse (W Ger 1959)

Kriegsgericht (W Ger 1959)
Jons und Erdme (W Ger 1959)
Bobby Dodd greift ein (W Ger 1959)
Keheimaktion Schwarze Kapelle (W Ger 1959)
Rosen für den Staatsanwalt (W Ger 1959)
Der Schatz vom Toplitzsee (W Ger 1959)
Strafbataillon 999 (W Ger 1959)
Die 1000 Augen des Dr. Mabuse (W Ger 1960)
Gauner in Uniform (W Ger-Aus 1960)
Schüsse im Morgengrauen (W Ger 1960)
Endstation "Rote Laterne" (W Ger 1960)
Denn das Weib ist schwacht (W Ger 1960)
Es muss nicht immer Kaviar sein (W Ger 1961)
The Counterfeit Traitor (Par 1961)
Diesmal muss es Kaviar sein (W Ger 1961)
Im Stahlnetz des Mabuse (W Ger 1961)
Unter Ausschluss der Öffentlichkeit (W Ger 1962)
Teppich des Grauens [Terror en la noche/Le terrore di notte]
    (W Ger-It-Sp 1962)
Die Türe mit den sieben Schlössern (W Ger 1962)
Die unsichtbaren Krallen des Dr. Mabuse (W Ger 1962)
Die endlose Nacht (W Ger 1962)
Das Feuerschiff (W Ger 1963)
Der Flucht der gelben Schlange (W Ger 1963)
Hipnosis [Ipnosi/Nur tote Zeugen schweigen] (Sp-It-W Ger 1963)
Das Geheimnis der schwarzen Witwie (W Ger-It-Sp 1963)
Der schwarze Abt (W Ger 1963)
Scotland Yard jagt Dr. Mabuse (W Ger 1963)
Die weisse Spinne (W Ger 1963)
Einer frisst den anderen [La morte vestita di dollari/Dog Eat
    Dog] (W Ger-It-USA 1964)
Die Gruft mit dem Rätselschloos (W Ger 1964)
Das Phantom von Soho (W Ger-Sp 1964)
Durchs wilde Kurdistan (W Ger-Sp 1964)
Die schwarzen Adler von Sante Fe (W Ger-Sp 1965)
Die Hölle von Macao [Les Corrompus/Il sigillo di Pechino/The
    Peking Medallion] (W Ger-It-Fr 1965)
Lotosblüten für Miss Quon (W Ger-It-Fr 1966)
Die Zeugin aus der Hölle (W Ger-Yug 1966)
Geheimnisse in goldenen Nylons [Deux Billets pour Mexico/Dead
    Run] (W Ger-It-Fr 1967)
Zucker für den Mörder [Un killer persua maestrà/Le Tueur
    aime les bonbons] (W Ger-It 1968)
Blonde Möder für den Mörder [La morte bussa due volte) (W
    Ger-It 1970)
Perrak (W Ger 1970)
Unter den Dächern von St. Pauli (W Ger 1970)
Die Tote aus der Themse (W Ger 1971)

PETIT, PASCALE (Anne-Marie Petit), b. Feb. 27, 1938
    Les Sorcières de Salem (Fr-It-W Ger 1956)
    Les Tricheurs [Youthful Sinners] (Fr-It 1958)
    Une Vie [End of Desire] (Fr-It 1958)

Faibles Femmes [Women Are Weak] (Fr-It 1959)
Julie la rousse (Fr 1959)
Une Fille pour l'été (Fr-It 1960)
Vers l'extase (Fr 1960)
L'Affaire d'une nuit [Night Affair] (Fr 1960)
La Novice (Fr-It 1960)
Le Démons de minuit (Fr-It 1961)
Bande de lâches (Fr-It 1961)
La Croix des vivants [The Cross of the Living] (Fr 1961)
Una regina per Cesare [A Queen for Caesar] (It-Fr 1962)
Comment épouser un premier ministre (Fr-It 1964)
Corrida pour un espion [The Spy Who Went Into Hell] (Fr-Sp-W Ger 1965)
Zwei Girls vom Roton Stern (W Ger-Fr-Aus 1966)
Un Soir à Tibériade (Fr-Israel 1966)
Gern hab' ich die Frauen gekillt [Killer's Carnival] (Aus-It-Fr 1966)
Suezanne--die Wirtin von der Lahn (Aus-It-Hun 1967)
Der Kommandant vom Molinette/Fast ein Held (W Ger-Yug 1967)
Mieux faire l'amour (Fr-It 1968)
Il mercenario (It-Sp 1968)
Joe--cercati un posto per morire [Joe--Go Find a Place to Die] (It 1968)
Suzanne à la coeur du roi (Fr-Aus 1969)
Die Weibchen (Fr-It-W Ger 1971)

PHILIPE, GERARD, b. Dec. 4, 1922, Cannes; d. Nov. 25, 1959
Les Petites du Quai aux Fleurs (Fr 1943)
La Boîte aux rêves (Fr 1945)
Le Pays sans étoiles (Fr 1945)
L'Idiot (Fr 1946)
Ouvert pour cause d'inventaire (Fr 1946)
Le Diable au corps (Fr-It 1947)
La Chartreuse de Parme (Fr 1948)
Une si jolie petite plage [Such a Jolly Little Beach] (Fr 1949)
Tout es les chemins mènent à Rome (Fr 1949)
Juliette, ou la clé des sanges (Fr 1950)
La Beauté du diable [Beauty and the Beast] (Fr-It 1950)
La Ronde [Circle of Love] (Fr 1950)
Souvenirs perdus (Fr 1950)
Fanfan, le tulipe (Fr-It 1951)
Les Belles de nuit (Fr-It 1952)
Les Sept Péchés capitaux (Fr-It 1952)
Villa Borghèse (It-Fr 1953)
Les Orgeilleux [The Proud Ones] (Fr-Mex 1953)
Si Versailles m'était conté (Fr 1953)
Knave of Hearts [Lovers, Happy Lovers] (ABP 1954)
Le Rouge et le noir [Scarlet and Black] (Fr-It 1954)
Si Paris nous était conté (Fr 1955)
La Meilleure Part (Fr-It 1955)
Les Grandes Manoeuvres [Summer Manoeuvres] (Fr-It 1955)
Les Aventures de Till l'Espiègle (Fr-Dut 1956)
Montparnasse 19 (Fr-It 1957)

La Vie à deux (Fr 1958)
Le Joueur [The Gambler] (Fr-It 1958)
Liasons dangereuses (Fr-It 1959)
La Fievre monte à El Paso (Fr-Mex 1960)

PICA, TINA (Concetta Annunziata Pica), b. March 31, 1884, Naples;
   d. 1968
Il delietto di San Giovanni a Teduccio (It 1933) [destroyed]
Il cappello a tre punte (It 1934)
Fermo con le mani (It 1937)
L'ha fatto una signora (It 1939)
Terra di nessuno (It 1939)
Sperduti nel buio (It 1947)
Proibito rubare (It 1948)
Fiamme sulla laguna (It 1949)
Il voto (It 1950)
Destino (It 1951)
Filumena Marturano (It 1951)
Porca miseria (It 1951)
La città canora (It 1952)
Marito e moglie (It 1952)
Processo alla città (It 1952)
I sette peccati capitali (It 1952)
Ergastolo (It 1952)
...e Napoli canta (It 1953)
Pane, amore e fantasia (It 1953)
Rimorso (It 1953)
Carosello napoletano (It 1953)
Siamo ricchi e poveri (It 1953)
L'oro di Napoli (ep "Il professore") (It 1954)
Pane, amore e gelosia (It 1954)
Ballata tragica (It 1954)
Cuore di mamma (It 1954)
Le signore dello 04 (It 1954)
Buonanotte...avvocato! (It 1955)
Destinazione Piovarolo (It 1955)
Le due orfanelle (It 1955)
Due soldi di felicità (It 1955)
Un eroe dei nostri tempi (It 1955)
Graziella (It 1955)
Io piaccio (It 1955)
Pane, amore e... (It 1955)
Piscatore è Posilleco (It 1955)
Il segno di Venere (It 1955)
Totò e Carolina (It 1955)
Cantate con noi (It 1955)
Da qui all'eredità (It 1955)
Un po' di cielo (It 1955)
Ci sposeremo a Capri (It 1956)
Napoli, sole mio! (It 1956)
Una pelliccia di visone (It 1956)
Arriva la zia d'America (It 1957)
Era di venerdi 17 (It 1957)

Il conte Max (It 1957)
Lazzarella (It 1957)
La nonna Sabella (It 1957)
La zia d'America va a sciare (It 1957)
E permesso maresciallo? (It 1958)
Fantasmi e ladri (It 1958)
La Pica sul Pacifico (It 1958)
La nipote Sabella (It 1958)
Mia nonna poliziotto (It 1958)
Non sono più guaglione (It 1958)
Amaramente (It 1959)
La duchessa di Santa Lucia (It 1959)
Non perdiamo la testa (It 1959)
La sceriffa (It 1959)
Il bacio del sole (It 1961)
Che femmina!...e che dolori! (It 1961)
Ieri, oggi, domani [Yesterday, Today and Tomorrow] (ep "Mara")
    (It 1963)

PICCOLI, MICHEL, b. Dec. 27, 1925, Paris
Le Point du jour (Fr 1949)
Parfum de la dame en noir (Fr 1949)
Sans laisser d'adresse (Fr 1950)
Rafles sur la ville [Trap for a Killer] (Fr 1953)
Interdit de séjour [The Price of Love] (Fr 1954)
French Can-Can (Fr-It 1954)
Tout chante autour de moi (Fr 1954)
Les Mauvaises Rencontres (Fr 1955)
Ernst Thaelmann, Führer seiner Klasse (E Ger 1955)
Marie Antoinette [Shadow of the Guillotine] (Fr-It 1955)
Le Mort en ce jardin [Evil Eden] (Fr-Mex 1956)
Les Sorcières de Salem [The Witches of Salem] (Fr-E Ger 1956)
Sylviane de Mes Nuits (Fr 1956)
Nathalie [The Foxiest Girl in Paris] (Fr-It 1957)
Tabarin (Fr-It 1958)
La Bête à l'affût (Fr 1959)
La Dragée haute (Fr 1959)
Le Bal des espions (Fr 1960)
Les Rendez-vous (Fr-It 1961)
La Chevelure (Fr 1961)
Le vergini di Roma (It-Fr-Yug 1961)
Climats [Climates of Love] (Fr 1962)
Le Doulos (Fr 1962)
Le Jour et l'heure [The Day and the Hour] (Fr-It 1962)
Le Mépris [Contempt] (Fr-It 1963)
Le Journal d'une femme de chambre [Diary of a Chambermaid]
    (Fr-It 1963)
La Chance et l'amour (Fr-It 1964)
Marie-Soleil (Fr 1964)
De l'amour [All About Loving] (Fr-It 1965)
Le Coup de grâce (Fr 1965)
Lady L (Fr-It 1965)
Compartiment tueurs [The Sleeping Car Murders] (Fr 1965)

Michel Piccoli in Les Choses de la vie (1970).

Les Ruses du diable (Fr 1965)
Les Créatures (Fr-Swe 1966)
Paris brûle-t-il? [Is Paris Burning?] (Fr 1966)
La Curée [The Game Is Over] (Fr-It 1966)
Les Demoiselles de Rochefort [The Young Girls of Rochefort]
  (Fr 1967)
Un Homme de trop [Shock Troops] (Fr-It 1967)
La Guerre est finie [The War Is Over] (Fr-Swe 1967)
La Voleuse (Fr-W Ger 1967)
Belle de Jour (Fr-It 1968)
Benjamin (Fr 1968)
Diabolik [Danger Diabolik] (It 1968)
Mon amour, mon amour (Fr 1968)
La Chamade [Heartbeat] (Fr-It 1968)
La Prisonnière [Women in Chains] (Fr-It 1968)
La Voie lactée [The Milky Way] (Fr-It 1968)
Dillinger è morto [Dillinger Is Dead] (It 1968)
Topaz (Univ 1969)
Gli invitati (It 1969)
Les Choses de la vie [The Things of Life] (Fr-It 1970)
L'invasione [The Invasion] (It-Fr 1970)
Max et les ferrailleurs (Fr 1970)
La Poudre d'escampette (Fr 1971)
La Décade prodigieuse [Ten Days Wonder] (Fr 1971)
L'udienza [The Audience] (It 1972)

Le Charme discret de la bourgeoisie [The Discreet Charm of
    the Bourgeoisie] (Fr-Sp-It 1972)
L'Attenat [The Plot] (Fr-It-W Ger 1972)
Themroc (Fr 1973)
La Femme en bleu (Fr-It 1973)
Les Noces Rouges [Blood Wedding] (Fr 1973)
Touche pas la femme blonche (Fr 1973)
La Grande Bouffe [Blow-Out] (Fr-It 1973)
Life Size (Fr-Sp-It 1973)
Le Trio infernal (Fr-W Ger-It 1974)
Vincent, François, Paul et les autres (Fr 1974)
Le Fantôme de la liberté [The Phantom of Liberté] (Fr 1974)
La Main occulte (Fr 1975) [made in 1972]
La Faille (Fr-W Ger-It 1975)
Léonor (Fr-Sp-It 1975)
7 Morts sur ordannance (Fr 1975)

PICCOLO, OTTAVIA, b. Oct. 9, 1949, Bolzano, Italy
Il gattopardo [Le Guépard] (It-Fr 1963)
Madamigella di Maupin [Le chevalier de Maupin] (It-Fr 1966)
Serafino (It 1968)
Una su tredici (It 1969)
Metello (It 1970)
La Veuve Couderc [L'evaso] (Fr-It 1971)
Bubù di Montparnasse (It 1971)
Trastevere (It 1971)
Un'anguilla da trecento milioni (It 1971)
Uccidere in silenzio (It 1972)
La cosa buffa (It 1972)
L'Histoire très bonne et très joyeuse de Colinot Trousse-Chemise
    [Colinot, l'alzasottane] (Fr-It 1973)
Orlando furioso (It 1974)
Antoine et Sébastien (Fr-It 1974)
Zorro (Fr-It 1975)

PIEL, HARRY, b. July 12, 1892, Düsseldorf; d. 1963
Das amerikanische Duell (Ger --)
Die grosse Wette (Ger --)
Ben Ali Bey (Ger 1913)
Police 1111 (Ger 1916)
Unter heisser Sonne (Ger 1916)
Das Auge des Götzen (Ger 1919)
Das Geheimnis des Zirkus Barre (Ger 1920)
Der grosse Coup (Ger 1919)
Über den Wolken (Ger 1919)
Das geheimnisvolle Telephon (Ger 1921)
Luftpiraten (Ger 1921)
Der brennende Berg (Ger 1921)
Das fliegende Auto (Ger 1921)
Der Fürst der Berge (Ger 1921)
Das Gefängnis auf dem Meeresgrunde (Ger 1921)
Das Geheimnis der Katakomben (Ger 1921)
Panik (Ger 1921)

Der Ritt unter Wasser (Ger 1921)
Die Todesfalle (Ger 1921)
Unus, der Weg in die Welt (Ger 1921)
Der Verächter des Todes (Ger 1921)
Das schwarze Kouvert (Ger 1922)
Die verschwundene Haus (Ger 1922)
Abenteuer einer Nacht (Ger 1923)
Der letzte Kampf (Ger 1923)
Menschen und Masken (Ger 1923)
Rivalen (Ger 1923)
Auf gefährlichen Spuren (Ger 1924)
Der Mann ohne Nerven (Ger 1924)
Abenteuer im Nachtexpress (Ger 1925)
Schneller als der Tod (Ger 1925)
Zigaro, der Brigant von Monte Diavolo (Ger 1925)
Achtung Harry! Augen auf! (Ger 1926)
Der schwarze Pierro (Ger 1926)
Was ist los im Zirkus Beely (Ger 1926)
Rätsel einer Nacht (Ger 1927)
Sein grösster Bluff (Ger 1927)
Mann gegen Mann (Ger 1928)
Panik (Ger 1928)
Seine stärkste Waffe (Ger 1928)
Männer ohne Beruf (Ger 1929)
Die Mitternachts-Taxe (Ger 1929)
Sein bester Freund (Ger 1929)
Achtung! Auto-Diebe! (Ger 1930)
Menschen im Feuer (Ger 1930)
Er oder ich (Ger 1930)
Bobby geht los (Ger 1931)
Schatten der Unterwelt (Ger 1931)
Der Geheimagent (Ger 1932)
Jonny stiehlt Europa (Ger 1932)
Das Schiff ohne Hafen (Ger 1932)
Sprung in dem Abgrund (Ger 1933)
Ein Unsichtbarer geht durch die Stadt (Ger 1933)
Die Welt ohne Maske (Ger 1934)
Artisten (Ger 1935)
90 Minuten Aufenthalt (Ger 1936)
Der Dschungel raft (Ger 1936)
Sein bester Freund (Ger 1937)
Menschen, Tiere, Sensationen (Ger 1938)
Der unmögliche Herr Pitt (Ger 1938)
Gesprengte Gitter (Ger 1940)
Panik (Ger 1940)
Der Mann im Sattel (Ger 1945)
Der Tiger Akbar (W Ger 1950)

PIEPLU, CLAUDE, b. May 9, 1923, Paris
Adorables démons (Fr 1956)
Du rififi chez les femmes (Fr 1959)
Le Caïd (Fr 1960)
L'Affaire d'une nuit (Fr 1960)

La Belle Américaine (Fr 1961)
Le Glaive et la balance (Fr 1962)
La Chambre ardente (Fr 1962)
Le Temps des copains (Fr 1962)
Les Pieds dans le plâtre (Fr 1964)
Cherchez l'idole (Fr 1964)
Une Souris chez les hommes (Fr 1964)
Faites sauter la banque (Fr 1964)
Les Copains (Fr 1964)
Le Gendarme de Saint-Tropez (Fr 1964)
La Bourse et la vie (Fr 1965)
Si j'étais un espion (Fr 1966)
Diaboliquement votre (Fr 1967)
L'Homme à la Buick (Fr 1967)
L'Ecume des jours (Fr 1968)
La Prisonnière (Fr 1968)
Le Diable par la Queue (Fr 1968)
Le Pistonné (Fr 1969)

Claude Pieplu

Clérambard (Fr 1969)
Et qu'ça saute! (Fr 1969)
Hibernatus (Fr 1969)
La Maison (Fr 1970)
La Coqueluche (Fr 1970)
Le Drapeau noir flotte sur la marmite (Fr 1971)
Le Charme discret de la bourgeoisie [The Discreet Charm of
    the Bourgeoisie] (Fr 1972)
Les Noces rouges (Fr 1972)
Sex shop (Fr 1972)
Les Aventures de Rabbi Jacob [The Mad Adventures of Rabbi

Prêtres interdits (Fr 1973)
Defense de savoir (Fr 1973)
Par le sang des autres (Fr 1973)
La Gueule de l'emploi (Fr 1973)
Un Nuage entre les dents (Fr 1973)
Le Fantôme de la liberté [Phantom of Liberty] (Fr 1974)
La Moutarde me monte au nez (Fr 1974)
Gross Paris (Fr 1974)
Section spéciale (Fr 1975)
Les Galettes de Pont-Aven (Fr 1975)
C'est dur pour tout le monde (Fr 1975)
La Meilleure façon de marcher (Fr 1975)
Calmos (Fr 1975)

PILBEAM, NOVA (Margery Pilbeam), b. Nov. 15, 1919, Wimbledon,
    England
    Little Friend (Gaumont 1934)
    The Man Who Knew Too Much (Gaumont 1934)
    Tudor Rose [Nine Days a Queen] (Gaumont 1936)
    Young and Innocent [A Girl Was Young] (GFD 1937)
    Cheer Boys Cheer (ABFD 1939)
    Pastor Hall (GN 1940)
    Spring Meeting (Pathe 1941)
    Banana Ridge (Pathe 1941)
    Next of Kin (UA 1942)
    Yellow Canary (RKO 1943)
    This Man Is Mine (Col Br 1946)
    Green Fingers (Anglo 1947)
    Counterblast (Pathe 1948)
    The Three Weird Sisters (Pathe 1948)

PLEASANCE, DONALD, b. Oct. 5, 1919, Worksop, England
    The Beachcomber (GFD 1954)
    Orders Are Orders (BL 1954)
    1984 (ABP 1956)
    The Black Tent (RFD 1956)
    The Man in the Sky [Decision Against Time] (MGM 1957)
    Manuela [Stowaway Girl] (RFD 1957)
    Barnacle Bill [All at Sea] (MGM 1957)
    A Tale of Two Cities (RFD 1958)
    Heart of a Child (RFD 1958)
    The Wind Cannot Read (RFD 1958)
    The Man Inside (Col 1958)
    The Two-Headed Spy (Col 1958)
    Look Back in Anger (ABP 1959)
    Killers of Kilimanjaro (Col 1959)
    The Battle of the Sexes (Bry 1959)
    The Shakedown (RFD 1960)
    The Flesh and the Fiends [Mania] (RFI 1960)
    Hell Is a City (WPD 1960)
    Circus of Horrors (AA 1960)
    Sons and Lovers (20th 1960)
    The Big Day (Bry 1960)

Suspect (BL 1960)
The Hands of Orlac (Britannia 1960)
A Story of David (BL 1960)
No Love for Johnnie (RFD 1961)
The Wind of Change (Bry 1961)
Spare the Rod (Bry 1961)
The Horsemasters (BV 1961)
What a Carve Up! (RFI 1961)
The Inspector [Lisa] (20th 1962)
Dr. Crippen (WPD 1962)
The Caretaker [The Guest] (BL 1963)
The Great Escape (UA 1963)
The Greatest Story Ever Told (UA 1965)
The Hallelujah Trail (UA 1965)
Fantastic Voyage (20th 1966)
Cul-de-Sac (Compton 1966)
Eye of the Devil [13] (MGM 1966)
The Night of the Generals (Col 1967)
You Only Live Twice (UA 1967)
Will Penny (Par 1969)
The Madwoman of Chaillot (WPD 1969)
Arthur, Arthur! (1969) [unreleased]
Soldier Blue (Avco Emb 1970)
THX 1138 (WB 1971)
Outback (Australia 1971)
The Jerusalem File (USA-Israel 1971)
The Pied Piper (GB-W Ger 1972)
Kidnapped (RFD 1972)
Henry VIII and His Six Wives (MGM-EMI 1972)
Wedding in White (Can 1972)
Dr. Jekyll and Mr. Hyde (ABC-TV 1973)
The Rainbow Boys (Can 1973)
Tales That Witness Madness (Par 1973)
From Beyond the Grave (Col-Warner 1974)
Malachi's Cove (Saga 1974)
The Black Windmill (CIC 1974)
...Altrimenti ci arabiamo [Watch Out, We're Mad] (Sp-It 1974)
Escape to Witch Mountain (BV 1974)
The Mutations (Col-Warner 1974)
Barry McKenzie Holds His Own (EMI 1975)
I Don't Want to Be Born (Fox-Rank 1975)

PLUMMER, CHRISTOPHER, b. Dec. 13, 1929, Toronto
Wind Across the Everglades (WB 1958)
Stage Struck (RKO 1958)
The Fall of the Roman Empire (Par 1964)
The Sound of Music (20th 1965)
Inside Daisy Clover (WB 1966)
The Night of the Generals (Col 1967)
Triple Cross (GB-Fr 1967)
Oedipus the King (RFD 1967)
Nobody Runs Forever [The High Commissioner] (Cin 1968)
Lock Up Your Daughters! (Col 1969)

Battle of Britain (UA 1969)
The Royal Hunt of the Sun (National General 1969)
Waterloo (It-USSR 1970)
The Pyx (Can 1973)
The Spiral Staircase (Col-Warner 1975)
The Return of the Pink Panther (UA 1975)
Conduct Unbecoming (BL 1975)

PODESTA, ROSSANA, b. Aug. 20, 1934, Zliten, Libya
Domani è un altro giorno (It 1949)
Strano appuntamento (It 1950)
Gli angeli del quartiere (It 1951)
Guardie e ladri (It 1951)
Sette nani alla riscossa [The Seven Dwarfs to the Rescue] (It 1951)
Il moschettiere fantasma (It 1952)
Don Lorenzo (It 1952)
Fanciulle di lusso (It 1952)
Io, Amleto (It 1952)
La Maison du silence [La voce del silenzio] (Fr-It 1952)
Addio, figlio mio (It 1953)
La Red (It 1953)
Ulisse [Ulysses] (It-USA 1953)
Viva la rivista (It 1953)
Helen of Troy (It 1953)
Nosotros, los hombres (Sp 1954)
Le ragazze di Sanfrediano (It 1954)
Canzoni di tutta Italia (It 1955)
Non scherzare con le donne (It 1956)
Nosotros dos (It-Sp 1956)
Santiago (WB-7 Arts 1956)
La Bigorne, caporal de France (Fr 1957)
Raw Wind in Eden (Univ 1958)
Playa Prohibita (Sp 1958)
L'Île du Bout du Monde [Temptation] (Fr 1958)
La spade e la croce (It 1958)
Un vaso de whisky (Sp 1958)
Ismael il conquistadore (It 1959)
La grande vallata (It 1960)
La furia dei barbari [Fury of the Pagans] (It 1960)
La schiava di Roma (It 1960)
Sodom and Gomorrah (USA-It 1961)
Solo contro Roma (It 1962)
Un aereo per Baalbek [Dernier Avion pour Baalbeck] (It-Fr-Leba-
    nese 1963)
La vergina di Norimberga [Horror Castle] (It 1963)
La freccia d'oro [The Golden Arrow] (It 1964)
Le ore nude (It 1964)
Sette uomini d'oro [Siete hombres de oro/Sept Hommes en or/
    Seven Golden Men] (It-Sp 1965)
Il grande colpo dei sette uomini do'oro (It 1966)
Il prete sposato (It 1970)
Homo eroticus (It 1971)
L'uccello migratore (It 1972)

Paolo il caldo (It 1973)

POEIRA, BARRETO (Domingos António Barreto Poeira), b. April
24, 1901, Vila Franca, Xira
A Portuguesa de Napóles (Por 1931)
A canção da terra (Por 1938)
O porto de abrigo (Por 1941)
Fátima, terra de fé (Por 1943)
O amor de perdição (Por 1943)
Um homem às direitas (Por 1944)
O diablo são Elas (Sp 1945)
Um homem do Ribatejo (Por 1946)
Cais sodré (Por 1946)
Rainha santa (Sp 1947)
Viela, a rua sem sol (Sp 1947)
Heróis do mar (Por 1949)
Vendaval maravilhoso (Por 1949)
Frei Luis de Sousa (Por 1950)
O trigo (Por 1965)
O joio (Por 1965)

Barreto Poeira

POLA, ISA (Maria Luisa Betti di Montesano), b. Dec. 19, 1909,
Bologna
Martiri d'Italia (It 1926)
Boccaccesca (It 1927)
Myriam (It 1929)
La canzone dell'amore (It 1930)

Terra madre (It 1930)
L'ultima avventura (It 1931)
La cantante dell'opera (It 1932)
Wally (It 1932)
La telefonista (It 1932)
Acciaio (It 1933)
Ragazzo (It 1933)
Creature della notte (It 1934)
L'albergo della felicità (It 1934)
Le scarpe al sole (It 1935)
L'anonoma Roylott [Gli avvoltoi della metropoli] (It 1936)
Sono stato io! (It 1937)
Gli uomini non sono ingrati (It 1937)
La vedova (It 1939)
Cavalleria rusticana (It 1939)
Il ponte di vetro (It 1940)
Lucrezia Borgia (It 1940)
Una signora dell'West (It 1942)
I bambini ci guardano (It 1943)
Circo equestre Za-Bum (It 1943)
Baruffe chiozzotte [Paese senza pace] (It 1943)
Furia (It 1947)
Margherita di Cortona (It 1950)
La rivale dell'imperatrice (It 1950)
Angelo tra la folla (It 1950)
Ombre sul Canal Grande (It 1951)
Tre storie proibite (It 1952)
La regina di Saba (It 1952)
Il moschettiere fantasma (It 1952)
La figlia del forzato (It 1954)
Amore e chiacchiere [Salvemos el paisaje] (It-Sp 1957)

POREL, MARC (Marc Landry), b. Jan. 3, 1949, Lausanne
Un Homme de trop [Shock Troops] (Fr 1966)
Des garçons et des filles (Fr 1967)
La Promesse (Fr 1969)
Le Clan des siciliens [The Sicilian Clan] (Fr 1969)
Le Dernier Saut (Fr 1969)
La Route de Salina [The Road to Salinas] (Fr-It 1970)
La Horse (Fr 1970)
Les Aveux les plus doux (Fr 1970)
Tumuc-Humac (Fr 1970)
Un Peu de soleil dans l'eau froide [Un po' di sole nell'acqua
   gelida] (Fr-It 1971)
Un Officier de police sans importance (Fr-It 1972)
Ludwig II [Crepuscule des dieux/Ludwig] (W Ger-Fr-It 1973)
Tony Arzenta [Big Guns/Les Grands Fusils] (It-Fr 1973)
Virilità (It 1973)
Nipoti miei diletti (It 1974)
Colpo in canna (It 1974)
Quand la ville s'éveille (Fr 1975)
Uomini nasce poliziotti si muore (It 1975)
Il Giustiziere in divisa (It 1975)

Marc Porel

PORTEN, HENNY, b. April 7, 1888, Magdeburg, Germany, d. 1960
Die Sieger (Ger 1906)
Apachentanz (Ger 1906)
Lohengrin (Ger 1907)
Meissner Porzellan (Ger 1907)
Desdemona (Ger 1908)
Tief im Böhmerwald (Ger 1908)
Wiegenlied (Ger 1908)
Der Kinderarzt (Ger 1910)
Liebesglück einer Blinden (Ger 1910)
Mütter, verzaget nicht (Ger 1910)
Verkannt (Ger 1910)
Adressatin verstorben (Ger 1911)
Die Blinder (Ger 1911)
Der Eindringling (Ger 1911)
Das gefährliche Alter (Ger 1911)
Die Magd (Ger 1911)
Maskierte Liebe (Ger 1911)
Ein schweres Opfer (Ger 1911)
Zwei Frauen (Ger 1911)
Des Pfarrers Töchterlein (Ger 1911)
Eva Feenhände (Ger 1911)
Gefangene Seelen (Ger 1911)
Kuss des Fürsten (Ger 1912)
Die Nacht des Grauens (Ger 1912)
Schatten des Meeres (Ger 1912)
Gräfin Küchenfee (Ger 1912)
Die grosse Sünderin (Ger 1913)
Heroismus einer Französin (Ger 1913)
Das Tal des Lebens (Ger 1914)

Um Haaresbreite (Ger 1914)
Ungarische Rhapsodie (Ger 1914)
Abseits vom Glück (Ger 1914)
Das Adoptivkind (Ger 1914)
Alexandra (Ger 1914)
Das Ende vom Lied (Ger 1914)
Hans, Hein und Henny (Ger 1914)
Nordlandlose (Ger 1914)
Tirol in Waffen (Ger 1915)
Geisterhof (Ger 1915)
Gelöste Ketten (Ger 1915)
Das Geschlecht deren von Ringwall (Ger 1915)
Der Schirm mit dem Schwan (Ger 1915)
En Überfall in Feindesland (Ger 1915)
Die Ehe der Luise Rohrback (Ger 1915)
Das wandernde Licht (Ger 1916)
Die Dame, der Teufel und die Probiermamsell (Ger 1917)
Die Faust des Riesen (Ger 1917)
Das goldene Kalb (Ger 1917)
Höheluft (Ger 1917)
Die blaue Laterne (Ger 1918)
Irrungen (Ger 1918)
Maskenfest der Liebe (Ger 1918)
Odysseus' Heimkehr (Ger 1918)
Rose Bernd (Ger 1919)
Fahrt ins Blaue (Ger 1919)
Ohr Sport (Ger 1919)
Die Lebende Tote (Ger 1919)
Monika Wogelsang (Ger 1919)
Anna Boleyn (Ger 1920)
Auf der Alm (Ger 1920)
Die blinden Gatten der Frau Ruth (Ger 1920)
Die eingebildete Kranke (Ger 1920)
Die goldene Krone (Ger 1920)
Kohlhiesels Töchter (Ger 1920)
Liebe auf den ersten Blick (Ger 1920)
Die Geierwally (Ger 1921)
Die Hintertreppe (Ger 1921)
Catherina Gräfin von Armagnac (Ger 1922)
Frauenopfer (Ger 1922)
Gespenster (Ger 1922)
Das grosse Schweigen (Ger 1922)
Minna von Barnhelm (Ger 1922)
Mona Lisa (Ger 1922)
Sie und die Drei (Ger 1922)
Das alte Gesetz (Ger 1922)
Das Geheimnis von Brinkenhof (Ger 1922)
Inge Larsen (Ger 1923)
I. N. R. I. (Ger 1923)
Der Kaufmann von Venedig (Ger 1923)
Die liebe einer Königin (Ger 1923)
Das Goldene Kalb (Ger 1923)
Gräfin Donelli (Ger 1924)

Mutter und Kind (Ger 1924)
Prater (Ger 1924)
Das Abenteuer der Sybille Brandt (Ger 1924)
Kammermusik (Ger 1924)
Tragödie (Ger 1924)
Die Flammen lügen (Ger 1926)
Rosen auf dem Süden (Ger 1925)
Wehe, wenn sie losgelassen (Ger 1925)
Die grosse Pause (Ger 1927)
Meine Tante--Deine Tante (Ger 1927)
Violanta (Ger 1927)
Liebe im Kuhstall (Ger 1927)
Liebfraumilch (Ger 1927)
Lotte (Ger 1928)
Zuflucht (Ger 1928)
Die Frau, die jeder liebt, bist Du! (Ger 1927)
Die Herrin und ihr Knecht (Ger 1928)
Mutterliebe (Ger 1929)
Skandal um Eva (Ger 1930)
Kohlhiesels Töchter (Ger 1930)
Luise, Königin von Preussen (Ger 1931)
24 Studen im Leben einer Frau (Ger 1932)
Mutter und Kind (Ger 1933)
Krach im Hinterhaus (Ger 1935)
Der Optimist (Ger 1935)
War es der in 3. Stock ? (Ger 1938)
Komödianten (Ger 1941)
Symphonie des Lebens (Ger 1942)
Wenn der junge Wein blüht (Ger 1943)
Familie Buchholz (Ger 1944)
Neigungsehe (Ger 1944)
Absender umbekannt (W Ger 1950)
Das Fraulein von Scüderi (W Ger-Swi 1955)
Carola Lamberti (W Ger 1955)

PORTMAN, ERIC, b. July 13, 1903, Halifax, Nova Scotia; d. Dec.
7, 1970
Maria Marten; or, The Murder in the Red Barn (MGM Br 1935)
Abdul the Damned (Wardour 1935)
Old Roses (Fox Br 1935)
Hyde Park Corner (Pathe 1935)
The Cardinal (Pathe 1936)
The Crimes of Stephen Hawke (MGM Br 1936)
Hearts of Humanity (AP & D 1936)
Moonlight Sonata (UA 1937)
The Prince and the Pauper (WB 1937)
49th Parallel [The Invaders] (GFD 1941)
One of Our Aircraft Is Missing (Anglo 1942)
Uncensored (GFD 1942)
Squadron Leader X (RKO Br 1942)
We Dive at Dawn (GFD 1943)
Escape to Danger (RKO Br 1943)
Millions Like Us (GFD 1943)

A Canterbury Tale (EL 1944)
Great Day (RKO Br 1945)
Wanted for Murder [A Voice in the Night] (20th 1946)
Men of Two Worlds (GFD 1946)
Daybreak (GFD 1946)
Dear Murderer (GFD 1947)
The Mark of Cain (GFD 1948)
Corridor of Mirrors (GFD 1948)
The Blind Goddess (GFD 1948)
The Spider and the Fly (GFD 1949)
Cairo Road (ABP 1950)
The Magic Box (BL 1951)
His Excellency (GFD 1952)
South of Algiers [The Golden Mask] (WB 1952)
The Colditz Story (BL 1955)
The Deep Blue Sea (20th 1955)
Child in the House (Eros 1956)
The Good Companions (ABPC 1957)
The Naked Edge (UA 1961)
Freud [The Secret Passion] (Univ 1962)
The Man Who Finally Died (Magna 1962)
West 11 (WPD 1963)
The Bedford Incident (Col 1965)
The Wrong Box (Col 1966)
The Whisperers (UA 1966)
The Spy with the Cold Nose (Par 1966)
The Whisperers (Col 1967)
Deadfall (20th 1968)
House of Cards (Univ 1968)

PRADA, JOSE MARIA, b. Toledo, Spain
Comicos (Sp 1952)
Curra Veleta (Sp 1956)
El verdugo (Sp-It 1963)
La tia tula (Sp 1963)
Crimen de doble filo (Sp 1964)
Tiempo de amor (Sp 1964)
De cuerpo presente (Sp 1965)
Amador (Fr-Sp 1965)
El arte de vivir (Sp 1965)
Aquella joven de blanco (Sp 1965)
La caza [The Hunt] (Sp 1965)
La barrera (Sp 1965)
Los flamencos (Sp 1966)
Adios cordera (Sp 1966)
La busca (Sp 1966)
Ultimo encuentro (Sp 1966)
Club de solteros (Sp 1966)
Ditirambo (Sp 1967)
Los invasores del Espacio (Sp 1967)
Oscuros sueños de agosto (Sp 1967)
Villa Rides (Par 1968)

Sangre en el Ruedo (Sp 1969)
Quadrilatero (Sp 1969)
El "Che" Guevara [Rebel with a Cause] (It 1968)
La Femme écarlate (Fr-It 1969)
Vivan los novios! (Sp 1970)
Goya (Sp 1970)
El proceso de las brujas (W Ger-It-Sp 1970)
Cao-xa (Sp 1971)

PREJEAN, ALBERT, b. Oct. 27, 1898, Paris
Les Trois Mousquetaires (Fr 1921)
Les Mauvais Garçon (Fr 1921)
Vingt Ans après (Fr 1922)
Gonzague (Fr 1923)
Jim Bougne, boxeur (Fr 1924)
Le Miracle de loups (Fr 1924)
Paris qui dort (Fr 1924)
Le Fantôme du Moulin-Rouge (Fr 1924)
Amour et carburateur (Fr 1925)
La Justicière (Fr 1925)
Le Voyage imaginaire (Fr 1925)
Le Bouif errant (Fr 1926)
Un Chapeau de paille d'Italie [The Italian Straw Hat] (Fr 1927)
Le Chauffeur de mademoiselle (Fr 1927)
Verdun versions d'histoire (Fr 1928)
Les Nouveaux Messieurs (Fr 1928)
Fécondité (Fr 1929)
Bluff (Fr 1929)
L'Aventure de Luna-Park (Fr 1929)
Le Reguin (Fr 1930)
Sous les toits de Paris (Fr 1930)
Le Chant du marin (Fr 1930)
L'Amoureuse Aventure (Fr-Ger 1930)
L'Opéra de quat'sous (Fr 1931)
Un Soir de rafle (Fr 1931)
Un Fils d'Amérique (Fr 1932)
Voyages de noces (Fr 1932)
Theodore et Cie (Fr 1932)
Rivaux de la piste (Fr 1933)
Les Bleus du ciel (Fr 1933)
Caprice de princesse (Fr 1933)
L'Homme inusable (Fr 1934)
Le Paquebot Tenacity (Fr 1934)
La Crise est finie (Fr 1934)
Volga en flammes (Fr 1934)
L'Auberge du Petit Dragon (Fr 1934)
Le Chauffeur de mademoiselle (Fr 1934)
Dédé (Fr 1934)
Le Secret d'une nuit (Fr 1934)
Toto (Fr 1934)
L'Or dans la rue (Fr 1935)
Le Contrôleur des wagon-lits (Fr 1935)
Quelle drôle de bosse (Fr 1935)

Princesse Tam-Tam (Fr 1935)
Paris-Canargue (Fr 1935)
Un Mauvais Garçon (Fr 1936)
Jenny (Fr 1936)
Moïse et Salomon Parfumeurs (Fr 1936)
Alibi (Fr 1937)
La Fessée (Fr 1937)
Neuf de trèfle (Fr 1937)
A Venise, me nuit (Fr 1937)
Mollenard (Fr 1938)
La Rue sans joie (Fr 1938)
La Piste du sud (Fr 1938)
Métropolitan (Fr 1938)
Place de la Concorde (Fr 1938)
L'Inconnue de Monte-Carlo (Fr 1938)
Nord-Atlantique (Fr 1938)
Pour le maillot jaune (Fr 1938)
L'Or du Cristobal (Fr 1938)
Dédé la musique (Fr 1938)
L'Etrange Suzy (Fr 1941)
Caprices (Fr 1941)
Picpus (Fr 1942)
Vie de plaisir (Fr 1943)
Au Bonheur des dames (Fr 1943)
Cécile est morte (Fr 1943)
Les Caves du majestic (Fr 1944)
L'Assassin n'est pas coupable (Fr 1945)
L'Homme de la nuit (Fr 1946)
La Kermesse rouge (Fr 1946)
Le Secret du Florida (Fr 1946)
Les Frères Bouquinquant (Fr 1947)
L'Idole (Fr 1947)
La Grande Volière (Fr 1947)
Pieges à hommes (Fr 1948)
Les Nouveaux Maîtres (Fr 1949)
Je n'ai que toi au monde (Bel 1950)
Le Désir et l'amour (Fr 1951)
Ils sont dans les vignes (Fr 1951)
Les Amants du Tage (Fr 1951)
Casse-cou mademoiselle (Fr 1951)
Chéri-Bibi (Fr 1951)
Un Missionaire (Fr 1955)
Le Circuit de minuit (Bel 1956)

PRESLE, MICHELINE (Micheline Chassagne), b. Aug. 22, 1922,
   Paris
As Micheline Michel:
   Vous seule que j'aime (Fr 1938)
   Je chante (Fr 1938)
   Petite peste (Fr 1939)
As Micheline Presle:
   Jeunes Filles en détresse (Fr 1939)
   Paridis perdu (Fr 1939)

Micheline Presle in <u>Under My Skin</u> (1950).

Fausse alerte (Fr 1939)
La Comédie du bonheur (Fr 1940)
Elles étaitent douze femmes (Fr 1940)
Parade en sept nuits (Fr 1941)
Le Soleil à toujours raison (Fr 1941)
Histoire de rire (Fr 1941)
La Nuit fantastique (Fr 1942)
Félicie Nanteuil (Fr 1942)
La Belle Aventure (Fr 1942)
Un Seul Amour (Fr 1943)
Falbalas (Fr 1944)
Boule de suif (Fr 1945)
Le Diable au corps (Fr-It 1947)
Les Jeux sont faits (Fr 1947)
Les Derniers Jours de Pompeï (Fr-It 1948)
Tous les chemins mènent à Rome (Fr 1948)
As Micheline Prelle in USA:
Under My Skin (20th 1950)

The Adventures of Captain Fabian (Rep 1951)
An American Guerilla in the Philippines [I Shall Return] (20th
    1950)
As Micheline Presle:
    La Dame aux camelias [Camille] (Fr-It 1952)
    Si Versailles m'était conté (Fr 1953)
    L'Amour d'une femme (Fr-It 1953)
    Casa Ricordi (It-Fr 1954)
    Napoléon (Fr 1954)
    Les Amants de Villa Borghèse (Fr-It 1954)
    Les Impures (Fr 1955)
    Treze à table (Fr 1955)
    Beatrice Cenci (It-Fr 1956)
    La Mariée est trop belle [The Bride Is Too Beautiful] (Fr-It
        1956)
    Les Louves (Fr 1958)
    Les Femmes sont marrantes (Fr 1958)
    Bobosse (Fr 1958)
    Christine (Fr-It 1958)
    Une Fille Pour l'été (Fr-It 1959)
    Blind Date [Chance Meeting] (RFD 1959)
    Le Baron de l'ecluse (Fr-It 1960)
    Interpol contre "X" (Fr 1960)
    Les Grandes Personnes (Fr-It 1960)
    Les Mystères d'Angkor (W Ger-Fr-It 1960)
    L'Amant de cinq jours [The Five Day Lover] (Fr-It 1961)
    Les Sept Péchés capitaux [Seven Capital Sins] (ep "La Luxure")
        (Fr-It 1961)
    I briganti italiani (It-Fr 1961)
    La Loi des hommes (Fr 1961)
    L'assassino [Lady Killer of Rome] (It-Fr 1961)
    Le Diable et les dix commandements (Fr-It 1962)
    Vénus impériale (Fr-It 1962)
    Coup de bambou (Fr 1962)
    If a Man Answers (Univ 1962)
    L'intrigo [Dark Purpose] (It-USA 1963)
    The Prize (MGM 1963)
    La Chasse à l'homme [Male Hunt] (Fr-It 1964)
    Les Pieds nickelés (Fr 1964)
    Je vous salue, Mafia [Hail Mafia!] (Fr-It 1965)
    Le Roi du coeur [King of Hearts] (Fr-It 1966)
    La Religeuse (Fr 1966)
    Peau d'âne [The Magic Donkey] (Fr 1970)
    Les Pétroleuses (Fr-Sp-It 1971)
    L'Oiseau rare (Fr-It 1973)
    L'Evenement le plus important depuis que l'homme à marche
        sur la lune (Fr 1973)
    Il diavolo nel cervello (It 1973)
    Eulalie quitte les champs (Fr 1973)
    La Gueule de l'emploi (Fr 1973)
    Bouche à bouche (Fr 1974)
    Deux Grandes Filles dans un pyjama (Fr 1974)

PREVOST, FRANÇOISE, b. 1930, Paris
  Jean de la lune (Fr 1948)
  Clara de Montargis (Fr 1950)
  Les Miracles n'ont lieu qu'une fois (Fr 1950)
  Nez de cuir (Fr 1951)
  Virgile (Fr 1953)
  Les Trois Mousquetaires (Fr 1953)
  Cette Nuit là (Fr 1958)
  Le Bel Age [Love Is Where You Find It] (Fr 1958)
  Paris nous appartient [Paris Belongs to Us] (Fr 1958)
  Par-dessus le mur (Fr 1960)
  La Récréation (Fr 1962)
  La Morte Saison des amours [The Season for Love] (Fr 1960)
  La Fille aux yeux d'or (Fr 1961)
  Payroll (AA 1961)
  Il proceso de Verona (It-Fr 1962)
  Les Egarements (Fr-It 1962)
  Il Mare (It 1962)
  Amours sans lendemain (Fr 1963)
  I sequestrati di Altona [The Condemned of Altona] (It-Fr 1963)
  Ein Mann im schonsten alter (W Ger 1964)
  La Cage de verre (Fr-Israel 1965)
  Via Macao (Fr-Port 1966)
  Galia (Fr-It 1966)
  Maigret und sein grösster Fall (Austria-It 1966)
  L'Une et l'autre (Fr 1967)
  La lama nel corpo [The Murder Clinic] (It-Fr 1967)
  Pronto...c'è una certa Giuliana per te (It 1967)
  Italian Secret Service (It 1968)
  Quella sporca storia del West [Johnny Hamlet] (It 1968)
  Histoires extraordinaires [Spirits of the Dead] (ep "Metzenger-
    stein"] (Fr-It 1968)
  Les Vieilles Lunes (Swi 1969)
  Häscher in der grube (W Ger 1969)
  Quarta parete [The Fourth Wall] (It-Fr 1969)
  Brucia, ragazzo, brucia [Burn, Boy, Burn] (It 1969)
  Mont-Dragon (Fr-Bel 1970)
  Una Maleta para un cadaver (Sp-It 1971)
  Auuando l'amore e sensualità (It 1973)
  Mais ou sont passées les jeunes filles en fleur (Fr 1974)
  Le Telephone rose (Fr 1975)

PRICE, DENNIS (Dennistoun Rose-Price), b. June 23, 1915, Twy-
    ford, England; d. Oct. 7, 1973
  A Canterbury Tale (EL 1944)
  A Place of One's Own (EL 1945)
  The Echo Murders (Anglo 1945)
  Caravan (GFD 1946)
  The Magic Bow (GFD 1946)
  Hungry Hill (GFD 1947)
  Dear Murderer (GFD 1947)
  Jassy (GFD 1947)
  Holiday Camp (GFD 1947)

Master of Bankdam (GFD 1947)
The White Unicorn [Bad Sister] (GFD 1947)
Easy Money (GFD 1947)
Snowbound (RKO Br 1948)
Good Time Girl (GFD 1948)
The Bad Lord Byron (GFD 1949)
Kind Hearts and Coronets (GFD 1949)
Helter Skelter (GFD 1949)
The Lost People (GFD 1949)
The Dancing Years (ABP 1950)
Murder Without Crime (ABP 1950)
The Adventurers [The Great Adventure/Fortune in Diamonds]
    (GFD 1951)
The Magic Box (BL 1951)
I'll Never Forget You [The House in the Square] (20th 1951)
Lady Godiva Rides Again (BL 1951)
Song of Paris [Bachelor in Paris] (Adelphi 1952)
The Tall Headlines [The Frightened Bride] (GN 1952)
Noose for a Lady (AA 1953)
Murder at 3 a.m. (Renown 1953)
The Intruder (BL 1953)
Time Is My Enemy (IFD 1954)
For Better, for Worse [Cocktails in the Kitchen] (ABP 1954)
That Lady (20th 1955)
Oh Rosalinda! (ABP 1955)
Private's Progress (BL 1956)
Charley Moon (BL 1956)
Port Afrique (Col 1956)
A Touch of the Sun (Eros 1956)
Fortune Is a Woman [She Played with Fire] (Col 1957)
The Naked Truth [Your Past Is Showing] (RFD 1957)
Danger Within [Breakout] (RFI 1958)
I'm All Right Jack (BL 1959)
Don't Panic Chaps! (Col 1959)
School for Scoundrels (WPD 1960)
Oscar Wilde (20th 1960)
Tunes of Glory (UA 1960)
Piccadilly Third Stop (RFD 1960)
The Millionairess (20th 1960)
The Pure Hell of St. Trinian's (BL 1960)
No Love for Johnnie (RFD 1961)
The Rebel (WPD 1961)
Five Golden Hours (Col 1961)
Double Bunk (Bry 1961)
Watch It Sailor! (Col 1961)
Victim (RFD 1961)
What a Carve Up! (RFI 1961)
Go to Blazes (WPD 1962)
Play It Cool (AA 1962)
The Pot Carriers (WPD 1962)
The Amorous Prawn (BL 1962)
Kill or Cure (MGM Br 1962)
The Wrong Arm of the Law (BL 1962)

The Cool Mikado (UA 1963)
The V. I. P. 's (MGM 1963)
The Cracksman (WPD 1963)
Doctor in Distress (RFD 1963)
Tamahine (WPD 1963)
The Comedy Man (BL 1963)
A Jolly Bad Fellow (Pax 1963)
The Horror of It All (20th 1964)
Murder Most Foul (MGM 1964)
The Earth Dies Screaming (20th 1964)
The Curse of Simba [Curse of the Voodoo] (Gala 1965)
Ten Little Indians (WPD 1965)
Just Like a Woman (Monarch 1966)
Jules Verne's Rocket to the Moon [Those Fantastic Flying
    Fools/Blast Off] (AA 1967)
The Haunted House of Horror (Tigon 1969)
The Magic Christian (CUE 1969)
Some Will, Some Won't (WPD 1970)
The Horror of Frankenstein (MGM-EMI 1970)
Twins of Evil (RFD 1971)
The Adventures of Barry McKenzie (Australian 1972)
Pulp (UA 1972)
Tower of Evil [The Horror of Snape Island] (MGM-EMI 1972)
Go for a Take (Fox-Rank 1972)
Alice's Adventures in Wonderland (Fox-Rank 1972)
Theatre of Blood (UA 1973)
Horror Hospital (Anthony Balch 1973)
That's Your Funeral (Fox-Rank 1973)

PULVER, LISELOTTE (Lilo Pulver), b. Oct. 11, 1929, Bern,
    Switzerland
Swiss Tour (Swi 1949)
Föhn (Swi-W Ger 1950)
Heidelberger Romanze (W Ger 1951)
Klettermaxe (W Ger 1952)
Fritz und Friederike (W Ger 1952)
Hab' Sonne im Herzen (W Ger 1952)
Von Liebe reden wir später (W Ger 1953)
Das Nachtgespenst (W Ger 1953)
Ich und Du (W Ger 1953)
Uli der Knecht (Swi 1954)
Männer im gefährlichen Alter (W Ger 1954)
Schule für Eheglück (W Ger 1954)
Der letzte Sommer (W Ger 1954)
Uli der Knecht (Swi 1954)
Griff nach den Sternen (W Ger 1955)
Hanussen (W Ger 1955)
Uli der Pächter/Und ewig ruft die Heimat (Swi 1955)
Ich denke oft an Piroschka (W Ger 1955)
Heute heiratet mein Mann (W Ger 1956)
Die Zürcher Verlobung (W Ger 1957)
Die Bekenntnisse des Hochstaplers Felix Krull (W Ger 1957)
Les Aventures d'Arsène Lupin (Fr 1957)

Le Joueur (Fr 1958)
Helden (W Ger 1958)
Reaching for the Stars (Br 1958)
Das schöne Abenteur (W Ger 1959)
Eskimo (It 1959)
Das Glas Wasser (W Ger 1959)
Die Buddenbrooks (I) (W Ger 1960)
Die Buddenbrooks (II) (W Ger 1960)
Das Spukschloss im Spessart (W Ger 1960)
Gustav Adolfs Page (W Ger 1961)
One Two Three (UA 1962)
Kohlliesels Töchter (W Ger 1962)
La Fayette [La Fayette, una spada per due bandiere] (Fr-It 1962)
Maléfices (Fr 1962)
A Global Affair (UA 1963)
Le Gentleman de Cocody [Donne, mitra e diamanti] (Fr 1963)
Ein fast anständiges Mädchen [Una chica casi formal] (W Ger-Sp 1963)
Frühstück im Doppelbett (W Ger 1963)
Monsieur (W Ger 1964)
Dr. med. Hiob Prätorius (W Ger 1965)
La Religieuse (Fr 1965)
Le Jardinier d'Argenteuil [Blüten, Gauner und die Nacht von Niza] (Fr-W Ger 1966)
O'Ombrellone (Fr-It-Sp 1966)
Hokuspokus, oder wie lasse ich meinen Mann verschwinden (W Ger 1966)
Herrliche Zeiten im Spessart (W Ger 1967)
Pistol Jenny (W Ger 1969)
Die Hochzeitsreise (W Ger-It 1969)
Peter Alexander präsentiert spezialitäten (W Ger 1969)
Le Trefle à cinq femelles (Fr 1973)
Monika und die Sechszehnjährigen (W Ger-Hun 1975)

QUAYLE, ANTHONY, b. Sept. 7, 1913, Ainsdale, England
Hamlet (GFD 1948)
Saraband for Dead Lovers (GFD 1948)
Oh Rosalinda! (ABP 1955)
The Battle of the River Plate [Pursuit of the Graf Spee] (RFD 1956)
The Wrong Man (WB 1957)
No Time for Tears (ABPC 1957)
Woman in a Dressing Gown (ABP 1957)
The Man Who Wouldn't Talk (BL 1958)
Ice Cold in Alex [Desert Attack] (ABPC 1958)
Serious Charge (Eros 1959)
Tarzan's Greatest Adventure (Par 1959)
The Challenge (RFD 1960)
The Guns of Navarone (Col 1961)
HMS Defiant [Damn the Defiant!] (Col 1962)
Lawrence of Arabia (Col 1962)
Fall of the Roman Empire (Par 1964)

East of Sudan (Col 1964)
Operation Crossbow [The Great Spy Mission] (MGM 1965)
A Study in Terror [Fog] (Compton 1965)
Incompreso [Misunderstood] (It 1967)
Before Winter Comes (Col 1969)
MacKenna's Gold (Col 1969)
Anne of the 1,000 Days (RFD 1970)
Everything You Always Wanted to Know About Sex ** but Were
    Afraid to Ask (UA 1972)
Bequest to the Nation [The Nelson Affair] (CIC 1973)
Q. B. VII (ABC-TV 1974)
The Tamarind Seed (Avco Emb 1974)
Moses [Moses, the Law Giver] (It-GB 1975)

RABAL, FRANCISCO (Francisco Valera), b. March 8, 1925, Aquilas,
    Murcia, Spain
La prodiga (Sp 1945)
La honradez de la cerradura (Sp 1950)
Luna de sangre (Sp 1950)
Duda (Sp 1951)
Hay un camino a la derecha (Sp 1953)
Todo es posible en Granada (Sp 1953)
Murio hace quince años (Sp 1954)
La picara molinera (Sp 1954)
El cante del gallo (Sp 1955)
Rivelazione (It-Sp 1955)
Saranno uomini (It-Sp 1955)
La gran mentira (Sp 1956)
Amenece en puerta oscura (It 1956)
Prisonero del mar (It-Sp 1957)
Le Gerusalemme liberata (It-Sp 1957)
La noche y el alba (Sp 1958)
L'amore più bello (It-Sp 1958)
Nazarín (Mexico 1958)
Los clarínes del miedo (Sp 1958)
Tal vez mañana (Sp-It 1958)
Diez fusiles esperan (Sp 1959)
Sonatas (Sp 1959)
El hombre de la isla (Sp 1959)
Azahares rojos (Sp 1960)
A las conco de la tarde (Sp 1960)
Tiro al piccone (It-Sp 1960)
Trio de dames (Sp 1960)
Hijo de hombre (Sp 1961)
La sed (Arg-Sp 1961)
Viridania (Sp-Mex 1961)
La mano en la trampa (It-Sp 1961)
L'Eclisse [The Eclipse] (It-Fr 1962)
Autopsia de un criminal (Sp 1962)
Setenta veces siete (It 1962)
Niche de verano (Sp-It 1962)
El conde Sandorff (Sp-It-Fr 1963)
La rimpatriata (It 1963)

Fra Diavolo (Sp-It 1963)
El diablo tambien llora (Sp-It 1963)
Llanto por un bandido (Sp 1964)
Maria Rosa (Sp 1964)
La otra mujer (Fr-It-Sp 1964)
Currito de la cruz (Sp 1965)
Marie Chantal contre le Dr. Kha (Fr-It-Morocco 1965)
España insolita (Sp 1965)
La Religieuse (Fr 1966)
Camino del Rocio (Sp 1966)
Das Vermachtnis des Inka (W Ger-It-Sp 1966)
Hoy como ayer (Sp 1966)
I lunghi giorni della vendetta (It 1966)
Cervantes (Sp 1967)
Oscuros sueños de agosto (Sp 1967)
El "Che" Guevara [Rebel with a Cause] (It 1968)
Sangre en el ruedo (Sp 1968)
Los desafíos (Sp 1969)
Simón Bolívar (Sp-It-Venezuela 1969)
El largo día del Aguila (Fr-It-Sp 1969)
Laia (Sp-It 1969)
Las gatas tienen frio (Sp 1969)
Cabesas cortadas (Sp-Br 1970)
Goya (Sp 1970)
Los largos días de la venganza (Sp-It 1970) [made in 1967]
Después del dilubio (Sp 1972)
Nada menos que todo un hombre (Sp 1971)
Las melancolías (Sp 1971)
La colonna infame (It 1973)
Il consigliori [The Counsellor] (It 1973)

RADDATZ, CARL, b. March 13, 1911, Mannheim, Germany
Urlaub auf Ehrenwort (Ger 1937)
Verklungene Melodie (Ger 1938)
Liebelei und Liebe (Ger 1938)
Silvesternacht am Alexanderplatz (Ger 1939)
12 Minuten nach 12 (Ger 1939)
Wir tanzen um die Welt (Ger 1939)
Zwielicht (Ger 1940)
Wunschkonzert (Ger 1940)
Golowin geht durch die Stadt (Ger 1940)
Befreite Hände (Ger 1940)
Über alles in der Welt (Ger 1941)
Stukas (Ger 1941)
Heimkehr (Ger 1941)
Der 5. Juni (Ger 1941)
Immensee (Ger 1941)
Das war mein Leben (Ger 1944)
Opfergang (Ger 1944)
Eine Frau für drei Tage (Ger 1944)
Unter den Brücken (Ger 1945)
Die Schenke der ewigen Liebe (Ger 1945)
In jenen Tagen (W Ger 1947)

Und finden dereinst wir uns wieder (W Ger 1947)
Zugvögel (W Ger 1947)
Wohin die Züge fahren (W Ger 1949)
Der Schatten des Herrn Monitor (W Ger 1950)
Epilog (W Ger 1950)
Gabriella (W Ger 1950)
Schatten der Nacht (W Ger 1950)
Taxi-Kitty (W Ger 1950)
Gift im Zoo (W Ger 1952)
Türme des Schweigens (W Ger 1952)
Geliebtes Leben (W Ger 1953)
Regina Amstetten (W Ger 1954)
Geständnis unter vier Augen (W Ger 1954)
Ouse (W Ger 1955)
Rosen im Herbst (W Ger 1955)
Nacht der Entscheidung (W Ger 1956)
Friederike von Barring (W Ger 1956)
Das Mädchen Marion (W Ger 1956)
Made in Germany (W Ger 1957)
Das Mädchen Rosemarie (W Ger 1958)
Jons und Erdme (W Ger 1959)
The Counterfeit Traitor (Par 1961)
Jeder stirbt für sich Allein (W Ger 1975)

RAIMU (Jules Muraire), b. Dec. 17, 1883, Toulon, France; d.
    Sept. 20, 1946
    L'Homme nu (Fr 1910)
    L'Agence cacahuète (Fr 1914)
    Le Blanc et le noir (Fr 1931)
    Mam'zelle nitouche (Fr 1931)
    Marius (Fr 1931)
    La Petite Chocolatière (Fr 1931)
    Fanny (Fr 1932)
    Les Gaîtes de l'escadron (Fr 1932)
    Théodore et Cie (Fr 1933)
    Ces Messieurs de la santé (Fr 1933)
    Charlemagne (Fr 1933)
    J'ai une idée (Fr 1934)
    Tartarin de Tarascon (Fr 1934)
    Minuit, Place Pigalle (Fr 1935)
    L'Ecole des cocottes (Fr 1935)
    Gaspard de Besse (Fr 1935)
    Le Roi (Fr 1936)
    Faisons un Rêve (Fr 1936)
    César (Fr 1936)
    Le Secret de Polichinelle (Fr 1936)
    Les Jumeaux de Brighton (Fr 1936)
    Vous n'avez rien à déclarer? (Fr 1937)
    Les Rois du sport (Fr 1937)
    Un Carnet de bal [Christine] (Fr 1937)
    Les Perles de la Couronne (Fr 1937)
    Le Fanteuil 47 (Fr 1937)
    Gribouille (Fr 1937)

La Chaste Suzanne (Fr 1937)
L'Etrange Monsieur Victor (Fr 1938)
Les Héros de la Marne (Fr 1938)
Les Nouveaux Riches (Fr 1938)
La Femme du boulanger [The Baker's Wife] (Fr 1938)
Noix de Coco (Fr 1939)
Monsieur Bretonneau (Fr 1939)
Dernière Jeunesse (Fr 1939)
Le Duel (Fr 1939)
L'Homme qui cherche la vérité (Fr 1940)
La Fille du puisatier (Fr 1940)
Un Tel père et fils [Heart of a Nation] (Fr-USA 1940) [completed
   in USA]
Parade en sept nuits (Fr 1941)
Les Petits Riens (Fr 1941)
L'Arlésienne (Fr 1942)
Les Inconnus dans la maison (Fr 1942)
Le Bienfaiteur (Fr 1942)
Monsieur la souris (Fr 1942)
Le Colonel Chabert (Fr 1943)
Les Gueux au paradis (Fr 1945)
L'Homme au chapeau rond (Fr 1946)

RASCEL, RENATO (Renato Ranucci), b. April 28, 1912, Rome
Pazzo d'amore (It 1942)
Botta e riposta (It 1949)
Figaro qua, figaro là (It 1950)
Amor non ho...pero, pero (It 1951)
Io sono il capataz (It 1950)
Bellezze in bicicletta (It 1951)
L'eroe sono io (It 1951)
Fiorenzo il terzo uomo (It 1951)
Marakatumba...ma non è una rumba (It 1951)
Napoleone (It 1951)
Canzoni di mezzo secolo (It 1952)
Il cappotto (It 1952)
Il bandolero stanco (It 1953)
Attanzio cavallo vanesio (It 1953)
Ho scelto l'amore (It 1953)
La passaggiata (It 1953)
Il matrimonio (It 1953)
Piovuto dal cielo [Voleur malgré lui] (It-Fr 1953)
Alvaro piuttosto corsaro (It 1954)
Gran varietà (It 1954)
Io sono la primula rossa (It 1954)
Questi fantasmi (It 1954)
Rosso e nero (It 1955)
Carosello di varieta (It 1955)
Montecarlo (It 1956)
I pinguini ci guardano (It 1956)
Rascel-fifi (It 1957)
Arrivederci Roma [The Seven Hills of Rome] (It-USA 1958)
Come te movi te fulmino (It 1958)

Rascel marine (It 1958)
Ferdinando I, re di Napoli (It 1958)
Policarpo, ufficiale di scrittura [Policarpo de tapetti] (It-Sp-Fr 1959)
Tempi duri per i vampiri (It 1959)
Anonima cocottes [Petites Femmes et hautes finances] (It-Fr 1960)
Il corazziere (It 1960)
Un militare e mezzo (It 1960)
L'Ours (Fr-It 1960)
Gli attendenti (It 1961)
Il giudizio universale [Le Jugement dernier] (It-Fr 1961)
Mani in alto [En pleine bagarre] (Fr-It 1961)
The Secret of Santa Vittoria (UA 1969)
Il trapianto [Trasplante a la italiana] (It-Sp 1970)

RASP, FRITZ, b. May 13, 1891, Bayreuth, Germany
Das Phantom der Oper (Ger 1915)
Das Sportsmädel (Ger 1915)
Die verkanfte braut (Ger 1915)

Fritz Rasp in <u>Lina Braake</u> (1975).

Teufelchen (Ger 1915)
Zucker und Zinit (Ger 1915)
Schuhpalast Pinkus (Ger 1916)
Hans Trutz im Schlaraffenland (Ger 1917)
Jugend (Ger 1922)
Der Mensch am Wege (Ger 1923)
This Is Money (Ger 1923)
Schatten, eine nächtliche Halluzination (Ger 1923)
Zwischen Abend und Morgen [Der Spuk siner Hacht] (Ger 1923)
Arabella, der Roman eines Pferdes (Ger 1924)
Komödianten (Ger 1925)
Ein Sommernachtstraum (Ger 1925)
Menschen am Meer (Ger 1925)
Die Puppe vom Lunapark (Ger 1925)
Goetz von Berlichingen zubenannt mit der eisernen Hand (Ger
     1925)
Das Haus der Lüge (Ger 1926)
Qualen der Nacht (Ger 1926)
Der Liebe Lust und Leid [Kellerkavaliere] (Ger 1926)
Überflüssige Menschen (Ger 1926)
Die Waise von Lowood (Ger 1926)
Metropolis (Ger 1927)
Kinderseelen Klagen euch an (Ger 1927)
Der letzte Walzer (Ger 1927)
Die Liebe der Jeanne Ney (Ger 1927)
Schinderhannes (Ger 1928)
Der geheimnisvolle Spiegel (Ger 1928)
Spione (Ger 1928)
Die Carmen von St. Pauli (Ger 1928)
Der Hund von Baskerville (Ger 1929)
Die Frau im Mond (Ger 1929)
Tagebuch einer Verlorenen (Ger 1929)
Die Drei um Edith (Ger 1929)
Frühlings erwachen (Ger 1929)
Die grosse Sehnsucht (Ger 1930)
Dreyfus (Ger 1930)
Tropennächte [Ger version of Dangerous Paradise] (Ger 1931)
Der Mörder Dimitri Karamasoff (Ger 1931)
Les Frères Karamazoff [Fr version of Der Mörder Dimitri
     Karamasoff] (Ger 1931)
Die Dreigroschenoper (Ger 1931)
Der Zinker (Ger 1931)
Die Pranke (Ger 1931)
Emil und die Detektive (Ger 1931)
Die Vier vom Bob 13 (Ger 1931)
Der Hexer (Ger 1932)
Die Grausame Freundin (Ger 1932)
Der sündige Hof [Lona und ihr Knecht] (Ger 1933)
Der Schuss am Nebelhorn (Ger 1933)
Der Judas von Tirol (Ger 1933)
Grenzfeuer (Ger 1934)
Charleys Tante (Ger 1934)
Klein Dorrit (Ger 1934)

Lockvogel (Ger 1934)
Lockspitzel Asew (Ger 1935)
Onkel Braesig (Ger 1936)
Die Leuchter des Kaisers (Ger 1936)
Der Hund von Baskerville (Ger 1937)
Togger (Ger 1937)
Einmal Werd' Ich dir Gefallen (Ger 1938)
Nanu, Sie kennen Korff noch nicht? (Ger 1938)
Es war eine Rauschende Ballnacht (Ger 1939)
Frau im Strom (Ger 1939)
Leidenschaft (Ger 1940)
Alarm (Ger 1941)
Paracelsus (Ger 1943)
Irgendwo in Berlin (W Ger 1946)
Skandal in der Botschaft (W Ger 1950)
Haus des Lebens (W Ger 1952)
Hokuspokus (W Ger 1953)
Die Mühle im Schwarzwälder Tal (W Ger 1953)
Der Cornet (W Ger 1955)
Magic Fire [Frauen um Richard Wagner] (USA-W Ger 1956)
Der Frosch mit der Maske [Froen med masken] (W Ger-Dan 1959)
Der rote Kreis (W Ger 1960)
Die Bande des Schreckens (W Ger 1960)
Das schwarze Schaf (W Ger 1960)
Die seltsame Gräfin (W Ger 1961)
Das Rätsel der Roten Orchidee (W Ger 1962)
Das schwarz-weiss-rote Himmelbett (W Ger 1962)
Der Zinker (W Ger 1963)
Dr. Med. Hiob Praetorius (W Ger 1965)
Lina Braake--die Interessen der Bank können nicht die interessen Sein, die Braake Hat (W Ger 1975)

REDGRAVE, LYNN, b. March 8, 1943, London
Tom Jones (UA 1963)
Girl with Green Eyes (UA 1964)
Georgy Girl (Col 1966)
The Deadly Affair (Col 1967)
Smashing Time (Par 1967)
The Virgin Soldiers (Col Br 1969)
Last of the Mobile Hot Shots [Blood Kin] (WB 1970)
Viva la muerta tua [Don't Turn the Other Cheek] (It-Sp 1972)
Every Little Crook and Nanny (MGM-EMI 1972)
Everything You Always Wanted to Know About Sex ** but Were Afraid to Ask (UA 1972)
The National Health (Col 1973)
The Happy Hooker (Cannon 1975)

REDGRAVE, MICHAEL, b. March 20, 1908, Bristol, England
The Lady Vanishes (MGM Br 1938)
Climbing High (MGM Br 1938)
Stolen Life (Par Br 1939)
A Window in London [Lady in Distress] (GFD 1939)

The Stars Look Down (GN 1939)
Kipps [The Remarkable Mr. Kipps] (20th Br 1941)
Atlantic Ferry [Sons of the Sea] (WB 1941)
Jeannie (GFD 1941)
The Big Blockade (UA 1942)
Thunder Rock (MGM Br 1942)
The Way to the Stars [Johnny in the Clouds] (UA 1945)
Dead of Night (ep "The Ventriloquist's Dummy") (EL 1945)
The Captive Heart (GFD 1946)
The Years Between (GFD 1946)
The Man Within [The Smugglers] (GFD 1947)
Fame Is the Spur (GFD 1947)
Mourning Becomes Electra (RKO 1947)
The Secret Beyond the Door (Univ 1948)
The Browning Version (GFD 1951)
The Magic Box (BL 1951)
The Importance of Being Earnest (GFD 1952)
The Green Scarf (BL 1954)
The Sea Shall Not Have Them (Eros 1954)
Confidential Report [Mr. Arkadin] (WB 1955)
The Night My Number Came Up (GFD 1955)
The Dambusters (ABPC 1955)
Oh Rosalinda! (ABP 1955)
1984 (ABP 1956)
The Happy Road (MGM 1957)
Time Without Pity (Eros 1957)
The Quiet American (UA 1958)
Law and Disorder (BL 1958)
Behind the Mask (BL 1958)
Shake Hands with the Devil (UA 1959)
The Wreck of the Mary Deare (MGM 1959)
No, My Darling Daughter (RFD 1961)
The Innocents (20th 1961)
The Loneliness of the Long Distance Runner (Bry 1962)
Young Cassidy (MGM 1965)
The Hill (MGM 1965)
The Heroes of Telemark (RFD 1965)
La Vingt Cinquieme Heure [The 25th Hour] (Fr-It-Yug 1967)
Assignment K (Col 1967)
Heidi (TVM 1968)
Oh! What a Lovely War (Par 1969)
Battle of Britain (UA 1969)
Goodbye, Mr. Chips (MGM 1969)
Connecting Rooms (London Screen 1969)
Goodbye Gemini (CIRO 1970)
The Go-Between (MGM-EMI 1971)
Nicholas and Alexandra (Col 1971)

REDGRAVE, VANESSA, b. Jan. 30, 1937, London
Behind the Mask (BL 1958)
Morgan--A Suitable Case for Treatment (BL 1966)
A Man for All Seasons (Col 1966)
Blow-Up (MGM 1967)

Camelot (WB 1967)
Sailor from Gibraltar (UA 1967)
Red and Blue (UA 1967)
The Charge of the Light Brigade (UA 1968)
Un tranquillo posto in campagna [A Quiet Place in the Country]
    (It-Fr 1968)
Isadora [The Loves of Isadora] (RFD 1969)
The Sea Gull (WPD 1969)
Dropout (It 1971)
The Devils (WB 1971)
The Trojan Women (Cin 1971)
Mary, Queen of Scots (RFD 1972)
Murder on the Orient Express (EMI 1974)
Out of Season (EMI 1975)

Vanessa Redgrave

REED, OLIVER, b. 1938, Wimbledon, England
    The Angry Silence (BL 1960)
    The League of Gentlemen (RFD 1960)

The Two Faces of Dr. Jekyll [House of Fright] (Col 1960)
Beat Girl [Wild for Kicks] (Renown 1960)
Sword of Sherwood Forest (Col 1960)
The Bulldog Breed (RFD 1960)
His and Hers (Eros 1961)
No Love for Johnnie (RFD 1961)
The Curse of the Werewolf (Univ 1961)
The Rebel (WPD 1961)
The Pirates of Blood River (Col 1962)
Captain Clegg [Night Creatures] (Univ 1962)
Paranoiac (Univ 1963)
The Damned [These Are the Damned] (Col 1963)
The Scarlet Blade (WPD 1963)
The System [The Girl Getters] (Bry 1964)
The Party's Over (Monarch 1965) [made in 1963]
The Brigand of Kandahar (WPD 1965)
The Trap (RFD 1966)
The Jokers (RFD 1966)
The Shuttered Room (WPD 1967)
I'll Never Forget What's 'is Name (RFD 1967)
Oliver! (Col 1968)
Hannibal Brooks (UA 1969)
The Assassination Bureau (Par 1969)
Women in Love (UA 1969)
Take a Girl Like You (Col 1971) [made in 1969]
La Dame dans l'auto avec des lunettes et un fusil [The Girl in
   the Car with Glasses and a Gun] (Fr 1971)
The Devils (UA 1971)
The Hunting Party (UA 1971)
Zero Population Growth [Z. P. G.] (Scotia-Barber 1971)
Sitting Target (MGM-EMI 1972)
Mordi e fugi [Bite and Run] (It-Fr 1972)
Revolver (It-Fr-W Ger 1972)
Un Uomo (It-GB 1973)
The Three Musketeers [The Queen's Diamonds] (20th 1973)
Il giorno del furore [Fury] (It-GB 1973)
Blue Blood (Nationwide 1974)
The Four Musketeers [The Revenge of Milady] (20th 1974)
Tommy (Hemdale 1975)
Royal Flash (Fox-Rank 1975)

REGGIANI, SERGE, b. May 2, 1922, Reggio-Emilia, Italy
   Le Voyageur de la toussaint (Fr 1942)
   Le Carrefour des enfants perdus (Fr 1943)
   François Villon (Fr 1945)
   Etoile sans lumière (Fr 1945)
   Les Portes de la nuit (Fr 1946)
   Coincidences (Fr 1946)
   Le Desus des cartes (Fr 1947)
   La Fleur de l'âge (1947) [unfinished]
   Les Amants de Vérone (Fr 1948)
   Manon (Fr 1949)
   Le Mystère de la chambre jaune (Fr 1948)

Retour à la vie [Return to Life] (Fr 1949)
Aux royaume des cieux [Woman Hunt] (Fr 1949)
Le Parfum de la dame en noir (Fr 1949)
Les Anciens de Saint-Loup (Fr 1950)
Une Fille à croquer (Fr 1950)
La Ronde [Circle of Love] (Fr 1950)

Serge Reggiani

The Secret People (GFD 1951)
Casque d'or [Golden Helmet] (Fr 1951)
Camicie rosse (It 1951)
La Bergère et la ramoneur (Fr 1952)
Les Anges déchus (Fr-It 1952)
Fille dangereuse (Fr-It 1952)
Act of Love (UA 1954)
Napoléon (Fr 1954)
Les Salauds vont en enfer (Fr 1955)
La Fille Eliza (Fr 1956)
Une Hectare de ciel (It-Fr 1956)
Echec au porteur (Fr-It 1957)
Les Misérables (Fr-It-E Ger 1957)
Le Passager clandestin (Fr-Australia 1957)
La donna del giorno (It-Fr 1957)
Marie-Octobre (Fr 1958)
Tutti a casa [Everybody Go Home] (It-Fr 1960)
Paris Blues (Par 1961)
La guerra continua (It-Fr 1961)
Il gattopardo [The Leopard] (It-Fr 1962)
Les Doulos (Fr 1962)
Bestiaire d'amour (Fr 1964)
Marie Chantal contre le Dr. Kha (Fr-Sp-It-Mor 1965)

Compartiment Tueurs [The Sleeping Car Murders] (Fr 1965)
The 25th Hour (MGM 1966)
Les Aventuriers [The Last Adventure] (Fr-It 1967)
Il giorno della civetta (It 1968)
I setti fratelli Cervi (It-Fr 1968)
Les Ruffians (Fr 1969)
Les Mains dans les poches (Fr-It 1969)
L'Amee des ambres (Fr-It 1969)
Comptes à rebours [Countdown] (Fr 1970)
Trois Milliards sans ascenseur (Fr-It 1972)
Les Caïds (Fr 1972)
Vincent, François, Paul et les autres (Fr-It 1974)
Le Bon et les mefiants (Fr 1975)
La Chat et la souris (Fr 1975)

REID, BERYL, b. 1918, Hereford, England
The Belles of St. Trinians (BL 1954)
The Extra Day (BL 1956)
Two-Way Stretch (BL 1960)
The Dock Brief [Trial and Error] (MGM Br 1962)
Star! [Those Were the Times] (20th 1968)

Beryl Reid in Entertaining Mr. Sloane (1970).

Inspector Clouseau (UA 1968)
The Killing of Sister George (Cin 1969)
The Assassination Bureau (Par 1969)
Entertaining Mr. Sloane (WPD 1970)
The Beast in the Cellar (Tigon 1970)
Dr. Phibes Rises Again (AIP 1972)
Psychomania (Scotia-Barber 1973)
Father, Dear Father (Fox-Rank 1973)
No Sex Please, We're British (Col-Warner 1973)

RENAUD, MADELEINE, b. Feb. 21, 1903, Paris
Vent Debout (Fr 1922)
La Terre qui meurt (Fr 1926)
Serments (Fr 1931)
Jean de la lune (Fr 1931)
La Belle Marinière (Fr 1932)
Mistigri (Fr 1932)
La Couturière de Lunéville (Fr 1932)
De Tunnel [Fr version of German film] (Fr 1933)
La Maternelle (Fr 1933)
Primerose (Fr 1933)
Le Voleur (Fr 1934)
Maria Chapdelaine (Fr 1934)
Coeur de Gueux (Fr 1935)
La Marche Nuptiale (Fr 1935)
Les Demi-Vierges (Fr 1936)
Les Petites Alliées (Fr 1936)
Hélène (Fr 1936)
L'Etrange Monsieur Victor (Fr 1938)
Remorques (Fr 1939)
Lumière d'été (Fr 1942)
L'Escalier sans fin (Fr 1943)
Le Ciel est à vous (Fr 1943)
Le Plaisir (Fr 1951)
Les Dialogue dés Carmélites (Fr-It 1959)
The Longest Day (20th 1962)
Le Diable par la queue (Fr-It 1969)
La Mandarine (Fr-It 1971)

RENNIE, MICHAEL, b. Aug. 25, 1909, Bradford, England; d. June
     10, 1971
The Secret Agent (Gaumont 1936)
Gangway (GFD 1937)
Bank Holiday [Three on a Weekend] (GFD 1938)
The Divorce of Lady X (UA 1938)
This Man in Paris (Par Br 1939)
Conquest of the Air (UA 1940) [started ca. 1936]
The Patient Vanishes (Pathe 1941)
Turned Out Nice Again (UA 1941)
Pimpernel Smith [Mister V] (Anglo 1941)
Dangerous Moonlight [Suicide Squadron] (RKO Br 1941)
The Tower of Terror (Pathe 1941)
Ships with Wings (UA 1941)

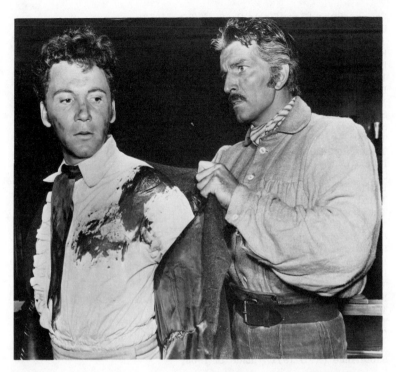

Michael Rennie (right) and Cameron Mitchell in Les Miserables (1952).

The Big Blockade (UA 1942)
I'll Be Your Sweetheart (GFD 1945)
The Wicked Lady (EL 1945)
Caesar and Cleopatra (EL 1946)
The Root of All Evil (GFD 1947)
White Cradle Inn [High Fury] (BL 1947)
Idol of Paris (WB 1948)
Uneasy Terms (Pathe 1948)
The Golden Madonna (WB 1949)
Miss Pilgrim's Progress (GN 1950)
The Body Said No! (Eros 1950)
Trio (ep "Sanatorium") (GFD 1950)
The Black Rose (20th 1950)
The 13th Letter (20th 1951)
The Day the Earth Stood Still (20th 1951)
I'll Never Forget You [The House in the Square] (20th 1951)
Phone Call from a Stranger (20th 1952)
5 Fingers (20th 1952)
Les Miserables (20th 1952)

Sailor of the King [Single-Handed] (20th 1953)
Dangerous Crossing (20th 1953)
The Robe (20th 1953)
King of the Khyber Rifles (20th 1954)
Demetrius and the Gladiators (20th 1954)
Princess of the Nile (20th 1954)
Desiree (20th 1954)
Mambo (Par 1955)
Seven Cities of Gold (20th 1955)
Soldier of Fortune (20th 1955)
The Rains of Ranchipur (20th 1955)
Teenage Rebel (20th 1956)
Island in the Sun (20th 1957)
Omar Khayyam (Par 1957)
Battle of the V 1 [Unseen Heroes] (Eros 1958)
Third Man on the Mountain (BV 1959)
The Lost World (20th 1960)
Mary, Mary (WB 1963)
Ride Beyond Vengeance (Col 1965)
Hondo and the Apaches (MGM 1967)
Hotel (WB 1967)
Bersaglio mobile [Death on the Run] (It 1967)
The Power (MGM 1968)
Nude...si muore [The Young, the Evil and the Savage] (It 1968)
The Devil's Brigade (UA 1968)
La battaglia di El Alamein [Desert Tanks] (It-Fr 1969)
Dracula--el hombre que vino de ummo [Dracula vs. Frankenstein]
    (Sp-W Ger 1971)
Subterfuge (RFD 1971) [made in 1968]

REY, FERNANDO (Fernando Casade Arambillet), b. Jan. 20, 1917,
    La Coruna, Spain
La gitanilla (Sp 1940)
Eugenia de Montijo (Sp 1944)
Los ultimos de Filipinas (Sp 1945)
Mision blanca (Sp 1945)
Reina santa (Sp 1947)
Don Quijote de la Mancha (Sp 1947)
Cocura de amor (Sp 1948)
Aventuras de Juan Lucas (Sp 1949)
Agustina de Aragon (Sp 1950)
Cielo negro (Sp 1951)
Bienvenido Mr. Marshall! (Sp 1952)
Comicos (Sp 1952)
Rebeldia (Sp 1953)
En alcalde de Zalamea (Sp 1953)
Un marido de ida y vuelta (Sp 1955)
Tangier Assignment (NR 1955)
Faustina (Sp 1956)
El Amor de Don Juan (Sp 1956)
Una Aventura de Gil Blas (Fr-Sp 1956)
La Venganza (Sp 1957)
Les Bijoutiers au clair de lune [Heaven Fell That Night] (Fr-
    Sp 1957)

Culpables (Sp 1958)
Los habitants de la casa deshabitada (Sp 1958)
Parque de Madrid (Sp 1958)
Sonatas (Sp 1959)
Operación Relampage (It-Sp 1959)
Fabiola (It-Sp 1960)
Los ultimos dias de Pompeya (Sp-It-W Ger 1960)
Don Lucio y el hermano pio (Sp 1960)
Viridania (Sp-Mex 1961)
Rebelión de los esclavos [Revolt of the Slaves] (It-Sp-W Ger 1961)
Shéhérazade (Fr-It-Sp 1962)
Rogelia (Sp 1962)
Goliat contra los gigantes (It-Sp 1962)
La casa del terror (Sp 1962)
Tierra brutal [The Savage Guns] (Sp-USA 1962)
El espontanes (Sp 1963)
Dios eligio sus viajeros (Sp 1963)
El diablo también llora (It-Sp 1963)
Los palomas (Sp 1964)
El espontaneo (Sp 1964)
El señor de la salle (Sp 1964)
La nueva cenicienta (Sp 1964)
Echappement libre (Fr-It-Sp 1964)
El hijo de pistolero (Sp 1965)
España insolita (Sp 1965)
Misión Lisboa (Fr-It-Sp 1965)
Zampo y yo (Sp 1965)
Cartas boca arriba [Cards on the Table] (Sp-Fr 1965)
Don Quijote (Fr-Sp-W Ger 1966)
Dulcinea del Tobosco (Fr-Sp-W Ger 1966)
Das Vermachtnis des Inka (W Ger-It-Sp 1966)
Campanadas a medianoche [Falstaff] (Sp-Swi 1966)
Los jeuces de la Biblia (It-Sp 1966)
Robo de Diamantes [Run Like a Thief] (Sp-USA 1967)
Joe, el implacable [Navajo Joe] (Sp-USA 1967)
Mas allá de las montañas (Sp-USA 1967)
Amor en el aire (Arg-Sp 1967)
Atraco al hampa (Fr-It-Sp 1967)
Cervantes (Sp 1967)
Guns of the Magnificent Seven (UA 1968)
Villa Rides (Par 1968)
Un sudario a la Medira (It-Sp 1969)
Satyricon [Fellini-Satyricon (It-Fr 1969)
Land Raiders (Col 1969)
The Adventurers (Par 1970)
Tristana (Fr-It-Sp 1970)
Muerte de un presidente (It-Sp 1970)
La colera del viente (Sp-It 1971)
The Light at the Edge of the World (Sp-Swi 1971)
Los compañeros (W Ger-It-Sp 1971)
The French Connection (20th 1971)
Los frios ojos del miedo (Sp-It 1971)
Historia de una traición (It-Sp 1971)

A Town Called Bastard (GB-Sp 1971)
Chicas de club (Sp 1972)
Antony and Cleopatra (GB-Sp 1972)
One Way (It-Mex 1973)
Zanna bianca (It-Sp-Fr 1973)
Cadeveri excellenti (It-Fr 1975)
La Grande Bourgeoise (It-Fr 1975)
French Connection II (20th 1975)
Seven Beauties (It 1975)

RIBEIRINHO (Francisco Carlos Lopes Ribeiro), b. Sept. 21, 1911,
    Lisbon
Revolução de maio (Por 1937)
O feitiço do império (Por 1940)
O pai tirano (Por 1941)
O pátio das cantigas (Por 1942)
A menina da rádio (Por 1944)
A vizinha do lado (Por 1945)
Três espelhos (Por 1947)
O grande elias (Por 1950)
O costa de Africa (Por 1954)
O primo basilio (Por 1959)
Aqui há fantasmas (Por 1963)

Ribeirinho

RIBEIRO, ALBERTO (Alberto Dias Ribeiro), Feb. 29, 1920, Er-
    mezinde, Portugal

Um homem do Ribatejo (Por 1946)
Capas negras (Por 1947)
Cantiga da rua (Por 1949)
Rosa de Alfama (Por 1953)
A canção da saudade (Por 1964)

Alberto Ribeiro

RICH, CLAUDE, b. Feb. 8, 1929, Orgeval, France
　　Les Grandes Manoeuvres [Summer Manoeuvres] (Fr-It 1955)
　　C'est arrivé à Aden [It Happened in Aden] (Fr 1956)
　　Mitsou (Fr 1956)
　　La Polka des Menottes (Fr 1956)
　　Ni vu...ni connu (Fr 1957)
　　La ligne de vie (Fr 1957)
　　La Française et l'amour [Love and the Frenchwoman] (ep "Le
　　　　Mariage"] (Fr 1960)
　　L'Homme à femmes (Fr 1960)
　　Ce Soir au jamais [Tonight or Never] (Fr 1960)
　　Tout l'or du monde [All the Gold in the World] (Fr-It 1961)
　　Les Sept Péchés capitaux [Seven Capital Sins] (ep "L'Avarice")
　　　　(Fr-It 1961)
　　La Chambre ardente [The Curse and the Coffin] (Fr-It 1961)
　　Les Petits Matins [Girl on the Road] (Fr-It 1962)
　　Le Caporal épinglé [The Vanishing Corporal] (Fr 1962)
　　Le Diable et les dix Commandements (Fr-It 1962)
　　Copacabana Palace (It-Fr-Braz 1962)
　　Les Tontons flinguers (Fr-It-W Ger 1963)
　　Comment trouvez-vous ma soeur? (Fr 1963)
　　Constance aux enfers [Web of Fear] (Fr-It-Sp 1963)

Le Repas des fauves (Fr-It-Sp 1964)
Les Copains (Fr 1964)
La Chasse à l'homme [Male Hunt] (Fr-It 1964)
Mata-Hari--Agent H 21 (Fr-It 1964)
L'Or du Duc (Fr-It 1965)
Un Milliard dans un billard (Fr-W Ger-It 1965)
M. le président directeur général/Appelez-moi maître (Fr 1966)
Paris brûle-t-il? [Is Paris Burning?] (Fr 1966)
Mona, l'étoile sans nom (Fr-Rum 1967)
Les Compagnons de la Marguérite [Order of the Daisy] (Fr-It
     1967)
Oscar (Fr 1967)
La Mariée était en noir [The Bride Wore Black] (Fr-It 1968)
Je t'aime, je t'aime (Fr 1968)
La Piscine [The Swimming Pool] (Fr-It 1968)
Le Corps de Diane (Fr-Czech 1969)
Une Neuve en or (Fr-W Ger-It 1969)
Stravisky (Fr 1973)
L'Ironie du Sort (Fr 1973)
Le Futur aux trousses (Fr 1975)
Adieu poulet (Fr 1975)

RICHARD, CLIFF (Harry Webb), b. 1940, India
The Young Ones (WPD 1961)
Serious Charge (Eros 1959)
Expresso Bongo (Britannia 1959)
Summer Holiday (WPD 1963)
Wonderful Life (Elstree 1964)
Finders Keepers (UA 1966)
Two a Penny (WW 1967)
Take Me High (MGM-EMI 1973)

RICHARDSON, RALPH, b. Dec. 19, 1902, Cheltenham, Gloucester-
     shire, England
The Ghoul (W & F 1933)
Friday the 13th (ep "Millie the Non-Stop Variety Girl") (Gaumont
     1933)
The Return of Bulldog Drummond (Wardour 1934)
Java Head (ABFD 1934)
The King of Paris (UA 1934)
Bulldog Jack [Alias Bulldog Drummond] (Gaumont 1935)
Things to Come (UA 1936)
The Man Who Could Work Miracles (UA 1936)
Thunder in the City (UA 1937)
South Riding (UA 1938)
The Divorce of Lady X (UA 1938)
The Citadel (MGM Br 1938)
Q Planes [Clouds over Europe] (Col Br 1939)
The Four Feathers (UA 1939)
The Lion Has Wings (UA 1939)
On the Night of the Fire [The Fugitive] (GFD 1939)
The Day Will Dawn [The Avengers] (GFD 1942)
The Silver Fleet (GFD 1943)

Sir Ralph Richardson

The Volunteer (Anglo 1943)
School for Secrets [Secret Flight] (GFD 1946)
Anna Karenina (BL 1948)
The Fallen Idol (BL 1949)
The Heiress (Par 1949)
Outcast of the Islands (BL 1951)
Home at Seven [Murder on Monday] (BL 1952)
The Sound Barrier [Breaking the Sound Barrier] (BL 1952)
The Holly and the Ivy (BL 1952)
Richard III (BL 1955)
Smiley (20th 1956)
The Passionate Stranger [A Novel Affair] (BL 1957)
Our Man in Havana (Col 1960)
Oscar Wilde (20th 1960)
Exodus (UA 1960)
Long Day's Journey into Night (20th 1962)
Woman of Straw (UA 1964)
Doctor Zhivago (MGM 1965)

Khartoum (UA 1966)
The Wrong Box (Col 1966)
Oh! What a Lovely War (Par 1969)
Battle of Britain (UA 1969)
The Bed-Sitting Room (UA 1969)
The Looking Glass War (Col 1969)
The Midas Run [A Run on Gold] (Cin 1969)
David Copperfield (20th 1969)
Eagle in a Cage (Cin 1970)
Whoever Slew Auntie Roo? (AIP 1972)
Tales from the Crypt (Cin 1972)
Lady Caroline Lamb (GB-It 1972)
Alice's Adventures in Wonderland (Fox-Rank 1972)
O Lucky Man! (Col-Warner 1973)
A Doll's House (MGM-EMI 1973)
Frankenstein: The True Story (CIC 1974)
Rollerball (UA 1975)

RIVA, EMMANUELLE (Emmanuele), b. Feb. 24, 1927, Chenimenil
      (Vosges), France
Hiroshima mon amour (Fr-Jap 1959)
Le Huitième Jour (Fr 1959)
Recours en grace [Appeal for Mercy] (Fr-It 1960)
Adua et ses compagnes (It-Fr 1960)
Kapo (It-Fr-Yug 1960)
Léon Morin, prête [Leon Morin, priest] (Fr-It 1961)
Climats [Climates of Love] (Fr 1961)
Thérèse Desqueyroux (Fr 1962)
Le ore dell'amore (It-Fr 1963)
Le Gros Coup (Fr-It 1964)
Thomas l'imposteur (Fr 1964)
Le Coup de grâce (Fr-Canada 1965)
Il momento della verità [The Moment of Truth] (It-Sp 1965)
Io uccido, tu uccidi (It-Fr 1965)
L'Or et le plomb (Fr 1965)
Soledad (Fr 1966)
Fruits amer [Bitter Fruit] (Fr-Yug-It 1967)
Les Risques du métier (Fr 1968)
La Modification (Fr-It 1970)
L'Homme du désir (Fr 1970)
Safari 5000 (Jap 1972)
Au long de Rivière Fango (Fr 1975)

ROBSON, FLORA, b. March 28, 1902, South Shields,
      England
A Gentleman of Paris (Gaumont 1931)
Dance Pretty Lady (Wardour 1932)
One Precious Year (Par 1933)
Catherine the Great (UA 1934)
Fire Over England (UA 1937)
Farewell Again [Troopship] (UA 1937)
I, Claudius [Unfinished 1937]
Wuthering Heights (UA 1939)

Poison Pen (ABPC 1939)
The Lion Has Wings (UA 1939)
We Are Not Alone (WB 1939)
Invisible Stripes (WB 1940)
The Sea Hawk (WB 1940)
Bahama Passage (Par 1941)
2,000 Women (GFD 1944)
Great Day (RKO Br 1945)
Caesar and Cleopatra (EL 1946)
Saratoga Trunk (WB 1946) [made in 1943]
The Years Between (GFD 1946)
Black Narcissus (GFD 1947)
Frieda (GFD 1947)
Holiday Camp (GFD 1947)
Good Time Girl (GFD 1948)
Saraband for Dead Lovers (GFD 1948)
Tall Headlines [The Frightened Bride] (GN 1952)
Malta Story (GFD 1953)
Romeo and Juliet (GFD 1954)
High Tide at Noon (RFD 1957)
No Time for Tears (ABPC 1957)
The Gypsy and the Gentleman (RFD 1958)
Innocent Sinners (RFD 1958)
Murder at the Gallop (MGM Br 1963)
55 Days at Peking (AA 1963)
Guns at Batasi (20th 1964)
Young Cassidy (MGM 1965)
Those Magnificent Men in Their Flying Machines; or, How I
    Flew from London to Paris in 25 Hrs and 11 Minutes (20th
    1965)
A King's Story (BL 1965) [documentary] (voice only)
Eye of the Devil [13] (MGM 1966)
The Shuttered Room (WPD 1967)
Cry in the Wind (GB-Gr 1967)
Fragment of Fear (Col 1970)
The Beloved (MGM-EMI 1971)

ROC, PATRICIA (Felicia Riese), b. June 7, 1918, Hampstead, Lon-
    don
The Gaunt Stranger [The Phantom Strikes] (ABFD 1938)
The Rebel Son (GB-Fr 1939)
The Missing People (GN Br 1939)
A Window in London [Lady in Distress] (GFD 1939)
Dr. O'Dowd (WB Br 1940)
Pack Up Your Troubles (Butcher 1940)
Gentlemen of Venture [It Happened to One Man] (RKO Br 1940)
Three Silent Men (Butcher 1940)
The Farmer's Wife (Pathe 1941)
My Wife's Family (Pathe 1941)
Let the People Sing (Anglo 1942)
Suspected Person (Pathe 1942)
We'll Meet Again (Col Br 1942)
Millions Like Us (GFD 1943)

2,000 Women (GFD 1944)
Love Story [A Woman Surrenders] (EL 1944)
Madonna of the Seven Moons (EL 1944)
Johnny Frenchman (EL 1945)
The Wicked Lady (EL 1945)
Canyon Passage (Univ 1946)
So Well Remembered (RKO Br 1947)
The Brothers (GFD 1947)
Jassy (GFD 1947)
Holiday Camp (GFD 1947)
When the Bough Breaks (GFD 1947)
One Night with You (GFD 1948)
The Perfect Woman (GFD 1949)
Man on the Eiffel Tower (RKO 1950)
L'Inconnue de Montreal (Fr-Can 1950)
Something Money Can't Buy (GFD 1952)
Le avventure di Cartouche [Cartouche] (It-USA 1953)
La vedova [The Widow] (It-Fr 1955)
The Hypnotist [Scotland Yard Dragnet] (AA 1959)
The House in the Woods (Archway 1959)
Bluebeard's Ten Honeymoons (WPD 1960)

RODRIGUES, AMALIA (Amália da Piedade Rebordão Rodrigues Sea-
    bra), b. June 23, 1920, Lisbon
    Capas negras (Por 1947)
    Fado a história de uma cantadeira (Por 1947)
    Sol e toiros (Por 1949)
    Vendaval maravilhoso (Por 1949)
    Os amantes do Tejo (Fr-Por 1954)
    Abril em Portugal (USA 1955) [documentary] (narrator)
    As canções unidas (Mex 1956)
    Sangue toureiro (Por 1958)
    Fado corrido (Por 1964)
    As ilhas encantadas (Por 1964)
    Os noivos (Sp-It 1965)
    Via Macau (Por-Fr 1965)

ROELS, MARCEL, b. Jan. 1, 1894, Antwerp; d. 1974
    Le Gentilhomme pauvre (Bel 1921)
    Ame belge (Bel 1922)
    La Libre belgique (Bel 1923)
    Le Mouton noir (Bel 1924)
    Le Masque du génie (Bel 1925) [unreleased]
    Un Clown dans la rue (Bel 1929)
    Prince d'une nuit (Bel 1929)
    En avant la musique (Bel 1935)
    C'était le bon temps (Bel 1936)
    Gardons notre sourire (Bel 1937)
    Bossemans et Coppenolle (Bel 1938)
    Zig-Zag (Bel 1940)
    La Maudite (Bel 1949)
    Fête de quartier (Bel 1954)
    Un Soir de joie (Bel 1954)
    L'Amour est quelque part (Bel 1955)

RÖKK, MARIKA, b. Nov. 3, 1913, Cairo
    Leichte Kavallerie (Ger 1935)
    Heisses Blut (Ger 1936)
    Und Du, mein Schatz, fährst mit (Ger 1936)
    Der Bettelstudent (Ger 1936)
    Gasparone (Ger 1937)
    Karussell (Ger 1937)
    Eine Nacht im Mai (Ger 1939)

Marika Rökk (center), Gunnar Möller, and Renate Ewart in Nachts
im grünen Kakadu (1957).

    Hall, Janine (Ger 1939)
    Es war eine rauschende Ballnacht (Ger 1940)
    Kora Terry (Ger 1940)
    Wunschkonzert (Ger 1940)
    Tanz mit dem Kaiser (Ger 1941)
    Frauen sind doch bessere Diplomaten (Ger 1941)
    Hab' mich lieb (Ger 1942)
    Die Frau meiner Träume (Ger 1944)
    Fregola, das Kind der Donau (W Ger 1948)
    Sensation in Sam Remo (W Ger 1950)
    Die Czardasfürstin (W Ger 1951)
    Maske in Blau (W Ger 1952)
    Die geschiedene Frau (W Ger 1953)

Nachts im grünen Kakadu (W Ger 1957)
Bühne frei für Marika (W Ger 1958)
Die Nacht vor der Premiere (W Ger 1959)
Mein Mann, das Wirtschaftswunder (W Ger 1962)
Die Fledermaus (W Ger 1962)
Hochzeitsnacht im Paradies (W Ger 1962)
Heute gehn wir bummeln (W Ger 1962)

ROMANCE, VIVIANE (Pauline Ortmans), b. July 4, 1912, Roubaix,
    France
Ciboulette (Fr 1933)
L'Epervier (Fr 1933)
Liliom (Fr 1934)
N'aimer que toi (Fr 1934)
Marchand d'amour (Fr 1935)
Les Yeux noirs (Fr 1935)
Princesse Tam-Tam (Fr 1935)
Retour au paradis (Fr 1935)
La Bandéra (Fr 1935)
La Belle Equipe (Fr-Ger 1936)
Les Deux Favoris (Fr 1936)
L'Ange du foyer (Fr 1936)
Mademoiselle docteur (Fr 1937)
L'Homme à abattre (Fr 1937)
Le Puritain (Fr 1937)
Le Club de aristocrates (Fr 1937)
Naples au baiser de feu (Fr 1937)
Prison des femmes (Fr 1937)
L'Etrange Monsieur Victor (Fr 1938)
Le Joueur (Fr 1938)
La Maison du maltais (Fr 1938)
Gibraltar (Fr 1938)
L'Esclave blanche (Fr 1939)
La Tradition de minuit (Fr-It 1939)
Rosa di sangue (It 1939)
La Vénus aveugle (Fr 1941)
Cartacalha (Fr 1941)
Une Femme dans la nuit (Fr 1941)
Feu sacrée (Fr 1942)
Carmen (It 1943)
La Boîte aux rêves (Fr 1943)
La Route du bagne (Fr 1945)
La Colère des dieux (Fr 1946)
Panique (Fr 1946)
La Maison sans la mer (Fr 1946)
L'Affaire du collier de la reine (Fr 1946)
Le Carrefour des passions (Fr-It 1947)
Maya (Fr 1949)
Passion (Fr 1950)
Au Coeur de la Casbah (Fr 1951)
Les Sept Péchés capitaux [Seven Capital Sins] (Fr-It 1952)
Les Femmes sont des anges (Fr 1952)
Legion etrangérè (It 1953)

La Chaîr et le diable (Fr 1953)
Le Tournant dangereux (Fr 1954)
Gueule d'ange (Fr-It 1955)
L'Affaire des poisons (Fr-It 1955)
L'Inspecteur connaît la musique (Fr 1955)
Pitié pour les vamps (Fr 1956)
Pelusa (Sp 1960)
Mélodie en sous-sol [The Big Snatch] (Fr-It 1963)
Nada (Fr-It 1973)

RONET, MAURICE, b. April 13, 1927, Nice
Rendez-vous à Juillet (Fr 1948)
Un Grand Patron (Fr 1951)
Les Sept Péchés capitaux [Seven Capital Sins] (ep "Luxure")
   (Fr-It 1952)
Horizon sans fin (Fr 1952)
La Jeune Folle [A Kiss for a Killing] (Fr 1952)
La Môme Vert-de-Gris [Gun Moll] (Fr 1952)
Lucrèce Borgia (It-Fr 1952)
Châteaux en Espagne (Fr-Sp 1953)
La Guérisseur (Fr 1953)
Casta Diva/Casa Ricordi (It-Fr 1954)
Gueule d'Ange (Fr 1955)

Maurice Ronet and Christa Lang in Le Scandale (1966).

Les Aristocrates (Fr 1955)
La Sorcière (Fr 1955)
Section des disparus (Fr 1956)
Celui qui dort mourir [He Who Must Die] (Fr-It 1956)
Ascenseur pour l'échafaud [Lift to the Scaffold] (Fr 1957)
Cette-Nuit-là (Fr 1958)
Ce Corps tant désiré [Way of the Wicked] (Fr 1958)
Plein soleil [Purple Noon] (Fr-It 1959)
Carmen de Grenade (Sp 1959)
Les Grandes Personnes [A Taste of Love] (Fr-It 1960)
Il peccato degli anni verdi (It 1960)
La récreation [Playtime] (Fr 1960)
Portrait Robot (Fr 1960)
Mi ultimo tango (Sp 1960)
Le Rendez-vous de minuit [Rendezvous at Midnight] (Fr 1961)
Liberté 1 (Fr-Senegal 1961)
La Dénonciation (Fr 1961)
Le Meurtrier [Enough Rope] (Fr-It-W Ger 1963)
Le Feu follet [Will o' the Wisp] (Fr 1963)
Das Todesauge von Ceylon (W Ger-It-Fr 1963)
The Victors (Col 1963)
Donde tu estés (Sp-Fr-It 1964)
Casablanca mid d'espions (Sp 1964)
Les Parias de la gloire (Fr-Sp-It 1964)
La Ronde [Circle of Love] (Fr-It 1964)
Le Voleur de Tibidabo (Fr-Sp-It 1965)
Trois Chambres à Manhattan (Fr 1965)
Amador (Fr-Sp 1965)
La Longue Marche (Fr 1966)
Lost Command (Col 1966)
La Ligne de démarcation (Fr 1966)
Le Scandale [The Champagne Murders] (Fr 1966)
Il giardino della delizie [The Garden of Delight] (It 1967)
La Route de Corinthe [The Road to Corinth] (Fr-It-W Ger 1967)
Les Oiseaux vont mourir au Perou [The Birds Come to Die in
    Peru] (Fr 1968)
Le Curieux impertinent (Fr-It 1968)
Un diablo bajo la almohada (Sp 1968)
How Sweet It Is! (WB 1968)
La Femme infidele [The Unfaithful Wife] (Fr-It 1968)
Delphine (Fr 1969)
La piscine [The Swimming Pool] (Fr-It 1969)
Les Femmes (Fr-It 1969)
Le Dernier Saut (Fr-It-Swi 1969)
La Femme écarlate [The Scarlet Woman] (Fr-It 1969)
Qui? (Fr-It 1970)
La Modification (Fr-It 1970)
Un peu, beaucoup passionement (Fr 1971)
Raphael ou la debauche (Fr 1971)
Il diavolo nel cervello (It 1973)
Crazy Capo (Fr-It 1973)
Le Cri du coeur (Fr 1974)
La Messe Dorfe (Fr-It 1974)

Seul le vent connait la reponse [Die Antwort kennt nur der
  Wind] (Fr-W Ger 1974)
Jackpot (Fr-It 1975)
Oh! mia bella matrigna (It 1975)

ROQUEVERT, NOËL, b. Dec. 18, 1894, Paris; d. Nov. 5, 1973
  L'Etroit mousquetaire (Fr 1922)
  Cartouche (Fr 1934)
  La Bandera (Fr 1935)
  Marthe Richard, au service de la France (Fr 1936)
  Tarass Boulba (Fr 1936)
  La Porte du large (Fr 1936)
  La Terre qui meurt (Fr 1936)
  Miarka, la fille à l'ourse (Fr 1937)
  Barnabé (Fr 1938)
  Thérèse Martin (Fr 1938)
  Entrée des artistes (Fr 1938)
  Trois Valses (Fr 1938)
  La Belle Revanche (Fr 1938)
  Les Otages (Fr 1939)
  Chantons quand même (Fr 1939)
  Moulin-Rouge (Fr 1939)
  Le Chasseur de chez Maxim's (Fr 1939)
  Paris-New York (Fr 1939)
  Les Musiciens du ciel (Fr 1939)
  Ils étaient cinq permissionnaires (Fr 1940)
  Parade en sept nuits (Fr 1941)
  Mam'zelle Bonaparte (Fr 1941)
  La Symphonie fantastique (Fr 1941)
  Le Journal tombe à 5 heures (Fr 1942)
  Les Inconnus dans la maison (Fr 1942)
  Le Voile blue (Fr 1942)
  Picpus (Fr 1942)
  L'Assassin habite au 21 (Fr 1942)
  Le Destin fabuleux de Désirée Clary (Fr 1942)
  Dernier Atout (Fr 1942)
  La Main du diable (Fr 1943)
  Le Corbeau (Fr 1943)
  La Vie de plaisir (Fr 1943)
  Pierre et Jean (Fr 1943)
  25 Ans de bonheur (Fr 1943)
  Sérénade aux nuages (Fr 1945)
  Le Dernier Sou (Fr 1946)
  L'Affaire du grand hôtel (Fr 1946)
  La Rose de la mer (Fr 1946)
  Histoire de chanter (Fr 1946)
  Dernier Refuge (Fr 1946)
  Antoine et Antoinette (Fr 1947)
  Le Village perdu (Fr 1947)
  Croisìere pour l'inconnu (Fr 1947)
  Du Guesolin (Fr 1948)
  Scandale aux Champs-Elysées (Fr 1948)
  Le Paradis des pilotes perdus (Fr 1949)

Retour à la vie (Fr 1949)
Ronde de nuit (Fr 1949)
Véronique (Fr 1949)
La Cage aux filles (Fr 1949)
Adémaï au poteau-frontière (Fr 1949)
Amour et Cie (Fr 1949)
Justice est faite (Fr 1950)
Méfiez-vous des blondes (Fr 1950)
Les Femmes sont folles (Fr 1950)
Andalousie (Fr 1950)
La Passante (Fr 1951)
Ma Femme est formidable (Fr 1951)
Rome-Paris-Rome [Signori, in carrozaa! (Fr-It 1951)
L'Agonie des aigles (Fr 1951)
Le Plus Joli Péché du monde (Fr 1951)
Pas de vacances pour monsieur le maire (Fr 1951)
Fanfan-la-tulipe (Fr 1952)
Elle et moi (Fr 1952)
Cent Ans de gloire (Fr 1952)
Le Trou normand (Fr 1952)
Le Rideau rouge (Fr 1952)
Deux de l'escadrille (Fr 1952)
Sidi Bel Abbes (Fr 1952)
Les Détectives du dimanche (Fr 1953)
Capitaine Pantoufle (Fr 1953)
Les Compagnes de la nuit (Fr 1953)
Dortoir des grandes (Fr 1953)
Maternité clandestine (Fr 1953)
Mon Frangin du Sénégal (Fr 1953)
C'est la vie parisienne (Fr 1953)
Le Secret d'Hélène Marimon (Fr 1953)
Mourez, nous ferons le reste (Fr 1953)
Cadet-Rousselle (Fr 1954)
Le Mouton à cinq pattes (Fr 1954)
Madame du Barry (Fr-It 1954)
Le Comte de Monte-Cristo [Il Tesoro di Monte-Cristo] (Fr-It 1954)
Les Diaboliques (Fr 1954)
Le Dossier noir [Fascicolo nero] (Fr-It 1955)
Napoléon (Fr 1955)
La Soupe à la grimace (Fr 1955)
Chantage (Fr 1955)
L'Impossible Monsieur Pipelet (Fr 1955)
Nana [Nana] (Fr-It 1955)
On déménage le colonel (Fr 1955)
Tant qu'il y aura des femmes (Fr 1955)
La Bande a papa (Fr 1955)
La Madelon (Fr 1955)
Toute la ville accuse (Fr 1956)
L'Auberge fleurie (Fr 1956)
Fernand cow-boy (Fr 1956)
Les Lumières du soir (Fr 1956)
La Terreur des dames (Fr 1956)

La Vie est belle (Fr 1956)
Ah! Quelle équipe (Fr 1956)
Club de femmes [Club di ragazze] (Fr-It 1956)
Nous autres à Champignol (Fr 1956)
Le Coin tranquille (Fr 1957)
Nuit blanche et rouge à lèvres [Quelle sacree soiree] (Fr 1957)
A pied, à cheval et en voiture (Fr 1957)
Fumée blonde (Fr 1957)
Ce Joli Monde (Fr 1957)
Bonjour toubib (Fr 1957)
Le Goût du massacre [Mademoiselle et son gang] (Fr 1957)
Une Nuit au Moulin-Rouge (Fr 1957)
Le Désir mène les hommes (Fr 1957)
Donnez-moi ma chance (Fr 1957)
Une Parisienne [Una parigina] (Fr-It 1957)
C'est la faute d'Adam (Fr 1958)
A pied, à cheval et un spoutnik (Fr 1958)
La Moucharde (Fr 1958)
Sacrée Jeunesse (Fr 1958)
La Loi, c'est la loi [La legge è legge] (Fr-It 1958)
Marie-Octobre (Fr 1958)
Suivez-moi, jeune homme (Fr 1958)
Archimède le clochard (Fr 1959)
Faibles femmes (Fr 1949)
Houla-Houla (Fr-It 1959)
Le Gendarme de Champignol (Fr 1959)
Soupe au lait (Fr 1959)
Nathalie, agent secret (Fr 1959)
Voulez-vous danser avec moi? (Fr-It 1959)
Marie des Isles (Fr-It 1959)
Certains l'aiment froide (Fr 1959)
A rebrousse-poil [Les piqués (Fr 1959)
La française et l'amour (ep "L'enfance") (Fr 1960)
Les Portes claquent (Fr 1960)
Jusqu'à plus soif (Fr 1960)
Cartouche (Fr-It 1961)
L'Assassin est dans l'annuaire [Cet imbécile de Rimoldi] (Fr
    1961)
Pas si folles, les guêpes [Cadavres en vacances] (Fr 1961)
Un Singe en hiver (Fr 1962)
Le Diable et les commandements (Fr-It 1962)
Les Mystères de Paris (Fr-It 1962)
Les Filles de La Rochelle (Fr 1962)
Le Masque de fer (Fr 1962)
Comment réussir en amour (Fr-It 1962)
Une Blonde comme ça (Fr-Argentine 1962)
Les Veinards (Fr 1962)
La Mer à boire [Mare matto] (Fr-It 1962)
Réglements de comptes (Fr 1962)
Snobs (Fr 1962)
La Chaste Suzanne [La casta Susana] (Fr-Sp 1963)
Clémentine chérie (Fr-It 1963)
Conduite à gauche (Fr 1963)

Coup de bambou (Fr 1963)
A toi de faire, mignonne (Fr-It 1963)
L'Assassin connait la musique (Fr 1963)
L'Honorable Stanislas agent secret (Fr 1963)
Le Majordome (Fr 1964)
Patate (Fr-It 1964)
L'Age ingrat (Fr 1964)
Les Combinards (Fr 1964)
Merveilleuse Angélique [Angélique, 2 Teil] (Fr-Ger-It 1965)
L'Or du duc (Fr 1965)
Un Milliard dans un billard (Fr 1965)
La Ligne de démarcation (Fr 1965)
Le Jardinier d'Argenteuil [Blüten, Gauner und die Nacht von
     Nizza] (Fr-Ger 1966)
Le Grand Restaurant (Fr 1966)
Pas de caviar pour Tanta Olga (Fr 1966)
Un Merveilleux Parfum d'oseille (Fr 1968)
La Honte de la famille (Fr 1969)
Jeunes Filles bien pour tous rapports (Swi 1970)
Mais qui donc m'a fait ce bébé? (Fr-Luxembourg 1971)
Le Viager (Fr 1971)

ROSAY, FRANÇOISE (Françoise de Naleche), b. April 19, 1891,
     Paris
Falstaff (Fr 1913)
Crainquebille (Fr 1922)
Gribiche (Fr 1925)
Les Deux Timides (Fr 1927)
La Femme en homme (Fr 1927)
Madame Récamier (Fr 1928)
Le Bouteau de verre (Fr 1928)
The One Woman Idea (Fox 1929)
Soyons Gai [Fr version of Let Us Be Gay] (Par Fr 1929)
Echec au roi [Fr version of The Royal Bed] (RKO Fr 1929)
Le Procès de Mary Dugan [Fr version of The Trial of Mary
     Dugan] (MGM Fr 1929)
La Petit Café [Fr version of Playboy of Paris] (Par 1930)
Buster se marié [Fr version of Parlor, Bedroom and Bath] (MGM
     Fr 1930)
Herr Casanova [Ger version of Parlor, Bedroom and Bath] (MGM
     Ger 1930)
Si l'empereur savait ça [Fr version of His Glorious Night] (MGM
     Fr 1930)
Jenny Lind [Fr version of A Lady's Morals] (MGM Fr 1930)
Quand on est belle [Fr version of The Easiest Way] (MGM 1931)
The Magnificent Lie
La Chance (Fr 1931)
Papa sans le savoir (Fr 1932)
Le Rosier de Madame Husson (Fr 1932)
La Pouponnière (Fr 1932)
Tambour battant [Fr version of Ger Des Jungen Dessauser's
     Grosse Lieber] (Fr 1932)
Vers l'abîme [Fr version of Ger Die Insel] (Fr 1933)

Jahre des Schweigens (Ger 1933)
L'Abbé Constantin (Fr 1933)
Le Grand Jeu (Fr 1934)
Coralie et Cie (Fr 1934)
Pension Mimosas (Fr 1934)
Remous (Fr 1934)
Gangster malgré lui (Fr 1934)
Tout par rien (Fr 1934)
Maternité (Fr 1935)
Marchand d'amour (Fr 1935)
Marie des Angoisses (Fr 1935)
La Kermesse heroïque (Fr 1935)
Die Klugen Frauen [Ger version of La Kermesse Heroïque]
    (Ger 1935)
Le Secret de Polichinelle (Fr 1936)
Jenny (Fr 1936)
Un Carnet du bal [Christine] (Fr 1937)
Drôle de drame (Fr 1937)
Le Fanteuil 47 (Fr 1937)
Paix sur le Rhin (Fr 1938)
Ramuntcho (Fr 1938)
Le Joueur d'echecs (Fr 1938)
Le Ruisseau (Fr 1938)
Les Gens du voyage [Fr version of Ger Fahrendes Volk] (Fr
    1938)
Serge Panine (Fr 1938)
La Symphonie des brigands (Fr 1938)
Die Hochzeitreise (Ger 1939)
Bizarre Bizarre (Fr 1939)
Elles étaient douze femmes (Fr 1940)
Une Femme disparait (Swi 1941)
The Halfway House (Ealing 1944)
Johnny Frenchman (EL 1945)
Macadam (Fr 1946)
La Môme de Haut-le-Bois (Fr 1947)
Saraband for Dead Lovers (GFD 1948)
Quartet (ep "The Alien Corn") (GFD 1948)
Le Mystère Barton (Fr 1948)
Les Vagabonds du rêve (Fr 1949)
On n'aime qu'une fois (Fr 1950)
Maria Chapdelaine [The Naked Heart] (Fr-GB 1950)
Femmes sans nom (It 1950)
September Affair (Par 1951)
L'Auberge rouge [The Red Inn] (Fr 1951)
Wanda la pécheresse (It 1951)
Il figli di nessuno (It 1951)
The 13th Letter (20th 1951)
K--Das Haus des Schweigens (Ger 1951)
Les Sept Péchés capitaux [Seven Capital Sins] (ep "L'Orgueil")
    (Fr-It 1952)
Sul ponte dei sospiri (It-Fr 1952)
Le Banquet des fraudeurs (Bel 1952)
Chi è senza peccato? (It-Fr 1953)

La Princesse d'Eboli (Sp 1953)
La Reine Margot (Fr-It 1954)
That Lady (20th 1955)
Jeunes Filles d'aujourd'hui (Fr 1955)
La Chasse aux Maris (It 1955)
Le Long des trottoirs (Fr 1956)
The Seventh Sin (MGM 1957)
Interlude (Univ 1957)
Me and the Colonel (Col 1958)
Le Joueur [The Gambler] (Fr-It 1958)
Du Rififi chez les femmes [Riff-Raff Girls] (Fr-It 1959)
Sans tambour ni trompette (Fr 1959)
The Sound and the Fury (20th 1959)
Les Yeux de l'amour (Fr-It 1959)
Les Bois des amants (Fr-It 1960)
Die Gans von Sedan (W Ger-Fr 1960)
Stefanie in Rio (W Ger 1960)
Stop Me Before I Kill! (Col 1961)
Le Cave se rebiffe (Fr-It 1961)
Frau Cheney's Ende (W Ger-Swi 1961)
Pourquoi Paris? (Fr-It 1962)
Up from the Beach (20th 1965)
La Métamorphose de Cloportes [Cloportes] (Fr-It 1965)
The 25th Hour (Fr-It-Yug 1965)
Faut pas prendre les enfants du Bon Dieu pas des canards
    sauvages (Fr 1969)
Un Merveilleux Parfum d'oseille (Fr 1970)
Pas folle la guêpe (Fr 1972)

ROSSI-DRAGO, ELEANORA (Palmina Omiccioli), b. Sept. 23, 1925,
    Genoa, Italy
I pirati di Capri [The Pirates of Capri] (It 1948)
Altura (It 1949)
Due sorelle amano (It 1949)
Persiane chiuse (It 1950)
Sensualità (It 1951)
Tre storie proibite (It 1951)
L'ultima sentenza (It 1951)
Verginità (It 1951)
La fiammata (It 1952)
La tratta delle bianche (It 1952)
I setti dell'Orsa Maggiore (It 1952)
Destini di donne [Destinées] (It-Fr 1953)
Vestire gli ignudi (It 1953)
L'Esclave [Schiavitù] (Fr 1953)
L'Affaire Maurizius [Il caso Maurizius] (Fr-It 1954)
Le amiche (It 1954)
Napoléon (Fr 1954)
Donne sole (It 1956)
Il prezzo della gloria (It 1956)
Suor Letizia (It 1956)
Kean, genio e sregolatezza (It 1957)
Tous pluvent me tuer [Tutti possono uccidermi] (Fr-It 1957)

La Tour prends garde! [Agli ordini del re/Cuvaj se La Tur] (Fr-It-Yug 1957)
Dagli Appennini alle Ande (It 1958)
Le fric [La grana] (Fr-It 1958)
Estate violenta [Violent Summer] (It 1959)
L'impiegato (It 1959)
Un maledetto imbroglio [The Facts of Murder] (It 1959)
La strada lunga un anno [Cesta duga godinu dana] (It-Yug 1959)
Vacanze d'inverno (It 1959)
David e Golia (It 1959)
La garçonnière (It 1960)
Die rote Hand [La mano rosso] (W Ger-It 1960)
Sotto dieci bandiere [Under Ten Flags] (It 1960)
Dox, caccia all'uomo (It 1961)
Rosmunda e Alboino [Sword of the Conqueror] (It 1961)
Aiboino (It 1961)
Tiro al piccione (It 1961)
L'amore a vent'anni [Love at Twenty] (It-Fr-W Ger-Jap-Pol 1962)
Anima nera (It 1962)
I dongiovanni della Costa azzura (It 1963)
Il giorno più corto (It 1963)
Ipnosi [Hypnosis] (It-Sp-W Ger 1963)
Tempesta su Ceylon (It 1963)
Il terrore di notte [Terror en la noche/Teppich des Grauens] (It-Sp-W Ger 1962)
Amore facile (ep "Il vedovo bianco") (It 1964)
I disco volante (It 1964)
Il diablo también llora (Sp 1964)
L'idea fissa [Love and Marriage] (It-Sp 1964)
Onkel Toms Hütte [Uncle Tom's Cabin] (W Ger 1964)
Se permette, parliamo di donne [Let's Talk About Women] (It 1964)
Il treno del sabato (It 1964)
El secreto de Bill North [Il segreto del vestito rosso/Assassination Made in Italy] (Sp-It 1965)
Io uccido, tu uccidi (It 1965)
Su e giù (ep "Il colpo del leone") (It 1965)
La bibbia [The Bible... in the Beginning] (20th 1966)
Il delitto di Anna Sandoval (It-Sp 1966)
Mano di velluto (It 1967)
El ultimo sabado (Sp 1967)
Il segreto del vestito rosso (It 1968)
L'età del malessere [Love Problems] (It 1968)
Camille 2000 (It 1969)
Las endemoniadas (Sp 1971)
Nelle pieghe della carne (It 1970)
Il dio chiamato Dorian [Das Bildnis des Dorian Gray/Dorian Gray] (It-W Ger 1970)

RÜHMANN, HEINZ, b. March 6, 1902, Essen, Germany
Das deutsche Mutterherz (Ger 1926)
Das Mädchen mit den fünf Nullen (Ger 1927)
Die Drei von der Tankstelle (Ger 1930)

Heinz Rühmann and Johanna Matz in Der Kapitän (1971).

Einbrecher (Ger 1930)
Der brave Sünder (Ger 1931)
Bomben auf Monte Carlo (Ger 1931)
Meine Frau, die Hochstaplerin (Ger 1931)
Man braucht kein Geld (Ger 1931)
Der Mann, der seinen Mörder sucht (Ger 1931)
Der Stolz der 3. Kompanie (Ger 1931)
Es wird schon wieder besser (Ger 1932)
Strich durch die Rechnung (Ger 1932)
Drei blaue Jungs--ein blondes Mädel (Ger 1933)
Lachende Erben (Ger 1933)
Ich und die Kaiserin (Ger 1933)
Es gibt nur eine Liebe (Ger 1933)
Heimkehr ins Glück (Ger 1933)
Die Finanzen des Grossherzogs (Ger 1934)
So ein Flegel (Ger 1934)
Pipin der Kurze (Ger 1934)
Heinz im Mond (Aus 1935)
Ein Walzer für Dich (Aus 1934)
Frasquita (Aus 1934)
Der Himmel auf Erden (Aus 1935)
Der Aussenseiter (Ger 1935)

Eva (Ger 1935)
Wer wagt--gewinnt' (Ger 1935)
Ungeküsst soll man nicht schlafen geh'n (Aus 1936)
Wenn wir alle Engel waren (Ger 1936)
Allotria (Ger 1936)
Der Mustergatte (Ger 1937)
Der Mann, won dem man spricht (Aus 1937)
Der Mann, der Sherlock Holmes war (Ger 1937)
Lumpazivagabundus (Aus 1937)
Nanu, Sie kennen korff noch nicht? (Ger 1938)
Die Umwege des schönen Karl (Ger 1938)
Fünf Millionen suchen einen Erben (Ger 1938)
Paradies der Junggesellen (Ger 1939)
Hurra! Ich bin Papa (Ger 1939)
Der Florentiner Hut (Ger 1939)
13 Stühle (Ger 1939)
Kleider machen Leute (Ger 1940)
Wunschkonzert (Ger 1940)
Der Gasmann (Ger 1941)
Hauptsache glücklich (Ger 1941)
Quax, der Bruchpilot (Ger 1941)
Ich vertraue Dir meine Frau an (Ger 1943)
Die Feuerzangenbowle (Ger 1944)
Quax in Fahrt (Ger 1945)
Sag' die Wahrheit (W Ger 1946)
Der Herr vom andern Stern (W Ger 1948)
Das Geheimnis der roten Katze (W Ger 1949)
Ich mach' Dich glücklich (W Ger 1949)
Das kann jedem passieren (W Ger 1952)
Schäm dich, Brigitte [Wir werden das Kind schon schaukeln]
    (Aus-W Ger 1952)
Keine Angst vor grossen Tieren (W Ger 1953)
Briefträger Muller (W Ger 1953)
Auf der Reeperbahn nachts um half eins (W Ger 1954)
Zwischenlandung in Paris [Escale à Orly] (W Ger-Fr 1954)
Wenn der Vater mit dem Sohne (W Ger 1955)
Charleys Tante (W Ger 1956)
Der Hauptmann von Köpenick (W Ger 1956)
Das Sonntagskind (W Ger 1956)
Vater sein dagegen sehr (W Ger 1957)
Es geschah am hellichten Tag (W Ger-Swi 1958)
Der eiserne Gustav (W Ger 1958)
Der Pauker (W Ger 1958)
Ein Mann geht durch die Wand (W Ger 1959)
Menschen im Hotel (W Ger-Fr 1959)
Der Jugendrichter (W Ger 1959)
Mein Schulfreund (W Ger 1960)
Der brave Soldat Schweik (W Ger 1960)
Das schwarze Schaf (W Ger 1960)
Der Lügner (W Ger 1961)
Er kann's nicht lassen (W Ger 1962)
Max, der Taschendieb (W Ger 1962)
Das Haus in Montevideo (W Ger 1963)

Meine Tochter und Ich (W Ger 1963)
Vorsicht, Mister Dodd (W Ger 1964)
Dr. med. Hiob Prätorius (W Ger 1965)
La Bourse et la vie [Geld oder Leben] (Fr-W Ger-It 1965)
Das Liebeskarussell (Aus 1965)
Ship of Fools (Col 1965)
Grieche sucht Griechin (W Ger 1966)
Hokuspokus--oder wie lasse ich meinen Mann verschwinden (W
    Ger 1966)
Maigret und sein grösster Fall [Il caso difficile del Commissario
    Maigret] (W Ger-It 1966)
Die Abenteuer des Kardinal Braun (W Ger 1967)
Die Ente klingelt um 1/2 8 (W Ger 1967)
Der Kapitän (W Ger 1971)
Oh Jonathan--oh, Jonathan (W Ger 1973)

RUTHERFORD, MARGARET (Margaret Taylor Rutherford), b. May
    11, 1892, London; d. May 22, 1972
Dusty Ermine [Hideout in the Alps] (Wardour 1936)
Talk of the Devil (UA 1936)
Beauty and the Barge (Wardour 1937)
Catch as Catch Can [Atlantic Episode] (Fox Br 1937)
Missing, Believed Married (B & D--Par Br 1937)
Spring Meeting (Pathe 1941)
Yellow Canary (RKO 1943)

Dame Margaret and Stringer Davis in <u>Murder Most Foul</u> (1965).

The Demi-Paradise [Adventure for Two] (GFD 1943)
English without Tears [Her Man Gilbey] (GFD 1944)
Blithe Spirit (GFD 1945)
Meet Me at Dawn [The Gay Duellist] (20th 1947)
While the Sun Shines (Pathe 1947)
Miranda (GFD 1948)
Passport to Pimlico (GFD 1949)
The Happiest Days of Your Life (BL 1950)
Her Favourite Husband [The Taming of Dorothy] (Renown 1950)
The Magic Box (BL 1951)
Curtain Up (GFD 1952)
Castle in the Air (ABP 1952)
The Importance of Being Earnest (GFD 1952)
Miss Robin Hood (ABFD 1952)
Innocents in Paris (IFD 1953)
Trouble in Store (GFD 1953)
The Runaway Bus (Eros 1954)
Aunt Clara (BL 1954)
Mad About Men (GFD 1954)
An Alligator Named Daisy (RFD 1955)
The Smallest Show on Earth (BL 1957)
I'm All Right, Jack (BL 1959)
On the Double (Par 1961)
Murder She Said (MGM 1961)
The Mouse on the Moon (UA 1963)
Murder at the Gallop (MGM 1963)
The V.I.P.s (MGM 1963)
Murder Most Foul (MGM 1965)
Campanadas a medianoche [Falstaff/Chimes at Midnight] (Sp-Swi 1966)
A Countess from Hong Kong (RFD 1966)
Arabella (It 1969)

SANCHO, FERNANDO, b. 1916, Zaragoza, Spain
Polizón a borde (Sp 1941)
Las inquietudes de Shanti-Andia (Sp 1946)
La sirena negra (Sp 1947)
La mies es mucha (Sp 1948)
Agustina de Aragon (Sp 1950)
La Señora de Fatima (Sp 1951)
That Lady (20th 1955)
Cuerda de presos (Sp 1955)
Suspenso en Comunismo (Sp 1956)
Torrepartida (Sp 1956)
Y eligio el infierno (Sp 1957)
Operation Popoff (It-Sp 1958)
Caravana de esclaves (Sp 1958)
Susana pura nata (It-Sp 1958)
El pequeño coronel (Sp 1960)
King of Kings (MGM 1961)
El pobre garcía (Sp 1961)
Un Taxi para Toubrouk [Taxi to Tobruk] (Fr-Sp 1961)
El hijo del Capitan Blood (Sp 1962)
Goliat contra los Gigantes (Sp-It 1962)

Madame sans gêne (Fr-It-Sp 1962)
No temas a la ley (Fr-Sp 1962)
Tres hombres huenos (Sp 1963)
Bienvenido Padre Murray (Sp 1963)
Crimen (Sp 1963)
El Sabor de la venganza (It-Sp 1963)
El Vengador de California (It-Sp 1963)
Minnesota Clay (It-Sp-Fr 1964)
Antes llega la muerte (It-Sp 1964)
El hijo de Jesse James (Sp 1964)
Cuateros (Sp 1964)
Echappement libre (Fr-It-Sp 1964)
Il ritorno di Ringo (It-Sp 1965)
Desafío en Río Bravo (Fr-It-Sp 1965)
El rostro del asesino (Sp 1965)
¡Que viva Carrancho! (It-Sp 1965)
Dos pistoleros (It-Sp 1965)
Dos toreros de Aupa (It-Sp 1965)
Django spara per primo (It 1966)
Totò de Arabia (It-Sp 1965)
Pistoleros de Arizona (W Ger-It-Sp 1965)
El salvaje Kurdistan (W Ger-Sp 1966)
Paris-Estambul sin regreso (Fr-It-Sp 1966)
Sangre sobre Texas (It-Sp 1966)
Siete dolares al rojo (It-Sp 1966)
Siete pistolas para los MacGregor (It-Sp 1966)
Siete pistolas para Timothy (It-Sp 1966)
3 S 3, agente especials (Fr-It-Sp 1966)
Un hombre y un Colt (It-Sp 1966)
Agente 3 S 3, pasaporte para el infierno (Fr-It-Sp 1966)
Cazador de recompensas (It-Sp 1967)
La resa dei conti (It-Sp 1967)
El aventurero de Guyanas (It-Sp 1967)
El magnifico Tony Carrera (Sp 1968)
Forajidos implacables (It-Sp 1969)
Tres crisantemos para los Clyde (Sp 1969)
Como robar un quintal de diamantes en Rusia (Sp 1969)
Amor a todo gas (Sp 1970)
Odio per odio [Hate for Hate] (It 1967)
La banda de los tres crisantemos (It-Sp 1969)
Tarzan en la gruta del oro (Puerto Rico-It-Sp 1969)
Simón Bolívar (It-Sp 1969)
Golpe de mano (Sp 1969)
La diligencia de los condenados (It-Sp 1970)
Abre tu fosa, amigo, Ilega Sabata (It-Sp 1970)
Las endemoniadas (It-Sp 1970)
Orloff y el hombre invisible (Fr-Sp 1971)
El mas fabulouso golpe del far West (Fr-It-Sp 1971)
Los heroes del Patibulo (Greece-Sp 1971)
Los buitros caravan tu fosa (It-Sp 1971)
Aquel maldito dia (It-Sp 1971)

SANDA, DOMINIQUE (Dominique Varaigne), b. March, 1948, Paris
Une Femme douce [A Gentle Creature] (Fr 1970)

Erste Leben [First Love] (W Ger-Swi 1970)
Il conformista [The Conformist] (It-Fr-W Ger 1970)
Sans mobile apparent (Fr-It 1971)
Giardino dei Finzi Contini [The Garden of the Finzi-Continis]
 (It 1971)
La notte dei fiori [Night of the Flowers] (It 1972)
The Mackintosh Man (Col-Warner 1973)
L'Impossible Objet [Impossible Object] (Fr 1973)
Der Steppenwolf (USA-Swi 1974)
Gruppo di famiglia in un interno [Conversation Piece] (It-Fr
 1974)
1900 (It 1975)
L'eredità ferramonti (It 1975)

SANDRELLI, STEFANIA, b. June 5, 1946, Viareggio, Italy
Divorzio all'italiano [Divorce, Italian Style] (It 1961)
Il federale [The Fascist] (It 1961)
Gioventù di notte (It 1962)
La bella di Lodi (It 1963)
Il fornaretto di Venezia [Le procès des doges] (It-Fr 1963)
Les Vierges [Le vergine (Fr-It 1963)
L'aîné des Ferchaux (Fr 1963)
Sedotta e abbandonata [Seduced and Abandoned] (It 1964)
La Chance et l'amour [L'amore e la chance] (ep "I fidanzati del-
 la fortuna") (Fr-It 1964)
Io la conoscevo bene [Ich hab' sie gut gehannt] (It-W Ger 1966)
Tendre voyou [Tender Scoundrel] (Fr 1966)
L'immorale [Beaucoup trop pour un seul homme/The Climax]
 (It-Fr 1967)
Partner (It 1968)
L'amante di Gramigna (It 1969)
Il conformista [The Conformist] (It 1969)
Brancaleone alle crociate (It 1970)
La tarantola dal ventre nero (It 1970)
Un estate con pentimento (It 1970)
Alfredo, Alfredo (It 1972)
Il diavolo nel cervello (It 1972)
Delitto d'amore (It 1973)
C'eravamo tanto amati (It 1974)
Les Magiciens (Fr-It-W Ger-Tunisian 1975)
Le Voyage de noces [Un giorno e una notte] (Fr-It 1975)

SANIPOLI, VITTORIO (Luciano Sanipoli), b. Oct. 27, 1915, Genoa
Il figlio del Corsaro Rosso (It 1941)
Gli ultimi filibustieri (It 1941)
Quartieri alti (It 1943)
Rocambole (It 1947)
Il corriere del Re (It 1947)
Una lettera all'alba (It 1948)
Biancaneve e i sette ladri (It 1949)
Cavalcata d'eroi (It 1949)
Turri il bandito (It 1950)
La vendetta di Aguila nera (It 1951)

Il mago per forza (It 1951)
Ultimo incontro (It 1951)
Canzone di primavera (It 1952)
Vedi Napoli e poi muori (It 1952)
La donna che invento amore (It 1952)
Il figlio di lagardere (It 1952)
Il boia di Lilla (It 1952)
Il romanzo della mia vita (It 1952)
La trappola di fuoco (It 1952)
I Piombi di Venezia (It 1953)
Amanti del passato (It 1953)
Spartaco (It 1953)
Il cavaliere di Maison rouge (It 1953)
Napoletani a Milano (It 1953)
L'età dell'amore [L'âge de l'amour] (It-Fr 1953)
Una donna prega (It 1953)
Il sacco di Roma (It 1953)
Gioventù alla sbarra (It 1954)
La domenica della buona gente (It 1954)
Napoli piange e ride (It 1954)
Vergine moderna (It 1954)
Touchez pas au grisbi [Grisbi] (Fr-It 1954)
La reine Margot [La regina Margot] (Fr-It 1955)
La donna del giorno (It 1956)
Orlando e i Paladini di Francia (It 1956)
Addio per sempre (It 1957)
La grande guerra (It 1959)
Costantino il Grande [Constantine and the Cross] (It 1961)
Rosmunda e Alboino [Sword of the Conqueror] (It 1961)
Morte di un bandito (It 1961)
I mongoli (It 1961)
Maciste il gladiatore più forte del mondo (It 1962)
Violenza segreta (It 1963)
I compagni (It 1963)
Maigret e i gangsters [Maigret voit rouge] (It-Fr 1964)
Il vendicatore mascherato (It 1964)
Le verdi bandiere di Allah (It 1964)
Agente 077...dall'Oriente con furore [Fureur sur le Bosphore]
    (It-Fr 1965)
Avventurieri per una rivolta [Estouffade à la caraibe] (It-Fr 1967)
El "Che" Guevara (It 1968)
Il vero e il falso (It 1970)
Pianeta venere (It 1970)
La Décade prodigieuse (Fr 1971)
Uomini duri [Three Tough Guys] (It 1975)

SANTANA, VASCO (Vasco António Rodrigues Santana), b. Jan. 28,
    1898, Lisbon; d. June 13, 1958
A menina endiabrada (Sp-Ger 1929)
Lisboa, crónica anedótica (Por 1930)
A canção de Lisboa (Por 1933)
O pai tirano (Por 1941)
O pátio das cantigas (Por 1942)

Camões (Por 1946)
Fado, a história de uma cantadeira (Por 1947)
Não há rapazes maus (Por 1948)
Ribatejo (Por 1949)
Eram duzentos irmãos (Por 1951)
O comissário da policia (Por 1952)
O costa de Africa (Por 1954)
O dinheiro dos pobres (Por 1956)

SCHELL, MARIA (Margarethe Schell-Noé), b. Jan. 15, 1926, Vienna
Steibruch/Gottesmühlen (Swi 1942)
Matura-Reise (Swi 1943)
Der Engel mit der Posaune (W Ger 1947)
Maresi (W Ger 1948)
Wiener Kavalkade (Aus 1948)
Nach dem Sturm (Swi-W Ger 1948)
Die letzte Nacht (W Ger 1948)
Der Angeklagte hat das Wort (W Ger 1949)
Es Kommt ein Tag (W Ger 1950)
The Angel with the Trumpet (BL 1950) [Eng lang version of Der
    Engel mit der Posaune]
Dr. Holl (W Ger 1951)
The Magic Box (BL 1951)
So Little Time (ABP 1952)
Bir wir uns wiedersehen (W Ger 1952)
The Heart of the Matter (BL 1953)
Der träumende Mund (W Ger 1953)
Solange Du da bist (W Ger 1953)
Das Tagebuch einer Verliebten (W Ger 1953)
Die letzte Brucke [The Last Bridge] (W Ger 1954)
Napoléon (Fr 1954)
Herr über Leben und Tod (W Ger 1955)
Die Ratten (W Ger 1955)
Gervaise (Fr 1955)
Liebe (W Ger 1956)
Rose Bernd (W Ger 1956)
Le notte bianche [Les Nuits blanches] (It-Fr 1957)
Ungarn in Flammen (W Ger 1957) (narrator only)
The Brothers Karamazov (MGM 1958)
Der Schinderhannes (W Ger 1958)
Une Vie (Fr 1958)
The Hanging Tree (WB 1959)
Raubfischer in Hellas (W Ger 1959)
Cimarron (MGM 1960)
The Mark (20th 1961)
Das Riesenrad (W Ger 1961)
Ich bin auch nur eine Frau (W Ger 1962)
End of Desire (Br 1962)
L'Assassin connait la musique (Fr 1963)
Zwei Whisky und ein Sofa (W Ger 1963)
Duel in the Forest (1963)
Who Has Seen the Wind? (United Nations 1964)
Le Diable par la queue [The Devil by the Tail] (Fr 1969)

99 mujeres [99 Women/99 donne/Der heisse Tod] (Sp-GB-It-W
    Ger 1969)
La Provocation (Fr 1969)
El proceso de las brujas [El juez sangriento/Der Hexentöter von
    Blackmoor/Il trono di fuoco/Night of the Blood Monster] (Sp-
    W Ger-It 1970)
Dans la poussière du soleil (Fr 1971)
.Marie (W Ger 1972)
Die Pfarrhauskomödie (W Ger 1972)
Mas alla de las montañas (Sp 1972)
The Odessa File (Col 1974)
Change (W Ger 1975)
So oder so ist das Leben (W Ger 1975)

SCHELL, MAXIMILIAN, b. Dec. 8, 1930, Wien, Switzerland
    Kinder, Mütter und ein General (W Ger 1955)
    Der 20, Juli (W Ger 1955)
    Reifende Jugend (W Ger 1955)
    Ein Mädchen aus Flandern (W Ger 1956)
    Die Ehe des Dr. Med. Danwitz (W Ger 1956)
    Ein Herz kehrt Heim (W Ger 1956)
    Die Letzten werden die Ersten sein (W Ger 1957)
    Das Glück auf der Alm [Ein wunderbaren Sommer] (Liech 1958)

Maximilian Schell and Sophia Loren in I sequestrati di Altona (1962).

Taxichauffeur Bänz (Swi 1957)
The Young Lions (20th 1957)
Judgment at Nuremberg (UA 1961)
Five Finger Exercise (Col 1962)
The Reluctant Saint (Col 1962)
I sequestrati di Altona [Les Séquestrés d'Altona/The Condemned
  of Altona] (It-Fr 1962)
Topkapi (UA 1963)
Return from the Ashes (UA 1965)
The Deadly Affair (Col 1966)
John F. Kennedy: Years of Lighting, Day of Drums (USA 1966)
  (Ger lang narrator for the documentary)
Mas allá de las montañas [Beyond the Mountains] (Sp-US 1966)
Counterpoint [Battle Horns] (Univ 1967)
The Desperate Ones (UE 1967)
Krakatoa--East of Java (Cin 1968)
Heidi kehrt Heim (W Ger-US TV 1968)
Das Schloss (W Ger 1967)
Simón Bolívar (It-Sp-Venezuelan 1969)
L'assoluto naturale (It 1969)
Erste Liebe [First Love/Premier Amour] (Swi 1970)
Paulina 1880 (W Ger 1971)
Pope Joan [The Devil's Imposter] (Col 1972)
Trotta (W Ger 1972) [script only]
Der Fussgänger [Le Piéton/The Pedestrian] (Swi 1973)
The Odessa File (Col 1974)
The Man in the Glass Booth (AFT 1975)
Der Richter und sein Henker [The End of the Game] (Swi-W Ger
  1975) (director, co-script only)
Assassination at Sarajewo (Yug 1975)

SCHIAFFINO, ROSANNA, b. Nov. 25, 1940, Genoa
Totò, lascia o raddopia (It 1956)
Orlando e i paladini di Francia (It 1956)
Un ettaro di cielo (It 1957)
La sfida (It 1958)
Il vindicatore (It 1958)
La notte brava [Les Garçons] (It-Fr 1959)
Ferdinando I, re di Napoli (It 1959)
Le Bal des espions (Fr 1960)
Teseo e il minotauro [The Minotaur] (It 1960)
L'onorata società (It 1961)
Le Crime ne paie pas [Il delitto non paga/Crime Does Not Pay]
  (ep "Le Masque") (Fr-It 1961)
Le Miracle des loups (Fr 1961)
La Fayette [La Fayette: Una spada per due bandiere] (Fr-It
  1961)
Il ratto delle Sabine (It 1961)
I briganti italiani (It 1961)
Two Weeks in Another Town (MGM 1962)
Axel Munthe, der Arzt von San Michele [La storia di San Mi-
  chele] (W Ger-It 1962)
The Victors (Col 1963)

Rogopag (ep "Illibatezza") (It 1963)
The Long Ships (Col 1963)
Sette contro la morte [The Cavern] (It 1963)
La corruzione (It 1963)
El Greco (20th 1964)
Das Geheimnis der rei Dschunken [009 Missione Hong-Kong/Red
 Dragon] (W Ger-It 1965)
La mandragola (It 1965)
Arriverderci Baby! (Par 1965)
La strega in amore [The Witch] (It 1966)
L'avventuriero [The Rover] (It 1966)
Violenza per una monaca [Encrucijada para una monja/A Nun at
 the Crossroads] (It-Sp 1967)
Simón Bolívar (It-Sp 1968)
Scacco alla regina (It 1969)
Sept Fois par jour (Can 1971)
La betia, ovvero nell'amore per ogni gandenzia ci vuole sofferen-
 za (It 1971)
Trastevere (It 1971)
Gli eroi (It 1973)
Lo chiamavano Mezzogiorno [The Man Called Noon] (It 1973)
Il magnate (It 1973)
L'assassino fra riservato 9 poltrone (It 1974)
Il testimone deve tacere (It 1974)
Cagliostro (It 1975)

SCHMITZ, SYBILLE, b. April 2, 1909, Duren, Germany; d. April
 13, 1955
Der Überfall (Ger 1928)
Tagebuch einer Verlorenen (Ger 1928)
Vampyr (Ger-Fr 1932)
F. P. I. antwortet nich (Ger 1932)
Rivalen der Luft (Ger 1934)
Musik im Blut (Ger 1934)
Abschiedswalzer (Ger 1934)
Der Herr der Welt (Ger 1934)
Stradivari (Ger 1935)
Ein idealer Gatte (Ger 1935)
Punks kommt aus Amerika (Ger 1935)
Oberwachtmeister Schwenke (Ger 1935)
Ich war Jack Mortimer (Ger 1935)
Wenn die Muik nicht wär (Ger 1935)
Die Leuchter des Kaisers (Aus 1936)
Die Unbekannte (Ger 1936)
Fährmann Maria (Ger 1936)
Die Kronzeugin (Ger 1937)
Signal in der Nacht (Ger 1937)
Tanz auf dem Vulkan (Ger 1938)
Die Umwege des schönen Karl (Ger 1938)
Hotel Sacher (Ger 1939)
Die Frau ohne Vergangenheit (Ger 1939)
Trenck, der Pandur (Ger 1940)
Wetterleuchten um Barbara (Ger 1941)

Clarissa (Ger 1941)
Vom Schicksal verweht (Ger 1942)
Titanic (Ger 1943)
Die Hochstaplerin (Ger 1943)
Das Leben ruft (Ger 1944)
Zwischen Gestern und Morgen (W Ger 1947)
Die letzte Nacht (W Ger 1949)
Die Lüge (W Ger 1949)
Der Fall Rabanser (W Ger 1950)
Kronjuwelen (W Ger 1950)
Sensation im Savoy (W Ger 1950)
Illusion in Moll (W Ger 1950)
Kuĉa na obali (Yug-W Ger-Aus 195?)

SCHNEIDER, MAGDA, b. March 7, 1909, Augsburg, Germany
Zwei in einem Auto (Ger 1932)
Das Lied einer Nacht (Ger Eng 1932)
Ein bisschen Liebe für Dich (Ger 1932)
Glück über Nacht (Ger 1932)
Sehnsucht 202 (Ger 1932)
Das Testament des Cornelius Gulden (Ger 1932)
Fräulein--falsch verbunden (Ger 1932)
Marion, das gehört sich nicht (Ger 1932)
Kind, ich freu' mich auf Dein Kommen (Ger 1932)
Glückliche Reise (Ger 1932)
Going Gay (Eng 1933)
Liebelei (Ger 1933)
Fräulein Liselott (Ger 1933)
Ein Mädel wirbelt durch die Welt (Ger 1933)
Ich kenn' Dich nicht und ich liebe Dich (Ger 1933)
G'schichten aus dem Wienerwald (Ger 1934)
Vergissmeinnicht (Ger 1934)
Die Katz im Sack (Ger 1934)
Winternachtstraum (Ger 1935)
Die lustigen Weiber (Ger 1935)
Eva (Aus 1935)
Geheimnis eines alten Hauses (Ger 1935)
Die Puppenfee (Ger 1936)
Rendezvous in Wien (Ger 1936)
Das Weg des Herzens (Ger 1936)
Frauenliebe--Frauenleid (Ger 1936)
Musik für Dich (Ger 1937)
Ihr Leibhusar (Ger 1937)
Die Frau am Scheidewege (Ger 1939)
Frülingsluft (Ger 1939)
Wer küsst Madeleine? (Ger 1939)
Das Recht auf Liebe (Ger 1939)
Mädchen im Vorzimmer (Ger 1940)
Herzensfreud--Herzensleid (Ger 1940)
Am Abend auf der Heide (Ger 1942)
Liebeskomödie (Ger 1942)
Zwei glückliche Menschen (Ger 1943)
Ein Mann für meine Frau (Ger 1943)

Die himmlichen Bräuten (Ger 1943)
Eines Tages (Ger 1944)
Ein mann gehört ins Haus (Ger 1945)
Die Sterne lügen nicht (W Ger 1950)
Wenn der weisse Flieder wieder blüht (W Ger 1953)
...und ewig bleibt die Liebe (W Ger 1954)
Mädchenjahre einer Königin (W Ger 1954)
Sissi, (W Ger 1954)
Die Deutschmeister (W Ger 1955)
Sissi, die junge Kaiserin (W Ger 1956)
Von allen geliebt (W Ger 1957)
Sissi, Schicksalsjahre einer Kaiserin (W Ger 1957)
Das Dreimäderlhaus (W Ger 1957)
Robinson soll nicht sterben (W Ger 1958)
Die Halbzarte (W Ger 1959)
Morgen beginnt das Leben (Aus 1961)

SCHNEIDER, ROMY (Rosemarie Albach-Retty), b. Sept. 23, 1938,
    Vienna
Wenn der weisse Flieder wieder blüht (W Ger 1953)
Mädchenjahre einer Königin [The Story of Vicki] (Aus 1954)
Feuerwerk (W Ger 1954)
Die Deutschmeister (Aus 1955)
Der letzte Mann (W Ger 1955)
Sissi (Aus 1955)
Kitty und die grosse Welt (W Ger 1956)
Sissi, die junge Kaiserin (Aus 1956)
Robinson, soll nicht sterben [The Girl and the Legend] (W Ger
    1957)
Monpti (W Ger 1957)
Sissi-Schicksaljahre einer Kaiserin (Aus 1957)
Scampolo (W Ger 1958)
Christine [L'amante pura] (Fr-It 1958)
Madchen in Uniform (W Ger 1958)
Die Halbzarte (Aus 1958)
Die Schöne Lugnerin (W Ger 1959)
Katia [Magnificent Sinner] (Fr 1959)
Ein Engel auf Erden [Mademoiselle Ange/Angel on Earth] (W
    Ger-Fr 1959)
Die Sendung der Lysistrata (W Ger 1961)
Le Combat dans l'île (Fr-It 1962)
L'Amour a la mer (Fr 1962)
Le Procès [Der Prozess/Il Processo] (Fr-W Ger-It 1963)
The Cardinal (Col 1963)
The Victors (Col 1963)
Good Neighbor Sam (Col 1964)
Le Train (Fr-It-USA 1964)
What's New, Pussycat? (UA 1965)
The Lost Command (Col 1966)
La Voleuse [Schornstein nr. 4] (Fr-W Ger 1966)
10:30 P.M. Summer (Lopert 1966)
Triple Cross [La Fantastique Histoire vrai d'Eddie Chapman]
    (GB-Fr 1966)

La Piscine [The Sinners] (Fr 1968)
Otley (Col 1968)
My Lover, My Son (MGM 1969)
Les Choses de la vie [The Things of Life] (Fr 1969)
Bloomfield [The Hero] (20th 1971) [made in 1969]
Boccaccio '70 (ep "Il Lavoro") (It 1970)
Qui? (Fr 1970)
Max et les ferrailleurs (Fr 1970)
La Califfa (It 1971)
César et Rosalie [Cesar and Rosalie] (Fr 1971)
The Assassination of Trotsky [L'Assassinat de Trotsky/L'As-
    sassino di Trotsky] (GB-Fr-It 1972)
Ludwig II [Le Crepuscule des Dieux/Ludwig] (W Ger-Fr-It 1973)
Le Mouton enragé (Fr 1973)
Un Amour de pluie [Love in the Rain] (Fr 1973)
Le Trio infernal [The Infernal Trio] (Fr 1973)
L'Important c'est d'aimer (Fr 1975)
Les Innocents aux maius sales (Fr 1975)
Le Vieux Fusil (Fr 1975)

SCHÖNER, INGEBORG, b. July 2, 1935, Wiesbaden
Der schweigende Engel (W Ger 1954)
Das verbotene Paradies (W Ger 1955)
Der Hauptmann und sein Held (W Ger 1955)
Du mein stilles Tal (W Ger 1955)
Der erste Frühlingstag (W Ger 1956)
Kuss mich noch einmal (W Ger 1956)
Die Stimme der Sehnsucht (W Ger 1956)
Herrscher ohne Krone (W Ger 1957)
El Hakim (W Ger 1957)
Souvenir d'Italie [It Happened in Rome] (It 1957)
Il Corsaro della mezzaluna (It 1957)
Il cocco di Mamma (It 1957)
Venezia, la luna e tu (It 1958)
Promesse di marinsio (It 1958)
Les Dragueurs (Fr 1959)
The Vikings (UA 1959)
Menschen im Netz (W Ger 1959)
La Vache et le prisonnier [Ich und die Kuh/The Cow and I] (Fr-
    W Ger 1959)
Liebe verboten--Heiraten erlaubt (W Ger 1959)
Heimat--deine Lieder (W Ger 1959)
Ja, die Frauen sind gefährlich (W Ger 1960)
Soldatensender Calais (W Ger 1960)
Weit ist der Weg (W Ger 1960)
Das grosse Wunschkonzert (W Ger 1960)
Der Landartzt (W Ger 1960)
Bankraub in der rue Latour (W Ger 1961)
An der Donau, wenn der Wein blüht (W Ger 1964)
Buffalo Bill, l'eroe del Far-West [Das war Buffalo Bill] (It-W
    Ger 1964)
I misteri della giungla nera [Das Geheimnis der Lederschlinge/
    The Mystery of Thug Island] (It-W Ger 1964)

Ingeborg Schöner (ca. 1959)

L'idea fissa (It 1964)
L'avventuriero della Tortuga (It 1965)
Letti sbagliati (It 1965)
Sperrbezirk (W Ger 1966)
...und so was muss um acht ins Bett (W Ger 1966)
Das Vermächtnis des Inka [El ultimo roy de los Incas/Sansone e il
    Tesoro degli Incas] (W Ger-Sp-It 1966)
Ich spreng'euch alle in die Luft--Inspektor Bloomfields Fall Nr. 1
    (W Ger 1968)
Peter und Sabine (W Ger 1968)
El invencible hombre invisible [L'inafferabile invincibile Mr.
    Superinvisible/Mr. Superinvisible] (Sp-It 1970)
Fegefeuer (W Ger 1971)
Kopf oder Zahl (W Ger 1972)
Über Nacht (W Ger 1972)
Tod eines Fremden (Israeli-W Ger 1973)
George (USA) (Capital 1973)

SCHRECK, MAX, b. 1870, Berlin; d. 1936
    Am Narrenseil (Ger 1921)
    Der Favorit der Königin (Ger 1922)
    Nosferatu--Eine Symphonie des Grauens (Ger 1922)
    Pique Ass (Ger 1922)
    Der Kaufmann von Venedig (Ger 1923)
    Die Strasse (Ger 1923)
    Dudu, ein Menschenschicksal (Ger 1923)
    Die Finanzen des Grossherzogs (Ger 1923)

Die gefundene Braut (Ger 1925)
Krieg im Frieden (Ger 1925)
Der rosa Diamant (Ger 1925)
Der alte Fritz (Ger 1927)
Am Rande der Welt (Ger 1927)
Dona Juana (Ger 1927)
Luther (Ger 1927)
Der Sohn der Hagar (Ger 1927)
Der Kampf der Tertia (Ger 1928)
Das Mädchen von der Strasse (Ger 1928)
Moderne Piraten (Ger 1928)
Rasputins Liebesabemeuer (Ger 1928)
Die Republik der Backfische (Ger 1928)
Ritter der Nacht (Ger 1928)
Serenissimus und die letzte Jungfrau (Ger 1928)
Wolga Wolga (Ger 1928)
Ludwig der Zweite (Ger 1929)
König von Bayern (Ger 1929)
Das Land des Lächelns (Ger 1930)
Im Banne der Berge (Ger 1931)
Muss man sich gleich scheiden Lassen? (Ger 1932)
Die Nacht der Versuchung (Ger 1932)
Ein Mann mit Herz (Ger 1932)
Die verkaufte Braut (Ger 1933)
Fürst Seppl (Ger 1933)
Peter Voss, der Millionendieb (Ger 1933)
Der Tunnel (Ger 1933)
Ein Kuss in der Sommernacht (Ger 1933)
Das verliebte Hotel (Ger 1933)
Roman einer Nacht (Ger 1933)
Eine Frau wie Du (Ger 1933)
Fraulein Hoffmanns Erzählungen (Ger 1933)
Der Schlafwagenkontrolleur (Ger 1935)
Donogoo Tonka (Ger 1936)
Die letzten Vier von Santa Cruz (Ger 1936)

SCHUBERT, KARIN, b. Nov. 26, 1944, Hamburg
Io ti amo (It 1968)
Willst du ewig Jung Frau bleiben? (W Ger 1969)
Pussycat, Pussycat, I Love You (UA 1969)
Vamos a matar, compañeros [Los compañeros/Lasst uns töten,
  compañeros] (It-Sp-W Ger 1969)
Ore di terrore (It-W Ger 1970)
Una spada per Brando (It 1970)
I due maghi del pallone (It 1970)
La Folie des grandeurs [Mania di grandezza/Die dummen
  Streiche der Reiceh/Delusions of Grandeur] (Fr-It-W Ger-Sp
  1971)
Satiricosissimo (It 1971)
La Punition (Fr 1971)
L'Etrange Histoire d'une peinture (Fr-It 1971) [Unreleased]
...Scusi, ma lei le paga le tasse? (It 1971)
L'attentat [L'attentato] (Fr-It 1972)

Blaubart [Barbablù/Barbe-Bleu/Bluebeard] (W Ger-It-Fr-USA 1972)
Quel gran pezzo dell'Ubaldo tutta nuda e tutta calda [Due bellissime donzelle] (It 1972)
Racconti proibiti di niente vestit (It 1972)
Gli occhi freddi della paura (It 1972)
Tutti per uno, botte per tutti (It-W Ger 1973)
Questa volta ti faccio ricco [This Time I'll Make You Rich] (It-Hong Kong 1973)
Samoa [Il pavone nero] (It 1974)
L'ammazzatina (It 1975)
Emanuella nera (It 1975)
L'uomo che sfido l'organizzazione [Angel Face Killer] (It-USA 1975)

SCOTT, JANETTE, b. Dec. 14, 1938, Morecambe, Lancashire, England
Went the Day Well? [48 Hours] (UA 1942)
The Lamp Still Burns (GFD 1943)
A Medal for the General (Anglo 1944)
2,000 Women (GFD 1944)
No Place for Jennifer (ABP 1950)
The Galloping Major (IFD 1951)
No Highway [No Highway in the Sky] (20th 1951)
The Magic Box (BL 1951)
Background (ABFD 1953)
As Long As They're Happy (GFD 1955)
Helen of Troy (WB 1956)
Now and Forever (ABP 1956)
The Good Companions (ABPC 1957)
Happy Is the Bride (BL 1958)
The Lady Is a Square (ABP 1959)
The Devil's Disciple (UA 1959)
School for Scoundrels (WPD 1960)
His and Hers (Eros 1961)
Double Bunk (Bry 1961)
Two and Two Make Six (Bry 1962)
The Day of the Triffids (RFD 1962)
Paranoiac (Univ Br 1963)
The Old Dark House (Col 1963)
The Siege of the Saxons (Col 1963)
The Beauty Jungle [Contest Girl] (RFD 1964)
Bikini Paradise (AA 1964) [Br release 1970]
Crack in the World (Par 1965)

SEBERG, JEAN, b. Nov. 13, 1938, Marshalltown, Iowa
Saint Joan (UA 1957)
Bonjour Tristesse (Col 1958)
The Mouse That Roared (Col 1959)
A bout de souffle [Breathless] (Fr 1959)
Let No Man Write My Epitaph (Col 1959)
Les Grandes Personnes (Fr-It 1961)
L'Amant de cinq jours [The Five Day Lover] (Fr-It 1961)

La Récreation (Fr 1962)
Congo Vivo (It-Fr 1962)
In the French Style (Col 1963)
Les Plus Belles escroqueries du monde (ep "Le grand Escroc")
    (Fr-It-Jap 1964) [made as part of the feature but shown
    separately]
Lilith (Col 1964)
Échappement libré (Fr-Sp-It 1964)
Un Milliard dans un billard (Fr-W Ger-It 1965)
A Fine Madness (WB 1966)
Estouffade à la Caraibe (Fr-It 1966)
Moment to Moment (Univ 1966)
La Ligne de démarcation (Fr 1966)
La Route de Corinthe [The Road to Corinth] (Fr-It-W Ger 1967)
Les Oiseaux vont mourir au Pérou [The Birds Come to Die in
    Peru] (Fr 1968)
Pendulum (Col 1968)
Paint Your Wagon (Par 1969)
Airport (Univ 1970)
Macho Callahan (Avco Emb 1970)
Ondata de Calore [Dead of Summer] (It-Fr 1970)
L'Attenat [Plot] (Fr-It-W Ger 1972)
Kill! [Kill Kill Kill] (Fr-Sp 1972)
La Corrupción de Chris Miller [The Corruption of Chris Miller]
    (Sp 1973)
Cat and Mouse (EMI 1974)
Ballad of the Kid (Fr 1974)
Les Hautes Solitudes (Fr 1975)
Le Grand Délire (Fr-It-W Ger 1975)

SELLERS, PETER, b. Sept. 8, 1925, Southsea, Hants, England
    Penny Points to Paradise (Adelphi 1951)
    Down Among the Z Men (NR 1952)
    Beat the Devil (IFD 1954) (dubbing only)
    Our Girl Friday [The Adventures of Sadie] (Renown 1954) (dub-
        bing only)
    Malaga [Fire over Africa] (BL 1954) (dubbing only)
    Orders Are Orders (BL 1954)
    John and Julie (BL 1955)
    The Lady killers (RFD 1955)
    The Man Who Never Was (20th Br 1956) (dubbing only)
    The Smallest Show on Earth (BL 1957)
    The Naked Truth [Your Past Is Showing] (RFD 1957)
    Up the Creek (WB 1958)
    Tom Thumb (MGM 1958)
    Carlton-Browne of the F O [Man in a Cocked Hat] (BL 1959)
    The Mouse that Roared (Col Br 1959)
    I'm All Right Jack (BL 1959)
    The Battle of the Sexes (Bry 1959)
    Two-Way Stretch (BL 1960)
    Climb Up the Wall (New Realm 1960)
    Never Let Go (RFD 1960)
    The Millionairess (20th 1960)

Peter Sellers and Sophia Loren in The Millionairess (1960).

Mr. Topaze [I Like Money] (20th 1962)
Only Two Can Play (BL 1963)
The Road to Hong Kong (UA 1963)
Waltz of the Toreadors (RFD 1963)
The Dock Brief [Trial & Error] (MGM 1963)
Lolita (MGM Br 1963)
The Wrong Arm of the Law (BL 1964)
Heavens Above! (BL 1964)
Dr. Strangelove; or, How I Learned to Stop Worrying and Love
    the Bomb (Col 1964)
The Pink Panther (UA 1964)
The World of Henry Orient (UA 1964)
A Shot in the Dark (UA 1964)
What's New, Pussycat? (UA 1965)
The Wrong Box (Bol 1966)
Caccia Alla Volpe [After the Fox] (It-USA 1966)
Casino Royale (Col 1967)
The Bobo (WB-7 Arts 1967)
Sept Fois femmes [Woman Times Seven] (It-USA 1967)
The Party (UA 1968)
I Love You, Alice B. Toklas! (WB-7 Arts 1968)
The Magic Christian (CUE 1969)
Hoffman (WPD 1970)

There's a Girl in My Soup (Col 1970)
Where Does It Hurt? (Cin 1972)
Alice's Adventures in Wonderland (Fox-Rank 1972)
Soft Beds, Hard Battles (Fox-Rank 1974)
The Optimists of Nine Elms [The Optimists] (Scotia-Barber 1974)
The Great McGonagall (Tigon 1975)
The Return of the Pink Panther (UA 1975)

SERATO, MASSIMO (Giuseppe Segato), b. May 31, 1916, Oderzo, Italy
Appuntamento allo zoo (It 1940)
L'ispettore Vargas (It 1940)
L'amore canta (It 1941)
Piccolo mondo antico (It 1941)
L'uomo venuto (It 1941)
Due cuori sotto sequestro (It 1941)
I sette peccati (It 1941)
Luisa San Felice (It 1942)
Giacomo l'idealista (It 1942)
La sorelle Materassi (It 1943)
Quartieri alti (It 1943)
La Fornarina (It 1944)
Il mondo vuole così (It 1946)
Il sole sorge ancora (It 1946)
Sangue a Ca'Foscari (It 1946)
L'apocalisse (It 1947)
Il coviere del re (It 1947)
La danse de mort [La pri gioniera dell'isola] (Fr-It 1947)
La signora dalla camelie (It 1947)
Il principe ribelle (It 1948)
I cavalieri della maschera nera (It 1948)
I pirati di Capri [The Pirates of Capri] (It 1948)
Marechiaro [Man of the Sea] (It 1949)
La strada buia (It 1949)
Il ladro di Venezia [The Thief of Venice] (It 1949)
Monastero di Santa Chiara (It 1949)
Rondini in volo (It 1950)
Domenica d'agosto (It 1950)
Amore e sangue (It 1950)
Il conte di Sant'Elmo (It 1950)
Incantesimo tragico [Olivia] (It 1951)
La rivale dell'imperatrice (It 1951)
Senza bandiera (It 1952)
I due derelitti (It 1952)
I piombi di Venezia (It 1953)
Amore rosso (It 1953)
Il boia di Lilla (It 1953)
Febbre di vivere (It 1953)
La figlia del diavolo (It 1953)
Il mercante di Venezia [Le marchand de Venise] (Fr-It 1953)
Lucrèce Borgia [Lucrezia Borgia/The Sin of the Borgias] (Fr-It 1953)

Dramma nella casbah [The Man from Cairo] (It 1953)
La provinciale (It 1953)
Gioventù alla sbarra (It 1954)
Pietà per chi cade (It 1954)
Opinione pubblica [Rumeur publique] (Fr-It 1954)
Madame du Barry (Fr-It 1954)
L'amante di Paride [Il giudizio di Paride] (It 1955)
Un emule de Cartouche [Le avventure di Cartouche/Cartouche]
    (It-Fr 1955)
Foglio di via (It 1955)
Il piccolo vetrato (It 1955)
La vedova (It 1956)
La trovatella di Milano (It 1956)
Il falco d'oro (It 1956)
Maruzzella (It 1956)
Carta a Sara (Sp 1956)
Tormento d'amore (It 1957)
Peppino, le modelle e... chella lla (It 1957)
The Silent Enemy (RFD 1957)
Suprema confessione (It 1958)
La grande ombra (It 1958)
Ora X: Gibralterra o morte (It 1958)
Afrodite, dea dell'amore (It 1958)
The Naked Maja (UA 1959)
La spada e la croce (It 1959)
Il cavaliere del castello maledetto (It 1959)
Capitan Fuoco (It 1959)
Tunisi Top Secret (It 1959)
Il magistrato [El magistrado] (It-Sp 1959)
La scimitarra del saraceno [La Vengeance du Sarrasin/The Pi-
    rate and the Slave Girl] (It-Fr 1959)
Il terrore dei barbari (It 1959)
David e Golia [David and Goliath] (It 1960)
Gli amori di Ercole [The Loves of Hercules] (It 1960)
Femmine di lusso [Love, the Italian Way] (It 1960)
La venere dei pirati [Queen of the Pirates] (It 1960)
Ti aspettero all'inferno (It 1960)
Costantino il Grande [Constantine and the Cross] (It 1961)
El Cid (AA 1961)
Ponce Pilate [Onzio Pilato/Pontius Pilate] (Fr-It 1962)
Marte, dio della guerra (It 1962)
55 Days at Peking (AA 1962)
Il colpo segreto di d'Artagnan [The Secret Mark of d'Artagnan]
    (It 1963)
Giacobbe ed Esau (It 1963)
Ipnosi [Hipnosis/Nur tote Zeugen schweigen/Hypnosis] (It-Sp-
    W Ger 1963)
Goliath e la schiava ribelle [Samson and the Slave Queen] (It
    1963)
Zorro contro Maciste (It 1963)
Il giorno più corto (It 1963)
Gli invincibili sette [Los invencibles/The Secret Seven] (It-Sp
    1964)

L'invincibile cavaliere mascherato [Terror of the Black Mask] (It 1964)
Brenno il nemico di Roma (It 1964)
Il leone di Tebe (It 1964)
Maciste alla corte dello zar [Samson vs. the Giant King] (It 1964)
La celestina (It 1965)
La rivolta dei sette (It 1965)
Il gladiatore che sfido l'impero (It 1965)
La decima vittima [The Tenth Victim] (It 1965)
Sfida a Rio Bravo [Desafio en Rio Bravo/Duel à Rio Bravo/Gunmen of the Rio Grande] (Sp-It-Fr 1965)
Delitto quasi perfetto [Rapt à Damao] (It-Fr 1966)
I criminali della galassia [Wild, Wild Planet] (It 1966)
FBI operazione Vipera gialla [Das Neot der gelben Viper] (It-W Ger 1966)
Superseven chiamo Cairo (It 1966)
Lo scatenato [Catch as Catch Can] (It 1967)
La notte pazza del conigliaccio (It 1967)
La mujer perdida (Sp-It 1967)
Il magnifico texano [Sangre sobre Texas] (It-Sp 1967)
Il bello, il brutto, il cretino (It 1967)
Rififi ad Amsterdam (It 1967)
Uno sceriffo d'oro (It 1967)
00/Ciak operazione mondo (It 1968)
E stato bello amarti (It 1968)
Camille 2000 (It-USA 1969)
Breve amore (It 1969)
La califfa (It 1970)
Una nuvola di polvere...un grido di morte...arriva Saratana (It 1970)
The Gambles (U-M Film Distributors 1970)
Il sergente Klems (It 1971)
Anda muchacho spara (Sp-It 1971)
Diario segreto di un carcere femminile (It 1972)
Historia de una traición (Sp 1972)
Un apprizzato professionista di siano avveruie (It 1972)
Llega sartana (Sp 1972)
Don't Look Now (Par 1973)
Macchie solari (It 1973)
Salvo d'Acquisto (It 1975)

SERVAIS, JEAN, b. Sept. 24, 1910, Anvers, Belgium; d. Feb. 22, 1976
Criminel (Fr 1931)
Mater Dolorosa (Fr 1932)
Les Misérables (Fr 1934) (3 roles)
Jeunesse (Fr 1934)
La Chanson de l'adieu (Fr 1934)
Angèle (Fr 1934)
Amok (Fr 1934)
La Voie sans visage (Fr 1934)
Bourrasque (Fr 1935)
La Dernière Heure (Fr 1936)

Rose (Fr 1936)
Les Réprouvés (Fr 1936)
Une Fille à Papa (Fr 1936)
La Valse éternelle (Fr 1936)
Police mondaine (Fr 1936)
La Vie est magnifique (Fr 1937)
L'Etrange nuit de Nöel (Fr 1938)
Quartier sans soleil (Fr 1939)
Ceux du ciel (Fr 1940)
Terre de feu (Fr 1940)
Fromant jeune et Risler aîné (Fr 1941)
Patricia, Malhia la métisse (Fr 1942)
Tornavara (It-Fr 1943)
Finance noire (Fr 1943)
La Vie de plaisir (Fr 1944)
La Septième Porte (Fr 1946)
La Danse de mort (Fr-It 1946)
Une si jolie petit plage [Such a Jolly Little Beach] (Fr 1949)
Le Furet (Fr 1949)
Mademoiselle de la Ferté (Fr 1949)
La Terre tremble (Fr 1949) (narrator)
Le Chateau de verre (Fr 1950)
Le Plaisir (Fr 1951)
Tourbillon (Fr 1952)
Nina de Vanghel (Fr 1952)
Rue de l'Estrapade [Françoise Steps Out] (Fr 1953)
Le Chevalier de la nuit (Fr 1953)
Du Rififi chez les hommes (Fr 1954)
Les Héros sont fatigués [The Heroes Are Tired] (Fr 1955)
Le Couteau sous la gorge [Cut Throat] (Fr 1955)
La Châtelaine du Liban (Fr-It 1956)
La Roue (Fr 1956)
Celui qui doit mourir [He Who Must Die] (Fr-It 1956)
Quand la femme s'en mêle (Fr-It 1957)
Tamango (Fr-It 1957)
Jeux dangereux (Fr-It 1958)
Cette nuit-là (Fr 1958)
La Fievre monte à El Pao [Republic of Sin] (Fr-Mex 1959)
Meutres en 45 jours (Fr 1960)
Le Sahara brûle (Fr 1960)
Vendredi 13 heures (W Ger-Fr-It 1961)
Le menteurs (Fr 1961)
Le jeu de la vérité (Fr 1961)
Les Frères corses (Fr-It 1961)
Le Crime ne paie pas (ep "L'Affaire Hugues") (Fr-It 1962)
The Longest Day (20th 1962)
Le cage (Fr 1962)
La soupe au poulets (Fr 1963)
Un soir, par hazard (Fr 1963)
L'homme de Rio (Fr-It 1964)
Thomas l'imposteur (Fr 1964)
Sursis pour un espion (Fr-It 1964)
Rififi en la ciudad (Fr-It 1965)

Avec la peau des autres [To Skin a Spy] (Fr-It 1966)
Lost Command (Col 1966)
L'assassino ha le ore (It-Fr 1967)
Qualcuno ha tradito (It-Fr 1967)
Coplan sauve sa peau [The Devil's Garden] (Fr-It 1968)
Requiem pour un canaille (Fr-It 1968)
Las Vegas 500 millions (Sp-Fr-W Ger-It 1968)
Meglio vedova (It-Fr 1968)
Seduto alla sua destra (It-Fr 1968)
Femme 100 têtes (Sp 1969)
La Notte più lunga del diavolo (It 1972)
Crazy Capo (Fr-It 1973)
Le Protecteur (Fr 1973)
Un Tueur, un flic, ainsi soit-il (Fr 1973)

SEVILLA, CARMEN (Maria del Carmen Garcia Galisteo), b. 1930,
    Seville
Jalisco canta en Sevilla (Sp 1948)
Filigrana (Sp 1949)
Cuentos de la Alhambra (Sp 1950)
Le Désir et l'amour (Fr-Sp 1951)
La hermana San Sulpicio (Sp 1952)
La bella de Cadiz (It-Sp 1953)
Un caballero andaluz (Sp 1954)
La fierecilla domada (Sp 1956)
El amor de Don Juan (Sp 1956)
La venganza (Sp 1957)
Secretaria para todo (Sp 1958)
Europa di notte (Sp-It 1959)
King of Kings (MGM 1961)
El secreto de Monica (Sp 1961)
El balcón de la luna (Sp 1962)
Crucero de verano (Sp 1963)
Camino del Rocio (Sp 1966)
La guerillera de Villa (Sp 1966)
Un adulterio decente (Sp 1969)
El Taxi des los Conflictos (Sp 1969)
El relicario (Sp 1970)
Enseñar a un sinverguenza (Sp 1970)
Una señora llamada Andres (Sp 1970)
El más fabuloso golpe del Far West (Fr-It-Sp 1971)
El techo de Cristal (Sp 1971)

SEYRIG, DELPHINE, b. April 10, 1932, Beirut
L'Année dernière a Marienbad [Last Year at Marienbad] (Fr-It
    1961)
Muriel, ou le temps d'un retour (Fr-It 1963)
Qui êtes-vous, Polly Magoo? (Fr 1965)
La musica (Fr 1967)
Accident (Lip 1967)
Mister Freedom (Fr 1968)
Baisers volés [Stolen Kisses] (Fr 1968)
La Voie lactée [The Milky Way] (Fr-It 1969)

Les Lèvres rouges [Daughters of Darkness] (Fr-Bel-W Ger 1970)
Peau d'âne [The Magic Donkey] (Fr 1970)
Le Journal d'un suicide (Fr 1972)
Le Charme discret de la bourgeoisie [The Discreet Charm of the
 Bourgeoisie] (Fr 1972)

Delphine Seyrig in Les Lèvres rouges (1970).

The Day of the Jackal (Univ 1973)
A Doll's House (GB 1973)
India Song (Fr 1974)
Dites-le avec des fleurs (Fr-Sp 1974)
Le Cri du coeur (Fr 1974)
Le Jardin qui bascule (Fr 1975)
Jeanne Dileman, 23 Quai du Commerce--1080 Bruxelles (Bel
 1975)
Aloise (Fr 1975)
Le Boucher, la star et l'orpheline (Fr 1975)
Voyage en Amérique (Fr 1975)
Je t'aime, tu danses (Fr 1975)
Caro Michele (It 1975)

SHAW, ROBERT, b. Aug. 9, 1927, Westhoughton, Lancashire, Eng-
 land
The Dam Busters (ABPC 1955)
A Hill in Korea [Hell in Korea] (BL 1956)
Sea Fury (RFD 1959)
The Valiant (GB-It 1962)

Tomorrow at Ten (Planet 1962)
The Caretaker [The Guest] (BL 1963)
From Russia with Love (UA 1963)
The Luck of Ginger Coffey (Can 1964)
Situation Hopeless--But Not Serious (Par 1965)
Battle of the Bulge (WB 1965)

Robert Shaw (right) and Leonard Whiting in The Royal Hunt of the
Sun (1969).

A Man for All Seasons (Col 1966)
Custer of the West (Cin 1967)
Battle of Britain (UA 1969)
The Royal Hunt of the Sun (RFD 1969)
The Birthday Party (Connoisseur 1970)
Figures in a Landscape (20th 1970)
A Town Called Bastard (GB-Sp 1971)
A Reflection of Fear (Col 1971)
Young Winston (Col 1972)
The Sting (Univ 1973)
The Hireling (Col 1973)
The Taking of Pelham One Two Three (UA 1974)
Jaws (Univ 1975)
Der Richter und sein Henker [Murder on the Bridge/The Judge
    and His Hangman] (Ger-It 1975)

SHIMKUS, JOANNA, b. Oct. 30, 1943, Nova Scotia
    Paris vu par... [Six in Paris] (ep "Montparnasse-Levallois")
      (Fr 1964)
    De l'Amour [All About Loving] (Fr-It 1965)
    Idoli contro luce (It 1966)
    Les Aventuriers [The Last Adventure] (Fr-It 1967)
    Tante Zita (Fr 1967)
    Ho! ["Ho" Criminal Face] (Fr-It 1968)
    Boom (Univ 1968)
    Gli invitati (It-Fr 1969)
    The Lost Man (Univ 1969)
    The Virgin and the Gypsy (London Screenplays 1970)

Joanna Shimkus and Richard Burton in Boom (1968).

SHINER, RONALD, b. June 8, 1903, London; d. June 30, 1966
    My Old Dutch (Gaumont 1934)

Doctor's Orders (Wardour 1934)
It's a Bet (Wardour 1935)
Royal Cavalcade [Regal Cavalcade] (Wardour 1935)
Gentleman's Agreement (B & D-Par Br 1935)
Once a Thief (B & D-Par Br 1935)
Squibs (Gaumont 1935)
Line Engaged (BL 1935)
Excuse My Glove (ABFD 1936)
King of Hearts [Little Gel] (Butcher 1936)
The Black Tulip (Fox Br 1937)
Beauty and the Barge (Wardour 1937)
Dreaming Lips (UA 1937)
Dinner at the Ritz (20th Br 1937)
A Yank at Oxford (MGM Br 1938)
St. Martin's Lane [Sidewalks of London] (ABPC 1938)
Prison without Bars (UA 1938)
They Drive by Night (FN Br 1938)
The Mind of Mr. Reeder [The Mysterious Mr. Reeder] (GN Br 1939)
Trouble Brewing (ABFD 1939)
Flying Fifty Five (RKO Br 1939)
The Missing People (GN Br 1939)
I Killed the Count [Who Is Guilty?] (GN Br 1939)
The Gang's All Here [The Amazing Mr. Forrest] (ABPC 1939)
Discoveries (GN Br 1939)
The Lion Has Wings (UA 1939)
Come On, George (ABFD 1939)
The Middle Watch (ABPC 1939)
Bulldog Sees It Through (ABPC 1940)
The Case of the Frightened Lady [The Frightened Lady] (BL
    1940)
Old Bill and Son (GFD 1940)
Major Barbara (GFD 1941)
The Seventh Survivor (Anglo 1941)
The Black Sheep of Whitehall (UA 1941)
South American George (Col Br 1941)
The Big Blockade (UA 1942)
Unpublished Story (Col Br 1942)
They Flew Alone [Wings and the Woman] (RKO Br 1942)
Those Kids from Town (Anglo 1942)
The Young Mr. Pitt (20th Br 1942)
Sabotage at Sea (Anglo 1942)
Squadron Leader X (RKO Br 1942)
King Arthur Was a Gentleman (GFD 1942)
The Balloon Goes Up (New Realm 1942)
Get Cracking (Col Br 1943)
Thursday's Child (Pathe 1943)
The Gentle Sex (GFD 1943)
Miss London Ltd (GFD 1943)
My Learned Friend (Ealing 1943)
The Butler's Dilemma (Anglo 1943)
Bees in Paradise (GFD 1944)
I Live in Grosvenor Square [A Yank in London] (Pathe 1945)
The Way to the Stars [Johnny in the Clouds] (UA 1945)

Caesar and Cleopatra (EL 1946)
George in Civvy Street (Col Br 1946)
The Man Within [The Smugglers] (GFD 1947)
The Ghosts of Berkeley Square (Pathe 1947)
Brighton Rock [Young Scarface] (Pathe 1947)
Worm's Eye View (ABFD 1951)
The Magic Box (BL 1951)
Reluctant Heroes (ABFD 1951)
Little Big Shot (ABFD 1952)
Top of the Form (GFD 1953)
Innocents in Paris (IFD 1953)
Laughing Anne (Rep 1953)
Up to His Neck (GFD 1954)
Aunt Clara (BL 1954)
See How They Run (BL 1955)
Keep It Clean (Eros 1956)
Dry Rot (IFD 1956)
My Wife's Family (ABP 1956)
Carry On, Admiral [The Ship Was Loaded] (Renown 1957)
Not Wanted on Voyage (Renown 1957)
Girls at Sea (ABPC 1958)
Operation Bullshine (ABPC 1959)
The Navy Lark (20th 1959)
The Night We Got the Bird (BL 1960)

SIGNORET, SIMONE (Simone Kaminker), b. March 25, 1921, Wies-
    baden
Le Prince Charmant (Fr 1942)
Les Visiteurs du Soir (Fr 1942)
Bolero (Fr 1942)
Adieu Léonard (Fr 1943)
L'Ange de la nuit (Fr 1943)
Beatrice devant le désir (Fr 1943)
Le Couple ideal (Fr 1945)
La Boîte aux rêves (Fr 1945)
Les Demons de l'Aube (Fr 1945)
Macadam (Fr 1946)
Fantômas (Fr 1947)
Dedée (Fr 1947)
Against the Wind (GFD 1948)
L'Impasse de deux anges (Fr 1948)
Four Days Leave [Swiss Tour] (Swi-USA 1949)
Manèges (Fr 1949)
La Ronde [Circle of Love] (Fr 1950)
Le Traque [Gunman in the Streets] (Fr-USA 1950)
Ombre et lumière (Fr 1950)
Casque d'or [The Golden Helmet] (Fr-It 1951)
Thérèse Raquin (Fr 1953)
Les Diaboliques [The Fiends] (Fr 1955)
Mutter Courage (W Ger 1955) [Unfinished]
La Mort et ce jardin [Evil Eden] (Fr-Mex 1956)
Les Sorcières de Salem [The Witches of Salem] (Fr-E Ger 1956)
Room at the Top (IFD 1959)

Simone Signoret in Le Jour et l'heure (1963).

Aduae le compagne (Fr 1960)
Les Mauvais Corps (Fr 1960)
Amours célébrés (ep "Jenny de Lacours") (Fr-It 1961)
Terms of Trial (WPD 1962)
Le Jour et l'heure [The Day and the Hour] (Fr-It 1962)
Dragées au poivre [Sweet & Sour] (Fr 1963)
Ship of Fools (Col 1965)
Compartiment tueurs [The Sleeping Car Murders] (Fr 1965)
The Deadly Affair (Col 1966)
Paris brûle-t-il? [Is Paris Burning?] (Fr 1966)
Games (Univ 1967)
The Sea Gull (WB-7 Arts 1968)
L'Armée des ombres (Fr-It 1969)
L'Américain (Fr 1969)
Le Chat (Fr 1970)
Comptes à rebours [Countdown] (Fr 1970)
La Veuve Couderc (Fr-It 1971)
Les Granges brulées (Fr-It 1973)
Rude Journée pour la reine (Fr-Swi 1973)
La Chaîr de l'orchidée (Fr-W Ger 1974)

SILVA, ANTONIO see DA SILVA, ANTONIO

SIM, ALASTAIR, b. Oct. 9, 1900, Edinburgh; d. Aug. 19, 1976
    The Riverside Murder (Fox Br 1935)
    The Private Secretary (TFD 1935)
    A Fire Has Been Arranged (TFD 1935)
    Late Extra (Fox Br 1935)
    Troubled Waters (20th Br 1936)
    Wedding Group [Wrath of Jealousy] (Fox Br 1936)
    The Big Noise (20th Br 1936)
    Keep Your Seats Please (ABFD 1936)
    The Man in the Mirror (Wardour 1936)
    The Mysterious Mr. Davis (RKO Br 1936)
    Strange Experiment (20th Br 1937)
    Clothes and the Woman (ABPC 1937)
    Gangway (GFD 1937)
    The Squeaker [Murder on Diamond Row] (UA 1937)
    A Romance in Flanders [Lost on the Western Front] (BL 1937)
    Melody and Romance (BL 1937)
    Sailing Along (GFD 1938)
    The Terror (ABPC 1938)
    Alf's Button Afloat (GFD 1938)
    This Man Is News (Par Br 1938)
    Climbing High (MGM Br 1938)
    Inspector Hornleigh (20th Br 1939)
    This Man in Paris (Par Br 1939)
    Inspector Hornleigh on Holiday (20th Br 1939)
    Law and Disorder (RKO Br 1940)
    Inspector Hornleigh Goes to It [Mail Train] (20th Br 1941)
    Cottage to Let [Bombsight Stolen] (GFD 1941)
    Let the People Sing (Anglo 1942)
    Waterloo Road (GFD 1945)
    Green for Danger (GFD 1946)
    Hue and Cry (GFD 1947)
    Captain Boycott (GFD 1947)
    London Belongs to Me [Dulcimer Street] (GFD 1948)
    The Happiest Days of Your Life (BL 1950)
    Stage Fright (WB 1950)
    Laughter in Paradise (ABP 1951)
    Scrooge [Christmas Carol] (Renown 1951)
    Lady Godiva Rides Again (BL 1951)
    Folly to Be Wise (BL 1952)
    Innocents in Paris (IFD 1953)
    An Inspector Calls (BL 1954)
    The Belles of St. Trinian's (BL 1954)
    Escapade (Eros 1955)
    Geordie [Wee Geordie] (BL 1955)
    The Green Man (BL 1956)
    Blue Murder at St. Trinian's (BL 1957)
    The Doctor's Dilemma (MGM 1959)
    Left, Right and Centre (BL 1959)
    School for Scoundrels (WPD 1960)
    The Millionairess (20th 1960)

The Anatomist (Br TV 1961) [released as feature only in USA]
The Ruling Class (Avco Emb 1972)
Royal Flash (Fox-Rank 1975)

SIMMONS, JEAN (Jean Merilyn Simmons), b. Jan. 31, 1929, Crouch
    Hill, London
Give Us the Moon (GFD 1944)
Mr. Emmanuel (EL 1944)
Kiss the Bride Goodbye (Butcher 1944)
Meet Sexton Blake (Anglo 1944)
The Way to the Stars [Johnny in the Clouds] (UA 1945)
Great Expectations (GFD 1946)
Hungry Hill (GFD 1946)
Black Narcissus (GFD 1947)
Uncle Silas [The Inheritance] (GFD 1947)
The Woman in the Hall (GFD 1947)
Hamlet (GFD 1948)
The Blue Lagoon (GFD 1949)
Adam and Evelyne [Adam & Evalyn] (GFD 1949)
So Long at the Fair (GFD 1950)
Trio (ep "Sanatorium") (GFD 1950)
Cage of Gold (GFD 1950)
The Clouded Yellow (GFD 1950)

Jean Simmons

Androcles and the Lion (RKO 1952)
Angel Face (RKO 1953)
Affair with a Stranger (RKO 1953)
The Actress (MGM 1953)
The Robe (20th 1953)
Young Bess (MGM 1953)
She Couldn't Say No (RKO 1954)
Demetrius and the Gladiators (20th 1954) (cameo)
The Egyptian (20th 1954)
Desiree (20th 1954)
A Bullet Is Waiting (Col 1954)
Guys and Dolls (MGM 1955)
Footsteps in the Fog (Col 1955)
Hilda Crane [The Many Loves of Hilda Crane] (20th 1956)
This Could Be the Night (MGM 1957)
Until They Sail (MGM 1957)
The Big Country (UA 1958)
Home Before Dark (WB 1958)
This Land Is Mine (Univ 1959)
Spartacus (Univ 1960)
Elmer Gantry (UA 1960)
The Grass Is Greener (Univ 1961)
All The Way Home (Par 1963)
Life at the Top (Col 1965)
Mister Buddwing [Woman Without a Name] (MGM 1966)
Divorce, American Style (Col 1966)
Rough Night in Jericho (Univ 1967)
Heidi (20th 1968) [orig. for TV; shown theatrically in Europe]
The Happy Ending (UA 1969)
Say Hello to Yesterday (Cin 1970)

SIMON, FRANÇOIS, b. Aug. 16, 1917, Geneva
Die Vier im Jeep (Swi 1949)
Bäckerei Zurrer (Swi 1957)
Charles mort ou vif (Swi 1969)
Le Fou (Swi 1970)
Où est passe Tom? (Fr 1971)
Corpo d'amore (It 1972)
L'Invitation (Swi 1973)
Lumière (Fr 1975)

SIMON, MICHEL (François Simon), b. April 9, 1895, Geneva; d.
   May 30, 1975
La Vocation d'André Carrel/La Puissance du travail (Swi 1925)
Feu Mathias Pascal (Fr 1925)
L'Inconnue des six jours (Fr 1926)
Casanova [The Prince of Adventurers] (Fr 1927)
La Passion de Jeanne d'Arc (Fr 1928)
Tire au flanc (Fr 1928)
Pivoine (Fr 1929)
L'Enfant de l'amour (Fr 1929)
On purge Bébé (Fr 1931)
La Chienne (Fr 1931)

Jean de la lune (Fr 1932)
Boudu sauvé des eaux [Boudu Saved from Drowning] (Fr 1932)
Miquette et sa mère (Fr 1933)
Du haut en bas (Fr 1933)
Léopold le bien-aimé (Fr 1933)
Lac aux dames (Fr 1934)
L'Atlante (Fr 1934)
Le Bonheur (Fr 1934)
Le Bébé de l'escadron/La Vie était belle (Fr 1935)
Ademaï au moyen age (Fr 1935)
Amants et voleurs (Fr 1935)
Sous les yeux d'Occident [Razumov] (Fr 1936)
Moutonnet (Fr 1936)
Les Jumeaux de Brighton (Fr 1936)
Le Morte en fuite (Fr 1936)
Jeune Filles de Paris (Fr 1936)
Faisons un rêve (Fr 1937)
La Bataille silencieuse/Le Poisson chinois (Fr 1937)
Naples au baiser de feu (Fr 1937)
Drôle de drame (Fr 1937)
Le Choc en retour (Fr 1937)
Boulot aviateur [Fripons, voleurs et Cie] (Fr 1937)
Mirages [Si tu m'aimes] (Fr 1937)
Le Disparus de Saint-Agil (Fr 1938)
Quai des brumes [Port of Shadows] (Fr 1938)
Les Nouveaux riches (Fr 1938)
La Chaleur du Sein (Fr 1938)
Belle étoile (Fr 1938)
Le Ruisseau (Fr 1938)
Eusebe Député (Fr 1939)
Le Dernier Tournant [The Postman Always Rings Twice] (Fr
   1939)
Noix de Coco (Fr 1939)
Derrière le façade (Fr 1939)
La Fin du jour (Fr 1939)
Cavalcade d'amour (Fr 1939)
Circonstances atténuantes (Fr 1939)
Fric-Frac (Fr 1939)
Paris-New York (Fr 1939)
Le Musicians du ciel (Fr 1939)
La Comédie du bonheur (Fr 1940)
La Tosca (It-Fr 1940)
Il Re si diverte (It 1942)
La Signora dell'ouest (It 1942)
Au bonheur du dames (Fr 1943)
Vautrin (Fr 1943)
Un Ami viendra ce soir (Fr 1945)
Panique (Fr 1946)
La Taverne du poisson couronne (Fr 1946)
Non Coupable (Fr 1947)
Les Amants du Point Jean (Fr 1947)
La Carcasse et le tord-cou (Fr 1947)
Fabiola (It-Fr 1948)

Le Beauté du diable (Fr 1949)
Les Deux Vérités (Fr-It 1950)
La Poison (Fr 1951)
La Fille au fouet (Fr 1952)
Brelan d'as (Fr 1952)
Monsieur Taxi (Fr 1952)
Le Rideau rouge [The Red Curtain] (Fr 1952)
Le Chemin de damas (Fr 1952)
La Vie d'un honnête homme (Fr 1952)
Le Marchand de Venise (Fr-It 1952)
Femmes de Paris [Women of Paris] (Fr 1952)
L'Etrange Désir de M. Bard (Fr 1953)
Saadia (MGM 1953)
Ungarische Rhapsodie [Par ordre du Tsar] (W Ger-Fr 1953)
Quelques pas dans la vie (Fr 1953)
Tempi nostri (ep "Casa d'altri") (It 1954)
L'Impossible Monsieur Pipelet (Fr 1955)
Les Mémoires d'un flic (Fr 1955)
La Joyeuse Prison (Fr 1956)
Les Trois font la paire (Fr 1957)
Un Certain Monsieur Jo (Fr-It 1957)
Es Geschah am hellichten Tag [Assault in Broad Daylight] (W
    Ger-Fr 1959)
Die Naakte und der Satan [The Head] (W Ger-Fr 1959)
Austerlitz (Fr-It-Yug 1960)
Pierrot la tendresse (Fr 1960)
Candide, ou la optimisme au XXe siecle (Fr 1960)
Le Bateau d'Emile (Fr-It 1961)
Le Diable et les dix commandements (Fr-It 1962)
Cyrano et d'Artagnan (Sp-It-Fr 1962)
Le Train [The Train] (Fr-It-USA 1963)
Il mondo di notto no. 3 [This Shocking World] (It 1963) (cameo)
Deux heures à tuer (Fr-Bel 1965)
Le Vieil Homme et l'enfant [The Two of Us] (Fr 1966)
Ce Sacré grand-père (Fr 1968)
Concerto pour trois flûtes (Fr 1970)
La Maison [The House] (Fr 1970)
Blanche (Fr 1971)
La Panne [La più bella serata della mia vita] (Fr-It 1972)
Le Boucher, la star et l'orpheline (Fr 1974)
L'Ibis rouge [The Red Ibis] (Fr 1975)

SIMON, SIMONE, b. April 23, 1914, Marseilles
Le Chanteur inconnu (Fr 1931)
La Petite Chocolatière (Fr 1931)
Mam'zelle Nitouche (Fr 1931)
Pour vivre heureux (Fr 1931)
Durand contre Durand (Fr 1931)
Le Roi des palaces (Fr 1932)
Prenez garde à la peinture (Fr 1932)
Un Fils d'Amérique (Fr 1932)
Tirè-au-flanc (Fr 1933)
L'Etoile de Valencia (Fr 1933)

Lac-aux-dames (Fr 1934)
Les Yeux noirs (Fr 1935)
Les Beaux Jours (Fr 1935)
Girls' Dormitory (20th 1936)
Ladies in Love (20th 1936)
Seventh Heaven (20th 1937)
Love and Kisses (20th 1937)
Josette (20th 1938)
La Bête humaine (Fr 1938)
Cavalcade d'amour (Fr 1939)
All That Money Can Buy [The Devil and Daniel Webster] (RKO 1941)
Cat People (RKO 1942)
Tahiti Honey (Rep 1943)
The Curse of the Cat People (RKO 1944)
Mademoiselle Fifi [The Silent Bell] (RKO 1944)
Johnny Doesn't Live Here Any More [And So They Were Married] (Mon 1944)
Petrus (Fr 1946)
Temptation Harbour (Pathe 1947)
Femmes sans nom (Fr 1950)
La Ronde (Fr 1950)
Olivia (Fr 1950)
Le Plaisir (Fr 1951)
Les Trois Voleurs (Fr 1954)
Double Destin (Fr 1954)
The Extra Day (BL 1956)
La Femme en bleu (Fr-It 1973)

SINDEN, DONALD, b. Oct. 9, 1923, Plymouth, Devon, England
The Cruel Sea (GFD 1953)
A Day to Remember (GFD 1953)
Mogambo (MGM 1953)
You Know What Sailors Are (GFD 1954)
Doctor in the House (GFD 1954)
The Beachcomber (GFD 1954)
Mad About Men (GFD 1954)
Simba (GFD 1955)
Above Us the Waves (GFD 1955)
An Alligator Named Daisy (RFD 1955)
Josephine and Men (BL 1955)
The Black Tent (RFD 1956)
Eyewitness (RFD 1956)
Tiger in the Smoke (RFD 1956)
Doctor at Large (RFD 1957)
Rockets Galore (RFD 1958)
The Captain's Table (RFD 1959)
Operation Bullshine (ABPC 1959)
Your Money or Your Wife (RFD 1960)
The Siege of Sidney Street (RFI 1960)
Twice Round the Daffodils (AA 1962)
Mix Me a Person (BL 1962)
Decline and Fall...of a Bird-Watcher! (20th 1968)

Villain (MGM-EMI 1971)
Rentadick (RFD 1972)
The National Health (Col-Warner 1973)
The Day of the Jackal (GB-Fr 1973)
Father, Dear Father (Fox-Rank 1973)
The Island at the Top of the World (BV 1973)
That Lucky Touch (Fox-Rank 1975)

SLAUGHTER, TOD (Carter Slaughter), b. March 19, 1885, New-
    castle, England; d. Feb. 19, 1956
    Maria Marten; or, The Murder in the Red Barn (MGM Br 1935)
    Sweeney Todd, the Demon Barber of Fleet Street (MGM Br 1936)
    The Crimes of Stephen Hawke (MGM Br 1936)
    Song of the Road (SC 1937)
    Darby and Joan (MGM Br 1937)
    It's Never Too Late to Mend (MGM Br 1937)
    The Ticket of Leave Man (MGM Br 1937)
    Sexton Blake and the Hooded Terror (MGM Br 1938)
    The Face at the Window (BL 1939)
    Crimes at the Dark House (BL 1940)
    Bothered by a Beard (GFD 1946)
    The Curse of the Wraydons (GFD 1946)
    The Greed of William Hart (Ambassador 1948)
    King of the Underworld (Ambassador 1952)
    Murder at Scotland Yard (Ambassador 1952)

SMITH, C. AUBREY (Charles Aubrey Smith), b. July 21, 1863, Lon-
    don; d. Dec. 20, 1948
    Builder of Bridges (Frohman Amusement Corp 1915)
    Red Pottage (Ideal 1918)
    The Face at the Window (Phillips 1920)
    Castles in Spain (Gaumont 1920)
    The Shuttle of Life (Phillips 1920)
    The Bohemian Girl (Astra 1922)
    Flames of Passion (Astra 1922)
    The Temptation of Carlton Earle (Phillips 1923)
    The Unwanted (Napoleon 1924)
    Birds of Prey [The Perfect Alibi] (Radio 1930)
    Such Is the Law (Butcher 1930)
    The Bachelor Father (MGM 1930)
    Guilty Hands (MGM 1931)
    Contraband Love (Par Br 1931)
    But the Flesh Is Weak (MGM 1932)
    Trouble in Paradise (Par 1932)
    Love Me Tonight (Par 1932)
    Tarzan, the Ape Man (MGM 1932)
    No More Orchids (Col 1932)
    Polly of the Circus (MGM 1932)
    The Barbarian (MGM 1933)
    They Just Had to Get Married (Univ 1933)
    Luxury Liner (Par 1933)
    Secrets (UA 1933)
    Adorable (Fox 1933)

Monkey's Paw (RKO 1933)
Morning Glory (RKO 1933)
Bombshell [Blonde Bombshell] (MGM 1933)
Queen Christina (MGM 1933)
We Live Again (UA 1934)
The House of Rothschild (UA 1934)
The Scarlet Empress (Par 1934)
Caravan (Fox 1934)
Cleopatra (Par 1934)
Bulldog Drummond Strikes Back (UA 1934)
Gambling Lady (WB 1934)
Curtain at Eight (Majestic 1934)
Madame Du Barry (WB 1934)
One More River [Over the River] (Univ 1934)
The Right to Live (WB 1935)
The Tunnel [Transatlantic Tunnel] (Gaumont 1935)
China Seas (MGM 1935)
The Crusades (Par 1935)
Jalna (RKO 1935)
The Firebird (WB 1935)
Clive of India (20th 1935)
The Gilded Lily (Par 1935)
Lives of a Bengal Lancer (Par 1935)
The Florentine Dagger (WB 1935)
Lloyds of London (20th 1936)
Little Lord Fauntleroy (UA 1936)
Romeo and Juliet (MGM 1936)
The Garden of Allah (UA 1936)
Wee Willie Winkie (20th 1937)
Thoroughbreds Don't Cry (MGM 1937)
The Prisoner of Zenda (UA 1937)
The Hurricane (UA 1937)
60 Glorious Years [Queen of Destiny/Queen Victoria] (RKO Br
   1938)
Four Men and a Prayer (20th 1938)
Kidnapped (20th 1938)
East Side of Heaven (Univ 1939)
The Four Feathers (UA 1939)
Five Came Back (RKO 1939)
The Sun Never Sets (Univ 1939)
Another Thin Man (MGM 1939)
Balalaika (MGM 1939)
Eternally Yours (UA 1939)
The Underpup (Univ 1939)
City of Chance (20th 1939)
A Bill of Divorcement (RKO 1940)
Rebecca (UA 1940)
Beyond Tomorrow (RKO 1940)
Waterloo Bridge (MGM 1940)
A Little Bit of Heaven (Univ 1940)
Maisie Was a Lady (MGM 1941)
Free and Easy (MGM 1941)
Dr. Jekyll and Mr. Hyde (MGM 1941)

Forever and a Day (RKO 1943)
Two Tickets to London (RKO 1943)
Flesh and Fantasy (Univ 1943)
Madame Curie (MGM 1943)
The White Cliffs of Dover (MGM 1944)
Adventures of Mark Twain (WB 1944)
Secrets of Scotland Yard (Rep 1944)
Sensations of 1945 (UA 1944)
And Then There Were None [Ten Little Niggers] (20th 1945)
Forever Yours (Mon 1945)
Scotland Yard Investigator (Rep 1945)
Cluny Brown (20th 1946)
Rendezvous with Annie (Rep 1946)
High Conquest (Mon 1947)
Unconquered (Par 1947)
An Ideal Husband (BL 1947)
Little Women (MGM 1949)

SMITH, MAGGIE, b. 1934, Ilford, Essex, England
Nowhere to Go (MGM Br 1958)
The V. I. P. 's (MGM 1963)
The Pumpkin Eater (Col 1964)
Young Cassidy (MGM Br 1965)
Othello (Eagle 1965)
The Honey Pot (UA 1967)
Hot Millions (MGM 1968)
The Prime of Miss Jean Brodie (20th 1969)
Travels with My Aunt (MGM 1972)
Love and Pain and the Whole Damn Thing (Col 1973)

SÖDERBAUM, KRISTINA, b. Sept. 5, 1912, Djursholm (Stockholm)
Onkel Bräsig (Ger 1936)
Jugend (Ger 1938)
Verwehte Spuren (Ger 1938)
Die Reise nach Tilsit (Ger 1939)
Das unsterbliche Herz (Ger 1939)
Jud Süss (Ger 1940)
Der grosse König (Ger 1942)
Die goldene Stadt (Ger 1942)
Immensee (Ger 1943)
Opfergang (Ger 1944)
Kolberg (Ger 1945)
Unsterbliche Geliebte (W Ger 1951)
Hanna Amon (W Ger 1951)
Die blaue Stunde (W Ger 1953)
Sterne über Colombo (W Ger 1953)
Die Gefangene des Maharadscha (W Ger 1954)
Verrat an Deutschland (W Ger 1955)
Zwei Herzen im Mai (W Ger 1958)
Ich werde Dich auf Händen tragen (W Ger 1958)
Die blonde Frau des Maharadscha (W Ger 1962)
Karl May (W Ger 1975)

SOLNADO, RAUL (Raul Augusto de Almeida Solnado), b. Oct. 19,
    1929, Lisbon
    O noivo das caldas (Por 1956)
    Perdeu-se um marido (Por 1956)
    Sangue toureiro (Por 1958)
    O Tarzan do 5.º esquerdo (Por 1958)
    As pupilas do Senhor Reitor (Por 1960)
    Sexta-feira 13 (Por 1961)
    Don Roberto (Por 1962)
    O milionário (Por 1962)

SOMMER, ELKE (Elke Schletz), b. Nov. 6, 1940, Berlin
    Ragazzi del juke box (It 1959)
    L'amico del giaguaro (It 1959)
    Uomini e nobiluomini (It 1959)
    Ti diro...che tu mi piaci (It 1959)
    La pica sul Pacifico (It 1959)
    Das Totenschiff (W Ger 1959)
    Am Tag als der Regen kam (W Ger 1959)
    Lampenfieber (W Ger 1960)
    Himmel, Amor und Zwirn (W Ger 1960)
    Urlatori alla sbarra (It 1960)
    Femmine di lusso (It 1960)
    ...und sowas nennt sich Leben (W Ger 1960)
    Don't Bother to Knock (WPD 1961)
    Geliebte Hochstaplerin (W Ger 1961)
    Zarte Haut in schwarzer Seide (W Ger-Fr 1961)
    Douce violence (Fr 1961)
    Auf wiedersehen in Arizona (W Ger 1962)
    Cafe Oriental (W Ger 1962)
    Caprici Borghesi (It 1962)
    Das Mädchen und der Staatsanwalt (W Ger 1962)
    Les Bricoleurs (Fr 1962)
    Un Chien dans un jeu de guilles (Fr 1962)
    Nachts ging das Telephon (W Ger 1962)
    Bahia de palma (Sp 1962)
    Ostrva [Verführung am Meer] (Yug-W Ger 1963)
    Denn die Musik und die Liebe im Tirol (W Ger 1963)
    The Victors (Col 1963)
    The Prize (MGM 1963)
    A Shot in the Dark (UA 1964)
    Le Bambole [Four Kinds of Love] (ep "Il trattato di Eugenetica")
        (It 1964)
    Unter Geiern [Medu Jastrebovina] (W Ger-It-Yug 1964)
    The Art of Love (Univ 1965)
    Hotel der toten Gäste (W Ger-Sp 1965)
    The Money Trap (MGM 1966)
    The Oscar (Emb 1966)
    Boy Did I Get a Wrong Number (UA 1966)
    Deadlier Than the Male (Univ 1966)
    Die Hölle von Macao [Il sgillo di Pechino/Les Corrompus/The
        Peking Medallion] (W Ger-It-Fr 1966)
    An einem Freitag in Las Vegas [Las Vegas 500 millones/Radio-

Elke Sommer in <u>Le bambole</u> (1964).

grafia di un colpo d'oro/Les Hommes de Las Vegas/They
   Came to Rob Las Vegas] (W Ger-Sp-It-Fr 1967)
The Venetian Affair (MGM 1967)
The Wicked Dreams of Paula Schultz (UA 1968)
The Wrecking Crew (Col 1968)
The Invincible Six [Heroes of Yucca] (Par 1968)
Zeppelin (WB 1971)
Percy (MGM-EMI 1971)
Gli orrori del castello di Norunberga [Baron Blood] (Sp-It 1972)
Lisa e il diavalo (It-Sp 1973)
Einer von uas beiden (W Ger 1973)
Die Reise nach Wien (W Ger 1973)
Percy's Progress (MGM-EMI 1974)
E poi non rimase nessuno [And Then There Were None] (It-GB
   1974)
The Swiss Conspiracy (USA-W Ger 1975)
Carry On Behind (Fox-Rank (1975)

SPIRA, CAMILLA, b. March 1, 1906, Hamburg
   Mutter und Sohn (Ger 1924)
   Das Herz am Rhein (Ger 1925)
   Die dritte Eskadron (Ger 1926)
   Brennende Grenze (Ger 1926)
   Die Perle des Regiments (Ger 1926)
   Die versunkene Flotte (Ger 1926)
   Wie einst im Mai (Ger 1926)
   An der Weser (Ger 1926)
   Liebeskarneval (Ger 1928)
   Sechzehn Töchter amd kein Papa (Ger 1928)
   Meine Schwester und ich (Ger 1929)
   Die Jugendeliebte (Ger 1930)
   Die lustigen Musikanten (Ger 1930)
   Die Faschingsfee (Ger 1931)
   Mein Leopold (Ger 1931)
   Der schönste Mann im Staate (Ger 1931)
   Gehetzte Menschen (Ger 1932)
   Die elf schill'schen Offiziere (Ger 1932)
   Ja, treu ist die Soldatenliebe (Ger 1932)
   Skandal in der Parkstrasse (Ger 1932)
   Grün ist die Heide (Ger 1932)
   Der Judas von Tirol (Ger 1933)
   Das Testament des Dr. Mabuse (Ger 1933)
   Sprung in den Abgrund (Ger 1933)
   Morgenrot (Ger 1933)
   Die Nacht im Forsthaus (Ger 1933)
   Die Buntkarierten (W Ger 1949)
   Epilog (W Ger 1950)
   Semmelweiss--Retter der Mütter (W Ger 1950)
   Die lustigen Weiber von Windsor (W Ger 1952)
   Stunde der Entscheidung (W Ger 1952)
   Drei Tage Angst (W Ger 1952)
   Pension Schöller (W Ger 1952)
   Der fröhliche Weinberg (W Ger 1952)

Emil und die Detektive (W Ger 1954)
Roman eines Franenartzes (W Ger 1954)
Des Teufels General (W Ger 1955)
Vatertag (W Ger 1955)
Der letzte Mann (W Ger 1955)
Himmel ohne Sterne (W Ger 1955)
Zwei blaue Augen (W Ger 1955)
Liebe (W Ger 1956)
Fuhrmann Henschel (W Ger 1956)
Made in Germany (W Ger 1957)
Der tolle Bomberg (W Ger 1957)
Das Herz von St. Pauli (W Ger 1957)
Nachtschwester Ingeborg (W Ger 1958)
Der Czardaskönig (W Ger 1958)
Vater, Mutter und neun Kinder (W Ger 1958)
Freddy, die Gitarre und das Meer (W Ger 1959)
Buddenbrooks (W Ger 1959)
Rosen für den Staatsanwalt (W Ger 1952)
Freddy unter fremden Sternen (W Ger 1962)
Vertauschtes Leben (W Ger 1961)
Piccadilly null Uhr Zwölf (W Ger 1961)

STAMP, TERENCE, b. July 22, 1939, Stepney, London
Term of Trial (WPD 1962)
Billy Budd (RFD 1962)
The Collector (Col 1965)
Modesty Blaise (20th 1966)
Far from the Madding Crowd (MGM 1967)
Poor Cow (AA 1967)
Histoires Extraordinaires [Spirits of the Dead] (ep "Il ne faut
     jamais parier sa tête avec le diable"/"Toby Dammit") (Fr-It
     1967)
Blue (Par 1968)
Teorema (It 1968)
The Mind of Mr. Soames (Col 1970)
Una stagione all'inferno (It-Fr 1971)
La divina creature (It 1975)

STEELE, TOMMY (Thomas Hicks), b. Dec. 17, 1936, Bermondsey,
     London
The Shiralee (MGM 1957) (sang title song)
Kill Me Tomorrow (Renown 1957)
The Tommy Steele Story [Rock Around the World] (AA 1957)
The Duke Wore Jeans (AA 1958)
Tommy the Toreador (WPD 1959)
Light Up the Sky (Bry 1960)
It's All Happening (Magna 1963)
The Happiest Millionaire (BV 1967)
Half a Sixpence (Par 1967)
Finian's Rainbow (WB-7 Arts 1968)
Where's Jack? (Par 1968)

Terence Stamp in _Teorema_ (1968).

STEPHENS, ROBERT, b. July 14, 1931, Bristol, England
    Circle of Deception (20th 1960)
    Pirates of Tortuga (20th 1961)
    A Taste of Honey (Bry 1961)
    The Queen's Guards (20th 1961)
    The Inspector [Lisa] (20th 1962)
    Lunch Hour (Bry 1962)
    The Small Sad World of Sammy Lee (Bry-7 Arts 1963)
    Cleopatra (20th 1963)
    Morgan--A Suitable Case for Treatment (BL 1966)
    Romeo and Juliet (Par 1968)
    The Prime of Miss Jean Brodie (20th 1969)
    The Private Life of Sherlock Holmes (UA 1970)
    Travels with My Aunt (MGM 1972)
    The Asphyx (Scotia-Barber 1973)
    Q B VII (ABC-TV 1974)

STEWART, ALEXANDRA, b. June 10, 1939, Montreal
    Les Motards (Fr 1959)

Tommy Steele

Deux Hommes dans Manhattan (Fr 1959)
Liasons dangereuses 1960 (Fr-It 1959)
L'Eau à la bouche (Fr 1959)
Le Bel Age [Love Is Where You Make It] (Fr 1960)
La Mort de belle (Fr 1960)
Les Distractions (Fr-It 1960)
Tarzan the Magnificent (Par 1960)
Exodus (UA 1960)
La Morte Saison des amours [The Season for Love] (Fr 1961)
Le Rendez-vous de minuit [Rendezvous at Midnight] (Fr 1961)
Le Mauvais Coups (Fr 1961)
Merci natercia (Fr 1962) [made in 1959]
Climats [Climates of Love] (Fr 1962)
Rogopag (It-Fr 1962)
Quatre Femmes pour un héros (Fr-Arg 1962)
Une Grosse Tête (Fr 1962)
Bekenntnisse eines möbilierten Herrn (W Ger 1962)
Vilenza Segreta (It 1962)
Dragées au poivre [Sweet & Sour] (Fr-It 1963)
Das grosse Liebesspiel (W Ger-Aus 1963)
Le Feu follet [Will O' the Wisp] (Fr 1963)
Volles Herz und leere Taschen (W Ger-It 1964)
La Brûlure de 1000 soleils [The Fire of a Thousand Suns] (Fr 1965)

La ley del forastero (W Ger-Sp 1965)
Thrilling (It 1965)
Sie nannten ihn Gringo [The Man Called Gringo] (W Ger-Sp 1965)
Mickey One (Col 1965)
Marcia nuziale (It 1966)
La Loi du survivant (Fr 1967)
Maroc 7 (RFD 1967)
L'Ecume des jours [Froth on the Daydram] (Fr 1967)
La Mariée était en noir [The Bride Wore Black] (Fr-It 1968)
Only When I Larf (Par 1968)
Waiting for Caroline (Canada 1968)
Obsessions (Dut 1969)
Bye Bye Barbara (Fr 1969)
Obsessions (Dut-W Ger 1969)
Umano no Umano (It 1969)
The Man Who Had Power Over Women (Avco Emb 1970)
Le Ciel est bleu (Fr 1970)
Ils (Fr 1970)
Valparaiso, Valparaiso (Fr 1971)
Ou est passé, Tom? (Fr 1971)
Zeppelin (WB 1971)
Les Soleils de l'Ïle de Pâques (Fr-Bra-Chile 1972)
Niet voor de Poesen [The Rape] (Dut-Bel 1973)
Black Moon (Fr 1974)
Un Animal odue de déraison (Bra-Fr 1975)

SULLIVAN, FRANCIS L. (Francis Loftus Sullivan), b. June 6, 1903,
        London; d. Nov. 19, 1956
    The Missing Rembrandt (PDC 1932)
    The Chinese Puzzle (W & F 1932)
    When London Sleeps (A P & D 1932)
    Called Back (Radio 1933)
    F. P. 1. [Secrets of F. P. 1.] (GB-Ger 1933)
    The Stickpin (Fox 1933)
    The Fire Raisers (W & F 1933)
    The Right to Live (Fox Br 1933)
    The Wandering Jew (Gaumont 1933)
    Red Wagon (Wardour 1934)
    Princess Charming (Gaumont 1934)
    The Return of Bulldog Drummond (Wardour 1934)
    Chu Chin Chow (Gaumont 1934)
    Jew Suss [Power] (Gaumont 1934)
    What Happened Then? (Wardour 1934)
    Cheating Cheaters (Univ 1934)
    Great Expectations (Univ 1934)
    Strange Wives (Univ 1935)
    The Mystery of Edwin Drood (Univ 1935)
    Her Last Affaire (PDC 1935)
    The Interrupted Honeymoon (BL 1936)
    A Woman Alone [Two Who Dared] (UA 1936)
    Spy of Napoleon (Wardour 1936)
    The Limping Man (Pathe 1936)
    Fine Feathers (BL 1937)

Action for Slander (UA 1937)
Non-Stop New York (GFD 1937)
Dinner at the Ritz (20th Br 1937)
The Gables Mystery (MGM Br 1938)
Kate Plus Ten (GFD 1938)
The Drum [Drums] (UA 1938)
Climbing High (MGM 1938)
The Citadel (MGM Br 1938)
The Ware Case (ABFD 1938)
The Four Just Men [The Secret Four] (ABFD 1939)
Young Man's Fancy (ABFD 1939)
21 Days [21 Days Together] (Col 1939) [made in 1937]
Pimpernel Smith [Mister V] (Anglo 1941)
The Foreman Went to France [Somewhere in France] (UA 1942)
The Day Will Dawn [The Avengers] (GFD 1942)
Lady from Lisbon (Anglo 1942)
The Butler's Dilemma (Anglo 1943)
Fiddlers Three (Ealing 1944)
Caesar and Cleopatra (EL 1946)
The Laughing Lady (Anglo 1946)
Great Expectations (GFD 1946)
The Man Within [The Smugglers] (GFD 1947)
Take My Life (GFD 1947)
Broken Journey (GFD 1948)
Oliver Twist (GFD 1948)
The Winslow Boy (BL 1948)
Christopher Columbus (GFD 1949)
The Red Danube (MGM 1949)
Night and the City (20th 1950)
Joan of Arc (RKO 1950) [made in 1948]
Behave Yourself (RKO 1951)
My Favorite Spy (Par 1951)
Caribbean (Par 1952)
Sangaree (Par 1953)
Plunder of the Sun (WB 1953)
Drums of Tahiti (Col 1954)
Hell's Island (Par 1955)
The Prodigal (MGM 1955)

SUZMAN, JANET, b. Feb. 9, 1939, Johannesburg, South Africa
Nicholas and Alexandra (Col 1971)
A Day in the Death of Joe Egg (Col 1972)
The Black Windmill (CIC 1974)

SYLVIE (Thérèse Sylvie), b. Jan. 3, 1885, Paris; d. Jan. 5, 1970
Britannicus (Fr 1912)
Germinal (Fr 1918)
La Fille du Peuple (Fr 1918)
Marie-Jeanne (Fr 1918)
Ursule Mironet (Fr 1918)
Le Coupable (Fr 1918)
Roger la Honte (Fr 1922)
La Cabane d'amour (Fr 1924

Crime et châtiment [Crime and Punishment] (Fr 1935)
Un Carnet de bal [Christine] (Fr 1937)
L'Affaire Lafarge (Fr 1938)
L'Esclave blanche (Fr 1939)
Montmartre-sur-Seine (Fr 1941)
Romance de Paris (Fr 1941)
L'Homme sans nom (Fr 1942)
Marie-Martine (Fr 1942)
Le Corbeau (Fr 1943)
Le Voyageur sans bagage (Fr 1943)
Les Anges du peché (Fr 1943)
L'Ile d'amour (Fr 1943)
Le Père Goriot (Fr 1944)
La Route du bagne (Fr 1945)
Le Pays sans étoiles (Fr 1945)
L'Idiot (Fr 1946)
Le Diable au corps (Fr 1946)
On ne meurt pas comme ca (Fr 1946)
Coincidences (Fr 1946)
Miror (Fr 1947)
La Revoltée (Fr 1947)
Deux Amours (Fr 1948)
Pattes blanches (Fr 1948)
Tous les deux (Fr 1949)
La Cage aux filles [Cage of Girls] (Fr 1949)
Dieu à besoin des hommes [Isle of Sinners] (Fr 1950)
Sous la ciel de Paris (Fr 1951)
Il piccolo mondo di Don Camillo [Le Petit Monde de Don Camil-
   lo] (It-Fr 1951)
Le fruit Défendu [Forbidden Fruit] (Fr 1952)
Nous sommes tous des assassins [We Are All Murderers] (Fr
   1952)
Adam est... Eve (Fr 1953)
Thérèse Raquin (Fr-It 1953)
Tempi Nostri (ep "Casa d'Altri") (It 1954)
Ulysse (It 1954)
Frou-Frou (Fr-It 1954)
Le Dossier noir (Fr-It 1955)
Michel Strogoff (Fr-It-Yug 1956)
Les Truands [Lock Up the Spoons] (Fr 1956)
Le Miroir à deux faces [The Mirror Has Two Faces] (Fr-It
   1958)
Quai du point du jour (Fr 1960)
Crésus (Fr 1960)
Cronica familiare (It 1962)
Château en Suède (Fr-It 1963)
Belphegorr (Fr TV 1964)
La Vieille Dame indigne [The Shameless Old Lady] (Fr 1965)
J'ai tué Raspoutine [I Killed Rasputin] (Fr-It 1967)
Le Ciel des fous (Fr 1969)

SYMS, SYLVIA, b. Jan. 6, 1934, Woolwich, London
   My Teenage Daughter [Teenage Bad Girl] (BL 1956)

No Time for Tears (ABPC 1957)
Woman in a Dressing Gown (ABP 1957)
The Birthday Present (BL 1957)
Ice Cold in Alex [Desert Attack] (ABPC 1958)
The Moonraker (ABPC 1958)
Bachelor of Hearts (RFD 1958)
No Trees in the Street (ABP 1959)
Ferry to Hong Kong (RFD 1959)
The Devil's Disciple (UA 1959)
Expresso Bongo (Britannia 1959)
Conspiracy of Hearts (RFD 1960)
The World of Suzie Wong (Par 1960)
Flame in the Streets (RFD 1961)
Le vergini di Roma (It-Fr-Yug 1961)
Victim (RFD 1961)
The Quare Fellow (Bry 1962)
The Punch and Judy Man (WPD 1962)
The World Ten Times Over (WPD 1963)
East of Sudan (Col 1964)
Operation Crossbow [The Great Spy Mission] (MGM 1965)
The Big Job (AA 1965)
Danger Route (UA 1967)
Hostile Witness (UA 1968)
Asylum (ep "Frozen Fear") (Cinema International 1972)
The Tamarind Seed (Avco Emb 1974)

TATI, JACQUES (Jacques Tatischeff), b. Oct. 9, 1908, Pecq, Seine-
    et-Oise, France
Sylvie et le fantôme (Fr 1945)
Le Diable au corps (Fr-It 1947)
Jour de fête (Fr 1949)
Les Vacances de Monsieur Hulot [Monsieur Hulot's Holiday] (Fr
    1953)
Mon Oncle (Fr-It 1958)
Playtime (Fr 1967)
Trafic [Traffic]
Parade (Fr-Swe 1974)

TEARLE, GODFREY, b. Oct. 12, 1884, New York; d. June 18,
    1953
The Fool (Pathe 1913)
Lochinvar (Gaumont 1915)
A Sinless Sinner [Midnight Gambols] (World 1919)
The March Hare (Ideal 1919)
Fancy Dress (Ideal 1919)
Nobody's Child (Butcher 1919)
Queen's Evidence (Moss 1919)
One Colombo Night (Stoll 1926)
If Youth But Knew (Reciprocity Films 1926)
Infatuation (Alpha 1930)
These Charming People (Par Br 1931)
The Shadow Between (Wardour 1931)
Puppets of Fate [Wolves of the Underworld] (UA 1933)

The 39 Steps (Gaumont 1935)
The Last Journey (TFD 1935)
East Meets West (Gaumont 1936)
Tomorrow We Live (ABFD 1936)
One of Our Aircraft Is Missing (Anglo 1942)
Undercover [Underground Guerillas] (UA 1943)
The Lamp Still Burns (GFD 1943)
Medal for the General (Anglo 1944)
The Rake's Progress [The Notorious Gentleman] (EL 1945)
The Beginning or the End (MGM 1947)
Private Angelo (ABP 1949)
White Corridors (GFD 1951)
I Believe in You (GFD 1952)
Mandy [Crash of Silence] (GFD 1952)
Decameron Nights (ep "Wager for Virtue") (Eros 1952)
The Titfield Thunderbolt (GFD 1953)

TEIXEIRA, VIRGILIO (Virgilio Gomes Delgado Teixeira), b. Oct.
    26, 1917, Funchal
    O costa do castelo (Sp 1943) (extra)
    A ave de arribação (Por 1943)
    Um homem às direitas (Por 1944)
    A noiva do Brasil (Por 1945)
    O José do talhado (Por 1945)
    Madelena, zero em compartamento (Por-Sp 1945)
    Ladrão (Por 1946)
    Precisa-se (Por 1946)
    Cais sodré (Por 1946)
    A mantilha de Beatriz (Por 1946)
    Três espelhos (Por 1947)
    Fado, a história de uma cantadeira (Por 1947)
    Rainha santa (Por-Sp 1947)
    Amanhã como hoje (Por-Sp 1947)
    Uma vida para dois (Por 1948)
    Estranho amanhecer (Sp 1948)
    The Bad Lord Byron (GFD 1949)
    Herois do mar (Por 1949)
    Ribatejo (Por 1949)
    A volta do José do Telhado (Por 1949)
    Vendaval (Sp 1949)
    Agostinha de Aragao (Sp 1950)
    O Verdugo (Sp 1950)
    A noite de sábado (Sp 1950)
    Alba de América (Sp 1951)
    Lola (Sp 1951)
    A piconerra (Sp 1951)
    A leoa de castela (Sp 1951)
    A filhoa do mar (Sp 1952)
    Cañas y barro (Sp 1952)
    Nazaré (Por 1952)
    Flor de lago (Sp 1953)
    Eu não sou a Mata-Hari (Sp 1953)
    Torturados (Sp 1953)

Virgilio Teixeira

Polvorilha (Sp 1953)
Zalacain (Sp 1954)
O Aventureiro (Sp 1954)
Padre Pitillo (Sp 1954)
Parabéns, Senhor Vicente (Por-Sp 1954)
O cerco do diabo (Sp 1955)
Um dia perdido (Sp 1955)
Perdeu-se um marido (Por 1956)
A irmã alegria (Sp 1956)
Alexander the Great (UA 1956)
Dos dias no paraiso (Por 1957)
A freira cigana (Sp 1957)
A estrela (Sp 1958)
The Seventh Voyage of Sinbad (Col 1958)
A tirana (Sp 1959)
Carta ao céu (Sp 1959)
Tommy the Toreador (WPD 1959)
Habanera (Sp 1959)
Rosa de Lima (Sp 1960)
The Boy Who Stole a Million (Par 1960)
Júlia e o celacanto (Sp 1961)
The Happy Thieves (UA 1962)
Balcão da lua (Sp 1963)
Tens ôlhos de mulher fatal (Sp 1963)
The Fall of the Roman Empire (Par 1964)
Ela o Medo (Sp 1964)
A voz do sangue (Por 1965)

Dr. Zhivago (MGM 1965)
Passagem de nível (Por 1965)
Return of the Seven (UA 1966)

THORNDYKE, SYBIL, b. Oct. 24, 1882, Gainsborough, Lincolnshire,
    England; d. June 18, 1976
Moth and Rust (Butcher 1921)
Tense Moments with Great Authors (ep "Nancy") (BEF 1922)
Tense Moments from Famous Plays (ep "Macbeth; Bleak House;
    Jane Shore; The Lady of the Camelias; The Merchant of
    Venice; Esmeralda and the Scarlet Letter") (BEF 1922)
[Saint Joan] (1927) (short, capturing her unique stage perform-
    ance)
Dawn (W & F 1928)
To What Red Hell (Tiffany 1929)
Hindle Wakes (Gaumont 1931)
A Gentleman of Paris (Gaumont 1931)
Tudor Rose [Nine Days a Queen] (Gaumont 1936)
Major Barbara (GFD 1941)
Nicholas Nickleby (GFD 1947)
Britannia Mews [The Forbidden Street] (20th 1949)
Stage Fright (WB 1950)
Gone to Earth [The Wild Heart] (BL 1950)
The Magic Box (BL 1951)
The Lady with a Lamp (BL 1951)
Melba (UA 1953)
The Weak and the Wicked (ABP 1954)
Smiley Gets a Gun (20th 1958)
Alive and Kicking (ABF 1958)
Jet Storm (Britannia 1959)
Shake Hands with the Devil (UA 1959)
Hand in Hand (WPD 1960)
The Big Gamble (20th 1961)

TILLER, NADJA, b. March 16, 1929, Vienna
Eroica (Aus 1949)
Marchen vom Glück (Aus 1949)
Kleiner Schwindel am Wolfgangsee (W Ger 1949)
Das Kind an der Donau (Aus 1950)
Wir werden das Kind schon schaukeln (Aus 1952)
Ich hab' mich so an Dich gewöhnt (Aus 1952)
Illusion in Moll (W Ger 1952)
Einmal keine Sorgen haben (W Ger-Aus 1953)
Die Kaiserin von China (W Ger 1953)
Ein tolles Früchtchen Schlagerparade (W Ger 1953)
Liebe und Trompetenblasen (W Ger 1954)
Mädchen mit zukunft (W Ger 1954)
Der letzte Sommer (W Ger 1954)
Ball im Savoy (W Ger 1955)
Gestatten, mein Name ist Cox (W Ger 1955)
Griff nach den Sternen (W Ger 1955)
Wie werde ich Filmstar? (W Ger 1955)
Hotel Adlon (W Ger 1955)

Die Barrings (W Ger 1955)
Reich mit die Hand mein Leben (Aus 1955)
Das Bad auf der Tenne (Aus 1956)
Ich suche Dich (W Ger 1956)
Friederike von Barring (W Ger 1956)
Fuhrmann Henschel (Aus 1956)
Spion für Deutschland (W Ger 1956)
Banktresor (W Ger 1957)
La Tour, prends garde! [Cuvaj se la tur] (Fr-Yug-It 1957)
Drei Mann auf einem Pferd (W Ger 1957)
El Hakim (W Ger 1957)
Le Désordre en la nuit [Night Affair] (Fr 1958)
Das Mädchen Rosemarie (W Ger 1958)
Labyrinth (W Ger 1959)
The Rough and the Smooth [Portrait of a Sinner] (Renown 1959)
Du Rififi chez les femmes [Rififi fra le donne/Riff Raff Girls]
    (Fr-It 1959)
Buddenbrooks (W Ger 1959)
An einem Freitag um halb Zwölf [Il mondo nella mia tasca/Vend-
    redi, 13 heures/The Word in My Pocket] (W Ger-It-Fr 1960)
Die Botschafterin (W Ger 1960)
L'Affaire Nina B (Fr-W Ger 1961)
Geliebte Hochstaplerin (W Ger 1961)
Anima nera (It 1962)
Lulu (Aus 1962)
La chambre ardente [Das brennende Gericht/I peccatori della
    foresta nera/The Burning Court] (Fr-W Ger-It 1962)
Das grosse Liebesspiel [And So to Bed] (W Ger-Aus 1963)
Moral 63 (W Ger 1963)
Schloss Gripsholm (W Ger 1963)
Tonio Kröger (W Ger-Fr 1964)
Erotica [L'amore difficile] (W Ger-It 1964)
Das Liebeskarussell (Aus 1965)
Rendezvous der Killer [Pleins feux sur Stanislas] (W Ger-Fr 1965)
L'estate (It 1966)
Das gewisse Etwas der Frauen [Come imparai ad amare le don-
    ne] (W Ger-It-Fr 1966)
Tendre Voyou [Un avventuriero a Tahiti/Tender Scoundrel] (Fr-
    It 1966)
Rififi in Paris [Du Rififi a Paname/Rififi Internationale/The Up-
    per Hand] (W Ger-It-Fr 1966)
Lady Hamilton (W Ger-It-Fr 1968)
Ohrfeigen (W Ger 1969)
Blonde Köder für den Mörder [La morte bussa due volte] (W Ger-
    It 1970)
L'occhio nel labirinto (It-W Ger 1972)
L'etrusco uccide ancora [The Dead Are Alive] (It 1972)
Le Moine [Il monaco] (Fr-It 1972)

TISSIER, Jean, b. April 1, 1896, Paris; d. March 31, 1973
Madame Sans-gêne (Fr 1925)
Le Monde où l'on s'ennui (Fr 1934)
Le Voyage imprévu (Fr 1934)

Les Hommes de la côte (Fr 1934)
Haut comme trois pommes (Fr 1935)
Retour au paradis (Fr 1935)
Soirée de gala (Fr 1935)
Les Gaîtés de la finance (Fr 1935)
Un Oiseau rare (Fr 1935)
Quelle drôle de gosse (Fr 1935)
La Mascotte (Fr 1935)
Veille d'armes (Fr 1935)
Les Jumeaux de Brighton (Fr 1936)
Blanchette (Fr 1936)
L'Ange du foyer (Fr 1936)
Enfants de Paris (Fr 1936)
Nitchevo (Fr 1936)
Les Gaietés du palace (Fr 1936)
Une Queule en or (Fr 1936)
La Garçonne (Fr 1936)
Le Chanteur de minuit (Fr 1936)
Alerte en Méditerranée (Fr 1937)
Le Grand Refrain (Fr 1937)
Boulot aviateur (Fr 1937)
Messieurs les ronds-de-cuir (Fr 1937)
Les Deux Combinards (Fr 1937)
Sarati le terrible (Fr 1937)
Ne tirez pas Dolly! (Fr 1937)
Hercule (Fr 1937)
L'Affaire du courrier de Lyon (Fr 1937)
Une Femme sans importance (Fr 1937)
Le Club des aristocrates (Fr 1937)
Le Puritain (Fr 1937)
Le Petit Chose (Fr 1938)
L'Ange que j'ai vendu (Fr 1938)
Les Femmes collantes (Fr 1938)
Le Grand élan (Fr 1938)
Carrefour (Fr 1938)
Le Monsieur de cinq heures (Fr 1938)
J'Etais une aventurière (Fr 1938)
L'Enfer des anges (Fr 1939)
Le Séducteur ingénu (Fr 1939)
Les Chevaliers de l'aventure (Fr 1939)
Le Millionnaire (Fr 1939)
Le Monde imprévu (Fr 1939)
Cas de conscience (Fr 1939)
Je chante (Fr 1939)
Quartier latin (Fr 1939)
Tourbillon de Paris (Fr 1939)
Irrésistible rebelle (Fr 1939)
Battement de coeur (Fr 1939)
Nuit de décembre (Fr 1939)
Fausse Alerte (Fr 1939)
Une Idée à l'eau (Fr 1939)
L'Homme qui cherche la vérité (Fr 1940)
L'Age d'or (Fr 1940)

Faut ce qu'il faut (Fr 1940)
L'Acrobate (Fr 1940)
Nous, les gosses (Fr 1941)
Premier Rendez-vous (Fr 1941)
Le Dernier des six (Fr 1941)
Ce n'est pas moi (Fr 1941)
Romance de Paris (Fr 1941)
Chèque au porteur (Fr 1941)
La Femme quie j'ai le plus aimée (Fr 1942)
La Maison des sept jeunes filles (Fr 1942)
Les Inconnus dans la maison (Fr 1942)
L'Amant de Bornéo (Fr 1942)
Le Lit a colonnes (Fr 1942)
L'Assassin habite au 21 (Fr 1942)
A vos ordres, Madame (Fr 1942)
Picpus (Fr 1942)
Adrien (Fr 1943)
Au bonheur des dames (Fr 1943)
25 Ans de bonheur (Fr 1943)
Coup de tête (Fr 1943)
Mon Amour est pres de toi (Fr 1943)
La Collection Ménard (Fr 1943)
Lucrèce [Comédienne] (Fr 1943)
Tête brûlée (Fr 1943)
Le Merle blanc (Fr 1944)
Le cavalier noir (Fr 1944)
Roger-la-honte (Fr 1945)
Son Dernier Rôle (Fr 1945)
Le Capitan (Fr 1945)
L'Extravagante Mission (Fr 1945)
La Femme coupée en morceau (Fr 1945)
Christine se marie (Fr 1946)
Lunegarde (Fr 1945)
24 Heures de perm' (Fr 1945)
L'Invité de la 11-eme heure (Fr 1945)
Le Roi des resquilleurs (Fr 1945)
Leçon de conduite (Fr 1945)
Rendez-vous à Paris (Fr 1946)
L'ennemi sans visage (Fr 1946)
Le Kermesse rouge (Fr 1946)
L'Homme traqué (Fr 1946)
Le Diamant de cent sous (Fr 1946)
On demande un ménage (Fr 1946)
Les Aventures de Casanova (Fr 1946)
La Revanche de Roger-la-Honte (Fr 1946)
Si jeunesse savait (Fr 1947)
La Dame d'onze heures (Fr 1947)
Une Mort sans importance (Fr 1947)
La Fleur de l'âge (Fr 1947) [Unfinished]
La Cité de l'espérance (Fr 1948)
Les Casse-pieds (Fr 1948)
Métier de fous (Fr 1948)
Toute la famille etait la (Fr 1948)

Ces Dames aux chapeaux verts (Fr 1948)
Gigi (Fr 1948)
La Veuve et l'innocent (Fr 1948)
Fandango (Fr 1948)
Le Furet (Fr 1949)
La Femme nue (Fr 1949)
Rome-Express [Signori, in carrozza! (Fr-It 1949)
La Voyageuse inattendu (Fr 1949)
Tête blonde (Fr 1949)
Sans tambour ni trompette (Fr 1949)
La Ronde des heures (Fr 1949)
Veronique (Fr 1949)
Vendetta en Camargue (Fr 1949)
La Porteuse de pain [La portatrice di pane] (Fr-It 1949)
Quai de Grenelle (Fr 1950)
Le Tampon du capiston (Fr 1950)
Minne, l'ingénue libertine (Fr 1950)
Sa Majesté M. Dupont [Prima Communione] (Fr-It 1950)
Cet Age est sans pitié (Fr 1950)
Coeur-sur-Mer (Fr 1950)
Les Maîtres-nageurs (Fr 1950)
Ce Coquin d'anatole (Fr 1950)
Trois Vieilles Filles en folie (Fr 1950)
Le Roi du bla-bla-bla [Les farfelus] (Fr 1950)
Les Petites Cardinal (Fr 1950)
Rendez-vous a Grenade (Fr 1951)
Et ta soeur! (Fr 1951)
Messaline [Messalina] (Fr-It 1951)
Descendez, oon vous demande (Fr 1951)
Un Caprice de Caroline chérie (Fr 1952)
Mon Gosse de pere (Fr 1952)
Quitte ou double (Fr 1952)
Quand te tues-tu? (Fr 1952)
L'Ile aux femme nues (Fr 1952)
Gangster en jupons (Fr 1952)
Hold-up en musique [Le Gang des pianos a bretellés] (Fr 1952)
Douze Heures de bonheur [Jupiter] (Fr 1952)
Tourbillon (Fr 1952)
La Belle de Cadix (Fr 1953)
La Rafle est pour ce soir (Fr 1953)
La Famille Cucuroux (Fr 1953)
Le Petit Jacques (Fr 1953)
Une Femme dans un lit (Fr 1953)
Ma Petite Folie (Fr 1953)
C'est la vie parisienne (Fr 1953)
Alerte au sud (Fr 1953)
Adam est... Eve (Fr 1953)
Si Versailles m'était conté (Fr 1953)
Fête de quartier [Bistro du coin] (Fr 1954)
Crime au Concert Mayol (Fr 1954)
Le Vicomte de Bragelonne [Il visconte di Bragelonne] (Fr-It
   1954)
Pas de souris dans le bizness (Fr 1954)

Papa, maman, la bonne et moi (Fr 1954)
Papa, maman, ma femme et moi (Fr 1955)
Pas de pitié pour les caves (Fr 1955)
La Môme Pigalle (Fr 1955)
Coup dur chez les mous (Fr 1955)
Ces Sacrées Vacances (Fr 1955)
Enquête aux Champs-Elysées (Fr 1955)
Alerte aux Canaries (Fr 1955)
Boulevard du crime (Fr 1955)
La Rue des bouches peintés (Fr 1955)
Un Policier pas comme les autres (Fr 1955)
Si Paris nous était conté (Fr 1955)
On Déménage le colonel (Fr 1955)
Mon Curé chez les pauvres (Fr 1956)
L'Inspecteur aime la bagarre (Fr 1956)
Printemps à Paris (Fr 1956)
Notre-Dame de Paris (Fr 1956)
Pas de grisbi pour Ricardo (Fr 1956)
L'Aventurière des Champs-Elysées (Fr 1956)
Et Dieu créa la femme (Fr 1956)
Baratin (Fr 1956)
Vacances explosives (Fr 1956)
Alerte au Deuxième Bureau (Fr 1956)
Le Colonel est de la revue (Fr 1956)
Police judiciaire (Fr 1957)
Une Nuit au Moulin-Rouge (Fr 1957)
La Blonde des tropiques (Fr 1957)
L'Amour descend du ciel (Fr 1957)
C'est arrivé à 36 chandelles (Fr 1957)
Maigret tend un piège (Fr 1957)
Les Gaîtés de l'escadrille (Fr 1957)
A pied, à cheval, et en voiture (Fr 1957)
Bistro du coin (Bel 1958)
Miss Pigalle (Fr 1958)
Bobosse (Fr 1958)
La Vie à deux (Fr 1958)
Visa pour l'enfer (Fr 1958)
Madame et son auto (Fr 1959)
Brigade des moeurs (Fr 1959)
Soupe au lait (Fr 1959)
Enigme aux folies-Bergère (Fr 1959)
Monsieur Suzuki (Fr 1959)
Vous n'avez rien a déclarer? (Fr 1959)
Marie des Isles (Fr-It 1959)
Mademoiselle Ange [Ein Engel auf Erden] (Fr-W Ger 1959)
Alibi pour un meurtre (Fr 1960)
Candide (Fr 1960)
Les Godelureaux (Fr-It 1961)
Vive Henri IV, Vive l'amour (Fr 1961)
La Bride sur le cou (Fr 1961)
Les Croulants se portent bien (Fr 1961)
Dossier 1413 (Fr 1961)
La Fille du torrent (Fr-It 1961)

Les Snobs (Fr 1961)
Seul...a corps perdu (Fr 1961)
Un Chien dans un jeu de quilles (Fr-It 1962)
Réglements de comptes (Fr 1962)
Clementine chérie (Fr-It 1962)
Strip-tease (Fr-It 1962)
Le Bon Roi Dagobert (Fr-It 1962)
Les Vierges [Le vergini] (Fr-It 1962)
Un Drôle de paroissien (Fr 1963)
L'Assassin viendra ce soir (Fr 1963)
Les Motorisées [Le motorizzate] (Fr-It 1963)
Le Sexe des anges [Le voci bianche] (Fr-It 1964)
Requiem pour un caid (Fr 1964)
Les Baratineurs (Fr 1965)
L'Or du duc (Fr 1965)
Le Jardinier d'Argenteuil [Bluten, Grauner und die Nacht von
    Nizza] (Fr-W Ger 1966)
Deux Billets pour Mexico [Geheimmsse in goldenen Nylous [Se-
    gretiche Scottano] (Fr-W Ger-It 1967)
La Veuve Couderc [L'evaso] (Fr-It 1971)
Sex Shop (Fr 1972)

TODD, ANN, b. Jan. 24, 1909, Hartford, Cheshire, England
    Keepers of Youth (Wardour 1931)
    These Charming People (Par Br 1931)
    The Ghost Train (W & F 1931)
    The Water Gypsies (Radio 1932)
    The Return of Bulldog Drummond (Wardour 1934)
    Things to Come (UA 1936)
    Action for Slander (UA 1937)
    The Squeaker [Murder on Diamond Row] (UA 1937)
    South Riding (UA 1938)
    Poison Pen (ABPC 1939)
    Danny Boy (Butcher 1941)
    Ships with Wings (UA 1941)
    Perfect Strangers [Vacation from Marriage] (MGM-London 1945)
    The Seventh Veil (GFD 1945)
    Gaiety George [Showtime] (GFD 1946)
    The Paradine Case [Selznick 1948]
    So Evil My Love (Par Br 1948)
    The Passionate Friends [One Woman's Story] (GFD 1949)
    Madeleine [The Strange Case of Madeleine] (GFD 1950)
    The Sound Barrier [Breaking the Sound Barrier] (BL 1952)
    The Green Scarf (BL 1954)
    Time Without Pity (Eros 1957)
    Taste of Fear [Scream of Fear] (Col 1961)
    The Fiend (Miracle 1972)

TODD, RICHARD (Andrew Palethorpe-Todd), b. June 11, 1919, Dub-
    lin
    For Them That Trespass (ABP 1949)
    The Hasty Heart (ABP 1949)
    The Interrupted Journey (BL 1949)

Stage Fright (WB 1950)
Portrait of Clare (ABP 1950)
Lightning Strikes Twice (WB 1951)
Flesh and Blood (BL 1951)
The Story of Robin Hood and His Merrie Men (RKO 1952)
24 Hours of a Woman's Life [Affair in Monte Carlo] (ABP 1952)
Venetian Bird [The Assassin] (GFD 1952)
Elstree Story (ABP 1952)
Secrets d'Alcove [The Bed] (ep "Le Billet de Logement") (Fr-It
    1953)
Rob Roy, the Highland Rogue (RKO 1953)
The Sword and the Rose (RKO 1953)
A Man Called Peter (20th 1955)
The Virgin Queen (20th 1955)
The Dam Busters (ABPC 1955)
Marie Antoinette [The Shadow of the Guillotine] (Fr-It 1955)
D-Day, the Sixth of June (20th 1956)
St. Joan (UA 1957)
Yangtse Incident [Battle Hell] (BL 1957)
Chase a Crooked Shadow (ABP 1958)
Naked Earth (20th 1958)
Intent to Kill (20th 1958)
Danger Within [Breakout] (BL 1959)
Never Let Go (RFD 1960)
The Long and the Short and the Tall (WPD 1961)
Don't Bother to Knock (WPD 1961)
The Hellions (Col 1961)
Le Crime ne paie pas [The Gentle Art of Murder] (ep "L'Homme
    de l'Avenue"/"The Man on the Avenue") (Fr-It 1962)
The Longest Day (20th 1962)
The Boys (Gala 1962)
The Very Edge (Garrick 1963)
Todestrommeln am grossen Fluss [Death Drums Along the River/
    Sanders of the River] (W Ger-GB 1963)
Operation Crossbow [The Great Spy Mission] (MGM 1965)
Coast of Skeletons (GB-W Ger 1965)
The Battle of the Villa Fiorita (WB 1965)
The Love-Ins (Col 1967)
The Last of the Long Haired Boys [Unreleased 1968]
Bildnis des Dorian Gray [Dorian Gray] (W Ger-It-Liecht 1970)
Asylum (ep "Frozen Fear") (Cinema International 1972)

TOLO, MARILU, b. May 17, 1943, Rome
Le adolescente (It 1961)
Shéhérazade [Scheherazade/La schiava di Bagdad] (Fr-Sp-It 1963)
Il magnifico gladiatore (It 1964)
Matrimonio all'italiana [Marriage à l'italienne] (It-Fr 1964)
Il figlio prodigo (It 1964)
La Celestina (It 1964)
Il trinfo di Ercole (It 1964)
Giulietta degli spiriti (It 1965)
Barbouze chérie [La muerte viaja en baul] (Fr-Sp-It 1965)
La Bourse et la vie (Fr-It 1965)

Le Chant du mone (Fr-It-W Ger 1965)
077--Intrigo a Lisbona (Sp-It 1965)
Avec la peau des autres (Fr-Aus-It 1966)
Le Judoka agent secret [Sciarada per quattro spie/Carnet per un
    morto] (Fr-It 1966)
Kiss the Girls and Make Them Die [Se tutte le donne del mondo/
    Operazione Paradiso] (USA-It 1966)
New York dans les ténèbres (It 1966)
Call-Girls (It 1966)
Sept Hommes et une garce (Fr-It-Rum 1966)
Un colpo da mille miliardi (It-Sp 1966)
Le notti della violenza (It 1966)
The Poppy Is Also a Flower (Comet 1966)
Casse-tête chinois (Fr-It-W Ger 1967)
Le Plus Vieux métier du monde [L'amore attraverso i secoli/Das
    älteste Gewerbe der Welt] (ep "Anticipation") (Fr-It-W Ger
    1967)
Se sei vivo spara (It 1967)
Le streghe [Les sorcières/The Witches] (ep "La steghe bruciata
    viva") (It-Fr 1967)
Face d'ange [Faccia d'angelo/Un killer per sua Maestà/The Kil-
    ler Likes Candy] (Fr-It-W Ger 1968)
Commandos (It-Sp-W Ger 1968)
Diabolik (It 1968)
Candy [Candy e il suo pazzo mondo] (USA-It-Fr 1968)
L'urlo dell'apocalisse [Las trompetas del Apocalipsis] (It-Sp
    1968)
Ore violente (It 1968)
Caldi amori di una minorenne (It 1968)
I dannati della terra (It 1969)
Gradiva (It 1969)
Roy Colt e Winchester Jack (It 1970)
Un Eté sauvage (Fr 1970)
Uccidete il vitello grasso e arrostitelo (It 1970)
Mio caro assassino (It 1970)
Confessione di un commissario di polizia al procuratore della
    Repubblica (It 1971)
Siamo tutti in libertà provvisoria (It 1971)
La controfigura (It 1971)
Romance of a Horse Thief (USA-It-Yug 1971)
Barbablù [Blaubart/Barbe-Bleue/Bluebeard] (It-W Ger-Fr-USA
    1972)
Viva la muerte...tua [Don't Turn the Other Cheek] (It-W Ger
    1972)
Jus primas noctis (It 1972)
Meo Patacca (It 1972)
Abuso di potere (It-W Ger-Fr 1972)
Le cinque giornate (It 1973)
Prigione di donne (It 1974)
Il trafficone (It 1974)
Au delà de la peur (Fr-It-W Ger 1975)

TOTO see DE CURTIS, ANTONIO

TOZZI, FAUSTO, b. 1921, Rome
Il caimano del Piave (It 1950)
La città si difende (It 1951)
Il brigante di Tacca del Lupo (It 1951)
Fratelli d'Italia (It 1952)
Carmen proibita [Siempre Carmen] (It-Sp 1952)
Musoduro (It 1953)
La corda d'acciaio (It 1953)
I cinque dell'Adamello (It 1954)
Nel gorgo del peccato (It 1954)
Casa Ricordi [House of Ricordi] (It 1954)
Divisione Folgore (It 1954)
Casta diva (It 1954)
Terroristi a Madrid [La ciudad perdida] (It-Sp 1954)
La ladra [Les Anges aux mains noires] (It-Fr 1955)
Il mantello rosso [Les Révoltes/Le Manteau rouge] (It-Fr 1955)
Canzoni di tutta Italia (It 1955)
Un po' di cielo (It 1955)
Beatrice Cenci (It 1956)
Quai des illusions (Fr 1956)
Il cielo brucia (It 1957)
El Alamein (It 1957)
La grande caccia [The Big Search/East of Kilimanjaro] (It-GB
    1957)
Dagli Appennini alle Ande (It 1958)
Quando gli angeli piangono (It 1958)
Un uomo facile (It 1959)
La notte del grande assalto (It 1959)
Storie d'amore proibite (It 1959)
Questo amore ai confini del mondo (It 1960)
Costantino il grande [Constantine and the Cross] (It 1960)
St. Tropez Blues (Fr-It 1960)
El Cid (AA 1961)
FBI contro dottor Mabuse [Im Stahlnetz des Dr. Mabuse/Le re-
    tour du Dr. Mabuse] (It-W Ger-Fr 1961)
Le meraviglie di Aladino [The Wonders of Aladdin] (It-USA 1961)
La congiura dei dieci [Lo spadacino di Sienna/Swordsman of
    Siena] (It-Sp 1962)
Marcia o crepa [Marcha o muore/Marschier oder krepier/Héros
    sans retour/Commando] (It-Sp-W Ger-Bel 1962)
La schiava di Bagdad [Scheherazade] (It-Fr-Sp-USA 1962)
Gibraltar [Spionaggio a Gibilterra/Misión en el estrecho] (It-Sp
    1963)
Il giorno più corto commedia umaristica [The Shortest Day] (It
    1963)
La vendetta della signora [La visita/Der Besuch/La Rancune/The
    Visit] (It-W Ger-Fr 1964)
The Agony and the Ecstasy (20th 1965)
I violenti di Rio Bravo (It 1965)
The Sailor from Gibraltar (UA 1967)
...e divenne il più spietato bandito del sud [El hombre que mató
    a Billy el niño] (It-Sp 1967)
I coltelli del vendicatore [Raffica di coltelli/Knives of the Aven-
    ger] (It 1967)

The Appointment (MGM 1969)
Sledge (It 1969)
Mazzabubu--quanta corna stanno quaggiu? (It 1970)
La Faute de l'abbé Mouret (Fr-It 1970)
Per grazia ricevuta (It 1970)
La spina dorsale del diavolo [The Deserter] (It 1971)
Joe Valachi--i segreti di Cosa Nostri [Cosa Nostri] (It-Fr 1972)
La mano spietata della legge (It 1973)
Valdez il mezzo sangue (It-Sp-Fr 1973)
Alyon-Oppio (Fr-It 1973)
Crazy Joe (Par 1973)
Il suo nome Faceva tremare Interpol in Allarme [L'Homme aux
    neuf d'acier] (It-Fr 1973)
Le guerriere dal seno nudo [The Amazons] (It 1974)
Street People (It-USA 1975)

TRINTIGNANT, JEAN-LOUIS, b. Dec. 11, 1930, Pont St-Esprit,
    Nîmes, France
Si tous les gars du Monde (Fr 1955)
La Loi des rues (Fr 1956)
Et Dieu créa la femme [And God Created Woman] (Fr 1956)
Club des femmes (Fr-It 1956)
Les Liasons dangereuses 1960 (Fr-It 1959)
L'estate violenta (It-Fr 1959)
Austerlitz (Fr-It-Yug 1960)
La Millième Fenêtre (Fr 1960)
Le Coeur battant (Fr 1961)
Pleins feux sur l'assassin (Fr 1961)
L'Antinea, la ante della città sepotta (It-Fr 1961)
Le Jeu de la vérité (Fr 1961)
Le Combat dans l'île (Fr 1961)
Il sorpasso (It 1962)
Horace '62 (Fr 1962)
Les Sept Péchés capitaux [Seven Deadly Sins] (Fr-It 1962)
Chateau en Suede (Fr-It 1963)
Angélique (Fr-W Ger-It-Sp 1964)
Les Pas perdus (Fr 1964)
Mata Hari--Agent H. 21 (Fr-It 1964)
Compartiment tueurs [The Sleeping Car Murders] (Fr 1965)
La Bonne Occase (Fr 1965)
Io uccido, tu uccidi (It-Fr 1965)
Merveilleuse Angélique (Fr-W Ger-It 1965)
La Longue Marche (Fr 1966)
Le Dix-Septième Ciel (Fr 1966)
Paris brûle-t-il? [Is Paris Burning?] (Fr 1966)
Un Homme et un femme [A Man and a Woman] (Fr 1966)
Safari diamants (Fr-W Ger 1966)
Trans-Europ Express (Fr 1967)
Un Homme à abattre [A Man to Kill] (Fr-Sp 1967)
La morte ha fatto l'uovo [Plucked] (It-Fr 1967)
Col cuore in gola [With Bated Breath] (It-Fr 1967)
Mon amour... mon amour (Fr 1967)
La matriaca [The Libertine] (It 1968)

Les Biches [The Does] (Fr-It 1968)
L'Homme qui ment [Shock Troops] (Fr-It 1968)
Il grande silenzio (It 1969)
Metti, una sera a cena [The Love Circle] (It 1969)
Le Voleur des crimes (Fr-It 1969)
Z (Fr-Alg 1969)
L'Américain (Fr 1969)
Ma Nuit chez Maud [My Night with Maud] (Fr 1969)
Il Conformista [The Conformist] (It-Fr-W Ger 1969)
Le Bateau (Fr 1970)
Par le sang versé (Fr 1970)
Le Voyou (Fr 1970)
La Course du lievre à travers ces champs [Cross My Heart and
    Hope to Die] (Fr-It 1971)
Sans Mobile apparent (Fr-It 1971)
L'Homme aux cerveau greffé (Fr-It-W Ger 1972)
L'Attenat [Plot] (Fr-It-W Ger 1972)
Un Homme est mort [The Outside Man] (Fr-It 1972)
Defense de savoir [Forbidden to Know] (Fr-It 1973)
Le Train (Fr-It 1973)
Une Journée bien remplie [A Well-Filled Day] (Fr 1973)
Les Violons du bal [Violins of the Ball] (Fr 1974)
L'Escapade (Fr-Swi 1974)
Le Mouton enragé [Love at the Top] (Fr 1974)
Le Secret (Fr 1974)
Le Jeu avec le feu [Playing with Fire] (Fr-It 1974)
L'Agression (Fr 1975)
Flic Story (Fr-It 1975)
Il Pleut sur Santiago (Fr-Bul 1975)
Le Voyage de noces (Fr 1975)
La donna della domenica (It-Fr 1975)

TSCHECHOWA, OLGA, b. April 26, 1896, Alexandropol, Russia
Todesreigen (Ger 1921)
Hochstapler (Ger 1921)
Schloss Vogelöd (Ger 1921)
Das Haus der Unseligen (Ger 1922)
Der Kampf ums Ich (Ger 1922)
Ein Puppenheim [Die Fahrt ins Gluck/Bub und Mary/Nora] (Ger
    1923)
Die Pagode (Ger 1923)
Tatjana (Ger 1923)
Der verlorene Schuh (Ger 1923)
Die Bacchantin (Ger 1924)
Die Fraum im Feuer (Ger 1924)
Soll und Haben (Ger 1924)
Das alte Ballhaus (Ger 1925)
Die Gesunkenen (Ger 1925)
Mädels von heute (Ger 1925)
Der Mann aus dem Jenseits (Ger 1925)
Die Millionenkompagnie (Ger 1925)
Soll man heiraten? (Ger 1925)
Die Stadt der Versuchung (Ger 1925)

Die Venus vom Montmartre (Ger 1926)
Der Feldherrenhügel (Ger 1926)
Brennende Grenze (Ger 1926)
Familie Schimeck (Ger 1926)
Der Mann im Feuer (Ger 1926)
Die Mühle von Sanssouci (Ger 1926)
Sein grosser Fall (Ger 1926)
Trude, die Sechzehnjährige (Ger 1926)
Das Meer (Ger 1926)
Der Meister der Welt (Ger 1927)
Die selige Excellenz (Ger 1926)
Marter der Liebe (Ger 1928)
Weib in Flammen (Ger 1928)
Blutschan die 173 St. G. B. (Ger 1929)
Diane (Ger 1929)
Die Liebe der Brüder Rott (Ger 1929)
Der Narr seiner Liebe (Ger 1929)
Stud. chem. Helene Willfüer (Ger 1929)
Der Detektiv der Kaisers (Ger 1920)
Die grosse Sehnsucht (Ger 1930)
Die Drei von der Tankstelle (Ger 1930)
Troika (Ger 1930)
Zwei Krawatten (Ger 1930)
Liebe im Ring (Ger 1930)
Ein Mädel von de Reeperbahn [Menschen im Sturm] (Ger 1930)
Liebling der Götter (Ger 1930)
Liebe auf Befehl [Ger version of Boudoir Diplomat] (Ger 1931)
Die Nacht der Entscheidung (Ger 1931)
Das Konzert (Ger 1931)
Panik in Chikago (Ger 1931)
Nachtkolonne (Ger 1931)
Mary (Ger 1931)
Spione im Savoy-Hotel (Ger 1932)
Trenck (Ger 1932)
Wege zur guten Ehe (Ger 1933)
Heideschulmeister (Ger 1933)
Uwe Karsten (Ger 1933)
Ein gewisser Herr Gran (Ger 1933)
Leibelei (Ger 1933)
Der Choral von Leuthen (Ger 1933)
Peer Gynt (Ger 1934)
Zwischen Zwei Herzen (Ger 1934)
Was bin ich ohne Dick (Ger 1934)
Regine (Ger 1934)
Maskerade (Aus 1934)
Die Welt ohne Maske (Ger 1934)
Abenteuer eines jungen Herrn in Polen (Ger 1934)
Der Polizeibericht meldet (Ger 1934)
Die ewige Maske [The Eternal Mask] (Aus-Swi 1935)
Liebesträume (Ger 1935)
Lockspitzel Asew (Ger-Aus 1935)
Künstlerliebe (Ger 1935)
Ein Walzer um der Stephansturm (Aus 1935)

Hannerl and ihre Liebhaber (Aus 1935)
Der Favorit der Kaiserin (Ger 1936)
Manja Valewska (Ger 1936)
Seine Tochter ist der Peter (Aus 1936)
Burgtheater (Aus 1936)
Unter Ausschluss der Öffentlichkeit (Ger 1937)
Gewitterflug zu Claudia (Ger 1937)
Liebe geht seltsame Wege (Ger 1937)
Die gelbe Flagge (Ger 1937)
Verliebtes Abenteuer (Ger 1938)
Rote Orchideen (Ger 1938)
Das Mädchen mit dem guten Ruf (Ger 1938)
Befreite Hände (Ger 1939)
Bel ami (Ger 1939)
Zwei Frauen (Ger 1939)
Ich verweigere die Aussage (Ger 1939)
Parkstrasse 13 (Ger 1939)
Die unheimlichen Wünsche (Ger 1939)
Leidenschaft (Ger 1940)
Angelika (Ger 1940)
Der Fuchs von Glenarvon (Ger 1940)
Andreas Schlüter (Ger 1941)
Menschen im Sturm (Ger 1941)
Mit den Augen einer Frau (Ger 1942)
Reise in die Vergangenheit (Ger 1943)
Gefährlicher Frühling (Ger 1943)
Der ewige Klang (Ger 1943)
Melusine (Ger 1944)
Mit meinen Augen (Ger 1944)
Der Mann, der zweimal leben wollte (W Ger 1950)
Eine Nacht im Séparée (W Ger 1950)
Kein Engel ist so rein (W Ger 1950)
Zwei in einen Anzug (W Ger 1950)
Maharadscha wider Willen (W Ger 1950)
Aufruhr im Paradies (W Ger 1950)
Die Perlenkette (W Ger 1951)
Eine Frau mit Herz (W Ger 1951)
Das Geheimnis einer Ehe (W Ger 1951)
Mein Freund, der Dieb (W Ger 1951)
Hinter Klostermauern (W Ger 1952)
Heute nacht passiert's (W Ger 1953)
Alles für Papa (W Ger 1953)
Rosen-Rösli (W Ger 1954)
Rittmeister Wronski (W Ger 1954)
Ich war ein hässliches Mädchen (W Ger 1955)
Die Barrings (W Ger 1955)
U-47 Kapitänleutnant Prien (W Ger 1958)
Frühling auf Immenhof (W Ger 1974)

TUSHINGHAM, RITA, b. 1940, Liverpool
A Taste of Honey (Bry 1961)
The Leather Boys (Garrick 1963)
A Place to Go (Bry 1963)

Girl with Green Eyes (UA 1964)
The Knack...and How to Get It (UA 1965)
The Trap (RFD 1966)
Smashing Time (Par 1967)
Diamonds for Breakfast (Par 1968)
The Guru (20th 1969)
Rachel's Man (Isr 1975)
Ragazzo di borgata (It 1975)

Michael York and Rita Tushingham

URE, MARY, b. Feb. 18, 1933, Glasgow; d. April 3, 1975
Storm Over the Nile (IFD 1955)
Windoms Way (RFD 1957)
Look Back in Anger (ABP 1959)
Sons and Lovers (20th 1960)
The Mind Benders (AA 1962)
The Luck of Ginger Coffey (Can-USA 1964)
Custer of the West (Cin 1967)
Where Eagles Dare (MGM 1968)
A Reflection of Fear (Col 1971)

URZI, SARO (Rosario Urzi), b. Feb. 24, 1913, Catania, Italy
Il sogno di Butterfly (It 1939)
Marco Visconti (It 1940)
Tosca (It 1940)
Un colpo di pistola (It 1941)
Inviati speciali (It 1942)
Girono di nozze (It 1942)
Harlem (It 1942)
Odessa in framme (It 1942)
La freccia nel fianco (It 1943)
La locandiera (It 1943)
Tombolo, paradiso nero (It 1947)
Emigrantes (It 1948)
In nome della legge (It 1948)
La mano della morta (It 1949)
Gente così (It 1949)
Barriera a settentrione (It 1949)
Ho sognato il pardiso (It 1949)
I fuorilegge (It 1949)
Lo sparviero del Nilo (It 1949)
Il cammino della speranza (It 1950)
Il bivio (It 1950)
I falsari (It 1950)
Trieste mia! (It 1951)
Il monello della strada (It 1951)
La vendetta del Corsaro (It 1951)
Slavate mia figlia (It 1951)
Il brigante di Tacca del Lupo (It 1951)
I falsari (It 1952)
Don Camillo (It 1952)
Fuoco nero (It 1952)
Fratelli d'Italia (It 1952)
Il ritorno di don Camillo (It 1952)
Paulde tragica (It 1953)
Io, Amleto (It 1953)
Cronaca di un delitto (It 1953)
Rivalita (It 1953)
Opinione pubblica (It 1953)
Il tesoro dell'Africa [Beat the Devil] (It-USA 1954)
La vendetta del corsaro (It 1954)
I cinque dell'Adamello (It 1954)
Cañas y barro [La palude del peccato] (Sp-It 1954)
Don Camillo e l'onorevole Peppone (It 1955)
La ladra (It 1956)
Il ferroviere [The Railroad Man] (It 1956)
Motivo in maschera (It 1956)
I fidianzati della morte (It 1956)
Liana, la schiava bianca (It 1957)
Marchands de filles (Fr 1957)
L'uomo di paglia (It 1957)
Dinanzi a noi il cielo (It 1957)
Nella città l'inferno [...And the Wild, Wild Women] (It 1958)
Il filgio del Corsaro rossa [Son of the Red Corsair] (It 1958)

Un maledetto imbroglio [The Facts of Murder] (It 1959)
Gli avventurieri dei tropici (It 1960)
Cavalcata selvaggia (It 1960)
I mafiosi (It 1960)
Les Filles sement le vent [The Fruit Is Ripe] (Fr-It 1961)
Un giorno da leoni (It 1961)
Ça va être ta fête (Fr 1961)
Don Camillo, monsignore...ma non troppo (It 1961)
Lo sgarro (It 1962)
Sedotta e abbandonate [Seduced and Abandoned] (It 1964)
Il compagno don Camillo (It 1965)
Le Corniaud [Colpo grosso ma non troppo] (Fr-It 1965)
Le Chant du monde (Fr-It 1965)
Modesty Blaise (20th 1965)
Io, io, io...e gli altri (It 1966)
La Fille de la Mer Morte (Fr 1966)
Una storia di notte (It 1967)
Kriminal Story (It 1967)
La Ronte de Corinthe [Who's Got the Black Box?] (Fr-It 1967)
Vivre la nuit [La ragazza della notte] (Fr-It 1968)
Serafino (It 1968)
Gente d'onore (It 1969)
Principe coronato cercasi per ricca ereditiera (It 1970)
La prima notte del Dr. Danieli, industriale col complesso del
   giocattolo (It 1970)
Alfredo Alfredo (It 1971)
Le inibizioni del dottor gaudenzi, vedor col complesso della
   buonanima (It 1971)
Torino nerva (It 1972)
Il caso Pisciotta (It 1973)
Il figlioccio del padrino (It 1973)

USTINOV, PETER, b. April 16, 1921, London
   Mein Kampf--My Crimes (Fr 1940)
   Hullo Fame! (British Films 1940)
   One of Our Aircraft Is Missing (Anglo 1942)
   Let the People Sing (Anglo 1942)
   The Goose Steps Out (UA 1942)
   The New Lot (AKC 1943)
   The Way Ahead (EL 1944)
   The True Glory (GB-USA 1945)
   School for Secrets [Secret Flight] (GFD 1946)
   Vice Versa (GFD 1948)
   Private Angelo (ABP 1949)
   Odette (BL 1950)
   Quo Vadis (MGM 1951)
   Hotel Sahara (GFD 1951)
   The Magic Box (BL 1951)
   Beau Brummel (MGM 1954)
   The Egyptian (20th 1954)
   We're No Angels (Par 1955)
   Lola Montez [Lola Montes] (Fr-W Ger 1955)
   Un angel volo sobra [An Angel over Brooklyn] (Sp 1955)

Peter Ustinov (right) toasts Robert Morley, in Hot Millions (1968).

Les Espions (Fr 1957)
Spartacus (Univ 1960)
The Sundowners (WB 1960)
Romanoff and Juliet (Univ 1961)
Billy Bud (RFD 1962)
Topkapi (UA 1964)
John Goldfarb, Please Come Home (20th 1964)
Lady L (Fr-It 1965)
The Comedians (MGM 1967)
Blackbeard's Ghost (BV 1967)
Hot Millions (MGM 1968)
Viva Max! (CUE 1970)
Hammersmith Is Out (Cin 1972)
Robin Hood (BV 1973) (voice only)
One of Our Dinosaurs Is Missing (BV 1975)

VALLI, ALIDA (Alida Maria Altenburger), b. May 31, 1921, Pola,
    Italy
Il Capello a tre punte (It 1935)
I due sergenti (It 1936)
Sono stato Io! [It Was I] (It 1937)
Il feroce Saladino (It 1937)
L'ultima nemica [The Last Enemy] (It 1938)
L'Amor mio non muore (It 1938)
L'ha fatto una signore (It 1938)
Mille lire al mese (It 1938)
La casa del peccato (It 1939)
Ballo al castello (It 1939)
Assenza ingiustficata (It 1939)
Manon Lescaut (It 1940)
Taverna Rossa (It 1940)
Oltre l'amore (It 1940)
La prima donna che passa (It 1940)
Piccolo mondo antico (It 1941)
Luce nelle tenebre (It 1941)
Ore nove lezione di Chimica [Schoolgirl Diary] (It 1941)
L'amante segreta (It 1941)
Catene invisibli (It 1942)
Noi vivi (It 1942)
Addio Kira [part II of Noi vivi] (It 1942)
Le due orfanelle [The Two Orphans] (It 1942)
Stasera niente di nuovo (It 1942)
I pagliacci [Laugh, Pagliacci] (It 1943)
T'amero sempre (It 1943)
Dieci minute di vita (It 1943) [Unreleased]
Apparizione (It 1944)
Il canto della vita (It 1945)
La vita ricominicia [Life Begins Anew/The Sin of Patricia] (It
    1945)
Circo equestre Za-Bum (It 1946) [made in 1944]
Eugenia Grandet (It 1946)
The Paradine Case (Selznick Releasing Organization 1947)
The Miracle of the Bells (RKO 1948)

Alida Valli and Steve Cochran in <u>Il grido</u> (1957).

The Third Man (Selznick Releasing Organization 1949)
The White Tower (RKO 1950)
Walk Softly, Stranger (RKO 1950)
I miracoli non si ripetono [Les Miracles n'ont lieu qu'une fois]
    (It-Fr 1950)
Ultimo incontro (It 1951)
Il mondo la condonna (It 1952)
Gli amanti di Toledo [Les Amants de Toledo/El tirano de Tole-
    do/The Lovers of Toledo] (It-Fr 1953)
La mano dello straniero [The Stranger's Hand] (It 1954)
Senso [The Wanton Countess] (It 1957)
La diga sul Pacifico [Barrage contre le Pacifique/The Sea Wall/
    This Angry Age] (It-Fr 1957)
La lunga strada azzurra [Un Dénommé Squarcio] (It-Fr-W Ger
    1957)
Il Grido (It 1957)
Les Bijoutiers du clair de lune [Gli amanti del chiaro di luna/
    The Night Heaven Fell] (Fr-It 1957)
L'amore più Gello [L'uomo dai calzoni corti/Tal vez manana]
    (It 1958)
Tal vez mañana (Sp 1958)

L'assegno (It 1959)
L'amore più bello [L'uomo dai calzoni corti] (It 1959)
Le Dialogue des Carmelites [I dialoghi delle carmelitane] (Fr-It 1960)
Le Gigolo [Il gigolo] (Fr-It 1960)
Les Yeux sans visage [Occhi senza volto/Eyes without a Face] (Fr-It 1960)
Il peccato degli anni verdi (It 1960)
Signé Arsène Lupin [Il ritorno di Arsene Lupin] (Fr-It 1960)
La Fille du torrent (Fr-It 1960)
L'inverno ti fara tornare [Une Aussi Longue Absence] (Fr-It 1960)
Il disordine [Disorder] (It 1962)
The Happy Thieves (UA 1962)
Ophélia (Fr 1962)
Homenaje a la hora de la siesta (Argentinia 1962)
Al otro lado de la ciudad (Sp 1962)
El valle de las espadas [The Castilian] (Sp-USA 1963)
L'Autre Femme [La otra mujer] (Fr-Sp-It 1965)
Humour noir [Umorismo nero/La muerte viaje demasiado] (Fr-It-Sp 1966)
Edipo re [Oedipus Rex] (It 1967)
Le champignon [L'Assassin frappe à l'aube] (Fr-Swi 1969)
Concerto per pistola solista (It 1970)
La strategia del ragno [The Spider's Strategy] (It 1970)
La prima notte di guiete [Le professeur] (It-Fr 1972)
L'occhio nel labirinto (It 1972)
Lisa e il diavolo (It 1972)
Diario di un italiano (It 1973)
La Grande Trouille (Fr 1974)
L'Anticristo (It 1974)
La Chaîr de l'orchidée (Fr-W Ger 1974)
Ce Cher Victor (Fr 1975)
No es Nada Mama, Solo un Juego (Sp-Venezuelan 1975)

VALLONE, RAF, b. Feb. 17, 1916, Tropea, Italy
Riso amaro [Bitter Rice] (It 1949)
Non c'è pace tra gli ulivi [Under the Olive Tree] (Ig 1950)
Il cammino della speranza [The Path of Hope] (It 1950)
Cuori senza frontiere [The White Line] (It 1950)
Cristo proibito [Strange Deception] (It 1951)
Anna (It 1952)
Roma ore 11 [Rome, 11 o'clock] (It 1952)
Camicie rosse [Les Chemises rouges] (It-Fr 1952)
Gli eroi della Domenica (It 1952)
Carne inquiete (It 1952)
Il bivio (It 1952)
Le avventure di Mandrin [Le Chevalier sans loi] (It-Fr 1952)
Thérèse Raquin [Teresa Raquin/The Adulteress] (Fr-It 1953)
Perdonami! (It 1953)
Destinées [Destini di donne/Daughters of Destiny] (Fr-It 1953)
La spiaggia [La Pensionnaire] (It-Fr 1954)
Vomini senza pace [Los ojos dejan huellas] (It-Sp 1954)
Delirio [Orage] (It-Fr 1954)

Domanda di grazia [Obsession] (It-Fr 1954)
Siluri umani (It 1955)
Il segno di Venere (It 1955)
Les Possédées [L'isola delle donne sole/Passionate Summer]
    (Fr-It 1955)
Andrea Chênier (Fr-It 1955)
Le Secret de soeur Angele [Il segreto di suor Angela] (Fr-It
    1956)
Uragano sul Po [Liebe] (It-W Ger 1956)
Rose Bernd [The Sins of Rose Bernd] (W Ger 1956)
Guendalina (It 1957)
La vendetta [Ho giurato di ucciderti/La Venganza] (It-Sp 1957)
Le Piège [La trappola si chiude/No Escape] (Fr-It 1958)
La Violetera (Sp 1958)
Recours en grâce [Tra due donne] (Fr-It 1959)
La garconnière (It 1960)
La ciociara [Two Women] (It 1960)
El Cid (AA 1961)
A View from the Bridge [Vu du pont] (Continental Distributing
    1962)
Phaedra (Lopert 1962)
The Cardinal (Col 1963)
The Secret Invasion (UA 1964)
Harlow (Par 1965)
Nevada Smith (Par 1966)
Se tutte le donne del mondo [Operazione Paradiso/Ramdam a
    Rio/Kiss the Girls and Make Them Die] (It-Fr 1966)
Volver a vivir (Sp-It 1968)
Más allá de la montañas [Beyond the Mountain] (Sp-US 1968)
La esclava del paraiso (Sp-It 1969)
The Italian Job (Par 1969)
The Kremlin Letter (20th 1970)
La morte risale a ieri sera [Death Occurred Last Night] (It
    1970)
Cannon for Cordoba (UA 1970)
A Gunfight (Par 1971)
Meurtres au soleil [Un verano para matar/The Summertime Kil-
    ler] (Fr-Sp-It 1973)
Honor Thy Father (CBS-TV 1973)
Simona [Histoire de l'oeil] (It-Fr-Bel 1973)
Rosebud (UA 1974)
That Lucky Touch (AA 1975)

VANAL, CHARLES (Marie-Charles Vanel), b. Aug. 21, 1892, Ren-
    nes, France
    Jim Crow (Fr 1912)
    L'Atre (Fr 1919)
    Du créspuscule à l'aube (Fr 1919)
    Miarka, la fille à l'ourse (Fr 1920)
    Créspuscule d'épouvante (Fr 1921)
    La Fille de la Carmargue (Fr 1921)
    Phrose (Fr 1922)
    La Maison du mystère (Fr 1922)

Tempêtes (Fr 1922)
Le Vol (Fr 1923)
Calvaire d'Amour (Fr 1923)
La Mendiante de Saint-Sulpice (Fr 1923)
L'Autre Aile (Fr 1924)
La Flambée des rêves (Fr 1924)
Pêcheur d'Islande (Fr 1924)
La Nuit de la revanche (Fr 1924)
Aime l'artiste (Fr 1925)
600,000 Francs par mois (Fr 1925)
Barocco (Fr 1925)
Le Réveil (Fr 1925)
La Flamme (Fr 1925)
L'Orphelin du cirque (Fr 1925)
Nitchevo (Fr 1926)
Martyre (Fr 1926)
La Proie du vent (Fr 1926)
Chanté (Fr 1927)
L'Esclave blanche (Fr 1927)
Maquillage (Fr 1927)
Feu! (Fr 1927)
Panane n'est pas Paris (Fr 1927)
Waterloo (Fr 1928)
Le Passager (Fr 1928)
La Femme rêvée (Fr 1929)
Feux Follets (Fr 1929)
La Plongée tragique (Fr 1929)
Les Fourchambault (Fr 1929)
Dans le nuit (Fr 1929)
Les 50 Ans de Don Juan (Fr 1930)
Le Capitaine jaune (Fr 1930)
Chiqué (Fr 1930)
Maison de danse (Fr 1930)
L'Obsession (Fr 1930)
La Maison jaune du Rio (Fr 1930)
Faubourg Montmartre (Fr 1932)
Au nom de la loi (Fr 1932)
Gitanes (Fr 1932)
Les Croix de bois (Fr 1932)
Le Roi de Camargue (Fr 1933)
Les Misérables (Fr 1934) (3 parts)
L'Enfant du Carneval (Fr 1934)
Au bout du monde (Fr-Ger 1934)
Le Grand Jeu (Fr 1934)
L'Impossible Aveu (Fr 1935)
L'Equipage (Fr 1935)
Domino vert (Fr 1935)
La Belle Equipe (Fr 1936)
Vertige d'un soir (Fr 1936)
Jenny (Fr 1936)
Les Grands (Fr 1936)
Port Arthur (Fr 1936)
Police Mondaine (Fr 1936)

S. O. S. Sahara (Fr 1936)
Michel Strogoff (Fr 1936)
L'Assaut (Fr 1936)
La Flamme (Fr 1936)
Courrier-sud (Fr 1936)
La Peur (Fr 1936)
Abus de confiance (Fr 1937)
Troika sur la piste blanche (Fr 1937)
L'Occident (Fr 1937)
Les Pirates du rail (Fr 1937)
Yamilé sous les Cèdres (Fr 1937)
Legions d'Honneur (Fr 1938)
La Femme du bout du monde (Fr 1938)
Carrefour (Fr 1938)
Les Bataliers de la Volga (Fr 1938)
Bar du Sud (Fr 1938)
La Sonate à Kreutzer (Fr 1938)
La Brigade sauvage (Fr 1939)
La Loi du nord (Fr 1939)
L'Or du Cristobal (Fr 1939)
La Nuit merveilleuse (Fr 1940)
Le Diamant noir (Fr 1940)
Le Soleil a toujours raison (Fr 1941)
Promesse à l'inconnue (Fr 1942)
Haut-le-vent (Fr 1942)
Les Affaires sont les affaires (Fr 1942)
Les Roquevillard (Fr 1943)
Le Ciel est à vous (Fr 1943)
La Ferme du pendu (Fr 1945)
Gringolet (Fr 1946)
Le Bateau à soupe (Fr 1946)
La Cabane aux souvenirs (Fr 1946)
Le Diable souffle (Fr 1947)
Le Pain des pauvres (Fr 1948)
La Femme que j'ai assassinée (Fr 1948)
Un nomma della legge (It 1949)
Les Mauvents (Sp 1949)
Le Secret des Mendovic (It 1949)
Jeunesse sur la Mer (Fr-It 1949)
La Brigade volante (It 1949)
Gli inesorabili (It 1950)
Il Bivio (It 1951)
Olivia (It-Fr 1951)
Plus fort que la haine (Fr 1951)
Ultima sentenzia (It-Fr 1951)
La Salaire de la peur (Fr-It 1953)
Cuori sul Marc (It-Fr 1953)
Si Versailles m'était conté (Fr 1953)
Maddelena (It-Fr 1953)
L'Affaire Maurizius (Fr-It 1954)
Les Gaîtés de l'escadron (Fr-It 1954)
Tam-Tam (It-Fr 1955)

To Catch a Thief (Par 1955)
Les Diaboliques [The Fiends] (Fr 1955)
Le Missionaire (Fr-It 1955)
La Femme scandeleuse (It-Fr 1956)
Le Mort en ce jardin [Evil Eden] (Fr-Mex 1956)
Le Feu aux poudres (Fr-It 1957)
Les Suspects (Fr 1957)
Rafles sur la ville (Fr 1958)
Le Gorille vous salue bien (Fr 1958)
Le Piège [The Trap] (Fr-It 1958)
Les Bataliers de la Volga (Fr-It-W Ger 1958)
Les Naufrageurs (Fr 1959)
Pêcheur d'Islande (Fr 1959)
La Valse du gorille (Fr 1959)
Maria, matricula de Bilboa (Sp 1960)
La Vérité [The Truth] (Fr-It 1961)
Tintin et le mystère de la toison d'or (Fr 1961)
La Steppe (Fr-It 1962)
Lo sgarro (It-Fr 1962)
Rififi à Tokyo (Fr-It 1962)
L'Ainé des Ferchaux [Magnet of Doom] (Fr-It 1963)
La Poursuite (Fr-It 1963)
Symphonie pour un massacre [The Corrupt] (It-Fr 1963)
Le Chant du monde (Fr 1965)
Les Tribulations d'un chinois en Chine [Up to His Ears] (Fr-It
    1965)
Un Homme de trop [Shock Troops] (Fr-It 1967)
Ballade par un chien (Fr 1968)
La Nuit bulgare (Fr 1970)
Ils (Fr 1970)
Comptes à rebours [Countdown] (Fr 1970)
L'Aventure c'est l'aventure [Money, Money, Money] (Fr 1972)
La panne [La più bella serata della mia vita] (It-Fr 1972)
7 Morts sur Ordannance (Fr 1975)

VAN AMMELROOY, WILLEKE (Willy Geertje van Ammelrooy), b.
    April 5, 1944
Mira (Dut 1971)
Louisa, een Woord van Liefde (Bel 1972)
De Inbreker (Dut 1972)
L'Assassino...è al Telefono [L'Assassin est au téléphone/The
    Killer Is on the Phone] (It-Bel 1973)
Frank en Eva (Dut 1973)
De Familie [The Family] (Dut 1973)
Help, de Dokter Verzuipt (Dut 1973)
Le Journal érotique d'un bûcheron (Fr 1973)
L'Amour aux trousses (Fr 1974)
Dakota (Dut 1974)
Alicia (Dut 1974)
Règlement de Femmes a O.Q. Corral (Fr 1974)
L'Arrière-train sifflera trois fois (Fr 1975)
Nelly Pile ou face (Fr 1975)

Mijn Nachten met Susan, Olga, Albert, Julie, Piet en Sandra
    (Dut 1975)
Het Jaar van de Kreeft (Dut 1975)
La Donneuse (Bel-Fr 1975)
Mens Erger Je Niet (Dut 1975)
Wan Pipel (Dut 1975)

VAN DER GROEN, DORA, b. 1927, Merksem, Belgium
    Meeuwen Streven in de Haven (Bel 1955)
    Vuur, Liefede en Vitam Inen (Bel 1956)
    Wat Doen We met de Liefde? (Bel 1957)
    Monsieur Hawarden (Bel-Dut 1969)
    Rolande met de bles (Bel 1970)
    Malpertuis (Bel-Fr-W Ger 1972)
    Camera Sutra (Bel 1972)
    La Maison sous les arbres (Fr 1972)
    Het Dwaallicht (Bel-Dut 1973)
    Dakota (Dut 1973)
    De Komst van Joachim Stiller (Bel 1974)
    Keetje Tippel (Dut 1974)
    Kind van de Zon (Dut 1974)
    Dr. Pulder Zaait Papavers (Dut 1975)

VAN DE VEN, MONIQUE, b. July 28, 1952, Uden, Netherlands
    Turks Fruit (Dut 1972)
    Verloren Maandag [Way Out] (Bel-Dut 1973)
    Dakota (Dut 1974)
    Keetje Tippel (Dut 1975)
    De Laatste Trein (Dut 1975)

VAN DOMMELEN, JAN (Johannes Sebastianus Engelbertus van Dom-
    melen), b. April 28, 1878, Amsterdam; d. Oct. 26, 1942
    Weergevonden (Dut 1914)
    De Vloek van het Testament (Dut 1915)
    De Vrouw Clasina (Dut 1915)
    Liefdesstrijd (Dut 1915)
    Het Geheim van den Vuurtoren (Dut 1916)
    Majoor Frans (Dut 1916)
    La Renzoni (Dut 1916)
    Het Geheim van Delft (Dut 1917)
    Madame Pinkette & Co. (Dut 1917)
    Gouden Ketenen (Dut 1917)
    Ulbo Garvema (Dut 1917)
    De Kroon der Schande (Dut 1918)
    Toen het Licht Verdween (Dut 1918)
    Oorlog en Vrede I--Erfelijk Belast (Dut 1918)
    Oorlog en Vrede II--1916--Ontvluchting (Dut 1918)
    Oorlog en Vrede III--1918--Gewetenswroeging (Dut 1918)
    Op Hoop van Zegen (Dut 1918)
    American Girls (Dut 1919)
    Een Carmen van het Noorden (Dut 1919)
    Het Goudvischje (Dut 1919)
    De Leugen van Pierrot (Dut 1920)

Schakels (Dut 1920)
Rechten der Jeugd (Dut 1921)
Bulldog Drummond [Het Geheimzinnige Sanatorium] (GB-Dut 1922)
Bleeke Bet (Dut 1923)
Moderne Landhaaien (Dut 1926)
Het Heksenlied (Dut 1928)
De Big van het Regiment (Dut 1935)
Boefje (Dut 1939)

VAN EYCK, PETER (Götz von Eick), b. June 6, 1912, Steinwehr,
    Pomerania, Germany; d. July 15, 1969
The Moon Is Down (20th 1942)
Five Graves to Cairo (Par 1943)
Hitler's Madman (MGM 1943)
Address Unknown (Col 1944)
The Imposter (Univ 1944)
Hallo Fräulein! (W Ger 1949)
Epilog (W Ger 1950)
Export in Blond (W Ger 1950)
Königskinder (W Ger 1950)
Der Dritte von rechts (W Ger 1950)
Opfer des Herzens (W Ger 1950)
Au coeur de la casbah (Fr 1951)
Le Salaire de la paura [The Wages of Fear] (Fr-It 1953)
Alerte au sud (Fr 1953)
La Chaîr et le diable [Il fuoco nelle vene] (Fr-It 1953)
Sailor of the King [Single-Handed] (20th 1953)
Le Grand Jeu [Il grande gioco] (Fr-It 1954)
Night People (20th 1954)
Sophie et le crime (Fr 1955)
A Bullet for Joey (UA 1955)
Mr. Arkadian (CAI 1955)
Tarzan's Hidden Jungle (RKO 1955)
Jump into Hell (WB 1955)
Der Cornet (W Ger 1955)
Attack (UA 1956)
Rawhide Years (Univ 1956)
Run for the Sun (UA 1956)
Fric-Frac en dentelles (Fr 1956)
Le Feu aux poudres (Fr-It 1957)
Retour de manivelle (Fr-It 1957)
Tous peuvent me tuer (Fr 1957)
Der gläserne turm (W Ger 1957)
Dr. Crippen lebt (W Ger 1958)
Schwarze Nylons--heisse Nächte [Indecent] (W Ger 1958)
Das Mädchen Rosemarie (W Ger 1958)
The Snorkel (Col 1958)
Schmutziger Engel (W Ger 1958)
Du gehörst mir (W Ger 1959)
Rommel ruft Kairo (W Ger 1959)
Foxhole in Cairo [Eng version of Rommel ruft Kairo] (W Ger
    1959)
Verbrechen nach Schulschluss [The Young Go Wild] (W Ger 1959)

Labyrinth (W Ger 1959)
Der Rest ist Schweigen (W Ger 1959)
Lockvogel der Nacht (W Ger 1959)
Abschied von den Wolken [Rebel Flight to Cuba] (W Ger 1959)
Geheimaktion schwarze Kapelle [I sicari di Hitler] (W Ger-It 1959)
Liebling der Götter (W Ger 1960)
Die 1000 Augen des Dr. Mabuse [Il diabolico Dr. Mabuse/Le Diabolique Dr. Mabuse/The 1000 Eyes of Dr. Mabuse] (W Ger-It-Fr 1960)
An einem Freitag un halb zwolf [Il mondo nella mia tasca/The World in My Pocket/Vendredi, 13 heures] (W Ger-It-Fr 1961)
Kriegesgesetz [Legge della guerra/La Loi de la guerre] (W Ger-It-Fr 1961)
Die Stunden, die Du glücklich bist (W Ger 1961)
La Fête espagnole [No Time for Ecstasy] (Fr 1961)
Finden Sie, dass Constanze sich richtig verhält? (W Ger 1962)
The Longest Day (20th 1962)
Endstation 13 Sahara (W Ger 1963)
Station Six, Sahara [Eng lang version of Endstation 13 Sahara] (AA 1964)
Im Namen des Teufels [Devil's Agent] (W Ger-GB 1962)
Ein Toter sucht seinen Mörder [Vengeance/The Brain] (W Ger-GB 1962)
Ein Alibi zerbricht (Aus 1963)
Das grosse Liebesspiel [And So to Bed] (W Ger-Aus 1963)
Scotland Yard jagt Dr. Mabuse (W Ger 1963)
Verführung am Meer [Ostrva/Seduction by the Sea] (W Ger-Yug 1963)
Kennwort: Reiher (W Ger 1964)
Die Todesstrahlen des Dr. Mabuse [I raggi mortali del Dottor Mabuse/Mission spéciale au Feuxième Bureau] (W Ger-It-Fr 1964)
Duell vor Sonnenuntergang (W Ger 1965)
The Spy Who Came in from the Cold (Par 1965)
Das Geheimnis der Lederschlinge [I misteri della giungla nera/The Mystery of Thug Island] (W Ger-It 1965)
Die Herren (Ger 1965)
Spione unter sich [La Guerre secrete/La guerra segreta/The Dirty Game] (W Ger-Fr-It 1965)
Der Chef schickt seine besten Mann [Requiem per un agente segreto/Consigna: Tanger 67] (W Ger-It-Sp 1966)
Karriere (W Ger-Fr 1966)
Sechs Pistolen jagen Professor Z [Comando de asesinos] (W Ger-Sp 1966)
L'Homme qui valait des milliards [L'uomo che valeva miliardi] (Fr-It 1967)
Shalako (Cinerama 1968)
Heidi [Heidi kehrt heim] (USA-W Ger 1968)
Tevye und seine sieben Töchter (W Ger-Isr 1968)
Rose rosse per il Führer (It 1968)
Assignment to Kill (WB 1968)
The Bridge at Remagen (UA 1969)

Peter van Eyck and Erica Beer in <u>Verbrechen nach Schulschluss</u> (1959).

VAN HOOL, ROGER, b. 1940, Antwerp
  Des garçons et des filles (Fr-Bel 1967)
  Oscar (Fr 1967)
  La Prisonnière (Fr 1967)
  A tout casser (Fr 1967)
  La Chamade (Fr 1968)
  Catherine [Il Suffit d'un Amour] (Fr 1968)
  Et qu'ça saute (Fr 1969)
  Louisa--een Woord van Liefde (Bel 1969)
  Le Soldat Laforet (Fr 1971)
  Rendez-vous à Bray (Bel-W Ger 1971)
  L'assassino e al telefono [L'Assassin est au téléphone] (It-Bel 1972)
  Verloren Maandag (Bel-Dut 1973)

VEIDT, CONRAD, b. Jan. 22, 1893, Berlin; d. April 3, 1943
  Der Spion* [In Die Wolken Verfolgt] (Ger 1917)
  Der Weg des Todes (Ger 1917)
  Furcht (Ger 1917)
  Das Ratsel von Bangalor (Ger 1917)
  Wenn Tote Sprechen (Ger 1917)
  Die Claudi von Geiserhof (Ger 1917)
  Das Tagebuch einer Verlorenen, Part I (Ger 1918)

Das Tagebuch einer Verlorenen, Part II: Dida Ibsens Geschichte
(Ger 1918)
Das Dreimaderlhaus (Ger 1918)
Colomba (Ger 1918)
Jettchen Geberts Geschichte, Part 1: Jettchen Geberts (Ger 1918)
Die Serenyi (Ger 1918)
Jettchen Geberts Geschichte, Part 2: Henriette Jacoby (Ger 1918)
Sundige Mutter (Ger 1918)
Opfer des Gesellschaft (Ger 1918)
Nocturno der Liebe (Ger 1918)
Der Japanerin (Ger 1918)
Opium (Ger 1919)
Gewitter im Mai (Ger 1919)
Die Reise um die Erde in 80 Tagen (Ger 1919)
Peer Gynt (Ger 1919) [shown in 2 parts]
Anders Als die Anderen (Ger 1919)
Die Prostitution (Ger 1919) [shown in 2 parts]
Die Mexikanerin (Ger 1919)
Die Okarina (Ger 1919)
Prinz Kuckuck [Prince Cuckoo] (Ger 1919)
Unheimliche Geschichten (Ger 1919)
Wahnsinn (Ger 1919)
Die Nacht auf Goldenhall (Ger 1920)
Nachtgestalten [Eleagabal Kuperus] (Ger 1920)
Satanas (Ger 1920)
Das Kabinet des Dr. Caligari [The Cabinet of Dr. Caligari]
(Ger 1920)
Der Reigen (Ger 1920)
Patience (Ger 1920)
Der Januskopf [Schrecken] (Ger 1920)
Liebestaumel (Ger 1920)
Die Augen der Welt (Ger 1920)
Kurfürstendamm [Der Teufel in Berlin] (Ger 1920)
Der Reigen (Ger 1920)
Moriturus (Ger 1920)
Abend-Nacht-Morgen (Ger 1920)
Manolescus Memoiren [The Memoirs of Manolescu] (Ger 1920)
Kunsterlaunen (Ger 1920)
Sehnsucht [Bajazzo] (Ger 1920)
Der Gang in die Nacht (Ger 1920)
Christian Wahnschaffe (Ger 1920) [shown in 2 parts]
Der Graf von Cagliostro (Ger-Aus 1920)
Das Geheimnis von Bombay (Ger 1920)
Menschen im Rausch (Ger 1920)
Die Liebschaften des Hektor Dalmore (Ger 1921)
Der Leidensweg der Inge Krafft (Ger 1921)
Landstrasse und Grosstadt (Ger 1921)
Lady Hamilton (Ger 1921)
Sündige Mutter (Ger 1921)
Das Indische Grabmal [Mysteries of India/Above All Law] (Ger
1921) [shown in 2 parts]
Lucrezia Borgia [Lucretia Borgia] (Ger 1922)
Paganini (Ger 1923)

Wilhelm Tell (Ger 1923)
Glanz gegen Gluck (Ger 1923)
Carlos und Elisabeth (Ger 1924)
Das Wachsfigurenkabinett [Three Waxmen] (Ger 1924)
Orlacs Hände [The Hands of Orlac] (Aus 1924)
Nju (Ger 1924)
Schicksal (Ger 1924)
Graf Kostja (Ger 1925)
Ingmarsarvet [In Dalarnia and Jerusalem] (Swe 1925)
Till Osterland (Swe 1925)
Liebe macht Blind [Love Is Blind] (Ger 1925)
Der Geiger von Florenz [Impetuous Youth] (Ger 1926)
Die Brüder Schellenberg [The Brothers Schellenberg] (Ger 1926)
Dürfen wir Schweigen? (Ger 1926)
Kreuzzug des Weibes (Ger 1926)
Der Student von Prag [The Man Who Cheated Life] (Ger 1926)
Die Flucht in die Nacht [The Flight in the Night] (It 1926)
The Beloved Rogue (UA 1927)
A Man's Past (Univ 1927)
The Man Who Laughs (Univ 1928)
The Last Performance [Erik the Great Illusionist] (Univ 1928)
Das Land ohne Frauen (Ger 1929)
Die letze Kompagnie [Thirteen Men and a Girl] (Ger 1930)
The Lost Company [Eng lang version of Die letze Kompagnie]
    (Ger 1930)
Die grosse Sehnsucht (Ger 1930)
Der Student von Prag (Aus 1930) [sound and music added to
    1926 version]
Menschen im Kafig [Ger version of Cape Folorn] (GB-Ger 1930)
The Virtuous Sin (USA 1930)
Der Mann, Der den Mord beging [The Man Who Committed the
    Murder] (Ger 1931)
Die Nacht der Entscheding [Ger version of The Virtuous Sin] (Par
    Ger 1931)
Der Kongress Tanzt (Ger 1931)
The Congress Dances [Eng lang version of Der Kongress Tanzt]
    (Ger 1931)
Rasputin (Ger 1931)
Die andere seite [Ger version of Journey's End] (Ger 1931)
Der Schwarze Husar [The Black Hussar] (Ger 1932)
Rome Express (Gaumont 1932)
FP1 [Secrets of F P 1] (GB-Ger 1933)
Ich und der Kaiserin (Ger 1933)
I Was a Spy (Gaumont 1933)
The Wandering Jew (Gaumont 1933)
Jew Suss [Power] (Gaumont 1934)
Wilhelm Tell [The Legend of William Tell] (Ger 1934)
Bella Donna (Gaumont 1934)
The Passing of the Third Floor Back (Gaumont 1935)
King of the Damned (Gaumont 1936)
Under the Red Robe (20th 1937)
Dark Journey [The Anxious Years] (UA 1937)
Tempete sur L'Asie (Fr 1938)

Le Joueur d'echecs [The Devil Is an Empress] (Fr 1938)
The Spy in Black [U-Boat 29] (Col 1939)
The Thief of Bagdad (UA 1939)
Contraband [Blackout] (Anglo 1940)
Escape (MGM 1940)
A Woman's Face (MGM 1941)
Whistling in the Dark (MGM 1941)
The Men in Her Life (Col 1941)
Nazi Agent (MGM 1942)
All Through the Night (WB 1942)
Casablanca (WB 1943)
Above Suspicion (MGM 1943)

VELASCO, CONCHITA, b. Valladolid, Spain
Los maridos no cenan en casa (Sp 1956)
Muchachas en vacaciones (Sp 1957)
Las chicas de la Cruz Roja (Sp 1958)
Crimen para recien casados (Sp 1959)
St. Valentine's Day (Sp 1959)
Sonatas (Sp 1959)
El indulto (Sp 1960)
Amor Baja Cero (Sp 1960)
Festival en Benidorm (Sp 1960)
Julia y el Celacanto (Sp 1960)
La Paz empieza nunca (Sp 1960)
Trampa para Catalina (Sp 1961)
Martes y trece (Sp 1961)
Mi noche de bodas (Sp 1961)
La boda era a las 12 (Sp 1962)
Sabian demasiado (Sp 1962)
La verbena de la Paloma (Sp 1963)
Casi un caballero (Sp 1964)
Historias de la television (Sp 1965)
El arte de Casarse (Sp 1965)
El arte de no casarse (Sp 1965)
Hoy como ayer (Sp 1966)
Maria y la otra (Sp 1966)
Pero...en que pais vivimos? (Sp 1967)
Viaje de novios a la Italiana (It-Sp 1967)
Los que tienen que servir (Sp 1967)
Relaciones casi publicas (Sp 1968)
Una vez al ano, ser "hippy" no hace dano (Sp 1968)
Cuata noches de boda (Sp 1969)
Susana (Sp 1969)
El alma se serena (Sp 1969)
Matrimonios Separados (Sp 1969)
Despues de los nueve meses (Sp 1970)
Juicio de faldas (Sp 1970)
La decente (Sp 1970)
En un lugar de la manga (Sp 1970)
Los Gallos de la Madrugada (Sp 1971)
Prestame quince dias (Sp 1970)
Medebes un muerto (Sp 1971)
En la red de mi canción (Sp 1971)

Le notti di Lucrezia (It-Fr 1959)
La Ligne de Mire (Fr 1959)
Ein Engel auf Erden (W Ger-Fr 1959)
Tirez sur le pianiste [Shoot the Pianist] (Fr 1959)
La Brune que voilà (Fr 1960)
Le Saint mene la danse (Fr 1960)
Goodbye Again [Aimez-vous Brahms?] (UA 1961)
Fury at Smugglers Bay (RFI 1961)
The Wonders of Aladdin (USA-It 1961)
I giustiziere del mari (It-Fr 1961)
Le prigioniere dell'isola del diavolo (It-Fr 1961)
Anni Ruggenti [Roaring Years] (It 1962)
Symphonie pour un massacre [The Corrupt] (It-Fr 1963)
I tre volti della paura [Black Sabbath] (It-USA 1963)
L'Ainé des Ferchaux [Magnet of Doom] (Fr-It 1963)
La Pupa [Every Night of the Week] (It 1963)
Via Veneto (It 1963)
Frenesia dell'estate (It-Fr 1963)
I giovedi (It 1963)
I mostri [Fifteen from Rome] (It 1963)
Alta Infedeltà (ep "Les Gens moderns") (It-Fr 1963)
A Global Affair (MGM 1964)
Angélique, marquise des anges (Fr-W Ger-It 1964)
Amore in quattro dimensione (It-Fr 1964)
Merveilleuse Angélique [The Road to Versailles] (Fr-W Ger-It
    1964)
Casanova '70 (It-Fr 1965)
I complessi (It 1965)
Le Tonnerre de Dieu [God's Thunder] (Fr-It-W Ger 1965)
Angélique et le roy (Fr-It-W Ger 1965)
La Seconde Vérité (Fr-It 1966)
I nostri mariti (It-Fr 1966)
Come imparai ad amare le donne [How I Learned to Love Women]
    (W Ger-Fr-It 1966)
Le Soleil noir [Black Sun] (Fr-It 1966)
Le Plus Vieux Métier du monde (ep "L'Amore nei Secoli") (Fr-
    W Ger-It 1967)
Indomptable Angélique (Fr-W Ger-It 1967)
Une Corde, un Colt (Fr-It 1968)
Angélique et le sultan (Fr-It-W Ger 1968)
Lady Hamilton (Fr-It-W Ger 1968)
Une Veuve en or (Fr-W Ger-It 1969)
You Can't Win 'em All (Col 1970)

MERIL, MACHA (Macha Gagarin), b. Sept. 3, 1940, Rabat, Morocco
La Main chaude (Fr-It 1960)
Adorable menteuse (Fr 1961)
Le Repos du guerrier [Love on a Pillow] (Fr-It 1962)
La Vie conjugale: Françoise (Fr-It 1963)
La Vie conjugale: Jean-Marc (Fr-It 1963)
Who's Been Sleeping in My Bed? (Par 1963)
Une Femme mariée (Fr 1964)
Der Ölprinz [Rampage at Apache Wells] (W Ger-Yug 1965)
L'Espion [Lautlose Waffen/The Defector] (Fr-W Ger 1967)

Les Grandes Gueules [The Wise Guys] (Fr-It 1965)
La Métamorphose des Cloportes [Cloportes] (Fr 1965)
Ne nous fâchons pas (Fr 1965)
Le Deuxième Souffle [Second Wind] (Fr 1966)
Avec la peau des autres [To Skin a Spy] (Fr-It 1966)
Les Aventuriers [The Last Adventure] (Fr-It 1966)
Le Rapace [Birds of Prey] (Fr-It-Mex 1968)
L'Armée des ombres (Fr-It 1969)
Dernier Domicile connu (Fr-It 1969)
Boulevard du rhum (Fr-It-Sp 1970)
Fantasia chez les ploucs [Diamond Bikini] (Fr 1971)
Laisse aller, c'est une valse (Fr 1971)
La Bonne Année (Fr-It 1973)
L'Emmerdeur (Fr 1973)
La Gifle (Fr-It 1974)
La Cage (Fr 1975)
Cadaveri eccellenti (It-Fr 1975)

VERLEY, BERNARD, b. Oct. 4, 1939, Lille, France
Les Honneurs de la guerre (Fr 1961)
Napoleon 11, l'aiglon (Fr 1962)
L'Amour à la mer (Fr 1964)
Berenice (Fr 1966)
Les Cracks (Fr 1967)
Au Pan Coupe (Fr 1967)
La Fille d'en face [The Girl Opposite] (Fr 1967)
La Voie lactée [The Milky Way] (Fr-It 1969)
L'Amour, l'après-midi [Love in the Afternoon] (Fr 1972)
Le Fantôme de la liberté [The Phantom of Liberté] (Fr 1974)
La Pieuvre (Fr-It 1974)

VILLARET, JOÃO (João Henrique Pereira Villaret), b. 1913; d. 1961
Bocage (Por 1936)
O pai tirano (Por 1941)
O violino de João (Por 1944)
Inês de Castro (Por 1945)
Camões (Por 1946)
Três espelhos (Por 1947)
Frei Louis de Sousa (Por 1950)
A garça (Por 1952)
A serpente (Por 1952)
O primo basilio (Por 1959)

VITTI, MONICA (Maria Luisa Ceccarelli), b. Nov. 3, 1931, Rome
Ridere, ridere, ridere (It 1954)
Una pellicia di visione (It 1956)
Le dritte (It 1958)
L'avventura (It 1960)
La notte (It 1960)
L'eclisse (It 1961)
Les Quatre Vérités [Le quattro verità] (ep "Le Lièvre et la tortue") (Fr-It 1962)
Dragées au poivre (Fr 1963)

João Villaret

Château en Suède (Fr 1963)
Alta infedeltà (ep "La sospirosa") (It 1963)
Il deserto rossa (It 1964)
Le bambole (ep "La minestra") (It 1964)
Modesty Blaise (20th 1966)
Le piacevoli notti (It 1966)
Le fate (It 1966)
Fai in fretta ad uccidermi, ho freddo (It 1967)
La cintura di castita [On My Way to the Crusades, I Met a Girl
    Who...] (It 1967)
Ti ho sposato per allegria (It 1967)
La ragazza con la pistola (It-GB 1967)
La Femme écarlate [La donna scarlatta] (Fr-It 1968)
Amore mio aiutami (It 1969)
Vedo nudo (It 1969)
Dramma della gelosia (It 1970)
La supertestimone (It 1971)
Nini Tirabuscio, la donna che invento la mossa (It 1971)
Le coppie (It 1971)
La pacifista (It 1971)
Gli ordini sono ordini (It 1972)
La Tosca (It 1972)
Noi donne siamo fatte così (It 1972)
Polvere di stelle (It 1973)
Teresa la ladra (It 1973)
Le Fantôme de la liberté [Il fantasma della libertà] (Fr-It 1974)
A mezzanotte va la ronda del piacere (It 1975)

Monica Vitti in Le bambole (1964).

VLADY, MARINA (Marina de Poliakoff-Baïdaroff), b. May 10, 1937,
    Clichy, France
    Due sorelle amano (It 1949)
    Idylle au château (Fr-It 1952)
    Grand Gala (It-Fr 1952)
    Penne Nere (It-Fr 1952)
    Faniculle di lusso (It-Fr 1952)
    Le infedeli (It-Fr 1952)
    La figlia del diavolo (It 1952)
    Canzoni, canzoni, canzoni (It 1953)
    Avant le déluge (Fr-It 1953)
    Des gosses de riches (Fr 1953)
    L'età dell'Amore (It-Fr 1953)
    Le avventure di Giacomo Casanova (It-Fr 1954)
    Giorni d'amore (It-Fr 1954)
    Musodoro (It-Fr 1954)

Sie (W Ger 1954)
Le Crâneur (Fr 1955)
Sinfonia d'amore (It-Fr 1955)
Les Salauds vont en Enfer [The Wicked Go to Hell] (Fr 1955)
Sophie et le crime (Fr 1955)
La Sorcière [The Sorceress] (Fr 1955)
Pardonnez nos offenses [Forgive Us Our Trespasses] (Fr 1956)
Crime et châtiment [Crime and Punishment] (Fr 1956)
La Liberté surveillée (Fr-Czech 1957)
Toi le venin (Fr 1958)
La Nuit des espions (Fr 1959)
La Sentence (Fr 1959)
Les Canailles (Fr 1960)
La Fille dans la vitrine (Fr-It 1960)
La Princesse de Clèves (Fr 1960)
Adorable menteuse (Fr 1961)
Les Sept Péchés [Seven Capital Sins] (ep "L'Orgueil") (Fr-It
    1961)
Le Steppe (Fr-It 1962)
Climats [Climates of Love] (Fr 1962)
La Cage (Fr-Gabon 1962)
Le Meurtrier [Enough Rope] (Fr-It-W Ger 1962)
Les Bonnes Causes (Fr-It 1963)
Dragées au pouvre [Sweet & Sour] (Fr-It 1963)
Ape Regina (It-Fr 1963)
Le Voleur de la Joconbe (Fr-It 1963)
Una moglie americana [Run for Your Wife] (It-Fr 1965)
Chimes at Midnight [Falstaff] (Sp-Swi 1966)
Mona, pour une étoile sans nom (Fr-Rum 1967)
A tout coeur à Tokyo pour OSS 117 [Terror in Tokyo] (Fr 1967)
Deux ou trois choses que je sais d'elle [One or Two Things I
    Know About Her] (Fr 1967)
Tema pour en lille novelle (USSR-Bel-Fr 1969)
Le Temps de vivre (Fr 1969)
Le Temps des loups [The Last Shot] (Fr-It 1969)
Sirocco d'hiver [Sirocco] (Hun-Fr 1969)
Pour un sourire (Fr 1969)
La Nuit bulgare (Fr 1970)

VOLONTE, GIAN MARIA, b. April 9, 1933, Milan
Sotto dieci bandiero [Under Ten Flags] (It-GB 1960)
La ragazza con la valigia (It 1961)
Antinea, l'amante della città sepolta [L'Atlantide/Journey Beneath
    the Desert] (It-Fr 1961)
Ercole alla conquista di Atlantide (It 1961)
A cavallo della tigre (It 1961)
Un uomo da bruciare (It 1962)
Le quattro giornate di Napoli (It 1962)
Il terrorista (It 1962)
Il peccato (It 1963)
Per un pugno di dollari [Por un puñado de dolares/Für eine
    Handvoll de dolares/For a Fistfull of Dollars] (It-Sp-W Ger
    1964)

Il magnifico cornuto [Le Cocu magni Figue] (It-Fr 1964)
Per qualche dollari in più [La Muerte tenia un precio/Für ein paar
    Dollar mehr] (It-Sp-W Ger 1965)
Svegliati e uccidi [Lutring, réveille-toi et meurs] (It-Fr 1965)
L'armeta Brancaleone (It 1966)
La strega in amore [The Witch] (It 1966)
Het Gangstermeisje (Dut 1967)
A ciascuno il suo (It 1967)
Faccia a faccia (It 1967)
Quien sabe? (It 1967)
I sette fratelli Cervi (It 1968)
Banditi a Milano (It 1968)
Summit (It 1968)
L'amante di Gramigna (It 1969)
Sotto il segno dello scorpione (It 1969)
Vento dell'est (It 1970)
Indagine su un cittadino al di sopra di ogni sospetto [Investigation
    of a Citizen above Suspicion] (It 1970)
Le Cercle rouge (Fr-It 1970)
12 dicembre (It 1970)
Vomini contro (It 1970)
Sacco e Vanzetti (It 1970)
La classe operaia va in paradiso (It 1971)
Il caso Mattei (It 1971)
L'attentat [L'attentato] (Fr-It 1972)
Sbatti il mostro in prima pagina (It 1972)
Lucky Luciano (It-Fr 1973)
Giordano Bruno (It 1973)
Il sospetto (It 1975)

VON STROHEIM, ERICH (Erich Oswald Stroheim), b. Sept. 22, 1885,
        Vienna; d. May 12, 1957
    Captain McLean (Triangle 1914)
    Ghosts (Mutual 1915)
    The Birth of a Nation (Epoch 1915)
    Old Heidelberg (Triangle 1915)
    Intolerance (Triangle 1916)
    The Social Secretary (Fine Arts 1916)
    His Picture in the Papers (Fine Arts 1916)
    Panthea (Selznick 1917)
    In Again, Out Again (Fine Arts 1917)
    Sylvia of the Secret Service (Pathe 1917)
    For France (Vitagraph 1917)
    Less Than the Dust (Par 1917)
    The Unbeliever (Edison-Kleine 1918)
    Hearts of the World (Artcraft 1918)
    The Hun Within (Artcraft 1918)
    The Heart of Humanity (Univ 1919)
    Blind Husbands (Univ 1919)
    Foolish Wives (Univ 1921)
    The Great Gabbo (Sono Art-World Wide 1929)
    Three Faces East (WB 1930)
    Friends and Lovers (RKO 1931)

The Lost Squadron (RKO 1932)
As You Desire Me (MGM 1932)
Crimson Romance (Mascot 1934)
Fugitive Road (Invincible 1934)
The Crime of Dr. Crespi (Rep 1935)
Marthe Richard (Fr 1937)
La Grande Illusion [Grand Illusion] (Fr 1937)
Mademoiselle Docteur (Fr 1937)
Alibi (Fr 1937)
Les Pirates du rail (Fr 1938)
L'Affaire Lafarge (Fr 1938)
Les Disparus de Saint-Agil (Fr 1938)
Ultimatum (Fr 1938)
Gibraltar (Fr 1938)
Derrière la façade (Fr 1939)
Rappel immédiat (Fr 1939)
Pièges (Fr 1939)
Le Monde tremblera/La Révolte des Vivants (Fr 1939)
Tempête sur Paris (Fr 1939)
Macao, l'enfer du jeu (Fr 1939)
Menaces (Fr 1939)
Paris--New York (Fr 1939)
I Was an Adventuress (20th 1940)
So Ends Our Night (UA 1941)
Five Graves to Cairo (Par 1943)
The North Star [Armored Attack] (RKO 1943)
The Lady and the Monster (Rep 1944)
Storm Over Lisbon (Rep 1944)
The Great Flamarion (Rep 1945)
Scotland Yard Investigator (Rep 1945)
The Mask of Dijon (PRC 1946)
La Foire aux chimères (Fr 1946)
On ne meurt pas comme ca! (Fr 1946)
La Danse de mort (Fr 1947)
Le Signal rouge (Fr 1948)
Portrait d'un assassin (Fr 1949)
Sunset Boulevard (Par 1950)
Alraune (W Ger 1952)
Minuit, Quai de Bercy (Fr 1953)
L'Envers du paradis (Fr-It 1953)
Alerte au sud (Fr-It 1953)
Napoléon (Fr 1954)
Série noire (Fr 1955)
La Madone des sleepings (Fr 1955)

WALBROOK, ANTON (Adolph Wohlbrück), b. Nov. 19, 1896, Vienna;
     d. Aug. 9, 1967
Der Fluch der Bosen Tat [Das Geheimnis auf Schloss Elmshoh]
     (Ger 1925)
Salto Mortale [Trapeze] (Ger 1931)
Der Stolz der 3 Kompagnie (Ger 1931)
Drei von der Stempelstelle (Ger 1932)
Die fünf verfluchten Gentlemen (Ger 1932)

Melodie der Liebe (Ger 1932)
Baby (Ger 1932)
Walzerkrieg [Waltz Time in Vienna] (Ger 1933)
Keine Angst vor Liebe (Ger 1933)
Viktor und Viktoria (Ger 1933)
Georges et Georgette [Fr version of Viktor und Viktoria] (Ger 1933)
Die vertauschte Braut (Ger 1934)
Maskerade [Maskerade in Vienna] (Aus 1934)
Eine Frau, die weiss, was sie will (Ger-Czech 1934)
Regine (Ger 1934)
Der Student von Prag (Ger 1934)
Die englische Heirat (Ger 1934)
Zigeunerbaron (Ger 1934)
Le Baron tzigane [Fr version of Zigeunerbaron] (Ger 1935)
Ich war Jack Mortimer (Ger 1935)
Der Kurier des Zaren (Ger 1936)
Michel Strogoff (Ger 1936) [Fr version of Der Kurier des Zaren]
Michael Strogoff [The Soldier and the Lady] (Ger-RKO Br 1936)
   [Eng lang version of Der Kurier des Zaren]
Allotria (Ger 1936)
Port Arthur [I Give My Life/Orders from Tokyo] (Ger-Czech 1936)
Port Arthur [Fr version of Port Arthur] (Ger-Czech 1936)
Victoria the Great (Radio 1937)
The Rat (Radio 1937)
Sixty Glorious Years [Queen of Destiny/Queen Victoria] (RKO Br 1938)
Gaslight [Angel Street] (Anglo 1940)
Dangerous Moonlight [Suicide Squadron] (Radio 1941)
The 49th Parallel [The Invader] (GFD 1941)
The Life and Death of Colonel Blimp [Colonel Blimp] (GFD 1943)
The Man from Morocco (Pathe 1945)
The Red Shoes (GFD 1948)
The Queen of Spades (ABP 1948)
La Ronde (Fr 1950)
König für eine Nacht (W Ger 1950)
Wiener Waltzer [Wien tänzt/Vienna Waltzes] (Aus 1951)
L'Affaire Maurizius (Fr 1954)
Lola Montez [Lola Montes] (W Ger-Fr 1955)
Oh, Rosalinda! (ABP 1955)
Saint Joan (UA 1957)
I Accuse! (MGM 1958)

WALLS, TOM, b. Feb. 16, 1883; Kingsthorpe, Northampton, England; d. Nov. 27, 1949
   Rookery Nook [One Embarrassing Night] (W & F 1930)
   On Approval (W & F 1930)
   Canaries Sometimes Sing (W & F 1930)
   Tons of Money (W & F 1931)
   Plunder (W & F 1931)
   A Night Like This (W & F 1932)
   Thark (W & F 1932)

Leap Year (W & F 1932)
The Blarney Stone [The Blarney Kiss] (W & F 1933)
Just Smith (W & F 1933)
A Cuckoo in the Nest (W & F 1933)
Turkey Time (W & F 1933)
A Cup of Kindness (Gaumont 1934)
A Lady in Danger (Gaumont 1934)
Dirty Work (Gaumont 1934)
Fighting Stock (Gaumont 1935)
Me and Marlborough (Gaumont 1935)
Stormy Weather (Gaumont 1935)
Foreign Affaires (Gaumont 1935)
Pot Luck (Gaumont 1936)
Dishonour Bright (GFD 1936)
For Valour (GFD 1937)
Second Best Bed (GFD 1938)
Strange Boarders (GFD 1938)
Crackerjack [The Man with a Hundred Faces] (GFD 1938)
Old Iron (BL 1938)
Undercover [Underground Guerillas] (UA 1943)
They Met in the Dark (GFD 1943)
The Halfway House (Ealing 1944)
Love Story [A Lady Surrenders] (EL 1944)
Johnny Frenchman (EL 1945)
This Man Is Mine (Col Br 1946)
Master of Bankdam (GFD 1947)
While I Live* [Dream of Olwen] (20th 1947)
Spring in Park Lane (BL 1948)
Maytime in Mayfair (BL 1949)
The Interrupted Journey (BL 1949)

WALSH, KAY, b. 1914, London
How's Chances (Fox 1934)
Get Your Man (B & D-Par Br 1934)
Smith's Wives (Fox Br 1935)
Luck of the Irish (Par 1935)
If I Were Rich (Radio 1936)
Secret of Stamboul* [The Spy in White] (GFD 1936)
All That Glitters (Radio 1936)
Keep Fit (ABFD 1937)
The Last Adventurers* [Down to the Sea in Ships] (SC 1937)
I See Ice (ABFD 1938)
Meet Mr. Penny (ABPC 1938)
The Mind of Mr. Reeder [The Mysterious Mr. Reeder] (GN 1939)
The Missing People (GN 1939)
All at Sea (BL 1939)
The Middle Watch (ABPC 1939)
Sons of the Sea (GN 1939)
The Chinese Bungalow [Chinese Den] (BL 1940)
The Second Mr. Bush (Anglo 1940)
In Which We Serve (BL 1942)
This Happy Breed (EL 1944)

The October Man (GFD 1947)
Vice Versa (GFD 1948)
Oliver Twist (GFD 1948)
Last Holiday (ABP 1950)
Stage Fright (WB 1950)
The Magnet (GFD 1950)
The Magic Box (BL 1951)
Encore (ep "Winter Cruise") (GFD 1951)
Hunted [The Stranger in Between] (GFD 1952)
Meet Me Tonight (ep "The Red Peppers") (GFD 1952)
Young Bess (MGM 1953)
The Rainbow Jacket (GFD 1954)
Lease of Life (GFD 1954)
Cast a Dark Shadow (Eros 1955)
Now and Forever (ABP 1956)
The Horse's Mouth (UA 1959)
Tunes of Glory (UA 1960)
Greyfriars Bobby (BV 1961)
Reach for Glory (Gala 1962)
Lunch Hour (Bry 1962)
80,000 Suspects (RFD 1963)
Dr. Syn--Alias the Scarecrow (BV 1963)
The Beauty Jungle [Contest Girl] (RFD 1964)
The Magnificent Showman [Circus World] (Par 1964)
He Who Rides a Tiger (BL 1965)
The Witches (WPD 1966)
The Virgin and the Gypsy (London Screenplays 1970)
Bikini Paradise (Golden Era 1970) [made in 1964]
Scrooge (20th 1970)
The Ruling Class (Avco Emb 1972)

WARNER, DAVID, b. 1941, Manchester, England
Tom Jones (UA 1963)
Morgan: A Suitable Case for Treatment (BL 1966)
Work Is a Four Letter Word (RFD 1968)
The Fixer (MGM 1968)
The Bofors Gun (RFD 1968)
The Sea Gull (WB-7 Arts 1968)
Michael Kolhaas--der Rebell [Michael Kolhaas] (W Ger 1969)
The Ballad of Cable Hogue (WB 1970)
Perfect Friday (London Screenplays 1970)
Straw Dogs (Cin 1971)
A Doll's House (GB-Fr 1973)
Little Malcolm and His Struggle Against the Eunuchs (Multi-
    cetera Investments 1974)

WARNER, JACK (John Waters), b. Oct. 24, 1900, Bromley-by-Bow,
    London
The Dummy Talks (Anglo 1943)
The Captive Heart (GFD 1946)
Hue and Cry (GFD 1947)
Dear Murderer (GFD 1947)
Holiday Camp (GFD 1947)

It Always Rains on Sunday (GFD 1947)
Easy Money (GFD 1948)
Against the Wind (GFD 1948)
My Brother's Keeper (GFD 1948)
Here Come the Huggetts (GFD 1948)
Vote for Huggett (GFD 1949)
The Huggetts Abroad (GFD 1949)
Train of Events (GFD 1949)
Boys in Brown (GFD 1949)
The Blue Lamp (GFD 1950)
Talk of a Million [You Can't Beat the Irish] (ABP 1951)
Valley of Eagles (GFD 1951)
Scrooge (Renown 1951)
Emergency Call [The Hundred Hour Hunt] (Butcher 1952)
Meet Me Tonight (ep "Ways and Means") (GFD 1952)
Those People Next Door (Eros 1953)
The Final Test (GFD 1953)
The Square Ring (GFD 1953)
Albert R N [Break to Freedom] (Eros 1953)
Bang! You're Dead [Game of Danger] (BL 1954)
Forbidden Cargo (GFD 1954)
Quatermass Experiment [The Creeping Unknown] (Ex 1955)
The Ladykillers (RFD 1955)
Now and Forever (ABP 1956)
Home and Away (Eros 1956)
Carve Her Name with Pride (RFD 1958)
Jigsaw (Britannia 1962)

WATTIS, RICHARD, b. Feb. 25, 1912, Wednesbury, Staffordshire,
    England; d. Feb. 1, 1975
A Yank at Oxford (MGM Br 1938)
The Happiest Days of Your Life (BL 1950)
The Clouded Yellow (GFD 1950)
The Importance of Being Earnest (GFD 1952)
Top Secret [Mr. Potts Goes to Moscow] (ABP 1952)
Made in Heaven (GFD 1952)
Top of the Form (GFD 1953)
Appointment in London (BL 1953)
Innocents in Paris (IFD 1953)
Background (ABFD 1953)
Blood Orange (Ex 1953)
The Intruder (BL 1953)
Small Town Story (GFD 1953)
Park Plaza 605 [Norman Conquest] (Eros 1953)
Hobson's Choice (BL 1954)
Doctor in the House (GFD 1954)
The Belles of St. Trinian's (BL 1954)
Lease of Life (GFD 1954)
The Crowded Day (Adelphi 1954)
The Colditz Story (BL 1955)
See How They Run (BL 1955)
The Time of His Life (Renown 1955)
I Am a Camera (IFD 1955)

A Yank in Ermine (Monarch 1955)
Simon and Laura (RFD 1955)
An Alligator Named Daisy (RFD 1955)
Jumping for Joy (RFD 1956)
The Man Who Never Was (20th 1956)
The Man Who Knew Too Much (Par 1956)
Eyewitness (RFD 1956)
It's a Wonderful World (Renown 1956)
The Iron Petticoat (MGM Br 1956)
The Silken Affair (RKO 1956)
A Touch of the Sun (Eros 1956)
Around the World in 80 Days (UA 1956)
The Prince and the Showgirl (WB 1957)
Second Fiddle (BL 1957)
The Abominable Snowman (WB 1957)
Barnacle Bill [All at Sea] (MGM 1957)
Blue Murder at St. Trinian's (BL 1957)
The Inn of the Sixth Happiness (20th 1958)
The Captain's Table (RFD 1959)
Left, Right and Centre (BL 1959)
The Ugly Duckling (Col 1959)
Ten Seconds to Hell (UA 1959)
Libel (MGM 1959)
Follow a Star (RFD 1959)
Your Money or Your Wife (RFD 1960)
Follow That Horse! (RFD 1960)
Very Important Person (RFD 1961)
Dentist on the Job [Get On With It!] (AA 1961)
Nearly a Nasty Accident (Britannia 1961)
Play It Cool (RFD 1962)
I Thank a Fool (MGM 1962)
Bon Voyage (BV 1962)
The Longest Day (20th 1962)
Come Fly With Me (MGM 1963)
The VIP's (MGM Br 1963)
Carry On Spying (AA 1964)
The Amorous Adventures of Moll Flanders (Par 1965)
Operation Crossbow [The Great Spy Mission] (MGM 1965)
The Battle of the Villa Fiorita (WPD 1965)
You Must Be Joking! (Col 1965)
Bunny Lake Is Missing (Col 1965)
The Alphabet Murders (MGM 1965)
Up Jumped a Swagman (Elstree 1965)
The Liquidator (MGM 1965)
The Great St. Trinian's Train Robbery (BL 1966)
Casino Royale (Col 1967)
Wonderwall (Cinencenta 1968)
Chitty Chitty Bang Bang (UA 1968)
Monte Carlo or Bust (Par 1969)
Games That Lovers Play (Border 1970)
Egghead's Robot (CFF 1970)
The Troublesome Double (CFF 1972)
The Devil's Widow [Tam Lin] (AIP 1972) [Made in 1969]

Sex and the Other Woman (Eagle 1973)
That's Your Funeral (Fox-Rank 1973)
Diamonds on Wheels (BV 1973)
Take Me High (MGM-EMI 1973)
Confessions of a Window Cleaner (Col-Warner 1974)

WEGENER, PAUL, b. Dec. 11, 1874, Bischdorf, Germany; d. Sept.
13, 1948
Der Student von Prague (Ger 1914)
Die Verführte (Ger 1914)
Die Augen des Ole Brandis (Ger 1914)
Evintrude, die Geschichte eines Abenteurers (Ger 1914)
Die Rache des Blutes (Ger 1914)
Peter Schlemihl (Ger 1915)
Der Golem (Ger 1914)
Rübezahls Hochzeit (Ger 1916)
Der Rattenfänger von Hameln (Ger 1916)
Der Yoghi (Ger 1916)
Der Golem und die Tänzerin (Ger 1917)
Hans Trutz in Schlaraffenland (Ger 1917)
Dörnroschen G 18, der fremde Fürst (Ger 1918)
Der Galeerensträfling (Ger 1918)
Nachtgestalten (Ger 1919)
Der Golem, wie er in die Welt kam (Ger 1920)
Medea (Ger 1920)
Steuermann Holck (Ger 1920)
Sumurun (Ger 1920)
Die Geliebte Roswolskys (Ger 1920)
Der verlorene Schatten (Ger 1921)
Das Weib des Pharao (Ger 1921)
Flammende Völker (Ger 1921)
Herzog Ferrantes Ende (Ger 1922)
Das Liebesnest (Ger 1922)
Lukrezia Borgia (Ger 1922)
Monna Vanna (Ger 1922)
Sterbende Völker (Ger 1922)
Vanina oder die Galgenhochzeit (Ger 1923)
Der Schatz der Gesine Jakobsen (Ger 1924)
SOS (Ger 1924)
Die Insel der Tränen (Ger 1925)
Lebende Buddhas (Ger 1925)
Der Mann aus dem Jenseits (Ger 1925)
Dagfin (Ger 1926)
Alraune (Ger 1927)
Arme kleine Sif (Ger 1927)
Glanz und Elend der Kurtisanen (Ger 1927)
Ramper, der Tiermensch (Ger 1927)
Svengali (Ger 1927)
Die Weber (Ger 1927)
Fundvogel (Ger 1930)
Marschall Vorwärts (Ger 1932)
Das Geheimnis um Johann Orth (Ger 1932)
Unheimliche Geschichten (Ger 1932)

Inge und die Millionen (Ger 1933)
Hans Westmar (Ger 1933)
Der Mann mit der Pranke (Ger 1935)
...nur ein Komödiant (Ger 1935)
In geheimer Mission (Ger 1938)
Stärker als die Liebe (Ger 1938)
Das Recht auf Liebe (Ger 1939)
Das unsterbliche Herz (Ger 1939)
Zwielicht (Ger 1940)
Das Mädchen von Fanö (Ger 1940)
Mein leben für Irland (Ger 1940)
Diesel (Ger 1942)
Der grosse König (Ger 1942)
Hochzeit auf Bärenhof (Ger 1942)
Wenn die Sonne wieder scheint (Ger 1943)
Zwischen Nacht und Morgen (Ger 1944)
Seinerzeit zu meiner Zeit (Ger 1944)
Der Fall Molander (Ger 1944)
Dr. phil. Döderlein (Ger 1945)
Tierarzt Dr. Vlimmer (Ger 1945)
Kolberg (Ger 1945)
Der grosse Mandarin (W Ger 1949)

WERNER, OSKAR (Oskar Josef Bschliessmayer), b. Nov. 13, 1922,
    Vienna [Note: As a schoolboy Werner played bits and walk-
    ons in Austrian films from 1938]
Der Engel mit der Posaune (Aus 1948)
Eroica (Aus 1949)
The Angel with the Trumpet (BL 1950)
Ein Wunder unserer Tage (Aus 1950)
Un Sourire dans la tempête (Fr 1950)
Das gestohlene Jahr (W Ger-Aus 1951)
Ruf aus dem Äther (W Ger 1951)
The Wonder Kid [Wonder Boy] (BL 1951)
Decision before Dawn (20th 1952)
Lola Montes [The Fall of Lola Montes] (Fr-W Ger 1955)
Spionage (Aus 1955)
Reich Mir die Hand, mein Leben [Mozart] (Aus 1955)
Die Letzte Akt [Ten Days to Die/The Last Ten Days] (Aus 1955)
Jules et Jim (Fr 1962)
Ship of Fools (Col 1965)
The Spy Who Came in from the Cold (Par 1965)
Fahrenheit 451 (RFD 1966)
Interlude (Col 1968)
The Shoes of the Fisherman (MGM-EMI 1968)

WERY, CARL, b. 1897, Trostberg, Germany; d. March 14, 1975
Drei Kaiserjager (Ger 1933)
Keinen Tag ohne Dich (Ger 1933)
Anna und Elisabeth (Ger 1933)
Königswalzer (Ger 1935)
Fasching (Ger 1939)
Der enige Quell (Ger 1939)

Oskar Werner and Julie Christie in Fahrenheit 451 (1966).

Gold in New Frisco (Ger 1939)
Wasser für canitoga (Ger 1939)
Was will Brigitte? (Ger 1940)
Feinde (Ger 1940)
Venus vor Gericht (Ger 1941)
Kameraden (Ger 1941)
Kleine Residenz (Ger 1942)
Die See ruft (Ger 1942)
Der verkaufte Grossvater (Ger 1942)
Via Mala (Ger 1944)
Frau Holle (Ger 1944)
Tromba (W Ger 1949)
Die seltsame Geschichte des Brandner Kaspar (W Ger 1949)
Susanna Jakobäa Krafftin (W Ger 1950)
Blaubart (W Ger-Fr 1951)
Dr. Holl (W Ger 1951)
In München steht ein Hofbräuhaus (W Ger 1952)
Das letzte Rezept (W Ger 1952)
Die grosse Versuchung (W Ger 1952)
Hab' Sonne im Herzen (W Ger 1953)
Ein Herz spielt falsch (W Ger 1953)
Ave Maria (W Ger 1953)
Liebeserwachen (W Ger 1953)
Hochzeitgloeken (W Ger 1954)
Konsul Strotthoff (W Ger 1954)

Columbus entdeckt Krähwinkel (W Ger 1954)
Heidi und Peter (Swi 1954)
Und der Himmel lacht dazu (W Ger 1954)
Es geschah am 20 Juli (W Ger 1955)
San Salvatore (W Ger 1956)
Rosen für Bettina (W Ger 1956)
Der Meineidbauer (W Ger 1956)
Ohne Dich wird es Nacht (W Ger 1956)
Schwarzwaldmelodie (W Ger 1956)
Nina (W Ger 1956)
Kleines Biest mit langen haaren (W Ger 1957)
Der Bauerndoktor von Bayrischzell (W Ger 1957)
Ein Amerikaner in Salzburg (W Ger 1958)
Meine schöne Mama (W Ger 1958)
Hab'ein schlofftief im Wald (W Ger 1958)
Die grünen Teufel von Monte Cassino (W Ger 1958)
Nackt wie Gott sie schuf (W Ger-Aus 1958)
Sebastian Kneipp (Aus 1958)
Kriegsgericht (W Ger 1959)
Arzt aus Leidenschaft (W Ger 1959)
Tränen in Deinen Augen (W Ger 1959)
Am Galgen hängt die Liebe (W Ger 1960)
Frau Irene Besser (W Ger 1960)
Kriegsgericht (W Ger-It-Fr 1961)
Ein Sommer, den man nie vergisst (W Ger 1961)
Mein Vaterhaus steht in den Bergen (W Ger 1961)
Kohlhiesels Töchter (W Ger 1962)
Trompeten der Liebe (W Ger 1962)
Lausbubengeschichten (W Ger 1964)

WESSELY, PAULA, b. Jan. 20, 1908, Vienna
Maskerade (Aus 1934)
So endete eine Liebe (Ger 1934)
Episode (Aus 1935)
Ernte (Aus 1936)
Die Julika (Ger 1936)
Die ganz grossen Torheiten (Ger 1937)
Spiegel des Lebens (Aus 1938)
Maria Ilona (Ger 1939)
Ein Leben lang (Ger 1940)
Heimkehr (Ger 1941)
Späte Liebe (Ger 1943)
Die kluge Marianne (Ger 1943)
Das Herz muss schweigen (Ger 1944)
Der Engel mit der Posaune (W Ger 1948)
Vagabunden der Liebe (Aus 1949)
Cordula (Aus 1950)
Maria Theresia (Aus 1951)
Ich und meine Frau (Aus 1953)
Das Licht der Liebe [Wenn Du noch eine Mutter hast] (Aus 1954)
Der Weg in die Vergangenheit (Aus 1954)
Die Wirtin zur goldenen Krone (Aus 1955)
Anders als Du und ich (W Ger 1957)

Unter 18 [Noch minderjährig] (Aus 1957)
Die unvollkommene Ehe (Aus 1959)
Der Bauer als Millionär (Aus 1961)
Jedermann (Aus 1961)

Paula Wessely and Adolf Wohlbrück in Maskerade (1934).

WHITE, CAROL, b. April 1, 1943, Hammersmith, London
    Circus Friends (CFF 1956)
    Carry On, Teacher (AA 1959)
    Never Let Go (RFD 1960)
    Linda (Bry 1960)
    Man in the Back Seat (AA 1961)
    A Matter of WHO (MGM 1961)
    Bon Voyage (BV 1962)
    Village of Daughters (MGM 1962)
    The Boys (Gala 1962)
    The Leather Boys (Garrick 1963)
    Ladies Who Do (Bry 1963)
    Slave Girls [Prehistoric Women] (WPD 1966)
    Poor Cow (AA 1967)
    I'll Never Forget What's 'is Name (RFD 1967)
    The Fixer (MGM 1968)
    Daddy's Gone a Hunting (National General 1969)
    Dulcima (MGM-EMI 1971)
    Something Big (20th 1971)
    Made (MGM-EMI 1972)
    Some Call It Loving (Pleasant Pastures 1973)

Carol White and Terence Stamp in Poor Cow (1967).

WHITTY, MAY, b. June 19, 1865, Liverpool; d. May 29, 1948
    Night Must Fall (MGM 1937)
    The 13th Chair (MGM 1937)
    Marie Walewska Conquest [Marie Walewska (MGM 1937)
    I Met My Love Again (UA 1938)
    The Lady Vanishes (Gaumont 1938)
    Raffles (UA 1940)
    A Bill of Divorcement (RKO 1940)
    One Night in Lisbon (Par 1941)
    Suspicion (RKO 1941)
    Mrs. Miniver (MGM 1942)
    Thunder Birds (20th 1942)
    Slightly Dangerous (MGM 1943)
    Forever and a Day (RKO 1943)
    Crash Dive (20th 1943)
    Stage Door Canteen (UA 1943)
    The Constant Nymph (WB 1943)
    Lassie Come Home (MGM 1943)
    Flesh and Fantasy (Univ 1943)
    Madame Curie (MGM 1944)
    Gaslight [Murder in Thornton Square] (MGM 1944)

The White Cliffs of Dover (MGM 1944)
My Name Is Julia Ross (Col 1945)
Devotion (WB 1946)
Green Dolphin Street (MGM 1947)
This Time for Keeps (MGM 1947)
If Winter Comes (MGM 1947)
The Sign of the Ram (Col 1948)
The Return of October (Col 1948)

WIAZEMSKY, ANNE, b. 1947, Berlin
Au hasard, Balthazar (Fr-Swe 1966)
La Chinoise (Fr 1967)
Week-end (Fr-It 1968)
Les Gauloises bleues (Fr 1968)
Teorema [Theorem] (It 1968)
One Plus One [Sympathy for the Devil] (Conn 1968)
Les Anarchistes; ou, La Bande à Bonnot (Fr-It 1968)
Porcile [Pigsty] (It-Fr 1969)
Vent d'est (It 1970)
Les Vieilles Lunes (Swi 1969)
Capricci (It 1969)
Il seme dell'uomo (It 1969)
Voices (Conn 1970) [documentary] [filmed in 1968 during making
    of One Plus One]
Moi Je (Fr 1973)
La Vérité sur l'imaginaire (Fr 1974)

WICKI, BERNHARD, b. Oct. 28, 1919, Sankt Polten, Austria
Der fallende Stern (W Ger 1950)
Junges Herz voll Liebe (W Ger 1953)
Rummelplatz der Liebe (W Ger 1954)
Die letzte Brücke (W Ger 1954)
Gefangene der Liebe (W Ger 1954)
Die Mucke (W Ger 1954)
Das sweite Leben (W Ger 1954)
Ewiger Waltzer (W Ger 1954)
Kinder, Mutter und ein General (W Ger 1955)
Es geschah am 20. Juli (W Ger 1955)
Du mein stilles Tal (W Ger 1955)
Rosen im Herbst (Ger 1955)
Frucht ohne Liebe (W Ger 1956)
Weil du arm bist, musst Du früher sterben (W Ger 1956)
Tierarzt Dr. Vlimmen (W Ger 1956)
Königin Luise (W Ger 1957)
Die Zürcher Verlobung (W Ger 1957)
Flucht in der Tropennacht (W Ger 1957)
Es wird alles wider gut (W Ger 1957)
Madeleine und er Legionär (W Ger 1958)
Frauensee (W Ger 1958)
Unruhige Nacht (W Ger 1958)
Eine Frau im besten Mannesalter (W Ger 1958)
La Chatte (Fr 1958)
Warum sind sie gegen uns? (W Ger 1958) (only director and
    script)

Lampenfieber (W Ger 1959)
Die Brücke (W Ger 1959) (only director)
Das Wunder des Malachias (W Ger 1961) (only director, co-script)
La Notte (It 1961)
Elf Jahre und ein Tag (W Ger 1961)
Erotica [L'amore difficile] (It 1961)
The Longest Day (20th 1962 (only co-director)
The Visit (20th 1964 (only director, co-script)
Deine Zärtlichkeiten (W Ger 1964)
Les Vacances portugaises (Fr 1964)
Morituri (20th 1965 (only director, co-script)
Transit (Swi 1966) [Unfinished]
Das falsche Gewicht (W Ger 1972) (only director)

WIECK, DOROTHEA, b. Jan. 3, 1905, Davos, Switzerland
Heimliche Sünder (Ger 1926)
Ich hab' mein Herz in Heidelberg verloren (Ger 1926)
Die kleine Inge und ihre drei Väter (Ger 1926)
Hast Du geliebt am schönen Rhein (Ger 1927)
Klettermaxe (Ger 1927)
Mein Heidelberg, ich kann Dicht nicht vergessen (Ger 1927)
Sturmflut (Ger 1927)
Valencia (Ger 1927)
Wenn die Schwalben heimwärts ziehen (Ger 1927)
Mädchen in Uniform (Ger 1931)
Gräfin Mariza (Ger 1932)
Theodor Körner (Ger 1932)
Trench (Ger 1932)
Teilnehmer antwortet nicht (Ger 1932)
Ein toller Einfall (Ger 1932)
Anna und Elisabeth (Ger 1933)
Cradle Song (Par 1933)
Miss Fane's Baby Is Stolen (Par 1934)
Liselotte von der Pfalz (Ger 1935)
Der Student von Prag (Ger 1935)
Der stählerne Strahl (Ger 1935)
Die unmögliche Frau (Ger 1936)
Die gelbe Flagge (Ger 1937)
Liebe kann lügen (Ger 1937)
Die Vierte kommt nicht (Ger 1939)
Dein Leben gehört mir (Ger 1939)
Gesprengte Gitter (Ger 1940)
Kopf hoch, Johannes (Ger 1941)
Andreas Schlüter (Ger 1942)
Panik (Ger 1942)
Der grüne Salon (Ger 1944)
Leb' wohl Christina (Ger 1945)
Mordprozess Dr. Jordan (W Ger 1949)
Fünf unter Verdacht (W Ger 1950)
Herz der Welt (W Ger 1952)
'Das seltsame Leben des Herrn Bruggs (W Ger 1952)
Hinter Klostermauern (W Ger 1955)
Der Mann meines Lebens (W Ger 1955)

Der Froschkönig (W Ger 1955)
Unternehmen Schlafsack (W Ger 1955)
Das Fräulein von Scüderi (W Ger 1955)
Das Forsthaus im Tirol (W Ger 1955)
Roman einer Siebzehnjährigen (W Ger 1955)
Anastasia, die letzte Zarentochter (W Ger 1956)
A Time to Love and a Time to Die (Univ 1958)
Aus dem Tagebuch eines Frauenarztes (W Ger 1959)
Menschen im Hotel (W Ger-Fr 1960)
Schachnovelle (W Ger 1960)
Morgen wirst Du um mich weinen (W Ger 1960)

WIEMAN, MATHIAS, b. 1902, Osnabrück, Germany; d. 1969
Potsdam, das Schicksal einer Residenz (Ger 1926)
Feme (Ger 1927)
Der fidele Bauer (Ger 1927)
Königin Luise (Ger 1927)
Mata Hari (Ger 1927)
Der Sohn der Hagar (Ger 1927)
Die Durchgängerin (Ger 1928)
Unter der Laterne (Ger 1928)
Tagebuch einer Kokotte (Ger 1928)
Das Land ohne Frauen (Ger 1929)
Sturme über dem Montblanc [Avalanche] (Ger 1930)
Rosenmontag (Ger 1930)
Zum goldenen Anker (Ger-Fr 1931)
Die Herrin von Atlantis (Ger 1932)
Die Gräfin von Monte Christo (Ger 1932)
Das blaue Licht (Ger 1932)
Mensch ohne Namen (Ger 1932)
Anna und Elisabeth (Ger 1933)
Das verliebte Hotel (Ger 1933)
Fräulein Hoffmanns Erzählungen (Ger 1933)
Achtung! Wer kennt diese Frau? (Ger 1934)
Klein Dorrit (Ger 1934)
Das verlorene Tal (Ger 1934)
Vorstadtvarieté (Ger 1934)
Der Schimmelreiter (Ger 1934)
Die ewige Maske [The Eternal Mask] (Aus-Swi 1935)
Viktoria (Ger 1935)
Patrioten (Ger 1935)
Unternehmen Michael (Ger 1937)
Togger (Ger 1937)
Anna Faverti (Ger 1938)
Michelangelo (Ger 1934) (narrator)
Kadetten (Ger 1941)
Ich klage an (Ger 1941)
Das andere Ich (Ger 1941)
Paracelsus (Ger 1943)
Man rede mir nicht von Liebe (Ger 1943)
Das Herz muss schweigen (Ger 1944)
Träumerei (Ger 1944)
Wie sagen wir es unseren Kindern? (Ger 1945)

Melodie des Schicksals (W Ger 1950)
Wenn eine Frau liebt (W Ger 1950)
Herz der Welt (W Ger 1951)
Solange Du da bist (W Ger 1952)
Königliche Hoheit (W Ger 1953)
Eine Liebesgeschichte (W Ger 1953)
Der letzte Sommer (W Ger 1954)
Angst (W Ger 1954)
Reifende Jugent (W Ger 1955)
Die Ehe des Dr. med. Danwitz (W Ger 1956)
Robinson soll nicht sterben (W Ger 1957)
Wetterleuchten um Maria (W Ger 1957)

WILDING, MICHAEL, b. July 23, 1912, Westcliff-on-Sea, Essex,
     England
Wedding Group [Wrath of Jealousy] (Fox Br 1936)
There Ain't No Justice (ABFD 1939)
Tilly of Bloomsbury (RKO Br 1940)
Sailors Don't Care (Butcher's 1940)
Convoy (ABFD 1940)
Sailors Three [Three Cockeyed Sailors] (ABFD 1940)
The Farmer's Wife (Pathe 1941)
Spring Meeting (ABPC 1941)
Kipps [The Remarkable Mr. Kipps] (20th Br 1941)
Cottage to Let [Bombsight Stolen] (GFD 1941)
Ships with Wings (UA 1941)
The Big Blockade (UA 1942)
Secret Mission (GFD 1942)
In Which We Serve (BL 1942)
Undercover [Underground Guerrillas] (UA 1943)
Dear Octopus [The Randolph Family] (GFD 1943)
English without Tears [Her Man Gilbey] (GFD 1944)
Piccadilly Incident (Pathe 1946)
Carnival (GFD 1946)
The Courtneys of Curzon Street [The Courtney Affair] (BL 1947)
An Ideal Husband (BL 1948)
Spring in Park Lane (BL 1948)
Maytime in Mayfair (BL 1949)
Under Capricorn (WB 1949)
Stage Fright (WB 1950)
Into the Blue [The Man in the Dinghy] (BL 1951)
The Lady with the Lamp (BL 1951)
The Law and the Lady (MGM 1951)
Derby Day [Four Against Fate] (BL 1952)
Trent's Last Case (BL 1952)
Torch Song (MGM 1953)
The Egyptian (20th 1954)
The Glass Slipper (MGM 1955)
The Scarlet Coat (MGM 1955)
Zarak (Col 1957)
Hello London (RFI 1958)
Danger Within [Break Out] (BL 1959)
The World of Suzie Wong (Par 1960)

The Naked Edge (UA 1962)
Best of Enemies (GB-It 1962)
Tamiko [A Girl Named Tamiko] (Par 1961)
The Sweet Ride (20th 1968)
Waterloo (It-USSR 1970)
Lady Caroline Lamb (GB-It 1972)
Frankenstein: The True Story [Dr. Frankenstein] (NBC-TV 1973)

WILLIAMS, EMLYN, b. Nov. 26, 1905, Mostyn, North Wales
The Frightened Lady [Criminal at Large] (Ideal 1932)
Men of Tomorrow (Par 1932)
Sally Bishop (BL 1932)
Friday the Thirteenth (ep "Blake, the Gentleman of Fortune")
    (Gaumont 1933)
My Song for You (Gaumont 1934)
Evensong (Gaumont 1934)
Roadhouse (Gaumont 1934)
The Man Who Knew Too Much (Gaumont 1934)
The Iron Duke (Gaumont 1935)
The Love Affair of a Dictator [Loves of a Dictator/For Love of
    a Queen] (Gaumont 1935)
The City of Beautiful Nonsense (Butcher's 1935)
Broken Blossoms (TFD 1936)
I, Claudius (UA 1937)
Dead Men Tell No Tales (ABPC 1938)
A Night Alone (Pathe 1938)
The Citadel (MGM Br 1938)
They Drive by Night (FN 1938)
Jamaica Inn (ABPC 1939)
The Stars Look Down (GN 1939)
Girl in the News (20th 1940)
You Will Remember (BL 1940)
This England [Our Heritage] (Anglo 1941)
Major Barbara (GFD 1941)
Hatter's Castle (Par Br 1941)
The Last Days of Dolwyn [Woman of Dolwyn] (BL 1949)
Three Husbands (WB 1950)
The Scarf (UA 1951)
Another Man's Poison (Eros 1951)
The Magic Box (BL 1951)
Ivanhoe (MGM Br 1952)
The Deep Blue Sea (20th 1955)
I Accuse! (MGM 1958)
The Wreck of the Mary Deare (MGM 1959)
Beyond This Place [Web of Evidence] (Renown 1959)
The L-Shaped Room (BL 1962)
Eye of the Devil [13] (MGM 1966)
The Walking Stick (MGM 1970)

WISDOM, NORMAN, b. Feb. 4, 1920, London
A Date with a Dream (GN 1948)
Trouble in Store (GFD 1953)
One Good Turn (GFD 1954)

As Long As They're Happy (GFD 1955)
Man of the Moment (RFD 1955)
Up in the World (RFD 1956)
Just My Luck (RFD 1957)
The Square Peg (RFD 1958)
Follow a Star (RFD 1959)
There Was a Crooked Man (UA 1960)
The Bulldog Breed (RFD 1960)
The Girl on the Boat (UA 1961)
On the Beat (RFD 1962)
A Stitch in Time (RFD 1963)
The Early Bird (RFD 1965)
The Sandwich Man (RFD 1966)
Press for Time (RFD 1966)
The Night They Raided Minsky's (UA 1968)
What's Good for the Goose (Tigon 1969)

WITHERS, GOOGIE, b. March 12, 1917, Karachi, India
The Girl in the Crowd (FN Br 1934)
The Love Test (Fox Br 1935)
Windfall (PDC 1935)
Her Last Affair (Fox Br 1935)
All at Sea (Fox Br 1935)
Crown v. Stevens (WB Br 1936)
King of Hearts [Little Gel] (Butcher 1936)
She Knew What She Wanted (Wardour 1936)
Accused (UA 1936)
Crime Over London (UA 1936)
Pearls Bring Tears (Col Br 1937)
Paradise for Two [The Gaiety Girls] (UA 1937)
Paid in Error (Col Br 1938)
If I Were Boss (Col Br 1938)
Kate Plus Ten (GFD 1938)
Strange Boarders (GFD 1938)
Convict 99 (GFD 1938)
The Lady Vanishes (Gaumont 1938)
You're the Doctor (BIED 1938)
Murder in Soho [Murder in the Night] (ABPC 1939)
Trouble Brewing (ABFD 1939)
The Gang's All Here [The Amazing Mr. Forrest] (ABPC 1939)
She Couldn't Say No (ABPC 1939)
Bulldog Sees It Through (ABPC 1940)
Busman's Honeymoon [Haunted Honeymoon] (MGM Br 1940)
Jeannie (GFD 1941)
Back Room Boy (GFD 1942)
One of Our Aircraft Is Missing (Anglo 1942)
The Silver Fleet (GFD 1943)
On Approval (GFD 1944)
They Came to a City (Ealing 1944)
Dead of Night (ep "The Haunted Mirror") (EL 1945)
Pink String and Sealing Wax (EL 1945)
The Loves of Joanna Godden (GFD 1947)
It Always Rains on Sunday (GFD 1947)

Miranda (GFD 1948)
Once Upon a Dream (GFD 1949)
Traveller's Joy (GFD 1949)
Night and the City (20th 1950)
White Corridors (GFD 1951)
The Magic Box (BL 1951)
Derby Day [Four Against Fate] (BL 1952)
Devil on Horseback (BL 1954)
Port of Escape (Renown 1956)
The Nickel Queen (Australia 1972)

WOOD, MONTGOMERY see GEMMA GIULIANO

WYNTER, DANA (Dagmar Wynter), b. June 8, 1929, London
White Corridors (GFD 1951)
Lady Godiva Rides Again (BL 1951)
The Woman's Angle (ABD 1952)
It Started in Paradise (GFD 1952)
The Crimson Pirate (WB 1952)
Colonel March Investigates (GB 1954)
The View from Pompey's Head [Secret Interlude] (20th 1955)
Invasion of the Body Snatchers (AA 1956)
Something of Value (MGM 1957)
Fraulein (20th 1958)
In Love and War (20th 1958)
Shake Hands with the Devil (UA 1959)
Sink the Bismarck! (20th 1960)
On the Double (Par 1961)
The List of Adrian Messenger (Univ 1963)
Companions in Nightmare (NBC-TV 1968)
Any Second Now (NBC-TV 1969)
Airport (Univ 1970)
Owen Marshall (ABC-TV 1971)
Santee (Col-Warner 1972)
The Connection (ABC-TV 1973)
The Questor Tapes (NBC-TV 1974)
The Lives of Jenny Dolan (NBC-TV 1975)

WYNYARD, DIANA (Dorothy Cox), b. Jan. 16, 1906, London; d. May
    13, 1964
Rasputin and the Empress (MGM 1933)
Reunion in Vienna (MGM 1933)
Cavalcade (Fox 1933)
Men Must Fight (MGM 1933)
One More River [Over the River] (Univ 1934)
On the Night of the Fire [The Fugitive] (GFD 1939)
Tom Brown's Schooldays (RKO 1940)
Gaslight [Angel Street] (Anglo 1940)
Freedom Radio [A Voice in the Night] (Col Br 1941)
The Prime Minister (WB Br 1941)
Kipps [The Remarkable Mr. Kipps] (20th Br 1942)
An Ideal Husband (BL 1948)
The Feminine Touch [The Gentle Touch] (RFD 1956)
Island in the Sun (20th 1957)

YANNE, JEAN (Jean Gouille), b. July 18, 1933, Paris
    La Vie à l'Envers [Life Upside Down] (Fr 1964)
    L'Amour à la chaîne [Victims of Vice] (Fr 1965)
    Monnaie de singe [Monkey Money] (Fr-Sp 1966)
    La Linge de démarcation (Fr 1966)
    Bang Bang (Fr-It 1967)
    Week-end (Fr-It 1968)
    Un Drôle de colonel (Fr 1968)
    Ces Messieurs de la famille (Fr 1968)
    Erotissimo (Fr 1969)
    Que la bête meure [This Man Must Die] (Fr-It 1969)
    Le Boucher [The Butcher] (Fr-It 1970)
    Etes-vous fiancée a un marin Grec ou a un pilote de ligne? (Fr
    Fantasia chez les Ploucs [Diamond Bikini] (Fr-It 1971)
    Laisser aller, c'est une valse [The Trouble Shooters] (Fr-It
      1971)
    Le Saut de l'ange [Cobra] (Fr 1971)
    Nous ne vieillons pas ensemble (Fr-It 1972)
    Tout le monde, il est beau, tout le monde, il est gentil (Fr
      1972)
    Moi y en a vouloir des sous (Fr 1973)
    Les Chinois à Paris (Fr-It 1974)
    Chobizenesse [Show Business] (Fr 1975)
    Ralbot (Fr 1975)

YORK, MICHAEL, b. March 27, 1942, Fulmer, Buckinghamshire,
    England
    The Taming of the Shrew (USA-It 1966)
    Accident (LIP 1967)
    Red & Blue (UA 1967)
    Smashing Time (Par 1967)
    Confessions of a Loving Couple (GB 1967) [not shown commer-
      cially]
    Romeo and Juliet (Par 1968)
    The Strange Affair (Par 1968)
    The Guru (USA-India 1968)
    Alfred the Great (MGM 1969)
    Justine (20th 1969)
    Something for Everyone [Black Flowers for the Bride] (National
      General 1970)
    Zeppelin (WB 1971)
    La Poudre d'escampette (Fr 1971)
    Cabaret (Cin 1972)
    England Made Me (Hemdale 1972)
    Lost Horizon (Col 1972)
    The Three Musketeers [The Queen's Diamonds] (20th 1973)
    Murder on the Orient Express (EMI 1974)
    The Four Musketeers [The Revenge of Milady] (20th 1974)
    Great Expectations (Scotia-Barber 1975)
    Conduct Unbecoming (BL 1975)

YORK, SUSANNAH, b. Jan. 9, 1939, London
    There Was a Crooked Man (UA 1960)

Susannah York and Dirk Bogarde in Sebastian (1967).

Tunes of Glory (UA 1960)
The Greengage Summer (Col 1961)
Freud [The Secret Passion] (Univ 1962)
Tom Jones (UA 1963)
The Seventh Dawn (UA 1964)
Sands of the Kalahari (Par 1965)
Scruggs (Juvenal 1965)
Kaleidoscope [The Bank Breaker] (WPD 1966)
A Man for All Seasons (Col 1966)
Sebastian (Par 1967)
Duffy (Col 1968)
The Killing of Sister George (Cin 1968)
Lock Up Your Daughters! (Col 1969)
Oh! What a Lovely War (Par 1969)
Battle of Britain (UA 1969)
They Shoot Horses, Don't They? (Cin 1970)
Jane Eyre (BL 1971)
Country Dance [Brotherly Love] (MGM 1971) [made in 1969]
Happy Birthday, Wanda June (Col 1971)
X, Y & Z [Zee & Co] (Col 1972)
Images (Hemdale 1972)
Gold (Hemdale 1974)
The Maids (AFT 1974)
That Lucky Touch (Fox-Rank 1975)
Conduct Unbecoming (BL 1975)

ZIEMANN, SONJA, b. Feb. 8, 1925, Eichwalde, Germany
Die Jungfern vom Bischofsberg (Ger 1943)
Beliebter Schatz (Ger 1943)
Ein Windstoss (Ger 1943)
Freunde (Ger 1944)
Eine reizende Familie (Ger 1945)
Eine kleine Sommermelodie (Ger 1944)
Hundstage (Ger 1944)
Spuk in Schloos (Ger 1944)
Liebe nach Noten (Ger 1945)
Sag' die Wahrheit (W Ger 1946)
Herzkönig (W Ger 1947)
Wege im Zwielicht (W Ger 1948)
Die Freunde meiner Frau (W Ger 1949)
Nach Regen scheint Sonne (W Ger 1949)
Nichts als Zufälle (W Ger 1949)
Nächte am Nil (W Ger 1949)
Nasenlänge (W Ger 1949)
Eine Nacht im Separee (W Ger 1950)
Maharadscha wider Willen (W Ger 1950)
Schwarzwaldmädel (W Ger 1950)
Die lustigen Weiber von Windsor (W Ger 1950)
Schön muss man sein (W Ger 1950)
Die Frauen des Herrn S. (W Ger 1950)
Johannes und die 13 Schönheitsköniginnen (W Ger 1951)
Grün ist die Heide (W Ger 1951)
Die Diebin von Bagdad (W Ger 1952)

Alle kann ich nicht heiraten (W Ger 1952)
Am Brunnen vor dem Tore (W Ger 1952)
Hollandmädel (W Ger 1953)
Mit siebzehn beginnt das Leben (W Ger 1953)
Die Privatsekretärin (W Ger 1953)
Bei Dir war es immer so schön (W Ger 1954)
Meine Schwester und ich (W Ger 1954)
Die 7 Kleider der Katrin (W Ger 1954)
Das Zarewitsch [Le Tzarévitch] (W Ger 1954)
Liebe ohne Illusion (W Ger 1955)
Grosse Star Parade (W Ger 1955)
Ich war ein hässliches Mädchen (W Ger 1955)
Mädchen ohne Grenzen (W Ger 1955)
Das Bad auf der Tenne (W Ger 1955)
Dany, bitte schreiben Sie (W Ger 1956)
Opernball (W Ger 1956)
Kaiserball (W Ger 1956)
Nichts als Ärger mit der Liebe (W Ger 1956)
Die Grosse Sünde (W Ger-It 1957)
Frauenarzt Dr. Bertram (W Ger 1957)
Frühling in Berlin (W Ger 1957)
Die Zürcher Verlobung (W Ger 1957)
Der achte Wochentag [Osmy dzien tygoduia] (W Ger-Pol 1958)
Gli italiani sono matti [Los italianos estan locos] (It-Sp 1958)
Menschen im Hotel (W Ger-Fr 1959)
Liebe auf krummen Beinen (W Ger 1959)
Tabarin (Fr-It 1959)
Abschied von den Wolken (W Ger 1959)
Nacht fiel über Götenhafen (W Ger 1960)
Strafbataillon 999 (W Ger 1960)
Denn dast Weib ist schwach (W Ger 1961)
The Secret Ways (Univ 1961)
Hunde, wollt ihr ewig leben (W Ger 1961)
Affäre Näbob (W Ger 1962)
Der Traum von Lieschen Müller (W Ger-It-Fr 1961)
Axel Munthe, der Arzt von San Michele (W Ger 1961)
Ihr schönster Tag (W Ger 1962)
Der Tod fährt mit (W Ger 1962)
Frühstück mit dem Tod (W Ger-Aus 1964)
2 mal 2 im Himmelbett [Halløj i himmelsengen] (W Ger-Dan 1964)

ZOU-ZOU, b. Nov. 29, 1943, Blida, Algeria
Comme un poisson dans l'eau (Fr 1959)
Hitler, connais pas (Fr 1961)
Marie pour mémoire (Fr 1967)
La Concentration (Fr 1968)
Le Lit de la vierge [The Virgin's Bed] (Fr 1970)
La Naissance (Fr 1970)
La Famille (Fr 1971)
L'Amour, l'après-midi [Love in the Afternoon] (Fr 1972)
S. P. Y. S. (EMI 1974)
L'Important c'est d'aimer (Fr 1974)
Lily aime-moi (Fr 1975)
Les Lolos de Lola (Fr 1975)

ABOUT THE COMPILERS

JAMES ROBERT PARISH, New York-based freelancer, was born in Cambridge, Massachusetts. He attended the University of Pennsylvania and graduated as a Phi Beta Kappa with an honors degree in English. A graduate of the University of Pennsylvania Law School, he is a member of the New York Bar. As president of Entertainment Copyright Research Co., Inc., he headed a major researching facility for the media industries. Later he was a reporter for Motion Picture Daily and Variety. He is the author of such books as The Fox Girls, The RKO Gals, Hollywood's Great Love Teams, The Tough Guys, and Actors' Television Credits (1950-72; and Supplement). Among his co-authorship credits are: The Cinema of Edward G. Robinson, Liza!, The Debonairs, The MGM Stock Company, Hollywood Players: The 30s, The Great Spy Pictures, The Great Western Pictures, and Film Directors: A Guide to Their American Pictures.

KINGSLEY CANHAM, London-based freelancer, was born in Port Elizabeth, South Africa, on February 18, 1945. A film buff from early childhood, he attended St. Andrew's College in Grahamstown and in 1962 came to England. He has contributed to many cinema journals, including Films, Focus on Film, Films in Review, Films and Filming, and Screen. His cinema research has been published by Tantivy Press, the British Film Institute, and the National Film Archive. He is the author of a number of books in the "Hollywood Professional" series and contributed to Film Directors Guide: Western Europe. He is currently the London correspondent for Filmquía, a Spanish cinema journal.

HERVÉ DUMONT was born in February 1943 in Berne, Switzerland, and attended schools in Sweden, Germany, and Spain, receiving his Ph.D. in 1970. For the cinema journal Travelling he has provided several articles, and has contributed to such Spanish film publications as Film Ideal and El Cine. He joined in the researching for Film Directors Guide: Western Europe. He is associated with the Swiss National Film Archive in Lausanne, Switzerland and is the author of W. S. Van Dyke (1975).

JEANNE PASSALACQUA was born in New York City and graduated from Baruch College. She has always been interested in the cinema and is a contributor to several cinema journals; she was research associate on Film Directors Guide: Western Europe. Her first job was working in a secretarial capacity for a major film

company. At present she is associated with one of the city libra-
ries. She is married and has one daughter.

LINDA J. SANDAHL was born in Jersey City, New Jersey,
and later moved to Morristown, New Jersey, where she attended
school and currently resides. Long interested in cinema scholar-
ship, she was a research associate on the book The Hollywood Re-
liables.

FLORENCE SOLOMON, born in New York, attended Hunter
College and then joined Ligon Johnson's copyright research office.
Later she was appointed director of research at Entertainment Copy-
right Research Co., Inc., and is presently a reference supervisor
at A. S. C. A. P. 's Index division in Manhattan. Ms. Solomon has
collaborated on such works as The American Movies Reference Book:
The Sound Era, TV Movies, The Swashbucklers, The Hollywood
Players: The Thirties, and Actors TV Credits (1950-72; and Sup-
plement). She is the niece of the noted sculptor, the late Sir Jacob
Epstein.